THE ROUTLEDGE COMPANION TO PICTUREBOOKS

Containing forty-eight chapters, *The Routledge Companion to Picturebooks* is the ultimate guide to picturebooks. It contains a detailed introduction, surveying the history and development of the field and emphasizing the international and cultural diversity of picturebooks. Divided into five key parts, this volume covers:

- Concepts and topics – from hybridity and ideology to metafiction and emotions;
- Genres – from baby books through to picturebooks for adults;
- Interfaces – their relations to other forms such as comics and visual media;
- Domains and theoretical approaches, including developmental psychology and cognitive studies;
- Adaptations.

With ground-breaking contributions from leading and emerging scholars alike, this comprehensive volume is one of the first to focus solely on picturebook research. Its interdisciplinary approach makes it key for both scholars and students of literature, as well as education and media.

Bettina Kümmerling-Meibauer is Professor in the German Department at the University of Tübingen, Germany. She recently co-edited *Learning from Picturebooks: Perspectives from Child Development and Literacy Studies* (Routledge, 2015).

ROUTLEDGE COMPANIONS TO LITERATURE SERIES

For further information on this series visit: www.routledge.com/literature/series/RC4444

THE ROUTLEDGE COMPANION TO PICTUREBOOKS

Edited by
Bettina Kümmerling-Meibauer

Routledge
Taylor & Francis Group

LONDON AND NEW YORK

First published 2018 by Routledge

2 Park Square, Milton Park, Abingdon, Oxon OX14 4RN

605 Third Avenue, New York, NY 10017

Routledge is an imprint of the Taylor & Francis Group, an informa business

First issued in paperback 2021

British Library Cataloguing-in-Publication Data
A catalogue record for this book is available from the British Library

Library of Congress Cataloging-in-Publication Data
Names: Kèummerling-Meibauer, Bettina editor.
Title: The Routledge companion to picturebooks / edited by Bettina Kèummerling-Meibauer.
Description: Milton Park, Abingdon, Oxon : New York : Routledge, 2018. | Includes index.
Identifiers: LCCN 2017016030| ISBN 9781138853188 (hardback : alk. paper) |
ISBN 9781317526599 (epub) | ISBN 9781317526605 (pdf) | ISBN 9781317526582 (kindle)
Subjects: LCSH: Children's literature—History and criticism. | Picture books for children—History. |
Picture books for children—Technique. | Picture books for children—Authorship. |
Children—Books and reading. | Narrative art. | Graphic novels—History and criticism. |
Illustrated books—History. | Young adult literature—History and criticism.
Classification: LCC PN1009.A1 R695 2018 | DDC 002–dc23
LC record available at https://lccn.loc.gov/2017016030

ISBN: 978-1-138-85318-8 (hbk)
ISBN: 978-1-03-217883-7 (pbk)
DOI: 10.4324/9781315722986

Typeset in Bembo
by Apex CoVantage, LLC

Printed in the United Kingdom
by Henry Ling Limited

CONTENTS

Contents

Contents

FIGURES

TABLES

CONTRIBUTORS

Cherie Allan is a Lecturer in the Faculty of Education at the Queensland University of Technology, Australia. She is Coordinator of the Children's and Young Adult Literature and Youth Popular Culture units within the postgraduate and undergraduate program. She is author of the book *Playing with Picturebooks: Postmodernism and the Postmodernesque* (Palgrave Macmillan, 2012). The focus of her current research is on digital fiction.

Ghada Al-Yagout holds a PhD from the University of Cambridge. Her PhD thesis explores picturebooks in series. She is currently an Assistant Professor of Children's Literature in the English Department of the College of Basic Education, PAAET, Kuwait.

Evelyn Arizpe is Senior Lecturer at the School of Education, University of Glasgow, UK, where she leads the MEd Programme in Children's Literature and Literacies. She has taught and published widely in the areas of literacy and children's literature and worked on a number of studies related to picturebooks and response.

Sandra L. Beckett is Professor Emeritus at Brock University, Canada. Her authored books include *Revisioning Red Riding Hood around the World: An Anthology of International Retellings* (Wayne State UP, 2014), *Crossover Picturebooks: A Genre for All Ages* (Routledge, 2012), *Crossover Fiction: Global and Historical Perspectives* (Routledge, 2009), *Red Riding Hood for All Ages: A Fairy-Tale Icon in Cross-Cultural Contexts* (Wayne State UP, 2008), *Recycling Red Riding Hood* (Routledge, 2002), and *De grands romanciers écrivent pour les enfants* (Presses Univ. de Montreal, 1997). She is the editor of several books including *Transcending Boundaries: Writing for a Dual Audience of Children and Adults* (Garland, 1999) and *Reflections of Change: Children's Literature Since 1945* (Greenwood Press, 1997).

Elizabeth Bird is the Collection Development Manager of Evanston Public Library, and the former Youth Materials Specialist of New York Public Library, USA. A regular reviewer for *Kirkus Reviews*, she hosts the children' literature site A Fuse #8 Production through *School Library Journal*. Her publications include the ALA Editions title *Children's Literature Gems: Choosing and Using Them in Your Library Career* (Am. Library Assoc. Ed., 2009) and a co-author credit on *Wild Things: Acts of Mischief in Children's Literature* (Candlewick Press, 2014).

Emma Bosch is a graphic designer and author who achieved a BA degree in Fine Arts and a PhD degree in Educational Sciences, both at the University of Barcelona, Spain. She teaches at the department of Visual Education and in the master's degrees in *Interdisciplinary Education of the Arts* (UB), *Books and Literature for Children and Young People* (UAB) and *School Library and Reading Promotion* (UB+UAB). Her research area covers picturebooks, illustration, and visual literacy.

Nina Christensen is Associate Professor and Head of the Centre for Children's Literature and Media at Aarhus University, Denmark. She writes and lectures on visual texts, children's literature and concepts of childhood, the history of children's literature, and children's texts between media. She co-edits the John Benjamins series "Children's Literature, Culture, and Cognition."

Karen Coats is Professor of English at Illinois State University, USA, where she teaches children's and young adult literature. Her publications include numerous articles and book chapters that relate contemporary theory to youth literature. She is author of *The Bloomsbury Introduction to Children's and Young Adult Literature* (Bloomsbury, 2017) *and Looking Glasses and Neverlands: Lacan, Desire, and Subjectivity in Children's Literature* (U of Iowa Press, 2004), and co-editor of *Handbook of Research on Children's and Young Adult Literature* (Routledge, 2011) and *The Gothic in Children's Literature: Haunting the Border* (Routledge, 2007).

Johanna Drucker is the Breslauer Professor of Bibliographical Studies in the Department of Information Studies at University of California, Los Angeles, USA. She has published widely on topics related to the history of the book, including her volume *The Century of Artists' Books* (Granary Press, 1995), and is also a well-known book artist.

Elina Druker is Associate Professor in Comparative Literature at Stockholm University, Sweden. Her research area is picturebook research and intermedia studies. She is the author and co-editor of several publications dealing with children's literature, co-author of *Swedish Children's Literature History* (forthcoming) and co-editor of the book series "Children's Literature, Culture and Cognition" (John Benjamins).

Jennifer Farrar is a final year doctoral candidate in the School of Education at the University of Glasgow, UK, with research interests in critical literacy, metafiction, and picturebooks. Her PhD study is exploring the responses of young children and their parents to metafiction in picturebooks.

Eva Gressnich is a teacher for German as a foreign language. Her main topics of research are the interfaces between language acquisition, literature acquisition, and literacy development. Her PhD thesis deals with the relationship between picturebooks and children's narrative development.

Nancy L. Hadaway is Professor Emerita, University of Texas at Arlington, USA. She has served on numerous book award committees including the Orbis Pictus Committee (NCTE), the Notable Books for a Global Society Committee (Children's Literature and Reading SIG/IRA), and the Outstanding International Books Committee (USBBY).

Naomi Hamer is Assistant Professor in the Department of English at Ryerson University, Canada. Her current research examines the cross-media adaptation of picturebooks. She is co-editor of *More Words about Pictures: Current Research on Picture Books and Visual/Verbal Texts for Young People* (Routledge, 2017, with Perry Nodelman and Mavis Reimer).

Erica Hateley is Professor of English in the Faculty of Education at Norwegian University of Science and Technology (NTNU) in Trondheim, Norway. She has published widely on issues of cultural values in children's literature, and is the author of *Shakespeare in Children's Literature: Gender and Cultural Capital* (Routledge, 2009).

Beatriz Hoster Cabo has a degree in Philology and a PhD in Science Education. She is a professor and the Academic Director of CEU "Cardenal Spínola," University of Seville, Spain. She lectures on subjects related to education, children's literature, and didactics. Since 1994 she is a member of the PAI research group "Marcas Andaluzas: Discourse and Literature" (University of Huelva, Spain).

Vanessa Joosen is Professor in English Literature at the University of Antwerp, Belgium, where she has specialized in children's literature. She is the author of *Critical and Creative Perspectives on Fairy Tales* (Wayne State UP, 2011) and *Wit als sneeuw, zwart als inkt* (Lannoo, 2014), a study on the Dutch reception of Grimm's fairy tales.

Bettina Kümmerling-Meibauer is a professor in the German Department at the University of Tübingen, Germany. She has been a guest professor at the University of Växjö, Sweden, and the University of Vienna. She is the author of four books, including an encyclopedia of international children's classics (Metzler, 1999) and a monograph on canon processes in children's literature (Metzler, 2003). Her recent (co-)edited books include *Learning from Picturebooks: Perspectives from Child Development and Literacy Studies* (Routledge, 2015), *Children's Literature and the Avant-Garde* (John Benjamins, 2015), *Canon Constitution and Canon Change in Children's Literature* (Routledge, 2017), and *Maps and Mapping in Children's Literature* (John Benjamins, 2017).

Tobias Kurwinkel is a lecturer and the Director of Children's and Youth Media Studies at the University of Bremen, Germany. In 2013 he published *Kinder- und Jugendfilmanalyse*, an introduction to the analysis of children's films (with Philipp Schmerheim). He is the Editor-in-Chief of KinderundJugendmedien.de, an interdisciplinary internet portal devoted to research on children's and youth media.

Megan Dowd Lambert is Senior Lecturer in Children's Literature at Simmons College, Boston, USA. She writes for *Kirkus Reviews* and *The Horn Book*. The author of *A Crow of His Own* (2015, illus. David Hyde Costello) and *Real Sisters Pretend* (2016, illus. Nicole Tadgell), she also wrote *Reading Picture Books with Children: How to Shake Up Storytime and Get Kids Talking about What They See* (Charlesbridge, 2015), introducing the Whole Book Approach.

Helma van Lierop-Debrauwer is Professor of Children's Literature at Tilburg University, the Netherlands. She is the coordinator of the Children's and Adolescent Literature Master's program at this university. She is a member of the editorial board of *Literatuur zonder leeftijd* (Literature without Age), the only academic journal on children's literature in the Netherlands. Her research interests are adolescent literature, life writing and the relation between children's literature and age studies. In 2014 she published, together with Rita Ghesquière and Vanessa Joosen, a new history on Dutch children's literature.

Marie-Pierre Litaudon has a PhD degree in Comparative Literature and is a member of the CELLAM laboratory, University Rennes 2, France. She dedicated her thesis to the history of ABC books (2014) and has deposited her collection of 1,200 English and French rare books at IMEC. Her work focuses on children's literature and cultural studies, book history and the text-image relationship.

María José Lobato Suero has a degree in Fine Arts and a PhD degree in Educational Sciences, both at the University of Seville, Spain. She is a professor and Coordinator of the Department of Education at CEU "Cardenal Spínola." She lectures in subjects related with education, visual culture, and didactics. Since 2007 she is a member of the PAI Research Group "Marcas Andaluzas: Discourse and Literature" (University of Huelva, Spain).

Margaret Mackey is Professor Emerita in the School of Library and Information Studies at the University of Alberta, Canada. She teaches and researches in the area of young people's literacies and literature, in print and other media. She recently published *One Child Reading: My Auto-bibliography* (University of Alberta Press, 2016).

Kerry Mallan is Professor Emerita in the Faculty of Education at Queensland University of Technology, Australia. She has published extensively on children's literature. Her most recent books are *Secrets, Lies and Children's Fiction* (Palgrave Macmillan, 2013) and an edited collection, *Picture Books and Beyond* (PETAA, 2014). She is a co-editor of the "Critical Approaches to Children's Literature" series (Palgrave Macmillan).

Julie McAdam is a lecturer in the School of Education, University of Glasgow, UK. She currently leads the TESOL Masters and works on the masters in Children's Literature and Literacies. Her current research is on narratives of change: a set of positive narratives that recount issues connected to identity, language, and migration.

Jörg Meibauer is Professor of German Language and Linguistics at the Johannes Gutenberg University Mainz, Germany, and Affiliated Professor at the University of Stockholm, Sweden. He wrote monographs on rhetorical questions, modal particles, pragmatics, and lying, and co-edited several collections, for instance, on sentence types, constructions, context, and pejoration. Currently, he is editing the *Oxford Handbook of Lying*. In particular, he is interested in the relation between linguistics and children's literature.

Nikola von Merveldt is Associate Professor of German Studies at the Department for Languages and Literatures of the World at the University of Montreal, Canada. Following her studies in medieval and comparative literature in Strasbourg, Neuchâtel, Cambridge (UK), and Munich, she now works on children's literature and explores the ways in which knowledge is presented in informational literature. She is a founding member of the interdisciplinary research group on book history, "Interacting with Print: Cultural Practices of Intermediality (1700–1900)," and associate fellow of the International Youth Library in Munich.

William Moebius has published a book of poetry and translations of ancient Greek poetry and drama; his writings about the picturebook have been published in the UK, Belgium, France, Germany, Canada, Venezuela, and China as well as the USA. Professor of Comparative Literature, he chairs the Department of Languages, Literatures, and Cultures at the University of Massachusetts in Amherst, USA.

Ann Montanaro Staples is the author of *Pop-up and Movable Books: A Bibliography* (Scarecrow Press, 1993). She is a founder of The Movable Book Society, a worldwide organization, begun in 1993 to provide a forum for enthusiasts to share and exchange information about pop-up and movable books. Until her retirement she was the libraries Director of Information Technology at Rutgers, the State University of New Jersey, USA.

Smiljana Narančić Kovač is an associate professor at the Faculty of Teacher Education, University of Zagreb, Croatia. Her research interests comprise children's literature, comparative literature, narrative theory, and applied linguistics. She serves as the principal investigator for the Croatian Science Foundation project about translations of children's literature (2015–2018). She is Editor-in-Chief of the journal *Libri & Liberi*.

Maria Nikolajeva is Professor of Children's Literature at the Faculty of Education, University of Cambridge, UK. Her most recent books are *Power, Voice and Subjectivity in Literature for Young Readers* (Routledge, 2010) and *Reading for Learning: Cognitive Approaches to Children's Literature* (John Benjamins, 2014). In 2005 she received the International Grimm Award for a lifetime achievement in children's literature research.

Riitta Oittinen holds a PhD in translation studies and is Adjunct Professor at the Universities of Tampere and Helsinki, Finland. She is a senior lecturer at the University of Tampere, with a special interest in literary translation, multimodal translation, and translating for children (child image, audience design). She is also an artist and has published books and articles as well as animated films.

Marilynn Olson is a professor and the Director of Advanced Studies in English at Texas State University, USA. She was Associate Editor and then Editor of the *Children's Literature Association Quarterly* from 1991–2000; her recent book is *Children's Culture and the Avant-Garde: Painting in Paris 1890–1915* (Routledge, 2012).

Åse Marie Ommundsen is Professor of Scandinavian literature in the Faculty of Education at Oslo and Akershus University College of Applied Sciences, Norway. She is also part-time Professor at Nord University, Norway. Her current interest is in contemporary Scandinavian children's literature, crossover picturebooks, and picturebooks for adults, on which she has published articles in Norwegian, English, French, and Dutch. She is the editor of *Looking Out and Looking In: National Identity in Picturebooks of the New Millenium* (Novus, 2013). Her current research project is "Challenging Picturebooks in Education: Rethinking Language and Literature Learning." In 2013 she was awarded *The Kari Skjønsberg Award* for her research on children's literature.

Nathalie op de Beeck is the author of *Suspended Animation: Children's Picture Books and the Fairy Tale of Modernity* (U Minnesota Press, 2010) and co-creator of the project *Little Machinery: A Critical Facsimile Edition* (Wayne State UP, 2009). Her essays have appeared in *Approaches to Teaching the Graphic Novel, Keywords for Children's Literature*, and the *Oxford Handbook of Children's Literature*, and in journals including *Children's Literature, The Lion and the Unicorn, Modern Fiction Studies*, and *Children's Literature Association Quarterly*. She directs the interdisciplinary program in Children's Literature and Culture at Pacific Lutheran University, Tacoma, USA, where she is an Associate Professor of English.

Clare Painter is Honorary Associate of the Department of Linguistics at the University of Sydney, Australia. Her chief research interests are in early child language and literacy development, systemic-functional linguistics, and multimodal discourse analysis. Her publications include *Learning through Language in Early Childhood* (Continuum, 1999) and *Reading Visual Narratives* (co-authored with J.R. Martin and Len Unsworth, Equinox, 2014).

Sylvia Pantaleo is a professor in the Faculty of Education at the University of Victoria, Canada. Her multiple classroom-based studies have explored how children ages six to thirteen respond to, understand, interpret, and analyze literary elements and elements of visual art and design in picturebooks, graphic novels, and other multimodal texts. She is the author of *Exploring Student Response to Contemporary Picturebooks* (University of Toronto Press, 2008) and the co-editor (with Lawrence Sipe) of *Postmodern Picturebooks: Play, Parody, and Self-Referentiality* (Routledge, 2008).

Nicolas Potysch is a post-doc research assistant and a scientific coordinator at the DFG Research Unit 2288: Journal Literature at Ruhr-University Bochum, Germany. He studied German Philology and Physics in Bochum and completed his dissertation at the interface of semiotics and literature studies in 2016 at the DFG Research Training Group 1808: Ambiguity at Tübingen University. His research focuses on narratology, intertextuality, intersemiotic and concepts of authorship, as well as on emblematic studies. He is leader of the section Language and Communicative Practices (SUKP) of the Kulturwissenschaftliche Gesellschaft (KWG).

Elaine Reese is Professor of Psychology at the University of Otago in Dunedin, New Zealand. She is an investigator on the Growing Up in New Zealand longitudinal birth cohort study. Her research focuses on the role of adult-child interaction in children's cognitive and social development.

Cornelia Rémi is Acting Chair of German Philology at the University of Tübingen and Assistant Professor of German Literature at Ludwig Maximilians University of Munich, Germany, where she has completed theses on early modern spiritual poetry and on functions of secrets and secrecy in nineteenth-century narrative fiction. In 2017 she was a jury member for the German Children's Literature Award. She regularly lectures on different aspects of literacy promotion.

Jessica Riordan is a doctoral candidate in Psychology at the University of Otago in Dunedin, New Zealand. Her research focuses on interventions for parents to support their children's transition to formal schooling with a particular focus on children's language and early literacy development.

Alberto Manuel Ruiz Campos has a PhD degree in Philology and is Professor of Language and Literature Teaching in the Department of Spanish Philology, University of Huelva, Spain. His main research focuses on the investigation of children's literature. He is the main investigator in the research group "Marcas Andaluzas: Discourse and Literature."

Donelle Ruwe is Professor of English at Northern Arizona University, USA, and Co-president of the Eighteenth- and Nineteenth-Century British Women Writers Association. She is the author of *British Children's Poetry in the Romantic Era: Verse, Riddle, and Rhyme* (Palgrave Macmillan 2014) and the editor of *Culturing the Child 1660–1830: Essays in Memory of Mitzi Myers* (Rowman & Littlefield, 2005). She is co-editing a collection of essays with James Leve on children and childhood in the Broadway musical. She is a published poet, and her chapbook *Condiments* (1996) won the Kinloch Rivers Award in 1999. A second chapbook, *Another Message You Miss the Point Of* (2005), won the Camber Press Prize in 2006.

Lara Saguisag is Assistant Professor of English at the City University of New York/College of Staten Island, USA. She is currently working on a monograph on constructions of childhood and citizenship in Progressive Era comic strips. Her work has appeared in *Children's Literature Association Quarterly, International Journal of Comic Art*, and *The Horn Book*.

Martin Salisbury is an illustrator and author of a number of books on illustration. He is Professor of Illustration at Cambridge School of Art at Anglia Ruskin University, UK, where he designed and leads the masters program in Children's Book Illustration and directs the Centre for Children's Book Studies.

Maria Cecilia Silva-Díaz is the academic coordinator of the International Master on Children's Books and Literature, organized by the Universitat Autònoma de Barcelona, Spain, and the Banco del Libro, Venezuela, where she also lectures. Previously she worked for the Banco del Libro in Caracas, directing the research department on children's books for a number of years, until she moved to Barcelona for her PhD thesis, which is about metafictional picturebooks. She combines academic lecturing and writing with editing picturebooks in Ediciones Ekaré.

John Stephens is Professor Emeritus at Macquarie University, Australia, a former president of the "International Research Society for Children's Literature," and Foundation Editor of *International Research in Children's Literature*. He is author of over a hundred articles, of *Language and Ideology in*

Children's Fiction (Longman, 1992) and co-author of *Retelling Stories, Framing Culture* (Routledge, 1998) and *New World Orders in Contemporary Children's Literature* (Palgrave Macmillan, 2008). He is editor of *Ways of Being Male: Representing Masculinities in Children's Fiction and Film* (Routledge, 2002), *Subjectivity in Asian Children's Literature and Film* (Routledge, 2012), and *The Routledge Companion to International Children's Literature* (Routledge, 2018). In 2007 he received the International Brothers Grimm Award and in 2013 the Anne Deveraux Jordan Award.

Johanna Tydecks studied General and Comparative Literature, Book Science, and German Language and Literature at the Johannes Gutenberg University in Mainz, Germany, and the Université de Bourgogne in Dijon, France. Her Ph.D. thesis investigates film adaptations of picturebooks. She is currently working as event manager and freelance dramaturge in Basel, Switzerland.

Ilgım Veryeri Alaca is an assistant professor and a practicing artist in the Media and Visual Arts Department at Koc University, Istanbul, Turkey. She recently contributed articles for *The Routledge Companion to International Children's Literature, The Routledge International Handbook of Early Literacy Education, Leonardo Journal*, and *International Journal of Education through Art*.

Jane Wattenberg is an author/artist of photo-illustrated books for children including the photo-montage, hip-hop retelling of *Henny-Penny* (2000), the Children's Choice Award winner *Never Cry Woof!* (2005), and the Baby Board Books *Mrs. Mustard's Baby Faces* (2007) and *Mrs. Mustard's Beastly Babies* (2012). A collector and historian of photo-illustrated books, a beekeeper and urban farmer, she lives in San Francisco, California, USA.

Lukas R. A. Wilde is a post-doc research associate at the Collaborative Research Center 923 "Threatened Order – Societies under Stress" at Tübingen University, Germany. He studied theatre and media studies, Japanese studies and philosophy at the Friedrich-Alexander-University Erlangen-Nürnberg, Germany, and the Gakugei University of Tokyo, Japan. In 2017, he completed a media studies-dissertation on the functions of 'meta-narrative characters' (kyara) within contemporary Japanese society. He is a member of the coordination team of the Comic Studies Board (AG Comicforschung) of the German Society of Media Studies (GfM) and editor for the German Society for Comic Studies (ComFor). His main areas of interest are visual communication, pictorial semiotics, comic book theory, and media theory.

Junko Yokota is the Director of the Center for Teaching through Children's Books and Professor Emeritus at National Louis University, Chicago, USA. Her research focuses on picturebook illustration and translation, multicultural and international literature, and digital storytelling. Her publications include co-authorship of six editions of *Children's Books in Children's Hands* (Pearson, 1997–2018) and numerous journal articles and book chapters. She was a Fulbright Scholar at the University of Wroclaw, Poland.

Terrell A. Young is Professor of Children's Literature at Brigham Young University in Provo, Utah, USA. He is a former president of both the IRA Children's Literature and Reading Special Interest Group and the Children's Literature Assembly of the National Council of Teachers of English. He has served on numerous book award committees including the USBBY Outstanding International Books and the American Folklore Society Aesop Prize.

Marlene Zöhrer is an editorial journalist and consultant for children's literature and media. She regularly holds lectureships for children's literature at the Universities of Munich, Erlangen-Nürnberg, Germany, and Innsbruck, Austria. Her research as well as her journalistic work and educational trainings focus on picturebooks and visual, digital, and transmedia storytelling.

INTRODUCTION

Picturebook research as an international and interdisciplinary field

Bettina Kümmerling-Meibauer

It is widely acknowledged that picturebooks play an important role in the international book market. Every year, innumerable picturebooks are newly released, whose variety of topics, genres, and artistic styles is compelling. Moreover, the picturebook audience has been extended, ranging from infants and preschool children up to children of primary school age, and even including young adolescents and adults. As a result, picturebook artists have developed techniques and strategies that drive the readers' sensations, thoughts, and feelings so that the story line and the intricate picture-text relationship keep them riveted to the page. Many picturebooks are replete with intertextual and interpictorial references to other works of art and incorporate visual codes that are typical of related multimedia art forms, such as artists' books, comics, and movies. Moreover, the picturebook as an art form can look back on a centuries-old history, with precursors in illustrated encyclopedias and picture stories for children. Although they are bound to the specific cultural, political, pedagogical, and aesthetic conditions of their time, some picturebooks convey a universal message, which contributes to their virtual longevity, even when they have vanished from bookshops. They open a window into a bygone era and at the same time surprise the reader by their timelessness and the anticipation of modern ideas. In order to fully grasp these complex relationships and to appreciate the sophisticated combination of text and images, picturebooks demand specific cognitive, linguistic, and aesthetic capacities on the part of the reader. Even picturebooks that seem to be quite simple at first glance reveal an astounding complexity, as is evident in the illustration on this companion book's cover.

What's in a picture?

The illustration shows six children sitting or lying in a meadow, each of them holding an open book in their hands or on their lap. Several items are spread across the meadow: an apple, a pear, two flowers, a basket with cherries, and a singing bird. The reader is able to look at the content of four books. While one has a written text only, three books display pictures of insects, flowers, and geometric figures, accompanied by some text lines. The deciphering of the image's content seems to be easy and apparently does not demand the acquisition of complex visual codes. However, this first impression is misleading for several reasons. First of all, the illustration itself includes visual information that requires a certain aptitude to decode the underlying meaning as well as a prior knowledge of the significance of the artistic style. On closer examination, the unusual depiction of the children, the objects, and the surrounding nature comes to the fore. All the items are presented in a rather abstract manner. The children's faces, hairstyles, and clothes are quite interchangeable. Besides the different colors of their clothes and hair, they have the same facial expression and haircut, and are wearing the same clothes: trousers, a jacket, socks, and loafers. The outlines of their bodies resemble simple geometrical forms, while their rigid postures remind us of wooden puppets. The main part of the background consists of a uniform light green surface. On the upper part of the illustration, a horizontal line delimits the green area from a small plane in light yellow. This visual strategy contributes to the impression of flatness, which is additionally stressed by the representation of the figures and objects. Although they cast shadows on the green surface and the books, the shadows are depicted in such an abstract manner that they evidently do not evoke the impression of central perspective and three-dimensionality.

This description demonstrates that the artist has obviously been inspired by children's drawings. Nevertheless, some details indicate that the illustration deviates from typical drawings created by children – for instance, the unusual depiction of the figures' noses and eyebrows and the use of shadows. As these observations show, the illustration is full of visual codes that have to be deciphered in order to understand their actual meaning. While it is not possible to decide whether the depicted children are boys or girls, only the two flowers and the bird indicate that the green surface can be interpreted as a meadow and not as a carpet in a room with yellow walls. Moreover, this picture presupposes knowledge of pictorial conventions, for instance, that the thin black outlines of the figures and items are not an essential feature of the objects themselves but serve to facilitate the distinction between foreground and background.

In addition, the artistic technique, the color scheme with light pastel colors, and the representation of the figures refer to specific artistic styles that emerged in the arts and in picturebooks in the 1920s. As a counterweight to Art Nouveau, avant-garde artists developed several new artistic movements during and after the First World War, the most relevant being Expressionism, Cubism, and New Realism (*Neue Sachlichkeit* in German). Interestingly, the illustration combines references to New Realism with allusions to Bauhaus. Moreover, like the contemporary artists Lyonel Feininger, Paul Klee, and Pablo Picasso, the artist shows an interest in children's drawings as a source of inspiration.

The artistic style and the pastel color application are the hallmarks of a picturebook artist of that time: Tom Seidmann-Freud (1892–1930), a niece of the famous psychoanalyst Sigmund Freud. Born in Vienna as Martha Gertrud Freud, the artist changed her first name to "Tom" at age 15. In 1920 she married the author Jakob Seidmann, with whom she founded the publishing house Peregrin in Berlin. Among the avant-garde works that came out with this publisher is one of Tom Seidmann-Freud's most famous picturebooks: *Die Fischreise* (1923; published in English as *Peregrin and the Goldfish* in 1929), from which the illustration on the book cover has been taken.

The picturebook story tells of the boy Peregrin, who undertakes a dream journey on the back of his goldfish in order to escape the chaotic and distressful situation in his homeland. He disembarks in an Eden-like country populated by children only. They live in peace together and selflessly contribute to the country's welfare by building houses; cultivating grain, vegetables, and fruits; and by caring for the youngest. On awakening Peregrin realizes that the exciting events he experienced with his goldfish have been a wonderful dream. As a result, he decides to take an active role in promoting a better society for mankind.

On his trip Peregrin comes across the six children in the meadow. As the accompanying text states, the children enjoy reading books, since they are attracted by the beautiful images and the stories, which provide knowledge about the world, tell of bygone historical events, and stimulate the children's imagination. Situated almost in the middle of the book, the doublespread emphasizes that a well-functioning society not only needs to provide food and shelter, but also education and mental stimulus, which find their equivalence in (picture) books.

This message reveals a double meaning when considering the contemporary historical situation in Europe after the First World War. On a superficial level, *Die Fischreise* depicts idyllic scenery as a counterpoint to the destruction and distress which had been caused by the war. As a deeper meaning, the picturebook presents a utopian children's republic which may serve as a model for a future peaceful and harmonious society with equal rights for everybody.

Tom Seidmann-Freud did not live to experience how this idea was thwarted by political develop-ments in the 1930s. During the world economic crisis in 1929, the couple's publishing house went bankrupt. Deeply distraught about the financial situation, Jakob Seidmann committed suicide. As a result, Tom Seidmann-Freud fell seriously ill and finally ended her life in 1930. Because of her Jew-ish descent and the avant-garde style of her artworks, her works were banned by the Nazi regime in 1937. Due to the world political situation, her picturebooks faded into oblivion. However, in the past few years German, English, and French publishers have rediscovered Tom Seidmann-Freud and released re-editions of her most recognized picturebooks, thus promoting these works as an essential part of the cultural heritage for children.

As this overview shows, a quite 'simple' picturebook may encompass artistic, historical, political, interpictorial, and cultural references that open up new ways of looking at the history and theory of the picturebook, thus broadening our knowledge of children's culture and conceptualizations of childhood. Delving deeper into these matters is one of the intriguing issues in picturebook research, which has now become a well-established field.

Picturebook research: perspectives and tendencies

A number of disciplines deal with picturebooks: children's literature research, literary didactics, art history, media studies, linguistics, education, developmental psychology, and picture theory, to name just a few. The increasing interest in this art form has led to the emergence of picturebook research as a special field within the broader discipline of children's literature research. Over nearly five decades, a significant number of academic volumes have addressed essential features of picturebooks, such as the way picturebooks present a realistic view of the world or the way we connect the characters portrayed. While some picturebook researchers have advocated a pedagogical approach as they are particularly interested in what happens when children look attentively at picturebooks and how picturebooks might foster the child's developing literacy skills, others have focused on the history of picturebooks or studied the visual codes implemented in the illustrations and the complex relation-ship between the text and the visuals. Still other scholars have tried to develop a consistent theory of the picturebook by considering theoretical frameworks of picture theory, art history, comic stud-ies, film studies, literacy studies, narratology, and most recently, cognitive studies, to name just a few significant disciplines and theoretical frameworks.

However, one question should be asked at the beginning of a discussion on this art form: what exactly is a picturebook? This is the kind of question that appears simple at first but upon further consideration can be quite controversial. As the term implies, the most significant characteristics are the medium (a book) and the content (pictures). The term does not imply that a picturebook also includes a text, although there is common agreement that picturebooks have both pictures and text. If this holds true, then all books with illustrations might be categorized as picturebooks, which has been disputed among children's literature scholars for a very long time. In actual academic discourse it is common to make a clear distinction between an illustrated book and a picturebook, the former being a book in which the text is more dominant than the illustrations, while the latter usually dis-plays a balance between text and visuals.

This controversy is still mirrored in the different spellings of the term 'picturebook.' While Eng-lish dictionaries clearly state that the notion should be written with two words as 'picture book,' scholars working in the realm of picturebook research suggest writing the term as one word in order to emphasize the inseparable unit of pictures and text. Since the wording 'picture book' evokes the association of a book that includes illustrations, whether an illustrated children's novel, a story collec-tion with images, or a picturebook – an association still observable in reviews and scholarly articles today – there is often confusion about the designation of the picturebook corpus. This becomes even more complicated in other languages, where a specific notion for 'picturebook' does not yet exist. In Spain and Portugal, for instance, the picturebook is still categorized as 'illustrated book' (*livro ilustrado*); that means, a distinction between a picturebook per se and an illustrated children's book is not made. In Spain and in Italy, the terms *libro ilustrado/libro illustrato* and 'album' are used interchangeably. French scholars mostly utilize the notion of 'album,' which indicates a book with images. In an English context, the term 'album' has different meanings: it refers either to a book with private photos (or other collective items) or to a record. In German and the northern European languages, the respective word for 'picturebook' is written as one word, for instance, *Bilderbuch* (Germany), *billedbog* (Denmark), *myndabók* (Iceland), and *bilderbok* (Sweden). However, it can at least be stated for the German context that the notion of *Bilderbuch* – which, according to the famous dictionary (1854ff.) of the Brothers Grimm is a translation of the Latin *liber imaginibus distinctus* – was interchangeably used for broadsheets, pictorial stories, and illustrated books until the beginning of the twentieth century and even later.

These observations point to a discussion which has not yet been fully resolved, but the numerous academic studies on picturebooks have shown that the picturebook in the strict sense of the term exists and presents a vast corpus which is distinguished by a specific relationship between text and visuals. Against this background, and to emphasize the particularities of the picturebook as a unique art form, this companion uses the one-word version, thus following the suggestions by renowned researchers in the field.

The first studies in the realm of picturebook research focused on the history of the picturebook (Doderer and Müller 1973; Bader 1976; Whalley and Chester 1988; Birkeland and Storaas 1993). Issues raised in this regard were the relationship between illustrated books and picturebooks, the history and improvement of printing techniques and their impact on the emergence of the modern picturebook, and the development of the picturebook within a specific country. Since the beginning of the new millennium, several books have followed in the footsteps of these early studies by investigating the history of the picturebook in different cultural contexts (Christensen 2003; Martin 2004; Druker 2008; op de Beeck 2010; Weld 2014; Druker and Kümmerling-Meibauer 2015; Boulaire 2016). Although there are still a lot of blank spots on the international picturebook map, these studies demonstrate that the investigation of the history of the picturebook is a promising undertaking which serves as an eye opener as far as the close connections of the picturebook with contemporary cultural, societal, artistic, and ideological shifts are concerned.

Picturebook theory experienced an upswing in the 1980s with the studies by Joseph Schwarcz (1982), Joseph Schwarcz and Chava Schwarcz (1988), and Perry Nodelman (1988), which have been complemented by the monographs of Ulla Rhedin (1993), Jane Doonan (1993), Barbara Kiefer (1995), Jens Thiele (2000), David Lewis (2001), and Maria Nikolajeva and Carole Scott (2001), among others. In this period, the notion of picture as an own aesthetic category as well as the significance of the symbolic meaning of text and image came to the fore. From the beginning, a core issue has occupied all scholarly investigations, namely the complex relationship between text and images. Based on actual debates in academia, quite different classifications have been developed in order to elucidate the multifarious aspects involved in the process of comprehending the meaning of the picturebook story.

The pleasures as well as the learning processes evoked by picturebooks have been addressed in book-length studies, edited volumes, and journal articles, whereby scholars from different disciplines have discovered the crucial role of the picturebook in the child's developing cognitive, linguistic, moral, and aesthetic capacities. In this regard, cutting-edge research has been done by scholars focusing on reader-response theory, who have called attention to the significance of reading picturebook stories aloud for the child's linguistic and cognitive development (Evans 1998, 2009; Arizpe and Styles 2003 [rev. 2016]). Other researchers have elaborated on these ideas and emphasized the impact of picturebooks on language acquisition and visual literacy as well as literary literacy (Kümmerling-Meibauer 2011; Kümmerling-Meibauer et al. 2015). These approaches highlight that children experience picturebooks, and that it is vitally important to understand as precisely as possible how children get involved as they jointly look at picturebooks. This is one of the crucial questions that have motivated the inclusion of cognitive studies in the realm of picturebook research. While this auspicious approach is still in its fledgling state, this orientation in contemporary scholarly discussions has led to an increasing interest in the narratological and aesthetic aspects of the picturebook (van der Linden 2007; Zaparaín and González 2010; Salisbury and Styles 2012; Kümmerling-Meibauer 2014). Grounded in semiotics and picture theory, the concept of visual narration has fertilized picturebook research to a considerable degree. This strand is strongly connected to the theoretical framework of multimodal analysis, initially developed by Gunther Kress and Theo van Leeuwen (1996) and further elaborated by the recent studies of Clare Painter, James R. Martin, and Len Unsworth (2013), John Bateman (2014), and Arsenio Jesús Moya Guijarro (2014).

No matter whether it concerns the increasing sophistication of the (post)modern picturebook (Sipe and Pantaleo 2008; Allan 2012), the double address of complex and boundary-crossing picturebooks (Beckett 2012), or even challenging and controversially discussed picturebooks (Evans 2015), the exploration of picturebooks proffers a multitude of potential approaches, as has been testified by numerous conference proceedings and edited volumes (Thiele 2007; Connan-Pinado et al. 2008; Colomer et al. 2010; Arizpe et al. 2013; Ommundsen 2013; Hamer, Nodelman and Reimer 2017). This condensed overview is far from complete, but gives a first insight into the variety and demanding scientific issues of current picturebook research.

Aims of this volume

This companion provides a critical survey of what is going on and what has already been done in international picturebook research by highlighting key ideas, significant terms, and current debates as well as drawing attention to new directions in which the study of picturebooks may expand. Consequently, the focus of this companion is exclusively theoretical; therefore chapters on the history of picturebooks in general and in diverse countries and regions in particular cannot be found – this would demand a totally different conceptualization and goes beyond the scope of this companion. In order to meet the internationality of the topic, the literature under consideration is transnational; the chapters explore a wide range of picturebooks from European as well as non-European countries. Moreover, the contributors to this companion – which include children's literature scholars, psychologists, art historians, linguists, educationalists, film scholars, and media scholars – come from various nations in Europe as well as North America, Asia, and Australia. The different kinds of writing should highlight the fact that there are different types of theoretical approaches being taken in the field of picturebook research, which contribute to the variety of attitudes and frameworks. The proximity of the entries in this volume creates interfaces between comparable frameworks, so that there are implicit dialogues between the chapters even though the contributors do not address each other explicitly.

The chapters to follow will elaborate and expand upon these and other issues. The companion is divided into five parts, each of which addresses a specific theme connected to the analysis of picturebooks. The first part focuses on the major concepts and key topics that have been discussed in picturebook research and which are essential for a better understanding of how picturebooks work. Starting with a chapter on the complex issue of the 'author-illustrator,' this section elaborates on subjects such as hybridity, interpictoriality, metafiction, paratext, and seriality, which shed new light on the often sophisticated level of the modern picturebook. Other entries concentrate on the material aspects of the picturebook by addressing the layout, montage, and collage as artistic devices, and materiality as a theoretical concept. One chapter is devoted to the fundamental issue of the relationship between text and visuals, while other chapters focus on cognitive, cultural, and ideological topics which influence the views, production, and reception of picturebooks – for instance, the depiction of emotions in picturebooks, the significance of gender issues, the impact of canon processes on the evaluation of picturebooks, and how ideological attitudes directly or subliminally affect the content and interpretation of picturebooks.

The second part introduces different picturebook categories, beginning with early-concept books and concept books, which are usually regarded as the first picturebooks very young children come in contact with. Also targeted at young children is the wimmelbook, a specific textless picturebook category which has experienced phenomenal success since the 1960s, while the ABC book can look back on a century-long tradition and a fascinating shift from instruction books to playful and typographically challenging picturebooks. The same applies to movable and pop-up books, whose emergence and artistic changes cannot be understood without a consideration of the evolving printing techniques. Wordless picturebooks address all age groups, from infants up to primary school and teenage readers, which is a reason for this picturebook category's broad range of themes and genres. The entry on postmodern picturebooks emphasizes the shifts in the picturebook medium since the 1990s, whereas the ensuing entries on crossover picturebooks and picturebooks for adults focus on the significant observation that picturebooks are not targeted at children only, but increasingly address young adults and grown-ups alike. The category of informational picturebook emphasizes the historical as well as the theoretical significance of non-fiction picturebooks, which has been mostly disregarded in previous research. Poetry in picturebooks is likewise a marginally investigated issue, although a vast number of picturebooks have texts written in rhyme or illustrate poems by renowned authors. Another chapter pays tribute to the growing interest in multilingual picturebooks due to the global shifts and the major migration waves all over the world. The rise of new technologies and digital media, finally, has initiated the emergence of digital picturebooks, which have already left their mark on the international book market.

The third part focuses on the interfaces between picturebooks and related art forms. As unique as picturebooks are as an art form, they have evolved from earlier traditions, most notably illustrated children's books. It is precisely for this reason that both art forms partially overlap, as is reflected in the somewhat confusing terminology still prevalent in different countries. Another entry investigates the close relationship between picturebooks and artists' books, since both art forms share a number of commonalities, including the fact that several renowned illustrators have created artwork in both realms. Since the invention of photography in the middle of the nineteenth century, picturebook artists have used this new medium as a specific means of expression, which has ultimately led to a vast production of photobooks for children, ranging from early-concept books and informational picturebooks to sophisticated artistic photobooks inspired by avant-garde movements. Comics and movies have frequently been an inspiration source for picturebook artists, thus calling attention to the tight connection between these different art forms and how comics and movies are contributing to the renewal of the picturebook. Two different chapters therefore discuss the influence of comics and movies on the artistic style, the page layout, the use of different perspectives and narrative voices, and the pacing of the story of picturebooks.

The fourth part deals with different theoretical frameworks and disciplines that focus on the analysis of picturebooks. The first domain covered in this part is the education of prospective picturebook artists, thus complementing the otherwise more theoretically focused chapters that follow. Since picturebook research emerged as a special field of study from children's literature research, one chapter reflects on the complex relationship between these two domains. Another significant framework is childhood studies, which provides new insights into the images of childhood represented in picturebooks. The chapters on literacy studies, developmental psychology, cognitive studies, and linguistics are linked to each other as they deal with the developmental processes that govern the child's understanding of picturebooks. These processes touch on cognitive, emotional, linguistic, and aesthetic matters, which form an indivisible unit when it comes to the attentive reading of picturebooks. This approach is complemented by a chapter that highlights the significance of narratology as a discipline that investigates the inherent narrative strategies on both the textual and the visual level. In recent years, the framework of multimodal analysis, which draws on semiotics as well as the linguistic and narrative analysis of picturebooks, has taken center stage and is therefore addressed in a separate chapter. Art history and picture theory mainly focus on the analysis of the visuals. While picture theory offers essential insights into the fundamental question of how pictures represent meaning via visual codes and the arrangement of visual elements, art history investigates the impact of art movements and specific artistic techniques on the picturebook. The chapter on media studies highlights the multiple remediation processes picturebooks are subjected to and also discusses the increasing effect of transmedia products on the conceptualization of picturebooks. The final chapter in this section – written from the perspective of translation studies – deals with the difficulties translators face with regard to picturebooks, since they have to respect the intricate text-picture relationship.

The final part of the book addresses adaptations and remediations of picturebooks. Fairy tales have been and still are prominent templates for picturebooks, whose illustrations add new meanings to the original story. A quite new tendency is the re-launch of world classics which were originally written for an adult audience in a picturebook format. Whether it concerns fairy tales or world literature, the adjustment to the design of a picturebook demands considerable changes to the original text in multiple respects. The related questions of the possible higher quality and authenticity of the source text are also relevant when it comes to remediation processes. The film adaptations of popular picturebooks are becoming increasingly important in a global media market, in which the printed book is just one medium among many. Moreover, this trend has led to the immersion of picturebooks in the merchandising industry, which increasingly influences the international reception and perception of picturebooks.

As this overview illustrates, picturebooks have become an indispensable part of our modern society. They are omnipresent in institutions, such as libraries, kindergartens, and schools, and in home settings, they are available in different media formats, and they appeal to all age groups. As a multimodal art form, the picturebook is attractive for many academic disciplines and theoretical frameworks. Whether the focus of interest is more historically or theoretically based, the picturebook reveals so many facets of possible scientific issues that it demands a field of its own. Picturebook research is a fast-growing discipline, which surely contributes to a better understanding of how picturebooks work and why they are so appealing to children and adults alike. Many words about pictures and texts in picturebooks have been written; many more words need to be written to gain insight into the multifaceted components and aspects that constitute the uniqueness of the picturebook. The chapters gathered in this volume testify to the coming-of-age of picturebook research by discussing the major achievements, current advances, and the state of research, but they also point out potential future directions, thus hopefully paving the way for further innovative studies in this significant and promising field.

References

Allan, Cherie (2012) *Playing with Picturebooks: Postmodernism and the Postmodernesque*, Basingstoke: Palgrave Macmillan.

Arizpe, Evelyn, Farrell, Maureen, and McAdam, Julie (eds) (2013) *Picturebooks: Beyond the Borders of Art, Narrative, and Culture*, New York: Routledge.

Arizpe, Evelyn, and Styles, Morag (2016) *Children Reading Picturebooks: Interpreting Visual Texts*, rev. ed., London: Routledge (first published 2003).

Bader, Barbara (1976) *American Picturebooks from Noah's Ark to the Beast Within*, New York: Macmillan.

Bateman, John A. (2014) *Text and Image. A Critical Introduction to the Visual/Verbal Divide*, New York: Routledge.

Beckett, Sandra L. (2012) *Crossover Picturebooks: A Genre for All Ages*, New York: Routledge.

Birkeland, Tone, and Storaas, Frøydis (1993) *Den norske biletboka*, Oslo: J.W. Cappelens Forlag.

Boulaire, Cécile (2016) *Les petits livres d'or: Des albums pour enfants dans la France de la guerre froide*, Tours: Presses Universitaires François Rabelais.

Christensen, Nina (2003) *Den danske billedbog 1950–1999: Teori, analyse, historie*, Frederiksberg: Center for Børnelitteratur/Roskilde Universitetsforlag.

Colomer, Teresa, Kümmerling-Meibauer, Bettina, and Silva-Díaz, Cecilia (eds) (2010) *New Directions in Picturebook Research*, New York: Routledge.

Connan-Pintado, Christiane, Gaiotti, Florence, and Poulou, Bernadette (eds) (2008) *L'album contemporain pour la jeunesse: nouvelles forms, nouveaux lecteurs?* Bordeaux: Presses Universitaires de Bordeaux.
Doderer, Klaus, and Müller, Helmut (1973) *Das Bilderbuch*, Weinheim: Beltz.
Doonan, Jane (1993) *Looking at Pictures in Picture Books*, Stroud: Thimble Press.
Druker, Elina (2008) *Modernismens bilder: Den moderna bilderboken i Norden*, Stockholm: Makadam.
Druker, Elina, and Kümmerling-Meibauer, Bettina (eds) (2015) *Children's Literature and the Avant-Garde*, Amsterdam: John Benjamins.
Evans, Janet (ed.) (1998) *What's in the Picture? Responding to Illustrations in Picture Books*, London: Paul Chapman.
Evans, Janet (ed.) (2009) *Talking Beyond the Page: Reading and Responding to Picturebooks*, London: Routledge.
Evans, Janet (ed.) (2015) *Challenging and Controversial Picturebooks: Creative and Critical Responses to Visual Texts*, London: Routledge.
Grimm, Jacob, and Grimm, Wilhelm (1854ff.) *Deutsches Wörterbuch*, Leipzig: Hirzel.
Guijarro, Arsenio Jesús Moya (2014) *A Multimodal Analysis of Picture Books for Children*, Sheffield: Equinox.
Hamer, Naomi, Nodelman, Perry, and Reimer, Mavis (eds) (2017) *More Words about Pictures: Current Research on Picture Books and Visual/Verbal Texts for Young People*, New York: Routledge.
Kiefer, Barbara (1995) *The Potential of Picturebooks: From Visual Literacy to Aesthetic Understanding*, Englewood Cliffs, NJ: Merrill Prentice Hall.
Kress, Gunther, and van Leeuwen, Theo (1996) *Reading Images: The Grammar of Visual Design*, London: Routledge.
Kümmerling-Meibauer, Bettina (ed.) (2011) *Emergent Literacy: Children's Books from 0 to 3*, Amsterdam: John Benjamins.
Kümmerling-Meibauer, Bettina (ed.) (2014) *Picturebooks: Representation and Narration*, New York: Routledge.
Kümmerling-Meibauer, Bettina, Meibauer, Jörg, Nachtigäller, Kerstin, and Rohlfing, Katharina (eds) (2015) *Learning from Picturebooks: Perspectives from Child Development and Literacy Studies*, New York: Routledge.
Lewis, David (2001) *Reading Contemporary Picturebooks: Picturing Text*, London: RoutledgeFalmer.
Martin, Michelle (2004) *Brown Gold: Milestones of African-American Children's Picture Books, 1845–2002*, New York: Routledge.
Nikolajeva, Maria, and Scott, Carole (2001) *How Picturebooks Work*, New York: Garland.
Nodelman, Perry (1988) *Words about Pictures: The Narrative Art of Children's Picture Books*, Athens: University of Georgia Press.
Ommundsen, Åse Marie (ed.) (2013) *Looking Out and Looking In: National Identity in Picturebooks of the New Millennium*, Oslo: Novus Press.
op de Beeck, Nathalie (2010) *Suspended Animation: Children's Picture Books and the Fairy Tale of Modernity*, Minneapolis: University of Minnesota Press.
Painter, Clare, Martin, James R., and Unsworth, Len (2013) *Reading Visual Narratives: Image Analysis of Children's Picture Books*, Sheffield: Equinox.
Rhedin, Ulla (1993) *Bilderboken: På väg mot en teori*, Stockholm: Alfabeta.
Salisbury, Martin, and Styles, Morag (2012) *Children's Picturebooks: The Art of Visual Storytelling*, London: Laurence King.
Schwarcz, Joseph (1982) *Ways of the Illustrator: Visual Communication in Children's Literature*, Chicago: American Library Association.
Schwarcz, Joseph, and Schwarcz, Chava (1988) *The Picture Book Comes of Age: Looking at Childhood Through the Art of Illustration*, Chicago: American Library Association.
Seidmann-Freud, Tom (1923) *Die Fischreise*, Berlin: Peregrin [*Peregrin and the Goldfish*, New York: Macmillan, 1929].
Sipe, Lawrence R., and Pantaleo, Sylvia (eds) (2008) *Postmodern Picturebooks: Play, Parody, and Self-Referentiality*, New York: Routledge.
Thiele, Jens (2000) *Das Bilderbuch: Ästhetik, Theorie, Analyse, Didaktik, Rezeption*, Oldenburg: Isensee.
Thiele, Jens (ed.) (2007) *Neue Impulse der Bilderbuchforschung*, Baltmannsweiler: Schneider Verlag Hohengehren.
van der Linden, Sophie (2007) *Lire l'album*, Le Puy-en-Velay: L'Atelier du poisson soluble.
Weld, Sara Pankenier (2014) *Voiceless Vanguard: The Infantilist Aesthetics of the Russian Avant-Garde*, Evanston, IL: Northwestern University Press.
Whalley, Joyce Irene, and Chester, Tessa Rose (1988) *A History of Children's Book Illustration*, London: John Murray with the Victoria & Albert Museum.
Zaparaín, Fernando, and González, Luis Daniel (2010) *Cruce de caminos: Albumes ilustrados: Construcción y lectura*, Valladolid: Ediciones de la Universidad de Castilla-la-Mancha.

PART I

Concepts and topics

1

AUTHOR-ILLUSTRATOR

Kerry Mallan

The concern of this chapter is not with the process of writing and illustrating a picturebook but with the concept of 'author-illustrator.' In exploring this concept I draw on two key texts – Roland Barthes's "The Death of the Author" (1968) and Michel Foucault's "What Is an Author?" (1969) – to examine the question of 'authorship' in its broadest sense, and to consider how the concept of author-illustrator can contribute to these discussions, especially at a time when author-illustrators need to participate in a wide range of public media spaces for their professional and artistic survival.

In the decades since "The Death of the Author" and "What Is an Author?" first appeared, the world has become more market driven and digitally sophisticated, changing how texts are written, illustrated, published, distributed, and transformed. Evolving digital technologies and software platforms are changing notions of the text, authorship, and reader-text interaction. In tandem with these digital transformations and spaces, publishers are also finding new ways to not only promote their authors in the public media but also brand their products (including their authors), and sell licenses of their books/book characters to toy, clothing, game, film, and DVD companies (see Hade and Edmondson 2003). All of these activities paradoxically reinscribe and erase the author in multiple ways.

Barthes's controversial essay "The Death of the Author" shifted attention away from the 'Author-God,' the creative genius who passed on truths that needed clever readers to uncover. For Barthes, the author did not exist once the work had moved into the public sphere. In his view, this removal or 'death' of the author created a space where readers were free to make their own meanings: "a text's unity lies not in its origin but in its destination" (1977: 148). Furthermore, each new reading of a text would elicit different meanings and significations. In raising the reader above the author, Barthes was challenging the idea of the 'authority' of the author that had long been interpreted as authorial intention. Readers were no longer expected to regard authorial intention as the true meaning of a text, but were now, in a sense, authors in their own right. In debunking the idea of the capital-A 'Author,' and revising the idea of authorship, Barthes also brought to readers' attention the processes that often were invisible in the creation of a text (such as consultation, collaboration, editing, layout, and design).

Foucault's response to Barthes argued that the idea of the death of the author and the killing of his or her 'authority' did not take account of the fact that the world is driven by cultural production and market forces; however, Barthes was well aware of "an increasingly *multi*mediated artistic culture" (Allen 2004: 495, emphasis original). Foucault's point was that authors and their books are commodities and the author's name performs a role both in the circulation and reception of texts and in narrative discourse (1998: 210). Rather than disappearing, Foucault felt that the author "seems always to be present, marking off the edges of the text, revealing, or at least characterizing, its mode of being" (211). Foucault suggested that the 'author-function' could be just as important in understanding texts as anything else.

I turn now to revisiting notions of author-illustrator as a way of examining how this dual identity has come to be understood and perpetuated in different contexts. I will then consider some of the key issues that arise from the work of Barthes and Foucault for this chapter, namely, the irony of the death of the author and changing notions of authorship and readers, and how a multimedia public sphere contributes to the evolving notion of author-illustrator.

What is an author-illustrator?

A simple answer to the question posed in this section's heading is that the designation 'author-illustrator' embodies an individual who writes and illustrates with equal or varying proficiencies of skill, creativity, and ingenuity. Achieving this dual identity for some comes after years of working in a different artistic field (for example, Eric Carle was formerly a commercial artist) or after illustrating other authors' works. Many author-illustrators continue to illustrate texts other than their own long after they have been successful in writing and illustrating their own books. Thus, the designation of author-illustrator is somewhat fluid as it is not necessarily a fixed attribution; nor is it unproblematic, especially when it is understood within a wider cultural context.

The designation 'author-illustrator' suggests an implied hierarchy – the elevation of writing over illustrating. How this designation appears on the cover and title page contributes to a tradition of unease between the verbal and the visual that dates back to Horace's famous observation: *Ut pictura poesis* ("as in painting, so is poetry") in his *Ars Poetica* (19–10 BC). Rather than, as Horace suggested, that the visual (painting) is prioritized over the verbal (poetry), subsequent debate continues to argue whether or not the verbal is the master discourse and the visual is subservient (Hay 2006: 51f.). This uneasy dialectic can be seen as continuing in picturebooks where the order and description of the attributions can appear on the cover and title page as: "written and illustrated by"; "words by [. . .] and pictures by [. . .]"; "by [. . .] illustrated by [. . .]." Rarely, if ever, is the reverse order given. This matter is of course not relevant when it is one person who assumes the role of author-illustrator (or illustrator-author). In the case of Dutch writer and illustrator Ted Van Lieshout, his diverse works include picturebooks, books for early readers, novels for children and young adults, poems, song lyrics, and television scripts. Illustration is integral to his work, so much so that even his collections of poems have been called "poetry picture books" (Duijx and Van Lierop-Debrauwer 2014: 96), which we could see as befitting Horace's *Ut pictura poesis*.

The placement of the author before the illustrator may seem to imply the dominance of the word over the image, but even taken as separate terms, 'author' is afforded a particular form of cultural capital which is implicit in how Sandywell defines 'author' as being 'typically' associated with the verbal: "the seminal point of origin, originator, producer, composer or efficient cause of anything, typically of a written text" (2011: 161). In a world where the image and visual forms of knowledge are produced and consumed with increasing voracity, the written text is perhaps becoming less typical as the source of authorship. The problem is complicated when one considers that the verbal medium is the predominant mode of critical and analytical discussions about art, literature, and indeed, picturebooks. It may simply be a case of established orthodoxy whereby the 'artist' as a composite term is variously defined and classified according to institutional or elitist criteria (for instance, publishers' or literary awards and funding for the arts). While we can see writers, illustrators, musicians, and performers coming under the category of artist, author-illustrators remain a specialized sub-group that seems to elide consideration outside of the world of children's literature.

Words and images are integral to the unity of the picturebook, as each brings together different semiotic structures that have different traditions, methods, and histories. How an author-illustrator develops a picturebook – from a written outline or a storyboard – is part of the idiosyncratic creative/artistic process. While the idea of an individual who functions as author and illustrator would seem to solve any problems where a text is let down by poor or inappropriate illustrations (or vice versa), there is no guarantee that the result will be always better than one that was produced collaboratively between an author and an illustrator (or between multiple authors and illustrators). However, some picturebooks are produced with little or no collaboration, with the publisher assigning an illustrator to undertake the illustrations. A lack of collaboration or teamwork can result in what Nikolajeva and Scott see as a "mismatch of text and image" (2006: 30). There are, of course, many examples of compatibility of text and image through successful collaborations such as Jon Scieszka and Lane Smith (*The Stinky Cheese Man and Other Fairly Stupid Tales* 1992); Allan Ahlberg and Janet Ahlberg (*The Jolly Postman* 1986); Libby Hathorn and Gregory Rogers (*Way Home* 1994). In the case of book awards, such as the CILIP Kate Greenaway Medal for "an outstanding book in terms of illustration for children and young people," the visual is prioritized, but the criteria for selection includes "a synergy of illustration and text" (www.carnegiegreenaway.org.uk), a point which addresses the 'mismatch' concern of Nikolajeva and Scott.

While some author-illustrators prefer to create this synergy of illustration and text in a state of solitariness, at some stage of the process others provide input. As Lawrence Sipe quite rightly says, a picturebook is the result of a process that involves multiple people including editors, designers, and technical experts (2011: 239). We could add to this list family, friends, and colleagues; even students provide ideas and advice on works in progress during author visits to schools, or in some instances, children and communities are credited as co-creators. For example, the picturebook *Going Bush* (2007) is a collaboration between Australian author Nadia Wheatley and illustrator Ken Searle along with sixteen students from eight schools across Sydney. The text showcases and credits some of the writing and illustrations made by the students, which are linked together by Searle who assumed artistic and design control, and Wheatley provided the narrative. Consequently, any text, no matter its provenance, is always co-created and mediated regardless of whether it is credited to a single author-illustrator or not.

This multiple input into the creation of a picturebook not only raises questions about ownership but also impacts on interpretation. For Nikolajeva and Scott, it also raises the matter of multiple intentionality which they consider could lead to "ambiguity and uncertainty" (2006: 29). The following discussion considers the complexity of authorship – single, dual, and multiple – in relation to the essays by Barthes and Foucault.

The author is (not) dead

As this section's heading implies, there is a certain paradox or irony that operates in the now familiar phrase 'the author is dead' when one considers how popular authors today are marketed in order to ensure that they are very much 'alive' in the eyes of the reader/book buyer, even if they have indeed died (the enduring popularity of the author Astrid Lindgren or author-illustrator Maurice Sendak long after their deaths are cases in point). Harold Love (2002: 7) points to another irony, in that writers, such as Barthes and Foucault, in asserting the death of the author were at the same time asserting their own 'heroic authorship' even in their questioning of it.

Barthes's metaphorical killing of the author attacked the modern tendency to treat authors as cultural icons, yet authors (including author-illustrators) continue to be marketed as celebrities with special book readings and school visits, ensuring that children can not only meet flesh and blood authors but also read/buy their books. Changing approaches to literacy teaching in schools have also encouraged children to become familiar with popular authors and illustrators, their works, their creative process, and even details of their personal lives. This process of author recognition or familiarity extends beyond the classroom and is aided by robust, distributive marketing strategies by publishers, as well as interest in authors at children's literature conferences, book signings, writers' festivals, and other cultural activities.

Central to Barthes's argument was that the death of the author, where the meaning of text was once no longer seen as controlled by the author, gave rise to the "birth of the reader" (1977: 148).

Without being limited by the biographical substance of the author or the idea of the author as authority figure or cultural hero, the reader, for Barthes, was free to be creative, to actively engage in the production of textual meaning. Young readers may be unaware of, or disinterested in, Barthes's capital-A 'Authors' (or indeed, 'Author-Illustrators'), but may readily participate in the creative co-production of meaning, interpretation, and appropriation of texts for their own purposes and enjoyment. Teachers, librarians, and other adults often encourage children's playful engagement with texts, and the part that postmodern or interactive texts play in encouraging reader participation or co-creation cannot be underestimated.

This form of reader-text interaction, however, is similar to Foucault's idea that writing itself is like a game (*jeu*) whereby rules and limits are transgressed, in order to create a space into which the author (or writing subject) disappears (1998: 206). In playing these writing and illustrating games, the 'author' of the source text disappears as new authors and illustrators create their own texts which in turn are the basis for further playful disruption, imitation, and redesign. Foucault's point is that writing is often seen as something completed by an author, rather than something that is a process or a practice that is constantly revised, edited, and appropriated.

Very young children are also offered opportunities for a different kind of playful engagement with books that feature inventive moveable parts (such as Jan Pieńkowski's *Dinner Time* (1980), produce light as in Eric Carle's *The Very Lonely Firefly* (1995), and sounds as in *Ocean* (2008) from Maurice Pledger's 'Sounds of the Wild' series of picturebooks), encouraging a multisensory exploration. This attention to the materiality of the text not only accentuates what Bettina Kümmerling-Meibauer sees as "the production process and the physical character of the book itself" (2015: 252), but also exploits the multimodal possibilities of the picturebook as a stimulus for reader interaction. This kind of multimodal artistic product is similar to the multimedia artistic culture that Barthes had in mind at the time of his writing. Allen (2004: 495) explains that Barthes chose to publish 'The Death' in an art magazine (*5+6 of Aspen: The Magazine in a Box*), where each issue was published in a box which included contributions in the form of posters, postcards, photographs, phonograph recordings, games, and among other objects, John Lennon's 'pocket diary of the future.' These various forms of reader engagement as game player, author, and illustrator demonstrate Barthes's birth of the reader and the seeming disappearance of the author, yet the paradox of the death of the author continues.

In the global marketplace, not only does the author's name become part of the brand to be promoted and sold, but also the work, or in some instances, the character (Clarice Bean, Madeline, Spot) displaces its author creator (Lauren Child, Ludwig Bemelmans, Eric Hill), achieving its own cultural status. Digital platforms and public media bring the text to an ever-eager consumer market that delights in novelty, nostalgia, and buying merchandise. As Hade and Edmondson point out, "the book, each spin-off piece of merchandise, and each retelling across another medium becomes a promotion for every other product based upon that story" (2003: 139).

Another promotional avenue of a text is through national and international book awards. Picturebook awards such as the Caldecott Medal, the CILIP Kate Greenaway Medal, Children's Book Council of Australia Picture Book of the Year, Feng Zikai Chinese Children's Picture Book Award, and many others not only ensure financial return for the publisher but, as Smith (2013) notes, when a book is awarded the Caldecott Medal, the 'Caldecott effect' has been significant in terms of career success for many illustrators (or author-illustrators). The iconic gold or silver sticker on the winning medal or honor books signifies the text's artistic standing in a highly competitive field, but its recognition as a marker of 'quality' is not always noticed by the intended readership, as Lisa Dennis, coordinator of Children's Collections at the Carnegie Library of Pittsburgh, observes: "Preschoolers tend to just like the shiny sticker, but of course their parents generally like the idea that the books are award winners" (cited in Smith 2013: 10). Awards may make the author-illustrator disappear and elevate the text, or the converse may be equally true; either way, a complex network of external sources and relations work together to shape the existence of the author-illustrator and the reception and dissemination of his/her works.

In examining the paradox that accompanies the death of the author, other ideas that Foucault raises, such as 'author-function' and 'the work' (*oeuvre*), which are intended to replace the privileged position of the author, may actually preserve it. As the following section illustrates, these ideas have relevance for understanding the concept of author-illustrator, especially in terms of multimedia publishing and the spin-off industry of children's literature.

What's in a name?

Does it matter who wrote/illustrated a picturebook? It is probably safe to say that for many children and adults there is an indifference towards the question of authorship. However, there is probably a corresponding number of others for whom there is a deal of interest in such matters of a text's creator(s). Regardless of any perceived ambivalence as to a text's authorship, the name of the author (or author-illustrator) continues to occupy a discursive space in children's literature publishing, criticism, and reception. Having the name of the author on the cover and title page enacts Foucault's 'author-function.'

For Foucault, an author's name "performs a certain role with regard to narrative discourse, assuring a classificatory function" (1998: 210). A classificatory function of author-illustrator might work at one level of recognition for individuals such as Allen Say, Colin Thompson, or Jeannie Baker, for whom we could classify respectively as the author-illustrator of picturebooks that explore Asian American identity, the author-illustrator of quirky picturebooks, or the author-illustrator who uses collage to create picturebooks about ecological issues. But these classifications are only superficial and do not convey the complexity and diversity of their works and other aspects of their creative output. (For example, Baker directs animated films of her books, and Thompson collaborates with other illustrators on a wide range of subjects.)

The classificatory function, according to Foucault, means that a 'name' enables one to group a number of texts together, define them, and differentiate them from others, thereby establishing a relationship among the texts and their multiple spin-offs. While many author-illustrators experiment with different literary and illustrative styles and subject matter, it is not only the name of the individual on the book cover that connects these different texts, but the works themselves always contain a number of signs referring to its creator. These might be the particular style of writing and illustrating, such as that used by Beatrix Potter that distinguishes her work from those that bear a close resemblance, such as Alison Uttley's *Little Grey Rabbit* series (1929–1973), illustrated by Margaret Tempest. However, the name 'Beatrix Potter' is not only identified with her characters or picturebooks, but her *oeuvre* carries over into merchandise (crockery, clothing, toys), a BBC dramatization of her life, a biopic, a ballet film (*The Tales of Beatrix Potter*, 1971), and her home, Hill Top Farm, which is open to the public. In these instances of enduring interest in the name, one could argue that the classificatory system breaks down or at least creates further classifications.

Brian Selznick's *The Invention of Hugo Cabret* (2007) is an example of how a classificatory system can also alter how a text such as a picturebook is defined as well as the notion of an author-illustrator. *The Invention of Hugo Cabret* breaches the conventions of picturebooks in terms of length (in this case, over five hundred pages instead of the standard thirty-two pages), yet it clearly shows the 'synergy' between image and text that is often a criterion for awards such as the Caldecott Medal, which this book won in 2008. Selznick's metacommentary, *The Hugo Movie Companion*, on his book's origins and its development from book to 3-D film with Martin Scorsese provides a further instance of a disruptive classificatory function, as Selznick's name participates in both print and filmmaking cultures. In Foucault's view, the author can be viewed as a function emerging from within multiplying technological, social, and cultural sites.

This circulating author-function also points to the fact that the author has become a brand name in a consumer market. While children may readily accept the name of the author-illustrator as it is written on the text (for instance, Dr. Seuss), older readers and critics may enjoy the game of discovering the real name of the author that the pseudonym displaces or disguises. In the case of the author Lemony Snicket, his official website makes no mention of Daniel Handler (his real name) but perpetuates and gives a truth to the pseudonym. By contrast, Dr. Seuss's website, which is similarly playful and interactive as Snicket's, offers visitors the opportunity to find out about Theodor Seuss Geisel, the name behind the pseudonym, through the 'Bio' window.

In some cases, the name of the author functions long after their (real) death. For example, the Seussville site (www.seussville.com/) in June 2015 announced the 100-day countdown to "A newer-than-new/New Dr. Seuss book!" The "never-ever-before-seen picture book by Dr. Seuss" is "told in Dr. Seuss's signature rhyming style." By imitating or appropriating the style of writing and illustrating that made the name of Dr. Seuss famous, this new text (and others that have been produced after his death in 1991) reinforce the concept of author, as Foucault notes, by the signs (in this instance, specific poetic meters, cartoon-style illustration, humor) that refer to the author. The fact that the author of the latest book is not Theodor Seuss Geisel is of little consequence as it is 'Dr. Seuss' who has enabled the possibilities for the formation of other texts that share the same characteristic signs, grammatical structures, and rhyming patterns that were established by the figure we know as the author. It also points to the fact that the author has become a brand name in a consumer market. He may be dead (literally and metaphorically), but Dr. Seuss's works live on, and the perpetuation of his name as 'author' have resulted in an excess that goes beyond the author figure, and one that the Seussville site flaunts.

Seussville serves as an example of multiple or collaborative authorship whereby unknown writers, editors, designers, illustrators, and web developers work to create and recreate the Dr. Seuss brand. A further point that can be made about this kind of collaborative authorship is that of the precursory author, someone who Love (2002) proposes is the source of the ideas and style of writing. We could see Theodor Seuss Geisel fulfilling this role of precursory author as the Dr. Seuss books (and posters, greeting cards, clothing, theme park, animations, and movies) created after his death appropriate and imitate his literary and visual style. However, the invisible 'authors' of the Dr. Seuss books and Seussville are also collectively part of the precursory authorship. I raise this point to highlight the complexity and indebtedness that attend the creation of a text (both print and digital) that draws on multiple sources and talents. Even Theodor Seuss Geisel borrowed from precursory authors in his use of poetic meter (anapestic tetrameter and trochaic meter were popular with many early English poets and playwrights such as Shakespeare). As Mensch and Freeman (1987) point out, the magicians chanting "shuffle, duffle, muzzle, muff" in *Bartholomew and the Oobleck* (1949) resembles the witches' chant in Shakespeare's *Macbeth* (ca. 1606).

A further example of Foucault's author-function occurs with Babar the elephant, a series of stories beginning with *Histoire de Babar, le petit éléphant* (*The Story of Babar, the Little Elephant* 1931), which is attributed to the author-illustrator Jean de Brunhoff, but was first created by his wife Cécile as a bedtime story for their children. After De Brunhoff's death, his son Laurent studied art under the same teacher as his father, and eventually continued to write and illustrate his own Babar stories using the style his father had developed. These stories, originally published in French, were translated into English, bringing a further collaborative authorship into play with the translator. Prior to writing his own Babar stories, Laurent, as a teenager, contributed to the works by coloring some of the pages of his father's books which he had left in black and white (Malarte-Feldman 2006). After his father's death, some of the titles carry the name Jean de Brunhoff, while others are under Laurent de Brunhoff. These declarations of the 'author' announce the owner or creator of the work, and part of the author-function in being named as the author is that one not only benefits from the work (royalties and prestige), but also shoulders the responsibilities (author rights, criticisms, and reviews).

In addition to being a collective creation of a digital persona, author websites also function as play spaces where children can answer quizzes, discover personal information about the author, play games and activities, and in some cases (for instance, Seussville) learn basic literacy skills. This attempt at reader engagement can be understood as achieving Barthes's idea that removing the author elevates the reader above the text. However, while author websites more often than not make direct address to readers and are interactive, they are nevertheless redefining the concept of the author as a brand, a commodity, a 'friend' (especially if the author has a social media presence).

Authors are no longer just names on a book, but individuals readers feel they 'know.' For example, Lane Smith's blog, Curious Pages, gives an extensive list of "Recommended texts for cool kids and young rebels." By enticing "cool kids and young rebels" as the ones who would enjoy these texts, Smith is implying that he too is a cool-rebel-kid, but is also subtly reinforcing his view that reading is cool and in a digitally saturated world it takes a rebel to read a print book. To support this thesis, Smith displays photographs of his own personal picturebook library and gives an account of how he went about producing his picturebook *It's a Book* (2011). However, he deflects any overt proselytizing by saying: "No heavy message, I'm only in it for the laffs." The author-blog is not so much a return to Barthes's 'Author-God' but a reflection of the commodification of the author and the author-function in a digital space. Lane's personal account offers readers an insight into the writing and illustrating of a particular text and the influences that shaped the process (other children's books – Smith's own and others, silent era films, Walt Disney animations). The intertextual reporting, however, is only partial as it gives readers tidbits of images and texts that may or may not have played a part in the composition of *It's a Book*.

The diversity of the author-function across print and multimedia characterizes the works that are produced (and reproduced, translated, digitally transformed, circulated) during and after an author's lifetime. Foucault asks the question: "How can one define a work amid the millions of traces left by someone?" (1998: 207). By 'traces' he is not referring solely to those traces within the text itself that Barthes had in mind, but to everything that bears traces of the author's life and work – ephemera, personal correspondence, snippets of writing, draft artwork, photographs, and so forth: the primary sources of biographies, author exhibitions, and museums (for instance, the Tomi Ungerer Museum in Strasbourg).

These and other enduring material productions and avenues of preservation and critique highlight the irony of the death of the author, as his/her 'authority' is not killed, but lives on in a world driven by global marketing and cultural (re)production. Authors, illustrators, and their books are commodities, and having a name on a product carries with it different significations. Furthermore, as Wernick (1991: 106) observes, the name circulates independently of the individual and carries with it a reputation or significance that the name has acquired, while it is always in competition with other names that are part of marketing and publicity aspects of promotional culture.

Conclusion

The concept of author-illustrator is part of a wider discursive field that extends beyond print texts and is embedded in a complex, commodified, and digitally shaped public sphere. Authors and illustrators and their works are part of a multimedia network that produces and distributes an extensive array of media products that often have their origins in a book. Sometimes authors of a work are removed from this process once contracts and licenses have been signed. At other times, individuals such as Jeannie Baker and Brian Selznick and many others play an active role in the transformation of their picturebooks into films, animations, and other products. Selznick is an example of how the concept of author-illustrator is changing as the notion of a picturebook similarly evolves. These changing spaces of authorship, text production, transformation, and distribution provide opportunities to revisit the earlier debates that were sparked by Barthes and Foucault. What has been missing from these debates to date is the consideration of the particular place that author-illustrators occupy and their potential to further challenge traditional orthodoxy, conventions, definitions, classifications, and author functions. Furthermore, the concept of author-illustrator may itself change to encompass a different kind of designation that is less attentive to the duality of the role and more responsive to the fluidity that currently characterizes its function in contemporary culture.

References

Ahlberg, Allan, and Ahlberg, Janet (2002) *The Jolly Postman, or, Other People's Letters*, London: Puffin (first published 1986).

Allen, Graham (2004) *Roland Barthes*, London: Routledge.

Barthes, Roland (1977) "The Death of the Author," in *Image-Music-Text*, selected and translated by Stephen Heath, New York: Fontana/Collins, 142–148 (originally published in French in 1968).

Brunhoff, Jean de (1937) *The Story of Babar, the Little Elephant*, New York: Random House (originally published in French in 1931).

Carle, Eric (1995) *The Very Lonely Firefly*, New York: Philomel Books.

Duijx, Toin, and Van Lierop-Debrauwer, Helma (2014) "'I am my work': Dutch Writer and Illustrator Ted van Lieshout," *Bookbird* 52.4: 93–97.

Foucault, Michel (1998) "What Is an Author?," in James D. Faubion (ed.) *Aesthetics, Methods, and Epistemology*, New York: The New Press, 205–222 (originally published in French in 1969).

Hade, Dan, and Edmondson, Jacqueline (2003) "Children's Book Publishing in Neoliberal Times," *Language Arts* 81.2: 137–144.

Hathorn, Libby (1994) *Way Home*, illus. Gregory Rogers, Milsons Point, NSW: Random House Australia.

Hay, Kenneth G. (2006) "Concrete Abstractions and Intersemiotic Translations: The Legacy of Della Volpe," in Katy Macleod and Lin Holdridge (eds) *Thinking Through Art: Reflections on Art as Research*, New York: Routledge, 51–58.

Kümmerling-Meibauer, Bettina (2015) "From Baby Books to Picturebooks for Adults: European Picturebooks in the New Millennium," *Word & Image* 31.3: 249–264. Doi: 10.1080/02666286.2015.1032519.

Love, Harold (2002) *Attributing Authorship: An Introduction*, Cambridge: Cambridge University Press.

Malarte-Feldman, Claire L. (2006) "Brunhoff, Jean de," in Jack Zipes (ed.) *The Oxford Encyclopedia of Children's Literature*, Oxford: Oxford University Press (ebook).

Mensch, Betty, and Freeman, Alan (1987) "Getting to Solla Sollew: The Existentialist Politics of Dr. Seuss," *Tikkun* 2.2: 30–34.

Nikolajeva, Maria, and Scott, Carole (2006) *How Picturebooks Work*, New York: Routledge.

Pieńkowski, Jan (1980) *Dinner Time*, London: Gallery Five.

Pledger, Maurice (2008) *Ocean*, San Diego: Silver Dolphin Books.

Sandywell, Barry (2011) *Dictionary of Visual Discourse: A Dialectical Lexicon of Terms*, Surrey: Ashgate.

Scieszka, Jon (1992) *The Stinky Cheese Man and Other Fairly Stupid Tales*, illus. Lane Smith, New York: Viking Penguin.

Selznick, Brian (2007) *The Invention of Hugo Cabret*, New York: Scholastic Press.

Selznick, Brian (2011) *The Hugo Movie Companion*, New York: Scholastic Press.

Seuss, Dr. (1949) *Bartholomew and the Oobleck*, New York: Random House.

Sipe, Lawrence R. (2011) "The Art of the Picturebook," in Shelby A. Wolf, Karen Coats, Patricia Enciso, and Christine A. Jenkins (eds) *Handbook of Research on Children's and Young Adult Literature*, New York: Routledge, 238–252.

Smith, Lane (2011) *It's a Book*, London: Palgrave Macmillan.

Smith, Vicky (2013) "The Caldecott Effect," *Children & Libraries* 11.1: 9–13.

Uttley, Alison (2013) *Little Grey Rabbit Treasury*, illus. Margaret Tempest, Surrey: Templar (first published 1929–1973).

Wernick, Andrew (1991) *Promotional Culture: Advertising, Ideology and Symbolic Expression*, London: Sage.

Wheatley, Nadia (2007) *Going Bush*, illus. Ken Searle, Crows Nest: Allen & Unwin.

2

PICTURE-TEXT RELATIONSHIPS IN PICTUREBOOKS

Nathalie op de Beeck

Elegant and ideological, playful and nostalgic, picturebooks can seem to be distillations of childhood and of universal advice for all children. Picturebooks are basic, short, compact. Reading a picture-book is easy, and word-and-picture sequences legible to emergent as well as experienced readers. From an early age, we are surrounded by verbal-visual communication in print and digital media, and making meaning from diverse texts feels second nature to us. The picture-text relationship in a picturebook is quite easily taken for granted. Yet it is productive to question the picture-text relationships in a picturebook, which are cultural expressions rather than natural statements of a timeless, generalized childhood.

One such questioning of the picture-text relationship began during a classroom conversation on picturebook history. My students asked whether twenty-first-century picturebooks operate the way nineteenth- and twentieth-century picturebooks do, and the students' choice of verb (*operate*) brought to mind the mechanics of the picture-text relationship. I reflexively ventured to say that effective picturebooks of any era synchronize visual imagery and verbal components in a multipage, interdependent series, and that any picturebook depends upon a satisfying vacillation among signi-fiers and signifieds. Presumably the juxtaposition of written text and visual imagery necessitates a specific reading strategy, whatever the era. The process of scanning a picturebook sequence and dis-cerning its narrative arc is a simple matter for the functionally literate reader.

Yet, as one who argues that picturebook history is intertwined with modernity and that we must beware of picturebook essentialism, I disputed the notion that picture-text sequences can be under-stood mechanistically. Such a formalist response neglects picturebooks' historicity and fails to account for picturebooks' holistic appeal. After all, every picturebook's words, pictures, and material compo-nents suggest much about available technologies and about prevailing definitions of childhood in a particular time and place. Even though we learn early on to decode word-and-picture combinations (A is for Apple, H is for House), we gradually discover that a text holds multiple meanings (whose House is pictured?), and that meaning arises from form *plus* connotations and materiality (does the House resemble my own home?). For example, Perry Nodelman explores how and why readers make meaning in alphabet books and suggests that an abecedary's ludic play among signifiers might be more salient than its educative intent (Nodelman 2001). He discusses how "once they are present, pictures tend to *claim* words," so that an arbitrary sign like *tree* can signify a large plant or a picture made to resemble that plant, symbolically and iconically (Nodelman 2010: 16). Building upon semi-otic and formal readings, the picturebook must be understood as a complex signifying system whose cultural meanings exceed its superficial information. So the question is not only what we encounter

– the sequence of pictures and words in a material text – but who we are, where we are, when we are, and how and why we interpret as we do. Reading a picturebook is not only a matter of engaging with the structure and subject matter in the pictures and the text. To the child and to the experienced reader alike, the picturebook is a normative space that signals implied readership, explicit and implicit ideology, and historical and cultural contexts.

Thus we must ask whether the picture-text relationship in picturebooks is stable or predictable over time, even as we accept structural and aesthetic analyses as useful in picturebook analysis. For decades, scholars have approached picturebook codes by way of semiotic theory (see Moebius 1986), as a system of signifiers and signifieds. We can say that the picturebook presents words and pictures in a "synergistic relationship" with which readers make meaning through sustained engagement with the text (Sipe 1998: 99). Picturebook readers encounter "juxtaposed pictorial and other images in deliberate sequence" (McCloud 1993: 9), and through "the drama of the turning of the page" (Bader 1976: 1) engage with a story or with compelling information. Beyond that generic interaction, readers negotiate the picturebook's normalizing content at the level of words and pictures. If we take into account the dynamically shifting readerships, ideologies, and contexts of the words and pictures in children's literature, we discover that our perceptions change over time. If so, the picturebook of the present day does not *operate* as picturebooks in the past once did, although its superficial properties remain familiar.

Outwardly at least, recognizable codes and systems of signification define what is and is not a picturebook. The compound word *picturebook* presupposes interdependent nonverbal imagery and written language (a title at minimum). A picturebook interpellates a young audience and advances notions of what is and is not childlike. A picturebook constructs an implied reader – the innocent or irreverent child, or the middle-class Anglo-American child – and excludes an implied Other. The picturebook also calls to mind material conventions that differentiate such a text from an illustrated book, a mass-market novel, a comic book, or an e-reader (although tablets and book apps complicate picturebook materiality, and we now debate how transmedia texts mimic or diverge from print). Commonly, a picturebook is recognized by its handheld format, its limited number of pages, its few words and pictures per page or spread, and its narrow paper and board binding.

At the levels of form and content, a picturebook blends written and nonverbal representations, typically cued to emergent literacy. Picturebook creators orchestrate visual-verbal sequences in a way often related to musical performance and improvisation. Maurice Sendak credits classical music and opera as inspirations for many of his picturebooks, and strives for a symphonic harmony among words and pictures (1988: 4). Chris Raschka crafts combinations of heard musical notes, seen watercolor hues, and felt rhythms in *Charlie Parker Played Be Bop* (1992), *Mysterious Thelonious* (1997), and *John Coltrane's Giant Steps* (2002), based on jazz compositions. Picturebook openings can nod to stage sets, movie stills, or art galleries, as in Sendak's *In the Night Kitchen* (1970) – part comic book, part stage design, and part cinematic allusion – and *Higglety Pigglety Pop! Or There Must Be More to Life* (1967), an existential chronicle involving a terrier, an avant-garde theatrical troupe, and mortality. D.B. Johnson's *Magritte's Marvelous Hat* (2012) involves transparent overlays that animate paintings by Belgian surrealist painter René Magritte, and Johnson's trompe l'oeil *Palazzo Inverso* (2010) takes readers on a tour of inside-out images inspired by M.C. Escher. Even so, a picturebook's tangible form and its varying closeups, long shots, and worm's-eye and bird's-eye views differ from those of stage or screen. Although a picturebook narrative proceeds spatially and temporally, a reader manipulates the pages and the timing. Print picturebooks and e-books alike depend upon a handler who guides the experience, whether clumsily or adroitly.

Examinations of the picture-text relationship often make comparisons between the picturebook and fine art or handicraft, and focus on the homespun, interactive qualities of the picturebook as a mode. David Lewis considers picturebooks "quasi-literary objects, more closely related to books than to paintings, prints and drawings" (2001: 102). Yet he cautions against the notion that pictures are "discrete entities that have an existence apart from the overall text within which they are embedded"

(102). He insists on the unique way in which the picturebook fuses qualities of the book and of the nonverbal artwork, and points to the sequentiality of the verbal/visual unit. Martin Salisbury and Morag Styles describe the picturebook as a blend of a book and a work of art because "[t]he art of the picturebook maker [. . .] involves thinking in, and communicating through, both pictures and words" (2012: 56). They differentiate between the illustrated book, in which pictures accompany but are not essential to the written text, and the picturebook, in which "words and pictures combine to deliver the overall meaning of the book; neither of them necessarily makes much sense on its own[,] but they work in unison" (89). Salisbury and Styles particularly revere picturebook artistry, writing, "The very best picturebooks become timeless mini art galleries for the home – a coming together of concept, artwork, design and production that gives pleasure to, and stimulates the imagination of, both children and adults" (50). Citing Maurizio Corraini, they claim picturebooks give readers "the opportunity to hold and feel what are essentially works of art" (50).

Barbara Kiefer, too, calls the picturebook "an art form rather than a teaching tool," and points to its "combination of image and idea presented in sequence" (2008: 10–11). While distancing the picturebook from the nursery and schoolroom contexts, Kiefer notes that the picturebook "as an art object [. . .] has undergone many changes over the centuries as a result of societal, technological, and other influence" (2013: 12). Even so, she believes picturebook creators share uniform tendencies – "What I find remarkable is that the personality or intent of the artist during these years has remained so similar" (12) – due to commonplace depictions of everyday life, animals, and favorite fables from Aesop. Her examples suggest not so much universal agreement among artists as a narrow definition of picturebook content across the centuries, notwithstanding genre-dissolving innovations. Picture-books that interpellate a plural audience or address ostensibly taboo topics threaten prescribed norms around childhood and frequently become targets for censorship (see, for instance, Evans 2015).

The picturebook sequence – like the art object or mass image – carries an excess of significa-tion, dealing in page-to-page, verbally/visually interdependent information. In his foundational 1964 essay, "Rhetoric of the Image," Roland Barthes decodes the messages in a pasta advertisement (Bar-thes 1977). Barthes identifies the ad's literal and symbolic, denotative and connotative, and perceptual and cultural elements. Whereas the linguistic details in the ad help "*fix* the floating chain of signifieds in such a way as to counter the terror of uncertain signs" (39), the coded and non-coded iconic mes-sages depend upon "the perceptual message and the cultural message," which destabilize the overall image (36). Barthes attends to what he calls the "operational" relation between the literal and the symbolic (42), and he acknowledges that individuals perceive this relation differently, depending on their cultural foundations. Yet he suggests that the operational activity itself is secure because the "common domain of the signifieds of connotation is that of *ideology*, which cannot but be single for a given society and history, no matter what signifiers of connotation it may use" (49). Much depends, then, on the understanding of ideology in this now antique theorization of signification.

Further, Barthes's use of the term *operational* precedes my students' choice of the term *operation* to describe the picture-text relationship. Here again is the rub: with growing awareness of intersection-ality and multiple ideologies within cultural contexts, and within children's culture specifically, we find that the relationship between linguistic and iconic is unpredictable in its operations, even when preliterate readers encounter pictures and texts in developmental stages. The picture-text relationship defies exclusively functional definitions, and not only in ways that might be categorized as poststruc-tural or postmodern. We might look here at two posthumous picturebooks by the American street artist Keith Haring – a counting book called *Ten* (1998a) and an adjective primer called *Big* (1998b). Both texts present sequences we might perceive as strictly literal from an operational standpoint. Yet we cannot but consider Haring's art-world career, political views, HIV status, and short life (1958–1990); the picturebooks' publication by Haring's estate in 1998; and our global sociopolitical context. Reception of the text shifts when we link *Ten*'s androgynous dancing figures, its rainbow theme, and its numbers in four languages (English, Spanish, French, German), to the gender, peace, and antiwar activism Haring embraced. Likewise, the adjective primer *Big* shares synonyms for "big," but with an understanding of Haring or of present-day debates around equity, its diverse cartoon children imply openness to difference. Haring's picturebooks function as colorful multilingual toys for babies, allusions to social justice, and collectable items for Pop Art connoisseurs, more than a quarter century after Haring's untimely death. We might argue that the picture-text relationship has changed because of how code switching informs our non-coded iconic signs.

Certain wordless and near-wordless picturebooks demonstrate this excess of picture-text signification too (Rowe 1996; Arizpe 2003, 2014; Beckett 2012, 2014; Bosch 2014). For instance, David Wiesner's surreal dreamscapes take advantage of the slippage among linguistic messages and visual imagery. Wiesner's near-wordless *Tuesday* (1991) enigmatically identifies the random weekday on which a bizarre event takes place, rather than mentioning the flying frogs who invade a quiet neighborhood as the sun sets. The amusing fantasy, which pictures 1990s technologies and quiet natural settings, could seem impossibly bucolic in our postindustrial millennium. Another near-wordless sequence, Wiesner's *Flotsam* (2006), references ocean wreckage in its title, without describing the resourceful boy who discovers an antique camera at the seashore and develops a series of startling photographs. Contemporary technologies make it possible for Wiesner to compose *Flotsam*, a text that draws attention to marine debris as well as the potential for layering visual information across a long span of years. The resolution even anticipates the selfie, which in 2006 was not yet the phenomenon it became in the 2010s. *Flotsam's* inquisitive boy takes the camera's outdated film to a boardwalk shop to be developed – a process once common in tourist sites and towns – and discovers that generations of children have photographed themselves and then tossed the mysterious camera back into the waves. The boy's interaction with the camera indicates a manipulation of the image that we might associate with post-1990s media and the palimpsest, and an old-fashioned facility with bulky hardware that may decline in an era of software and nanotech gadgetry.

Everywhere we see complex variations on picturebook form and content, suggesting that the picture-text relationship is fluid and adaptable. Structuralist analysis still applies, yet seeing the picturebook in terms of a formal picture-text relationship diminishes its potential vitality. For example, twenty-first-century innovations like Shaun Tan's wordless refugee tale, *The Arrival* (2007), Peter Sís's autobiographical *The Wall: Growing Up Behind the Iron Curtain* (2007), and Brian Selznick's groundbreaking *The Invention of Hugo Cabret* (2007) challenge conventional expectations. Tan's *The Arrival* appeared as a portrait-layout hardcover from Hodder Children's Books in Australia and from Arthur A. Levine/Scholastic in the United States, yet its shadowy, tightly packed panels and melancholy ambience mark it as a graphic narrative or comic, not necessarily a picturebook for children. Sís's verbally and visually dense *The Wall* – presented in a picturebook binding and format – introduces young readers to mid-twentieth-century Czech politics, acknowledging childhood as a period of historical and ideological uncertainty. Notwithstanding that picturebook and cinematic montage are quite different modes (see Nodelman 1988: 183), Selznick's *The Invention of Hugo Cabret* pictures a curtained proscenium and silent cinema screen, depends upon sequential duotone sketches and film stills to conjure an illusion of the movement image, and alternates full-bleed wordless sequences with pictureless chapters. When the American Library Association awarded the 2008 Caldecott Medal to the 533-page hardcover *Cabret*, this departure from picturebook conventions brought both acclaim and controversy (see Maughan 2011; Sutton 2014), signaling a redefinition of picturebook norms.

Picture-text scholarship – switching the codes

As of my writing this piece, the picturebook scholar is still a person born pre-2000, schooled in an era of print culture and digital transition. Such a scholar might be at a loss to conceptualize how a person born after the turn of the millennium historicizes technology and understands picture-text relationships. I count myself among those pre-2000 writers, having explored American picturebooks from the twentieth-century interwar period and having noticed time-specific attitudes toward industry, environment, race, ethnicity, and gender encoded in picturebook tropes. My observations depend on my own limited standpoint, for my first studies of picturebooks took place in the 1990s, just as US picturebook publishing and graphic narrative production expanded, and before digital media were taken for granted. Hindsight shed light on how older picturebooks demonstrated dominant attitudes and prior technologies, and helped me discover how picturebooks materially and thematically belong to their eras even when we reread them in ours.

In her influential *Radical Change: Books for Youth in a Digital Age* (1999), Eliza Dresang considered this generational divide and said that we have witnessed a paradigm shift away from once commonplace print technologies such as newsprint, pamphlets, broadsheets, periodicals, and bound books. Dresang focused on the potentials of children's multimedia and how interactivity changes picturebooks and children's reading, writing that "both Radical Change and postmodernism can be viewed as parallel theoretical approaches to explicate many of the same observed changes, each surfacing from a different historical and societal perspective" (2008: 44). Whereas postmodernism involves "pastiche and parody, bricolage, irony and playfulness" – qualities that arise from picturebook elements including formal structure and content, allusive peritexts, and inventive book packaging – Radical Change "emphasizes handheld hypertext and digital design that are related to the interactivity, connectivity, and access of the digital environment" in terms of "both text and reader" (44).

For any child, of course, childhood is a period of first encounters with cultural information, and those fluent in multiple media might underestimate the novelty of even a standard-issue print picturebook (or any visual-verbal medium) for the child. Writing on children's adaptability, Margaret Mackey argues that "the apparatus of the book itself is radically more visible to children of a very young age who are at home with contrasting formats" (2008: 103). Mackey, in an essay on postmodern picturebooks' play with print media, observes how children perceive the textual artifact and meta-commentaries in ways older readers may not fully appreciate. Nodelman also attends to picturebooks' imaginative abstractions and word/picture puzzles. While indebted to fine art and to postmodern phenomena, he says, picturebooks belong to young readers and to concepts of childhood:

> The picturebook is, I believe, the one form of literature invented specifically for audiences of children – and despite recent claims for a growing adult audience for more sophisticated books, the picturebook remains firmly connected to the idea of an implied child-reader/viewer.
>
> *2010: 11–12*

The term *picturebook* – whatever material form the textual object takes – further suggests participatory, shared reading practices between that "implied child reader/viewer" and a more experienced reader who, according to Joe Sutliff Sanders, "chaperones the words." Sanders writes, "This is the design of picture books, a design with ideological implications" because "the speaker inevitably *performs* the words in a way that narrows their meaning even as the words fix the meaning of the images" (2013: 62–63). Sanders provides a way to think about the picturebook's longstanding associations with teaching literacy, gatekeepers, and expert supervision. He also raises questions of the picturebook's implicit didacticism and its potential to reinforce (or subvert) norms. Nodelman observes that in picturebooks, "the insistence on illustration confirms an urge to explain things, to have the words account for and reveal the important meanings of the pictures and the pictures account for and reveal the basic significant thrust of the words" (2012: 444). Nodelman asks whether this codependent "illustrational dynamic" means that picturebook conventions are "inherently and already didactic even before authors make specific didactic use of them, or, for that matter, even when authors choose not to use them for didactic purposes" (444). These provocative theories of chaperoning, and of inherent disciplinary measures, suggest how central didacticism has been to the picturebook in Western cultural conceptions of the mode.

Picturebook critics of our millennium, then, interpret the picture-text relationship at the level of form, but increasingly in terms of coded values and didactic norms. Among the best evidence of this re-evaluation is the US-based We Need Diverse Books movement, established in 2014 as a Twitter campaign. We Need Diverse Books calls attention to assumptions, representations, and material realities contributing to a lack of racial and ethnic diversity in children's publishing. Within the movement, picturebooks have come under scrutiny for the ways coded picture-text relationships depend on antiquated hierarchies. Putting aside for the purpose of this article the issues of authorship, marketing, librarianship, curricula, and other related concerns of the movement, taken-for-granted picture-text relationships must be scrutinized afresh.

In a case that galvanized public and professional sentiment around We Need Diverse Books, author Emily Jenkins and illustrator Sophie Blackall's picturebook *A Fine Dessert: Four Centuries, Four Families, One Delicious Treat* received generous reviews when it was published by Random House Children's Books in March 2015 (Jenkins 2015a). Debate flared around *A Fine Dessert*, however, when the popular readership questioned the picturebook's representation of smiling African American slaves preparing and serving food, then secretly licking the bowl while white masters enjoyed the fine dessert. Journalists, scholars, publishing insiders, teachers, and parents weighed in, and a furious debate arose about the pros and cons of such casual, uncritical representation of slave history in a children's picturebook (see Schuessler 2015). Jenkins apologized in a comment on the blog *Reading While White:*

> I have come to understand that my book, while intended to be inclusive and truthful and hopeful, is racially insensitive. I own that and am very sorry. For lack of a better way to make reparations, I donated the fee I earned for writing the book to We Need Diverse Books.
>
> *2015b: n. pag.*

Blackall wrote on her own blog, "The way we look at pictures is incredibly complicated. I cannot ensure my images will be read the way I intended, I can only approach each illustration with as much research, thoughtfulness, empathy and imagination as I can muster" (2015: n. pag.). *A Fine Dessert* remains available for purchase. A few months later, in January 2016, readers revisited the controversy with the publication of Ramin Ganeshram and Vanessa Brantley-Newton's *A Birthday Cake for George Washington* (Ganeshram 2016). In the nonfiction-based tale, a slave named Hercules and his daughter Delia prepare a cake at Mount Vernon, home of the first US president. Amid outcry about the representation of contented slaves, and the erasure of the fates of the actual Hercules and Delia, Scholastic suspended publication. Professional and amateur commentators alike raised questions of censorship and the eye of the beholder, both central to the picture-text correspondence: children of color (and their gatekeepers) confronting the text have no choice but to reckon with slave history and coded iconic messages of racism, while white children (and their gatekeepers) opening the book might choose to overlook the discriminatory text and subtext, coding the iconic signifiers in ways that elide institutional racism.

Sanders's chaperoning metaphor lends powerful insight here, suggesting how emergent readers and chaperones decode picture-text relationships in ideologically freighted sequences. In any picturebook, readers and chaperones negotiate aesthetic appreciation and political content, however benign; the pictorial and literary imagery may be artfully constructed and otherwise appealing, yet stands for implicit or explicit ideologies. The text implies some ideal readers and excludes others. As texts' chaperones diversify and shed light on explicit and implicit picturebook ideologies, potential readings of picturebook texts broaden and ways of reading adapt. Although picture-text relationships are foundational to picturebooks, our ways of interpreting them – in traditional bound texts, in e-media, as mainstays of preschool and elementary school, as bedtime stories – must expand and change.

Thus, when asked whether picturebooks today operate as did those of the late nineteenth and early twentieth centuries, we can ask whether picturebooks today are the same artifacts they once were. Nostalgia for an ephemeral, often idealized childhood might leave readers inclined to read words and pictures formally and aesthetically, and reluctant to historicize picture-text relationships, especially when anachronistic picturebooks misrepresent lived experience (or represent lived experience from a dominant position, failing to account for other voices). This question of changing picture-text relationships therefore is an important and sticky one, not least because today's scholars have decades of hindsight with regard to picturebooks of earlier periods. Certain exemplary picturebook models retain classic status and are still read by children, while most picturebooks of the past are relegated to special collections plumbed by scholars and seldom seen by child audiences today. All picturebooks demonstrate generational codes that are influenced by such things as public education policy, understandings of developmental literacy, industrialization, globalization, perceptions of environment, and ways of describing human difference, to name just a few factors. We might ask how historical context and ideology inform and change the picture-text relationship, and how our culturally determined reading strategies change the picturebook.

Even the past twenty years have brought enormous technological developments that challenge the former twentieth-century relationship of words to pictures, and redefine reading itself as a multimodal practice. In areas including publishing, education, and communication, we have a changed understanding of how words and pictures work together, and younger scholars gain early fluency in specialized design vocabulary (see, for instance, Sipe 1998). Developments in graphic narrative storytelling and studies of the language of comics by Thierry Groensteen (2013), Charles Hatfield (2005), Hilary Chute (2010), and Nick Sousanis (2015) enrich picturebook criticism. And, of course, the reproducibility of the text has shifted. With all-digital production, there is no lost original; when the reproducibility of the text shifts, so do the interpretability and political ideology of that text, as theorists like Walter Benjamin and John Berger remind us.

A generic picture-text relationship may seem to be a given, the unquestionable and universal essence of the picturebook throughout the history of this mode of production. Yet picturebook scholars are wise to question the picture-text relationship. The relation between picture and text is not a stable signifier/signified combination, and our shifting methods of interpreting information and perceiving childhood change the very picture-text relationship itself. Depending on a reader's interaction with the text, a picturebook might be perceived as an artwork or a tool of literacy, as a zone of safe play or a polarizing political commentary. The picturebook's signature elements – word and picture – have altered over the decades, and we must question the historicity, predictability, and function of the picture-text relationship in our contemporary contexts.

References

Arizpe, Evelyn (2003) "Meaning-Making from Wordless (or Nearly Wordless) Picturebooks: What Educational Research Expects and What Readers Have to Say," *Cambridge Journal of Education* 43.2: 163–176.

Arizpe, Evelyn (2014) "Wordless Picturebooks: Critical and Educational Perspectives on Meaning-Making," in Bettina Kümmerling-Meibauer (ed.) *Picturebooks: Representation and Narration*, New York: Routledge, 91–106.

Bader, Barbara (1976) *American Picturebooks from Noah's Ark to The Beast Within*, New York: Macmillan.

Barthes, Roland (1977) "Rhetoric of the Image," in Roland Barthes (ed.) *Image-Music-Text*, trans. Stephen Heath, New York: Hill and Wang (first published 1964).

Beckett, Sandra L. (2012) *Crossover Picturebooks: A Genre for All Ages*, New York and London: Routledge.

Beckett, Sandra L. (2014) "The Art of Visual Storytelling: Formal Strategies in Wordless Picturebooks," in Bettina Kümmerling-Meibauer (ed.) *Picturebooks: Representation and Narration*, New York: Routledge, 53–70.

Blackall, Sophie (2015) "Depicting Slavery in *A Fine Dessert*," *Sophie Blackall Illustration*, blog, (October 23, 2015), http://sophieblackall.blogspot.com/2015/10/depicting-slavery-in-fine-dessert.html (accessed July 20, 2016).

Bosch, Emma (2014) "Texts and Peritexts in Wordless and Almost Wordless Picturebooks," in Bettina Kümmerling-Meibauer (ed.) *Picturebooks: Representation and Narration*, New York: Routledge, 71–90.

Chute, Hilary L. (2010) *Graphic Women: Life Narrative and Contemporary Comics*, New York: Columbia University Press.

Dresang, Eliza (1999) *Radical Change: Books for Youth in a Digital Age*, New York: H.W. Winston.

Dresang, Eliza (2008) "Radical Change Theory, Postmodernism, and Contemporary Picturebooks," in Lawrence R. Sipe and Sylvia Pantaleo (eds) *Postmodern Picturebooks: Play, Parody, and Self-Referentiality*, London: Routledge, 41–54.

Evans, Janet (ed.) (2015) *Challenging and Controversial Picturebooks: Creative and Critical Responses to Visual Texts*, New York: Routledge.

Ganeshram, Ramin (2016) *A Birthday Cake for George Washington*, illus. Vanessa Brantley-Newton, New York: Scholastic.

Groensteen, Thierry (2013) *Comics and Narration*, trans. Ann Miller, Jackson: University Press of Mississippi.

Haring, Keith (1998a) *Ten*, New York: Hyperion.

Haring, Keith (1998b) *Big*, New York: Hyperion.

Hatfield, Charles (2005) *Alternative Comics: An Emerging Literature*, Jackson: University Press of Mississippi.

Jenkins, Emily (2015a) *A Fine Dessert: Four Centuries, Four Families, One Delicious Treat*, illus. Sophie Blackall, New York: Random House.

Jenkins, Emily (2015b) "Untitled Comment," *Reading While White: Allies for Racial Diversity and Inclusion in Books for Children and Teens*, blog (November 1, 2015), http://readingwhilewhite.blogspot.com/2015/10/on-letting-go.html?showComment=1446389284847%23c7763644794125015907 (accessed July 20, 2016).

Johnson, D. B. (2010) *Palazzo Inverso*, New York: Houghton Mifflin.

Johnson, D. B. (2012) *Magritte's Marvelous Hat*, New York: Houghton Mifflin.

Kiefer, Barbara (2008) "What Is a Picturebook, Anyway?" in Lawrence R. Sipe and Sylvia Pantaleo (eds) *Postmodern Picturebooks: Play, Parody, and Self-Referentiality*, New York: Routledge, 9–21.

Kiefer, Barbara (2013) "What Is a Picturebook? Across the Borders of History," in Evelyn Arizpe, Maureen Farrell, and Julie McAdams (eds) *Picturebooks: Beyond the Borders of Art, Narrative and Culture*, London: Routledge, 6–22.

Lewis, David (2001) *Reading Contemporary Picturebooks: Picturing Text*, London: RoutledgeFalmer.

Mackey, Margaret (2008) "Postmodern Picturebooks and the Material Conditions of Reading," in Lawrence R. Sipe and Sylvia Pantaleo (eds) *Postmodern Picturebooks: Play, Parody, and Self-Referentiality*, New York: Routledge, 103–116.

Maughan, Shannon (2011) "And the Winner Is …," *Publishers Weekly* (December 5, 2011), www.publishersweekly.com/pw/by-topic/childrens/childrens-book-news/article/49729-and-the-winner-is.html (accessed July 20, 2016).

McCloud, Scott (1993) *Understanding Comics: The Invisible Art*, Northampton, MA: Kitchen Sink Press.

Moebius, William (1986) "Introduction to Picture Book Codes," *Word & Image* 2.2: 141–158.

Nodelman, Perry (1988) *Words about Pictures: The Narrative Art of Children's Picture Books*, Athens: University of Georgia Press.

Nodelman, Perry (2001) "A Is for … What? The Function of Alphabet Books," *Journal of Early Childhood Literacy* 1.3: 235–253.

Nodelman, Perry (2010) "Words Claimed: Picturebook Narratives and the Project of Children's Literature," in Teresa Colomer, Bettina Kümmerling-Meibauer, and Cecilia Silva-Díaz (eds) *New Directions in Picturebook Research*, New York: Routledge, 11–26.

Nodelman, Perry (2012) "Picture Book Guy Looks at Comics: Structural Differences in Two Kinds of Visual Narrative," *Children's Literature Association Quarterly* 37.4: 436–444.

Raschka, Chris (1992) *Charlie Parker Played Be Bop*, New York: Orchard.

Raschka, Chris (1997) *Mysterious Thelonious*, New York: Orchard.

Raschka, Chris (2002) *John Coltrane's Giant Steps*, New York: Atheneum.

Rowe, Anne (1996) "Voices Off: Reading Wordless Picture Books," in Eve Bearne, Morag Styles, and Victor Watson (eds) *Voices Off: Texts, Contexts, Readers*, London: Cassell, 219–234.

Salisbury, Martin, and Styles, Morag (2012) *Children's Picturebooks: The Art of Visual Storytelling*, London: Laurence King.

Sanders, Joe Sutliff (2013) "Chaperoning Words: Meaning-Making in Comics and Picture Books," *Children's Literature* 41: 57–90.

Schuessler, Jennifer (2015) "'A Fine Dessert': Judging a Book by the Smile of a Slave," *New York Times* (November 6, 2015), www.nytimes.com/2015/11/07/books/a-fine-dessert-judging-a-book-by-the-smile-of-a-slave.html (accessed July 20, 2016).

Selznick, Brian (2007) *The Invention of Hugo Cabret*, New York: Scholastic.

Sendak, Maurice (1967) *Higglety Pigglety Pop! Or There Must Be More to Life*, New York: Harper & Row.

Sendak, Maurice (1970) *In the Night Kitchen*, New York: Harper & Row.

Sendak, Maurice (1988) *Caldecott and Co.: Notes on Books and Pictures*, New York: Michael di Capua/Farrar, Straus and Giroux.

Sipe, Lawrence R. (1998) "How Picture Books Work," *Children's Literature in Education* 29.2: 97–108.

Sís, Peter (2007) *The Wall: Growing Up Behind the Iron Curtain*, New York: Farrar, Straus and Giroux.

Sousanis, Nick (2015) *Unflattening*, Cambridge, MA: Harvard University Press.

Sutton, Roger (2014) "As Pretty Does," *The Horn Book Magazine* (February 28, 2014), www.hbook.com/2014/02/opinion/editorials/editorial-pretty/ (accessed July 20, 2016).

Tan, Shaun (2007) *The Arrival*, New York: Arthur A. Levine/Scholastic.

Wiesner, David (1991) *Tuesday*, New York: Clarion.

Wiesner, David (2006) *Flotsam*, New York: Clarion.

3

PICTUREBOOKS AND PAGE LAYOUT

Megan Dowd Lambert

Picturebook scholar Barbara Bader's oft-quoted assertion that the success of the picturebook "as an art form [...] hinges on the interdependence of pictures and words, on the simultaneous display of two facing pages, and on the drama of the turning of the page" (1976: 1) invites consideration of multimodality, the impact of page-layout decisions, and pacing. When one also attends to the materiality of the picturebook codex, these components attain greater complexity as the reader engages with the physical nature of the book and perhaps even comes to value the unique potentials of the codex in the digital age. Film critic James Monaco refers to this materiality as "the 'thing-ness of a book'" (1977: 15), while children's literature scholar Aidan Chambers refers to "the book-as-object" (1983: 174). We thus arrive at the intersection of the picturebook as form *and* as object, with page layout emerging as an especially rich area of inquiry since the "simultaneous display of two facing pages" must accommodate, and can even exploit, the three-dimensional space of the physical, material book.

About facing pages

This physical space is defined in part by the sequential facing pages of the picturebook codex – verso on the left, recto on the right, with the gutter dipping down in between – which hold myriad page layout possibilities. Each of these, in turn, provides fodder for critical assessment and interpretation of the multimodal text and its material presentation. First, artists must choose whether to illustrate single- or doublespreads; in other words, they decide whether or not their art will cross the gutter at a particular page opening. The most traditional layout places text on the verso with art on the facing recto, as in Virginia Hamilton and Leo and Diane Dillon's *The Girl Who Spun Gold* (2000). Other picturebooks reverse this design, positioning illustration on the verso and text on the facing recto – see, for example, the first seven page openings in Jon Klassen's *I Want My Hat Back* (2011) – but this is a less common occurrence. Whether words or pictures appear on the verso or recto, the dual modes of communication are kept neatly apart in their visual presentation and in the physical space of the book-as-object, with the gutter acting like a part of a frame delineating halves of the whole spread. Both layouts offer formal arrangements of words and pictures, and Doonan describes "[t]he resulting visual rhythm" as "a series of strong beats" (1993: 85).

The display of facing, single-page pictures with text accompanying each one is another, less formal layout choice, with each page presenting a distinct moment in the multimodal text. In the fifth page opening of George Shannon and Laura Dronzek's *Tippy-Toe Chick, Go!* (2003), Big Chick confronts Dog, and this layout has an undeniable impact on pacing as a spread presents not one but two distinct moments in a story. Big Chick first musters up the courage to challenge Dog on the verso, and then he chickens out, so to speak, and hides under Hen's wing when Dog barks and lunges at him. This spread is a fine example of what Maria Nikolajeva and Carole Scott describe when they write that "quite often the verso establishes a situation, while the recto disrupts it; the verso creates a sense of security, while the recto brings danger and excitement" (2006: 151). Furthermore, the close causal and temporal relationship between the two facing images is underscored by their physical proximity in the material picturebook codex (the pictures face each other across the gutter instead of being separated by a page turn), even as the gutter firmly separates the two moments in time.

Likewise, picturebooks such as Brian Pinkney's *The Adventures of Sparrowboy* (1997) or Joseph Bruchac and Wendy Anderson Halperin's *My Father Is Taller Than a Tree* (2010) borrow from comic conventions to incorporate sequences of panel illustrations. This allows the art to compress the depicted temporal space of a narrative within the material space of the codex by showing a series of moments over time in individual spreads. While Pinkney's use of this layout overtly supports his story's grounding in superhero comics, in the case of Bruchac and Halperin's work, panel illustrations enable the picturebook to deepen the slice-of-life depictions of a diverse array of fathers and sons since each spread includes not just one shared moment in each relationship but several. Another technique that achieves such a compression of time is simultaneous succession, which one can observe in the penultimate spread of Wanda Gág's *Millions of Cats* (1928). Reflecting on how such a layout speeds up the pacing in a spread from her *Emma and Julia Love Ballet* (2016), author-illustrator Barbara McClintock states, "Viewing several small images in quick succession can be like looking at a flip-book that gives the impression of fast, fluid motion" (qtd. in Bircher 2016).

Although not all picturebooks follow explicitly linear plots in which every image progresses chronologically from one event to the next, most do. Furthermore, Nikolajeva and Scott note that

> various deviations from straight, chronological order, the so-called anachronies, are traditionally regarded as unsuitable for children, and have only recently become prominent in children's novels. Complex temporality is often limited in picturebooks because of their compact nature, which excludes long time spans. The vast majority of picturebooks have a short story time, often just one day or less.
>
> *2006: 165*

Regardless of the degree of complexity that a narrative employs, artists must decide whether to compress time (as in the preceding examples from Pinkney, Bruchac and Halperin, Gág, and McClintock) or to expand it in a given spread as the reader moves toward the turn of the page. Depicting at least one moment on the verso and one on the facing recto compresses the progression of time so that the reader moves along from one moment to the next in the space of one doublespread.

On the other hand, art that crosses the gutter creates the perception of expanding a given moment in time as it invites the reader to linger on the larger picture. If space equals time, it is as though the picture is taking a long time (occupying a lot of space) to convey what it needs to say. McClintock notes,

> Broad, dramatic scenes create a sense of mood and establish place; and fuller, detailed pictures slow the reader down at significant moments by creating an environment that invites investigation. That lingering pause can give majesty to a scene or narrative concept.
>
> *qtd. in Bircher 2016, n. pag.*

In my debut picturebook illustrated by David Hyde Costello, *A Crow of His Own* (2015b), Clyde the rooster clears his throat as he perches atop the chicken coop on the secure verso page of a full-bleed spread depicting the sunrise (Figure 3.1).

Figure 3.1 Illustration by David Hyde Costello from Megan Dowd Lambert's *A Crow of His Own*. Watertown, MA: Charlesbridge Publishing, 2015.

Reprinted by permission of Charlesbridge Publishing.

This creates a sense of anticipation for the triumphant, climactic scene in which Clyde finally crows a crow of his own in the subsequent full-bleed spread featuring an intraiconic "COCK-A-DOODLE-DOO!"

The expansion of time created by a full-bleed spread is enhanced when a *wordless* double-page picture occurs at the climax of a story, evoking a contemplative moment for the reader to reflect upon the scene and relate it back to the words and images that preceded it. Brian Selznick frequently includes this pacing and layout choice in picturebooks he illustrates. See, for example, his wordless doublespread toward the end of *When Marian Sang* (2002) by Pam Muñoz Ryan, which depicts Marian Anderson's 1939 Easter Sunday concert on the steps of the Lincoln Memorial. The prior spread is a powerful close-up of Anderson's face, and this subsequent wordless spread shifts perspective to position the reader within the massive crowd assembled to bear witness to her triumph and to participate in her defiance against bigotry.

Mind the gutter!

One way that Selznick invites allegiance with the crowd in this illustration is by positioning a child facing out at the reader to act as what Nikolajeva and Scott call an "'intrusive' visual narrator" (2006: 119). The eye is drawn to her figure because she is positioned in an empty space on the recto that extends from the gutter. Though rarely acknowledged in critical discussion of picturebook art, the gutter – the vertical seam between the verso and recto, where the pages are bound together – plays a tremendously important role in informing page layout and in helping the reader progress toward, or resist the pull of, Bader's "drama of the turning of the page." This production element of the codex impacts the success of each page opening's layout because it creates an interruption of the picture space. Picturebook artists therefore must, at the very least, accommodate the gutter in their compositions to avoid having important details obscured. In the case of Selznick's wordless picture of the crowd at Anderson's concert, the gutter is artfully accommodated as he depicts a space in the crowd assembled to hear the famed contralto and draws the eye away from the center of the picture at the gutter to focus on the little girl, her eyes closed in a contemplative, rapturous mood that guides the reader to experience a similar state.

Likewise, in her commentary on Uri Shulevitz's achievement in *The Fool of the World and the Flying Ship* (1968), Lyn Ellen Lacy notes that "he demonstrates absolute control in avoiding the annoying slice of the gutter" (1986: 189). And yet, artists may push beyond mere avoidance of the gutter to enhance a visual separation between the verso and recto and exploit the gutter as a visual or physical barrier in a composition created for the material picturebook codex. The title page of Marla Frazee's *Hush, Little Baby: A Folk Song with Pictures* (1999) does just this (Figure 3.2).

"Those parents are like a circle of love around the baby, and the sister is all the way over there on the other page," remarked a preschooler when I read this book with her class a few years ago. I was using the Whole Book Approach, a co-constructive storytime model I developed as an educator at the Eric Carle Museum of Picture Book Art (www.carlemuseum.org) and which I write about in *Reading Picture Books with Children: How to Shake Up Storytime and Get Kids Talking about What They See* (2015a). Whole Book Approach storytimes ask children to make meaning of picturebook para-texts, art, and design during a reading, and the child who made these observations about Frazee's title page composition was clearly experiencing what Doonan refers to as the "crucial role in the psychological effect" (1993: 85) that layout plays.

Indeed, by placing the jealous girl on the verso and the other characters on the recto, with the gutter between them in this doublespread illustration, Frazee heightens the dramatic tension of the picture to a degree that merely separating them in a single-page picture would not achieve. This is just one instance where the gutter is not merely the physical site of the binding, or a facet of book production that must be accommodated to avoid having it interrupt the visual continuity of a doublespread; instead, it is another physical and visual component of the book for readers to consider as they engage with the picturebook as a visual art form.

In Koen Van Biesen's *Roger Is Reading a Book (2015)*, the gutter is explicitly used as a division between the verso and recto because the artist makes this element of book production read as the wall separating two apartments. A little girl named Emily is noisily playing on the verso, while "Roger is reading a book" on the recto. She disturbs him when she bounces a ball against the wall-that-is-the-gutter, and then he strides purposefully over to it and pounds his fist to get her attention. "KNOCK/Roger knocks" reads the text, and the illustration employs the comic convention of depicting multiple, fading forms to convey the repeated motion of his hand knocking against the wall-that-is-the-gutter. A series of small curved lines emanates from the place where he knocks and onto the verso to represent the sound of that knocking, and small Emily stands still, looking up in their direction.

Other examples of such purposeful layout in consideration of the gutter as a part of the material-ity of the picturebook codex abound. Although he does not make the gutter into a wall separating his characters, Chris Raschka isolates two boys in *Yo! Yes?* (1993) on facing pages with the gutter between them. In the front matter pages, the boy on the recto even acts as what Nikolajeva and

Figure 3.2 Title page of *Hush Little Baby: A Folksong with Pictures* by Marla Frazee. New York: Harcourt, 1999. Reprinted by permission of Houghton Mifflin Harcourt.

Scott call a "pageturner" (2006: 152) with his dogged progression to the right, but the other boy's salutation "Yo!" stops him in his tracks and prompts the reader to consider the dynamic between the boys instead of simply moving on to the next page. The boys remain on facing pages until the story's resolution, when the shy child on the recto accepts the other boy's gestures of friendship and crosses the gutter to join him on the verso. In a feat of perfect pacing that starts with a single recto title page, the book ends with a single verso-page illustration depicting the now united boys jumping hand in hand in an exuberant celebration of their new friendship.

The impact of frames, borders, and bleeds

Illustrator Barbara McClintock notes, "The size and shape of the illustrations is all about creating a sense of time, movement, emotion, and place" (qtd. in Bircher 2016, n. pag.), and Raschka underscores the boys' emotional bond on the final page by merging the shapes of the white spaces that had acted as separate spotlights amid expressive washes of color on previous pages. The resulting shape of the picture in the culminating layout visually asserts a heartwarming resolution to the story, but it still keeps the viewer at a distance; even now, the merged white space around the characters acts as a visual reminder of the separation between the world of the book and the world of the reader. Ultimately, using a frame or border to enclose an image, or defining it by negative space (as in *Yo! Yes?*), impacts the viewer's perception. For example, like the animals depicted before her in the picturebook, the teacher in Bill Martin Jr. and Eric Carle's *Brown Bear, Brown Bear, What Do You See?* (1967) is not enclosed by a frame or by defined negative space. Carle simply situates the figures in this book against the empty white space of the page (or, in the case of the white dog, empty black space) to create a presentation of the art that is free of visual barriers between the viewer and the pictures. The impact is one of welcoming viewers into the world of the picturebook to make them feel like participants in the scene rather than spectators on the outside looking in. As Nikolajeva and Scott write, "Frames normally create a sense of detachment between the picture and the reader, while the absence of frames (that is, a picture that covers the whole area of a page or a doublespread) invites the reader into the picture" (2006: 62).

This effect is even more pronounced when fully detailed backgrounds (as opposed to empty pages like those noted in Carle's work) bleed off the page without a frame or border to enclose them within the picture plane. Full-bleed page designs can result in a dynamic, inviting presentation that obscures awareness of the perceptual line between the reader's reality and the world of the book, thus creating a greater sense of intimacy in the reading. Illustrator Aaron Becker uses this technique to great advantage in his Caldecott Honor Book, *Journey* (2013), immersing the reader in full-bleed, fantastic landscapes at key points in his protagonist's adventure as she moves from one setting to another and brings the reader along with her. When he visited a course I teach on the picturebook at Simmons College, Becker acknowledged that his framing choices were inspired by his study of Maurice Sendak's *Where the Wild Things Are* (1963), which famously uses diminishing and expanding air frames (white space around the picture, without any lines or decorative embellishments to define the frame). This influence is quite apparent in Becker's enclosed, small picture of the forlorn protagonist in her bedroom before she embarks on her fantastic adventures.

When she does set out on the eponymous journey, a key visual pageturner helps guide the reader from one spread to the next, and from reality and into the realm of fantasy. On an empty, white recto page, a series of three pictures moving from the top left to the lower right shows the girl using her red pencil to draw a doorway. The third image shows that door opened with the girl partway through it as she enters a partially visible, lush, green world beyond the doorway. Positioned behind and above the girl, the reader can only see part of her body as she exits through the doorway, and this helps provoke the dramatic page-turn to see where it leads.

In her essay, "Verbal and Visual Pageturners in Picturebooks," Eva Gressnich notes that

the layout of words and pictures is intentional and purposeful. A text sequence is related to a picture or a set of pictures and the arrangement of both on the page or the double spread is never coincidental. The page is thus not only a means to carrying the text and the pictures, but an element that influences the way we read the story.

2012: 169

Her ensuing analysis of the various kinds of pageturners in picturebooks emphasizes their potential impact on the pacing of a reading and underscores how they can support children in their engagement with sequential narratives. With regard to verbal pageturners (or PTs as she calls them), Gressnich emphasizes their efficacy for very young readers and notes that "Two kinds of verbal PTs are used frequently in the corpus books: split question-answer sequences and split sentences. In several books, the answer to a question asked on a spread is given on the subsequent spread" (169).

The example of Becker's work exemplifies how a visual rather than a verbal pageturner can heighten anticipation and create dramatic movement from one spread to the next by obscuring part of a character's body as she leaves one setting and one moment in time and enters another. The eighth spread in Rukhsana Khan and Sophie Blackall's *Big Red Lollipop* (2010) functions similarly, but without depicting a shift from reality to fantasy; indeed, the story's portrayal of sibling rivalry may seem all too real to anyone who's been a sibling or has parented them. On the verso, an outraged big sister Rubina holds her mostly eaten, no-longer-so-big red lollipop and glares across the gutter at the culprit who ate it, her little sister Sana on the recto. Instead of showing Sana in full, Blackall picks up on the text's first-person narration, reading, "When she sees me, she runs away," and illustrates only Sana's pajama-clad legs and bare feet as she flees her big sister's wrath.

The rest of her body is unseen in this picture, which renders her as a visual pageturner that provokes quick progression to the next spread, where an aerial perspective shows Rubina in hot pursuit of her lollipop-stealing sister as they race through the rooms of their house.

Typography

The outrage that Rubina expresses before taking off after Sana is conveyed not only by her facial expression and rigid stance, but also in her cry of "SANA!" The force of this utterance is communicated to the reader with its exclamation point, the use of all capital letters, and also through the following typographic choices: the little sister's name is dropped halfway down the page, isolated from the block of narrative text above it, the letters are in a larger size than the rest of the text on the page, and they adopt a bold typeface. These elements combine to fix the reader's attention on this single bit of text, and to cue a reading in a loud voice to express Rubina's anger and the blame she places on Sana.

Placement of text and typographic features such as size and weight are indeed an important part of layout, and scholars Frank Serafini and Jennifer Clausen note that "the typography of written language not only serves as a conduit of verbal narrative [. . .] it serves as a visual element and semiotic resource with its own meaning potentials" (2012: 23). This latter point heralds exciting possibilities for inquiry into typography as a bearer of meaning unto itself. Illustrator Laura Vaccaro Seeger has reflected on how children respond to typography in *Bully* (2013), her picturebook about friendship between animals overcoming a young bull's bullying behavior. Borrowing from comic art conventions, the spare text is presented as speech-balloon dialogue between the protagonist bully of a bull and other animals. The bully's words grow larger as the bull ramps up his cruelty, until a determined goat speaks up against him. At a dinner hosted by her publisher at the American Library Association's annual conference in 2013, Seeger recounted how she invites children to read the text aloud: "The great thing is that kids know that the bigger the word is, the louder their voices should be, and vice versa," she said. But the insights into typography and its impact on verbal expression do not stop there. When the heroic goat shames the bully of a bull and he apologizes, Seeger said that she asks the children if they believe that the bull is truly sorry. And they do. They read sincerity into his apology because of the small tear rolling from his eye in the picture, yes, but also because the single word of text, "Sorry . . .," appears small on the page, especially compared to the larger words bursting with bullish bravado that precede it in the text.

Typography choices can indicate or convey other elements of characterization, as well. In their essay about *Fox* (2000) by Margaret Wild and Ron Brooks, Bettina Kümmerling-Meibauer and Jörg Meibauer write,

> Brooks has handwritten the whole text in block letters, using a penholder with a thick black pen. He created spiky capitals and shaky letters by writing the text with his left hand. In this manner, Brooks gives the impression that the handcrafted lettering was made by a child or somebody who is not used or able to write regular letters and to keep to the line.
>
> *2015: 147*

This analysis underscores how typographic decisions can reinforce character development achieved through illustration and narrative text. In a similar example, Yuyi Morales concludes *Just a Minute: A Trickster Counting Book* (2003) with a farewell letter ostensibly penned by Señor Calavera. It appears as an epistolary moment of intraiconic text, with black hand-lettering on a white sheet of paper illustrated against a dark background. The lettering itself looks as if it were written with a shaky hand and stands in stark contrast with the Barcelona and Posada typefaces used for the display type and narrative text throughout the picturebook. This appearance reinforces the conceit that Señor Calavera wrote the letter and left it for Grandma Beetle, while also recalling his bony hands (*calavera* translates to "skull" in English and the character is depicted as a skeleton). The letters themselves have long ascenders and descenders (the parts of the letters that slope down or reach up in characters like *d* or *y*) that mimic the long, thin limbs of the skeleton.

Other picturebooks use varying typographic choices to denote different levels of text simultaneously at work. Douglas Martin discusses Shirley Hughes's foray into incorporating comic conventions into her picturebooks in his analysis of *Chips and Jessie* (1985), which includes a story within a story as Jessie regales Chips. Martin writes, "The text of the story which she's telling appears above. Chips's interjections as he gets more and more gripped by the story are given in speech balloons" (1989: 159). The typefaces for these two different levels of text differ, with the main text in a serif font and the speech balloon text in a faint type that looks closer to hand-lettering. Melissa Stewart, Allen Young, and Nicole Wong's *No Monkeys, No Chocolate* (2013) uses three different typefaces to help the reader navigate the three kinds of text in this nonfiction picturebook about chocolate. The concise main text is the largest type on the page and is bolded to highlight its dominance. The more in-depth supplemental nonfiction content appears to be the same serif type, but it is smaller in size and lighter in weight, which indicates its secondary status. Finally, humorous asides are delivered in a small, sans-serif, full-caps font in speech-balloons that are attributed to anthropomorphic worms who comment on the other levels of text while munching a chocolate bar.

A more traditional approach to typography does not regard it as a 'semiotic resource,' but as an element that should avoid drawing attention to itself. In his cleverly titled *Horn Book Magazine* essay, "Give 'Em Helvetica," Leonard S. Marcus asserts that "harmoniousness and understatement are clearly among the watchwords in picture-book type selection and design" (2012: 42). In other words, typography should not be a distraction from the art that conveys its own meaning, and it should seamlessly integrate into the visual layout of the page. How to achieve this? In Sendak's *Where the Wild Things Are* and in many other picturebooks, white space outside of the pictures, also known as air frames, provides room on the page for text. In the case of full-bleed art that extends out to all sides, the type must be especially well-integrated into the design of the page. Jerry Pinkney's nearly wordless Caldecott Medalist, *The Lion and the Mouse* (2009), incorporates intraiconic, onomatopoeic sounds in various images (owl hoots, the sounds of a jeep driving through the African savannah, and of course, squeaking mice and a lion's roar). This creates a text that functions something like a soundtrack, with sounds that seem to emanate from the world of the animals and that allow readers to immerse themselves into the wild, natural setting he has created.

Another excellent example of such seamless integration of text arises not from intraiconic text, but from the artful accommodation of narrative text in Trina Schart Hyman's version of *The Sleeping Beauty* (1977). This old fairy tale about a girl crossing the metaphorical threshold to womanhood has archways, windows, doors, mirrors, and patches of sky that seamlessly provide open spaces in illustrations for blocks of text. In his very different fairy tale retelling of *Goldilocks and the Three Bears* (1988), James Marshall similarly uses a mirror to hold the text in one of the crowded interior scenes set in the house of the Three Bears.

Such layout decisions eschew having typography take center stage as a site of meaning, but in order for text to convey any meaning at all, its words must be legible. Martin and Carle's *Brown Bear, Brown Bear, What Do You See?* (1967) includes a spread with a white dog, set against a black background. All the other spreads in the picturebook use the plain white of the page as a background, which would not work for this image since, in the words of Molly Bang, "contrast enables us to see" (2000: 80). And yet, the achievement of color contrast with this illustration change creates a new typographical challenge, since all other pages have text printed in black type, which would disappear against the dog's black background. The solution? White lettering on the dark background, which is also called reverse type or knockout type, provides contrast to allow readers to decode the "White dog, white dog" refrain.

The use of color with typography is handled differently in my second picturebook, *Real Sisters Pretend* (2016), illustrated by Nicole Tadgell (Figure 3.3). The text is entirely comprised of dialogue spoken between two sisters, which is delivered in speech balloons.

Figure 3.3 Illustration by Nicole Tadgell from Megan Dowd Lambert's *Real Sisters Pretend*. Lewiston, MA: Tilbury House Publishers, 2016.

Reprinted by permission of Tilbury House Publishers.

Taking a cue from Mo Willems's Elephant and Piggie beginning reader books (see for example, *Today I Will Fly!* (2007)), Tadgell embedded the hand-lettered text into color-coded speech balloons that correspond with the respective colors of each girl's clothing – purple for one sister and green for another.

Conclusion

While we might be inclined to think of children opening their ears to picturebook texts read aloud at storytime, guiding them to open their eyes to *see* the expressive nature of the visible text on the page, and perhaps to consider how typographic choices can even covey voice or character, affords additional opportunities for engagement. Indeed, any reader, whether engaging in a shared or an independent reading transaction with a picturebook, has much to gain from considering typography and many other design choices in page layout that can and do provide them with occasions to make meaning of all they behold in the picturebook codex as form and object. As books leave the page and take root on various kinds of screen readers, critics, artists, readers, designers, and others will doubt-lessly ask new questions about what constitutes successful design on these platforms; meanwhile, the picturebook codex affords ongoing, rich opportunities for experimentation and interpretation of the layout possibilities created by the meeting of verso and recto at the gutter of the book, and, more importantly, created by the meeting of the reader with the book in hand.

References

Bader, Barbara (1976) *American Picturebooks from Noah's Ark to the Beast Within*, New York: Palgrave Macmillan.

Bang, Molly (2000) *Picture This: How Pictures Work*, San Francisco: Chronicle Books. (Originally published as *Picture This: Perception and Composition*, Boston: Little, Brown).

Becker, Aaron (2013) *Journey*, Somerville: Candlewick Press.

Bircher, Katie (2016) "Five Questions for Barbara McClintock," www.hbook.com/2016/01/authors-illustrators/five-questions-for-barbara-mcclintock/ (accessed January 13, 2016).

Bruchac, Joseph (2010) *My Father Is Taller Than a Tree*, illus. Wendy Anderson Halperin, New York: Dial Books.

Chambers, Aidan (1983) *Introducing Books to Children*, 2nd ed., Boston: The Horn Book (first published 1973).

Doonan, Jane (1993) *Looking at Pictures in Picturebooks*, Stroud: Thimble Press.

Frazee, Marla (1999) *Hush Little Baby: A Folksong With Pictures*, New York: Houghton Mifflin Harcourt.

Gág, Wanda (1928) *Millions of Cats*, New York: Penguin Young Readers Group.

Gressnich, Eva (2012) "Verbal and Visual Pageturners in Picturebooks," *International Research in Children's Literature* 5.2: 167–183.

Hamilton, Virginia (2000) *The Girl Who Spun Gold*, illus. Leo and Diane Dillon, New York: Scholastic.

Hughes, Shirley (1985) *Chips and Jessie*, London: Bodley Head.

Hyman, Trina Schart (1977) *The Sleeping Beauty*, New York: Little, Brown.

Khan, Rukhsana (2010) *Big Red Lollipop*, illus. Sophie Blackall, New York: Viking.

Klassen, Jon (2011) *I Want My Hat Back*, Somerville: Candlewick Press.

Kümmerling-Meibauer, Bettina, and Meibauer, Jörg (2015) "*Beware of the fox!* Emotion and Deception in *Fox* by Margaret Wild and Ron Brooks," in Janet Evans (ed.) *Challenging and Controversial Picturebooks: Creative and Critical Responses to Visual Texts*, New York: Routledge, 144–159.

Lacy, Lyn Ellen (1986) *Art and Design in Children's Picture Books: An Analysis of Caldecott Award-Winning Illustrations*, Chicago: American Library Association.

Lambert, Megan Dowd (2015a) *Reading Picture Books with Children: How to Shake Up Storytime and Get Kids Talking about What They See*, Watertown, MA: Charlesbridge.

Lambert, Megan Dowd (2015b) *A Crow of His Own*, illus. David Hydee Costello, Watertown, MA: Charlesbridge.

Lambert, Megan Dowd (2016) *Real Sisters Pretend*, illus. Nicole Tadgell, Lewiston, MA: Tilbury House.

Marcus, Leonard S. (2012) "Give 'Em Helvetica: Picturebook Type," *The Horn Book Magazine* (Sept./Oct. 2012): 40–45.

Marshall, James (1988) *Goldilocks and the Three Bears*, New York: Dial Books for Young Readers.

Martin, Bill, Jr. (1967) *Brown Bear, Brown Bear, What Do You See?*, illus. Eric Carle, New York: Henry Holt.

Martin, Douglas (1989) *The Telling Line: Essays on Fifteen Contemporary Book Illustrators*, New York: Delacorte Press.

McClintock, Barbara (2016) *Emma and Julia Love Ballet*, New York: Scholastic.

Monaco, James (1977) *How to Read a Film: Movies, Media, Multimedia*, 3rd ed., New York: Oxford University Press.

Morales, Yuyi (2003) *Just a Minute: A Trickster Counting Book*, San Francisco: Chronicle Books.

Nikolajeva, Maria, and Scott, Carole (2006) *How Picturebooks Work*, New York: Routledge.

Pinkney, Brian (1997) *The Adventures of Sparrowboy*, New York: Simon and Schuster.

Pinkney, Jerry (2009) *The Lion & the Mouse*, New York: Little Brown Books.

Raschka, Chris (1993) *Yo! Yes?*, New York: Scholastic.

Ryan, Pam Muñoz (2002) *When Marian Sang*, illus. Brian Selznick, New York: Scholastic.

Seeger, Laura Vaccaro (2013) *Bully*, New York: Roaring Brook Press.

Sendak, Maurice (1963) *Where the Wild Things Are*, New York: HarperCollins.

Serafini, Frank, and Clausen, Jennifer (2012) "Considering Typography as a Semiotic Resource in Contemporary Picturebooks," *Journal of Visual Literacy* 31.2: 22–38.

Shannon, George (2003) *Tippy-Toe Chick, Go!*, illus. Laura Dronzek, New York: HarperCollins.

Shulevitz, Uri (1968) *The Fool of the World and the Flying Ship*, New York: Farrar, Straus and Giroux.

Stewart, Melissa, and Young, Allen (2013) *No Monkeys, No Chocolate*, illus. Nicole Wong, Watertown, MA: Charlesbridge.

Van Biesen, Koen (2015) *Roger Is Reading a Book*, New York: Eerdmans Books.

Wild, Margaret (2000) *Fox*, illus. Ron Brooks, St. Leonards, NSW: Allen & Unwin.

Willems, Mo (2007) *Today I Will Fly!*, New York: Disney-Hyperion.

4

PARATEXTS IN PICTUREBOOKS

Sylvia Pantaleo

Gérard Genette (1997a) introduced the concept of the paratext in his book, *Palimpsests*. He described the paratext as a threshold, an "undefined zone between the inside and the outside, a zone without any hard and fast boundary on either the inward side (turned toward the text) or the outward side (turned toward the world's discourse about the text)" (2). Authors and/or publishers can be responsible for the making of paratexts, or a third party may be involved in the production of certain paratexts (referred to as allographic paratexts). Paratexts can be official, semiofficial, or unofficial. According to Genette (1997b), paratexts create a "zone not only of transition but of transaction," strategically composed to influence a better reception and interpretation of the text by the public (2). In addition to describing the diverse and evolving nature of paratexts, which reflect the time "period, culture, genre, author, work, and edition" (3), Genette emphasized the need for the simultaneous attention to the paratextual characteristics of where, when, how, from, and to whom, and "to do what" (4). Furthermore, Genette described the noncompulsory nature of the inclusion of various paratextual elements in texts, and of reader attention to or engagement with the paratext.

Although privileging the linguistic mode (both oral and written language) in his discussion of paratextual elements in fiction, Genette wrote that "other types of manifestation" such as "iconic (illustrations)" (7) are to be considered as well. In *Paratexts: Thresholds of Interpretation*, Genette (1997b) acknowledged how his nascent theorizing and exploration of the paratext would provide a "provisional service" (15) to others who further studied the concept. Indeed, as well as criticizing Genette's narrow meaning of the term 'text' (print books) and his focus on literary works, scholars have applied the concept of the paratext to audiovisual forms and digitized media (Stanitzek 2005; Birke and Christ 2013; Kümmerling-Meibauer 2013; McCracken 2013; Leavenworth 2015), noting the impact of technological advancements on textual composition and production with respect to the role and function of authors, illustrators, publishers, and readers.

The paratext = the epitext + the peritext

Genette conceptualized the overarching category of the paratext as constituted by epitexts and peritexts. Epitexts are located outside a book: "any paratextual element not materially appended to the text within the same volume but circulating, as it were, freely, in a virtually limitless physical and social space" (1997b: 344). Public epitexts include public statements or critiques (oral or written) about the work by the author or publisher, interviews or lectures by the author, reviews of the work by the author, and public responses to critics by the author. With respect to private epitexts, Genette described two categories: the confidential epitext, "in which the author addresses one (or more rarely, several) confidant(s), either in writing (correspondence) or orally"; and the intimate epitext, such as a journal or diary "in which the author addresses himself" (372).

Most of Genette's *Paratexts: Thresholds of Interpretation* is devoted to the explication of various peritextual elements. Genette described the publisher's peritext as "the whole zone [spatial and material] of the peritext that is the direct and principal (but not exclusive) responsibility of the publisher" (16). Other individuals have used different terms to refer to the elements of the publisher's peritext. Jane Doonan (1993), for example, used the term *front matter* to describe "the title page (including title, name of author, illustrator, publisher), copyright page and any other printed material placed before the opening of a book's main text. Often called prelims" (84). Lawrence Sipe (1998) also used the term front matter but in a semantically different way than Doonan. He differentiated between the terms *front matter* and *publishing information* using the former to refer solely to the publication information, the fine print attended to by a paucity of readers, and the latter to describe the placement of the publishing and copyright information at the back of a book. The fine print typically includes Library of Congress information regarding the cataloguing of the book (the ISBN); information about the copyright, typeface, illustrative media, and techniques; and a summary statement about the book. Some people refer to this page as the copyright page. In some books, additional information is included on the fine print or dedication page, such as citations of sources of original material included in the book or an illustration.

Most of the following peritextual elements are explicated below in the analysis of three picturebooks: cover, dust jacket, endpapers, frontispiece, full title page, half-title page, dedication page, address of publisher, copyright date, price, typesetting style, choice of paper, table of contents, prefaces, intertitles, and footnotes. A few picturebooks feature footnotes, and this periextual element can provide commentary or additional information including explication of vocabulary, as in *Fungus the Bogeyman* (2012) by Raymond Briggs. Although some peritextual elements may be part of the inner story, the placement, function, and purpose of specific peritextual elements can vary across picturebooks. For example, internal titles or intertitles in a picturebook may or may not be initially featured in a table of contents. In *Hooray for Amanda and Her Alligator* (2011) by Mo Willems, a table of contents lists the titles of the short stories in the picturebook. However, the four internal titles in Anthony Browne's *Voices in the Park* (1998), which identify the particular character's point of view being conveyed, are not depicted in a table of contents.

Scholarship on paratexts in picturebooks

In their chapter on paratexts in picturebooks in *How Picturebooks Work* (2001), Maria Nikolajeva and Carole Scott state that "almost nothing has been written about the paratexts of picturebooks" (241). However, since 2001, several scholars have written about the multiple dimensionality and meaning potential of various peritextual elements in picturebooks. For example, Sipe and Caroline McGuire (2006) examined a collection of picture storybooks and created a typology of picturebook endpapers based on two main dimensions: "whether the endpapers are illustrated or unillustrated, or whether the front and back endpapers are identical or dissimilar" (293). Teresa Duran and Emma Bosch (2011) also classified picturebook endpapers, but their scheme focused on the function of endpages "in the context of the story" (124). Their two main categories of epitextual and peritextual endpapers were subdivided on a secondary level as well (plain, patterned, and illustrated). The categorization scheme developed by Duran and Bosch demonstrates the multifaceted nature and meaning-making potential of picturebook endpapers.

Sandra L. Beckett (2012) discussed the significant role of peritextual components, especially the title, in wordless picturebooks. She also explained how information provided by publishers' inserts, such as prefaces and afterwords, can assist or guide readers as they engage with wordless picturebooks. Similarly, Bettina Kümmerling-Meibauer and Jörg Meibauer (2013) noted how the "foreword, afterword and blurb" in Pop Art picturebooks "play significant roles, since they attempt to lead the audience's reception in specific directions" (106).

Multiple classroom-based studies conducted by Lawrence Sipe and myself have featured attention to peritextual elements in picturebooks. Of the five conceptual categories revealed by Sipe's (2008) data analysis of young children's responses to picture storybook read-alouds, the analytical category, which accounted for nearly three-quarters of the children's conversational turns, included "peritextual analysis" (91). Sipe's data revealed how the children's observations and interpretations denoted a deep understanding of how meaning was communicated by peritextual elements in picturebooks.

During my research in elementary classrooms I have taught 6- to 12-year-old students (and their teachers) about peritextual elements in picturebooks (Pantaleo 2003; 2008a; 2008b; 2010). Classroom observations revealed how students quickly understood the significance of various peritextual elements and appropriated the corresponding metalanguage when talking and writing about the literature. Indeed, analysis of elementary students' responses to picturebooks indicated that instruction focused on developing student knowledge and appreciation of the illustrator's intentional use of elements of visual art and design to represent and communicate meaning contributed to students' sophisticated understandings of and responses to various peritextual elements. Furthermore, the data revealed that once students developed their knowledge about peritextual elements, they anticipated the purposeful inclusion of these features in the literature.

Below, I describe and analyze specific peritextual elements in three picturebooks. Throughout the analysis of the first picturebook, *Tuesday* (1991) by David Wiesner, I also include explanations about the nature of particular peritextual elements.

Tuesday

In 1992 David Wiesner was awarded the Caldecott Medal for *Tuesday* (1991), a wordless picturebook about airborne amphibians who invade a town one Tuesday evening. The aerial invasion is foreshadowed by the artwork on the dust jacket.

A dust jacket (sometimes called a book jacket or a wrapper or case cover) is the removable paper cover wrapped around the outside of the front and back hard covers (called the case) and folded inside the covers to secure it. The two boards used for trade and library editions make picturebooks more durable. Although not all trade editions have a dust jacket, "the library edition, which has a stronger binding, frequently omits the dust jacket, reproducing the same illustration on the front cover" (Sipe 1998: 69). The front and back of a dust jacket may or may not be identical to the front and back hard cover of the picturebook. Finally, in many picturebooks creative visual experimentation with the barcode on the back of the cover or dust jacket makes a unique contribution to the narrative, often in a humourous way.

Generally the artwork on a dust jacket and/or front cover provides readers with their first impressions of the story, and is "often an integral part of the narrative, especially when the cover picture does not repeat any of the pictures inside the book" (Nikolajeva and Scott 2001: 241). With respect to *Tuesday*, Wiesner's use of a bird's-eye point of view for the dust jacket's artwork situates readers as accompanying the frogs on their flight (Figure 4.1). The scene includes the town clock, which reads 8:58, and numerous shadows of airborne frogs created by the illumination of a full moon. From a lighted walkway, Rusty the dog peers up in wonderment as frogs on green lily pads descend upon the town. Although chronologically, the events depicted in the painting occur after a few openings in the picturebook, the cover artwork is not repeated in the picturebook. A white border frames the image and a black border frames the white border. This double framing serves to distance readers from the events. The pale yellow and white capitalized title is centered in the framed artwork. David Wiesner's name is also capitalized and centered, but the typeface is white and placed in the black border at the bottom of the cover, outside of the 'events' depicted in the painting.

Figure 4.1 Dust jacket of *Tuesday* by David Wiesner. New York: Clarion Books, 1991.

Copyright © 1991 by David Wiesner. Reprinted by permission of Clarion Books, an imprint of Houghton Mifflin Harcourt Publishing Company.

The back of a dust jacket and hard cover may or may not have illustrations and/or other information such as reviews, a synopsis, and/or a text excerpt. The framed image on the black back of the dust jacket of *Tuesday*, which is exclusive to the dust jacket, positions readers at the initial setting of the visual narrative, peering through a stand of cattails. Readers view a lone frog on a lily pad rising above the water with a brilliant full moon shining in the background. The white framing of the image makes the artwork resemble a photograph that was snapped by someone who witnessed this mystical event.

In addition to protecting the book, the dust jacket usually features information about the picturebook's contents (and sometimes the price) on the front flap, and facts about the author and/or illustrator on the back flap. The dust jacket flaps of *Tuesday* are white. On the front flap of *Tuesday*, the black text warns readers that if they disbelieve the events in the book, there is always another Tuesday. This counsel contributes to the mysterious atmosphere that is created by the events visually depicted on the dust jacket. The back flap features information about David Wiesner and some of his other picturebooks.

Two elements exclusive to hard cover editions of some picturebooks are die-cuts on the front and/or back cover and stamping, where images or letters are pressed into the front or back covers. "If the image is simply stamped without any color, it is called blind stamping; if it is pressed in gold or another color, it is called foil stamping" (Sipe 1998: 71). Removal of the dust jacket of *Tuesday* reveals blind stamping of the word 'Tuesday' on the front pale green cover, and a plain back cover. Bosch (2014) describes the title as the "most important peritext" in "pure wordless picturebooks" (80), but in *Tuesday*, although the title of the book is repeated on the hard cover, the word provides limited information about the nature of the visual narrative. The green-colored cover is similar in hue to the lily pads; the lily pads provide the medium for the frogs' adventure and Wiesner's green hard cover picturebook affords readers with an amazing visual adventure.

The endpages of *Tuesday* are plain and light yellow in color. As well as serving the pragmatic function of connecting "the book's cover to the text block" (Sipe and McGuire 2006; 292) in hard cover editions, endpapers, also called endpages, are like "stage curtains, framing the performance of a play" (Sipe 1998: 69). Endpapers consist of two pages; the pastedown is pasted or adhered to the front and back cover, and the flyleaf faces the pastedown. The particular colors, designs, and/or illustrations chosen for the endpapers often complement the text, and can be significant in foreshadowing information about the picturebook's plot, characters, setting, themes, and/or mood. In *Tuesday*, perhaps the design and color choice of the endpages is to capture the subtle glow of a full moon. As noted earlier, the moon is full the night the frogs take flight.

The frontispiece of *Tuesday* precedes the fine print and full title page. A frontispiece is an illustration on the page that faces or immediately precedes the title page of a book or magazine. Although Kathy Short, Carol Lynch-Brown, and Carl Tomlinson (2014) state the frontispiece "is intended to establish the tone and to entice the reader to begin the story" (60), this particular peritextual element can be used for other functions, such as introducing characters or beginning the narrative. Agnes Bjorvand (2014) uses the terms 'prologue pictures' and 'epilogue pictures' to describe the artwork found on the frontispiece, front and back endpapers, title page, 'half-title page' (a page facing the front flyleaf featuring only the title and sometimes an illustration) (Sipe 1998: 71), and back cover. On the frontispiece in *Tuesday*, three air framed illustrations, banded horizontally to depict the passing of time, foretell events as three sleeping frogs on lily pads become three airborne amphibians (Figure 4.2).

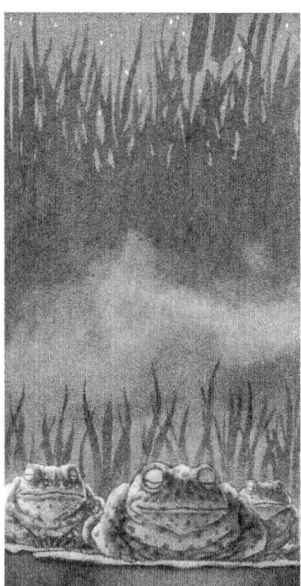

Figure 4.2 Frontispiece of *Tuesday* by David Wiesner. New York: Clarion Books, 1991.

A quick perusal of a number of picturebooks reveals how they differ with respect to the sequence of the half-title page, the full title page, and other fine print (Galda, Cullinan and Sipe 2006). In *Tuesday*, the fine print page, which contains the dedication and other publication information, facts about the typeface, illustrative media, paper choice, and book designer, precedes the title page. The dedication on *Tuesday* reads, "For Tom Sgouros," an individual identified by Wiesner as the most important person in his creative development. Thus, dedications, which can be included on the fine print page or have an entire page devoted to them, are important to authors and/or illustrators and should be considered by readers.

The full title page in *Tuesday* features the title of the book, the author, the illustrator, and the name and location of the publisher. Some picturebooks have an illustration on the full title page and this artwork can achieve varying and multiple purposes. In *Tuesday* the title page includes a lily pad, further foreshadowing the water plant's salience to the story.

When paperback editions of picturebooks are published, various peritextual elements can be both eliminated and/or altered. For example, soft cover versions omit the dust jacket and often the endpapers, and the artwork on a dust jacket may or may not be reproduced on the cover of the paperback edition. When compared to the dust jacket of the trade edition, the paperback version of *Tuesday* (1991) has identical front cover artwork but the back cover is different. For example, it

Figure 4.3 Dust jacket of the anniversary edition of *Tuesday* by David Wiesner. New York: Clarion Books, 2001.

features excerpts from reviews and lists five awards. A black frame and five airborne frogs on lily pads border the black textual information printed on white. The paperback version has no endpapers, so when readers open the book they see the frontispiece. Thus, although the paperback edition includes additional information, the missing peritextual elements are significant to the overall visual narrative.

As well as modifications made to the peritextual elements in a paperback version when compared to the hard cover version, the design of dust jackets and covers of translated picturebooks, or even English language picturebooks published in different countries or at different times, may differ from the original versions. Some peritextual elements were changed when the twentieth anniversary version of *Tuesday* was published (the publication date remained 1991). The typeface used on the dust jacket for the title and for David Wiesner's name is embossed and golden, perhaps symbolizing and celebrating the picturebook's literary achievement. The artwork on the dust jacket is a full bleed, no longer framed by two borders (Figure 4.3). Thus, as well as visually positioning readers in the sky with the airborne amphibians, Wiesner's page design choice further engages readers as participants in the events they are viewing because an illustration that bleeds to all four edges communicates that life continues beyond the confines of the page. In personal communications with Wiesner, he explained to me how by 2006 his cover design preferences began to change, and in addition to creating dust jackets without a border, he began to include paintings related to the narrative. Wiesner also described how the experience of creating full-bleed covers led to the decision to remove the borders from the original artwork on *Tuesday* for the anniversary version, and as is described later, to make other changes to the case cover.

The dust jacket's flaps on the anniversary edition are golden brown. Compared to the original, additional information on the inside jacket flap conveys that this rendering celebrates the twentieth anniversary of Tuesday in print and includes "new digital reproductions of the original watercolor illustrations." Additional information about *Tuesday* and some of Wiesner's more recent picturebooks is included on the back flap. The back of the dust jacket is identical to the 1991 publication.

With respect to the hard front and back case covers, the anniversary edition also has a vertical band of black that wraps around the book's spine (Figure 4.4). However, on the left-hand side of the front cover 'Tuesday' is written in white capitals parallel to the spine of the book (so 'T' is at the bottom of the cover) in the 6 cm black band. A white vertical line near the edge of the black band seems to underline the title. One of the framed images of the airborne amphibians from the verso of opening 4 is featured in the middle of the pale green (celadon, perhaps) front cover. The artwork is framed

Figure 4.4 Cover of the anniversary edition of *Tuesday* by David Wiesner. New York: Clarion Books, 2001.

twice – a thin black line frames the white border outlining the image. As is evident in Figure 4.4, in the black band on the back of the hard cover 'Tuesday' is written in the mirror image of the text on the front cover. The back cover also features an image – the caped flying frogs depicted on the verso of opening 8 – and it is framed similarly as the image on the front.

The endpapers are a yellowish tan color in the twentieth anniversary edition, complementing the golden text on the front dust jacket. Amendments to the text on the fine print page reflect changes to the ownership of the publishing company. These changes are also indicated on the title page.

The preceding descriptions and analyses of various peritextual elements in three editions of *Tuesday* reveal the intentionality of their inclusion and design with respect to communicating and representing meaning. Next, the analyses of peritextual elements in two other picturebooks provide further examples of the significant role of these multimodal and design components.

Mr. Tiger Goes Wild

In *Mr. Tiger Goes Wild* (2013), Peter Brown tells the story of a tiger's search for his identity when the male protagonist dares to be different. The dust jacket features the main character, Mr. Tiger, dressed in formal attire standing in foliage native to "the wildness" he flees to in order to escape the suffocating way of life of his Victorian-like city. This image, which portrays the juxtaposition of Mr. Tiger's experiences, is exclusive to the cover. On the dust jacket's back flap, Peter Brown, who has depicted himself similarly dressed and contextualized as the anthropomorphized tiger, directly addresses readers both visually (demand image) and verbally. The text in his speech bubble foreshadows narrative events: "Hello. I am Peter Brown and it is my professional opinion that everyone should find time to go a little wild."

The title of a picturebook is not always included on both the dust jacket and the hard cover. Indeed, the title appears on only the dust jacket of *Mr. Tiger Goes Wild*. Removal of the dust jacket, which can be viewed as a visual metaphor for the main character shedding his clothing on opening 10 and discovering his "inner self," reveals a close up of Mr. Tiger's fur. Together, the front and back vertically textured hard covers feature eight large and long black stripes on orange that nearly reach the white furry edge that borders the bottom of the covers. The artwork on the endpapers is both contrastive and symbolic in nature. The sepia-toned brick wall (although many reviewers describe the bricks as gray), which constitutes the front endpapers, is not only the building material of the structurally identical houses in Mr. Tiger's city, but also the bricks convey conformity, systematic arrangement, and monotony. A mixture of plant life indigenous to the landscape where Mr. Tiger travels to during his quest for self-actualization covers the back endpapers; the foliage could be interpreted as symbolizing freedom, diversity, growth, and change.

The fine print page, similar in color to the hills outside of Mr. Tiger's monochromatic city, features the metaphorical dedication "For tigers everywhere," as well as other publication information. Further fine print details regarding the illustrative media, typeface, paper choice and design, and production are located on the back flyleaf. By reading this publication information, readers learn that it was necessary to add special orange ink when the picturebook was being printed (because most books are printed using only four colors) (Wind 2014: para. 10). In *Mr. Tiger Goes Wild*, Brown uses Rockwell typeface for the text and hand-lettering for the display text. Typically in picturebooks, the title page presents the typeface that is used for the text, and generally the typography is selected for its appropriateness for the story content, the historical period, the mood of the book, or the intended audience. On the title page of *Mr. Tiger Goes Wild*, the publication information is rendered in Rockwell typeface, but the title, which is completed in uppercase letters, and Peter Brown's name, which is completed in lowercase letters, are hand-lettered. The varying typeface style and size can be inferred as symbolizing the range of events, experiences, and emotions that transpire during the narrative. The use of lowercase letters for Brown's name on both the dust jacket and the title page could be interpreted as representing and foreshadowing Mr. Tiger's deliberate opposition to societal conventions.

Thus, as well as contributing to the overall visual aesthetics of the picturebook, Brown's purposeful design of peritextual elements in *Mr. Tiger Goes Wild* conveys information about the literary elements of character, plot, setting, and theme.

Journey

Journey, a wordless book by Aaron Becker (2013) and a 2014 Caldecott Honor award winner, visually tells the story of a girl who embarks on a magical journey when she draws a door on her bedroom wall with her literally red crayon. Upon stepping through the open door, the girl discovers a fantastical world and begins her imaginative adventure.

The full-bleed artwork on the front dust jacket is unique, although the girl floating down a canal in her red boat to a city-sized castle is depicted in other paintings in the book (opening 5) (Figure 4.5). However, the purple phoenix featured in the cover artwork foreshadows her encounter with the bird. Becker uses color to create textual cohesion in several ways on the dust jacket. The red color of the title's capitalized typeface is the same hue as the girl's red crayon and boat. Furthermore, the back of the dust jacket and the spine are red in color – the same hue as the title, crayon, and boat.

The center alignment and uppercase font of the title communicate the power and importance of the word 'journey.' Becker's name is placed in the bottom right-hand corner, is midnight blue in color, and completed in title case. Unfortunately, information about the typeface is not provided on the fine print page – a missed opportunity for meaning-making. The text on the dust jacket spine is completed in the same typefaces but the title is white, again creating textual cohesion with respect to typography. Three lanterns, similar to those hanging in the magical forest the girl enters when she first opens the door in her bedroom, four excerpts from book reviews typed in black typeface, and the ISBN and price information are featured on the back dust jacket. The dust jacket's flaps are white; the text summarizing the story on the front flap begins with an illuminated red letter. Information about Aaron Becker is presented on the back flap, and his black capitalized name is rendered in the same typeface as the title of the picturebook.

Removal of the dust jacket reveals a midnight blue hard cover with a blind stamp image of the main character, with crayon in hand, floating in a hot air balloon. The centered, stamped impression foreshadows the girl's flight in the hot air balloon on the verso of opening 8. Only the spine features printed text: the title and the name of the author and publisher are foil-stamped in gold. The choice of gold may be to symbolize the worth and importance of journeys, whether they be literal or figurative in nature.

A pattern is created by the faint black drawings of various forms of transportation depicted on the identical front and back red endpapers. These multiple physical forms of traveling can be

Figure 4.5 Dust jacket of *Journey* by Aaron Becker. Sommerville, MA: Candlewick Press, 2013.

contrasted with the girl's use of imagination to travel on a journey. A red flyleaf faces the full title page; the color choice connects with the girl's red kickboard scooter depicted on the adjacent title page. Other than the girl's scooter and a hanging blue lantern, which is similar to those in the enchanted forest, sepia is the dominant color used for the art on the title page. Although the same typeface is used for the title as on the dust jacket, the title is black on the title page. The narrative seems to begin on the title page and the girl on her scooter serves as a vector, a leading line encouraging readers to turn the page and journey into the book. A page turn reveals a full-bleed doublespread of the girl's city neighborhood as well as a cutaway depiction of her house. The girl's red kickboard scooter, a boy's purple crayon, and muted colors on a stoplight and walk signal are in contrast to the otherwise sepia-toned scene. Becker's color scheme simultaneously differentiates the children from the setting and connects them with each other. The significance of the presence of the boy with the purple crayon, who is positioned with his back to readers on the fine print page, is realized on the penultimate opening when the girl returns from her journey accompanied by the purple phoenix. The fine print page features a dedication and most of the typical information included on this peritextual element.

As is evident by the preceding descriptions, Becker's intentional use of various elements of visual art and design in *Journey* create peritextual elements that convey a range of literal and symbolic meaning. Furthermore, recognition of the synergy among the peritextual elements in *Journey*, as well as in all picturebooks, is fundamental to both respecting and appreciating this format of literature as an art object.

Discussion

Genette (1997b) described the paratext as "only an assistant, only an accessory of the text" (410). However, as is evident by the preceding descriptions, in many picturebooks the peritextual elements are not merely assistive or accessorial – they constitute part of 'the' text. In the picturebooks by Wiesner, Brown, and Becker, peritextual elements simultaneously achieve multiple functions and purposes, such as introducing readers to main characters and settings, foreshadowing plot events, and establishing or contributing to the creation of a particular mood or atmosphere. Readers also view and read symbolic and metaphorical images and text in the peritextual elements that are central to the themes or plot events of the stories. Specific visual art choices used for peritextual elements exemplify the intentionality of design to represent and communicate meaning. For example, Wiesner, Brown, and Becker use color in various peritextual elements to convey information about characters and events, connote relationships, create textual cohesion, and rouse aesthetic appreciation. In addition, the artists use color to create emphasis, variety, and harmony in various peritextual elements. Thus, the descriptions and analyses of the peritextual elements convey their significance to the materiality and narrative of the picturebooks and of the reading experience itself.

Both scholarly and pedagogical consideration of picturebook paratexts has been, and should continue to be, approached from varying theoretical and conceptual frameworks such as narratology, reader-response, visual literacy, art appreciation, semiotics, and multimodality. As described previously, researchers have documented how knowledge about and interpretation of peritextual elements can contribute to students' aesthetic appreciation for and cognitive and literary understandings of picturebooks. Teaching students the language of peritextual elements provides them with a metalanguage that is fundamental to their abilities to analyze, critique, and interpret the affordances of these literary and artistic elements, and to their overall understanding of how picturebooks are intentionally designed and constructed to convey meaning. As authors, illustrators, and publishers continue to explore and experiment with peritextual elements in picturebooks, it is important that readers understand these critical and synergistic elements. Furthermore, students can apply and transfer their paratextual competencies to other print, multimodal, and multimedia texts.

References

Becker, Aaron (2013) *Journey*, Sommerville: Candlewick Press.

Beckett, Sandra L. (2012) *Crossover Picturebooks: A Genre for All Ages*, New York: Routledge.

Birke, Dorothee, and Christ, Birthe (2013) "Paratext and Digitized Narrative: Mapping the Field," *Narrative* 21.1: 65–87.

Bjorvand, Agnes-Margrethe (2014) "Prologue and Epilogue Pictures in Astrid Lindgren's Picturebooks," in Bettina Kümmerling-Meibauer (ed.) *Picturebooks: Representation and Narration*, New York: Routledge, 213–226.

Bosch, Emma (2014) "Texts and Peritexts in Wordless and Almost Wordless Picturebooks," in Bettina Kümmerling-Meibauer (ed.) *Picturebooks: Representation and Narration*, New York: Routledge, 71–90.

Briggs, Raymond (2012) *Fungus the Bogeyman: 35th Anniversary Edition*, London: Puffin (first published 1977).

Brown, Peter (2013) *Mr. Tiger Goes Wild*, New York: Little, Brown.

Browne, Anthony (1998) *Voices in the Park*, London: Picture Corgi Books.

Doonan, Jane (1993) *Looking at Pictures in Picture Books*, Stroud: The Thimble Press.

Duran, Teresa, and Bosch, Emma (2011) "Before and After the Picturebook Frame: A Typology of Endpapers," *New Review of Children's Literature and Librarianship* 17.2: 122–143.

Galda, Lee, Cullinan, Bernice E., and Sipe, Lawrence R. (2006) *Literature and the Child*, Independence, KY: Wadsworth.

Genette, Gérard (1997a) *Palimpsests: Literature in the Second Degree*, trans. C. Newman. Doubinsky, Lincoln: University of Nebraska Press (Original French ed. published 1982).

Genette, Gérard (1997b) *Paratexts: Thresholds of Interpretation*, trans. J. Lewin, New York: Cambridge Press (Original French ed. published 1987).

Kümmerling-Meibauer, Bettina (2013) "Paratexts in Children's Films and the Concept of Meta-Filmic Awareness," *Journal of Educational Media, Memory, and Society* 5.2: 108–123.

Kümmerling-Meibauer, Bettina, and Meibauer, Jörg (2013) "On the Strangeness of Pop Art Picturebooks: Pictures, Texts, Paratexts," in Evelyn Arizpe, Maureen Farrell, and Julie MacAdam (eds) *Picturebooks: Beyond the Borders of Art, Narrative and Culture*, New York: Routledge, 23–41.

Leavenworth, Maria Lindgren (2015) "The Paratext of Fan Fiction," *Narrative* 23.1: 40–60.

McCracken, Ellen (2013) "Expanding Genette's Epitext/Peritext Model for Transitional Electronic Literature: Centrifugal and Centripetal Vectors on Kindles and iPads," *Narrative* 21.1: 105–124.

Nikolajeva, Maria, and Scott, Carole (2001) *How Picturebooks Work*, New York: Garland.

Pantaleo, Sylvia (2003) "'Godzilla Lives in New York': Grade 1 Students and the Peritextual Features of Picture Books," *Journal of Children's Literature* 29.2: 66–75.

Pantaleo, Sylvia (2008a) "Ed Vere's *The Getaway*: Starring a Postmodern Cheese Thief," in Lawrence R. Sipe and Sylvia Pantaleo (eds) *Postmodern Picturebooks: Play, Parody, and Self-Referentiality*, New York: Routledge, 238–255.

Pantaleo, Sylvia (2008b) *Exploring Student Response to Contemporary Picturebooks*, Toronto: University of Toronto Press.

Pantaleo, Sylvia (2010) "Emily Gravett's Postmodern Picturebook *Wolves*," *Journal of Children's Literature* 36.1: 51–59.

Short, Kathy G., Lynch-Brown, Carol, and Tomlinson, Carl (2014) *Essentials of Children's Literature*, 8th ed., Upper Saddle River: Pearson Education.

Sipe, Lawrence R. (1998) "Learning the Language of Picturebooks," *Journal of Children's Literature* 24.2: 66–75.

Sipe, Lawrence R. (2008) *Storytime: Young Children's Literary Understanding in the Classroom*, New York: Teachers College Press.

Sipe, Lawrence R., and McGuire, Caroline (2006) "Picturebook Endpapers: Resources for Literary and Aesthetic Interpretation," *Children's Literature in Education* 37.4: 291–304.

Stanitzek, Greg (2005) "Texts and Paratexts in Media," trans. Ellen Klein, *Critical Inquiry* 32.1: 27–42.

Wiesner, David (1991) *Tuesday*, New York: Clarion Books.

Willems, Mo (2011) *Hooray for Amanda and her Alligator*, New York: Hyperion Books for Children.

Wind, Lee (2014) "Peter Brown on 'Mr. Tiger Goes Wild' – The 2014 Golden Kite Interviews," *scbwi: The Blog – The Official Blog of the Society of Children's Book Writers and Illustrators* (June 12, 2014), http://scbwi.blogspot.ca/2014/06/peter-brown-on-mr-tiger-goes-wild-2014.html.

5

COLLAGE AND MONTAGE IN PICTUREBOOKS

Elina Druker

Picturebook collage and the avant-garde

The term 'collage,' from the French *coller* (to glue), refers to the process of assembling fragments of different material to create a composite image. There is a long tradition of textual and visual collage – the cutting out and combining of elements from various contexts – within the arts. Both forms have been centrally involved in various shifts within Western art history, especially within avant-garde movements such as Cubism, Dada, and Surrealism. In 1912 Georges Braque and Pablo Picasso created the first *papiers collés*, an innovation regarded as a major turning point in the evolution of Cubism, and thus in the whole development of modernist art at the beginning of the twentieth century (Greenberg 1989: 70). Collage and other combination techniques were used in the search for new modes of expression, but were also a means of questioning the nature and value of art itself (Taylor 2006). This chapter utilizes the terms 'collage' and 'montage' to denote a broad aesthetic principle of combination and synthesis. This principle includes a variety of practices ranging from textual and visual collage to photomontage and digital montage.

Several connections can be traced between avant-garde art and the use of collage in picturebooks. One early example is the collaboration between Margaret Wise Brown and Esphyr Slobodkina, who produced the works *The Little Fireman* (1938) and *Sleepy ABC* (1953). Slobodkina was born in Russia in 1908 and lived in China as a young girl, studying painting and architecture before immigrating to the United States in 1928. She is best described as an abstract artist, working with painting, collage sculptures, and installations which integrated a variety of materials and everyday objects. She was one of the founding members of the American Abstract Artists, a group that was instrumental in drawing attention to the American abstract art movement at a time when abstract art was primarily considered to be the province of European artists (Kraskin et al. 2009). In *The Little Fireman*, striking colors and reduced, geometric shapes interact with straightforward text about the little fireman and his dog, which saves "fifteen little fat ladies" and later enjoys "a very little dish of pink ice cream." The setting consists of modern, urban scenery and is described through immediate sensory experiences, such as the wail of fire truck sirens or the visual image of the trucks moving through the city streets. The simplified collage technique was thought to allow children points of entry to the text, emphasizing their own imaginative participation. The aesthetic techniques employed by Slobodkina and Wise Brown – the use of an everyday setting, the play with sounds and colors – reflect modern ideas pertaining to children's literature, pedagogy, and art. The ideas that inform *The Little Fireman* are consistent with, for instance, Lucy Sprague Mitchell's influential *Here and Now Story Book* (1921), in which the author calls for a more child-centered approach to children's literature, a sense of the "here and now." Slobodkina may also be regarded as a predecessor to Ezra Jack Keats, who used India ink, patterned paper cutouts, different fabrics, and oilcloth in the collage illustrations of several of his picturebooks, including *The Snowy Day* (1962) or *Peter's Chair* (1967).

Several early twentieth-century picturebooks employing collage also feature connections to the worlds of painting and graphic design. The Dutch-Italian Leo Lionni's experimental picturebook, *Little Blue and Little Yellow* (1959), consists of simple, abstract shapes and features two characters – blue and yellow – playing together. Lionni, a painter, art director for *Fortune* magazine, and graphic designer, found inspiration for the book while entertaining his grandchildren during a long train ride. Using a copy of *Life* magazine, he tore out circles of yellow and blue from its pages to tell the story (1997: 214). The radically simplified picturebook features connections to the fields of commercial art and design, but also to De Stijl. Lionni's later works often take the form of animal fables, such as *Frederick* (1968) or *Alexander and the Wind-Up Mouse* (1969), in which he continues to play with the contrasts between shapes with torn edges and forms with sharply cut edges.

Another influential picturebook artist who utilizes cutouts and painted materials is Eric Carle, who often paints and dyes transparent tissue paper for his collage images. The painted or sponge-stippled watercolor surfaces are then formed into sharp-edged collages. The classic picturebook *The Very Hungry Caterpillar* (1969) guides the reader in counting the days of the week, naming different foods, and learning about a butterfly's life stages. Here, the pedagogical theme is combined with experimental and colorful illustrations and holes (ostensibly "eaten" by the caterpillar) in the pages. Several of Carle's books, including *Do You Want to Be My Friend?* (1971) and *The Mixed-Up Chameleon* (1975), feature these well-defined, sharp-edged shapes, and colorful, patterned surfaces against a white background.

Picturebook artists and authors like Slobodkina, Lionni, and Carle do not merely incorporate the aesthetic techniques of the avant-garde or contemporary graphic design into the picturebook; they also actively work to challenge and activate their readers in ways significant to the development of the picturebook medium as a whole. All three artists are concerned with the search for a new language and new images. Innovative pedagogical theories may be regarded as a precondition for the evolution of picturebook aesthetics in the twentieth century, yet it must also be remembered that this evolution took place during a revolutionary period in European graphic design and art. Within the arts, graphic design, and picturebooks, breaking with the past involves a renegotiation of how pictures are constructed, but also a reconsideration of the interrelation of text and image. Interest in the material aspects of art also entails treating books as physical objects. In a book such as Carle's *The Very Hungry Caterpillar*, for instance, the artist explores the material and conceptual qualities of the book, as well as the book as a three-dimensional spatial construction, in different ways.

Describing the postmodern world

While Leo Lionni and Eric Carle worked with layers of cut paper of different textures and colors, thus emphasizing the form and materiality of the figures created, many contemporary illustrators select their materials thematically. This latter approach recycles can and styles and creates new combinations of images, a method expressive of an attitude that can be termed postmodern. The choice of collage technique is of central importance to the picturebooks of German artist Wolf Erlbruch, whose work has had a significant influence on the aesthetics of contemporary European picturebooks more generally. Valérie Dayre's *Die Menschenfresserin* (The Ogress 1996) and Erlbruch's interpretation of Karl Philipp Moritz's *Das Neue ABC-Buch* (The New ABC-Book 2001) both employ a variety of materials, in combination with drawings created with pencil or wax pencil, as well as distinct cutout shapes. In the fashion of early picturebook artists, such as those mentioned above, cutouts are used to create strong, dynamic forms and expressive body language. Several of Erlbruch's picturebooks, for instance, *Nachts* (At Night 1999), feature a central contrast between playful and simple elements and shapes, and more mundane materials, such as newspaper clippings, timetables, and mathematic formulas.

Erlbruch's *Ente, Tod und Tulpe* (Duck, Death and the Tulip 2007) is a large picturebook which narrates the story of a duck who meets Death. The story can be read as an interpretation of the motif of the 'danse macabre,' a late-medieval allegory concerned with the universality of death, intended to remind people of the vanity of earthly life. Regardless of one's social position, the dance of death unites all: emperors and paupers, the mighty and the powerless, young and old. After the outbreak of the Black Death in Germany, the danse macabre spread in the form of plays and paintings, both forms aimed at the illiterate, as a reminder of the necessity to lead a Christian life. Among the most famous representations were the woodcuts designed by Hans Holbein the younger and executed by Hans Lützelburger (1538). In these representations, class distinctions are neutralized by Death, who treats everybody equally – an interesting socio-critical comment expressed through the motif.

The idea that death is an inevitable and natural part of life is central to Erlbruch's story. The use of small collage elements, such as engravings of trees and flowers resembling old book illustrations, emphasize the intertextual connection between the medieval motif and Erlbruch's interpretation of it (Figure 5.1). Throughout the book, Death and the duck are engaged in a dialogue in which physical movements and gestures are of central importance. Death is depicted as kind and thoughtful, almost apprehensive. The stark simplification of shapes, the sparse collage elements, and the scarce use of color or background elements place primary focus on the motif itself – a gentle dance of death. Color is gradually introduced in the book only after the duck has died. A deep blue begins to infuse the pages in the form of the night sky and the river that finally carries the duck away.

The work of Shaun Tan, an Australian picturebook artist, combines a pronounced interest in traditional painting and illustration with a postmodern approach to motif and technique. Tan employs a variety of artistic materials and methods: painting, lead pencil, India ink, and a variety of print and collage techniques. *The Red Tree* (2001) features a series of stunning, self-contained images, loosely connected to the interrelated themes of identity, language, solitude, even depression and anxiety. Collage techniques generally entail a dissolving of narrative and syntactic relationships, a fragmentation characteristic of *The Red Tree*. The book's sparse and poetic text, featuring only a few words or sentences per doublespread, does not form a traditional sequential narrative, but functions as a complement to and foundation for the complex and multifaceted images.

The Red Tree examines the theme of language and communication in a variety of ways. In the doublespread featuring the text that reads "without sense or reason," the main character is depicted standing on a ladder, surrounded by layers of fragmented words, signs, and texts. The chaotic collage illustration is created with oils, acrylics, wax pencil, and collage using newspaper clippings and stamps. The diminutive figure of the girl seems virtually drowned in the surrounding layers of signs and fragments of words and text. The scene can be interpreted as an image of alienation or as an expression of the difficulty of articulating emotion in words, even when one is surrounded by text and language.

While emphasizing the materiality of the medium, its seams and contours, a collage also reveals the conditions of its construction. Norwegian artist Svein Nyhus's *Snill* (Gentle 2002), with text by Gro Dahle, combines painting, drawing, and collage, generating a coherent and integrated mode of expression which simultaneously highlights the materials used and what they represent. In a fashion reminiscent of Wolf Erlbruch's books, collage material is used thematically in a number of key scenes. The first images a reader encounters in *Snill* feature sheets of graph paper and ruled paper situated behind the controlled and well-behaved main character (Gentle), signifying the underlying tension and rigidity of her strictly regulated life. The Italian-French artist Beatrice Alemagna's *Un lion à Paris*

Figure 5.1 Illustration from Wolf Erlbruch's *Ente, Tod und Tulpe*. Munich:Verlag Antje Kunstmann, 2007.
Copyright © Wolf Erlbruch. Used by permission of Verlag Antje Kunstmann.

(A Lion in Paris 2006) also utilizes collage in its background settings in order to create shapes or to introduce small, yet important details and fragments in the painted and drawn images. Alemagna's picturebook describes the experience of being a stranger in a new city, but the collage technique is also used to express the theme of belonging and the process of coming to understand one's own identity.

Collage and folk art

The work of Swedish painter and picturebook artist Jockum Nordström features a connection to painting but also a pronounced interest in folk art and cutout techniques. Nordström has written and illustrated a series of picturebooks whose readership includes children and adults alike. The absurd humor and naivety of *Sailor och Pekka gör ärenden på stan* (Sailor and Pekka Busy in Town 1993) is characteristic of Nordström's picturebooks. The story is simple, almost trivial: on their way to town, Sailor and Pekka meet a sad clown who has lost his trumpet. In town, Sailor buys a new shirt and Pekka, the dog, gets a tattoo. They incidentally recover the lost trumpet and return the instrument to its owner. The playfulness and ease of the nonsensical story is reflected in the rudimentary illustrations. In his paintings, Nordström utilizes a variety of techniques, from complicated cut-paper collages to simple line drawings. His picturebook illustrations also include photographic elements. The cartoonish, slightly clumsy characters and the simplicity of the stories embrace the irrational and childlike.

Sailor and Pekka Busy in Town employs a variety of different graphic materials, including structural designs, drawings, paintings, maps, wallpapers, and photographs. The images feature explicit influences from film, jazz music, cartoons, and popular culture, creating a world of strangely timeless settings and characters. This naïve approach is distinct from avant-garde collage techniques, recalling instead the way in which materials and techniques are combined within global and Nordic folk art. Folk art is usually created out of whatever material is at hand: illustrations and text from books, newspapers, and other printed matter, ornaments from fabrics, or photographs. It can consist of illustrations produced for private use and amusement. In "The Invention of Collage," Marjorie Perloff emphasizes this function of the collage technique, this impulse "[t]o collage elements from impersonal, external sources – the newspaper, magazines, television, billboards [. . .], to establish continuity between one's own private universe and the world outside, to make from what is already there something that is one's own" (Perloff 1998: 43). This tension between the private and the public, the naïve and high art, is characteristic of Nordström's painting in general.

With respect to his paintings and drawings, Nordström often divides the canvas or the sheet of paper in complex ways. A similar interest in complex composition is expressed in his picturebooks; but here the book medium offers other spatial and narrative opportunities, ranging from more fluid use of perspective to a range of alternative narrative and artistic strategies. The images in his picturebooks alternate between panoramic landscape views and precise close-ups. Every now and then, cartoonlike sequences are used to alter the pace of the story. Here, the particular choice of collage technique seems to be connected to the narrative possibilities offered to the artist by the book form.

Moreover, Nordström's settings often feature spacious avenues, industrial buildings, or public housing complexes, reminiscent of images of modernist, progressive city planning – standing for order and harmony, functionality, and organization. Yet, the town described in *Sailor and Pekka Busy in Town* is situated in an exotic environment, surrounded by palm trees, mountains, and romantic ocean views. Hence, the precise place and time in which the stories unfold remains ambiguous. Furthermore, the carefully constructed buildings are sometimes employed to form decorative patterns or abstract shapes on the page. They are used as ornamental surfaces, rather than solid, three-dimensional forms. This slight instability between the figurative and the abstract evokes a peculiar sense of spatial alienation. The illusory perception of surfaces and depth is explored playfully, yet precisely. The sensual and physical approach to the picturebook medium – connected to folk art, but expanded and narrated in Nordström's books – is also evident in his later work *Vart ska du?* (Where Are You Going? 2013), an accordion book which again incorporates different perspectives and materials and moves between simplicity and meticulous artistic craftsmanship.

Digital collage and montage

The introduction of new digital illustration techniques and the development of digital imaging software such as Adobe Photoshop have effected a series of fundamental transformations in graphic design and picturebook aesthetics. And yet, although it has become increasingly commonplace to import and recycle visual elements from different contexts in painting, propaganda, or commercials, this is by no means a new phenomenon (Druker 2008). In the late nineteenth century, for instance, the photographic collage and montage became the ideal creative medium for expressing new possibilities for the perception and interpretation of what was described as the 'New World,' a world dramatically transformed by the impact of modern technology.

The Norwegian graphic designer and artist Stian Hole's work represents an interesting development within the postmodern picturebook, a development in evidence from his very first work. *Den gamle mannen og hvalen* (The Old Man and the Whale 2005) is a story about two elderly brothers who meet again after years of disagreement. Here, Hole's digital photomontage illustrations include large numbers of items and objects from everyday life but also incorporate fantasy elements and images with intertextual references. Although strikingly decorative and elegant in their expression, his illustrations do not so much emphasize the flawless technical possibilities of the digital medium, but rather establish and play with the meeting ground between the separate collage elements. Moreover, Hole's picturebooks may be regarded as an interesting example of the distinction between montage and collage. In collage, the content of the material used is often secondary to the aesthetic arrangement, or else this content may be fragmented or illogical. By contrast, Hole's works emphasize the meaning associated with the individual picture elements; the use of photomontage thus creates explicit key connotations relating to the theme of the story.

Beginnings and endings are the main motif of another of Hole's works, *Garmanns sommer* (Garmann's Summer 2007). The summer vacation is almost over, and Garmann is feeling anxious. He is nervous about starting school in the next few days, and begins to ruminate about life, time, aging, and death. Garmann's thoughts about aging and change are mainly expressed through his dialogues with three old ladies visiting his family. Martin Salisbury describes the book as "both postmodern and Romantic," with "a hauntingly evocative, nostalgic visual tone" (2008: 29–30). The photographic image is essential for Hole's particular mode of expression. Both the settings and characters of his works are distinguished by a slight visual distortion, featuring somewhat exaggerated body proportions and distinctive facial expressions created with layers of photographic images.

Although Hole's montages are based primarily on photographic images, his mode of expression has little to do with documentary. Instead, his style relies on a tension between different visual contexts. The images in the book are still and motionless, often reflecting the inner thoughts of the main character, rather than describing narrative actions. The flat, stationary spatial construction and the somewhat distorted photographic portrait of the young boy generate a scenic, almost stage-like effect.

In *Garmanns sommer*, the young protagonist's thoughts about identity, time, and growth are reflected in the lighthearted, nostalgic, or banal objects scattered over the pages. Again, the distorted characters, surrounded by a myriad of items and objects from different time periods and contexts, are particularly interesting from a postmodern standpoint. Nina Christensen describes how the collage of objects and text elements in the *Garmann* books gives the reader "a strange feeling of 'being present,'" while simultaneously generating "a form of estrangement or *Verfremdung* in the viewer" (Christensen 2014: 118).

The construction of photographic images comprising disconnected segments of items, bodies, and objects, originally used in the aesthetic systems of Constructivism and Surrealism, is technically seamless in Hole's Photoshop images, but it is, to a certain extent, based on the same technique. Although produced digitally, the interplay of reality and illusion in Hole's illustrations functions in a similar way to the early avant-garde photographic collage works of the 1920s. The slight distortion and deformation is essential to his method. Instead of utilizing the documentary qualities of the camera, the surrealists regarded the camera as a tool of the imagination. There is, however, a distinct difference between the surrealist use of photo-based montages and collages, and the digital images in Hole's work. While surrealist and dadaist collage techniques aimed to shock, to explore the subconscious through unsettling combinations of images, Hole's digital montages could be described as a distortion of reality, rather than an attempt to create *surreality*.

Photography also forms part of the creative process for the Norwegian artist and illustrator Øyvind Torseter. In *Eg kan ikkje sove no* (My Father's Arms Are a Boat 2008), with text by Stein Erik Lunde, the artist works with a variety of different materials: layers of torn and cut paper, cardboard and wallpaper, metal thread, and folded paper objects. His illustration technique combines traditional drawing, paper art, and collage with digital technology. This method is developed further in Torseter's later books, in which he continues to build miniature scenes and figures from paper and cardboard, photographs them, experiments with various lighting schemes, and then modifies the images in Photoshop.

In collaboration with Kurt Johannesen, Torseter created the picturebook *Eg er ein frosk* (I Am a Frog 2010), a whimsical story about a girl's imaginative play, in which a nonsensical rhyme produces a series of transformations in the book's images (Figure 5.2). As new animals and items are introduced in the girl's poem, they correspondingly appear in the book's images. The spatial organization and structure of the book expresses a strong sense of three-dimensionality reminiscent of theater books, puppet theaters, or dioramas. Here too, the use of collage bears a relation to earlier avant-garde ideas in which collage, in both painting and photography, was used as part of a methodical examination of the relationship between painting and sculpture. In Torseter's illustrations, the technique of the diorama is explored and developed by activating the picturebook's spatiotemporal properties. The dreamlike string of words is dynamically connected to the fantastic, surreal transformation of images that takes place when the reader turns the pages. Since a picturebook tells a story through a combination of text and images, the diorama or photomontage functions here as a point of departure that is reshaped and transformed in the picturebook medium.

Conclusion

A wide range of collage techniques and methods are utilized within the picturebook medium, and an increasing number of illustrators and artists experiment with combinations of materials

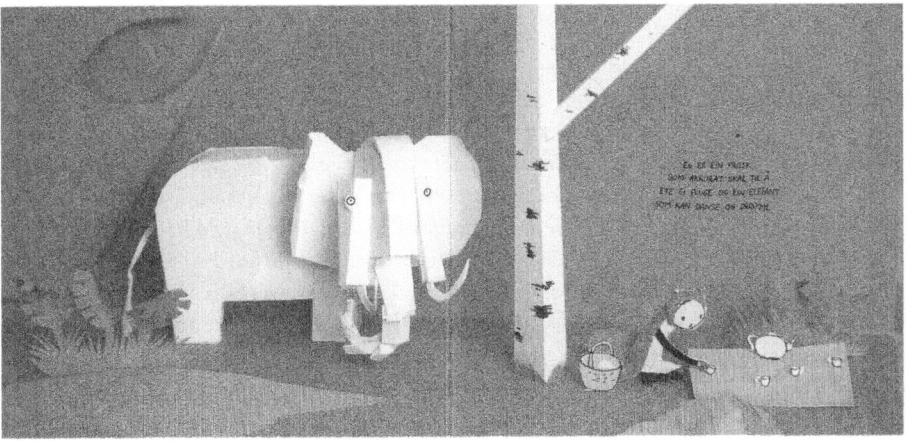

Figure 5.2 Illustration by Øyvind Torseter from Kurt Johannesen's *Eg er ein frosk*. Oslo: Omnipax, 2010.

Figure 5.3 Illustration by Linda Bondestam from Ulf Stark's *Diktatorn*. Helsinki: Söderström: 2010.

Copyright © Linda Bondestam. Reprinted by permission of Linda Bondestam.

and techniques. While Wolf Erlbruch interprets a medieval motif of life and death through the understated aesthetics of *Duck, Death and the Tulip*, similar concerns are manifested in Stian Hole's sophisticated, digitally created picturebooks. The playful oscillation between different levels of pictorial representation draws attention to the image and the medium at hand, and to the seams or boundaries between different materials and contexts. The use of collage or montage techniques also allows for a form of spatiotemporal fluidity, whereby older images and styles are recycled and recovered. This form of recycling and recomposing of material from earlier periods may be used playfully or ironically to create a nostalgic or poetic tone, as in Stian Hole's picturebooks, or to infuse settings with exotic, spatiotemporal ambiguity, as in Jockum Nordström's stories. As these two examples demonstrate, the collage techniques applied in picturebooks often generate the effect of 'defamiliarization,' helping the reader to see common objects or situations in unfamiliar or unusual ways.

The frequent use of collage and montage in contemporary picturebooks is in some ways a reflection of the creative possibilities facilitated by digital illustration techniques, and may also be regarded as one expression of a general trend towards media crossover. While many of the early collage artists searched for a new visual vocabulary (new forms and images through collage), it seems that collage in the contemporary picturebook is not based on discarding older visual traditions – quite the opposite. A telling example of this tendency is Shelley Jackson's *Mimi's Dada Catifesto* (2010), a children's book about the Dada movement. Here, basic ideas and concepts from the interwar avant-garde art movement are presented through a story about a cat searching for an owner and a home. As Philip Nel writes, the book emphasizes play rather than shock, but through an emphasis on the playful, oppositional spirit of Dada, Jackson's book, with its collage and mixed-media illustrations, also embodies avant-garde aesthetics, forms, and ideas (Nel 2015: 276).

The illustrators of many contemporary picturebooks utilize a range of styles and motifs, derived from high art and popular culture, combining them in unexpected ways. One example of this kind of whimsical (but also potentially provocative) commingling of motifs, colors, and styles is the picturebook *Diktatorn* (The Dictator 2010), by the Swedish author Ulf Stark and the Finnish-Swedish illustrator Linda Bondestam, which features an abundance of Soviet-inspired motifs and patterns in its collage images (Figure 5.3). The book can be read as the simple story of a strong-willed child behaving like a miniature tyrant, but the book's pointed fascination with historically inspired political imagery also suggests a darker, satirical undertone. The book's multilayered narrative evokes a sense of seriousness through references to current and historical dictators and rulers. Thus, the political dimension of avant-garde collage techniques is evoked in this work, however ambivalently.

While the use of collage was a vital part of the development of the picturebook, utilized both in avant-garde children's literature and as part of the child-centered approach inspired by new pedagogical ideas in the early to mid-twentieth century, collage and montage remain essential components of postmodern picturebook aesthetics. With their intermingling of motifs and styles, these works are firmly instantiated within a contemporary trend of media crossover. The works explored in this chapter reflect the ongoing, multi-directional interaction between picturebooks and other forms of art and literature. The artist's choice of collage technique, in examples from the 1930s as well as contemporary works, reveals an engagement between children's and adult literature on the one hand, and between picturebook illustration and other visual media on the other. Esphyr Slobodkina's interest in sculptures and installations, Jockum Nordström's intricate collage paintings, Øyvind Torseter's interest in digitally created dioramas – all suggest the picturebook artist's fascination with the boundaries between and creative possibilities inherent in a variety of media, materials, techniques, and styles. In this context, the picturebook functions as an alternative medium, a potential site for playful stylistic experiments, free from the rigorous strictures of the adult literary and artistic worlds.

References

Alemagna, Beatrice (2006) *Un lion à Paris*, Paris: Autrement jeunesse [*A Lion in Paris*, London: Tate, 2014].

Carle, Eric (1969) *The Very Hungry Caterpillar*, New York and Cleveland: World.

Carle, Eric (1971) *Do You Want to Be My Friend?*, New York: Philomel.

Carle, Eric (1975) *The Mixed-Up Chameleon*, New York: Harper Collins.

Christensen, Nina (2014) "'Thoughts and dreams are heavenly vehicles': Character, *Bildung*, and Aesthetics in Stian Hole's Garmann Trilogy (2006–2010)," in Bettina Kümmerling-Meibauer (ed.) *Picturebooks: Representation and Narration*, New York: Routledge, 109–120.

Dahle, Gro (2002) *Snill*, illus. Svein Nyhus, Oslo: Cappelen.

Dayre, Valérie (1996) *Die Menschenfresserin*, illus. Wolf Erlbruch, Wuppertal: Peter Hammer Verlag.

Druker, Elina (2008) "From 'Avant-garde' to Digital Images: Collage in Nordic Picturebooks," *Bookbird* 46.3: 45–51.

Erlbruch, Wolf (1999) *Nachts*, Wuppertal: Peter Hammer Verlag.

Erlbruch, Wolf (2007) *Ente, Tod und Tulpe*, Munich: Verlag Antje Kunstmann [*Duck, Death and the Tulip*, Wellington, NZ: Gecko Press, 2011].

Greenberg, Clement (1989) *Art and Culture: Critical Essays*, Boston: Beacon Press (first published 1961).

Hole, Stian (2005) *Den gamle mannen og hvalen*, Oslo: Cappelen.

Hole, Stian (2007) *Garmanns sommer*, Oslo: Cappelen [*Garmann's Summer*, Grand Rapids, MI: Eerdmans Publ., 2008].

Jackson, Shelley (2010) *Mimi's Dada Catifesto*, New York: Clarion Books.

Johannesen, Kurt (2010) *Eg er ein frosk*, illus. Øyvind Torseter, Oslo: Omnipax.

Keats, Ezra Jack (1962) *The Snowy Day*, New York: Viking Press.

Keats, Ezra Jack (1967) *Peter's Chair*, New York: Harper & Row.

Kraskin, Sandra, Cantor, Karen, and Marcus, Leonard S. (2009) *Rediscovering Slobodkina: A Pioneer of American Abstraction*, New York: Hudson Hills.

Lionni, Leo (1968) *Frederick*, New York: Pantheon Books.

Lionni, Leo (1969) *Alexander and the Wind-Up Mouse*, New York: Knopf.

Lionni, Leo (1997) *Between Worlds: The Autobiography of Leo Lionni*, New York: Knopf.

Lunde, Stein Erik (2008) *Eg kan ikkje sove no*, illus. Øyvind Torseter, Oslo: Det Norske Samlaget [*My Father's Arms Are A Boat*, Brooklyn, NY: Enchanted Lion Books, 2013].

Mitchell, Lucy Sprague (1921) *Here and Now Story Book*, New York: E.P. Dutton.

Moritz, Karl Philipp (2001) *Das Neue ABC-Buch*, illus. Wolf Erlbruch, Munich: Verlag Antje Kunstmann.

Nel, Philip (2015) "Surrealism for Children: Paradoxes and Possibilities," in Elina Druker, and Bettina Kümmerling-Meibauer (eds) *Children's Literature and the Avant-Garde*, Amsterdam: John Benjamins, 267–283.

Nordström, Jockum (1993) *Sailor och Pekka gör ärenden på stan*, Stockholm: Rabén & Sjögren.

Nordström, Jockum (2013) *Vart ska du?*, Stockholm: Rabén & Sjögren.

Perloff, Marjorie (1998) "The Invention of Collage," in *The Futurist Moment: Avant-Garde, Avant-Guerre, and the Language of Rupture*, Chicago: University of Chicago Press, 42–79.

Salisbury, Martin (2008) "The Artist and the Postmodern Picturebook," in Lawrence R. Sipe and Sylvia Pantaleo (eds) *Postmodern Picturebooks: Play, Parody, and Self-Referentiality*, London: Routledge, 22–40.

Stark, Ulf (2010) *Diktatorn*, illus. Linda Bondestam, Helsinki: Söderström.

Tan, Shaun (2001) *The Red Tree*, Melbourne: Lothian Books.

Taylor, Brandon (2006) *Collage: The Making of Modern Art*, New York: Thames & Hudson.

Wise Brown, Margaret (1938) *The Little Fireman*, illus. Esphyr Slobodkina, New York: W.R. Scott.

Wise Brown, Margaret (1953) *Sleepy ABC*, illus. Esphyr Slobodkina, New York: Lothrop, Lee and Shepard Co.

6

MATERIALITY IN PICTUREBOOKS

Ilgim Veryeri Alaca

Introduction

This chapter examines physical, sensory, and metaphoric qualities of materials and structures in picturebooks. Material interactions are increasingly sought after in printed as well as digital picturebooks due to multimodal literacies that are expanding via technological innovations. Baby books, toy books, novelty books, and books for the disabled are extensively exploring the possibilities of different materialities. Additionally, experimentations in materiality in artists' books and new media enable cross-pollination with picturebooks.

From battledores to iPads, systems that make up a picturebook may be organized for practicality, entertainment, and to enhance narrative. Perry Nodelman (1988) suggests that the material aspects of a book create an atmosphere that regulates readers' expectations and responses to a narrative. Bettina Kümmerling-Meibauer (2011) mentions the increasing production of picturebooks as playthings on the book market, whose heightened materiality and "synesthetic quality" might attract or even confuse young children (3). Maria Nikolajeva (2008) describes the covers of picturebooks as "gateways that alert curiosity" and includes the back cover as "a possible narrative space" (60). Material aspects can trigger postmodern games, positioning the reader in book systems and advancing a literary awareness: "to read these books coherently, it is necessary to know these systems and to bring their possibilities and constraints into play" (Mackey 2008: 115).

Nikolajeva (2008) comments that, "in postmodern picturebooks, playfulness is often expressed through their materiality, their quality as an artifact" (57). Hannah Field (2018) notes that "the *modus legendi* for novelty books – in which the child understands books materially, is a physicalized and embodied reader" (30). Cintia Rodriguez (2015) argues that objects are primers for language, drawing attention to the physical significance of the book (101).

Materiality in picturebooks is at its height when form-related aspects are intertwined into narratives to further the meaning, a strategy that at times extends to inviting the reader to actually contribute to the narrative. Materials can engage the child in a unique experience of performative reading, bringing "the book to life" (Scott 2014: 40). Play involving the book's material form enables the readers to put their own preferences into action through experimentation. Materiality, often a vehicle used to deliver a narrative, becomes a narrative by means of added or omitted parts, or through the use of different materials that stimulate the senses, challenging reading experiences (Do Rozario 2012). So far, the materiality of picturebooks has often been overlooked partly because non-standard applications raise the costs of printing or are simply impossible to produce. Moreover, materiality can give the illusion of a constraint when compared to the content, "drawing the reader inward in an endlessly expanding experience of sensation and association" (Drucker 2004: 359). However, as stated by Kümmerling-Meibauer (2014), materiality initiates intermediality via "the participation of more than one medium in a given work of art," configuring a hybrid genre that overarches spatial, time-based, and visual arts (4).

Materiality and technology

The origin of the word 'book,' like that of codex, may be interpreted as "a surface for writing" (Haslam 2006). This gives us a chance to explore novel ways to alter traditional books, that is, books printed with ink on rectangular paper. The materiality of picturebooks is closely tied to innovations in printing (for instance, woodcut, intaglio, lithography, screen-printing, inkjet, and UV lithography) and printable surfaces (for instance, papyrus, rice paper, tablet, and chips). Today, materiality increasingly attracts attention, boosted by a tug-of-war between printed and digital media that expands the frontiers of the reading experience. Dematerialization has also emerged as a result of new types of consumption of content and reading, especially by means of tablets and smartphones. These new types of consumption, according to Margaret Mackey (2008), have actually heightened our awareness of the physicality of books (105).

While current printed picturebooks alongside those stemming from ICT (information and communication technology) invite fresh insights into the potentials of the picturebook by means of play with its material forms, experimentation with interactivity already has a long history. For example, volvelles, utilized mostly for astrology in ancient times, made use of a turning disc to reveal configurations of their contents. Paper doll books presented around 1810 by S. and J. Fuller enabled children to play with different costumes and figures in the book. Movable books expanded in the nineteenth century with the publications of Dean & Son, which included plates that changed by means of a Venetian blind system. British publisher S. Louis Giraud created books that could be viewed from four different sides. These books were crafted by hand by paper engineers with at times up to a hundred workers configuring folds, flaps, and tabs, as well as three-dimensional paper constructions (Montanaro 2005).

Current interactive reading experiences on electronic devices enable children to manipulate text, explore hypertext, and adjust preferences such as sound. Texts are transformable and penetrate into diverse spaces, for instance with the help of air screens (Platzner 2005). Ghada Al-Yaquot and Nikolajeva (2015) address the amplified sensory and interactive aspects of electronic picturebooks, especially when originally designed for digital platforms (1f.). They review theories of transforming picturebooks, pointing out differences and similarities between printed and digital picturebooks. They mention for instance the role of spines in printed picturebooks, which are informative of the content of the book but which do not exist in digital books (although they are somewhat recalled by app icons). The augmented reality of picturebooks presents interactions between printed books and digital platforms, the two formats working together. In *What Lola Wants Lola Gets* (2011) by David Salariya and Carolyn Scrace, the book shown onto a computer screen with a camera reflects an augmented reality story that echos the printed one.

In *Magik Play* (2015), created by MagikBee, a tangible interface invites the child to position wooden blocks onto the screen to complete shapes like that of a ladder, for instance. This physical act is then identified by iPad sensors enabling a digital action, like climbing up the ladder to the hot air balloon. Transmedia, the telling of a story across different mediums and material interactions, promises new and emerging possibilities involving the integration of new technologies with storytelling (Kümmerling-Meibauer 2015; Serafini, Kachorsky and Aguilera 2015). For children who are digital natives, but who still need to make sense of the physical world and their own presence in it, the materiality of picturebooks synthesized with new technologies may be an essential reservoir of meaning, introducing new literacies appropriate for a digitally immersive world.

Books with unusual formats and parts

From portfolios to a French door format, the compilation of pages and the preference of bindings present a spectrum of options in terms of a book's material form. Volvelle, codex, fan, and Venetian blind, as depicted in Figure 6.1, are some of the book forms that have also been used

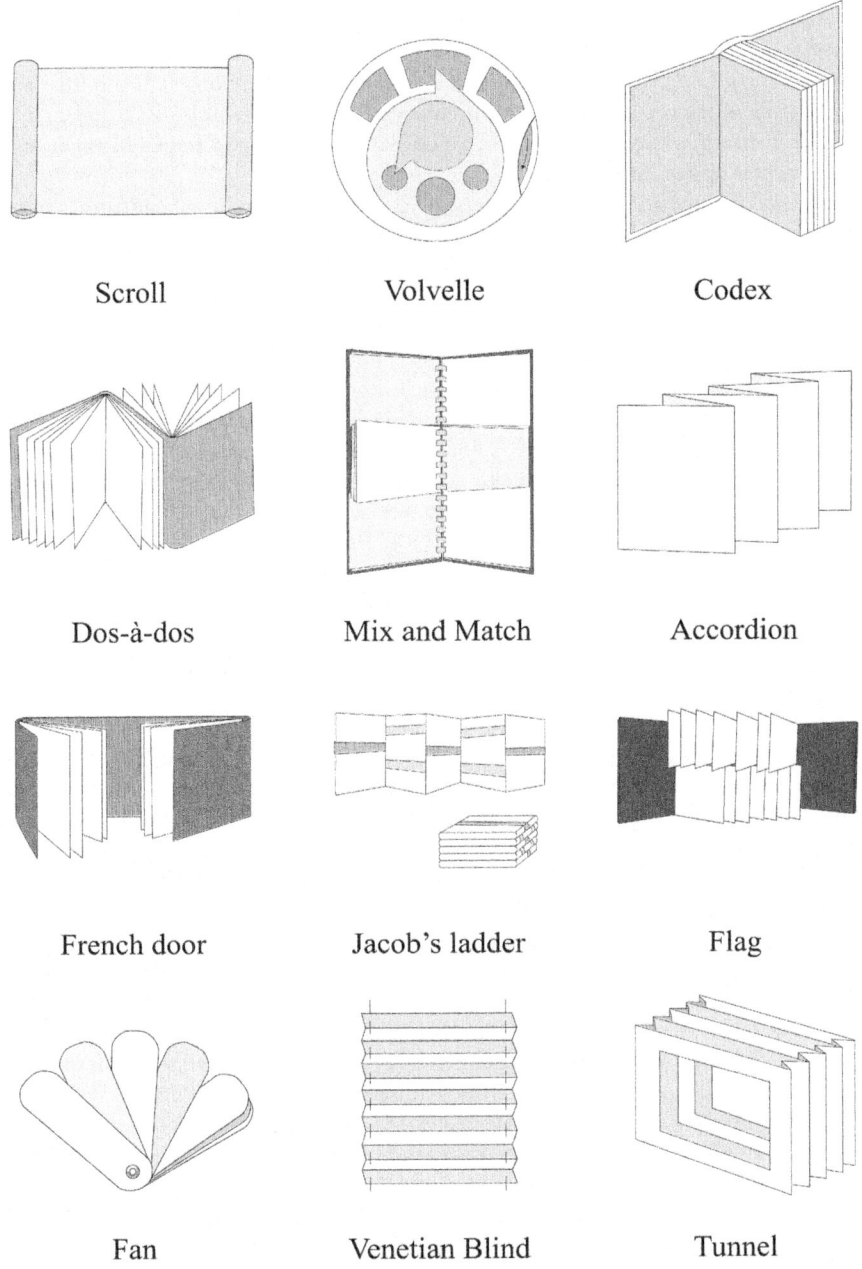

Scroll   Volvelle   Codex

Dos-à-dos   Mix and Match   Accordion

French door   Jacob's ladder   Flag

Fan   Venetian Blind   Tunnel

Figure 6.1 Illustration of selected picturebook formats, 2016.

© İpek Onmuş.

for picturebooks. According to Keith Smith (2003), elements of the book are "pages, binding, text and/or pictures, the revelation, and display" (412). Sewn and tied bindings, punched holes, knots (for instance, square knots) and stitches, crown bindings, piano hinge bindings, stick bindings, and perfect bindings mark different ways of gathering the pages (Golden 2010). Some books do not utilize any binding, presenting the book pages in leaflets for creative combinations and storytelling. Tunnel books or peep shows offer an accordion viewing perfect for depicting depth. In terms of orientation, the picturebook is typically in portrait, landscape, or square format, but can at times be cut into a certain shape such as a car or a purse with handles. Alternatively, some artists focus on a single format. Most of Dick Bruna's books are in a square format, supportive of minimal illustrations and an easy-to-follow narrative. The complementary relation between book shape and content is not new, as this concept was expressed for instance with heart-shaped books in medieval times to narrate the inner self (Jager 2000: 45).

When the classic picturebook is dissected, the parts include the spine, a headband, a hinge, a head square, a front pastedown, a cover, a fore edge square, a front board, a tail square, an endpaper, a head, leaves, a back pastedown, a back cover, a fore edge, a turn-intail, a flyleaf, and a foot (Haslam 2006). Each of these sections, including the foot and the gutter, can be altered innovatively according to the narrative. While these elements rarely transform into active agents of the book, considered usually to be limited to practical functions, they bear an untapped potential in terms of turning into narrative space. As soon as a component of a typical book is altered, the perception of the book shifts and the reader's perception expands. For instance, in *1536 Grimaces: Album à Transformations Comiques* (1898) by Lothar Meggendorfer, called a 'slice book' or 'mix and match,' each page is cut into three parts, inviting the viewer to make combinations of faces. In *The Slant Book* (1910) by Peter Newell, the slope that the baby slides from is accentuated by means of the tilted format of the book. *Libro Illeggibile MN 1* (Unreadable Book MN 1, 1984) by Bruno Munari has no words, but instead different shapes and colors for every page, which compels the viewer to contemplate the relation of each color to each abstract shape (see Beckett 2014: 54). In *Wave* (2008) by Suzy Lee, the gutter supports the meaning of the story, as this physical border describes the periphery between the girl and the sea. The girl's arm, which extends towards the ocean, is cut abruptly by the gutter, indicating this borderline. At last, the girl goes over the line (gutter) and intermingles with what lies beyond, overcoming fear.

Play with the size along with the format has a long historical geneology. Miniature books for children, starting with thumb Bibles, emerged in the sixteenth and seventeenth centuries. Sometimes a series of miniature books specifically designed to fit the palm of a child's hand have been presented on a book shelf or in a bus-shaped box. John Marshall produced miniature libraries for children like *The Infant's Library* (1800), which encouraged children to read by means of sixteen illustrated volumes housed in a wooden bookcase in the shape of a toy house (Bromer and Edison 2007).

In contrast, large books similar to ancient scrolls have been designed for the purposes of group reading sessions. An extended landscape format is found in scrolls like Toba Sojo's *Chōjū giga* (*Scroll of Animals*, twelfth and thirteenth centuries) from Japan, approximately 30 cm high and 1,100 cm wide, depicting animals from right to left. Similarly, Dean & Son's *Playtime Panorama* (nineteenth century) depicts a continuous narrative of a child's activities, but this time folded into a page structure. The panorama itself is illustrated in the book mise en abyme on the floor together with other toys, indicative of this object as part of play (Field 2018). Accordion books or panoramic books may not present a narrative but group similar objects such as birds or flowers. They also come in various shapes, such as figures holding hands, rooftops, and trees. Accordion books can be read/viewed page by page or as a whole; they are particularly suitable for topics that benefit from such shifting linearity, such as transformations, journeys, or trains. Sandra L. Beckett (2014) highlights how Warja Lavater's book-objects have been named "Imageries" in France and "folded stories" in Germany, focusing on her choice of format as she heavily concentrated on accordion books (61). While most accordion books are horizontal, some of Lavater's works are vertical, having hooks for mounting the book on the wall, thus acting as "mural books" (62). Similarly, *Migrar* (2011) by José Manuel Matéo and Javier Pedro features a vertical format, introducing a certain type of dynamism as well as tension to the journey that the migrants depicted in the book take.

In *Umi No Boken* (Adventure in the Sea 1993) by Katsumi Komagata, presented in a cardboard slip case, the accordion format makes note of the deep sea, first by means of a cutout hole revealing repetitive pages underneath, and second via pages that unfold irregularly in changing directions. The *leaf flow*, described as "pagination" by Smith (2003), is altered in this case by the orderly acts of the reader (413). Instead of a linear sequence, a random structure unfolds into different shapes, ultimately making a large square when the sixteen pages are fully opened. This creates a flexible space like that of the sea that the child can play with, on, and underneath, enabling them to follow the route of the leaping fish and encouraging the use of prepositions. The light blue and dark blue sides of the book and its unsettled page structure stimulate multiple readings.

Books with parts added

Additional elements in picturebooks primarily enable the viewer to organize and play with content via finger puppets, stickers, magnets, holograms, puzzles, removable folding structures for origami, or mirrors made out of aluminum foil to create reflective imagery (Yokoyama 1989). Second, enclosed artifacts can highlight plot elements, and have included postcards, maps, and flaps that alter narrative time. Third, enclosed visual gadgets such as glasses or screens can enhance the imagery of a book by, for instance, enabling three-dimensional vision. Finally, added parts, like a leash coming out of the spine in Art Spiegelman's *Open Me . . . I'm a Dog!* (1997) can pose a metafictive question involving whether the book is a dog or not.

Flaps in picturebooks typically facilitate a surprise, a question and answer, or changing states of forms, at times supported by Velcro parts or buttons attached to fabric. Anatomic illustrations in the fourteenth century were made out of layered plates similar to today's lift-the-flap books, giving information about the body as well as its inner organs. Similar to lift-the-flaps, printed acetate pages present an alternative way to reveal a transformed or hidden image underneath. Most of these interactive techniques were utilized in picturebooks in the eighteenth and nineteenth centuries, including in harlequinades, *paignion*, and toy theater. Harlequinades (also called turn-ups or metamorphoses) with their flaps, introduced by Robert Sayer, represented means of changing scenes in staged pantomimes (Reid-Walsh 2008). Harlequinades foreshadowed the lift-the-flap format of picturebooks that came to be popular in the twentieth century.

Optical illusions have been of interest as an additional feature in picturebooks for the purposes of heightened perception. *Gallop!* (2007) by Rufus Butler Seder is a scanimation picturebook, a format using a technique originally derived from the kinetoscope that depicts a moving image on the surface by means of a swift movement of that surface. Ordinary vision can be altered via inserted glasses in picturebooks, offering new ways of perceiving. Ana Pez's *Mon petit frère invisible* (My Little Invisible Brother 2014) offers red-filtered glasses that cancel out text and illustrations printed in red. A double narrative is created and the gap between them is filled by the children's interpretation as they read the story. Likewise, Isol's *Nocturne: Dream Recipes* (2012) is a bedtime picturebook that utilizes glow-in-the-dark ink with an additional texture, besides ordinary ink, creating a secondary imagery when the book is observed at night. The book has a backing at the bottom of the textblock so that the spiral bound pages can be set up by the child, to be observed before falling asleep. The book, a metaphor for light, substitutes for a bedside lamp. Isol's book recalls an older miniature book, *Les surprises* (The Surprises 1820), consisting of a set of twelve cards with hidden images in watermarks, which were revealed under light (Bromer and Edison 2007). Experimentations with inks can be further alternated via embossed, cut-out, and inkless surfaces.

Books with parts omitted

Papercutting, a traditional art form, is increasingly seen in picturebooks, by means of the use of die-cut technology. Tove Jansson's *Hur gick det sen* (Moomin, Mymble and Little My 1952) is a landmark in terms of the use of cutout forms, using them throughout the book, ending with a peephole punched into the back cover. This book depicts the difficult task of cutting in the endpaper by illustrating the bookmaker with a pair of scissors in his hand. The narrative indicates that a split has been created by the character Fillyjonk. This embeds the physical act of tearing into the narrative as the character not only alters narrative space but physical space (Scott 2014).

While many picturebooks utilize the front cover to place a hole, slit, window, or a door in, Emily Gravett makes use of a hole at the back cover to exaggerate the climax in *Again!* (2013). In this book, the child dragon breathes fire, thus burning through the back cover. This occurrence heightens the impact of the surprise ending and the child dragon's outburst of fury resulting from not being able to hear the story again and again before falling asleep. In contrast to the packed away hole in *Again!*, Hervé Tullet uses a face cut-out board, with a large cut-out circle at the spine functioning as an instrument of performativity in *The Book with a Hole* (2011). The cut-out circle calls for a new substitution into each page by the child, for instance for an empty plate, an open mouth, or abstract shapes. The requests are made with the support of simple instructions. *Hullet* (*The Hole* 2013) by Øyvind Torseter is also a bold design, featuring a single hole punched through the book by hand. This book's postmodern narrative hints at the physicality of the book. The hole disturbs the segregated space of the book by way of going through from the front to the back cover. The book, when held closed, acts as a peephole and a wall all at once. The hole in the story poses a repeated question in relation to its presence as it changes its role vis-à-vis the illustrations of each page. The illustrated figure in this wordless book attempts to make sense of the presence of the hole, much like the viewer; he tries to catch it, then takes it to the laboratory, while the hole transforms itself from an eye to a balloon, a street light to a traffic lamp, as the book proceeds. The cyclical pattern of the narrative ends in an unresolved vagueness as to the physical and symbolic function of the hole.

The Game of Shadows (2013) by Hervé Tullet, a black book with die-cut silhouettes, is a bedtime shadow book, adapting shadowgraphy that actively interacts with space with the help of a flashlight. *The Game of Sculpture* (2012) by Tullet introduces an accordion book format with easy to remove geometric parts that can be inserted randomly into the holes and openings of the cardboard pages to narrate a new story by the child. The reader can construct the pages each time and make an installation out of the given materials, adapting them onto slits and different shaped holes in the accordion format, turning the book into a sculpture.

Picturebooks made out of different materials

Picturebooks with a design that appeals to the senses create sensory stimuli via the integration of taste, touch, smell, and sound into their design, often supported by the utilization of appropriate materials. *Pat the Bunny* (1940) by Dorothy Kunhardt is a classic that invites the young child to a well-rounded sensory experience. The child can pat the bunny's fur and smell the flowers on the page, with assorted flowery scents evident. Margaret Wise Brown was a pioneer in thinking of an edible book that could be printed on fruit leather for children to take on the plane, a frequently stressful mode of travel for children and their parents (Marcus 2011). *I Prelibri* (The Pre-books 1980) by Munari is a landmark for preschool children with a set of twelve (10 × 10 cm) books made out of different materials such as cardboard, cloth, wood, and plastic, all bound in different ways. These books present a reading sampler to children for experiential viewing of book structure and texture.

In terms of sound, most picturebooks are silent while some offer buttons for special sound effects, audio recordings, or music. Maurice Pledger's *Sounds of the Wild: Jungle* (2008) introduces the soundscape of a forest, integrating animal sounds introduced in the pages in detail. By means of a battery, as soon as the page is turned, tropical sounds amaze and engage the child. This book is a reminder of the landmark *The Speaking Picturebook* (1880) by Theodor Brand, which when the strings with tassels embedded in the fore edge are pulled allows different sounds to be heard (Quayle 1983). The crackle book, a new type of sound-enhanced book, is described as a "picturebook made out of cloth filled with tiny pellets that make a crackling noise when the pages are touched and turned" (Kümmerling-Meibauer 2015: 252). In apps, similar to audio books and films, "diegetic and non-diegetic sounds" are embedded, relating directly to the narrative or user choice (Serafini, Kachorsky and Aguilera 2015: 19).

Paper, the major element of picturebooks, ranges from light to heavyweight, vellum to kraft, glossy to matte, and can involve alterations in how the colors appear, adding a tactile responsiveness, status, and value to the book. The paper also serves a practical purpose, such as durability as in the case of board books for babies. Details like deckled edges can give a fore edge a natural, handmade look. Yet papers made out of cotton, natural fibers, and synthetic materials with chemicals raise ecological concerns that have led the way towards the use of recycled paper or paperless reading. Anne Decis Gusti's *Mi papa estuvo en la selva* (My Dad Was in the Jungle 2008) has jacaranda seeds in its handmade paper, contributing to the content, as the picturebook can be planted after it is read.

While most books utilize one kind of paper throughout, making the book suitable for mass printing, some books involve different types of papers in a single picturebook, as in the case of the Grimms' *Hänsel und Gretel* (Hansel and Gretel 2011) by Sybille Schenker. The clear acetate cover sheet creates a frail protection for the laser-cut cover, enabling a further layering and protection of the book such that it looks handmade, a look further enhanced by its visible stab binding with orange linen. The book has black imprinted vellum pages with simple graphics balanced with colored opaque pages, also layered with vellum, which together create a theatrical atmosphere which surrounds Hansel and Gretel as they become lost. "The physical act of turning a page," pointed out by Smith (2003), is playful in this book due to the use of the vellum, which casts shadows as the pages turn.

While computer-generated imagery becomes easier to process via mass printing, handmade books, such as those created by Tara Books from India, present a process-based experience, particularly by means of delicate surface paper and with the additional application of a screen-printing technique. The production is an example of sustainable design since handmade papers made out of cotton rags and recycled waste paper are utilized. The paper's ink coating is visible to the eye and can be felt by the hand, in contrast to the uniform surface of mass-printed picturebooks (Tara Books 2015). These books not only transmit local cultural heritage via text and image, but also through their handmade look.

Books read in unconventional ways

In most cases, books are read in a single direction, pages read top to bottom and left to right, pages turned from right to left, proceeding from the front to the back of the book. Linear order is altered at times with juxtaposed, upside down, or circular narratives on one or more pages. For instance, Tom Schamp's Otto books are called *loop books*, such as *Otto in de Sneeuw* (Otto in the Snow 2008). Visual composition (Figure 6.2) in these books encourages a new way of reading by turning pages in a loop in order to follow the narrative (Kümmerling-Meibauer 2015). Shaun Tan's *The Lost Thing* (2000) requires the viewer to turn the horizontal doublespread page vertically because the change of direction in the illustration supports a dramatic spin to the story. This interruption invites the viewer to re-orient his body and the book physically. This act is a reminder of the change that comes in the narrative by means of this key page.

The double orientation in a single book is at its height in books with double covers, as two interrelated stories start from the front and the back. The dual narrative in *It's Useful to Have a Duck*

Figure 6.2 Illustration from Tom Schamp's *Otto in de Sneeuw*. Tielt: Lannoo, 2008.
© Lannoo Publishers.

(2007) by Isol features the same imagery on both sides accompanied by two different texts, reflecting the boy's and duck's perspectives, respectively, comparing their two different points of view. Angela Yannicopoulou (2013) mentions "upside down books, reversible books or tête-bêche (head to toes)" books with two covers. She describes

> a 'dos à dos' (from the French, meaning 'back-to-back') format where two, or even more separate books were bound together so one book faces outwards and the other inwards. This binding style, that dates back to sixteenth to seventeenth centuries in England and was used for books needed together, e.g. the New Testament and Psalter during church services, was considered ideal for stressing the fact that for every question there is more than one answer.
>
> *12*

Tactile books are essential for children with special needs, a unique way of processing narrative for others. Anette Diesen's *Vers pa tvers* (Lines and Rhymes 2007) utilizes velvet surfaces against plain paper synthesized with elastic strings, flaps, and sliding structures, prioritizing the perception of the visually impaired in the story formation and interactions during reading. Menena Cottin and Rosana Faría's *The Black Book of Colors* (2008) is a significant example that transmits the perception of a visually impaired person to the reader with its minimal design and embossed and glossy surfaces on black paper. The color selected for this book, black, is noteworthy in terms of how it allows children to experience the colors in their imagination without the use of eyesight.

Conclusion

In this chapter, the use of materiality in picturebooks was reviewed, drawing connections to changing technologies and diverse needs. First, materiality in picturebooks was presented as a third narrative system, alongside text and images, in ways that deepen children's understandings of a story, initiate play, and make connections to the real world. This enriches the book reading experience, honing spatial literacy into overarching new media literacies. Materials can be valuable catalysts, helping children to get into a story with a postcard or a folding-out box shape. Second, the benefit of the challenges that the materialities may pose was discussed. Inventive uses of materiality confront the child, with novel problems presented to them about handling the form that need to be solved in order to move on with the narrative. Materiality encourages multimodal communication as one finds order in chaotic structures, as in Komagata's work, or enables the development of an art work, as in *Game of Sculpture* (Serafini 2010). This type of materiality empowers and encourages the reader to take the lead, decide, create, and configure, erupting into an inquiry into the constitution and mediation of narrative. It is evident that materialities need to be explored further as developments in technology, ICTs, and new media promise multimodal literacies that connect to everyday life, merging the material phenomenon of books with that of the digital.

References

Al-Yagout, Ghada, and Nikolajeva, Maria (2015) "Re-Conceptualising Picturebook Theory in the Digital Age," *BLFT: Nordic Journal of ChildLit Aesthetics* 6. Doi: http://dx.doi.org/10.3402/blft.v6.26971 (accessed August 12, 2015).

Anonymous (1800) *The Infant's Library*, London: John Marshall.

Anonymous (1820) *Les surprises*, Paris: Marcilly.

Anonymous (1880–1900) *Playtime Panorama*, London: Dean & Son.

Beckett, Sandra L. (2014) "The Art of Visual Storytelling: Formal Strategies in Wordless Picturebooks," in Bettina Kümmerling-Meibauer (ed.) *Picturebooks: Representation and Narration*, New York: Routledge, 53–71.

Brand, Theodor (1880) *The Speaking Picturebook: A New Picturebook With Characteristic Voices*, London: Germany, Grevel.

Bromer, Anne C., and Edison, Julian I. (2007) *Miniature Books: 4000 Years of Tiny Treasures*, New York: Abrams.

Cottin, Menena (2008) *The Black Book of Colors*, illus. Rosana Faría, Toronto and Berkeley: Groundwood Books.

Diesen, Anette (2007) *Vers pa tvers*, Norway: International Board on Books for Young People.

Do Rozario, Rebecca-Anne (2012) "Consuming Books: Synergies of Materiality and Narrative in Picturebooks," *Children's Literature* 40.1: 151–166.

Drucker, Johanna (2004) *The Century of Artists' Books*, New York: Granary Books.

Field, Hannah C. (2018) *Novelty Value: The Child Reader and the Victorian Material Book*, Minneapolis: University of Minnesota Press.

Golden, Alisa (2010) *Making Handmade Books*, New York: Lark Crafts.

Gravett, Emily, (2013) *Again!* New York: Simon & Schuster.

Grimm, Jakob and Wilhelm (2011) *Hänsel und Gretel*, illus. Sybille Schenker, Bargteheide: Miniedition.

Gusti, Anne Decis (2008) *Mi papa estuvo en la selva*, Buenos Aires: Pequeño Editor.

Haslam, Andrew (2006) *Book Design*, New York: Harry N. Abrams Books.

Isol (2007) *It's Useful to Have a Duck; It's Useful to Have a Boy*, Toronto: Groundwood Books.

Isol (2012) *Nocturne: Dream Recipes*, Toronto: Groundwood Books.

Jager, Eric (2000) *The Book of the Heart*, Chicago: University of Chicago Press.

Jansson, Tove (1952) *Hur gick det sen*, Stockholm: Geber.

Komagata, Katsumi (1993) *Umi No Boken*, Tōkyō: Kaiseisha.

Kümmerling-Meibauer, Bettina (2011) "Emergent Literacy and Children's Literature," in Bettina Kümmerling-Meibauer (ed.) *Emergent Literacy: Children's Books from 0 to 3*, Amsterdam: John Benjamins, 1–17.

Kümmerling-Meibauer, Bettina (2014) "Introduction: Picturebooks Between Representation and Narration," in Bettina Kümmerling-Meibauer (ed.) *Picturebooks: Representation and Narration*, New York: Routledge, 1–15.

Kümmerling-Meibauer, Bettina (2015) "From Baby Books to Picturebooks for Adults: European Picturebooks in the New Millenium," *Word & Image* 31.3: 249–264.

Kunhardt, Dorothy (1940) *Pat the Bunny*, New York: Simon & Schuster.

Lee, Suzy (2008) *Wave*, San Francisco, CA: Chronicle Books.

Mackey, Margaret (2008) "Postmodern Picturebooks and the Material Conditions of Reading," in Lawrence R. Sipe and Sylvia Pantaleo (eds) *Postmodern Picturebooks: Play, Parody, and Self-Referentiality*, New York: Routledge, 103–117.

Magikbee (2015) *Magik Play*, www.magikbee.com/ (accessed December 12, 2015).

Marcus, Leonard S. (2011) "Touchy: Picture Books and the Feel of the Page," *The Horn Book Magazine* 87.6: 34.

Mateo, José Manuel (2011) *Migrar*, illus. Javier Martinez Pedro, Mexico, D.F.: Ediciones Tecolote.

Meggendorfer, Lothar (1898) *1536 Grimaces: Album à Transformations Comiques*, Paris: Nouvelle Librairie de la Jeunesse, Louis Westhausser éditeur.

Montanaro, Ann (2005) "Movable Books (Pop-Up Books)," in Bernice E.B. Cullinan and Diane Goetz Person (eds) *Continuum Encyclopedia of Children's Literature*, London: Continuum, http://0search.credoreference.com. libunix.ku.edu.tr/content/entry/kidlit/movable_books_pop_up_books/0 (accessed September 1, 2015).

Munari, Bruno (1980) *I Prelibri*, Milan: Danese.

Munari, Bruno (1984) *Libro Illeggibile MN 1*, Mantova: Corraini Edizioni.

Newell, Peter (1910) *The Slant Book*, New York: Harper and Brothers.

Nikolajeva, Maria (2008) "Play and Playfulness in Postmodern Picturebooks," in Lawrence R. Sipe and Sylvia Pantaleo (eds) *Postmodern Picturebooks: Play, Parody, and Self-Referentiality*, New York: Routledge, 55–75.

Nodelman, Perry (1988) *Words about Pictures: The Narrative Art of Children's Picture Books*, Athens: University of Georgia Press.

Pez, Ana (2014) *Mon petit frère invisible*, Paris: l'Agrume.

Platzner, Rebecca (2005) "Book Design," in Bernice E B. Cullinan and Diane Goetz Person (eds) *Continuum Encyclopedia of Children's Literature*, London: Continuum, http://0search.credoreference.com.libunix.ku.edu. tr/content/entry/kidlit/book_design/0 (accessed April 1, 2015).

Pledger, Maurice (2008) *Sounds of the Wild: Jungle*, San Diego, CA: Silver Dolphin Books.

Quayle, Eric (1983) *Early Children's Books*, New York: Barnes and Noble Books.

Reid-Walsh, Jacqueline (2008) "Harlequin Meets the Sims: A History of Interactive Narrative Media for Children and Youth From Early Flap Books to Contemporary Multimedia," in Kirsten Drotner and Sonia Livingstone (eds) *International Handbook of Children, Media and Culture*, London: Sage, 71–86.

Rodriguez, Cintia (2015) "The Connection Between Language and the World: A Paradox of the Linguistic Turn?" *Integrative Psychological & Behavioral Science* 49.1: 89–103.

Salariya, David (2011) *What Lola Wants Lola Gets*, illus. Carolyn Scrace, Brighton: Scribbler Books.

Schamp, Tom (2008) *Otto in de Sneeuw*, Tielt: Lannoo.

Scott, Carole (2014) "Artists' Books, Altered Books, and Picturebooks," in Bettina Kümmerling-Meibauer (ed.) *Picturebooks: Representation and Narration*, New York: Routledge, 37–52.

Seder, Rufus Butler (2007) *Gallop!: A Scanimation Picture Book*, New York: Workman.

Serafini, Frank (2010) "Reading Multimodal Texts: Perceptual, Structural and Ideological Perspectives," *Children's Literature in Education* 41: 85–104.

Serafini, Frank, Kachorsky, Dani, and Aguilera, Earl (2015) "Picturebooks 2.0: Transmedial Features Across Narrative Platforms," *Journal of Children's Literature* 41.2: 16–24.

Smith, Keith A. (2003) *Structure of the Visual Book*, New York: Keith Smith Books.

Sojo, Toba (12th–13th Century) *Chōjū giga*, Japan.

Spiegelman, Art (1997) *Open Me . . . I'm a Dog!* New York: Joanna Cotler Books.

Tan, Shaun (2000) *The Lost Thing*, Melbourne: Lothian Children's Books.

Tara Books, www.tarabooks.com/ (accessed January 12, 2015).

Torseter, Øyvind (2013) *Hullet*, Oslo: Cappelen Damm [*The Hole*, New York: Enchanted Lion Books, 2013].

Tullet, Hervé (2011) *The Book With a Hole*, London: Tate.

Tullet, Hervé (2012) *The Game of Sculpture*, London: Phaidon Press.

Tullet, Hervé (2013) *The Game of Shadows*, London: Phaidon Press.

Yannicopoulou, Angela (2013) "The Materiality of Picturebooks: Creativity Activities," in Triantafyllos Kotopoulos (ed.) *1st International Conference on "Creative Writing" Proceedings*, http://cwconference.web.uowm.gr/archives/giannikopoulou.pdf (accessed September 1, 2015).

Yokoyama, Tadashi (1989) *Tachiagaru non-Ugoku non/The Best of 3D Books*, Tokyo: Rikuyo-sha.

7

PICTUREBOOKS AND METAFICTION

Maria Cecilia Silva-Díaz

Metafiction, also called "fiction about fiction," "theoretical fiction" (Currie 1995), "critical fiction" (Lodge 1992), "self-referential fiction" (Jablon 1997), or "self-conscious fiction" (Waugh 1984), refers to the capacity of fiction to reflect on its own ontological status as an artifact, a construction. One of the most widely quoted definitions is that by Patricia Waugh:

> Metafiction is a term given to fictional writing which *self-consciously* and *systematically* draws attention to its status as an artifact in order to pose questions about the relationship between fiction and reality. In providing a critique of their own methods of construction, such writings not only examine the fundamental structures of narrative fiction, they also explore the possible fictionality of the world outside the literary fictional text.
>
> *1984: 2; italics added*

Metafiction shows the gap between the world represented in literature and reality and with that aim lays bare the conventions with which realist fiction builds the world of fiction, demonstrating that narratives are word constructions and not a reflection of reality. Unveiling the ontological status of fiction can lead to questioning reality, as well as to questioning the individual coherence of the subject that perceives it and constructs it.

Although metafiction is an ahistorical phenomenon present in works such as Miguel de Cervantes's *Don Quixote*, it has become a hallmark of postmodern literature that seeks to break with literary realism, exposing its illusionist mechanisms. Postmodern thought posits that reality is not subsumable in a single coherent interpretation and raises a special awareness of the arbitrary nature of language and representation. Metafiction meets literary postmodernism in the rejection of realism, as well as in the rejection of totalizing and closed versions of great narratives. It also meets postmodernism in the questioning of hierarchies (among them the authority of the narrator, notions of gender, and the differentiation of high and low culture), its linguistic consciousness, and a desire to cause perplexity. This questioning impulse violates the canonical story, producing instability and turning the reader into a participant of the construction of the work.

Metafiction is probably the main feature of literary postmodernism to the extent that the terms are frequently used interchangeably despite their differences, as Linda Hutcheon states:

> I explicitly rejected the term 'postmodernism' and opted instead for the more descriptive one of metafiction. Although I would still stand behind my objections to the label, it seems

to have stuck, and it would be foolish to deny that metafiction is today recognized as a manifestation of postmodernism.

1984: xiii

For children's literary criticism, metafiction can be an independent category – "children's metafiction" – present in narratives in which there is almost always a narrator who reflects on the act of narrating, as is the case in *The Story of the Treasure Seekers* (1899) by Edith Nesbit (Moss 1985). It can also group works of contemporary fiction that violate the canonical story as "metafictional texts" (Moss 1990); in other cases, metafiction is a *characteristic* of broader categories such as "experimental works" (McCallum 1996), "postmodern narrative" (Colomer 2001; Pantaleo 2014), or "radical change literature," which alludes to narrations influenced by technological change (Dresang 2008).

In children's literature studies, it is in picturebook theory where we find the most in-depth theory on how metafiction is presented to children. In general, the theory of metafiction in picturebooks is framed within postmodern culture – postmodernity – and some scholars establish a relationship between these books and the postmodern art project – postmodernism (see Lewis 2001: 88; Stephens 2008: 90). This theoretical corpus approaches different aspects such as the delimitation of the object of study and its place with regard to mainstream production, metafictional devices in multimodal texts, and the participation of readers, implicit and real, in the construction of meaning.

As metafictional fiction, picturebooks also tend to challenge conventions. Considered "the richest area of experimentation in children's literature" (Styles 1996: 36), the experimental tendency of picturebooks can be explained by their specific features as material objects (Moss 1990: 66; Colomer 1998: 91; Hunt 2001: 288). Picturebooks are manufactured and manipulable objects (materiality) that host a multimodal discourse comprising words and pictures, in which meaning comes about through the combination of both (dialogism) (Nodelman 1988; Trites 1994; Allan 2012). Thus the meaning is built in a non-linear manner, as it stems from the gaps between what the text tells and what the images tell (discontinuity). Although each of them communicate different narrative levels (multidiegesis) (Pantaleo 2010: 15), the visual narration and the textual narration coexist in the space of the double page (simultaneity), where there may even be more than two visual narrations at the same time (multilayered or multistranded stories) (Nodelman 1988: 153). Materiality, dialogism, discontinuity, simultaneity, and multidiegesis are inherent features of picturebooks that favor metafictional strategies. Creators, aware of the opportunities offered to them by the picturebook, have made the most of the tendency of these books towards openness and flexibility (Lewis 2001: 76) and through metafiction have challenged the canonical narratives and questioned the realism of fiction.

Metafiction, by calling the attention of the reader to the artifact of canonical fiction, joins the experimental impulse of the picturebook. However not all forms of experimentation are metafictional and not all metafictional strategies are perceived as innovation since some of them have become part of tradition. Metafictional experiments go back to books published long ago. *The Hole Book* (1908) by Peter Newell explores the materiality of the book with the introduction of a die-cut hole, which goes through the pages and blurs the limits between reality and the space of fiction in a similar manner to the die-cut bite on the back cover of *The Incredible Book Eating Boy* (2006) by Oliver Jeffers. In *Harold and the Purple Crayon* (1955) by Crockett Johnson, the narrative of illustrations enables the character to take a pencil and draw the world of fiction, thus violating the narrative levels by making the character into the implicit author; almost three decades later, the little bear in Anthony Browne's *A Bear-y Tale* (1989) takes the pencil and recreates the world of fairy tales in a similar way.

However, it is since the 1980s that metafictional experiments have become increasingly radical and frequent: narrative strands are multiplied through different stories told in parallel; genres are mixed; experiments are made with the text and the illustrations to render visible the stitches that hold together the coherence of the fictional world; narrative planes are confused and intertextual references are exacerbated. Picturebooks such as *Come Away from the Water, Shirley* (1977) by John Burningham, *Black and White* (1990) by David Macaulay, *The Stinky Cheese Man and Other Fairly Stupid Tales* (1992) by John Sciezka and Lane Smith, *Voices in the Park* (1998) by Anthony Browne, and *The Three Pigs* (2001) by David Wiesner are just some of the most widely quoted books by critics that systematically defy the canon of storytelling and explore new possibilities. Although some of these picturebooks seem more aware than others of their condition as artifacts, all of them use metafictional strategies typical of postmodern fiction. They have even been considered "a new subgenre" characterized by multiple story lines, perspectives, and contradictions, allowing the reader to be privy to the act of the book creation (Goldstone and Labbo 2004: 203).

The first critical works that studied these books preferred to talk of metafictional picturebooks (Lewis 1990; Moss 1990). It has to be noted, however, that nowadays "postmodern picturebooks" is the term most widely used (see Anstey 2002; Sipe and Pantaleo 2008; Allan 2012). Even though the terms are now generally used indistinctly and there are many instances where they are exchangeable, it is important to clarify that "metafictional" refers to narrative strategies that are not necessarily linked to a historical moment or to a literary project, whereas "postmodern" makes reference to the relationships between these works and postmodernism and to the context of production and reception that characterize postmodernity. Hence, most postmodern picturebooks employ metafictional devices because the metafictional strategies used in picturebooks generate the self-reflective condition that characterizes postmodern fiction.

In metafictional picturebooks addressed to children, the theoretical aspect of fiction differs from the type of theory included in self-reflective works directed to adults. Considered "*désopilants petits traités de fiction*" (hilarious fiction treatises) (Tauveron 2011), there seems to be agreement that in metafictional picturebooks, play imposes itself over theory (Moss 1990; Lewis 2001; Allan 2012). Play as a distinctive characteristic ensures that these books become, without abandoning the relativistic spirit of postmodernism, "a playful initiation to relativism" (Derrien 2005: 187). This relativism, however, is not as radical as that which uses postmodern fiction to attack humanist values; for example, Lewis sees no clear line of continuity that relates the radical poetics of literary postmodernism and these books for children (Lewis 2001: 99f.). In this respect, Cherie Allan (2012) holds that children's postmodern fiction does not attack the great narratives in the same way in which the postmodern literary project does: her argument is that even in very relativistic narratives such as *Voices in the Park*, humanist values are maintained because the implicit author orders the four stories in accordance with the sympathy he has for the narrators and thus constructs a position for the reader. Along the same lines, Deborah Kaplan (2003) considers that in a picturebook such as *Black and White*, in which all four parallel stories cannot be reconstructed into a single narrative, the constructive and purposive principle prevails over the attack on the coherence of the story typical of adult postmodernism: the reader of this work is actively engaged in the construction.

Without giving up entirely the possibility of meaning-making in postmodern picturebooks, the coherence of the story is violated systematically and the contrived mechanisms of fiction are left exposed through metafictional strategies. Metafictional strategies exacerbate the inherent features of the picturebook as a multimodal text causing an instability which is, in turn, an invitation to the reader to participate in the reconstruction of the sense, almost always in a playful way. In *Caperucita Roja (tal como se la contaron a Jorge)* (Little Red Riding Hood (As It Was Told to Jorge), 1996) by Luis María Pescetti and O'Kif, instability does attack the coherence of the canonical story (Figure 7.1).

Each opening of this picturebook presents four narrative strands: a textual narration that reproduces the tiresome and standardized version of the story of "Little Red Riding Hood" told by the

aperucita salió y empezó a cruzar el bosque.

13

Figure 7.1 Illustration by O'Kif from Luis María Pescetti's *Caperucita Roja (tal como se la contaron a Jorge)*. Buenos Aires: Alfaguara, 1996.

father to Jorge, and three visual narratives that take place in parallel: the narrative situation, the story as imagined by the father, and the story as imagined by Jorge. Both narrative strands within bubbles take place in a mental landscape and are subordinated to the main story. These two nested stories compete against each other and produce instability in the narration, which seeks to question the hegemony of the traditional story: which is the story that was actually told to Jorge? The reader must take part to try and clarify the story line, as Frank Serafini says: "Postmodern picturebooks challenge readers with metafictive and literary devices" (2012: 5). The traditional story splits into two strands to question the hegemony of the classic story, and the reconstructions encourage the reader's participation.

Metafictional strategies

Explicit self-consciousness in picturebooks in which books and reading are the theme is perhaps the most evident metafictional strategy. These books openly reflect on their own constructive process through the text, images, or the material condition. So, for instance, the text refers to the process of creation of text or images, or the book itself or its parts become the theme of the narrative. In these cases the self-consciousness is explicit, as occurs in Emily Gravett's *Wolves* (2006): "The author would like to point out that no rabbits were eaten during the making of this book. It is a work of fiction. And so, for more sensitive readers, here is an alternative ending" (n. pag.).

One type of self-consciousness is turning the book as a material object into a theme, such as in Lane Smith's *It's a Book* (2010) or Hervé Tullet's *Un livre* (*Press Here* 2010), where two picturebooks with parodic comparisons to apps reflect on the interaction between book and reader in printed books. Illustrations could also be self-conscious of their ontological status as printed matter when they represent the book and its pages as the chronotope where the story takes place, as in Monique Felix's *Histoire d'une petite souris qui était enfermée dans un livre* (Story of a Little Mouse Trapped in a Book 1981) and the rest of her Mouse Books Series published in the United States or in Jörg Müller's *Das Buch im Buch im Buch* (The Book in the Book in the Book 2001).

In Chris Van Allsburg's *Bad Day at Riverbend* (1995), the reader realizes that the cowboy story he is reading takes place in a coloring book that a girl is reading. This overlapping of narrative planes creates a mise en abyme that incorporates the reader's act into the fiction.

However, most of the metafictional works do not show explicit awareness of their fictional condition. Instead, it is the reader who, while reading, finds visible stitches, inconsistencies, collisions, loans, and jumps in levels that compel her to realize that the narrative is an artifact of fiction. If these encounters are systematic throughout the reading, it is possible for the reader to become metafictionally aware: thus, when metafiction is implicit, the self-consciousness transfers to the readers. In these cases, the metafictional strategies *intentionally* and *systematically* seek to awaken the reader's consciousness. Although the idea of intention was for a long time banished from the language of literary criticism, it has been recovered in criticism of postmodern works. Douglas states that to discuss when something departs from convention, it is essential to come out of the narrative framework and construct the author's probable intentions (1994: 186).

Consequently, non-thematic metafiction exists in a liminal space between a constructive intentional principle and an effect in the reader: the principle is the metafictional intention – that is, what the work attempts to violate or discover with regard to the canonical fiction – while the effect is a perceptible systematic instability. This potential space between production and reception has been addressed by scholars such as Andrea Schwenke-Wyile (2006) from the perspective of the reader's performance. I have organized metafictional picturebooks in four principle-effects that work alone or in combination and with each of which different metafictional strategies are associated (Silva-Díaz 2005).

Short circuit

This term was used by David Lodge and taken up by Anita Moss (1990). It refers to a shake-up that takes place when the levels of narrative are violated. In rhetoric, this figure is known as metalepsis (Pantaleo 2010; Ruiz Domínguez 2012). Picturebooks organized around this principle use strategies that dissolve the boundaries between fiction and reality, author and characters, enunciation and the enunciated. The effect of short circuit is often produced by using tangible elements, such as the hole produced by the dragon's fire in Gravett's *Again!* (2011), that draw attention to the materiality of the books, allowing fiction to become part of the reader's world and, in doing so, merging the boundaries between reality and fiction.

Under the effect of short circuit, hierarchies of the different narrative levels are attacked. Author, characters, and readers shift places from one narrative plane to another: characters who discuss the story with the author, insecure narrators who have doubts about their writing, characters who are conscious of their fictional condition, and so forth – they all cause the short-circuit effect. For example, in *The Bravest Ever Bear* (1999) by Allan Ahlberg and Paul Howard, the characters are not satisfied with the narrator, so they take over and become narrators of their own stories while being criticized by the other characters.

A very frequently used graphic strategy in metafictional picturebooks organized around the short-circuit principle is to show the character drawing the fictional work. In this case, the character becomes the visual narrator as in *Harry and the Purple Crayon* and other books such as *Chigüiro y el lápiz* (Capybara and the Pencil 1985) by Ivar Da Coll (Figure 7.2).

A variation of this strategy occurs in *Chester* (2007) by Mélanie Watt. Here, Chester is a cat writer who interferes with the role of the visual narrator, competes with the narrator/author, and usurps its role to manipulate the story, hence becoming a co-author. To achieve this, the images show the

Figure 7.2 Illustration from Ivar Da Coll's *Chigüiro y el lápiz*. Bogotá: Norma, 1985 (Reprint Babel Libros, 2005).
© Babel Libros, 2005. Reprinted by permission of Babel Libros.

strikeouts and modifications that the co-author inserts in the original author's text. The setbacks at various levels of the narration cause the illusion of reality to vanish and reveal the fictional artifact. Through this device, a questionable truth arises that is conditioned by the interests and positions of those that construct it.

Indeterminacy

This is applicable to the cases where metafiction generates ambiguities, vagueness, or contradictions in an intentional and systematic manner. Unlike what happens in a canonical narration, in the meta-fictional variant the reader may not be able to reconstruct the plot. It is possible that the narration dilutes into different stories or that there are opposing aspects that dissipate the meaning, or that there is a lack or an excess of information. Metafictional narrations where indeterminacy predominates place the reader in the active role of resolving the ambiguity, or can show her the importance of dealing with uncertainty, as it occurs in Macaulay's *Black and White* or *Voices in the Park* by Anthony Browne. The strategies that create the effect of indeterminacy include the breakdown of causal logic, narrative discontinuity, stories without an ending or with many endings, stories that branch out in multistranded narratives, multiple narrators or multiple focalizers, and multiple illustrative styles that destabilize the representation.

In *Els nens del mar* (Children of the Sea 1991) by Jaume Escala and Carme Solé Vendrell, a poet reads to a group of street children. In just one doublespread two chronotopes are represented: the dreamlike images evoked by the poet contrast with the violence of the children's mental landscapes (Figure 7.3). These two planes cause doubts as to the reality constructed through narration and make the reader think about the way readers construct meaning based on their own experiences.

Figure 7.3 Illustration by Carme Solé Vendrell from Jaume Escala's *Els nens del mar*. Barcelona: Siruela, 1991 [First published in French: *Les enfants de la mer*, París: Syros, 1991].

Reprinted by permission of Carme Solé Vendrell.

As in *Come Away from the Water, Shirley* by John Burningham, the presence of two chronotopes, one real and the other arising from imagination, creates a lack of definition and instability in the fiction and calls upon the reader to reconstruct the story. Strategies based on the principle-effect of indeterminacy defy the certainties of conventional storytelling. However, from the reader's point of view, particularly that of a child's, metafictional indeterminacy is more difficult to identify since uncertainty is part of any reader's experience with literature, especially when such a reader is developing her interpretative skills, and therefore it can be perceived as a non-intentional feature of the story or of the reading process.

Resonance

In this case, the elements of the narration that were bound together in canonical narrations tend to spill over because they are associated with other narrations or discourses. Fiction does not seem an original reality, but rather a reproduction of existing discourses in the manner of a pastiche. Other discourses are echoed in the words of the text, often with parodic intent, as occurs in *The Stinky Cheese Man and Other Fairly Stupid Tales* by Sciezka and Smith. In this picturebook, for example, a doublespread contains the deconstructed story of a giant presented as an image with text (icon-text); the image visually quotes fragments of famous fairy tales and children's classics such as *Der Struwwelpeter* (*Slovenly Peter*), *Beauty and the Beast*, and "The Ugly Duckling," which randomly fall upon the page. The presence of these loans causes an effect of resonance that amplifies the story. This principle-effect tends to relate to the saturation of intertextual relations and to the overcoding of some aspects of the narrative.

Another example of resonance is found in Patrick J. Lewis and Roberto Innocenti's *The Last Resort* (2002), a picturebook about a creative crisis that can only be solved when the artist gets in touch with creations from the past. The main character, a painter who is the alter-ego of Innocenti, visits a strange hotel where characters and authors from classic literary works are the guests. Among others he meets Andersen's Little Mermaid, Twain's Huck Finn, Stevenson's Long John Silver, Emily Dickinson, and Antoine de Saint-Exupéry. The picturebook addresses metaphorically the idea that stories are constructed by recycling other stories.

The metafictional strategies associated with the principle-effect of resonance include characters or chronotopes recycled from other narrations: mixes of genres, discursive and illustrative styles, modes of narration and modes of representation, parodic appropriations of other texts and discourses, and narration based on verbal and graphic intertextuality.

Play

Postmodern works turn readers into players because they require their participation in creating the meaning, and in this sense play is a feature common to almost all postmodern narrations. Play wrecks the coherence of the canonical narration: language and image stop having a referential function, allowing the pleasure of the signifier (leisure) to impose itself on the tyranny of the signification (work). This may be achieved by inviting the reader to participate in the game of constructing the meaning, as occurs in *Black and White* by Macaulay. Likewise, Tullet's *Un livre* engages the reader in a game in which the physical interaction recalls and functions as a metaphor for the intense relationship between readers and books and the participation of readers in the construction of meaning.

In Olivier Douzou's *Luchien* (2000), Madam Ida walks the city searching for her lost dog Luchien. In the last doublespreads, guided by typography and layout, the reader is invited to read the book upside down just to realize that the dog has been hiding in all the pictures (Figure 7.4). The game of turning the book around to find the dog calls attention to the relativism of representation.

Figure 7.4 Doublespread from Olivier Douzou's *Luchien*. Rodez: Éditions du Rouergue, 2000.

© Éditions du Rouergue, 2000. Reprinted by permission of Éditions du Rouergue.

Strategies related to this principle-effect include narration, where linguistic games and the use of forms of play such as sequences and accumulation bring out the text as an artifact, unusual designs and layouts or typographic experiments that call attention to the book as an object, and illustrative framing devices that play with embedded illustrations to question the reality presented by the image, as seen in *Zoom* (1995) by Istvan Banyai.

Lessons from metafictional picturebooks

Reading picturebooks that use metafictional strategies can help readers to develop an awareness of some of the most crucial theoretical aspects involved in the reading of literature. As we have seen, some of the picturebook narratives are not explicitly self-conscious, but through their strategies they create a distant and reflective position for their readers that favor this type of consciousness. As Linda Hutcheon states: "self-conscious metafiction today is a most didactic form. As such, it can teach us much about the ontological status of fiction (all fiction) and also the complex nature of reading (all reading)" (1984: xi–xii).

The reading of metafictional picture books can involve an element of unease that obliges readers to leave their comfortable spectator armchair to experience the backstage workings of fiction, but it also has a playful side that invites the reader to participate in a game. Metafictional picturebooks have been seen as opportunities to experience different ways of reading, such as distanced reading and critical reading focusing on the ideological construction of the text (see Goldstone 1998; Bull 2002; Anstey 2002; Sanders 2009). They have also been explored as means of building literary knowledge (Allan 2012; Pantaleo 2014).

Some metafictional picturebooks combine familiar elements typical of the canonical story with strategies that attack certain conventions and thus help the recognition of metafiction and the extension of expectations regarding what fiction can offer. Considering the limited and non-linear experience of young readers with different forms of fiction present in books and on screens, a question emerges regarding to what extent it is necessary for the reader to have a representation of the conventional in narrations in order to recognize metafiction as a violation of convention.

With regard to this defamiliarization process, Allan warns that in a changing culture it may not be surprising that new generations find discontinuity and fragmentation familiar strategies (Allan 2012: 4).

Reception studies have shown the ways in which readers engage in metafictional picturebooks (e.g., Pantaleo 2004; Serafini 2005; Sipe 2008; Arizpe, Styles et al. 2008; Swaggerty 2009), highlighting the sense of challenge, play, and participation offered by these books. One study in particular by Arizpe, Styles et al. (2008) shows how children with little reading experience and from different cultural traditions are able to build and appropriate these texts in an enjoyable way.

Finally, metafictional picturebooks are above all related to postmodern culture: they incorporate a form of adapted and necessary reading for these times when discourses proliferate and coexist, mix, and reproduce randomly.

References

Ahlberg, Allan (1999) *The Bravest Ever Bear*, illus. Paul Howard, London: Walker Books.

Allan, Cherie (2012) *Playing with Picturebooks: Postmodernism and the Postmodernesque*, Basingstoke: Palgrave Macmillan.

Anstey, Michelle (2002) "More than Cracking the Code: Postmodern Picture Books and New Literacies," in Michelle Anstey and Geoff Bull (eds) *Crossing the Boundaries*, Sydney: Pearson, 87–105.

Arizpe, Evelyn, Styles, Morag (with M. Cowan, K. Mallouri, M. Wolpert) (2008) "The Voices Behind the Pictures: Children Responding to Postmodern Picturebooks," in Lawrence R. Sipe and Sylvia Pantaleo (eds) *Postmodern Picturebooks: Play, Parody and Self Referentiality*, New York: Routledge, 207–222.

Banyai, Istvan (1995) *Zoom*, New York: Viking.

Browne, Anthony (1989) *A Bear-y Tale*, London: Hamish Hamilton.

Browne, Anthony (1998) *Voices in the Park*, London: Doubleday.

Bull, Geoff (2002) "The Postmodern Picture Book: Its Place in Post-Literate Pedagogy," in Michelle Anstey, and Geoff Bull (eds) *Crossing the Boundaries*, Sydney: Pearson, 46–64.

Burningham, John (1977) *Come Away From the Water, Shirley*, London: Jonathan Cape.

Colomer, Teresa (1998) *La formación del lector literario: Narrativa infantil y juvenil actual*, Madrid: Fundación Germán Sánchez Ruiperez.

Colomer, Teresa (2001) "Una literatura infantil y juvenil de calidad: El proyecto de un siglo," Supplement from Boletín Libre de *Enseñanza* 42–43.

Currie, Mark (ed.) (1995) *Metafiction*, New York: Longman.

Da Coll, Ivar (1985) *Chigüiro y el lápiz*, Bogotá: Norma (2nd edition: Bogotá: Babel Libros, 2005).

Derrien, Marie (2005) "Radical Trends in French Picturebooks," *The Lion and the Unicorn* 29.2: 171–189.

Douglas, J. Yellowlees (1994) "Plucked From the Labyrinth: Invention, Interpretation, and Interactive Narratives," in Mike Hayhoe, Bill Corcoran, and Gordon Pradl (eds) *Knowledge in the Making. Challenging the Text in the Classroom*, Portsmouth: Boynton/Cook, 179–192.

Douzou, Olivier (2000) *Luchien*, Rodez (France): Éditions du Rouergue.

Dresang, Eliza (2008) "Radical Change Theory, Postmodernism and Contemporary Picturebooks," in Lawrence R. Sipe and Sylvia Pantaleo (eds) *Postmodern Picturebooks: Play, Parody and Self Referentiality*, New York: Routledge, 41–54.

Escala, Jaume (1991) *Els nens del mar*, illus. Carme Solé Vendrell, Barcelona: Siruela.

Felix, Monique (1981) *Histoire d'une petite souris qui était enfermée dans un livre*, Paris: Gallimard-Tournesol.

Goldstone, Bette (1998) "Ordering the Chaos: Teaching Metafictive Characteristics of Children's Books," *Journal of Children's Literature* 24.2: 48–55.

Goldstone, Bette, and Labbo, Linda (2004) "The Postmodern Picture Book: A New Subgenre," *Language Arts* 81.3: 196–204.

Gravett, Emily (2011) *Again!*, London: Macmillan.

Gravett, Emily (2006) *Wolves*, London: Macmillan.

Hunt, Peter (2001) *Children's Literature*, Oxford: Blackwell.

Hutcheon, Linda (1984) *Narcissistic Narrative: The Metafictional Paradox*, New York: Methuen.

Jablon, Madelyn (1997) *Black Metafiction: Self-Conciousness in African American Literature*, Iowa City: University of Iowa Press.

Jeffers, Oliver (2006) *The Incredible Book Eating Boy*, London: Harper Collins.

Johnson, Crockett (1955) *Harold and the Purple Crayon*, New York: Harper Collins.

Kaplan, Deborah (2003) "Read All Over: Postmodern Resolution in Macaulay's *Black and White*," *Children's Literature Association Quarterly* 28.1: 37–41.

Lewis, David (1990) "The Constructedness of Texts: Picture Books and the Metafictive," *Signal* 62: 130–146.

Lewis, David (2001) *Reading Contemporary Picturebooks: Picturing Text*, London: RoutledgeFalmer.

Lewis, Patrick J. (2002) *The Last Resort*, illus. Roberto Innocenti, Mankato, MI: The Creative Editions.

Lodge, David (1992) *The Art of Fiction*, London: Secker and Warburg.

Macaulay, David (1990) *Black and White*, Boston, MA: Houghton Mifflin.

McCallum, Robyn (1996) "Metafiction and Experimental Work," in Peter Hunt (ed.) *The International Companion Encyclopedia of Children's Literature*, London: Routledge, 138–150.

Moss, Anita (1985) "Varieties of Children's Metafiction," *Studies in the Literary Imagination* 18.2: 79–92.

Moss, Geoff (1990) "Metafiction, Illustration and the Poetics of Children's Literature," in Peter Hunt (ed.) *Literature for Children: Contemporary Criticism*, London: Routledge, 44–66.

Müller, Jörg (2001) *Das Buch im Buch im Buch*, Aarau: Sauerländer.

Nesbit, Edith (1899) *The Story of the Treasure Seekers*, London: Fisher Unwin.

Newell, Peter (1908) *The Hole Book*, New York: Harper & Brothers.

Nodelman, Perry (1988) *Words about Pictures: The Narrative Art of Children's Picture Books*, Athens: University of Georgia Press.

Pantaleo, Sylvia (2004) "Young Children Interpret the Metafictive in Anthony Browne's *Voices in the Park*," *Journal of Early Childhood Literacy* 4.2: 211–233.

Pantaleo, Sylvia (2010) "Mutinous Fiction Narrative and Illustrative Metalepsis in Three Postmodern Picturebooks," *Children's Literature in Education* 41.1: 12–27.

Pantaleo, Sylvia (2014) "The Metafictive Nature of Postmodern Picturebooks," *The Reading Teacher* 67.5: 324–332.

Pescetti, Luis María (1996) *Caperucita Roja (tal como se la contaron a Jorge)*, illus. O'Kif, Buenos Aires: Alfaguara.

Ruiz Domínguez, Ma. del Mar (2012) "Metalepsis and Hypertext: Analysis of the Metafictional Processes in Two Picturebooks," *Anuario de Investigación en Literatura Infantil y Juvenil* 10: 155–171.

Sanders, Joe Sutcliff (2009) "The Critical Reader in Children's Metafiction," *The Lion and the Unicorn* 33.3: 349–361.

Schwenke-Wyile, Andrea (2006) "The Drama of Potentiality in Metafictive Picture Books: Engaging in Pictorialization in *Shortcut*, *Ohh-la-la* and *Voices in the Park* (with occasional assistance from A. Wolf's *True Story*)," *Children's Literature Association Quarterly* 31.2: 176–196.

Scieszka, Jon (1992) *The Stinky Cheese Man and Other Fairly Stupid Tales*, illus. Lane Smith, New York: Penguin.

Serafini, Frank (2005) "*Voices in the Park*, Voices in the Classroom: Readers Responding to Postmodern Picture Books," *Reading Research and Instruction* 44.3: 47–65.

Serafini, Frank (2012) "Interpreting Visual Images and Design Elements of Contemporary Picturebooks," *Connecticut Reading Association Journal* 1.1: 3–8.

Silva-Díaz, Maria Cecilia (2005) *Libros que enseñan a leer: Álbumes metaficcionales y conocimiento literario*. PhD, thesis, Departament de Didàctica de la Llengua, de la Literatura i de les Ciències Socials, Bellaterra: Universitat Autònoma de Barcelona.

Sipe, Lawrence R. (2008) "First Graders Interpret David Wiesner's *The Three Pigs*: A Case Study," in Lawrence R. Sipe and Sylvia Pantaleo (eds) *Postmodern Picturebooks: Play, Parody and Self Referentiality*, New York: Routledge, 223–237.

Sipe, Lawrence R., and Pantaleo, Sylvia (eds) (2008) *Postmodern Picturebooks: Play, Parody and Self Referentiality*, New York: Routledge.

Smith, Lane (2010) *It's a Book*, New York: Roaring Brook Press.

Stephens, John (2008) "They Are Always Surprised at What People Throw Away: Glocal Postmodernism in Australian Picturebooks," in Lawrence R. Sipe and Sylvia Pantaleo (eds) *Postmodern Picturebooks: Play, Parody and Self Referentiality*, New York: Routledge, 89–102.

Styles, Morag (1996) "Inside the Tunnel: a Radical Kind of Reading Picture Books and Postmodernism," in Victor Watson and Morag Styles (eds) *Talking Pictures: Pictorial Texts and Young Readers*, London: Hodder & Stoughton, 23–47.

Swaggerty, Elizabeth (2009) "'That Just Really Knocks Me Out': Fourth Grade Students Navigate Postmodern Picture Books," *Journal of Language and Literacy Education* 5.1: 9–31 www.coe.uga.edu/jolle/2009_1/postmodernpicturebooks (accessed March 30, 2014).

Tauveron, Catherine (2011) "Trois petits traités ludiques de fiction," *Strenæ* 2.2, URL: http://strenae.revues.org/348; DOI: 10.4000/strenae.348 (accessed April 6, 2015).

Trites, Roberta Seelinger (1994) "Manifold Narratives: Metafiction and Ideology in Picture Books," *Children's Literature in Education* 25: 225–242.

Tullet, Hervé (2010) *Un livre*, Paris: Bayard Jeunesse. [*Press Here*, San Francisco: Chronicle Books, 2011].

Van Allsburg, Chris (1995) *Bad Day at Riverbend*, Boston: Houghton Mifflin Harcourt.

Watt, Mélanie (2007) *Chester*, Toronto: Kids Can Press.

Waugh, Patricia (1984) *Metafiction: The Theory and Practice of Self-Conscious Fiction*, New York: Methuen.

Wiesner, David (2001) *The Three Pigs*, New York: Clarion Books.

8

HYBRIDITY IN PICTUREBOOKS

Helma van Lierop-Debrauwer

Introduction

Scholars involved in picturebook research unanimously agree that picturebooks are a unique art form, because they combine two modes of communication: words and images (cf. Sipe 1998; Nikolajeva and Scott 2001). This synergy between verbal and visual language makes picturebooks a hybrid, which is defined by *The Oxford English Dictionary* as "a thing made by combining two different elements." In this sense, hybridity is more or less synonymous with collage, bricolage, and fusion, terms that will be used interchangeably throughout this chapter. The origin of the term hybrid goes back centuries, to the realm of biology, where it refers to offspring that is the result of crossbreeding. Nowadays, 'hybrid' and its derivative 'hybridity' are used to refer to all kinds of phenomena that are a mixture of two or more elements. In the humanities, "hybridity has become a master trope across many spheres of cultural research, theory and criticism" (Kraidy 2002: n. pag.). More specifically, scholars working in the field of postcolonial studies and social scientists interested in globalization processes have adopted the concept to discuss cultural exchanges and interferences in general and encounters between colonized and colonizing cultures in particular. Its deployment in postcolonial studies is influenced by Mikhail Bakhtin's theory of linguistic hybridity: "a mixture of two social languages within the limits of a single utterance" (Bakhtin 1981: 358). In *The Dialogic Imagination* (1981), he makes a distinction between 'organic' hybridity, which is a major characteristic of the evolution of every language, and 'intentional' hybridity, which refers to a political use of language: "Intentional semantic hybrids are inevitably internally dialogic [. . .]. Two points of view are not mixed, but set against each other dialogically" (360), thus resisting the authority of one voice and accepting the inclusion of differences. As a result, the notion of hybridity in cultures and languages has been the subject of much debate, always involving value judgments in relation to issues of purity, power, and (in)equality.

In the following sections I will discuss the most important forms of hybridity that can be distinguished in picturebooks, the most obvious and characteristic form being their semiotic hybridity, already referred to in the first lines of this chapter. Another typical form is their genre hybridity. Right from the start, the picturebook as a multimodal art form has formed combinations with well-known children's book genres such as animal stories, adventure stories, and poetry, just to name a few. Since postmodernism found its way into Western art and thus also into children's literature during the last decades of the twentieth century, these two more traditional forms of mixing elements in the picturebook have stood out more and have become more challenging, and new forms of bricolage have gained ground. Although over the years postmodernism has been used in a range of contexts and for different purposes, most scholars agree on its main features being indeterminacy, fragmentation, decanonization, irony, participation, and hybridization in the sense of the blurring or even dissolution of boundaries (Lewis 2001: 88–91). New forms of hybridity that will be discussed are material and medial bricolage, the fusion of artistic styles and the blurring of low and high art, the hybridity of address, and, last but not least, cultural hybridity.

Semiotic hybridity

The various and dynamic relationships between words and pictures in picturebooks have been amply described by researchers (Schwarcz 1982; Golden 1990; Lewis 2001; Nikolajeva and Scott 2001). Words and pictures can offer the reader more or less the same information, as is the case in many alphabet books for very young readers; they can complement each other by filling each other's gaps, or they can be counterpointing. The latter is the case "as soon as words and images provide alternative information or contradict each other in some way" (Nikolajeva and Scott 2001: 17). Counterpointing picturebooks thus leave room for more than one interpretation, and by doing so they are often intentionally hybrid in the Bakhtinian sense of the word, making the reader aware that there are different views of the world that surrounds them. The dialogue between the visual and the verbal invites the reader to take a critical stance and to become actively engaged in the construction of meaning. A case in point is *Der Struwwelpeter* (Slovenly Peter), a worldwide classic, published in 1845 by Heinrich Hoffmann. In this picturebook, as Katrien Vloeberghs (2000: 9–11) argues, the pictures are subversive and undermine the extremely authoritarian content of the verbal text, in which disobedient children are severely punished for their behavior. In contrast to the words, the pictures form an alliance with the child. The images represent Slovenly Peter and the other children as self-aware and energetic rebels, making them "heroes with whom the reader wants to stand together" instead of "bad examples" (10).

Although words and pictures in picturebooks always convey meaning together, each of the two sign systems has its own potential in contributing to the story, in expressing temporality, spatiality, narrative perspective, and characterization (Nikolajeva and Scott 2001). This different potential of words and images for providing information raises the question of how readers deal with the semiotic hybridity of picturebooks. An interesting answer to this is offered by Lawrence Sipe's theoretical concept of transmediation, which helps to understand how people give meaning to picturebooks, interpreting "the text in terms of the pictures and the pictures in terms of the text in a potentially never-ending sequence" (1998: 102). Sipe makes this process more concrete by applying it to Maurice Sendak's classic picturebook *Where the Wild Things Are* (1963). In order to construct the meaning of Sendak's story about Max and the monsters, readers constantly move back and forth across the two sign systems. This process of transmediation illustrates that the visual and verbal texts are equally important for the interpretation of picturebooks. Through the intricate combination of two semiotic systems, this multimodal art form plays an important role in children's social learning, in the development of their verbal and visual literacy, and in their literary competence. The latter is also facilitated by the second form of hybridity in picturebooks, the mixing of genres.

Genre hybridity

Looking at picturebooks from a genre perspective reveals that this art form covers almost all other genres distinguished within children's literature. The picturebook includes genres such as alphabet books, poetry, fairy tales, nonfiction, realistic stories, autobiographies, and fantastic stories. Due to the combination of words and images, picturebooks add a new dimension to these well-known genres.

Moreover, through the code switching between the two sign systems picturebooks sometimes also mix genres within one and the same story. Maria Nikolajeva and Carole Scott (2001: 24) give several examples of what they call a "counterpoint in genre or modality," picturebooks in which the verbal text "may be 'realistic' while images suggest fantasy" or the other way around. A humorous example of this mixing of genres is the Dutch picturebook *Ridder Prikneus* (Knight Pricknose 2003) by Daan Remmerts de Vries, which is discussed by Vanessa Joosen and Katrien Vloeberghs (2008). While the words tell the story of a knight who saves the princess from a dragon, the pictures show a boy with his dog and his little sister in an everyday setting, suggesting that the verbal text is the product of the child's imagination.

From a hybridity point of view, autobiographical and biographical picturebooks are particularly interesting genres, because they are characterized by a combination of elements on different levels: a mix of fact and fiction, an interanimation of pictures and words, and sometimes, a blending with the fine arts (van der Heijden and van Lierop-Debrauwer 2014). Life writing is a genre that in the past few decades has been gaining more and more ground in children's literature, including in picturebooks (Kümmerling-Meibauer 2010). A well-known example of an autobiographical picturebook is *The Wall: Growing Up Behind the Iron Curtain* (2007) by Peter Sís, a 2008 Caldecott Honor Book. In this book Peter Sís tells and draws his own life story, growing up in Czechoslovakia in the 1950s and 1960s. In fact, *The Wall* is not only an autobiography but also a graphic memoir, as it touches upon the history of Eastern Europe during the Cold War.

With regard to biographical picturebooks two forms can be distinguished: the fact-oriented biographical picturebook and the so-called art fantasy. An example of the former is *A Picture Book of Anne Frank* (1993), written by David Adler and illustrated by Karen Ritz. This book, which is part of the Picture Book Biography Series, is about the brief life of this Jewish girl who became famous worldwide because of the diary she kept during the years she lived in hiding. In words and watercolor pictures based on well-known photographs, it tells the story of what happened to her, from her childhood in Germany, to the family hiding in the Amsterdam attic, to her deportation to Bergen-Belsen.

Art fantasies can be defined as "fantasies that bring to life past masters (and their works) in new, exciting – even surprising – contexts" (Nikola-Lisa 1995: 35). Well-known examples are *Pish, Posh, Said Hieronymus Bosch* (1991), with a text by Nancy Willard and illustrations by Leo, Diane, and Lee Dillon, and *Keepvogel en Kijkvogel in het spoor van Mondriaan* (Coppernickel Goes Mondrian 2011) by Dutch artist Wouter van Reek. The former is a fantasy story about fifteenth-century painter Hieronymus Bosch told by his housekeeper, who is very much annoyed by the presence of the many bizarre imaginary beings in the painter's household. *Coppernickel Goes Mondrian* is a work of biographical fiction elaborating on facts known through more scholarly biographies by making use of novelistic techniques such as the addition of fictional characters, imagined monologues, dialogues, and thoughts, and deviations from the chronological order (Figure 8.1). Moreover, van Reek's deliberate use of the interplay between words and images to inform about the life and work of Piet Mondrian and his experimenting with Mondrian's visual language amplify the possibilities of highlighting the artistic development the painter went through as well as the changes in his emotional well-being.

The picturebook not only mingles, renews, or recycles well-known genres, it also creates genres, like the so-called wimmelbooks, "textless picturebooks with doublespreads that present a panorama of characters and detailed 'pluriscenic' landscapes composed of various scenes" (Kümmerling-Meibauer 2015: 249). Because of their robust physical appearance and because they activate readers to participate in picturebook reading, they share certain features with puzzle and game books, genres that will be discussed in the next section on material and medial hybridity. An important difference however is that, unlike the game book, the wimmelbook is not characterized by rules or instructions (Rémi 2011: 117).

Figure 8.1 Illustration from Wouter van Reek's *Keepvogel en kijkvogel in het spoor van Mondriaan*. Amsterdam: Leopold B.V., 2011.

Material and medial hybridity

Although contemporary picturebooks often appeal to adult readers as much as they do to children, the implied reader of many picturebooks used to be and still is the child as an emergent reader. As a consequence, picturebook makers have always taken into consideration the young child's need for play by emphasizing the material aspects of the book, as is the case with the *knisperboek*, known in English as the 'crackle book,' which can be described as "a picturebook made of cloth filled with tiny pellets that make a crackling noise when the pages are touched and turned" (Kümmerling-Meibauer 2015: 252). To make their first books attractive for them, books for babies and toddlers often function as toys in disguise. On the contemporary book market there are books that are shaped like a house, a train, or a car, an example of the latter being *Maisy Drives* (2001) by Lucy Cousins.

Picturebooks for somewhat older children accentuate their materiality in a slightly different way than the books for the youngest readers. Instead of combining picturebook features with toy aspects, these books engage children in active book reading through a combination of picturebook characteristics and game or puzzle elements. The child is invited to press buttons and lift flaps in pages, preferably in a certain order by following the plot, to find an object or one or more characters, as is the case in the well-known *Spot* series by Eric Hill. In *Where's Spot?*, first published in 1980, the concept of lifting flaps is used to challenge the young reader to find out where Spot the dog is hiding. More innovative picturebook-game combinations are the books by Flemish picturebook artist Tom Schamp. In an overview of postmodern Flemish picturebooks, Sara Van Meerbergen characterizes his work using the term *lusboeken* (translated in English as 'loop books'). In *Otto rijdt heen en weer* (Otto Drives Back and Forth 2007), *Otto in de stad* (Otto in the City 2008), and *Otto in de sneeuw* (Otto in the Snow 2010), the circular structure allows readers to read in two directions. The large format of the books and the thick cardboard pages make them look like "a game board or a play mat for cars that can easily be spread out, for example on the floor, while the young reader follows Otto on his journeys and is able to turn the books in whichever direction" (Van Meerbergen 2012: n. pag.).

An intriguing example of a picturebook-puzzle story is *Ik wil naar verder* (I Want to Go to Further 2016) by Flemish artists Anne Provoost and An Candaele. The book consists of full- and half-size lengthwise cardboard pages and tells about Little Fish, Kitten, Girl, Little Ghost, and Little Creature leaving their parents in search of "further." The journey starts when the reader turns the title page, and she sees a picture extending over one and a half pages. What the reader has to figure out is that previous pictures return on the next pages and how this intravisuality contributes to the meaning of the story as a whole. The sphere is a recurrent metaphor, underlining that this is a story about finding out about the world people live in, about chasing dreams, and endless possibilities.

The most recent development in the mixing of elements of (traditional and computer) games with picturebook features is the picturebook app. Although children's book apps are very popular (Horne 2012), they are still in their infancy technologically. Junko Yokota and William Teale (2014) argue in favor of developing apps that use sound effects and employ the possibilities of interactivity for storytelling better than most apps do now in order to make reading an overall experience. To stimulate the literary and artistic quality of picturebook apps, the International Book Fair in Bologna introduced the Bologna Ragazzi Digital Award in 2012. The first winner of the award was *Dans mon rêve* (In My Dream 2011) by Stephane Khiel. The app is a visual and interactive twist on the well-known children's game "head, shoulders, knees, and toes." To create new images children have to slide the upper, middle, and lower panels on the screen. As in computer games, the child is put in charge of the story's direction, because as soon as the image changes, so does the line of text at the bottom of the screen. When the child touches the screen, the newly formed sentence is read aloud by the narrator. Moreover, the app includes features like a moon icon, which changes images from day to night, and a star-shaped window, which glides over the page when the iPad is turned from portrait to landscape mode. The child can also save favorite combinations of words and pictures.

The picturebook app also touches upon another aspect of the hybridity of the picturebook, which is not entirely new, but which is undoubtedly fueled by postmodernism: its multimediality. Picturebooks make use of photography and blend visual codes from media such as film, comics, graphic novels, and manga (Kümmerling-Meibauer 2013: 100). Although photography was used in picturebooks long before postmodernism influenced the genre, the blurring of media and visual styles characteristic of this art movement has provoked a more creative deployment of this medium. *Juul* (1996), a Flemish picturebook by Gregie de Maeyer and Koen Vanmechelen, is a tragic story about a boy who is bullied at school. The book catches our eye through its illustrations consisting of photographs of wooden sculptures, which represent Juul, who starts to mutilate himself as the bullying gets worse.

An example of a book employing a combination of picturebook and film codes is *The Invention of Hugo Cabret* (2007) by Brian Selznick, winner of the Caldecott Medal in 2008. The book has been characterized as a "cinematic, movielike book, evocative of early black-and-white films" (Evans 2015: 109). Although its length of over five hundred pages strongly deviates from the traditional picturebook format of thirty-two pages, the book retains picturebook features such as the brightly illustrated front cover on the dust jacket and the synergy between words and pictures. The form of the illustration on the front cover resembles a movie poster, which ties in with the story told, because the book consists of at least two interrelated story lines: one about orphan Hugo, who wants to be a magician, and one about the forgotten film maker and magician Georges Méliès. Cinematic motives are the red colored endpapers, which resemble the curtain in front of the movie screens in cinemas in the old days, and a credits section including information about the film stills and photographs used in the book. The story itself also challenges readers to use their knowledge of cinematic language, because in the images Selznick includes film stills referring to Méliès's movies and he applies several film techniques to convey information, such as medium shots and close-ups.

A pioneer in the blending of picturebook and comic is Raymond Briggs. In *The Snowman* (1978), he arranges picture sequences in panels to tell the story of a boy and a snowman who comes alive on the stroke of midnight. They play games together and the snowman takes him on a journey through the air, flying over the landscape, highlighted in the book by a doublespread with a view of the British coast. Bettina Kümmerling-Meibauer argues that readers of the wordless picturebook have to decode comic conventions to understand "that the panels are not separate images of different boys but a series of images of the same boy that should be read from left to right and from top to bottom, unfolding over time" (2013: 104). Differences in panel sizes function as narrative devices, to suggest time shifts for example, or to depict repetitive action.

The influence of manga is particularly visible in many adaptations of children's classics, such as Kinoshita Sakura's version of *Alice in Wonderland* (2006). What is specifically interesting in this manga-picturebook hybrid is that Alice looks different on every page because her clothes and hair-style vary, which can be interpreted as a reference to a form of manga focusing on "a CosPlay motif" (Kümmerling-Meibauer 2013: 108). The most obvious manga characteristics in this picturebook based on Lewis Carroll's famous story are Alice's oversized eyes, her almond-shaped face, and the exaggerated facial expressions.

Because picturebook artists are increasingly exploring the possibilities of other media, the distinctions traditionally made between book types consisting of both words and images are becoming less useful. Janet Evans therefore proposes creating a new category she refers to as "the 'fusion' text" (2015: 97), which synthesizes aspects of all art forms, media, and genres mentioned. Sipe suggests taking them together as forms of "sequential art," and he argues that new theories of sequential art are needed, because without them "we will be left trying to fit new and ground-breaking works of visual/verbal art into Procrustean beds of our old definitions of these forms and formats" (2011: 249). These theories will also shed new light on hybridity, as this concept no longer encompasses all the creative departures from the standard formats of the traditional categories discussed. Referring to them merely as hybrids fails to do justice to their innovative quality.

Artistic hybridity

Picturebooks have always been characterized by a variety of artistic styles, because many picturebook artists have had a formal art training, so that they have learned to apply diverse styles, techniques, and materials (Serafini 2015: 439). They make pictures using pencil, water-based paint, acrylics, or other materials, or they use the computer to make their drawings. This, however, is not the form of artistic hybridity that is foregrounded in contemporary picturebooks. Influenced by postmodernism and its blurring of the distinctions between popular and high culture as well as its tendency towards intertextuality and intervisuality, the most prominent characteristic of picturebooks published in the past few decades is the "often highly sophisticated, visual allusions to art works. Many of today's pic-turebook creators are master recyclers of art" (Beckett 2010: 83). Some illustrators mimic one specific style, whereas others blend two or more artistic movements, a phenomenon referred to by critics as a "scavenging of styles" (Nodelman 1988: 83). Moreover, many picturebook artists also allude to specific paintings or art works (Beckett 2012). An intriguing example of the employment of different artistic styles in combination with allusions to particular paintings is *Op zoek naar mij* (The Quest for Myself 2013) by Flemish writer Ed Franck and Flemish illustrator Kris Nauwelaerts, the latter being not only an illustrator but also an art educator and a picturebook researcher, who analyzed his own picturebooks in a PhD thesis about the relation between picturebooks and the development of children's visual literacy (2015). In *The Quest for Myself*, he uses distinct artistic styles to tell the story of Kitoko, an adopted black boy who becomes emotionally disturbed when his white adoptive mother gets pregnant. To give expression to the boy's anxieties, sadness, and happiness, Nauwelaerts uses different artistic styles on each doublespread, alluding to well-known paintings and painters. For example, when Kitoko's war experiences are visualized in one of his dreams, Nauwelaerts alludes to Pablo Picasso and *Guernica* (1937), the oil painting in gray, black, and white that Picasso painted as a response to the bombing of the Basque village of the same name during the Spanish Civil War (Figure 8.2). When the little boy dreams of being happily reunited with his sister Ayosha, Nauwelaerts draws a picture in the exotic style of Paul Gauguin (Figure 8.3).

Figure 8.2 Illustration by Kris Nauwelaerts from Ed Franck's *Op zoek naar mij*. Wielsbeke: De Eenhoorn, 2013. Reprinted by permission of De Eenhoorn.

Figure 8.3 Illustration by Kris Nauwelaerts from Ed Franck's *Op zoek naar mij*. Wielsbeke: De Eenhorn, 2013. Reprinted by permission of De Eenhoorn.

Hybridity of address

Although several researchers have expressed their doubts about the capacity of young children to decode the many allusions to the fine arts in contemporary picturebooks, others emphasize the opportunities these books offer for art education and the developing visual literacy of child readers (Serafini 2015: 450). This does not affect the observation that artistic hybridity is one of the aspects of picturebooks that appeals to adult readers as well. Another important factor responsible for the hybridity of address of picturebooks in the new millennium is the increase in so-called cross-generational themes (Beckett 2012) – that is, themes that are of interest to both adult and child readers. Although dark, disturbing, and complex themes are not new to children's books, even to those for the youngest readers, the number of picturebooks dealing with painful and difficult subjects has increased considerably since the 1970s. In the last few decades many authors, illustrators, and publishers have come to feel that books should provide a proper introduction to all stages of life. As a result, subjects that used to be taboo are now no longer avoided in picturebooks, ranging from death (of a [grand]parent, for instance), nudity, and sexuality to abuse and domestic violence. The latter is dealt with for example in the Norwegian picturebook *Sinna Man* (Angry Man 2003) by Gro Dahle and Svein Nyhus. It is about a young boy who sees his father transform into a violent monster. Although he does not quite understand the situation, the little boy empathizes with his father, feeling that his father's evil side is not his real self. Painful subjects such as violence and sexuality attract the attention of adult readers who read these books themselves but who at the same time feel uncomfortable about giving them to children. However, discussing picturebooks with children can help them become resilient and well-equipped to cope with the hard facts of life. One of the harsh realities for many children today is growing up in a country that is not originally their own. Contemporary picturebooks therefore sometimes explicitly address cultural encounters and the emotions that go with being torn between two cultural identities.

Cultural hybridity

Cultural hybridity can be discussed from different angles. One of the perspectives that can be taken is that of the picturebook's blending with manga, which I already hinted at earlier in the section on genre hybridity. The fusion of the picturebook with this originally Japanese genre is discussed at length by Bettina Kümmerling-Meibauer, who considers the coexistence of picturebook features and elements characteristic of manga in picturebooks to be "part of a global approach to the indigenization of foreign cultures [. . .], when one cultural space absorbs and transforms elements from another" (2013: 116). The same goes for the second form of cultural hybridity, which we find in so-called multicultural picturebooks. Although multicultural literature is defined in different ways, most definitions share the description that "multicultural literature is about groups of people that are distinguished racially, culturally, linguistically and in other ways from the dominant white" (Cai 2002: 5). As a result, multicultural children's books in general and multicultural picturebooks in particular tend to be political in nature, claiming space for minority groups in society and giving them a voice. These picturebooks are intentionally hybrid in the way Bakhtin (1981: 360) defined the term, establishing a dialogue between cultures and questioning imbalances in power. A representative example of a multicultural picturebook, interesting also from the point of view of artistic hybridity, is the aforementioned *The Quest for Myself* by Ed Franck and Kris Nauwelaerts. This book is not only a cultural hybrid because the plot is about the coexistence of cultures, but also because the multiculturalism of the story line is mirrored in the diversity of artistic styles employed in the illustrations, ranging from references to a colonial painting by the Belgian painter Gustave Vanaise and African statues, to allusions to Western artists such as Marc Chagall, Salvador Dalí, M.C. Escher, and Pablo Picasso.

Conclusion

Although some forms of hybridity have always been characteristic of the picturebook, others are the result of technological and artistic innovations. Together they are responsible for the fact that nowadays picturebooks are no longer perceived as a multimodal art form intended for and enjoyed by young children only. The many forms of hybridity characterizing contemporary picturebooks are aimed at a broad audience of all ages. The sophisticated use of both art and new media and the ways they discuss cultural similarities and differences in a global world make picturebooks increasingly meaningful cultural artifacts which "stand both in the traditional historical evolution of children's literature, and are poised to be on the cutting edge, promoting all types of new literacies" (Sipe 2011: 250).

References

Adler, David A. (1993) *A Picture Book of Anne Frank*, illus. Karen Ritz, New York: Holiday House.
Bakhtin, Mikhail (1981) *The Dialogic Imagination: Four Essays*, Austin and London: University of Texas Press.
Beckett, Sandra L. (2010) "Artistic Allusions in Picturebooks," in Teresa Colomer, Bettina Kümmerling-Meibauer, and Cecilia Silva-Díaz (eds) *New Directions in Picturebook Research*, New York: Routledge, 83–100.
Beckett, Sandra L. (2012) *Crossover Picturebooks: A Genre for all Ages*, New York: Routledge.
Briggs, Raymond (1978) *The Snowman*, New York: Random House.
Cai, Mingshui (2002) *Multicultural Literature for Children and Young Adults: Reflections on Critical Issues*, Westport and London: Greenwood Press.
Cousins, Lucy (2001) *Maisy Drives*, London: Candlewick.
Dahle, Gro (2003) *Sinna Man*, illus. Svein Nyhus, Oslo: Cappelen.
Evans, Janet (2015) "Fusions Texts – The New Kid on the Block: What Are They and Where Have They Come From?," in Janet Evans (ed.) *Challenging and Controversial Picturebooks: Creative and Critical Responses to Visual Texts*, London: Routledge, 97–120.
Franck, Ed (2013) *Op zoek naar mij*, illus. Kris Nauwelaerts, Wielsbeke: De Eenhoorn.
Golden, Joanne M. (1990) *The Narrative Symbol in Childhood Literature: Explorations in the Construction of Text*, Berlin and New York: Mouton de Gruyter.
Heijden, Ingrid, van der, and van Lierop-Debrauwer, Helma (2014) "A Threefold Hybridity. Picturebook Art Fantasies as Life Writing," *European Journal of Life Writing* 3: 63–81. Doi: http://dx.doi.org/10.5463/ejlw.3.119 (accessed December 28, 2015).
Hill, Eric (1980) *Where's Spot?*, New York: G.P. Putnam's Sons.
Hoffmann, Heinrich (1845) *Der Struwwelpeter oder lustige Geschichten und drollige Bilder*, Frankfurt: Literarische Anstalt.
Horne, Lasse K. (2012) "Apps: A Practical Approach to Trade and Co-Financed Book Apps," *Publishing Research Quarterly* 28: 17–22.
Joosen, Vanessa, and Vloeberghs, Katrien (2008) *Uitgelezen jeugdliteratuur: Ontmoetingen tussen traditie en vernieuwing*, Tielt and Den Haag: Lannoo Campus/Biblion.
Khiel, Stephane (2011) *Dans mon rêve*, Paris: e-Toiles éditions.
Kraidy, Marwan M. (2002) "Hybridity in Cultural Globalization," *Communication Theory* 12.3: 316–339. Doi: http://dx.doi.org/10.1111/j.1468-2885.2002.tb00272.x (accessed December 28, 2015).
Kümmerling-Meibauer, Bettina (2010) "Remembering the Past in Words and Pictures. How Autobiographical Stories Become Picturebooks," in Teresa Colomer, Bettina Kümmerling-Meibauer, and Cecilia Silva-Díaz (eds) *New Directions in Picturebook Research*, New York: Routledge, 205–216.
Kümmerling-Meibauer, Bettina (2013) "Manga/Comics Hybrids in Picturebooks," in Jaqueline Berndt and Bettina Kümmerling-Meibauer (eds) *Manga's Cultural Crossroads*, New York: Routledge, 100–120.
Kümmerling-Meibauer, Bettina (2015) "From Baby Books to Picturebooks for Adults: European Picturebooks in the New Millennium," *Word & Image* 31.3: 249–264. Doi: http://dx.doi.org/10.1080/02666286.2015.1032519 (accessed January 4, 2016).
Lewis, David (2001) *Reading Contemporary Picturebooks: Picturing Text*, London: RoutledgeFalmer.
de Maeyer, Gregie (1996) *Juul*, illus. Koen Vanmechelen, Averbode: Altiora Averbode.
Nauwelaerts, Kris (2015) *Onderzoek naar de relatie tussen prentenboeken en de ontwikkeling van de beeldende geletterdheid bij kinderen*, Dissertation, Hasselt: Universiteit Hasselt.
Nikolajeva, Maria, and Scott, Carole (2001) *How Picturebooks Work*, New York: Garland.

Nikola-Lisa, William (1995) "I Spy: A Place for the Arts in Children's Picture-Books," *Journal of Children's Literature* 21.2: 52–56.

Nodelman, Perry (1988) *Words about Pictures: The Narrative Art of Children's Picture Books*, Athens: University of Georgia Press.

Provoost, Anne (2016) *Ik wil naar verder*, illus. An Candaele, Wielsbeke: De Eenhoorn.

Reek, Wouter van (2011) *Keepvogel en kijkvogel in het spoor van Mondriaan*, Amsterdam: Leopold B.V. [*Coppernickel Goes Mondrian*, New York: Enchanted Lion Book, 2012].

Rémi, Cornelia (2011) "Reading as Playing. The Cognitive Challenge of the Wimmelbook," in Bettina Kümmerling-Meibauer (ed.) *Emergent Literacy: Children's Books from 0 to 3*, Amsterdam: John Benjamins, 115–140.

Remmerts de Vries, Daan (2003) *Ridder Prikneus*, Amsterdam: Querido.

Sakura, Kinoshita (2006) *Alice in Wonderland*, Tokyo: Gentosha Comics.

Schamp, Tom (2007) *Otto rijdt heen en weer*, Tielt: Lannoo.

Schamp, Tom (2008) *Otto in de stad*, Tielt: Lannoo.

Schamp, Tom (2010) *Otto in de sneeuw*, Tielt: Lannoo.

Schwarcz, Joseph (1982) *Ways of the Illustrator: Visual Communication in Children's Literature*, Chicago: American Library Association.

Selznick, Brian (2007) *The Invention of Hugo Cabret*, New York: Scholastic.

Sendak, Maurice (1963) *Where the Wild Things Are*, London: The Bodley Head.

Serafini, Frank (2015) "The Appropriation of Fine Art Into Contemporary Narrative Picturebooks," *Children's Literature in Education* 46: 438–453.

Sipe, Lawrence R. (1998) "How Picture Books Work: A Semiotically Framed Theory of Text-Picture Relationships," *Children's Literature in Education* 29.2: 97–108.

Sipe, Lawrence R. (2011) "The Art of the Picturebook," in Shelby A. Wolf et al. (eds) *Handbook of Research in Children's and Young Adult Literature*, New York: Routledge, 238–252.

Sís, Peter (2007) *The Wall: Growing Up Behind the Iron Curtain*, New York: Farrar, Straus and Giroux.

Van Meerbergen, Sara (2012) "Play, Parody, Intertextuality and Interaction. Postmodern Flemish Picture Books as Semiotic Playgrounds," *BLFT: Nordic Journal of Childlit Aesthetics* 3: n.pag, www.childlitaesthetics.net/index.php/blft/article/view/20075/25159 (accessed January 10, 2016).

Vloeberghs, Katrien (2000) "Rebellie zonder een woord: Over de ondermijnende kracht van illustraties in prentenboeken," *Literatuur zonder leeftijd* 14.51: 5–16.

Willard, Nancy (1991) *Pish, Posh, Said Hieronymus Bosch*, illus. Leo, Diane, and Lee Dillon, San Diego, CA: Harcourt, Brace.

Yokota, Junko, and Teale, William H. (2014) "Picture Books and the Digital World," *The Reading Teacher* 67.8: 577–585.

9

INTERPICTORIALITY IN PICTUREBOOKS

Beatriz Hoster Cabo, María José Lobato Suero,
and Alberto Manuel Ruiz Campos

The picturebook is a place of communication where readers perceive visual as well as verbal signs. Furthermore, readers are invited to explore them, thus making their own hypothesis regarding the picturebook's meaning. In this regard, interpictorial references emphasize the artistic strategies that are involved in the creation of a picturebook. A striking example of this strategy is the overarching influence of Maurice Sendak's *Where the Wild Things Are* (1963), particularly regarding the depiction of the archetypical figure of the monster (Figure 9.1).

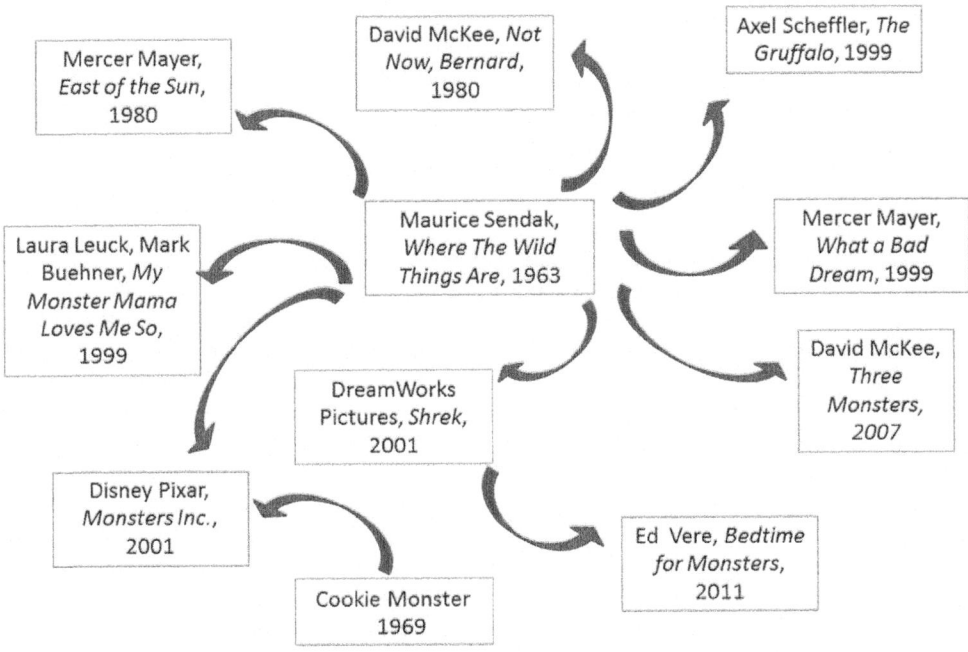

Figure 9.1 Maurice Sendak's *Wild Things* as a model for other picturebook and movie characters.

The impact of Sendak's image of the "Wild Things" is visible in the picturebooks *Not Now, Bernard* (1980) by David McKee and *The Gruffalo* (1999) by Julia Donaldson with illustrations by Axel Scheffler, among others, but it also influenced the depiction of monsters in animation films, such as *Monsters Inc.* (2001) and *Shrek* (2001) (see http://didacticaytextos.blogspot.es for a detailed synopsis of this schema).

Delimitation of the notions of interpictoriality, intervisuality, and intertextuality

The idea that texts and art works refer to other texts and art works is not new and has been discussed in literary studies for many centuries. However, the notion of 'intertextuality' as an adequate term to describe this phenomenon was introduced by Julia Kristeva in 1967 (see Kristeva 1980). Based on Mikhail Bakhtin's idea that all texts enter into a dialogue with each other, Kristeva maintains that intertextuality is the reference of one text to other texts (see Todorov 1984). Considering this, one of the most important tasks in the process of interpretation is to identify these intertextual references. As Kristeva affirms in reference to intertextuality:

> Yet, what appears as a lack of rigour is in fact an insight first introduced into literary theory by Bakhtin: any text is constructed as a mosaic of quotations; any text is the absorption and transformation of another.
>
> *1986: 37*

Many scholars have investigated the concept of intertextuality commencing with Bakhtin, but Michael Riffaterre (1980) has achieved the most popular definition. He considers intertextuality as the recognition of the relationship between a work of art and its preceding ones by the reader.

Therefore, the reader is asked to decipher the relationship between the present text and its pre-texts. The success of this task depends on the reader's intertextual knowledge, although connecting a text with other previous texts is not imperative. However, the ability to recognize the connection between the text and previous works gives the reader many interesting clues that are fundamental in order to discover the complete meaning of the text (Allen 2011). In the particular case of picture-books, this capacity is even more demanding due to the combination of a verbal and a pictorial discourse. In this regard, three different types of intertextual references can be distinguished: from text to text, from text to image, and from image to image. Traditionally, studies relating to the analysis of literature and art have used the general term 'intertextuality' to refer indistinctively to these multiple references. Generally, intertextual references encompass all cultural artifacts, ranging from folklore and literature – whether for children or adults – to paintings, films, and other art forms.

Since Kristeva's seminal study, a vast number of scholars have investigated the impact of inter-textuality on the analysis of literary texts, transferring these findings to other media forms such as films and comics (Barthes 1957; Derrida 1972; Eco 1979; Mendoza 1994). Gerard Genette (1997) has developed an elaborated system of intertextual references, which constitutes a complex web of concepts, the most relevant being 'hypotext' and 'hypertext.' A hypotext is an earlier text, which serves as a source of a subsequent text ('hypertext'). Therefore, a hypertext derives from hypotext(s) through a process, which Genette calls 'transformation': the hypertext evokes the hypotext without necessarily mentioning or quoting it.

Within this process, the readers have a central role of active participation, since they are required to discover the open and hidden references to other literary texts. Very often hypertexts include intertextual markers that call the reader's attention to the respective hypotexts.

In this way, readers have to positively use their interpretation skills, relying on their literary knowledge as well as their knowledge of other art forms such as painting, music, or sculpture. Similarly, readers are invited to update their previous knowledge during the interpretation, which induces a complex web of associations, thus enabling them to get a better access to the overall meaning of the literary work.

While 'intertextuality' initially refers to literary works only, the notion has been expanded to refer to artistic allusions in other media and art forms as well. In order to develop more distinctive frameworks, art historians have advocated using the term 'interpictoriality' (some have even suggested 'intericonicity') instead (Rose 2011). This notion refers to the process of an image referring to another image, whether a painting, an illustration in a book, or a movie. Concerning the analysis of interpictorial references in picturebooks, Maria Nikolajeva (2008: 67) proposed the term 'intervisuality.' This term has a double meaning as it encompasses pictorial references to images in general and to works of art in particular. Nevertheless, recent studies prefer the notion of 'interpictoriality' whenever references of images to other images are analyzed.

The discussion around the terminology is extensive. Liliana Louvel (2011) has taken Gerard Genette as a reference to propose her complementary terminology. Among these are the following: *transpictoriality* (a general term similar to transtextuality proposed by Genette), which makes references to semiotic systems (pictorial and verbal); *interpictoriality* shows the relationship between two or more pictorial texts that are in a work, either cited explicitly or alluded to; *parapictoriality* concerns the paratext (cover, front/back, frames, mottoes, etc.). *Metapictoriality* takes place when a system (for example a pictorial system) entices interpretations about another one (mainly the same pictorial system), for example, when an artist uses an illustration to reflect on the pictorial processes, or to define and to interpret the pictorial system; finally, *mnemopictoriality* evokes "the imaginary museum" in the viewer's mind.

Although the previous critical studies have generated a substantial amount of terminology on the subject, we opt to use the term 'interpictoriality' to refer to the relationship between pictorial texts, including the illustrations of picturebooks, while we use the notion of intertextuality to refer to interconnections between texts and pictures.

Finally, in the same way that the literary competence requires the readers' progressive understanding of the intertext, so does pictorial competence require an increase in their capacity of interpictorial reading. Hence, the understanding of interpictoriality is determined by pictorial-visual knowledge, that is, strategies and resources that the reader uses to better interpret texts, which contain a combination of pictorial and verbal codes (Mendoza 2001).

Different forms of intertextuality and interpictoriality in picturebooks

Intertextual and interpictorial references in picturebooks are not a new phenomenon, but their significance increased with the emergence of postmodern picturebooks and crossover picturebooks (Beckett 2012). Although some picturebook researchers have already analyzed the diverse functions of interpictorial references in picturebooks (Beckett 2001, 2010; Valleau 2006; Nikolajeva 2008; Nières-Chevrel 2009; Kokkola 2011; Lobato and Hoster 2011, 2014; Van Meerbergen 2012, Kümmerling-Meibauer 2015), the historical development of this intricate issue as well as the theoretical and educational implications of this artistic procedure still await academic investigation. Moreover, the tight connection between intertextual and interpictorial references in picturebooks has been largely neglected in these studies, which primarily focus on the interpictorial references. Whenever scholars discuss interpictorial issues in relation to picturebooks, they usually refer to the same illustrator, Anthony Browne.

This prolific artist not only incorporates many references to other authors and illustrators, but also often links his picturebooks with his own previous work, so that his entire picturebook collection seems like an interpictorial continuum. Additionally, scholars have shown that Browne has developed different levels of re-elaboration of the references: literally reproduced, subtly re-elaborated, or completely reworked (Hateley 2009; Lobato and Hoster 2014). Equally, there are differences in relation to the hypotext: it is either partially or entirely evoked in the illustration. Finally, it is possible to identify different intentions in the use of these interpictorial references.

Sandra Beckett (2001: 178, 192–195) has described Browne as one of the artists who has defied the usual concept of the picturebook because he has explored and developed the possibilities of this art form, in which the parodical metadiscourse about art plays an important role. According to this interpretation, Browne could be perceived as a "recycler of culture" (see Bruel 2001). In order to demonstrate this artistic strategy, we will distinguish different types of interpictorial references by a close analysis of the picturebook *The Visitors Who Came to Stay* (1984), written by Annalena McAfee and illustrated by Anthony Browne.

Interpictorial references to Magritte's artworks

The Visitors Who Came to Stay focuses on the conflicting feelings and the vicissitudes of Katy, who lives with her father and Earl, her cat, in a big house by the sea. Their life is harmonious but unchanging. Both father and daughter dedicate all their time to each other. Their activities are simple and family oriented: quiet walks along the beach, sharing moments of intimacy while sitting before the television, and visits to her mother at the weekend. Both have a routine and easygoing life until the visitors arrive: Mary, who is supposedly the new girlfriend of Katy's father, and Sean, her son. It seems, for Katy, that they may have the intention of staying. Discretion and order are not qualities of the newcomers. Hence, Katy realizes that her individual situation is changing even though she does not want this to happen. The girl perceives the visitors as intruders who have come to alter their intimate space and the close relationship with her father. Seen from Katy's perspective, readers are stimulated to interpret the visitors as invaders. However, over time, the situation changes; the visitors leave and Katy regains her interior harmony, but something is seemingly lacking. Surprisingly, she realizes that she misses the "invaders." Finally, all is resolved in a new situation, which is satisfactory for everyone. Katy, her father, Mary, and Sean are reunited due to the insistence of Katy herself, who is already accustomed to Sean's jokes and even shares them.

Considering the interpictorial preferences, it is evident that René Magritte is the favorite reference source in this picturebook. Browne appeals systematically to this artist in order to illustrate his ideas and to simultaneously empower his expressivity.

One illustration (Figure 9.2) shows the moment in which Katy, just returning from visiting her mother, finds two strangers in her peaceful home, whom she immediately perceives as "invaders." The bookshelf in front of her seems to contain an orderly collection of items she loves. On closer consideration, readers perceive that Browne has inserted references to several paintings of René Magritte by building up a transtextual relationship with the verbal discourse.

Stunned like her cat and teddy bear, Katy is about to experience a fragmentation of her mental order and, consequently, her personal values. This is evident when one notices the titles of Magritte's works contained in the illustration. The train, which refers to *Time Transfixed* (1939), has departed in search of new horizons and possibly has brought three new smiling inhabitants to the home. While Katy is paralyzed, time moves on for the others, and the everyday objects, including the birds, have escaped from the prison, which the bookshelf symbolizes. *The Reckless Sleeper* (1927) refers to Katy's father, who seems to awaken after a long episode of motionlessness and standstill. The items displayed in the bookshelf below the sleeping person indicate that the personal values are in disorder (*Personal Values*, 1951). The reference to Magritte's *Golden Legend* (1958) puts Katy's former steady worldview into question, while *The Explanation* (1952) and *The Listening Room* (1952) indicate that Katy and her father have to communicate about the new situation, which is completely changing their household. The circumstances are not hopeful for Katy: the white seagulls have left the cage and one of them is partially covering the male character, which represents *The Man in the Bowler Hat* (1965). All these interpictorial references to Magritte symbolically exemplify the emotion-laden and provoking situation caused by the encounter with the visitors.

Other details support this interpretation. Upon the arrival of Mary and Sean, the interior of the room provides clues about her father's feelings: the wallpaper is furnished with hearts and the chair

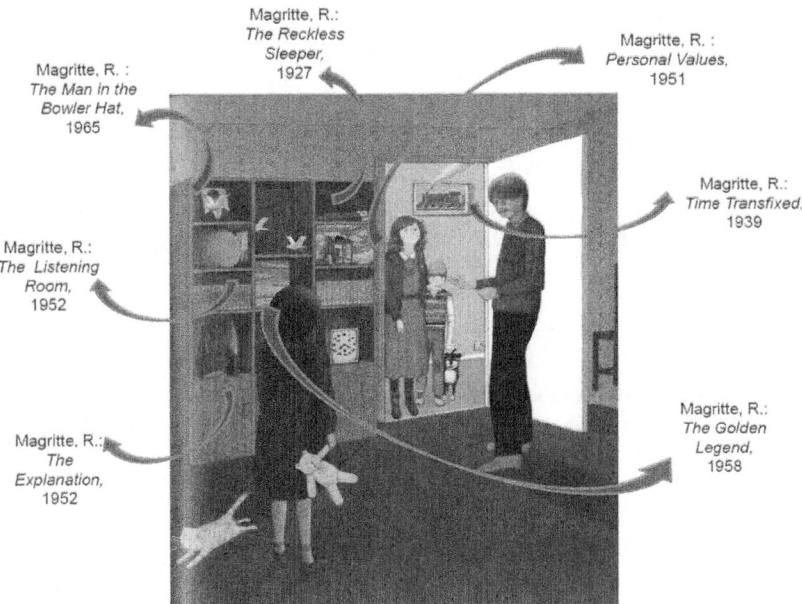

Figure 9.2 Interpictorial references to several paintings by René Magritte. Illustration by Anthony Browne from Anna-Lena McAfee's *The Visitors Who Came to Stay*, London: Hamilton, 1984.

Used by permission of Anthony Browne.

is floating in the air like a lover suspended in the air by a passionate relationship. Katy, meanwhile, remains apart from the group, rigid and paralyzed, while her father has a relaxed posture. In addition, he stands closer to Mary and Sean than to Katy. While he turns his face to Katy, he gestures invitingly towards Mary and Sean, thus attempting to build a bridge between his daughter and the newcomers. The visitors are highlighted by vibrant colors and bright lighting. By contrast, Katy stands in the shadowy part of the room, unable to advance towards the group. Moreover, her father and Sean are dressed in a similar way, which implies that Browne is establishing a link between them.

Interpictoriality and parapictoriality

The analysis of the front and back covers shows an interpictorial as well as parapictorial relationship with another illustration inside the picturebook, which sheds new light on the hypotexts that Browne incorporates in his works.

The three images show that Browne is using re-elaborated interpictorial references to his own works in addition to external references (see Figure 9.3). Furthermore, the three illustrations capture the chronological sequence of the fundamental events in an inverted way. The logical order of the events would begin with the picture on the back cover, which depicts the loneliness of father and daughter, until they meet the new visitors. The new situation is depicted as an insinuation on the front cover. Paradoxically, this arrangement of illustrations gives the picturebook a certain circularity, which presupposes that despite the acceptance of the new inhabitants Katy will not lose the stability and close relationship with her father she previously enjoyed. Moreover, these intrapictorial references transgress the main picturebook story, since they appear in the paratexts, thus constituting a parapictorial relationship on two levels: between the illustrations in the paratexts and between these illustrations and the images within the picturebook. On closer consideration, the different shades of colors reveal

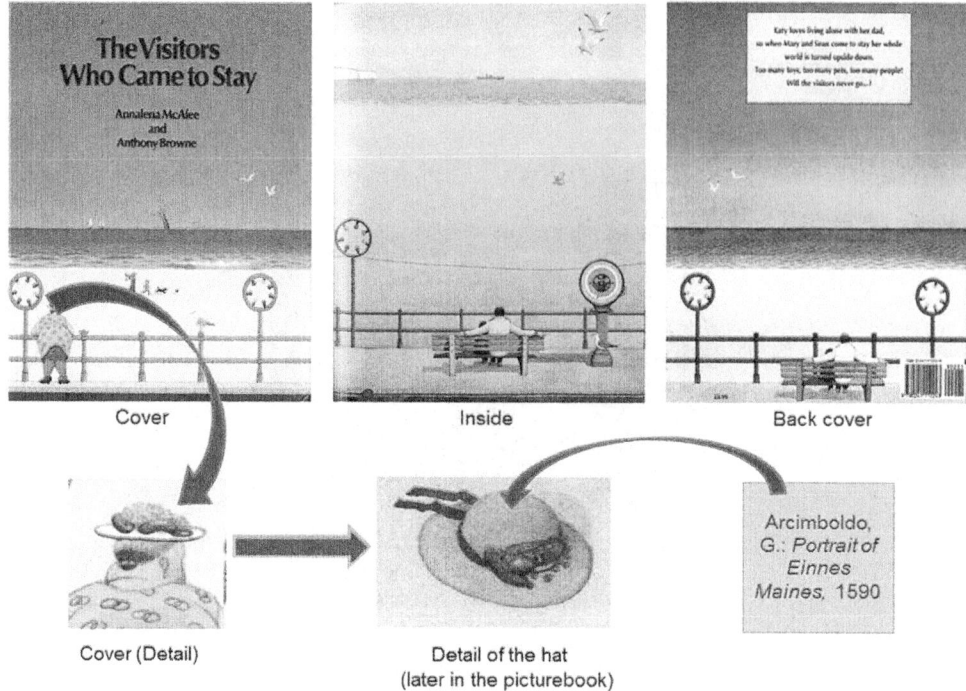

Cover

Inside

Back cover

Cover (Detail)

Detail of the hat
(later in the picturebook)

Arcimboldo,
G.: *Portrait of
Einnes
Maines*, 1590

Figure 9.3 Interpictorial references to the author–illustrator's own works.

Illustrations by Anthony Browne used by permission of Anthony Browne.

the attitudes of the characters as they face their daily lives. The image on the back cover is dominated by somber colors, which refer to the calm and serene atmosphere at the beach. The front cover, however, shows an abundance of items which are spread on the beach. The color scheme is dominated by bright colors, which emphasize the joy of living. Some details in this illustration suggest events to take place in the future, such as the compass (Figure 9.3, center), which symbolizes a forthcoming change. In the same way, the ball visualizes metonymically the imminent arrival of new characters. Finally, the seagull, which is the permanent witness of Katy's various emotional changes, represents the transformation of the main characters (in regard to the seagull, see also the analysis of Figure 9.5).

Another significant element is the fat lady's neck. As Browne frequently does, he camouflages in the neck the face of a lady gorilla, thus creating a figure with a duplicated face or a double face. In turn, the lady is wearing a fancy hat, which consists of a typical English dish: sausage, potatoes, and ketchup. The painting *Einnes Maines* (The Reversible Anthropomorphic Portrait of a Man), by Guiseppe Archimboldo, is obviously the model for this strange distortion, which becomes more evident in the depiction of the same hat inside the picturebook: the fat lady indicates the surreal atmosphere of the book, which is charged with the depiction of an emotional turmoil (with respect to Katy).

Intervisuality: constituting a network of interpictorial references

Images from other media, such as advertising or films, also represent a creative source for Browne. A case in point is the illustration that depicts Katy and Sean secretly watching a movie on television together (Figure 9.4). The scene on the television screen originates from the famous film *Gone with the Wind* (1939), starring Vivien Leigh and Clark Gable, and mirrors the romance of Katy's father

Figure 9.4 Intervisual reference to a movie in an illustration by Anthony Browne from Anna-Lena McAfee's *The Visitors Who Came to Stay*. London: Hamilton, 1984.

Reproduced by permission of Anthony Browne.

and Sean's mother. As a mere spectator, Katy cannot prevent the film from continuing according to the script, which clearly parallels the relationship of the new couple (see, in this regard, the hearts on the wallpaper). Since this is the first shared activity with Sean, Katy seems to accept this changed situation.

Interpictoriality is not limited to the method by which an author occasionally incorporates elements from previous works. Reprocessing of such references most often goes even further and, through devices such as metaphors and symbols, they can take on new meanings, depending on the various contexts in which the interpictorial references are placed. Moreover, such appropriations can reconnect with other hypotexts, thus increasing the complexity of the interpictorial references.

This procedure is not only an instance of appropriation of a new text, but achieves a complex remodeling, which implies a definite reinterpretation of the present story (Lobato and Hoster 2011, 2014). A notable example is the seagull that continuously appears in Browne's picturebook.

Possibly inspired by Magritte's paintings, the seagull is a prominent topic that can be found in different picturebooks created by Browne. This motif often merges with references to other works of art, ranging from Magritte's paintings to one of Pink Floyd's album covers and even referring to Browne's own works. Figure 9.5 shows some examples from Browne's *The Visitors Who Came to Stay* with information about the original sources.

The seagull repeatedly reappears throughout the picturebook in order to highlight its symbolic value as a witness of the successive changes experienced by the main character, from the initial rejection of the visitors to the girl's surprising affection for them in the end. The seagull connects the diverse personal experiences of Katy, thus underscoring the deeper levels of meaning of the picturebook story. Figure 9.5.5 displays three different types of interpictorial relations concerning the use of the seagull motif. The vertical axis shows an illustration from the picturebook, a detail from this illustration, and the hypotext it refers to: one of Browne's other picturebooks, a painting, the cover of a music album, and so forth. The horizontal axis indicates the type of the relationship: intrapictorial, interpictorial, or transpictorial.

The intrapictorial relationship (Figure 9.5.2) depicts a flying bear with the wings of a seagull. This motif appears when the visitors leave the house. After their departure, the picture is bleak and the cat wanders in the corners and avoids the girl. The stuffed bear also seems to prefer to leave with them. On closer consideration, the flying bear is a reference to the teddy bear in Browne's *A Bear-y Tale* (1989).

The parapictorial relationship (Figure 9.5.3) occurs when Katy feels that something is missing. There are images of the sky and the sea at the beach inside the question mark, alluding to previous days which, in contrast, are now surprisingly remembered, to the point that it raises a new question. Magritte's painting *The Promise* represents the outline of a dove with clouds inside. The bird, in this case, is part of the solution, which the question already indicates. Katy seems to miss the visitors' lack of inhibition and open-mindedness.

The scene on the beach contains a flying pig as evidence of several transpictorial allusions (Figure 9.5.4). The expression "When pigs fly" (a verbal phrase) refers to the impossibility of something happening, which could be interpreted as Katy's questioning of her father's relationship. Furthermore, the image of the flying pig is associated with the inflatable pig on the cover of Pink Floyd's album *Animals*, as well as with the beach scene portrayed as a 'pigsty' with an untidy display of objects on the beach, not unlike the dining room at breakfast time. Finally, an example of an interpictorial relationship

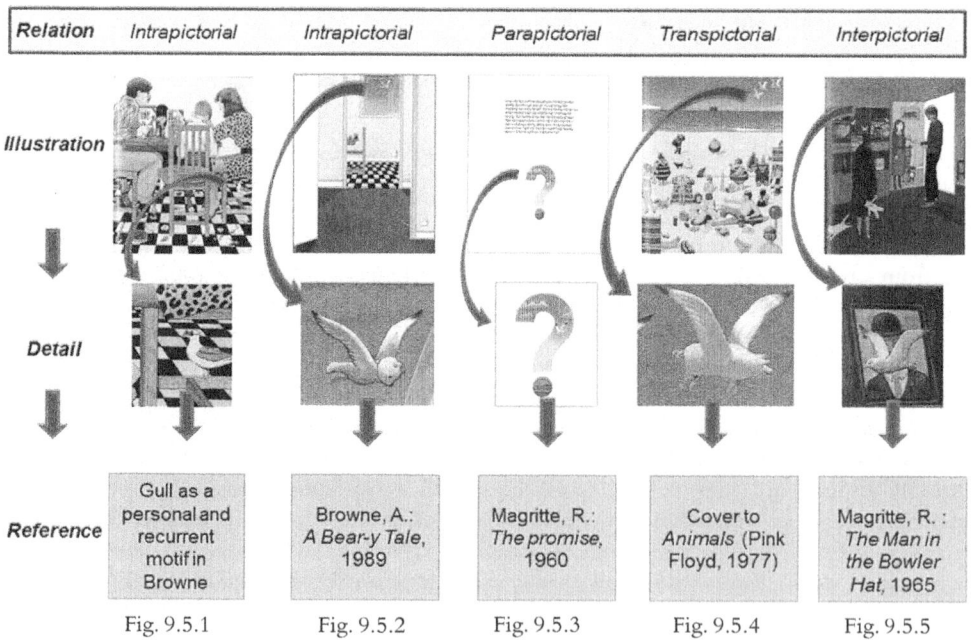

Different types of relations based in *The Visitors Who Came to Stay,* by A. Browne

Relation	Intrapictorial	Intrapictorial	Parapictorial	Transpictorial	Interpictorial
Illustration					
Detail					
Reference	Gull as a personal and recurrent motif in Browne	Browne, A.: *A Bear-y Tale,* 1989	Magritte, R.: *The promise,* 1960	Cover to *Animals* (Pink Floyd, 1977)	Magritte, R.: *The Man in the Bowler Hat,* 1965
	Fig. 9.5.1	Fig. 9.5.2	Fig. 9.5.3	Fig. 9.5.4	Fig. 9.5.5

Figure 9.5 Different types of relations in illustrations by Anthony Browne from Anna-Lena McAfee's *The Visitors Who Came to Stay*. London: Hamilton, 1984.

Reproduced by permission of Anthony Browne.

(Figure 9.5.5) is the carbon copy of Magritte's *The Man in the Bowler Hat* (1965) in the bookshelf. The bird that partially hides the man's face implies the changes that will occur very soon. It is important to note that the bird is coming from outside, as it is outside the picture frame and is flying freely.

As the analysis of the seagull motif in Browne's picturebook has shown, the interpictorial references are quite complex, inviting the viewer to participate in a visual game which consists in recognizing the motif's multiple levels of meanings.

Beyond Anthony Browne

Picturebooks readers can enjoy numerous and excellent opportunities to practice the game of discovery explained in the previous section. Evidence of this is provided by several research studies, which have also tracked the intertextual relationships between literature and painting in the context of picturebooks. Meanwhile, Sandra Beckett (2010) refers to Jean Claverie, Frédéric Clément, Maurice Sendak, and Chris Van Allsburg, among others, as artists who use this type of references. In other studies conducted by Lobato and Hoster (Lobato 2013; Lobato and Hoster 2011: 113–117; 2014), there is an initial approximation in which different forms of the presence of works of art or artists in picturebooks are suggested. Alluding to "works of art, which are hidden in the illustrations," they highlight *The Nightingale* (2002) by Stephen Mitchell with illustrations by Bagram Ibatoulline, which reminds the reader of Japanese Ukiyo-e; *The Three Goats* (2004), with a text by Olalla González and illustrations by Federico Fernández, which contains Picassian traits; or *I Am Marc Chagall* (2006) by Bimba Landmann, which represents the sun, candles, goats, musical instruments, and other motifs typical of Marc Chagall. The Spanish picturebook *El traje nuevo del rey* (The King's New Clothes 2001) by Xosé Ballesteros with illustrations by Joao Caetano is filled with interpictorial references to famous works of art. One illustration, for instance, refers to the painting *St. Jerome in His Study* (1442) by Jan Van Eyck (Figure 9.6). St. Jerome, with his attributes – the lion, the books, the writing instruments, and

Joao Caetano: *El traje nuevo del rey* (2001)

Van Eyck: *St. Jerome in His Study* [1442]

Figure 9.6 Interpictorial reference to Jan Van Eyck in an illustration by Joao Caetano from Xosé Ballesteros's *El traje nuevo del rey*. Sevilla: Kalandraka, 2001.

the enclosed study – builds up a contrast to the manipulating dressmakers. The insertion of the St. Jerome figure points to the transience of man and the strategies to deceive another person.

Interpictoriality and visual literacy

These artists' illustrations can configure an interesting imaginary set in the minds of their audience, full of connotations and metacognitive allusions, which involves in a playful manner the need to expand our visual and reading intertext. In the end, the interpretation of cultural references converts picturebooks into a potential resource for education in visual culture (Schritter 2005; Guerrero and García Gutiérrez 2006).

Picturebooks require a competent reader who is able to recognize the clues that refer to the essence of the story, which is not always explicit. In addition, since many picturebooks refer to other picturebook stories and works of art, readers must also be able to notice these references and to decipher their impact on the respective picturebook's meaning. In order to recognize these possible references, three hypotheses are put forward: First, the reader's competence depends on the breadth of her knowledge of other artworks and books. Second, the reader's competence is tightly connected with her capacity to detect unknown references in a first step and to understand their significance for the interpretation of the picturebook story in a next step. Finally, the reader's competence generally increases with each re-reading, since a multiple reading of the same picturebook gradually reveals several layers of references to other art works and texts. Several authors use the term *synergy* to refer to the interaction between words and images to build "mutually dependent narratives," while other scholars prefer the notions of *duets, contrast, interferences, polysystemy*, and *congruency* (Silva-Díaz 2005: 37; Duran 2007: 31–32; Kümmerling-Meibauer 2012).

Picturebooks elicit the capacity to switch between the visual and verbal codes, because the illustration, complemented by the text, contains what the painting alone is missing as a means of total understanding, with its open and polysemic communicative content (Klibanski 2006: 8). Therefore, it seems logical to use picturebooks as a medium that is especially attuned to aiding preschool children in acquiring visual literacy (Bajour 2010: 124). In our society, governed by mass media, text and image are combined, and the picturebook can interlace references to numerous discourses from different sources. The picturebook constitutes a basic resource for training the child as a reader, because it stimulates the extension of his intertext and guarantees the early development of metapictorial competence (Amo 2005: 63; Kümmerling-Meibauer 2012: 33). This peculiar textual arrangement claims and presupposes the child's active participation in the process of decoding. This process consists of establishing activities of identification, association, and connection, which will allow the child to reconstruct the meaning of the work (Nikolajeva and Scott 2001: 228; Styles 2010: 158). When this capacity is acquired, the reader gets what Catherine Tauveron calls a "euphoric compensation" (quoted in Azevedo 2008: 76).

References

Allen, Graham (2011) *Intertextuality*, New York: Routledge.

Amo, José Manuel (2005) "El papel del album en el desarrollo del intertexto lector," *Campo Abierto: Revista de Educacion* 28: 61–80.

Azevedo, Fernando (2008) "A intertextualidade como mecanismo auxiliador da formaçao de lectores: alguns exemplos da literature infantile contemporanea," *Lenguaje y Textos: Revista de la Sociedad Española de Didáctica de la Lengua y la Literatura* 28: 75–82.

Bajour, Cecilia (2010) "El arte de la sorpresa: la metonomia de la imagen en los libros-álbum," in Teresa Colomer, Bettina Kümmerling-Meibauer, and Cecilia Silva-Díaz (eds) *Cruces de miradas: nuevas aproximaciones al libro album*, Barcelona: Banco del libro, 116–126.

Ballesteros, Xosé (2001) *El traje nuevo del rey*, illus. Joao Caetano, Sevilla: Kalandraka.

Barthes, Roland (1957) *Mythologies*, Paris: Seuil.

Beckett, Sandra L. (2001) "Parodic Play With Paintings in Picture Books," *Children's Literature* 29: 175–195.

Beckett, Sandra L. (2010) "Artistic Allusions in Picturebooks," in Teresa Colomer, Bettina Kümmerling-Meibauer, and Cecilia Silva-Díaz (eds) *New Directions in Picturebook Research*, New York: Routledge, 83–98.

Beckett, Sandra L. (2012) *Crossover Picturebooks: A Genre for All Ages*, New York: Routledge.

Browne, Anthony (1989) *A Bear-y Tale*, London: Walker Books.

Bruel, Christian (2001) *Anthony Browne*, Paris: Éditions Être, Collection Boîtazoutils.

Derrida, Jacques (1972) *La dissemination*, Paris: Seuil.

Donaldson, Julia (1999) *The Gruffalo*, illus. Axel Scheffler, London: Macmillan.

Duran, Teresa (2007) "El álbum: un modelo de narratología postmoderna," *Primeras noticias: Revista de literatura* 230: 31–38.

Eco, Umberto (1979) *Lector in fabula: La cooperazione interpretativa nei testi narrativi*, Milan: Bompiani.

Genette, Gerard (1997) *Palimpsests: Literature in the Second Degree*, Ann Arbor: University of Michigan Library.

González, Olalla (2004) *The Three Goats*, illus. Federico Fernández, Sevilla: Kalandraka Ediciones Andalucía.

Guerrero, Pedro, and García Gutiérrez, María Estrella (eds) (2006) *Literatura y artes plásticas: La educación literaria*, Murcia: Consejería de Educación y Cultura de la Región de Murcia, Dirección General de Formación e Innovación Educativa, vol. II, www.educarm.es/templates/portal/ficheros/websDinamicas/154/VI.2.guerreroart.pdf (accessed February 19, 2016).

Hateley, Erica (2009) "Magritte and Cultural Capital: The Surreal World of Anthony Browne," *The Lion and the Unicorn* 33.3: 324–348.

Klibanski, Monica (2006) "El origen de una especie: los libros album de Anthony Browne," *CLIJ: Cuadernos de literatura infantile y juvenile* 19.190: 7–14.

Kokkola, Lydia (2011) "Interpictorial Allusion and the Politics of 'Looking Like' in Allison and Emma's Rug by Allen Say," *Children's Literature Association Quarterly* 36.1: 47–63.

Kristeva, Julia (1967) *Bachtine, le mot, le dialogue et le roman*, Paris: Seuil ["Word, Dialogue, and Novel," in Julia Kristeva, *Desire in Language*, Oxford: Blackwell, 1980, 64–91].

Kristeva, Julia (1980) *Desire in Language: A Semiotic Approach to Literature and Art*, Oxford: Blackwell (first published 1969).

Kristeva, Julia (1986) *The Kristeva Reader*, New York: Columbia University Press.

Kümmerling-Meibauer, Bettina (2012) "Bilder intermedial. Visuelle Codes erfassen," in Anja Pompe (ed.) *Literarisches Lernen im Anfangsunterricht*, Baltmannsweiler: Schneider Verlag Hohengehren, 19–33.

Kümmerling-Meibauer, Bettina (2015) "From Baby Books to Picturebooks for Adults: European Picturebooks in the New Millennium," *Word & Image* 31.3: 249–264. Doi: 10.1080/02666286.2015.1032519 (accessed February 19, 2016).

Landmann, Bimba (2006) *I Am Marc Chagall*, Grand Rapids, MI: William B. Eerdmans.

Lobato, María José (2013) "Intertestualità e intericonicità. Una valida risorsa per il giovane lettore," in Marnie Campagnaro and Marco Dallari (eds) *Incanto e Racconto nel Labirinto delle Figure: Albi illustrati e relazione educativa*, Trento: Edizioni Erickson, 183–226.

Lobato, María José, and Hoster, Beatriz (2011) "Acercamiento a los museos, al arte y al artista a través del álbum ilustrado," *EARI – Educación Artística Revista de Educación*, n° 2. ISSN: 1965–8403, http://artemaestrosymuseos.wordpress.com y http://issuu.com/eari/docs/revista_eari_numero_2_2011_completa_web (accessed February 19, 2016).

Lobato, María José, and Hoster, Beatriz (2014) "An Approximation to Intertextuality in Picturebooks: Anthony Browne and his Hypotext," in Bettina Kümmerling-Meibauer (ed.) *Picturebooks: Representation and Narration*, New York: Routledge, 165–183.

Louvel, Liliane (2011) *Poetics of the Iconotext*, Farnham: Ashgate.

McAfee, Annalena (1984) *The Visitors Who Came to Stay*, illus. Anthony Browne, London: Hamilton.

McKee, David (1980) *Not Now Bernard*, London: Andersen Press.

Mendoza, Antonio (1994) *Literatura comparada e Intertextualidad*, Madrid: La Muralla.

Mendoza, Antonio (2001) *El intertexto lector*, Cuenca: Ediciones de la Universidad de Castilla-La Mancha, www.cervantesvirtual.com/obra-visor/el-intertexto-lector-0/html/01e1dd60-82b2-11df-acc7-002185ce6064_2.html (accessed February 19, 2016).

Mitchell, Stephen (2002) *The Nightingale*, illus. Bagram Ibatoulline, New York: Candlewick Press.

Monsters, Inc. (2001) film, dir. Pete Docter, Lee Unkrich, and David Silverman, USA: Pixar Animation Studios.

Nières-Chevrel, Isabelle (2009) "Doubles images, double lecteurs: l'inter-inconicité dans le tunnel d'Anthony Browne," in Christiane Connan-Pintado, Florence Gaiotti, and Bernadette Poulou (eds) *Modernites 28. L'album contemporain pour la jeunesse: nouvelles forms, nouveaux lectures*, Bordeaux: Presses universitaires de Bordeaux, 89–100.

Nikolajeva, Maria (2008) "Play and Playfulness in Postmodern Picturebooks," in Lawrence R. Sipe and Sylvia Pantaleo (eds) *Postmodern Picturebooks: Play, Parody and Self-Referentiality*, New York: Routledge, 55–74.

Nikolajeva, Maria, and Scott, Carole (2001) *How Picturebooks Work*, New York: Garland.

Riffaterre, Michael (1980) *Semiotics of Poetry*, London: Methuen.

Rose, Margaret (2011) *Pictorial Irony, Parody, and Pastiche: Comic Interpictoriality in the Arts of the Nineteenth and Twentieth Centuries*, Bielefeld: Aisthesis.

Schritter, Istvan (2005) *La otra lectura: La ilustración en los libros para niños*, Buenos Aires: Lugar Editorial.

Sendak, Maurice (1963) *Where the Wild Things Are*, New York: Harper & Row.

Shrek (2001) film, dir. Andrew Adamson and Vicky Jenson, USA: Dreamwork Pictures.

Silva-Díaz, Cecilia (2005) *Libros que enseñan a leer: Álbumes metaficcionales y conocimiento literario*, Ph D thesis, Universidad Autónoma de Barcelona.

Styles, Morag (2010) "Me encanta Lauren Child': Las voces de las imágenes. Los niños relenan los silencios en los libros-álbum," in Teresa Colomer, Bettina Kümmerling-Meibauer, and Cecilia Silva-Díaz (eds) *Cruce de miradas: nuevas aproximaciones al libro-álbum*, Barcelona: Banco del Libro, 154–161.

Todorov, Tzvetan (1984) *Mikhail Bakhtin: The Dialogical Principle*, Minneapolis and London: University of Minnesota Press.

Valleau, Genevieve (2006) "Degas and Seurat and Magritte! Oh My! Classical Art in Picturebooks," *The Looking Glass: New Perspectives on Children's Literature* 10.3, www.lib.latrobe.edu.au/ojs/index.php/tlg/issue/view/7 (accessed February 19, 2016).

Van Meerbergen, Sara (2012) "Play, Parody, Intertextuality and Interaction. Postmodern Flemish Picture Books as Semiotic Playgrounds," *BLFT: Nordic Journal of Childlit Aesthetics* 3, www.childlitaesthetics.net/index.php/blft/article/view/20075 (accessed February 19, 2016).

10

SERIALITY IN PICTUREBOOKS

Bettina Kümmerling-Meibauer

Nowadays it is common practice in the international book market to commission and produce series of popular picturebooks, although this phenomenon is not quite new if one takes the renowned *Children's Tales* series (24 vols, 1902–1930) by Beatrix Potter and the *Railway Series* (26 vols, 1945) by Wilbert Vere Awdry into account. Picturebook series cover all genres and age groups, ranging from books for toddlers, such as Dick Bruna's *Miffy* books (24 vols, 1964–2007), and wordless picturebooks, for instance Suzy Lee's *Trilogy of the Limit* (2003–2010), to crossover picturebooks, such as the *Journey* books (6 vols, 1978–2003) by Mitsumasa Anno (Beckett 2012). Moreover, series are quite popular in the realm of informational picturebooks. Prominent examples are the *This Is* books by the Czech Miroslav Sasek (18 vols, 1959–1974), genuine travelogues for children, and the *My Village* series, a string of photobooks about the everyday life of children all over the world (15 vols, 1956–1974), created by Tim Gidal in tandem with his wife Sonia Gidal.

Mostly these series focus on the main character(s) and the adventures they experience over the course of time. Following the unspoken rule of typical mainstream series for children, the characters in these series do not grow up or change in a significant way. Therefore, beginning readers are invited to share further experiences with characters they are already familiar with. Famous examples are the picturebooks about the monkey Curious George, authored and illustrated by the couple H.A. and Margaret Rey (6 vols, 1941–1966), the *Eloise* books (five vols, 1955–2002) by Kay Thompson with illustrations by Hillary Knight, and the *Pettson and Findus* series by the Swede Sven Nordqvist (10 vols, 1986–2014). Other picturebook series, however, concentrate on thematic issues, such as the succession of the seasons in the *Wimmelbuch* sequence (2003–2008) by Rotraut Susanne Berner (Rémi 2011). The success of these and other picturebook series has spawned a merchandising franchise, which includes spin-offs, toys, card games, and media adaptations, such as movies and computer games.

By contrast, in recent decades picturebook artists have developed more sophisticated serial forms in which the characters undergo a developmental process, as in the three picturebooks about the boy Garmann (*Garmanns sommer* (2006), *Garmanns gate* (2008), *Garmanns hemmelighet* (2010)) by the Norwegian Stian Hole (Christensen 2014). In other picturebook series, the focus shifts to quite abstract aesthetic strategies by showing the same objects or events from multiple visual and narrative perspectives. A case in point is the picturebook trilogy *Zoom* (1995a), *Re-Zoom* (1995b), and *REM: Rapid Eye Movement* (1997) by Istvan Banyai, which focuses on three different modes of perception. Despite this increasing complexity of picturebook series, scholars working in the realm of picturebook research have virtually neglected this expanding picturebook corpus. This tendency certainly has to do with the fact that series are often regarded as inferior to standalone works. Such an attitude has hampered the serious scholarly investigation of series for a considerably long time. If considered at all, the analysis of series and their impact on the reader has been restricted to popular studies and cultural studies, which initially concentrated on mainstream series targeted at an adult audience (Allen and van den Berg 2014). This situation has changed during recent decades, primarily due to the increasing production of sophisticated TV and movie series as well as graphic novels, which have inspired the emergence of seriality studies. Scholars working in this field investigate the production and reception of series as well as their aesthetic, emotional, and social conditions and how they impact on the development of new narrative strategies, including transmedia storytelling and multimodal discourse. They consider series as an aesthetic form with a specific narrative and formal structure, as a practice of production and publication linked to historical and material conditions, and as a mode of connecting and structuring sets of similar, related, or repeating events or occurrences. Picking up on this ongoing process, seriality is coming to the fore as a genuine field of study, which will definitely enhance picturebook research.

So far just a few children's literature scholars have analyzed children's fiction series, by focusing on the aesthetic and narrative aspects of seriality as well as the reception and global distribution of children's series (Sheldrick 2011; Sands-O'Connor and Frank 2014; Kümmerling-Meibauer 2017), but picturebook series have virtually gone unnoticed (with the exception of Al-Yaquot 2011).

Different concepts of serialization

Series typically include an accumulation of books, whose number varies from two up to a hundred books and even more, and can come into being as a result of a further demand for a sequel, most often in the case of successful novels and movies, but also picturebooks. It may also happen that authors develop a story line in advance that expands over more than one book. Moreover, a series raises certain expectations on the part of the reader and covers all elements: setting, characters, plot, theme, and narrator's voice. The most prominent concept is the sequel that resumes the story developed in the original work. This often happens when a book or film has had unforeseen success, which impels publishers to ask authors and illustrators to write an extension of the first book. While the sequel tells a story of what happens after the end of the original work, a prequel, however, focuses on what occurs before the beginning of the first book. Telling the prehistory of the story developed in the first book still seems to be nonexistent in the domain of picturebooks, whereas the sequel, which continues the narrative and presents a further development of the main characters, is an established format in the international picturebook market. Since picturebook stories are quite short, sequels usually do not have summaries of the previous books in the beginning. They just tell another story about the same characters, whereby references to prior adventures may be found in order to update the readers' memory and potentially give some hints about what may await them in the new story.

When picturebook artists decide to write more than one sequel, they often create a trilogy, such as Peter Sís's picturebooks about the girl Madlenka and her experiences in New York City (2000–2010). However, most picturebook series comprise four to thirty books, depending on the economic success of the books and the willingness of the artists to devote their creative power to the further development of the same characters, as the popular *Old Bear and Friends* series (13 vols, 1986–2016) by Jane Hissey shows. In some cases, picturebook series are continued by other artists: the world-famous *Babar the Elephant* books (5 vols, 1934–1941) by French Jean de Brunhoff (Weber 1989) were carried on by his son Laurent de Brunhoff almost until the present (38 vols, 1948–2011).

While sequels are usually written and illustrated by the author(s) of the original work within a manageable time span of one to three years in order to attract the readers, it might principally be the case that authors who did not aspire to create a sequel, since they consider their book to be complete, change their mind for different reasons, producing a sequel after a time span of ten or more years. A case in point is Chris Van Allsburg's classic picturebook *Jumanji* (1981). The open ending of the story finally incited the author to release a sequel after more than twenty years. *Zathura* (2002) extends the original story by focusing on other characters who briefly appear at the end of the first book, driving the plot in new directions.

Seriality as a poetic and narrative strategy

The investigation of series is closely related to issues of repetition and continuity, singularity and iterability, sequences and episodes, and unity and open-endedness. Problems that arise from these issues touch on the relationship between single installments in a series and how narrative continuity may overcome or derive from the interruptions between these single works. In order to be efficient, a series requires a certain readiness on the part of the reader to learn more about the same characters. In view of this observation, the question arises as to why many readers have a preference for serial forms. An often proposed argument is the feeling of security, which is especially attractive for children, whose literacy competencies are still progressing (Mackey 1990). In line with Nodelman's (1985) assertion that sameness is an essential feature of children's literature, many critics complain about the monotony of series targeted at children, pointing to the fact that the characters do not change or grow older and the story line follows the same sequence of events (Deane 1991). In contrast, other scholars maintain that reading about the same characters may introduce children to schemas and scripts, which serve as a scaffold, thus gradually preparing them for the comprehension of more complex structures and topics (Watson 2000, 2004; Nikolajeva 2013).

The apparent sameness of the story line and the characters in picturebook series points to the paradigm of repetitiveness, which is a significant property of serial narratology (Reimer et al. 2014). However, it should be mentioned that repetition as a stylistic feature of literary texts in general cannot be regarded as a rhetorical instrument restricted to serial texts only. Nevertheless serial narratives are particularly characterized by a counterbalance of repetition and variation. The common pleasure of a series consists in the expectation that readers will encounter the same characters again and again. This joy of repetition is complemented by variations that may range from slight changes of the setting, the plot line, and the genre conventions up to the characterization of the protagonists (Sielke 2013). A sophisticated balance of repetition and variation is discernible in Eugène Ionesco's picturebook quartet, whose titles simply begin with the notion of 'story,' followed by the numbers one to four (1968–1973). The Pop Art illustrations by Etienne Delessert (the first two books), Philippe Corentin (third book), and Jean-Michel Nicollet (fourth book) ingeniously capture the surrealistic atmosphere of the picturebooks, which focus on the silly stories a father tells his daughter Jacqueline (Kümmerling-Meibauer 2015). The frame story – Jacqueline is bored and goes into her parents' bedroom in order to be entertained by her father, while her mother is either too tired or too busy to deal with her daughter – remains almost the same in all four picturebooks, while the inner stories become increasingly complex and weird, drawing the reader into an imaginative cosmos in which strange characters make their appearance and unexpected things happen. The questions and objections by Jacqueline propel the father's stories, which are based on wordplay, enumerations of ill-matched objects and actions, and travels into surreal places, thus evoking a dreamlike mood. While readers recognize the composition and the main characters in all four picturebooks, the inner stories and the dialogues between father and daughter deviate from the repetition pattern, thus inviting the reader to carefully look for the variations and changes, both on the verbal and the visual level, within the quartet.

As this example shows, picturebooks within a series are serially independent: each book can be read on its own and is complete in itself, but matches with the other books in the series. This fact elucidates that a series has to follow the principle of connection rather than the principle of unity. This issue reveals a paradoxical relationship: a series seems to be indefinitely extensible, but often comes to an unprompted end. Moreover, a series appears over time, but can later be assembled into a finished work. It is open but also in a certain way closed. In view of this, a poetics of serial narration touches on the nature of beginnings and endings, which is frequently linked with the topic of meeting and thwarting expectations. While the reading order of mainstream picturebook series is quite insignificant by virtue of the trend towards representing static characters and replaceable plots, other series demand that readers respect the correct sequence in order to comprehend the development of the characters and the connections of particular incidents to events presented in previous books. Whereas single books generally complete the representation of a character's development in a certain manner, the extension of the original story in a series offers readers the opportunity to understand the further growth of characters they have grown accustomed to. This process enables readers to remain within an already familiar frame of reference, while simultaneously broadening their knowledge and aesthetic pleasure. As a result, readers may interpret the previous books within a series in light of the new one, which probably gives rise to altered meanings. In this regard, a series satisfies the readers' interest in a possible storyworld beyond the single picturebook story.

Regardless of these issues, there are some essential narrative features that establish a connection between picturebooks within a series, for instance, parallelism, open-endedness, and circularity (Kümmerling-Meibauer 1997). Parallelism points to certain correspondences between single books in order to categorize them as a series. Parallel aspects can touch on all significant elements that constitute a narrative, such as the setting, the story line, the characters, and the narrative voice. In Aaron Becker's wordless trilogy, *Journey* (2013), *Quest* (2014), and *Return* (2016), the sequels refer to the characters and scenes of the first book in multiple respects. All three books start with child characters, who are able to escape their everyday world by drawing magic doors onto walls which lead them into a fantastic world full of wonder and adventures. By means of their red or purple markers they can draw vehicles that carry them on a journey in a fanciful landscape where they meet hostile soldiers, rescue a king, and set an encaged phoenix-like bird free. While the first book introduces a little girl who is feeling lonely and ignored by her father, in the second and third volumes she is accompanied by a boy whom she met at the end of the first book. In addition, her father secretly sneaks into the fantastic world in the final book, supporting the two children's efforts to reinstall the peaceful kingdom of the abducted king. The parallels between these three books trigger readers to carefully look out for the variations that distinguish each book from the other ones. The most obvious change is the introduction of a further main protagonist in each volume, so that the girl is finally joined by a boy the same age and her father.

As Becker's trilogy demonstrates, to a certain degree, a serial text must not provide the idea of completeness as a single text necessitates. The single text thus becomes an episode within a series and is embedded in a bigger context. Hence, picturebook artists are confronted with a situation in which they need to close each book in a satisfying way by leaving the ending open to facilitate the creation of a sequel. In this respect, the three picturebooks by Becker smoothly merge into each other, as the last doublespread of the previous book can be regarded as the first illustration of the subsequent book at the same time. Although readers are able to interpret each picturebook story on its own, the bigger idea behind the trilogy can only be revealed when the whole sequence is read from cover to cover: while the girl undertakes a journey into an unknown fantastic world in the first volume, she and the boy set out on a quest in the second book, prompted by the king, who has handed them a mysterious map. The last volume, eventually, assembles the loose ends of the previous volumes and also leads the girl to turn her back on the world of imagination in order to happily return with her father to her real home.

As a matter of fact, sequels contradict the limitations of literary art by expanding the storyworlds before and after the original book. In addition, sequels and series refer to the aporia of ending, pointing to the fact that it is rather impossible to determine whether a story is actually complete or solely ends. As scholars in the domain of narratology have demonstrated, closure in the text is a relational notion, since it can always be reopened in an ensuing text (Kermode 1967; Herman 2002). In this regard, the authors usually choose between two options: they either use cliffhangers to suggest that the story has only been fractionally completed, or they create an open ending, which leaves some gaps. These gaps stimulate the reader to think about the potential continuation of the story. Consequently, the gaps propel the reader's imagination as well as the author's chance to resume the story, without committing either to just one possible solution. Hence, the phenomenon of aperture, which is a predominant characteristic of modern and postmodern (children's) literature, is also present in picturebook series.

As the parallels between books within a series and the tight link between the openings and endings of the single picturebooks imply, a series can also modify the idea of a prescribed chronological order of the reading, as readers may move between different books in a series by comparing the key elements, the depiction of the characters, and the story line. This possible reading behavior points to the narrative strategy of circularity, which contradicts the assumed linearity and one-dimensionality of picturebook series.

Conclusion: why picturebook series matter

A comprehensive understanding of the cognitive, narrative, and aesthetic affordances of picturebook series demands an interdisciplinary approach that includes findings from literary studies, multimodal discourse, developmental psychology, pedagogy, literacy studies, and narratology. While seriality studies focuses on a wide range of literary genres and media formats, this emerging field has completely disavowed picturebook series, although they introduce children to the series concept, which plays an increasingly dominant role in our media driven times. A thorough investigation of the various facets of serial narration in picturebooks on the verbal as well as the visual level will be pertinent to the relevant topics in picturebook research for years to come. It is common knowledge that children enjoy reading or listening to the same (picturebook) story again and again. By offering them sequels to the story lines and beloved characters they are familiar with, picturebook series may expand their comprehension of the storyworld concept in a smooth manner, gradually extending their already acquired knowledge about literary paradigms. In this regard it might be a promising undertaking to find out in what way the combination of text and visuals contributes to the recognition effect and thus supports the series' encompassing concept as well as in what manner series potentially add something new and even alter the reader's comprehension of the story and attitude towards the characters.

Hence, the potential impact of any future seriality studies in the realm of picturebooks may consist in opening up a discussion across disciplinary borders by highlighting the complex narratological and aesthetic features of serialized picturebooks, whose significance for the child's cognitive, linguistic, and aesthetic development has been completely underrated.

References

Allen, Rob, and van den Berg, Thijs (eds) (2014) *Serialization in Popular Culture*, London: Routledge.

Al-Yaquot, Ghada (2011) "From Slate to Slate: What Does the Future Hold for the Picturebook Series?" *New Review of Children's Literature and Librarianship* 17.1: 57–77.

Anno, Mitsumasa (1978–2003) *Journey* books, 6 vols, London: Bodley Head (first Japanese eds. 1977–2002).

Awdry, Wilbert Vere (1945–1972) *Railway Series*, 26 vols, London: Edmund Ward.

Banyai, Istvan (1995a) *Zoom*, New York: Viking.

Banyai, Istvan (1995b) *Re-Zoom*, New York: Viking.

Banyai, Istvan (1997) *REM: Rapid Eye Movement*, New York: Viking.

Becker, Aaron (2013) *Journey*, London: Walker.

Becker, Aaron (2014) *Quest*, London: Walker.

Becker, Aaron (2016) *Return*, London: Walker.

Beckett, Sandra L. (2012) *Crossover Picturebooks: A Genre for All Ages*, New York: Routledge.

Berner, Rotraut Susanne (2003–2008) *Wimmelbuch* series, 5 vols, Hildesheim: Gerstenberg.
Bruna, Dick (1964–2007) *Miffy* books, 24 vols, London: Methuen (first Dutch eds. 1963–2006).
Brunhoff, Jean de (1934–1941) *Babar the Elephant* books, 5 vols, New York: Harrison Smith and Robert Haas, later: New York: Random House (first French eds. 1931–1941).
Brunhoff, Laurent de (1948–2011) *Babar the Elephant* books, 38 vols, New York: Random House.
Christensen, Nina (2014) "'Thought and dream are heavenly vehicles': Character, *Bildung*, and Aesthetics in Stian Hole's Garmann Trilogy (2006–2010)," in Bettina Kümmerling-Meibauer (ed.) *Picturebooks: Representation and Narration*, New York: Routledge, 109–119.
Deane, Paul (1991) *Mirrors of American Culture: Children's Fiction Series in the Twentieth Century*, Metuchen, NJ: Scarecrow Press.
Gidal, Tim, and Gidal, Sonia (1956–1974) *My Village* series, 15 vols, New York: Pantheon.
Herman, David (2002) *Story Logic: Problems and Possibilities of Narrative*, Lincoln: University of Nebraska Press.
Hissey, Jane (1986–2016) *Old Bear and Friends* series, 13 vols, Brighton: Salariya Books.
Hole, Stian (2006) *Garmanns sommer*, Oslo: J.W. Cappelens [*Garmann's Summer*, Cambridge, MA: Eerdmans Books for Young Readers, 2008].
Hole, Stian (2008) *Garmanns gate*, Oslo: Cappelen Damm [*Garmann's Street*, Cambridge, MA: Eerdmans Books for Young Readers, 2010].
Hole, Stian (2010) *Garmanns hemmelighet*, Oslo: Cappelen Damm [*Garmann's Secret*, Cambridge, MA: Eerdmans Books for Young Readers, 2011].
Ionesco, Eugène (1968) *Story Number 1*, illus. Étienne Delessert, New York: Harlin Quist.
Ionesco, Eugène (1971a) *Story Number 2*, illus. Étienne Delessert, New York: Harlin Quist.
Ionesco, Eugène (1971b) *Story Number 3*, illus. Philippe Corentin, New York: Harlin Quist.
Ionesco, Eugène (1973) *Story Number 4*, illus. Jean-Michel Nicollet, New York: Harlin Quist.
Kermode, Frank (1967) *The Sense of an Ending: Studies in the Theory of Fiction*, New York: Oxford University Press.
Kümmerling-Meibauer, Bettina (1997) "The Status of Sequels in Children's Literature," in Sandra L. Beckett (ed.) *Recent Changes: The Last 50 Years of Children's Literature*, Westport, CN: Greenwood Press, 53–70.
Kümmerling-Meibauer, Bettina (2015) "Just What Is It That Makes Pop Art Picturebooks So Different, So Appealing?" in Elina Druker, and Bettina Kümmerling-Meibauer (eds) *Children's Literature and the Avant-Garde*, Amsterdam: John Benjamins, 241–265.
Kümmerling-Meibauer, Bettina (2017) "Seriality," in Clémentine Beauvais and Maria Nikolajeva (eds) *The Edinburgh Companion to Children's Literature*, Edinburgh: Edinburgh University Press.
Lee, Suzy (2003) *Mirror*, New York: Chronicle Books.
Lee, Suzy (2008) *Wave*, New York: Chronicle Books.
Lee Suzy (2010) *Shadow*, New York: Chronicle Books.
Mackey, Margaret (1990) "Filling the Gaps: 'The Baby-Sitters Club,' the Series Book and the Learning Reader," *Language Arts* 67.5: 484–489.
Nikolajeva, Maria (2013) "Beyond Happily Ever After. The Aesthetic Dilemma of Multivolume Fiction for Children," in Benjamin Lefevre (ed.) *Textual Transformations in Children's Literature: Adaptations, Translations, Reconsiderations*, New York: Routledge, 197–213.
Nodelman, Perry (1985) "Interpretation and the Apparent Sameness of Children's Literature," *Studies in the Literary Imagination* 18.2: 5–20.
Nordqvist, Sven (1986–2014) *Pettson and Findus* series, 10 vols, Stroud: Hawthorn Press (first Swedish eds. 1984–2012).
Potter, Beatrix (1902–1930) *Children's Tales* series, 24 vols, London: Frederick Warne.
Reimer, Mavis, Ali, Nyala, England, Deanna, Unrau, Melanie, and Girard, Justin (eds) (2014) *Seriality and Texts for Young People: The Compulsion to Repeat*, Basingstoke: Palgrave Macmillan.
Rémi, Cornelia (2011) "Reading as Playing. The Cognitive Challenge of the Wimmelbook," in Bettina Kümmerling-Meibauer (ed.) *Emergent Literacy: Children's Books from 0 to 3*, Amsterdam: John Benjamins, 115–139.
Rey, H. A., and Rey, Margaret (1941–1966) *Curious George* series, 6 vols, Boston: Houghton Mifflin.
Sands-O'Connor, Karen, and Frank, Marietta A. (eds) (2014) *Internationalism in Children's Series*, Houndmills: Palgrave Macmillan.
Sasek, Miroslav (1959–1974) *This Is* books, 18 vols, New York: Palgrave Macmillan.
Sheldrick Ross, Catherine (2011) "Dime Novels and Series Books," in Shelby A. Wolf, Karen Coats, and Patricia Enciso (eds) *Handbook of Research in Children's and Young Adult Literature*, New York: Routledge, 195–206.
Sielke, Sabine (2013) "Joy in Repetition, or: The Significance of Seriality in Processes of Memory and (Re)Mediation," in Russell J.A. Kilbourn and Eleanor Tye (eds) *The Memory Effect: The Remediation of Memory in Literature and Film*, Waterloo, ON: Wilfrid de Laurier Press, 37–50.

Sís, Peter (2000) *Madlenka*, New York: Farrar, Straus and Giroux.

Sís, Peter (2002) *Madlenka's Dog*, New York: Farrar, Straus and Giroux.

Sís, Peter (2010) *Madlenka Soccer Star*, New York: Farrar, Straus and Giroux.

Thompson, Kay (1955–2002) *Eloise* books, 5 vols, illus. Hillary Knight, New York: Simon & Schuster.

Van Allsburg, Chris (1981) *Jumanji*, Boston: Houghton Mifflin.

Van Allsburg, Chris (2002) *Zathura*, Boston: Houghton Mifflin.

Watson, Victor (2000) *Reading Series Fiction: From Arthur Ransome to Gene Kemp*, London: Routledge.

Watson, Victor (2004) "Series Fiction," in Peter Hunt (ed.) *International Companion Encyclopedia of Children's Literature*, 2nd ed., London: Routledge, 532–541.

Weber, Nicholas Fox (1989) *The Art of Babar: The Work of Jean and Laurent de Brunhoff*, New York: Harry N. Abrams.

11

EMOTIONS IN PICTUREBOOKS

Maria Nikolajeva

In the recent explosion of children's literature research based on cognitive criticism, only a few studies specifically address the representation of emotions in picturebooks, where multimediality should be taken into consideration (Nikolajeva 2012, 2013, 2014a, 2014b, 2014c: 94–126; Kümmerling-Meibauer and Meibauer 2015; Silva-Diaz 2015). Yet as picturebooks are likely to be the first kind of books that emerging readers encounter, they may potentially offer a powerful tool for understanding one's own and other people's emotions, in particular for pre-literate readers with a limited ability to make connections between the experiencing of an emotion and its verbal signifier. The multimedial nature of picturebooks invites a contemplation of the difference in cognitive-affective responses to words and images, and thus of the potential synergetic effect of the two media.

As thoroughly explored elsewhere in the present volume, the common misconception about picturebooks is that they are simply books for very young children, with few words and with images that complement the words and have a predominantly decorative function. This assumption is frequently expressed through the loose and unscientific claim that "children like pictures." While the ostensible straightforwardness can be easily dismissed by a closer look at complex contemporary picturebooks, there are indeed good reasons why young readers enjoy pictures and why they are likely to engage with them cognitively and particularly emotionally. There are so far no published results of empirical research on children's understanding of emotions in picturebooks employing cognitive approaches; however, extensive reader-response scholarship demonstrates that even very young children are able to assess characters' emotions from images (see, for instance, Arizpe and Styles 2015). While the present chapter is not grounded in empirical evidence, it considers the implications of current cognitive-affective literary scholarship for better insights into children's engagement with picturebooks. It focuses on the ways cerebral hemispheres process verbal and visual emotionally charged information, and it suggests how picturebooks can enhance children's emotional literacy.

Brain laterality and picturebooks

In his study of brain laterality, *The Master and His Emissary: The Divided Brain and the Making of the Western World* (2008), Iain McGilchrist proposes a hypothesis about the preference of historical periods for different art forms and directions as a result of the interaction between cultural development and the evolution of the human brain. One of his observations points at the tangible trend toward the dominance of the left cerebral hemisphere over the right one, beginning in the fifteenth century in the Western world, when written language gradually gained supremacy over oral and visual communication. Drawing partially on McGilchrist's book, Hugh Crago's *Entranced by Stories. Brain, Tale and Teller, from Infancy to Old Age* (2014) offers a fascinating overview of readers' engagement with fiction, connected to individual rather than historical brain development, in particular the varying dominance of right or left cerebral hemispheres at different ages. (Regrettably, Crago does not address picturebooks as a specific literary form.) While not fully subscribing to Crago's claims, I believe that a combination of these two approaches has far-reaching consequences for general thinking about the representation of emotions in picturebooks.

Without going into a complicated discussion of brain functions, for which I have no qualification, let me offer a summary based on McGilchrist's arguments. It is, inevitably, a simplified model, since the brain structure is substantially more complex than can be sketched in a few sentences and certainly does not adhere to any strict binaries. While a neuroscientist would find such categorization too primitive, for the sake of my argument, the basic distribution of cerebral features is helpful. Thus, the right hemisphere is emotional, while the left is rational; the right is concrete, while the left is abstract; the right sees the whole in a context, while the left attends to details out of context; the right explores, while the left categorizes; and, perhaps most relevantly, the right hemisphere prioritizes novelty, change, plurality, and ambiguity. As McGilchrist suggests, the left hemisphere accumulates knowledge, while the right generates wisdom. Both are equally important in our perception of the world, yet each perceives the world differently, and we need to combine their views.

While we should be cautious about making definite statements before we have reliable experimental research, it is plausible to reflect on how brain laterality potentially affects readers' preferences for visual or verbal narratives and how the cerebral hemispheres process visual and verbal information in different manners. Brain research, which McGilchrist accounts for, dismisses earlier views that brain plasticity discontinues after adolescence. It also demonstrates that the clearly separated functions of the hemispheres are inaccurate: both hemispheres process visual as well as verbal information, and both are essential for emotion as well as reason. The corpus callosum, which provides the connection and interaction between the hemispheres, effectively inhibits the interference of one hemisphere with the other. Yet recent research has also shown that the hemispheres develop at a different pace and that in infanthood and childhood, the right hemisphere dominates over the left. Further, the right hemisphere has firmer connectivity with the more ancient and lower parts of the brain that manage immediate sensory perceptions and affective response to these, while the left hemisphere communicates better with the newer and higher parts, which support our analytical skills, abstract thinking, and partially language.

The implication for picturebook research is that any emotionally charged verbal and visual information offered by picturebooks is received and processed by different parts of the brain and at different speeds (see, for instance, Evans 2001: 25ff.). Evolutionarily, our brains respond to external stimuli in two ways: through the very quick "low path," short-cutting the rational part of the brain, and a slower but more accurate "high path," where, among other things, language is situated. The difference is measured in fractions of seconds, yet the initial affective response seems to take the short-cut. If so, then the image on a picturebook doublespread will be processed a split second quicker than the corresponding verbal statement, even if it is read by an adult while the young reader is looking at the image. Further, it seems that an emotionally laden visual stimulus is not only quicker, but stronger than a verbal one. Since visual perception is evolutionarily inherent to our brain, while language, especially written language, in evolutionary terms a recent cerebral improvement, is not, it should logically imply that reading visually represented emotions comes naturally, while understanding verbal statements about emotions, whether oral or written, must be learned. Pre-literate readers are likely to rely on images rather than words, since images are direct and immediate, while words need longer processing times. There is, however, no empirical research so far to confirm such hypotheses; therefore, the following discussion must necessarily express reservations in terms of "likely," "potentially," and so on.

Yet both in human evolution and in individual development, visual function precedes language. Our ancestors could communicate with visual signs before they invented language (see, e.g., Wolf

2007), and pre-verbal children are fully capable of understanding complex visual imagery long before they can articulate their responses verbally. Moreover, cognitive linguistics claims, in opposition to previous theories, particularly formalism, that figurative language precedes everyday language, that we think in metaphors even before we master verbal language (Lakoff and Johnson 1980).

Since it is the right hemisphere that processes the whole and engages with the context, the synergetic multimedial meaning-making is likely to be performed predominantly by the right hemisphere, which is more advanced in young children. The cognitive response (on the simplest level, "I recognize and understand what I see") comes from the left hemisphere, while the immediate emotional response (for instance, "I don't know what I see, but it makes me glad") is generated by the right hemisphere. The left hemisphere seeks isolated, disconnected details and sorts them in relation to previous knowledge, for instance into the categories 'glad,' 'distressed,' 'angry,' 'frightened,' and 'disgusted,' the five basic emotions (see Oatley 1992; LeDoux 1996; Evans 2001). The right hemisphere detects unpredictable elements, unfamiliar images, and, not least, incongruence between words and images, which the left hemisphere eschews. The direct connection between the image and its linguistic signifier ("I know that what I see is called a boy"), based on denotative language, is performed by the left hemisphere, while the lack of such a connection, when the image does not correspond directly to any linguistic sign ("It seems that this character, whoever it is, is happy") and involves connotative language ("This character is smiling, therefore I believe that he is happy, and besides the sun is shining, and the character is stroking a furry animal who rubs against his leg"), keeps the right hemisphere occupied. Naturally, as already mentioned, the hemispheres are not isolated from each other; they interact and may even compete in their responses, therefore the total response will result from this interaction. However, if in young children, whom picturebooks ostensibly target, the right hemisphere is dominant and better developed, then young children's fascination with visual narratives becomes understandable, as does their remarkable capacity to infer fictional characters' emotional states from images and to respond adequately, through non-verbal signs (see Arizpe and Styles 2015). Moreover, older children's gradual loss of interest in visual narratives in favor of verbal ones also becomes explicable as the left hemisphere catches up. Yet the right hemisphere's attraction to visual images never disappears, as can be seen from adolescents' and adults' devotion to comics, graphic novels, video games, and films. It is merely subdued by the left hemisphere's verbal orientation. Further, the right hemisphere continues to prioritize novelty, complexity, and ambiguity. It also continues to engage with texts emotionally. Since emotional engagement with fiction is just as beneficial for our intellectual and social development as cognitive engagement, it is valuable to encourage older readers to peruse visual and multimedial texts rather than focus exclusively on verbal literacy.

The iconotext and the brain

The difference in the way and the speed with which words and images are processed creates great potential for picturebooks to support individual affective development. The brain activity involved includes perception, attention, imagination, memory, reasoning, decision-making, and learning. While all fiction, as recent cognitive literary studies convincingly demonstrate (see Zunshine 2006; Keen 2007), enhances brain activity, the multimedial meaning-construction is arguably particularly beneficial for "the emotional brain" (LeDoux 1996). Let us consider some kinds of cognitive-affective processes that picturebooks potentially trigger (I would once again like to emphasize "potentially" since at the moment there is no reliable empirical research to support this argument).

First, as already mentioned, verbal information received by the brain is delayed by fractions of a second as compared to visual information. Thus, an emotionally charged cover image of a picturebook is ostensibly perceived before the title and affects the reader more strongly. The left hemisphere lingers on the title, trying to categorize it semantically, while the right hemisphere connects the title and the image, particularly if it discovers something unusual and surprising. Similarly, throughout the text, the left hemisphere makes sense of it through recognition of pre-existing schemas, scripts, and other simplified conceptual models (see Hogan 2003). The difference between schemas and scripts is that the former are singular and static objects, characters, situations, or events, while the latter are dynamic micro-plots. Schemas frequently include basic emotions such as joy, distress, fear, or anger, while scripts may be based on social, or higher-cognitive, emotions such as love or jealousy, which involve more than one character and imply emotional interaction between characters. In both cases, the left hemisphere relates the encountered patterns to those stored in its repertoire. The right hemisphere instead explores disruptions of universal patterns, focusing on the unique, the implicit, the undefinable, and the unknowable. The ambiguity typically created by the text/image tension, the iconotext, is favored by the right hemisphere, which possibly makes young readers more accepting and comfortable with this ambiguity. The left hemisphere, which prefers clarity, resists and pushes the reader toward an ostensibly more comprehensible and less equivocal verbal narrative. The interplay of the hemispheres supports comprehension.

Images are more efficient than words in representing something unfamiliar, something that deviates from readers' previous experience, whether lived or mediated, which alerts readers' attention. The right hemisphere is open and vigilant, always looking for something new, without necessarily rationalizing it. The new can be settings, characters, or objects that readers simply have not yet encountered in real life, but it can also be images that lack referents in real life: fantastic settings or creatures, anthropomorphized animals, and animated objects. The left hemisphere is more concerned with inanimate objects, while the right hemisphere is focused on the living. The living are more likely to have emotions; therefore we tend to endow the living with sentience, that is, to anthropomorphize. Anthropomorphizing, which cognitive criticism identifies as the way the brain interprets the world, seems a natural response for a young child. The abundance of anthropomorphic characters in picturebooks is therefore not a coincidence, but a conscious or intuitive device. As pointed out repeatedly in picturebook research, clever picturebooks allow text and image to fill each other's gaps, especially when one medium is better suited for conveying a particular type of information. Paradoxically, images seem to be far superior to words in representing interiority.

Thus, in addition to schema and script disruptions occurring in literary fiction, picturebooks afford an interaction of disruption and confirmation in the tension between two media. Any additional effort is beneficial for readers' cognitive-affective development. Surprise is an important factor, since counterpoint or ambiguity in the iconotext will make the brain work harder. Surprise is an emotion that is evolutionarily conditioned and aimed at assisting our ancestors in making quick decisions when confronted with new situations, such as to flee or to fight. In picturebook design, surprise is enhanced by pageturning. Picturebooks frequently contain verbal pageturners of the type "What do you think happened next?," prompting readers to turn the page. However, a more subtle way is a visual pageturner, an element typically positioned in the bottom right corner, pointing toward the next spread (in reverse in cultures employing a right-to-left order of writing). Whether visual or verbal, a pageturner is a cognitive-affective attractor. It creates anticipation, in which the left hemisphere will expect a confirmation of something it knows, while the right hemisphere will be prepared to explore something unusual and unfamiliar. The left hemisphere will look for a conspicuous detail, for instance, a bright patch of color, and connect it to a previously stored schema (for instance, red = danger). The right hemisphere will consider the patch in the context of the whole doublespread. Pageturning (or screen swiping in a digital picturebook) is a powerful affective stimulus because it is an embodied response – active participation – supported by the right hemisphere.

Through the doublespread layout, picturebooks determine the duration and pace of engagement with the narrative. Words may prompt readers to hurry, in order to follow the plot and confirm the emotional resolution, while the abundance of visual details encourages readers to stay on the spread and explore, possibly discovering clues not revealed by the words that add to the overall emotional experience. This minute exploration is supported by the right hemisphere, while the left hemisphere sorts and categorizes details for further recall and recognition. The composition of verso and recto suggests a temporal and occasionally causal sequence that demands the right hemisphere's attention, for instance, when a change in a character's emotional state occurs. With its narrow focus, the left hemisphere cannot fully process the non-linearity of an image or a sequence of images on a doublespread because it processes them as separate and disconnected. Ostensibly, it also considers words and images in isolation, without putting them together. Further, the left hemisphere sorts and orders information on each individual doublespread, but does not notice any development or change, while the right hemisphere compiles the whole narrative from disparate doublespreads, making connections between them, which demands attention, imagination, and memory. To put it simply, the right hemisphere is the only one of the two that can make sense of a narrative flow and thus the emotional development of the story.

Picturebook scholars have repeatedly claimed that complex, counterpointing picturebooks are more engaging for young readers than simple and symmetrical ones, that is, books where words and images duplicate each other. Educators, on the other hand, tend to question young children's capacity to make meaning out of complex picturebooks. With support from cognitive criticism, we can confidently state that complex picturebooks are beneficial for young readers' cognitive-affective development because they offer the brain something to work on.

Picturebooks and emotional literacy

Cognitive criticism offers new ways of thinking about picturebooks as an efficient implement to increase young readers' emotional intelligence (see Nikolajeva 2013), and here again the right hemisphere plays the leading role. Young readers not only lack the experience of a full range of human emotions (that is, emotional schemas and scripts that the left hemisphere tries to recognize), but have not yet fully developed their theory of mind and empathy skills. Theory of mind refers to the ability to understand how other individuals think. Empathy refers more specifically to understanding how other people feel (see, for instance, Doherty 2009). Both theory of mind and empathy are arguably the most important capacities that distinguish human beings from other living organisms (they are predominantly governed by frontal lobes, prominent in human beings). They are also essential social skills. However, they do not appear automatically, but develop gradually and can be enhanced and trained. Picturebooks have a great potential for such training. Like all fiction, picturebooks represent fictional characters' emotions as well as their interpretation of each other's emotions. However, unlike novels, picturebooks evoke emotional engagement through images as well as words, through amplification of words by images, and through ambiguity created in the interaction between media when conveying a character's emotional state. Once again, picturebooks appeal to the right hemisphere to a great extent.

Emotionally charged images in picturebooks are in most cases complemented by verbal statements: "He was sad," "She was frightened." Verbal statements are signifiers and therefore abstractions; they are labels – schemas – used by the left hemisphere to categorize what it already knows. However, emotions themselves are non-verbal. They are considerably less precise than any verbal language can adequately convey. Words can supply nuances and degrees of emotions, such as happy, glad, and exhilarated, sad and upset, angry and furious; however, there is no way words can represent these emotions effectively. Since the left hemisphere avoids anything imprecise and implicit, the burden of engaging with the representation of emotions falls primarily on the right hemisphere. Figurative language, especially metaphor, is a powerful device to approximate the nebulosity of emotion. For instance, "He froze in horror" is presumably stronger than the schema "He was scared," and "She boiled with fury" is stronger than the schema "She was angry." Yet visual images carry a more powerful potential. Thus viewing a person's facial expression or bodily posture sends a stronger and more immediate signal to the brain than reading the verbal schema-statement "This person is happy, sad, angry, or frightened." Picturebooks frequently utilize images, including wordless doublespreads, to convey strong emotions for which words would be insufficient and inadequate. There are also picturebooks that are wordless, or almost wordless, except for the title and occasional intraiconic texts; such picturebooks frequently contain emotionally disturbing or at least ambiguous plots. When words and images collaborate, they may be mutually complementary or enhancing. They can even be contradictory; for instance, words can state that a character is happy, while the images show them upset. This is where picturebooks offer a unique opportunity to engage with empathy and mind-reading, circumventing the inadequacy of language. For instance, children's false-belief capacity can be enhanced through picturebooks (see Silva-Díaz 2015). Clever picturebooks make use of the ambiguity created in the interaction between media when conveying a character's emotional state. Images can furthermore represent emotions of which young readers have limited or no experience, emotions for which the left hemisphere finds no recall in its schema database. A young reader may not know the exact meaning of verbal signifiers such as "He was sad" or "She was frightened" (predominantly the left hemisphere's function), but they will be able to respond to images evoking distress or fear, even though or perhaps precisely because they have no direct experience of these emotions.

Limited experimental research, registering brain reactions, has investigated children's affective responses to single – and typically simple – emotionally charged images and simple verbal descriptions of mental states. However, such experiments access extradiegetic emotions, triggered in a subject's brain by the image itself. A child feels joy seeing images of a smiling face, a bright sunlit landscape, or a cute animal, and they experience fear seeing a scary monster. Such responses are not substantially different from responses to real-life experience, even though a visual representation of a monster is not exactly the same as a real-life monster. Direct affective responses are hard-wired in the lower parts of the brain, connected with the right hemisphere, and evolutionarily conditioned. Although a picture of a monster presents no danger to the viewer, the brain, through mirror neurons, responds to the image as if it were real, since the brain is evolutionarily trained to alert to possible danger. Moreover, young children may not yet perceive a representation as different from its referent in real life. Horror movies are built on the premise that representations of scary creatures or things affect the viewer just as if they were real. Educators frequently claim that certain picturebook images can be scary for children, while literary scholars tend to dismiss such allegations far too easily, ignoring the fact that the right hemisphere makes little distinction. A young child who smiles seeing a happy face in a picturebook, or starts moving at the sight of a fictional character running and jumping, who cries over a picture of a dead animal or shudders at the gaping jaws of a giant dinosaur is truly experiencing the emotions as if they were real. In fact, they are real and only become rationalized as representations when the left hemisphere interferes.

The same mechanism allows us to engage vicariously with fictive characters' emotions. In readers' involvement with picturebooks, these two kinds of emotions, diegetic (textual) and extradiegetic (extratextual), inevitably interact. Readers can be directly frightened by images of creatures that they believe are dangerous, such as dinosaurs, bears, or wolves. They can also be frightened by certain settings, such as dark woods. The danger, however, threatens fictional characters rather than readers. As soon as the reader acknowledges, prompted by the left hemisphere, that the schema or script is fictional, the emotional engagement is shifted onto the characters: theory of mind and empathy are activated. Thus readers should be able to read the character's fear even if they do not experience the same emotion when looking at the image, or to understand that the character is sad without feeling distressed themselves.

Empirical studies confirm that even very young children understand emotional dimensions in picturebooks and respond to them independently of their own emotions (e.g., Arizpe and Styles 2015). Non-verbal response methods, such as drawing, collage, play, or performance, successfully circumvent young informants' lack of verbal skills to articulate their comprehension. Close observations during experiments, including recording children's facial expression, body language, gaze movement, and the duration of time spent on each spread, allow for reliable accounts of their engagement with multimodal texts, not least because the right hemisphere is firmly connected with the body. It is therefore natural that responses to emotionally charged images are best expressed through embodied rather than verbal activity. The idea of 'verbalizing' an image is a self-contradiction. Empirical research confirms that children respond more strongly to visual emotion representation when it is not supported by words (Arizpe 2013).

Obviously, picturebooks contain images that, alone or in combination with words, express a wide range of basic as well as social emotions, treating them in a range from simple, literal, and straightforward (left hemisphere) to elaborate and metaphorical (right hemisphere). Basic emotions, which include joy, distress, fear, anger, and disgust, are universal and independent of verbal language, thus are mainly processed by the right hemisphere. Physical manifestations of basic emotions, such as facial expression, body posture, and gestures, normally do not require any special training. Our emotional response to emotionally charged images is possible because we have stored, albeit inaccurate and fragmented, memories of the represented emotion, either from real-life experience or from an earlier experience of fiction, whether verbal, visual, or multimedial. We may not have a direct experience of extreme distress or extreme fear, but the little experience we have is sufficient to trigger the memory. When reading images, the left hemisphere is looking for recognizable external tokens of emotions, schemas once again. At the same time, the right hemisphere responds to embodied emotions, connected to body movements and spatial position. Indeed, we recognize emotions, in real life as well as in visual representations, through body language.

Unlike basic emotions, social or higher-cognitive emotions, such as love, guilt, shame, pride, envy, and jealousy, are not innate, or at least considerably less innate than basic emotions; and they may be culturally dependent, that is, perceived in a broader context. The concept of social emotions emphasizes that they involve more than one individual and are thus subject to negotiations. Although surprisingly many picturebooks feature one single character, most of them involve at least two, which immediately brings in social emotions. Social emotions are not directly connected to external expressions and are thus more difficult to communicate visually. While there are emoticons for all shades and degrees of joy, sadness, or anger (the left hemisphere's way of categorization), it is problematic to create a universal facial expression for envy or pride. If we need unequivocal visual signifiers for social emotions, we have to use symbols rather than icons, such as a stylized heart for love or a skull for hatred; again, something based on previous knowledge, something that the left hemisphere will recognize. For the right hemisphere, it is easier to infer that two people in close embrace love each other and are happy together; however, an emotional response to such an image also involves recognition of an emotional schema or script, which the left hemisphere will eagerly perform.

Picturebooks involving several characters encourage young readers to engage in a more complex mind-reading, or high-order mind-reading of the type: "A thinks that B thinks that A thinks. . . . " In this process, readers are asked not only to understand what characters think and feel but also what they think and feel about each other's thoughts and feelings. In real life, the main incentive of mind-reading is predicting and anticipating other people's actions and reactions through understanding their thoughts. Picturebooks depict conflicts between characters based on misunderstanding, misinterpretation, and misdirection of emotions; they also depict characters developing empathy toward other characters. Such representations demand more sophisticated emotional responses, and, since they are ambiguous, appeal to the right hemisphere. However, since the left hemisphere will respond to something previously learned, including artistic conventions, it is equally necessary for a rounded experience.

In summary, a cognitive-affective approach to the representation of emotions in picturebooks provides understanding of how multimediality is particularly beneficial for stimulating young readers' brain activity in terms of theory of mind and empathy. Theory of mind typically develops around the age of four, when picturebook reading is perhaps most intensive. However, the ability to empathize, that is, understand other individuals' emotions rather than project our own feelings onto them, is not fully developed until adolescence. It is, therefore, desirable that even older children be given opportunities to read multimedial narratives, be it picturebooks, graphic novels, or comics. While McGilchrist acknowledges the current dominance of the left hemisphere in Western culture, he strongly favors a return to the wisdom of the right hemisphere in its holistic, embodied, and emotional view of the world. For a picturebook scholar, this appeal supports greater attention to visual literacy as the right hemisphere's domain.

What is new?

What then does cognitive-affective criticism offer to support our understanding of emotions portrayed in picturebooks? First, it explains, anchored in experimental research, why we can engage with fictional emotions at all and particularly why we can be strongly affected by emotionally charged visual images even when we know that they are mere representations. Second, it provides fascinating insights, which still need to be confirmed experimentally, about the ways in which brain laterality governs our emotional engagement with multimedial narratives, as well as the particular appeal of picturebooks to young readers because of the right cerebral hemisphere's dominance at a young age. Third, cognitive criticism confirms claims that have been previously made without indisputable scientific evidence: reading multimedial texts is not only beneficial but is indispensable for our emotional development. Finally, cognitive criticism convincingly demonstrates that visual images are powerful means to invite readers to engage emotionally with texts, and that picturebooks are perfect training fields for young people's theory of mind and empathy. With this understanding, the importance of picturebooks reaches far beyond being reading matter for emergent readers. The common belief that picturebooks are intended for very young children and that school-based literacy should primarily involve the mastery of verbal, written language – that is, the supremacy of the verbal over the visual in formal Western education – regrettably results in children yielding to the demands of the left hemisphere and losing their innate ability to engage with images. Ultimately, then, cognitive criticism provides scholars and educators with concrete, easy-to-use implements for studying both young readers' emotional engagement with picturebook texts and picturebook texts' affordances that enable such engagement.

References

Arizpe, Evelyn (2013) "Meaning-Making from Wordless (or Nearly Wordless) Picturebooks: What Educational Research Expects and What Readers Have to Say," *Cambridge Journal of Education* 43.2: 163–176.

Arizpe, Evelyn, and Styles, Morag (2016) *Children Reading Picturebooks: Interpreting Visual Texts*, 2nd ed., London: Routledge.

Crago, Hugh (2014) *Entranced by Stories: Brain, Tale and Teller, From Infancy to Old Age*, New York: Routledge.

Doherty, Martin J. (2009) *Theory of Mind: How Children Understand Others' Thoughts and Feelings*, Hove: Psychology Press.

Evans, Dylan (2001) *Emotions. A Very Short Introduction*, Oxford: Oxford University Press.

Hogan, Patrick Colm (2003) *The Mind and Its Stories: Narrative Universals and Human Emotions*, Cambridge: Cambridge University Press.

Keen, Suzanne (2007) *Empathy and the Novel*, Oxford: Oxford University Press.

Kümmerling-Meibauer, Bettina, and Meibauer, Jörg (2015) "Beware of the Fox! Emotion and Deception in *Fox* by Margaret Wild and Ron Brooks," in Janet Evans (ed.) *Challenging and Controversial Picturebooks, Creative and Critical Responses to Visual Texts*, New York: Routledge, 144–159.

Lakoff, George, and Johnson, Mark (1980) *Metaphors We Live By*, Chicago: University of Chicago Press.

LeDoux, Joseph (1996) *The Emotional Brain: The Mysterious Underpinnings of Emotional Life*, New York: Touchstone.

McGilchrist, Iain (2008) *The Master and His Emissary: The Divided Brain and the Making of the Western World*, New Haven, CT: Yale University Press.

Nikolajeva, Maria (2012) "Reading Other People's Minds Through Words and Images," *Children's Literature in Education* 43.3: 273–291. Doi: 10.1007/s10583-012-9163-6.

Nikolajeva, Maria (2013) "Picturebooks and Emotional Literacy," *The Reading Teacher* 67.4: 249–254. Doi: 10.1002/trtr.1229.

Nikolajeva, Maria (2014a) "'The Penguin Looked Sad.' Picturebooks, Empathy and Theory of Mind," in Bettina Kümmerling-Meibauer (ed.) *Picturebooks: Representation and Narration*, New York: Routledge, 121–138.

Nikolajeva, Maria (2014b) "Emotion Ekphrasis: Representation of Emotions in Children's Picturebooks," in Davidd Machin (ed.) *Visual Communication*, Berlin: De Gruyter Mouton, 711–729.

Nikolajeva, Maria (2014c) *Reading for Learning: Cognitive Approaches to Children's Literature*, Amsterdam: John Benjamins.

Oatley, Keith (1992) *Best Laid Schemes: The Psychology of Emotions*, Cambridge: Cambridge University Press.

Silva-Díaz, Maria Cecilia (2015) "Picturebooks, Lies and Mindreading," *BLFT: Nordic Journal of ChildLit Aesthetics* 6. Doi: http://dx.doi.org/10.3402/blft.v6.2697.2.

Wolf, Maryanne (2007) *Proust and the Squid: The Story and Science of the Reading Brain*, New York: HarperCollins.

Zunshine, Lisa (2006) *Why We Read Fiction: Theory of Mind and the Novel*, Columbus: Ohio State University Press.

12

GENDER IN PICTUREBOOKS

Karen Coats

The scholarly study of gender in picturebooks did not begin with literary critics. In fact, most formalist studies of picturebooks that teach literary critics how to read the complex interactions between words and images in picturebooks, including those by William Moebius (1986), David Lewis (2001), and Clare Painter, J.R. Martin, and Len Unsworth (2013), among others, give almost no attention to the portrayals of gender. While Perry Nodelman (1988) devotes a few pages to the differential postures of the naked child in light of artistic conventions of the female and male nude (121–124), and Maria Nikolajeva and Carole Scott (2001) make some interesting claims that I will discuss in what follows, most of the early studies of gender in picturebooks have been undertaken by feminist sociologists working to understand the persistence of sex-role stereotypes. This makes sense, given that gender criticism belongs more to cultural studies than formalist metholodogies. However, by invoking the insights of cognitive psychologists that "perception occurs in the brain rather than in the eye" (Nodelman 1988: 8) and reminding us that we have "*to learn to see*" images in picturebooks (Williams 1961: 18), even theorists interested primarily in form have implicitly suggested the need for an interdisciplinary understanding that focuses on the way brains process texts within a cultural context – that is, a cognitive cultural studies that views mental activity not as rational brains processing information in autonomous, detached isolation, but as minds and bodies responding to cultural artifacts in active, reactive, and interactive ways.

Cognitive literary criticism is multifaceted, attending to all of the processes through which we construct and manipulate mental models while reading, and how style, character, and themes evoke emotional responses, among other things. Many of its areas of inquiry offer productive insights that map readily onto formalist studies of picturebooks, as well as onto newer approaches afforded through multimodal discourse analysis. However, given that my topic is limited to the depiction of gender in picturebooks, I will focus on the concept of schemas and scripts, which offers us a way to understand how texts participate in conveying and challenging prevalent social ideologies, as well as a way to consider why changing the way children understand gender might be so difficult.

To begin, then, we need some definitions. A cognitive schema is an associative cluster of ideas and knowledge about objects or situations that we acquire and develop through repeated experience, and then use to incorporate, organize, and understand new instances that are related in some way to a particular schema. Script is a term that describes a sequence of actions that we expect to happen based on the schema that has been evoked (Schank and Abelson 1977). So, for instance, when Western readers hear or see the words "once upon a time," a fairy tale schema is evoked that will probably involve a quasi-medieval setting and certain character types, with an ensuing script that follows a sequence of stasis, the introduction of trouble or a problem, heroic action, and a resolution that involves a marriage and some sort of boon for the heroes and punishment for the villains. While Schank (1999: 89) contends that we do not tell stories about scripts, but rather about scenarios where expected scripts are disrupted or violated, I would argue that children's picturebooks are one of the many cultural vehicles that instantiate schemas and scripts in their readers by setting expectations for the way literary texts represent objects, relationships, and patterns in the world.

However, Schank's observation reminds us that schemas and scripts ultimately exist in minds, not texts; that is, they are something we bring to our understanding of stories, and what we find there is conditioned by them in important ways. While Schank and Abelson (1977) proved that invoking the proper schema at the outset of a reading could improve recall and comprehension of stories, cognitive theorists have also determined that schemas can be so strong that they lead to false beliefs about situations, as study participants see what they expect to see, rather than what is really there (Brewer and Treyens 1981). This becomes especially problematic when we realize that stereotypes are a type of schema. Several studies have shown that people process information that accords with their stereotypes more quickly, and remember it better, than information that disrupts existing schema (Hugenberg and Bodenhausen 2004; Johnson and Macrae 1994; O'Sullivan and Durso 1984). More important for consideration with visual media such as picturebooks is the fact that people locate visual images within existing schema, including stereotypes, more quickly than associated verbal text (Lieberman, Hariri and Bookheimer 2001); this finding may indicate that images are more powerful than words, or at least more automatic, in invoking schema and setting expectations for scripts.

The transmission of gender scripts and schemas through picturebooks

The concern with the automatic recognition of the fairy tale schema and script in terms of gender is well-known; the cast of characters I invoked earlier will almost always be further specified with a passive young female valued for her physical beauty, an evil and ugly older female, and an active, skilled male. The question for feminist theorists is how children acquire such uneven binary gender schemas and scripts, and whether and how they might be changed. It should come as no surprise, then, that serious consideration of the representation of gender in picturebooks began with the work of feminist sociologists during the heyday of second-wave feminism. Linguist Mary Ritchie Key published a provocatively titled piece in 1971, "The Role of Male and Female in Children's Books: Dispelling All Doubt," wherein she reported that in children's books through the 1960s, male characters were more often featured in active roles that included cleverness, adventure, and earning money, while females were portrayed as victims, onlookers, or caught in situations where they were unable to achieve their goals without help. John Stephens (1996) notes similar characteristics in his list of schema clusters for masculinity and femininity; he adds such qualities as transgressive, independent, and analytical on the side of masculinity, and obedient, self-effacing, and emotional as characteristics invoked through a schema for femininity.

More often cited in the education and social science literature is "the Weitzman study," "Sex-Role Socialization in Picture Books for Preschool Children" (Weitzman, Eifler, Hokada, and Ross 1972); in fact, many of the studies since that article appeared include "an update" or "a change" in their subheading as an implicit nod to its landmark status (see Collins et al. 1984; Williams et al. 1987; Kortenhaus and Demerast 1993). Rather than focus on the picturebook as an artistic form, Weitzman and her colleagues saw it in the ways that many literary critics see it today, as a purveyor of ideology to a particularly impressionable population:

> Picture books play an important role in early sex-role socialization because they are a vehicle for the presentation of societal values to the young child. Through books, children learn about the world outside of their immediate environment: they learn about what other boys and girls do, say, and feel; they learn what is right and wrong; and they learn what is

expected of children their age. In addition, books provide children role models – images of what they can and should be like when they grow up.

1972: 1126

This might be read as a statement of faith regarding the power of literature in young children's lives to help them sort the enormous amount of social information they receive daily into usable schemas and scripts. While Weitzman et al. acknowledge that the link between literary representations and social norms may not be as direct as they assert, and that in fact literature may represent alternative values, they still believe that picturebooks communicate images that not only reflect existing conditions, but also have the potential to produce effects on individual identities and expectations. Their study of Caldecott winners from the '40s, '50s, and '60s revealed that images of males were overwhelmingly more prevalent than images of females; in fact, in one five-year sample of winners and honor books, boys were pictured over ten times more frequently than girls. But, like Key, they also noted a difference in the activities and attributes of female characters and the aspirations they were encouraged to have. In general, they found that "the girls and women depicted in these books are a dull and stereotyped lot" whose "future occupational world is presented as consisting primarily of glamour and service" (1146). Consider, then, the schemas shared by the researchers themselves that underwrite this conclusion: they view careers in glamour and service as limiting and devalued activities, unworthy of aspiration by anyone, and most especially by girls.

The most inclusive (though narrowly quantitative) study of representations of gender in picturebooks to date surveyed an impressive 5,618 picturebooks published throughout the twentieth century (McCabe, Fairchild, Grauerholz, Pescosolido and Tope 2011), finding that males were represented twice as frequently as females in titles, and 1.6 times as often as central characters. Greater degrees of parity were achieved during social activist periods such as 1900–1929 and 1970–2000, while disparities were greatest during the gender traditionalism of 1930–1969. They also found that the boy/girl ratio of central child characters was more equitable when the characters were human rather than animals.

The sheer number of the books surveyed in this study argues for its validity, but I decided to put it to an informal test to see how we were faring in the twenty-first century which is, arguably, seeing another wave of feminist activism. My wholly unscientific study was conducted at a local bookstore that featured an entire wall of picturebooks faced out on display. In each of the three separate bays, there were approximately 20–28 books. In the first bay, I was encouraged to see *I Am Jazz* (Herthel and Jennings 2014), a picturebook biography of a transgender child, as well as two books about nontraditional families. But of the remaining twenty-five books in that section, nine had human boys as protagonist, while only three featured girls. Seven showed ambiguously gendered animals, but upon reading, I discovered that only one was female. The other two bays delivered similarly disparate results, with human boys represented twice as often as human girls, and male animal characters outnumbering females by even greater ratios. While John Stephens asserts that "processes whereby the cognitive instruments of schema and script are textually modified have played a central function in positive representations of cultural diversity" (2011: 12), it is arguable, with these vast disparities still in evidence, that a similar positive transformation is taking place with regard to gender. While close readings of particular books certainly reveal challenges to certain attributes in a schema cluster, in order for gender schemas and scripts to be challenged or disrupted on a societal level, sufficient numbers of stories with girl protagonists are required to normalize a broad range of female experience, and they must be widely read. As we noted earlier, schemas exist in minds, and are only represented in texts that children engage with; hence a few books that seek to disrupt existing schemas are more likely to be dismissed as irrelevant data points, or played up as sites of humor, as in, for instance, *Naughty Mabel* (2015) by Nathan Lane and Devlin Elliott. This book challenges the prevalent picturebook animal schema by presenting its main character, a dog, as a girl.

It violates the girl schema by having the very active Mabel behave in outrageous ways, including clearing a fancy party by loudly passing gas. It also violates the 'bad behavior leads to punishment' script when Mabel receives no rebukes for her behavior, and instead is welcomed into her human parents' bed after the party. However, it still evokes certain visual stereotypes with regard to gender, as Mabel wears a bathing suit in the pool, spa attire with cucumbers on her eyes while relaxing, and a pink tutu, necklace, and high heels to the party. Stephens suggests that the reason picturebooks can function as something of a bellwether for cultural shifts in attitude is because "such modifications are an expression within story worlds of wider transformations of social mentalities" (1996: 12). If this is true, and I am not convinced that it is, the schemas we hold for gender are not necessarily seeing such wider transformations of social mentalities, for reasons I will elaborate in what follows.

The development and persistence of gender schemas

I suggest that greater parity in representations of boys and girls is needed to normalize female experience because that is what the ubiquity of books about boys has done for our understanding of childhood gender; it has made boys, and the schemas that attach to their behavior, the norm. Formal and informal studies have shown that when an animal character is ungendered in a picturebook, most parents and children gender it male in their reading (Arthur and White 1996). Nikolajeva and Scott (2001) suggest that the likely reason that most of the books in their formalist study feature boy protagonists and that "in those that have girls, the protagonist's gender is in many cases not essential" is because

> picturebooks usually address the reader at an age when gender identity is not relevant yet; Maurice Sendak's Max, Babro Lindgren and Eva Eriksson's Sam and the Wild Baby are not really boys, while John Burningham's Shirley or Tove Jansson's Susanna are not really girls – rather, they are merely children, genderless and often ageless.
>
> *108*

Such a claim is problematic given what cognitive theorists tell us about the development of gender identity. Since 1966, developmental psychologists have been testing Lawrence Kohlberg's strong cognitive claim that children develop a sense of gender identity – that is, the ability to label themselves and others – by around three years of age, and achieve gender constancy by age seven, with an awareness of gender stereotypes quickly following. What newer research indicates, however, is that gender constancy emerges as early as five and a half years of age, and that, in contradiction with Kohlberg's claims, children's awareness of social gender stereotypes is well in hand before they have achieved gender constancy (Coddington and Wiebers 2002). Certainly, then, the specific gender portrayals in children's picturebooks do matter insofar as they are informing very young children's gender schemas and social scripts. Moreover, Nikolajeva and Scott note being able to find only one exceptional picturebook where a "very male-oriented story is subverted by its illustrations" (2001: 108). Combined with the research cited earlier that indicates the power of pictures to more readily invoke schema associations, this suggestion that gender schemas are typically preserved and reinforced at both the verbal and visual levels may account for the earlier acquisition of gender stereotypes (Turner-Bowker 1996; Hamilton et al. 2006).

In fact, very young children are "gender detectives" (Martin and Ruble 2004: 67), actively seeking clues from their culture as to how gender is performed and valued. Cognitive theorists have observed that children's early intellectual achievements involve sorting things into categories that depend initially on a single trait, and that these traits are emotionally linked to the object's relation to the self. Anatomical sex differentiation is a category distinction that is thus rendered important to children's self-concept through their interactions with others, who inform them repeatedly of their gender and instruct them in the use of pronouns and socially normative behaviors. What is initially a self-oriented categorical distinction of boy/girl develops into a cognitive schema that accretes modes of appearance, emotion, and behavior into a developing understanding of their own and others' gender identities.

Not all categories develop into cognitive schemas, however. We do not, for instance, sort people into left-handed and right-handed and develop expectations for appearance based on that physical distinction (Fine 2010: 210). Psychologist Sandra Lipsitz Bem (1983), who developed the idea of gender schema theory, argues that social categories develop into cognitive schema when

> (a) the social context makes it the nucleus of a large associative network, that is, if the ideology and/or the practices of the culture construct an association between that category and a wide range of other attributes, behaviors, concepts, and categories; and (b) the social context assigns the category broad functional significance, that is if a broad array of social institutions, norms, and taboos distinguishes between persons, behaviors, and attributes on the basis of this category.
>
> *608*

Bem's point is that while sorting things into categories is an inescapable cognitive process, schema formation depends on the social and cultural context; despite the claim of Nikolajeva and Scott, gender differentiation is nearly always salient in picturebooks. Girls and boys are visually coded by the color of their clothing, and the presence or absence of features such as jewelry or even prominent eyelashes, which female animals have and male animals, apparently, do not. They are also coded by their size, with males almost always being larger than females. Charlie is older, taller, and wiser than Lola in Lauren Child's sibling series (Child 2000–ongoing), and Gerald the male Elephant is larger and taller than pink, female Piggie in Mo Willem's early reader series. The silent Sally is shorter (and thus presumably younger) than her unnamed brother in Dr. Seuss's *The Cat in the Hat* (1957). What these brief descriptions indicate is that multiple codes are in play that invoke and reinforce our gender schema; we expect boys to be bigger, for instance, and we expect girls to be quieter. Bem's hope as a feminist is that this schematic division is contingent and thus open to intervention. If children could be enabled to learn about sex differences without the associated cultural norms and signifiers, such as "division of labor, [. . .] personality attributes [. . .] [or even] the angularity or roundness of an abstract shape" (603), that accrete to those differences, then perhaps our schema would be more accommodating of variations within and between genders. And in fact, the books mentioned do in some measure challenge signifiers traditionally associated with gender – Piggie is the braver of the pair and more apt to solve problems, for instance, and Gerald is in fact quite round and emotionally dependent on Piggie. Still, the male character has a proper name, while the female does not.

However, the problem with sex-associated traits is that they are more often presented as natural, inevitable, and ideal traits that have no inherent connection to gender distinction, which is what seems to underlie (and give the lie to) Nikolajeva and Scott's assertion of gender neutrality. Max's aggressive behavior and his coronation as King in *Where the Wild Things Are* (1963) *is* part of a masculinity schema, as Nodelman (2002: 4) points out, such that when he and his students transformed Max into Maxine, they found that they responded differently to her behavior; the behavior that in Max was naughty and annoying, albeit normal for a boy, was considered brave and worthy of emulation when performed by Maxine. The "jeer pressure" (Fine 2010: 218) that Morris Micklewhite is subjected to when he appears "in drag" in *Morris Micklewhite and the Tangerine Dress* (2014) reminds us that gender schemas are neither neutral nor easy to change, but that within them gender is a socially policed, performative act. As Judith Butler (1993) describes it:

> To claim that all gender is like drag, or is drag, is to suggest that "imitation" is at the heart of the *heterosexual* project and its gender binarisms, that drag is not a secondary imitation that

presupposes a prior and original gender, but that hegemonic heterosexuality is a constant and repeated effort to imitate its own idealizations.

127

These idealizations are realized in and through cognitive schemas and scripts. While Bem argues that anatomy and reproductive capabilities should be the only things that differentiate gender, Butler goes even further to suggest that even these two attributes are the result of a series of socially negotiated performances. Picturebooks like Leslea Newman's *Heather Has Two Mommies* (1989), with its discussion of artificial insemination, *And Tango Makes Three* (2005) by Justin Richardson and Peter Parnell, and *I Am Jazz* (2014) by Jessica Herthel and Jazz Jennings do not violate schema for laughs, and thus deconstruct naturalized connections between gender, reproduction, and anatomy, revealing ways that they could be performed differently; in so doing, these books function to disrupt the reproduction and gender constancy schemas that readers bring to them. Peter Stockwell (2002) suggests that schema disruption occurs when "conceptual deviance offers a potential challenge" (80) to existing knowledge. Schema disruption requires a response; a reader must refresh or completely restructure his or her schema, or enlarge it to accommodate the new information. At their best, this is what stories can do: present conceptual information that forces readers to confront and reconsider their expectations, with the result of modifying schemas and scripts that have limiting social and intellectual effects.

In their different ways, both Bem and Butler argue that the host of associations that make the binary gender schema salient and functional are the result of social forms processed through cognitive structures, and in this they differ from both social constructivists and biological essentials. Social learning theory posits children as passive recipients of whatever messages their culture feeds them; ergo, picturebooks and other artifacts of children's culture matter enormously in the construction of gender identity, and can, over time, change our attitudes about gender.

Biological essentialists, which include a new crop of neuroscientists, argue that "infants have, quite literally, made up their minds [about gender] in the womb, safe from the legions of the social engineers who impatiently await them" (Moir and Jessel 1989: 20); in this view, gender is always already salient in terms of what children are naturally drawn to, so that picturebook representations only matter insofar as they affirm and reinforce what is considered socially good about each gender's inherent proclivities, which amount to relationships and empathy for girls and system-building and physical activity for boys (see Fine, 2010, introduction).

Picturebooks like *Morris Micklewhite and the Tangerine Dress* (2014), *Jacob's New Dress* (2014) by Sarah and Ian Hoffman, and *My Princess Boy* (2010) by Cheryl Kilodavis, which all feature boys who want to wear dresses, focus on a re-evaluation of the boy schema. The gender-normed secondary characters in these texts visually and verbally espouse the majority view of how boys and girls should dress. The characters of Morris, Jacob, and Dyson, respectively, and the fact that these books even exist, may suggest a shift in social mentalities, as Stephens proposes, but at the very least they challenge readers to rethink gender performance as a rigidly defined binary system. Books that present such views are thus to some degree acts of faith on behalf of social constructivists; they operate out of the belief that picturebooks can make a difference in terms of social learning, dispelling stereotypes with regard to gender and supporting children whose subjectivities are not comfortably seated within hegemonic norms and well-established schemas. But they also have something to offer with regard to gender schema theorists. One of the premises of schema theory is that the rigidity with which children hold to categorical distinctions "wax[es] and wane[s] across development" (Martin and Ruble 2004: 68). Trautner et al. (2005) found that:

a developmental pattern emerges that can be characterized by three ordered steps. First, there is a phase of learning about gender-related characteristics, mainly taking place during the preschool years. Second, the newly acquired gender knowledge is consolidated in a rigid either-or fashion, reaching its peak of rigidity between 5 and 7 years. Third, after that peak of rigidity, a phase of relative flexibility follows.

366

These steps offer a way for social learning to intervene in a cognitive schema. By positioning their characters in elementary school, picturebooks can showcase both rigid views and more expansive ones, thus hitting readers right at the zone of proximal development, that is, the point between what they can understand on their own and what they can come to understand with the help of these stories. When Becky tells Morris that boys do not wear dresses, Morris responds with "This boy does" (Baldacchino 2014: n. pag.), indicating not that he has completely undermined the binary gender schema, but that he has undergone what is known as schema accretion with regard to boys' dress options, "where new facts are added to an existing schema, enlarging its scope and explanatory power" (Stockwell 2002: 79); the hope is that readers will do likewise with their own gender schema.

Gender schema disruption and accretion is nothing new for women, who have been actively seeking to dispel limiting stereotypes throughout the twentieth and twenty-first centuries. But while there is a long tradition in children's literature of girls transgressing gender norms by behaving as tomboys (Abate 2008), there is no similar tradition for boys behaving in ways that have traditionally been coded feminine. In fact, Eve Kosofsky Sedgwick (1991) has coined the term "effeminophobia" (20) to highlight the fact that when boys behave in ways culturally construed as feminine, they are considered pathological, whereas girls engaging in activities generally associated with masculinity are often celebrated. With the exception of such standouts as Munro Leaf's *The Story of Ferdinand* (1936), which features a young male bull actively resisting the aggression and violence expected of his gender, and Charlotte Zolotow's *William's Doll* (1972), which tells the story of a boy who wants a doll to nurture and care for, most picturebooks invoke gender schema not only through modes of appearance, but also through modes of behavior and activity. Even Morris Micklewhite does not challenge the boy schema articulated by Stephens (1996) when it comes to his behavior; his desire to wear a dress is not because he is focused on building relationships through empathy and identification with the girls in his class, nor does he demonstrate care, a desire to please others, or an ability to share. Rather, he behaves like a competitive, independent, rapacious, active person, who also wants to wear a dress. Most of the images show him alone and physically separate from his peers, which may serve to highlight the fact that he is a bullied and lonely victim, if not for the picture where he sits triumphant atop an elephant in a world that he has imagined for himself; his ideal imaginary world, like Max's, only includes creatures over which he is sovereign. By contrast, Jazz clearly empathizes and desires relationships with other girls, and is often shown in close physical contact with family members and peers, or joyfully involved in group activities. In fact, the only time where she is depicted as sad and alone, off to the side of activity, is when she is forced to dress like a boy; her transition from boy to girl implies a full embrace of the traditional girl schema.

The strongly normative gender schemas and scripts that children acquire in early childhood are thus invoked through both verbal and visual representations in picturebooks, even in texts that seek to disrupt those schemas; the best these texts seem to be able to do is facilitate schema accretion, allowing children to choose which schema – boy or girl – they wish to perform. While Stephens concludes that schemas and scripts in diverse picturebooks can "function as transformative instruments" (2011: 34), it seems that with regard to gender, there are still binaries that matter.

References

Abate, Michelle Ann (2008) *Tomboys: A Literary and Cultural History*, Philadelphia: Temple University Press.

Arthur, April G., and White, Hedy (1996) "Children's Assignment of Gender to Animal Characters in Pictures," *The Journal of Genetic Psychology* 157: 297–301.

Baldacchino, Christine (2014) *Morris Micklewhite and the Tangerine Dress*, illus. Isabelle Malenfant, Toronto: Groundwood.

Bem, Sandra Lipsitz (1983) "Gender Schema Theory and Its Implication for Child Development: Raising Gender-Aschematic Children in a Gender-Schematic Society," *Signs* 8: 598–616.

Brewer, William F., and Treyens, James C. (1981) "Role of Schemata in Memory for Places," *Cognitive Psychology* 13: 207–230.

Butler, Judith (1993) *Bodies That Matter: On the Discursive Limits of Sex*, New York: Routledge.

Child, Lauren (2000–ongoing) *Charlie and Lola* series, Somerville, MA: Candlewick.

Coddington, Tara M., and Wiebers, Todd (2002) "Kohlberg Redux: Gender Concept Formation and Cognitive Processes in Preschool Children," *Psi Chi Journal of Undergraduate Research* 7.4: 171–175.

Collins, Laura J., Ingoldsby, Bron B., and Dellmann, Mary M. (1984) "Sex-Role Stereotyping in Children's Literature: A Change from the Past," *Childhood Education* 60: 278–285.

Fine, Cordelia (2010) *Delusions of Gender: How Our Minds, Society, and Neurosexism Create Difference*, New York: W.W. Norton.

Hamilton, Mykol C., Anderson, David, Broaddus, Michelle, and Young, Kate (2006) "Gender Stereotyping and Under-Representation of Female Characters in 200 Popular Children's Picture Books: A Twenty-First Century Update," *Sex Roles* 55: 757–765.

Herthel, Jessica, and Jennings, Jazz (2014) *I am Jazz*, illus. Shelagh McNicholas, New York: Dial.

Hoffman, Sarah, and Hoffman, Ian (2014) *Jacob's New Dress*, illus. Chris Case, Park Ridge, IL: Albert Whitman.

Hugenberg, Kurt, and Bodenhausen, Galen (2004) "Ambiguity in Social Categorization: The Role of Prejudice and Facial Affect in Race Categorization," *Psychological Science* 15.5: 342–345.

Johnston, Lynden, and Macrae, C. Neil (1994) "Changing Social Stereotypes: The Case of the Information Seeker," *European Journal of Social Psychology: General* 107: 420–435.

Key, Mary Ritchie (1971) "The Role of Male and Female in Children's Books: Dispelling All Doubt," *Wilson Library Bulletin* 46: 167–176.

Kilodavis, Cheryl (2010) *My Princess Boy*, New York: Aladdin.

Kohlberg, Lawrence (1966) "A Cognitive-developmental Analysis of Children's Sex-role Concepts and Attitudes," in Eleanor E. Maccoby (ed.) *The Development of Sex Differences*, Standford, CA: Stanford University Press.

Kortenhaus, Carole M., and Demerast, Jack (1993) "Gender Role Stereotyping in Children's Literature: An Update," *Sex Roles* 28.4: 219–232.

Lane, Nathan, and Elliott, Devlin (2015) *Naughty Mabel*, illus. Dan Krall, New York: Simon & Schuster.

Leaf, Munro (1936) *The Story of Ferdinand*, illus. Robert Lawson, New York: Viking.

Leiberman, Matthew D., Hariri, Ahmed, and Bookheimer, Susan (2001) "Controlling Automatic Stereotype Activation: An fMRI Study," Paper presented at meeting of the Society for Personality and Social Psychology, San Antonio, TX.

Lewis, David (2001) *Reading Contemporary Picturebooks: Picturing Text*, London: RoutledgeFalmer.

Martin, Carol Lynn, and Ruble, Diane N. (2004) "Children's Search for Gender Cues: Cognitive Perspectives on Gender Development," *Current Directions in Psychological Science* 13.2: 67–70.

McCabe, Janice, Fairchild, Emily, Grauerholz, Liz, Pescosolido, Benice A., and Tope, Daniel (2011) "Gender in Twentieth Century Children's Books: Patterns of Disparity in Titles and Central Characters," *Gender and Society* 25.2: 197–226.

Moebius, William (1986) "Introduction to Picture Book Codes," *Word & Image* 2.2: 141–151.

Moir, Ann and Jessel, David (1989) *Brain Sex: The Real Difference Between Men and Women*, London: Michael Joseph.

Newman, Leslea (1989) *Heather Has Two Mommies*, illus. Diana Souza, Los Angeles, CA: Alyson.

Nikolajeva, Maria, and Scott, Carole (2001) *How Picturebooks Work*, New York: Garland.

Nodelman, Perry (1988) *Words about Pictures: The Narrative Art of Children's Picturebooks*, Athens: University of Georgia Press.

Nodelman, Perry (2002) "Making Boys Appear: The Masculinity of Children's Fiction," in John Stephens (ed.) *Ways of Being Male: Representing Masculinities in Children's Literature and Film*, New York: Routledge, 1–14.

O'Sullivan, Carmel S., and Durso, Frank T. (1984) "Effect of Schema-Incongruent Information on Memory for Stereotypical Attributes," *Journal of Personality and Social Psychology* 47.1: 55–70.

Painter, Clare, Martin, J. R., and Unsworth, Len (2013) *Reading Visual Narratives: Image Analysis in Children's Picture Books*, Sheffield: Equinox.

Richardson, Justin, and Parnell, Peter (2005) *And Tango Makes Three*, illus. Henry Cole, New York: Simon & Schuster.

Schank, Roger C. (1999) *Dynamic Memory Revisited*, Cambridge: Cambridge University Press.

Schank, Roger C., and Abelson, Robert P. (1977) *Scripts, Plans, Goals and Understanding*, Hillside, NJ: Lawrence Erlbaum Associates.

Sedgwick, Eve Kosofsky (1991) "How to Bring Your Kids Up Gay," *Social Text* 29: 18–27.

Sendak, Maurice (1963) *Where the Wild Things Are*, New York: Harper & Row.

Seuss, Dr. (1957) *The Cat in the Hat*, New York: Random House.

Stephens, John (1996) "Gender, Genre and Children's Literature," *Signal* 79: 17–30.

Stephens, John (2011) "Schemas and Scripts: Cognitive Instruments and the Representation of Cultural Diversity in Children's Literature," in Kerry Mallan and Clare Bradford (eds) *Contemporary Children's Literature and Film: Engaging with Theory*, Basingstoke: Palgrave Macmillan, 12–35.

Stockwell, Peter (2002) *Cognitive Poetics: An Introduction*, New York: Routledge.

Trautner, Hanns M., Ruble, Diane N., Cyphers. Lisa, Kirsten, Barbara, Behrendt, Regina, and Hartmann, Petra (2005) "Rigidity and Flexibility of Stereotypes in Childhood: Developmental or Differential?" *Infant and Child Development* 14: 365–381.

Turner-Bowker, Diane (1996) "Gender Stereotyped Descriptors in Children's Picture Books: Does 'Curious Jane' Exist in the Literature?" *Sex Roles* 35.7/8: 461–487.

Weitzman, Lenore, Eifler, Deborah, Hokada, Elizabeth, and Ross, Catherine (1972) "Sex-Role Socialization in Picture Books for Preschool Children," *American Journal of Sociology* 77: 1125–1150.

Willems, Mo (2007–2015) *Elephant and Piggie* series, New York: Random House.

Williams, J. Allen, Vernon, JoEtta A., Williams, Martha C., and Malecha, Karen (1987) "Sex Role Socialization in Picture Books: An Update," *Social Science Quarterly* 68: 148–156.

Williams, Raymond (1961) *The Long Revolution*, London: Chatto & Windus.

Zolotow, Charlotte (1972) *William's Doll*, illus. William Pene du Bois, New York: Harper & Row.

13

CANON PROCESSES AND PICTUREBOOKS

Erica Hateley

Canonical works are understood to have intrinsic and historical significance. They exemplify an artistic or aesthetic achievement according to prevailing norms, and transcend those norms to reach wider audiences. While the intrinsic value of a canonical work is often asserted on aesthetic grounds, such qualitative judgments are readily extended to abstract philosophical or metaphysical judgments, loftily if tenuously described as insight into the human condition (Bloom 1994). Many literary scholars have a paradoxical relationship with the concept of a canon: on the one hand, we desire a tradition and an aesthetically rewarding reading experience to form the core of our practice; on the other hand, we are suspicious of norms becoming normative, and of every inclusion entailing exclusions. While canonical thinking survives within professional reading communities it often does so in the breach: today, it is the new norm to understand the canon as always-already problematic, but this means that canonicity remains a productive force within children's literature studies.

Children's literature is understood by many people – perhaps especially those who remain committed to the idea of a stable and secure literary canon – as 'lesser' or 'simpler' than general literature. This may be because the literary and sociocultural values that have long been associated with the literary canon are logically distinct from (are even defined by distinction from) childhood, inexperience, lack of education, or immaturity. Even within children's literature studies, there occasionally persists a notion that picturebooks are for the youngest of readers, and are thus somehow simpler than novels. Thus, it could be said that from a canonical perspective, picturebooks are doubly marginalized as a 'lesser' form of a 'lesser' form of literary art (see Kümmerling-Meibauer 2003: 17ff.).

This chapter takes for granted that neither children's literature in general nor picturebooks in particular are 'lesser' than any other form of literature. It considers how such hierarchies might operate within the field of picturebooks. Pierre Bourdieu's sense of 'field' refers to the many institutions, practices, dispositions, and actors who shape the norms and possibilities of cultural production:

> At stake in the literary field, and more specifically in the field of criticism is, among other things, the authority to determine the legitimate definition of the literary work and, by extension, the authority to define those works which guarantee the configurations of the literary canon.
>
> *Johnson 1993: 20*

The field extends beyond criticism, though, and

> includes sites and actors as varied as places of exhibition such as galleries and museums; institutions of consecration like academies and salons; institutions for "the reproduction of producers" themselves such as schools and universities; and other, specialized agents, including dealers, critics and art historians. The vast array of official forms of recognition includes government arts councils, literary prizes, academic exegeses, and authorized biographies, not to mention translations and publication in multiple editions.
>
> *Kolbas 2001: 62*

Even this list fails to take into account the popular cultural means by which canonicity is performed and extended. Not only are picturebooks translated from one language to another, but often from one medium to another as they are adapted for films, plays, video games, and increasingly, for digital applications. The picturebook creations of H.A. Rey, Jean de Brunhoff, Maurice Sendak, and Dick Bruna anchor massive merchandising and multimedia industries. Nonetheless, while popular esteem retains potency, canons are usually about 'quality' rather than popularity.

Defining canon

The scholarly 'canon' derives etymologically from the Greek *kanon*, meaning 'rod' or 'law', and institutionally from the religious practices of textual scholarship which designated particular books of the Bible as genuine for the purposes of Church dogma ("Canon" entry in OED). As a concept canonicity is thus concerned with ideals and norms, and is a "standard of judgement or authority; a test, criterion, means of discrimination" ("Canon"). Canon is also connected with institutional and cultural structures of power, as judgment and discrimination must be wielded by someone who has authority within a particular institutional or cultural structure. There is a

> close relation between the character of an institution and the needs it satisfies by validating texts and interpretations of them. The desire to have a canon, more or less unchanging, and to protect it against charges of inauthenticity or low value (as the Church protected Hebrews, for example, against Luther) is an aspect of the necessary conservatism of a learned institution.
>
> *Kermode 1979: 77*

Just as churches needed an agreed-upon biblical canon to anchor their hermeneutic and institutional practices, secular literary scholars required a textual canon to anchor their hermeneutic and institutional practices.

With the rise of English studies through the nineteenth and twentieth centuries, canonicity came to apply to particular groups of sacred secular texts – a contradictory phrase which reflects the extent to which liberal humanist literary scholarship shared the structures and practices of their religious forebears. Canon came to designate the genuine works of a particular author, as with the (still occasionally contested) list of plays written by William Shakespeare. More importantly, canon also came to apply to specific works of literature which formed the core of disciplinary knowledge and practice in English studies. Hypothetically, the canon is a body of literary works which – if read according to the institutional and hermeneutic norms of the discipline – would provide one with a knowledge and understanding of the essential history and highest aesthetic achievements of literature per se. In turn, the acquisition and exercise of such institutional and hermeneutic norms would usher the reading subject into a hallowed position of authority both dependent on and derived from the survival of that canon.

Canons as productive and problematic

The cultural authority which derives from mastery of and servitude to the literary canon is closely tied up with academe. Unsurprisingly, as the product of a profession comprising largely middle-class, classically trained men, the (somewhat stable) literary canon that emerged and was maintained in the nineteenth and twentieth centuries in English studies was itself populated largely by middle-class, classically trained male writers. The lives and works of canonical authors and academics alike appeared to be organized around a narrow set of shared or desired cultural and social values. Hence, the shorthand for the canon: "dead, white European males" (Kolbas 2001: 37).

Within academe, what came to be called the canon wars were precipitated by increased participation in higher education by previously subordinated or excluded groups. Just as first-wave feminism and civil rights movements enabled the opening up of social and educational opportunities to women and non-white people, so too did the literatures by and for these newly enfranchised groups become possible tools of education and objects of study. The new citizens of academia observed that the Western literary canon could be interpreted as an exemplification and tool of the same cultural hegemony that had previously made academe the province of a narrow and privileged social cohort. Defenders of the canon not only agreed but also argued for a continuation of such narrowness: "literary criticism, as an art, always was and always will be an elitist phenomenon" (Bloom 1994: 17).

Debates about canons and canon formation tend to split between, crudely, the aesthetic and the political. The aesthetic model of canonicity emphasizes intrinsic textual values, and sees the canon as an effective tool for the preservation and continuation of cultural heritage. The political model of canonicity emphasizes the social and ideological production, circulation, and reception of texts – including canonicity itself as a tool thereof – and critiques the role of the canon as a tool for the preservation and continuation of a particular culture heritage. Canon wars are fought less over the idea of a canon per se than over who or what is included in a given canon, and who or what determines such inclusion.

Canon wars and children's literature

The incursion of children's literature into English studies could be seen as part of the canon wars themselves: the inclusion of previously excluded or under-represented populations and works which challenged the Dead White Male syndrome of the Western Canon. The 1970s and 1980s witnessed both the canon wars – most visibly fought along lines of gender and race – and the migration of children's literature studies into English programs (while never abandoning its disciplinary roots in pedagogical and library studies). What is true of children's literature studies is also true within children's literature studies: canons are contentious.

Children's literature scholars find themselves engaged in a range of (somewhat contradictory) canonical enterprises. Children's literature can be legitimized as a field by integrating children's literature into the traditional canon and constructing a canon of children's literature. However, such strategies are necessarily subject to the same possibilities and problematics of any canon. The children's literary canon is further complicated by its long history outside the academy, its affective canon or "paracanon" (Stimpson 1990): those books which are loved, cherished, and passed from generation to generation within domestic cultures.

Even the most straightforward enterprises of canonicity are complicated when applied to picturebooks. While the Modern Language Association (MLA) volume *Teaching Children's Literature: Issues, Pedagogy, Resources* (1992) includes material about picturebooks, its essays about canonicity remain firmly focused on traditions of folktales and novels for young people. For example, in an essay called "Canon Formation: A Historical and Psychological Perspective," J.D. Stahl calls for "a process of discovery and analysis concerning which works serve best to exemplify the cruxes of children's literature" (1992: 20), but makes no mention of picturebooks. Presumably, this omission derives from wider norms of literary canonicity than from anything that inheres in the field of children's literature itself. In 2005, *The Norton Anthology of Children's Literature: The Traditions in English* (Zipes et al. 2005) was added to Norton's juggernaut of pedagogical canonicity. Comparing it with other Norton anthologies, however, Karin Westman finds that "the organizing principle is form rather than the passage of time. As a result, it is challenging to build a picture, let alone a canon, of children's literature" (2007: 284). Picturebooks are one of the forms given a section within the Norton anthology, and readers can see a chronological canon for picturebooks there ranging from Heinrich Hoffmann to Lane Smith but, as Westman suggests, may not readily see connections between picturebooks and children's literature more generally, let alone the wider literary tradition. Norton's canon of picturebooks does exemplify the paradoxes of canon formation: every inclusion indexes many exclusions, it serves as an introduction to and overview of a particular literary tradition, and it invites any number of criticisms along both aesthetic and ideological lines.

Canon processes

The competing and complementary logics of canonicity described as aesthetics (that which is in the work) and politics (that which imbricates the work), or more simply text and context, also inform the 'symptoms' of canonical reputation. It is useful to think in terms of canon processes – what Kenneth Kidd calls "canonical architecture" (2007: 169) and Deborah Stevenson calls canonical "accelerants" (2009: 118) – than committing to either an aesthetic or a sociopolitical perspective on how texts become canonized. Canon processes all seek (consciously or not) to celebrate something inherent within a literary work. However, by virtue of deeming such celebration necessary, also suggest that that 'something' may not be inherent, or at least not inherently valuable in and of itself. Rather, canonical processes are cumulative, and confer that which they claim to recognize: canonicity.

Prizing

The most commonplace and recognizable processes of 'legitimizing' picturebooks are by way of awards and 'best of' lists. As Kidd notes, prizing traffics in the cultural logic of canonicity with "the selection process an ostensible simulation of the test of time" (2007: 169). Over time, prestigious prizes accrue metrics of longevity and quality, particularly if their designation of instant classics is confirmed by long-standing interest in or influence of a winning title. In turn, such prizing strategies accredit the arbiters as well as the chosen books. When national prizes for children's literature are instituted, companion prizes/categories for illustration or picturebooks soon follow. This could be seen as a continued subordination of picturebooks to prose literature (a consequence of canonical traditions in the wider literary field), or more productively, might be interpreted as a sign of the impossibility of taking seriously children's literature as an art form without including picturebooks. In the United States, the Newbery Medal was instituted in 1921 and was joined by the Caldecott Medal in 1938. In the United Kingdom, the Carnegie Medal was established in 1936 followed by the Greenaway Medal in 1955. Australia's national awards for children's literature, administered by the Children's Book Council of Australia, first offered a general award in 1946 and added an award for picturebooks in 1955 (see Hateley 2017). While each award is marked by specific agendas or mandates, they share an intention to identify high quality picturebooks. They thus construct canons of picturebooks and also potentially contribute to wider canons of literature in their respective nations.

International prizes have followed suit: the International Board on Books for Young People's prestigious Hans Christian Andersen Award for writing was first given in 1956, and since 1966 there has also been a Hans Christian Andersen Award for illustration. The Bologna Children's Book Fair, first held in 1963, confers BolognaRagazzi Awards to picturebook illustrators from around the world. More recently, the Astrid Lindgren Memorial Award (currently the richest prize in children's literature), which is not exclusively focused on picturebook art, nonetheless gave two awards in its first year (2003): one to a writer and one to a picturebook creator.

Even this small selection of national and international prizes for picturebooks indicates not only that there is a serious industry of 'accrediting' picturebooks as canonical art, but that this industry has been accelerating through the latter half of the twentieth century. This is in keeping with prizing culture more broadly, but also with the increased presence of children's literature within the academy. Prize culture also serves to reinforce the connections between literary history, reception, and evaluation as intertwined mechanics of canonicity. Key early figures such as John Newbery and Randolph Caldecott are remembered in the prestigious awards. In turn, award winners are not infrequently used as the exemplary corpus for content analysis and criticism in educational and literary studies.

Professional readers and readings

There are a number of genres that align with canon formation including lists and anthologies of best, great, essential, or classic children's books. Probably because illustrations are expensive and complicated to reproduce, it is less common to see anthologies of picturebooks, although there are any number of illustrated collections of historical or classic children's literature – frequently called "Treasuries," signaling the multiple forms of capital and symbolic value being circulated within and by them. Despite Peter Hollindale's assertion that "only an academic madman (not, perhaps, too rare a creature) would dream of preparing a detailed scholarly edition of *The Tale of Peter Rabbit* (1993: 24), there has been at least one sustained scholarly treatment of a picturebook in Philip Nel's *The Annotated Cat: Under the Hats of Seuss and His Cats* (2007). In recent decades, a proliferation of scholarly editions of children's books; biographies of picturebook creators, editors, and publishers; monographs, edited collections, and journal articles about picturebooks has marked the increasing canonicity of picturebooks.

One influential scholarly intervention into the canon of picturebooks was the Children's Literature Association's *Touchstones* project. In 1980, the Association formed a committee to explore "Developing a Canon in Children's Literature" and in the years immediately following produced a canonical list (1982–1983) and then three volumes of criticism called *Touchstones: Reflections on the Best in Children's Literature*. The third volume was dedicated to picturebooks, and Perry Nodelman's introduction exemplifies the tensions which characterize any thoughtful canonical undertaking in the post-canon wars era. On the one hand, there is the desire for a shared and authoritative point of reference and tradition for scholars to build on. On the other hand, Nodelman is clearly conscious of the cultural myopia and elitism which so often accompanies canon-making:

> in naming touchstones the ChLA did not intend to make pronouncements from on high, to prescribe for certain and forever which children's books are to be considered the important ones. In fact, the intention was to open discussion rather than to close it.
>
> *Nodelman 1989: 3*

With some hindsight, ChLA's canon of picturebooks seems at once intuitive and restricted. They include pioneering figures such as Randolph Caldecott, Walter Crane, and Arthur Rackham, but the list overall tends – unsurprisingly, given the majority population of the ChLA – towards an Anglophone and predominantly North American tradition. But then, so too did Barbara Bader's influential contribution to constructing a tradition (and thus arguably a canon) of picturebooks which both reflected and shaped the rapidly consolidating field of children's literature scholarship in English, *American Picturebooks from Noah's Ark to the Beast Within* (1976). Equally logically, histories of picturebooks such as Brian Alderson's *Sing a Song of Sixpence: The English Picture-Book Tradition and Randolph Caldecott* (1986) and Joyce Irene Whalley and Tessa Chester's *A History of Children's Book Illustration* (1988) advanced British histories that articulated national traditions and fed international canons.

European histories and criticism of picturebooks also appeared in recent decades, and scholars of several national traditions of picturebooks are well-served by them (see Doderer and Müller 1973; Birkeland 1993; Christensen 2003; Druker 2008; de Bodt 2015).

What all of this 'canonical architecture' shares is its *mediating* function. These canon processes make visible the competing and complementary interests of the professional communities which 'use' children's literature, including librarians, teachers, and scholarly critics. In practice, they are all mutually constitutive and affirming. Prizes are named for publishers and given by librarians; prize-winning books are then used by scholars as core samples for content analysis, teaching, and the production of professional readings. Prizes, teaching, and analyses encourage publishers to keep books in print; parents, teachers, and librarians purchase award-winning books, and so on. John Guillory's extended critique of the mutually constitutive practices of canonicity and education, *Cultural Capital: The Problem of Literary Canon Formation* (1993), makes a compelling case that the machinery of canonicity is connected with education as a system of social and cultural reproduction. Guillory argues that "the distinction between the canonical and the noncanonical can be seen not as the form in which judgments are actually made about individual works, but as an effect of the syllabus as an institutional instrument" (30). Thus, the most powerful marker of increasing canonicity for picturebooks might be that unlike many other types of literature, they are now present in all stages of formal (and informal) education from early childhood to postgraduate university education.

A picturebook canon of the moment?

Having rehearsed the complexities and contradictions (perhaps even impossibilities?) of a canon of picturebooks, the temptation to take a scholarly risk is great – to follow in the footsteps of the canonists who have come before, and to offer a canon of one's own. And so, a gambit: reflecting on canonical processes and picturebooks today suggests the following figures (in alphabetical order) as a concentrated canon of picturebook makers of the late twentieth and early twenty-first century: Mitsumasa Anno, Anthony Browne, Roberto Innocenti, Maurice Sendak, Shaun Tan, and Tomi Ungerer. This is not to naïvely assert a consistent nor even universal canonicity of these figures. Rather, it is to suggest that these picturebook creators offer useful case studies (something which is beyond the purview of this chapter) for the flow of aesthetic, socio-cultural, economic, and associated symbolic capitals in an international context.

It may be that in the early twenty-first century, Maurice Sendak is *the* canonical picturebook creator, as even a brief consideration of the canonical markers accrued by him and his best-known picturebook *Where the Wild Things Are* (1963) shows. From 1966–2014, a significant collection of Sendak's original artwork and associated materials were deposited with and curated by the Rosenbach Museum in Philadelphia. There have been numerous exhibitions in galleries and museums around the world organized around Sendak's life and work ("Maurice Sendak Collection"). In 1988 a special exhibition dedicated to Sendak was mounted at the Bologna Children's Book Fair as part of its twenty-fifth anniversary celebrations. In 2013, a large touring exhibition was mounted to mark both the fiftieth anniversary of *Where the Wild Things Are* and the death of Sendak; *Maurice Sendak: The Memorial Exhibition* is scheduled to tour the United States into 2019 and perhaps beyond ("Sendak Memorial Exhibition"). Such markers of national and international esteem have been matched by book awards. *Where the Wild Things Are* received the 1964 Caldecott Medal, and Sendak would later be awarded the National Book Award (in 1982, for *Outside Over There* (1981)). Internationally, he won the 1970 Hans Christian Andersen Award for illustration and was the illustrator who won one of the first two Astrid Lindgren Memorial Awards ever given, in 2003. Sendak's works have been adapted for stage, television, and cinema; *Where the Wild Things Are* has had both an animated and a live-action adaptation. Perhaps more canonically significant is the extent to which Sendak's work has been taken up by other picturebook creators. Isabelle Nières has described the ways that intertextual and interpictorial allusions in picturebooks constitute a creative history of the genre, and notes that:

> it should not be difficult to compose a collective homage to Maurice Sendak from the picturebooks written and illustrated by Etienne Delessert (*Story number 1*), Tomi Ungerer (*The Beast of Monsieur Racine*), Mitsumasa Anno (*U.S.A.*), Susan Varley (*The Monster Bed*), Claude Ponti (*Adéle et la Pelle*), Mem Fox and Vivienne Goodman (*Guess What?*), Beatrice Poncelet (*T'aurais tombé*), and Gwen Strauss and Anthony Browne (*The Night Shimmy*).
>
> *Nières 1995: 55*

These could be seen as creative canonical architecture: picturebook makers designating a canon of their chosen form. In turn, many of the examples cited by Nières were produced by picturebook illustrators who are themselves canonical figures, confirming that to engage in a canonical enterprise is often simultaneously a gesture of self-canonization.

In *Making Mischief: A Maurice Sendak Appreciation* (2009), Gregory Maguire notes Sendak's *own* tendency towards intertextual play and "visual conversations" with other artists (5). *Making Mischief* is just one of several recent books which both observe and extend Sendak's work as a reflection and extension of much wider traditions. While Sendak's long career was marked by a number of critical and popular marks of esteem, it was the 1980s – the decade of canon wars and consolidating children's literature scholarship – that saw an escalation in Sendak's canonicity. Selma Lanes published a large, illustrated account of Sendak's work in 1980, *The Art of Maurice Sendak* (in 2003, this was updated and extended by Tony Kushner's *The Art of Maurice Sendak: From 1980 to the Present*). As mentioned earlier, the 1980s saw Sendak receive a National Book Award in the United States and enjoy Guest of Honor status and an exhibition dedicated to his work at the Bologna Children's Book Fair in 1988. The same year, Sendak published a collection of his own essays about children's literature, *Caldecott and Co.: Notes on Books and Pictures*, and further located himself within a canonical tradition.

The scholarly industry of Sendak analysis, and thus of cumulative canonicity, has accelerated in recent years. In early 2015, the *MLA International Bibliography* listed over one hundred separate works of criticism dealing with Sendak's work. Following Sendak's death in 2012, the *New York Times* obituary called him "the most important children's book artist of the 20th century" (Fox 2012). Since then, three major scholarly monuments to Sendak's canonicity have appeared: Leonard Marcus edited *Maurice Sendak: A Celebration of the Artist and His Work* in 2013 (a companion volume for an exhibition curated by Justin G. Schiller and David M.V. Dennis); *The Comics Journal* published an eighty-page interview with Sendak (Groth 2013), along with essays about Sendak's life and work; and, in 2014, the highly esteemed literary studies journal *PMLA* included a tribute to Maurice Sendak with contributions from eight scholars.

Perhaps the greatest indicator of Sendak's canonical status is the extent to which many of these markers can operate without reference to Sendak's actual work. Like other great canonical artists, it is possible to recognize the cultural value of Sendak's name without necessarily having direct knowledge of his work; in this sense, he may well be the Shakespeare or the Dickens of picturebooks. Like other canonical figures, of course, to know only the reputation is to miss out on wonderful reading experience, and the greatest achievement of *Where the Wild Things Are* is the book itself.

Sendak and the others on this chapter's canonical short list have created books that exemplify what it is to be a picturebook: a complex and complete (which is not to say difficult or closed) narrative or readerly experience which is understood most fully when visual and verbal elements are each attended to (both separately and together). Further, these visual and verbal elements will attain high aesthetic levels, and will both reflect and shape their histories and contexts of production. They may be iconoclastic, but it will be an iconoclasm borne of mastery. They will speak to readers of many ages, and from many times and places. And often, they will do so in just thirty-two pages.

The works of Mitsumasa Anno, Anthony Browne, Roberto Innocenti, Maurice Sendak, Shaun Tan, and Tomi Ungerer are useful for thinking about canon processes in picturebooks, with an eye to both the national and the international, to the aesthetic and the political, and to both child and adult audiences: their books are great artistic achievements; all are firmly rooted in specific historical or cultural contexts, but also transcend them; all access the general through the particular, and thus create unique work which is accessible by many. Even this very short list, though, reveals biases on the part of the listmaker. Even as these picturebook makers may have experienced varied forms of cultural and social marginalization connected with their particular cultural, national, religious, sexual, or other subjectivities, the list privileges the Global North, has only male artists, and is lacking in ethnic or cultural diversity. The same patriarchal and Anglocentric logics that have shaped canon formation historically seem also to have shaped, consciously or not, the maker of this short canonical list. It is difficult to engage in canon formation without recourse to existing canon processes, especially when those processes were used as measures for inclusion on the list.

The figures chosen *are* obviously canonical when viewed through the lens of canonical architecture, accelerants, or markers. Pro-canonists would presumably suggest that such markers are quite rightly attached to great works of art. Critics of canons might suggest that nothing attracts one canonical marker like already having accrued such a marker, and that the literary field depends on such mediations to constitute and justify its own existence. The commonalities of canonical markers accrued by these picturebook creators should not be mistaken for a one-size-fits-all recipe for canonicity. More importantly, they should not allow us to be blinded to other creators' works, or to other works of the canonized. The great risk of consensus canons is critical apathy: a taking-for-granted that a work is "great," that it rewards close (re)reading, or that it has something new to tell us about ourselves or the world in which we live, rather than undertaking a close and conscious (re)reading of the books themselves. The paradox of desiring and distrusting canons should lead us to further research into particular histories of canonization and decanonization; the effects of crossover picturebooks, artists' books, and picturebooks for adults on the literary field; the prevalence of fiction over nonfiction in canonized works; negotiations between national and international contexts; and the many and varied ways in which canonicity exerts pressures both productive and problematic in picturebook cultures.

References

Alderson, Brian (1986) *Sing a Song for Sixpence: The English Picture Book Tradition and Randolph Caldecott*, Cambridge: Cambridge University Press.

Bader, Barbara (1976) *American Picturebooks from Noah's Ark to the Beast Within*, New York: Macmillan.

Birkeland, Tone, and Storaas, Frøydis (1993) *Den norske biletboka*, Oslo: Cappelen.

Bloom, Harold (1994) *The Western Canon: The Books and School of the Ages*, Orlando, FL: Harcourt, Brace.

"Canon, *n*.," *Oxford English Dictionary*.

Christensen, Nina (2003) *Den danske billedbog, 1950–1999*, Roskilde: Roskilde Universitetsforlag.

de Bodt, Saskia (2015) *De verbeelders: Nederlandse boekillustratie in de twintigste eeuw*, Nijmegen: Vantilt.

Doderer, Klaus, and Müller, Helmut (eds) (1973) *Das Bilderbuch: Geschichte und Entwicklung*, Weinheim: Beltz.

Druker, Elina (2008) *Modernismens bilder: Den moderna bilderboken i Norden*, Stockholm: Makadam.

Fox, Margalit (2012) "Maurice Sendak, Author of Splendid Nightmares, Dies at 83," *New York Times* (May 8, 2012), www.nytimes.com/2012/05/09/books/maurice-sendak-childrens-author-dies-at-83.html.

Groth, Gary (2013) "Maurice Sendak Interview," *The Comics Journal* 302: 30–109.

Guillory, John (1993) *Cultural Capital: The Problem of Literary Canon Formation*, Chicago: University of Chicago Press.

Hateley, Erica (2017) "Visions and Values: The Children's Book Council of Australia's Prizing of Picturebooks in the Twenty-First Century," in Bettina Kümmerling-Meibauer and Anja Müller (eds) *Canon Constitution and Canon Change in Children's Literature*, New York: Routledge, 205–221.

Hollindale, Peter (1993) "Peter Pan: The Text and the Myth," *Children's Literature in Education* 24.1: 19–30.

Johnson, Randal (ed.) (1993) "Editor's Introduction," *The Field of Cultural Production: Essays on Art and Literature* by Pierre Bourdieu, New York: Columbia University Press, 1993, 1–25.

Kermode, Frank (1979) "Institutional Control of Interpretation," *Salmagundi* 43: 72–86.

Kidd, Kenneth (2007) "Prizing Children's Literature: The Case of Newbery Gold," *Children's Literature* 35: 166–190.

Kolbas, E. Dean (2001) *Critical Theory and the Literary Canon*, Boulder, CO: Westview.

Kümmerling-Meibauer, Bettina (2003) *Kinderliteratur, Kanonbildung und literarische Wertung*, Stuttgart and Weimar: Metzler.

Lanes, Selma G. (1980) *The Art of Maurice Sendak*, New York: Abradale Press/Harry N. Abrams.

Maguire, Gregory (2009) *Making Mischief: A Maurice Sendak Appreciation*, New York: William Morrow.

Marcus, Leonard S. (ed.) (2013) *Maurice Sendak: A Celebration of the Artist and His Work*, New York: Abrams.

"Maurice Sendak Collection," *The Rosenbach of the Free Library of Philadelphia*, www.rosenbach.org/learn/collections/maurice-sendak-collection.

Nel, Philip (2007) *The Annotated Cat in the Hat: Under the Hat of Seuss and His Cats*, New York: Random House.

Nières, Isabelle (1995) "Writers Writing a Short History of Children's Literature Within Their Texts," in Maria Nikolajeva (ed.) *Aspects and Issues in the History of Children's Literature*, Westport: Greenwood Press, 49–56.

Nodelman, Perry (1989) "On Words and Pictures, Neglected Noteworthies, and Touchstones in Training," in Perry Nodelman (ed.) *Touchstones: Reflections on the Best in Children's Literature*, Vol. 3: *Picture Books*, West Lafayette, IN: Children's Literature Association, 1–13.

Sendak, Maurice (1963) *Where the Wild Things Are*, New York: Harper & Row.

Sendak, Maurice (1981) *Outside Over There*, New York: Harper & Row.

Sendak, Maurice (1988) *Caldecott & Co.: Notes on Books and Pictures*, New York: Farrar, Straus and Giroux.

"Sendak Memorial Exhibition," *Maurice Sendak Memorial Exhibition*, http://sendakexhibition.com.

Stahl, John Daniel (1992) "Canon Formation: An Historical and Psychological Perspective," in Glenn Sadler (ed.) *Teaching Children's Literature: Issues, Pedagogy, Resources*, New York: Modern Language Association, 12–21.

Stevenson, Deborah (2009) "Classics and Canons," in M.O. Grenby, and Andrea Immel (eds) *The Cambridge Companion to Children's Literature*, Cambridge: Cambridge University Press, 108–123.

Stimpson, Catharine R. (1990) "Reading for Love: Canons, Paracanons, and Whistling Jo March," *New Literary History* 21.4: 957–976.

Westman, Karin E. (2007) "Children's Literature and Modernism: The Space Between," *Children's Literature Association Quarterly* 32.4: 283–286.

Whalley, Joyce Irene, and Chester, Tessa Rose (1988) *A History of Children's Book Illustration*, London: John Murray with the Victoria & Albert Museum.

Zipes, Jack et al. (eds) (2005) *The Norton Anthology of Children's Literature: The Traditions in English*, New York: W.W. Norton.

14
PICTUREBOOKS AND IDEOLOGY

John Stephens

All aspects of textual discourse, from story outcomes to the expressive forms of language and pictorial representation, are informed and shaped by ideology. In books for children, as in wider society, ideology functions as a cognitive framework that shapes, among other things, "knowledge, opinions and attitudes, and social representations" (van Dijk 2008: 34). In its broadest form, core elements of this cognitive framework are shared by members of a community or society such that social practice is built upon a complex of norms, values, and goals which, it is tacitly assumed, constitute the best kind of society. Notions of social cohesion are premised on this assumption about best social practice, and hence value judgments as to what constitutes the desirable behavior of individuals will be grounded here.

Ideologies are necessary for the functioning of social life, since a society cannot exist without structure. If children are to become competent members of society, they need to be able to operate within the various social and linguistic codes used by society to order itself. Embedded in ideology, texts produced for children serve to sustain, and sometimes redefine, social values that are assumed to be shared by text and audience, and they perform the cognitive function of supplying a meaningful organization of the social attitudes and relationships which constitute narrative plots. When we set out to examine the ideological dimension of texts, we are thus concerned with the ideological practices and assumptions which determine a society's sense of meaning and value, with how individual selfhood is constructed, and with the mechanisms which regulate interpersonal relationships and social hierarchies. Because ideologies are made up of widely shared assumptions and are inscribed textually as an aspect both of *story* and *significance*, they are often virtually invisible, and may lie at a level of meaning deeper than the notion of 'theme' which is often the endpoint of interpretation.

The significance deduced from a text – its theme, moral, insight into behavior, and so on – is never without an ideological dimension or connotation. Less overtly, ideology is implicit in the way the story an audience derives from a text is oriented towards the actual world: such orientation resides in the assumptions an author makes about the nature of the world, of good and evil, of what is valuable and desirable human experience, and of what kind of person a child should aspire to be. Even if the story's events are wholly or partly impossible in actuality, narrative sequences, character inter-relationships, processes of inferencing, aspects of visual modality, and so on will be shaped according to recognizable forms, and that shaping can in itself express ideology insofar as it implies assumptions about the forms of human existence. Stereotypical sexual, racial, and class attitudes, with concomitant social practices, have long been implicitly inscribed in this way: since at least the early 1970s, picturebooks such as Anthony Browne's *Piggybook* (1986), Chris Van Allsburg's *The Widow's*

Broom (1992), and many others have sought to make visible and hence challenge some cultural gender assumptions. Because ideology is thus present as an implicit secondary meaning at two levels – story and significance – narrative must be regarded as a special site for ideological effect, with a capacity not only to encourage audiences to internalize social norms but also to develop affective and nuanced interactions with those norms.

What any given society assumes to be meaningful and valuable in the practices of its social life, and the notions it accepts about how it is structured, about what constitutes proper authority, and about what is a desirable individual selfhood, are all aspects of social ideology. The literary fictions written within a society are situated within or against those practices and notions, and books for children tend to be firmly within the domain of cultural practices which exist for the purpose of socializing children. This socializing purpose has been most overt through the past half century in such domains as gender, race, and multiculturalism, and more recently environmental sustainability, all of which have inspired self-consciously ideological texts ranging from the very subtle to the very heavy-handed. Strategically, these areas reflect how one of the strongest influences from postmodernist thought upon children's literature has been the focus on the idea of the 'other' – especially the marginalized or excluded 'other' – since this overlaps with a general concern of picturebooks, the expansion of childhood experience from the domestic sphere into a wider world and hence an encounter with otherness.

Picturebooks as ideological artifacts

Picturebooks express the ideology of a society both verbally and visually. The interaction of the dual semiotic codes can work to produce an ideological conjunction, either because a reader's action in filling the gaps between visual and verbal discourses or in instantiating the third meaning prompted by the interaction will have an ideological effect, or because where the interaction is ironic the ideological effect will be more marked. Since picturebooks were first analyzed as ideological artifacts (Nodelman 1988 [by implication]; Stephens 1992, 1994; Trites 1994; McCallum 1997; Kanatsouli 2005; Stephens and McCallum 2011), there has been a steady, though not prolific, stream of scholarship, mostly focused on US-produced books (for example, Bernstein 2011; op de Beeck 2010) or generalizing American ideology to other regions (Zornado 2001, for example). Victoria Flanagan usefully argues that because picturebooks establish "the cognitive schemata for normative categories of identity and forms of behaviour" (2013: 14), they can play a significant role in reflecting an uninterrogated ideology. Hence Jackie Stallcup identifies simple acceptance of "a hierarchical view of the adult-child relationship" (2002: 141), and Christina Desai's analysis of picturebooks about Christopher Columbus discloses an underlying ideology that "condones conquest and exploitation of the weak by the strong" and affirms a Eurocentric concept of the world (2014: 194). In a similar vein, Flanagan illustrates how whiteness functions as a privileged racial category in Australian picturebooks.

Such picturebooks may unthinkingly reflect the common assumptions of a society, but more self-consciously propagandistic functions are as old as the genre itself and continue into the present. In many cases the line between implicitly and overtly articulated ideologies seems indistinct – it is not always clear, for example, whether the representation of a particular social ecology aims to inculcate its underpinning ideology. Further, as George Lakoff points out, not everyone has a coherent ideology (2002: 14) and an individual may invoke different ideological models in, for example, the domains of nationalism and multiculturalism. In her study of the depictions of migration and adoption in recent Spanish children's books, Macarena García González (2015) deploys Lakoff's (2002) argument that the conceptual metaphor Nation-as-Family is "one of the most common ways we have of conceptualizing what a nation is." A conceptual metaphor is the systematic projection of elements from one conceptual domain (the "vehicle" domain) onto elements of another (the "topic" domain). Like other such metaphors, they are part of everyday cognition and may be internalized by children from their mostly unmarked presence in picturebooks, especially if Allbritton, McKoon, and Gerrig are correct in arguing that "the framework created by a conceptual metaphor can aid in the comprehension of new information" (1995: 612). An especially pertinent example is the social positioning of the idea of multiculturalism within concepts of nation.

Ideologies of multiculturalism were prominently and optimistically advocated in Western children's literature through the second half of the twentieth century, especially in line with liberal political stances, but came under challenge, especially in the United States, when 9/11 shifted the balance in the Nation-as-Family metaphor away from Nurturant Parent morality. As Jo Lampert puts it,

> one of the key features of the 9/11 picture books is the complicated competition which emerges between the pre-9/11 ideologies of multiculturalism (with its urge to represent an idealized culturally diverse world) and a post-9/11 protectionism, as represented by a white American desire for centrality and dominance within that world.
>
> *2010: 48*

While the ideology of multiculturalism was never monolithic or unchanging either between or within countries, 9/11 and the subsequent War on Terror constituted probably the greatest impact upon it since its emergence from the 1960s Civil Rights movement.

The 9/11 picturebooks are ideologically nationalistic, although, as Lampert (2010) and Paula Connolly (2008) observe, they often deal with events by telling analogous stories. A good example is Mary Pope Osborne's *New York's Bravest* (2002), a story about Mose, a nineteenth-century New York fireman and folk hero. Pope adapts her own earlier retelling of the story so that the folk hero both reflects the Nation-as-Family metaphor (Mose not only rescues babies but people from all walks of life) and takes on some of the attributes of a superhero. As Jason Dittmer argues with reference to Captain America, a wide range of Americans interpret the actions of the nationalist superhero "as conforming to their ideal of America" (2012: 182). The superhero offers a sense of power and unity to a fragmented society and "interpellate[s] readers as national subjects" (182). The plain narrative style with some shifts to tall tale exaggeration (for instance, "Eight feet tall, Mose had hands as big as Virginia hams") declare the text an American discourse, and the use of numerous low angle perspectives emphasizes Mose's heroic stature. The book's peritext declares it to be a response to 9/11, so that the superhero ideology readily transfers to that event and opposes a symbol of American power to the assault on the fabric of the country.

The Nation-as-Family metaphor appears also within a different domain of multicultural ideology which seems to have been unaffected by 9/11 discourses, although it is grounded in the same caring affluence that reaffirms American power in the face of the vulnerability disclosed by 9/11 (see Lampert 2010: 116–119). This is the ideology which underpins picturebooks about the adoption of a baby from an orphanage in a foreign country. Such books may be based on a recount of an adopter's experience, and hence have some correspondence to the physical reality of international adoption, although as Macarena García González and Elisabeth Wesseling note, adoption narratives are also shaped by narrative scripts (2013: 259). A *script* is a frequently occurring action pattern which underlies a variety of everyday activities, but further refers to standard actions, situations, or familiar narrative forms which enable readers to make predictions about a recognizable sequence of events on the basis of some key components or schemas. Like conceptual metaphors, scripts are, or readily become, part of everyday cognition and hence can be ideologically powerful in their teleological assumptions. The stories of adopting a baby girl from China told in *The Red Blanket* (2004) by Eliza Thomas and Joe Cepeda, and *Just Add One Chinese Sister* (2005) by Patricia McMahon, Conor Clarke McCarthy, and Karen A. Jerome, have many script commonalities, but most notably the books share retrospective second person address: that the narratee is the adopted child is a common narrative device which, ostensibly striving to assist an adoptee audience in identity formation, interpellates its audience within a particular culture. The Nation-as-Family metaphor appears in both books as an effusive US community which celebrates the adoption and showers the adoptee with gifts on her arrival: no other picturebook genre presents so many smiling faces. The implied adoptee reader is thereby assured that children in other countries who have been abandoned for whatever reason will find a welcome and a permanent, loving home in the United States. Such acts of care begin with the arduous journey ("Two days and three nights later, I reached the orphanage" – *The Red Blanket*) and the effort to connect with a physically and emotionally undernourished infant (PanPan in *The Red Blanket* is "small and thin" and has "skinny little feet," and shares her cot with three other babies). In contrast, the US "home" is drenched in middle class affluence: a house of many rooms, a piano, and a crib "piled high with stuffed animals and toys that friends had brought for you." These friends embody the Nation-as-Family metaphor, but only one of the books includes a (token) non-white face: both books depict a society in which the norm is to be white, and it is assumed that the baby will be effortlessly absorbed into that society. These are well-meaning books, but express an overt, albeit surprisingly limited, multicultural ideology.

Ideology and the fluidity of affect

Ideology may be expressed as social ecology or habitus in such a way that it permeates visual and verbal discourses without becoming overt. Because ideology is not fixed, the function of stories both to make the world intelligible and to shape it in desirable forms must necessarily be fluid and flexible. How the operation of ideology in picturebooks is to be understood has been challenged by the (re-)turn to affect in critical theory in the twenty-first century, in that attention to affect shifts the interpretation of the relationship both between audiences and texts and between audiences and the social. Affect is a loose concept referring to bodily forces other than conscious knowing and not reducible to a simple understanding of emotion or to a contrast between biology and culture (Gregg and Seigworth 2010: 1f.), but which may also imbricate desires, memories and other kinds of feeling. The dual semiotic mode of picturebooks is thus particular powerful because of the interplay of word and image and because of a viewer's affective, more than cognitive, responses to tensions between familiarity and difference inherent in images. The reading experience is further complicated by two related issues. First, as Clare Painter and colleagues point out, existing schemes that explain picture-book structure assume that only one kind of text and image relationship pertains throughout a book, whereas interactions may be much more variable (2013: 6). Second, any presumption that the normal viewing position for a picturebook image is centered on the horizontal and vertical axes and represented participants are at full-figure distance, is apt to be ruptured by uses of perspective that move away from central position. When perspective is made overt, viewers are positioned ambiguously: they are offered a particular point of view, literally and conceptually, but may affectively embrace or resist the challenge to perceptual and hence ideological norms.

Presuppositions and multiple levels of ideology

A frequent strategy in picturebooks is to suggest a possibility that the audience knows more than the protagonist, a situation which may variously confirm internalized conceptions or make space to question the imposition of ideology onto form. Picturebooks may thus exploit audience knowledge in order to resist an ideological imaginary form, as we can see with *Nina Bonita* (1994), by Ana Maria Machado and Rosana Faría. Sometimes the ideological import of a text is simply disclosed in response to the question, "What is this text about?" Here there is an obvious story answer: a white rabbit wants to find out how Nina got her beautiful black skin, because he hopes one day to have a daughter with fur that black. He finally learns the answer – Nina has a black grandmother – and so he marries a black rabbit. Underlying the rabbit's quest are two conceptual metaphors which thread through the book: Discovery Is a Journey and Logical Relations Are Causal Relations. The first is made apparent by repetition of a variant of the formula, "The rabbit went to Nina Bonita's house and asked. . . ." The second lies in Nina's dependence on false premises and confusion of correlation with causation (for example, "eating blackberries will turn your skin black"), and hence the absurdity of her premises encourages the book's audience to formulate a more accurate version of the relation between logic and causality. Both metaphors have an ideological function to convey a particular understanding about the world, and contribute to more thematic answers to the question, "What is this book about?" – for example, the book presents an image of a harmonious life in the multi-ethnic, multicultural societies of Brazil and Venezuela. Higher level content answers include information about inter-racial marriage and genetics, which identify the book as a multicultural book. At a more abstract level, however, *Nina Bonita* is a book about the ideological bases of concepts of transcendent beauty.

Nina Bonita was originally published in Spanish and Portuguese in 1994, and in English in 1996. An international children's literature adult audience can be expected to have some familiarity with multicultural and postcolonial studies, but would have been unlikely in the 1990s to have recognized the book's magical realist elements, especially the hesitation over the ontological status of the rabbit, who is simultaneously human-like and a rabbit. That is, he captures the principle of conflicting, but internally coherent, perspectives which is a core of magical realism: in this case, a rational view of reality confirms that the rabbit is a rabbit, but his human-like behavior is simply accepted as another part of everyday reality. This ambiguity is unlikely to bother children, however, who are generally happy with the idea of talking animals. The meeting of the two rabbits is depicted in opening 9: their status in the visual scene is that of pets, but their reciprocal glance across the page enacts a "love at first sight" cliché. At the same time, the verbal text modulates comically from human to rabbit: "[the black rabbit] thought the white rabbit was quite charming. They fell in love, got married and started having bunnies, lots of them, because when rabbits start having babies, they never seem to stop" (n. pag.). Nina dominates this picture: she is deep black against the white clothes of the characters who surround her, and is much larger (in other pictures she is just a small girl). Nina is the key object of beauty throughout the book, and we can identify one function of the narrative as affectively reinforcing or modifying a reader's schema for what is a beautiful human body.

Nina Bonita is very concept rich, but young readers do not need access to complex cultural or literary concepts for it to have its effect, as this can be explained in terms of scripts and schemas. A *schema* is a memory structure that organizes categories of information; a mental structure of preconceived ideas. These may range from simple objects to abstract concepts. A schema consists of several components and is activated either by naming the object or concept or naming some components, or, in illustration, by visual representation of key components. An assumption underlying *Nina Bonita* is that audiences will already have internalized a schema for female beauty derived from white, ethnically European values. This schema is interrogated from opening 1, which informs readers that "[Nina's] eyes were like two shiny black olives. Her hair was curly and pitch black, as if made of unwoven threads of the night. Her skin was dark and glossy, just like a panther in the rain," and Faría's illustrations complement this poetic evocation by depicting Nina as lithe, muscular, and active. She is also quite unselfconscious about her appearance. Readers will know that all the answers Nina gives the rabbit are wrong, and will use their grasp of scripts to anticipate, first, that eventually the correct answer will emerge, and second, that it will probably be genetic. Because narrative both evokes scripts and schemas and has a capacity to modify their components, readers may develop a new cognitive map that interrogates their internalized ideology. Readers' affective investment in the rabbit's quest, reinforced by amusement at his folly in pursuing Nina's eccentric explanations, serves to undermine the propensity for affect to allow ideology "to seem real, natural, undeniable" (Jenkins 2013: 590). On the contrary, Machado and Faría show a different and more diverse version of subjectivity in everyday life.

Altruism as a global ideology

Many social assumptions are reiterated in picturebooks from diverse regions of the world, which suggests that various elements of an ideology of childhood are global and serve to sustain, and sometimes redefine, social values that are assumed to be shared by texts and audiences. The iteration of represented behavioral scripts for altruism, resilience, or self-awareness demonstrates the potential desirability of internalizing a moral attitude through enjoying an imaginary world of image-objects and agentic actions. Moral perspectives are in turn sustained by ideologies which frame notions of how to live well. For example, most societies formally eschew a life impelled predominantly by self-interest and they favor instead behavior which is capable of prioritizing the interests of others over those of the self. Empathic reaching out to an abjected other, as in Aaron Blabey's *The Ghost of Miss Annabel Spoon* (2011), can be represented within a simple moral fable, for instance. Ghosts may perform a useful function in such narratives, in that they readily embody liminality, but ghost stories are also rich sites on which to explore the imbrications of ideology and affect, since they readily invoke universal emotions such as anger, fear, sadness, disgust, and shame, and link these under the umbrella of the well-lived life.

The Ghost of Miss Annabel Spoon is a humorous book about difference, and particularly the tendency for people to fear those who are different, those we do not know or understand. The emotion of fear is clearly asserted on the opening page, primarily through comically excessive language – "The village … was haunted and cursed … plagued by a ghost" (ellipses added) – and an illustration depicting empty landscape, leafless trees and overcast, gray sky. As this illustration shows, visual images in picturebooks can express affect symbolically, especially through metonymy (a conjunction of literal and symbolic meanings). The absence of human figures or other living creatures – quite unusual in picturebooks, which normally focus on human figures and their body language – is explained by the inference that people are too afraid to leave their houses. Social well-being is generally posited on intersubjective interactions, so when social normality is restored and the same setting is repeated at opening 15, the symbolism is reversed: the page depicts not only a blue sky and trees with leaves, but a human *happiness*-schema, indicated by the presence of many people, laughing faces, games being played, community fun, absence of decorum.

This happy outcome has been reached through the enactment of an ideological position which underlies many of the representations of moral behavior in picturebooks, that is, that the common social assumption that the norm of human behavior is self-interest must be resisted. The affirmation of a set of social and moral concerns that shape elements such as identity, self-perception, and worldview in order to produce altruistic and empathic subjects points to a core ideology in picturebooks. Altruistic behavior – "Behavior designed to benefit another, even when this may risk sacrificing the actor's own welfare" (Monroe 1994: 861) – is the pivot of *The Ghost of Miss Annabel Spoon*. The story is set vaguely in the late nineteenth century, when decisions about local governance were made by the wealthy or educated members of the community. Thus a town meeting depicted in opening 4 identifies, visually and/or verbally, the mayor and "baker," "teacher" and "doctor," with the parish priest indicated by his church robes, his Bible, and his bad haircut. In its focus on the problem of the ghost, their debate is histrionic and authoritarian, but interrupted and redirected by a cinder-lad figure, "young Herbert Kettle." Herbert's suggestion that they should "just ask the poor ghost why it's here" abruptly shifts the notion of care and responsibility from self-interest to other-regardingness. He is the only person who has recognized that "the poor ghost" is suffering, and is prepared to breach a common folktale interdiction against speaking with a ghost and thus risking one's own life. Herbert overcomes his own fear and, performing a common "freeing-the-ghost" script, goes to the derelict cottage deep in the woods where the ghost dwells, discovers that she is both desperately lonely and "as nice as can be," and forges a friendship with her.

Self-perception and the move from negative to positive affect states

The conjunction of affect and ideology in the outcome of *Miss Annabel Spoon* accords with Patrick Colm Hogan's argument that story structures are shaped and oriented by emotion systems (2011: 1). Visual texts may invoke subsystems such as facial expression, body posture, or represented vocalization to indicate a version of the emotion system associated with fear, for example, as when

Herbert approaches Annabel's cottage. Conversely, because a basic emotion (or emotion 'prototype') is characterized by an action tendency (a physical response), an orientation toward objects (what causes fear), and a goal orientation (to escape from or overcome an averse emotion) (Smith 1999: 104), the emotion system structures the narrative both on micro and macro levels. As with the performance of the 'freeing-the-ghost' script, picturebook structures often confirm an altruistic or comparable worldview by following a trajectory from a negative affect state to a positive affect state. This trajectory may involve self-perception rather than altruism, although a basic understanding is that empathic and altruistic behaviors can only stem from healthy self-awareness.

The progression from a negative affect state to a positive affect state is only one way in which affect plays a significant role in ideologically motivated picturebooks. Starting from schema theory, David S. Miall (1989) argued that readers modify or create schemas to capture a text's complex of unfolding and shifting meanings. *Affect* is central to this procedure because it provides a principle for guiding the comprehension process in three ways: affect allows experiential and evaluative aspects of the reader's self-concept to be applied to the task of comprehension; it enables cross-domain categorization of text elements; and it is anticipatory, pre-structuring the reader's understanding of the meaning of a text early in the reading process. As Miall argues, self-reference is most apparent when readers align their own cognitive and affective processes with the experience and motives of the main character or characters in a narrative. In a sense, a reader "comes to share a character's feelings and goals" (62), but, further, draws on his or her prior experience and concerns to provide a range of potential contexts for attributing meaning to text elements.

A forceful example of this structure is offered by Jackie French and Bruce Whatley's *Flood* (2011), a faction picturebook about floods which swept through the Australian state of Queensland in 2011, and about the everyday heroism of ordinary people in their efforts to cope with one of Australia's extreme weather events. The book begins with two openings that depict how natural events suddenly shift from benign to destructive. Opening 1, illustrated in soft greens and blues, captures a positive affect state in its account of gentle rain nourishing the dry earth, the grass, and the trees, and by the positive emotion aroused by looking at a soft green landscape that includes a stretch of water. The only jarring moment is the comment, "It was strange not to play outside," a perception that the illustration attributes to a cattle dog surveying the scene, and which serves as a reminder that in times of extended drought an Australian child – or in this case, dog – can be two or three years old and have never seen rain. French's verbal text nowhere mentions a dog, so its appearance in over half of Whatley's illustrations transforms the text from third person omniscient narration to a character focalized narration that has the potential to strengthen audience empathy with the people dealing with the flood. In other words, the illustrations express an affect not as strongly present in the verbal text, but which lays some groundwork for the text's ideological basis in its expression of Australian relationships with an environment which can be unpredictable and harsh.

The second opening reverses the affect: the language introduces negative affect in the language describing the flood ('savage, slashed, giant wave swept across'), and the conceptual metaphor THE LAND IS A CONTAINER expresses negative excess, as the land is unable to absorb the vast quantity of water flowing across it. A still more negative emotion is evoked by depicting the rising floodwater in a limited brown and gray palette, and Whatley's technique of allowing the paint to run down the page suggests dissolution of things and impending chaos. The negative affect is intensified by an underpinning *helplessness* emotion schema. A reader may thus contextualize the scene in relation to any situation where one feels helpless or overwhelmed by circumstances beyond control. Negative affect governs the next four openings, until another reversal at opening 7 initiates a narrative of heroism and hope, and from this point a positive affect state becomes dominant. Opening 11, for example, describes how "strangers" offer assistance to the victims of the flood. The depicted "bucket brigade" (a human chain where items are passed from one stationary person to the next) consists of people standing in muddy water with their backs to the viewer or with occluded faces. By standing in the water, these anonymous people physically enact empathy, but metaphorically they also rise above the flood and help move the situation towards a positive outcome. The behavior of these strangers in a time of calamity is, of course, not unique to Australia, but is presented as a core element of Australian social ideology. An exemplary narrative, based on an actual event, recounts how a kilometer-long boardwalk is wrenched free by the flooded river, but is then pushed and nudged by "a tiny tugboat" until it is swept out to sea and can do no harm. As well as recounting the story, the picturebook conveys an ideological perspective that has long pervaded Australian literature, including children's literature. The essence of this ideology was expressed for example in Colin Thiele's short story, "The Water Trolley" (1966), which represents a confrontation with natural forces as a crucial rite of passage: Paul, a twelve-year-old boy, "had gone out a boy, but he was a boy no longer. For a whole day a continent had hurled itself at him, and he had beaten it back" (68; for further discussion, see Stephens and McCallum 1999).

Ideology and empathy

The confluence of affect and ideology pivots on the production of empathy, which is the endpoint of reader self-reference. Empathy is tied up with two categories of reader affect: the inferences readers make about characters' emotions, and readers' emotional responses to texts (Smith 1999; Izard 2009). The inferences readers draw can be activated and influenced by perceptual processes and cognitive appraisal – that is, readers interpret and assess the depicted scene and experience empathic engagement on two levels: as an emotion felt by characters within the story, and as empathy felt by readers toward those characters. As the picturebooks discussed in this chapter clearly show, however, such empathy has its basis in social ideology. Empathy in the close of a text may therefore function as a chain, which is a very familiar textual practice. One character enacts empathy for another; readers feel empathy with the represented empathic character and through him or her empathize with the object of the character's empathy. In a picturebook, this seems a useful strategy for augmenting the limitations of the dominant form, situational empathy, which is focused on aspects of plot and circumstance, and depends more on recognition of an experience than imaginative role taking. Affect in a picturebook is largely the product of how its dual semiotic system organizes information across the two systems to enable reader inferencing and hence attribution of affect. Both the inferences drawn and the attributed affect, however, are inevitably nuanced by contemporary ideology.

References

Allbritton, David W., McKoon, Gail, and Gerrig, Richard J. (1995) "Metaphor-Based Schemas and Text Representations: Making Connections Through Conceptual Metaphors," *Journal of Experimental Psychology: Learning, Memory, and Cognition* 21.3: 612–625.

Bernstein, Robin (2011) *Racial Innocence: Performing American Childhood From Slavery to Civil Rights*, New York: New York University Press.

Blabey, Aaron (2011) *The Ghost of Miss Annabel Spoon*, Melbourne: The Penguin Group.

Browne, Anthony (1986) *Piggybook*, London: Julia MacRae Books.

Connolly, Paula T. (2008) "Retelling 9/11: How Picture Books Re-Envision National Crises," *The Lion and the Unicorn* 32.3: 288–303.

Desai, Christina (2014) "The Columbus Myth: Power and Ideology in Picturebooks About Christopher Columbus," *Children's Literature in Education* 45.3: 179–196.

Dittmer, Jason (2012) *Captain America and the Nationalist Superhero: Metaphors, Narratives, and Geopolitics*, Philadelphia: Temple University Press.

Flanagan, Victoria (2013) "A Similarity or Difference: The Problem of Race in Australian Picture Books," *Bookbird* 51.2: 13–25.

French, Jackie (2011) *Flood*, illus. Bruce Whatley, Lindfield, NSW: Scholastic.

García González, Macarena (2015) "Imagining Transnational Orphanhoods: Nation-as-Family in Recent Spanish Children's Books," *Children's Literature Association Quarterly* 40.4: 322–338.

García González, Macarena, and Wesseling, Elisabeth (2013) "The Stories We Adopt By: Tracing 'The Red Thread' in Contemporary Adoption Narratives," *The Lion and the Unicorn* 37.3: 257–276.

Gregg, Melissa, and Seigworth, Gregory J. (2010) *The Affect Theory Reader*, Durham, NC: Duke University Press.

Hogan, Patrick Colm (2011) *Affective Narratology: The Emotional Structure of Stories*, Lincoln and London: University of Nebraska Press.

Izard, Carroll E. (2009) "Emotion Theory and Research: Highlights, Unanswered Questions, and Emerging Issues," *Annual Review of Psychology* 60: 1–25.

Jenkins, Eric S. (2013) "Another Punctum: Animation, Affect, and Ideology," *Critical Inquiry* 39.3: 575–591.

Kanatsouli, Meni (2005) "Ideology in Contemporary Greek Picture Books," *Children's Literature* 33: 209–223.

Lakoff, George (2002) *Moral Politics: How Liberals and Conservatives Think*, 2nd ed. Chicago: University of Chicago Press.

Lampert, Jo (2010) *Children's Fiction About 9/11: Ethnic, National and Heroic Identities*, New York: Routledge.

Machado, Ana Maria (1996) *Nina Bonita*, illus. Rosana Faría, Brooklyn and La Jolla, CA: Kane/Miller (first published 1994).

McCallum, Robyn (1997) "Cultural Solipsism, National Identities and the Discourse of Multiculturalism in Australian Picture Books," *Ariel* 28.1: 101–116.

McMahon, Patricia, and McCarthy, Conor Clarke (2005) *Just Add One Chinese Sister*, illus. Karen A. Jerome, Honesdale, PA: Boyds Mills Press.

Miall, David S. (1989) "Beyond the Schema Given: Affective Comprehension of Literary Narratives," *Cognition and Emotion* 3.1: 55–78.

Monroe, Kristen Renwick (1994) "A Fat Lady in a Corset: Altruism and Social Theory," *American Journal of Political Science* 38.4: 861–893.

Nodelman, Perry (1988) *Words about Pictures. The Narrative Art of Children's Picture Books,* Athens: University of Georgia Press.

op de Beeck, Nathalie (2010) *Suspended Animation: Children's Picture Books and the Fairy Tale of Modernity*, Minneapolis: University of Minnesota Press.

Osborne, Mary Pope (2002) *New York's Bravest*, New York: Alfred A. Knopf.

Painter, Clare, Martin, J.R., and Unsworth, Len (2013) *Reading Visual Narratives: Image Analysis of Children's Picture Books*, Sheffield: Equinox.

Smith, Greg M. (1999) "Local Emotions, Global Moods, and Film Structure," in Carl Plantinga and Greg M. Smith (eds) *Passionate Views: Film, Cognition, and Emotion*, Baltimore: Johns Hopkins University Press, 103–126.

Stallcup, Jackie (2002) "Power, Fear, and Children's Picture Books," *Children's Literature* 30: 25–58.

Stephens, John (1992) *Language and Ideology in Children's Fiction*, London and New York: Longman.

Stephens, John (1994) "Illustrating the Landscape in Australian Children's Literature," in Wendy Parsons (ed.) *Landscape and Identity: Perspectives from Australia*, Blackwood: Auslib Press, 69–83.

Stephens, John, and McCallum, Robyn (1999) "Unbronzing the Aussie: Heroes and SNAGs in Fiction and Television for Australian Adolescents," in Dudley Jones and Tony Watkins (eds) *A Necessary Fantasy: The Heroic Figure in Children's Popular Culture*, New York: Garland, 343–362.

Stephens, John, and McCallum, Robyn (2011) "Ideology and Children's Books," in Shelby Wolf, Karen Coats, Patricia Enciso, and Christine Jenkins (eds) *Handbook of Research on Children's and Young Adult Literature*, New York: Routledge, 359–371.

Thiele, Colin (1974) "The Water Trolley," in *The Rim of the Morning*, Adelaide: Rigby (first published 1966).

Thomas, Eliza (2004) *The Red Blanket*, illus. Joe Cepeda, New York: Scholastic Press.

Trites, Roberta Seelinger (1994) "Manifold Narratives: Metafiction and Ideology in Picture Books," *Children's Literature in Education* 25.4: 225–242.

Van Allsburg, Chris (1992) *The Widow's Broom*, New York: Houghton Mifflin.

van Dijk, Teun A. (2008) *Discourse and Power*, Basingstoke: Palgrave Macmillan.

Zornado, Joseph L. (2001) *Inventing the Child: Culture, Ideology and the Story of Childhood*, New York: Garland.

PART II

Picturebook categories

15

EARLY-CONCEPT BOOKS AND CONCEPT BOOKS

Bettina Kümmerling-Meibauer and Jörg Meibauer

Introduction

Picturebooks for children aged twelve to eighteen months typically show pictures of common, everyday objects of the young child's surroundings, such as balls, dolls, shoes, bananas, or chairs. These books are made of thick cardboard, but also of plastic, wood, and cloth ('rag books'). They usually have a handy format and fewer than ten pages. Their titles often refer to the implied users (*Baby's First Book*, *Pictures for the Little Ones*), the depicted objects (*First Things*, *What Is That?*), or the child's ownership (*My First Picturebook*). These picturebooks contain no text, with the possible exception of a single word denoting the object that is pictorially represented. The pictures are either color drawings or photographs in black and white or color.

The most common term for this book type is 'baby book' (Nodelman 1988). This notion is far too general, though, since it refers to all picturebooks targeted at young children before the age of three, ranging from simple board books to I Spy books and wimmelbooks. More suitable terms may be 'object book,' the Swedish *sakbok* (thing book) and *pekbok* (pointing book), or the Dutch *anwijsboek* (instruction book), since they emphasize a major characteristic of this book type.

Considering the fact that this book type is quite prominent on the international book market and generally has high print runs, one may wonder why there is so little research on this increasing picturebook corpus. One reason may be that these books do not display an intricate text-picture relationship, nor do they contain a story, which are typical features of picturebooks targeted at children older than three years of age. Another reason may be that people are unsure about their classification: since they just show images of single objects without any story, librarians and educationalists maintain that they neither belong to the category of 'literature' nor can they be clearly assigned the status of 'book.' Instead they suggest terms such as 'pre-literature' or 'learning toys' (Apseloff 1987). The latter points to the fact that some 'baby books' have gadgets, such as a tiny puppet, a button to push in order to make different noises, or diverse materials that imitate the surface of the depicted objects.

Among the first studies that have taken this book type seriously are the monographs by Perry Nodelman (1988) and Gunther Kress and Theo van Leeuwen (1996), which each devote a chapter to picturebooks for young children. Only in recent years have two edited volumes called attention to these picturebooks and how they contribute to young children's emergent literacy (Kümmerling-Meibauer 2011; Kümmerling-Meibauer et al. 2015).

Early-concept books: some typical features

In an article published in 2005, we proposed the more specific term 'early-concept book,' because the basic function of this book type consists in depicting early concepts (Kümmerling-Meibauer and Meibauer 2005). A concept contains the verbal knowledge that a person needs in order to correctly refer to a given entity. For example, the concept CAR enables the child to refer to cars, and the picture of a car has the intention to stimulate the child's acquisition of this concept. Early concepts belong to the young child's early lexicon and are usually acquired between twelve and eighteen months of age. These early concepts not only comprise nouns, but also verbs, adjectives, deictic expressions, and forms of greeting (Clark 1993; Barrett 1995).

The early-concept book has prominent precursors, such as Johann Amos Comenius's *Orbis Sensualium Pictus* (The Visible World 1658) and Friedrich Justin Bertuch's *Bilderbuch für Kinder* (Picturebook for Children 1790–1830), since they also show pictures of everyday objects. However these books were intended for primary school children and conveyed an encyclopedic knowledge of the world. In contrast, early-concept books that address young children emerged in the last two decades of the nineteenth century. Prominent examples are the cloth books from the British publishing house Dean's Rag Book since the beginning of the twentieth century and the books by Dick Bruna, which revolutionized this book type in the 1960s (see Figure 15.1). Edward Steichen and Mary Steichen

Figure 15.1 Book cover of Dick Bruna's *Erste Bilder*. Ravensburg: Ravensburger Buchverlag, 1973.

Calderone's photobook *The First Picture Book* (1930) and its follow-up *The Second Picture Book* (1931) influenced the emergence of early-concept books with photographs in the United States, the UK, Germany, France, and other European countries (see Figure 15.2). Since then, several renowned artists such as Keith Haring, Tana Hoban, Tom Seidmann-Freud, Emmanuel Sougez, and Andy Warhol have created early-concept books, which are now regarded as rare collectibles (Kümmerling-Meibauer and Linsmann 2009).

When closely looking at a modern version of this book type, some visual features come to the fore. One object is usually depicted on each page, but sometimes two to five objects constitute a scene. A black line frames the object in order to distinguish it from the background. Moreover, the viewer is at eye level with the object, which is either shown from the front or from one angle. The objects are depicted in bright colors with a predominance of primary colors (Werner 2011). The hue is consistent and modulations of colors are lacking. The objects are surrounded by an empty white or single-colored background so that they seem to float in a negative space. They are always static and are never shown in movement. Moreover, the objects usually do not cast a shadow and sources of light are not discernible. These facts contribute to the reduction of the objects' three-dimensionality. The proportions are noticeable, since the objects seem to be of the same size, even though they may

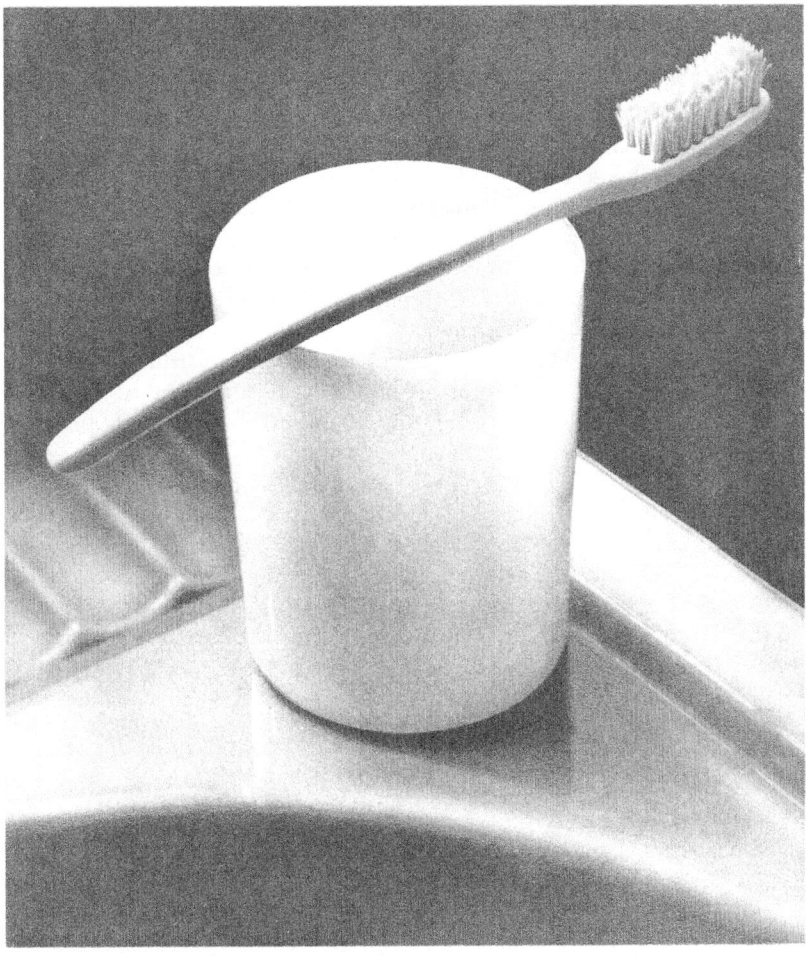

Figure 15.2 Photo from Erich Retzlaff's *Das erste Bilderbuch*. Frankfurt: Wolfgang Metzner Verlag, 1949.

have different actual sizes. This description illustrates that the objects are not presented in a natural manner. Due to their stylized representation, the majority of early-concept books show a certain degree of abstraction.

Early-concept books and emergent literacy

On closer consideration, the supposed simplicity of the illustrations reveals a remarkable complexity, which demands that young children have acquired some basic skills of perception in order to understand the visuals. These skills concern (1) the differentiation between figure and background, (2) the recognition of lines, colors, and patterns as inseparable parts of the represented objects, (3) the understanding that two-dimensional objects represent three-dimensional objects, and (4) the acquisition of learned visual schemata (Nodelman 1988: 35f.; Kümmerling-Meibauer and Meibauer 2011: 94).

These four essential skills demonstrate that pictures comprise visual codes which are not innate but must be learned (Kress and van Leeuwen 1996: 22–24). By attentively looking at early-concept books, children are encouraged to acquire these conventions, which constitute a sort of "visual grammar" (18). Psychological studies in picture perception stress that children at an early age develop a surprising ability to understand visual signs and codes, which is a significant stepping-stone in the acquisition of visual literacy (Thomas et al. 2001; Nikolajeva 2003).

The intensive consideration of the images in early-concept books not only fosters visual literacy, but enhances language acquisition as well. Children learn their first words when they are about one year old. By eighteen months, they have acquired a repertoire of roughly fifty words, which constitutes the 'early lexicon.' Nouns play a significant role in the early lexicon; approximately 45 percent of the first fifty words are nouns (Bloom 2000). It is not purely coincidental that the objects presented in early-concept books are labeled through nouns. In this regard, this book type perfectly matches with the young child's language acquisition. As research in language acquisition has demonstrated, the understanding of the meaning of words is not automatic and challenges young children in multiple respects. First of all, children have to learn the prototypical features of a concept in order to avoid overextension and underextension (Murphy 2002). Prototype theory emphasizes that prototypes are crucial for categorization (Gelman 2006). Robins are more prototypical for the category 'birds' than ostriches, while an apple appears to belong to the category 'fruit' rather more than a pear (Taylor 2004). In language acquisition, prototypes are relevant for conceptual development and the acquisition of lexical knowledge. Hence, we argue that the illustrators have most probably considered what objects should represent a prototype for the child. An overview of the typical objects recurring in early-concept books gives some evidence that the illustrators intend to provide conceptual information that is relevant for young children. Of prime interest are therefore objects in the child's immediate surroundings: toys, animals, food, and clothes, among other things.

Jointly looking at early-concept books is a different learning process, since it is determined by explicit instructions by the caretakers. A typical situation consists in a pointing and naming game: the adult points to the picture and simultaneously asks the child what the picture shows, expecting to get the correct answer. If the child gives the wrong answer, the adult may correct her. This observation is in line with case studies in language acquisition and literacy studies that show that looking at these picturebooks with a caregiver supports the young child's lexical acquisition (Dromi 1987; Larson and Marsh 2014).

The process of understanding the picture-word relationship in early-concept books is quite complex. Figure 3 shows the relevant aspects of the word 'apple' in relation to conceptual development and how images may enhance the acquisition of mental pictures.

Children know a word when they have acquired a consistent mapping between form and concept, which is called a lexeme (that is, an element that is permanently stored in the child's mental lexicon). A concept is a set of properties of a lexeme that enables the reference to a referent, for instance, a specific apple. Part of the concept APPLE is that it can be eaten, is a fruit, is round, grows

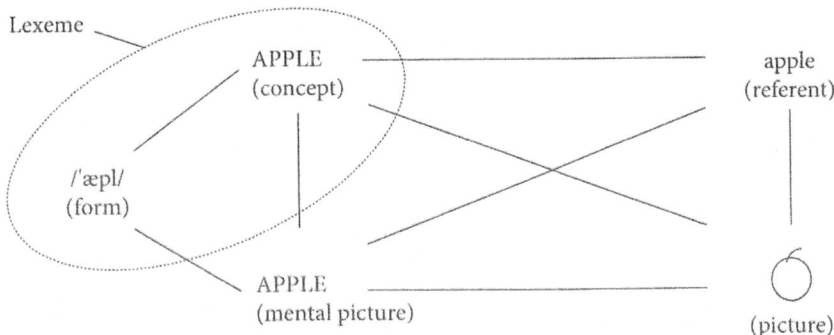

Figure 15.3 Relevant aspects of the lexeme apple.
© Bettina Kümmerling-Meibauer and Jörg Meibauer.

on trees, has a stem, and is red, green, or yellow. Pictures are two-dimensional visual representations of referents. Another significant step in the child's early cognitive development is the ability to create mental pictures, that is, a mental pictorial representation (Damasio 2001). Knowledge of a concept and knowledge of a mental picture are independent of each other, since it is possible to have a mental picture without the knowledge of a referent (for example, the unicorn) as well as to acquire conceptual knowledge without pictorial knowledge (for instance, when children have not seen pictures of referents yet). Nevertheless, both domains impact on each other. This observation evidently demonstrates that early literacy cannot be restricted to one domain but has to consider the connection between two or more domains.

Consequently, we assume that children may learn something by looking at early-concept books: First, they are introduced to the so-called rules of book behavior (Lewis 2001: 78), that is, sitting still, holding the book in the correct position, turning the pages, and attentively looking at the images. Second, they are gradually accustomed to visual codes, thus fostering their visual literacy. Third, they learn new words as well as develop a consistent mapping between the prototypical features of a concept and its referent. Finally, the pointing and naming game and the adult's possibility to invent short narratives related to the depicted objects are a seminal step in the acquisition of literary literacy and prepare the young child for listening to picturebook stories read aloud (Kümmerling-Meibauer and Meibauer 2011).

Early-concept books depicting different word categories

A step ahead are those early-concept books that show on each doublespread an object on one side and an activity that could be done with the object on the other, as shown in Helen Oxenbury's popular board books, such as *Playing* (1981) and *Working* (1981). These books most often depict a character – either a child or an animal – that is busying itself with the object, for instance, throwing a ball into the air, eating a slice of bread, cuddling a doll, or looking intensively at a picturebook.

Besides nouns and verbs, children between twelve and eighteen months of age already know other word categories as well, for instance, adjectives, deictic expressions, pronouns, personal-social words, and onomatopoetic words. These categories, as well as abstract concepts such as 'love' are not easy to depict. Nevertheless, since the 1970s early-concept books focusing on these word categories have captured the book market. In Vladimir Radunsky's *square, triangle, round, skinny* (2002), the properties are arranged in accordance with the contrast principle of antonyms and illustrated by objects that present the respective properties. Onomatopoetic words expressed by noises turn up in Soledad Bravi's *Le livre des bruits* (The Book of Noises 2004), while Annette Langen's *Noch mal! Meine ersten*

Lieblingswörter (Once Again! My First Favorite Words 2012) has a mixture of deictic expressions, verbs, salutations, adverbs, and onomatopoetic words. In order to visualize these word categories, the presence of objects is essential. Activities, properties, and noises are generally depicted with respect to objects, since it is quite impossible to depict them as such. Although the majority of words presented in these early-concept books still belong to the child's early lexicon, these books have a transitional effect, since they prepare children for more complex book types.

Concept books

In contrast to early-concept books, which display objects from different conceptual domains, concept books go a step further in that they depict objects that belong to the same conceptual domain or class, for instance, animals, vehicles, and toys. Typical examples of this book type are Chez Picthall's *Baby Sees Farm Animals* (2008) and Helmut Spanner's *Mein Spielzeug* (My Playthings 1979). There are even concept books that display abstract concepts, such as colors, shapes, letters, and numbers. Tana Hoban's *Shapes, Shapes, Shapes* (1986), Bruno Munari's *ABC* (1960), and Keith Haring's *Ten* (1998) are prominent examples. Like early-concept books, concept books usually do not contain any text; sometimes single words denote the objects or the objects' features. Concept books show objects that refer to nominal concepts, but in comparison to early-concept books these concepts mostly do not belong to the child's early lexicon. They are usually acquired later, when children are approximately eighteen to twenty-four months of age and even older. While most children have a repertoire of fifty words by the age of eighteen months, the lexicon seems to 'explode' after that age. Then children acquire new words on a daily basis, which enlarges their knowledge about concepts at an astonishing pace.

Concept books support children's ability to categorize objects, but also properties and activities, according to conceptual domains, which is a crucial precondition for the capacity to store a bigger lexicon in the brain as well as for the facility to see the connections between individual objects which belong to the same or a different domain (Carey 1985). Thus, children may learn that a ball belongs to the conceptual domain of 'toys,' like a doll, a teddy bear, a pull toy, building blocks, or a board game. Moreover, children may also be introduced to a hierarchy of conceptual domains: an apple belongs to the general conceptual domain of 'food' as well as the particular conceptual domain of 'fruit.' In this regard, one might also distinguish between fruits that grow on trees, bushes, or near the ground. By this, children are enabled to quickly categorize things, thus establishing a network of categories and conceptual domains. Acquisition of conceptual domains not only expands the child's lexicon, but also supports the understanding of coherence, that is, the coordination of objects that belong to the same conceptual domain (Rakison and Oakes 2003). Some concept books even have commonalities with picture dictionaries as they show several objects on a page with labels printed below or beside the depicted objects. Picture dictionaries, however, present a transition from concept books to more complex picturebooks which introduce children to further linguistic and cognitive aspects, such as scripts and frames.

Picturebook spurt: scripts, frames, and early narratives

When children outgrow early-concept books and concept books, they are offered an increasing variety of different book types, ranging from picturebooks depicting scenes, I Spy books, and wimmelbooks (Rémi 2011) to descriptive picturebooks with a short text (Meibauer 2015). Just as studies in language acquisition emphasize children's vocabulary spurt from the age of twenty-four months onwards, a picturebook spurt is recognizable as well, since children from the age of two years onwards encounter an increasing range of topics, themes, genres, and styles. Picturebook artists create book types that serve diverse purposes at the same time. They may encourage a question-and-answer dialogue, stimulate a pointing and naming game, invite the child to search for hidden things, support the comprehension of deixis and speech acts, and introduce children to basic poetic features, such as rhyme and rhythm. Nevertheless, these picturebooks, which usually do not tell an elaborate story or any story at all, still focus on the depiction of concepts and conceptual domains.

One prominent picturebook type is those books which depict simple scenes, such as going shopping, gardening, and playing in the kindergarten. Most often these books are a combination of scenes with single items from the scenes depicted on the opposite page, as in Paul Stickland's *A Child's Book of Things* (1990). This book type engages the child in two activities: naming and describing the objects and activities represented in the scene as well as searching for the individual items displayed on the opposite page. The child is encouraged to attentively look at a complex image that connects objects belonging to one or two conceptual domain(s). Thus, the child becomes accustomed to 'descriptive frames,' which interact with the category of conceptual domains by putting these into a broader context.

Picturebooks that focus on 'scripts,' however, show detailed pictures of people and objects that are in the same location or setting, such as a kindergarten, a farmyard, or a train station. Most often, these picturebooks contain texts that describe the main events discernible in the illustrations. This book type fosters the ability to categorize, that is, the mapping of a conceptual domain to a frame (Jones 1996). Moreover, these picturebooks have some commonalities with concept books and picturebooks focusing on frames: viewers can look at each page or doublespread on its own, since the text usually does not build up a connection to the previous or subsequent pages. The overarching frame, however, connects the images, thus constituting a sequence of images.

More complex are those picturebooks that focus on 'narrative scripts,' such as train rides, doctor's visits, or birthday parties. These picturebooks also emphasize the significance of conceptual domains, but the text-picture relationship is more complex. This book type combines different conceptual issues, namely categorization, coherence, and cohesion, which concern the visual as well as the linguistic level. The essential cohesive features are pageturners and recurring visual aspects, such as characters and objects that turn up on every doublespread, thus enticing the viewer to page forward and backward in order to discover the repeating visual cues (Gressnich 2012). This procedure is supported by recurrent linguistic items, such as deictic references and anaphor, as well as by *wh*-questions and direct speech which compel the reader to turn the page.

The presented book types have two common features: they focus on objects and on what can be done with these objects. The latter requires the incorporation of characters. This crucial trait highlights that these book types belong to the category of 'nonfiction picturebook,' since they familiarize young children with real objects, the properties of objects, the correct handling of objects, and in which way these objects are related to everyday settings as well as frames and scripts. Although these picturebooks seem to be simple at first glance, they play a crucial role in the child's cognitive development, because they gradually accustom the child to more complex nonfiction books as well as to fictional picturebook stories (see Kümmerling-Meibauer and Meibauer 2015 for an elaborated overview of this fundamental issue).

The underlying question of how children manage the transition from concept books and picturebooks focusing on scripts and frames to narratives, which are a core feature of fictional picturebooks, has not yet been fully investigated and demands cooperative efforts of picturebook researchers, cognitive psychologists, linguists, and scholars working in the realm of literacy studies.

References

Apseloff, Mary (1987) "Books for Babies: Learning Toys or Pre-literature?" *Children's Literature Association Quarterly* 12: 63–66.

Barrett, Martyn (1995) "Early Lexical Development," in Paul Fletcher and Brian MacWhinney (eds) *The Handbook of Child Language*, Oxford: Blackwell, 362–292.

Bertuch, Friedrich Justin (1790–1830) *Bilderbuch für Kinder*, Weimar: Verlag des Industrie-Comptoirs.

Bloom, Harold (2000) *How Children Learn the Meaning of Words*, Cambridge, MA: MIT Press.

Bravi, Soledad (2004) *Le livre des bruits*, Paris: L'école des loisirs.

Bruna, Dick (1973) *Erste Bilder*, Ravensburg: Ravensburger Buchverlag.

Carey, Susan (1985) *Conceptual Change in Childhood*, Cambridge, MA: MIT Press.

Clark, Eve (1993) *The Lexicon in Acquisition*, Cambridge: Cambridge University Press.

Comenius, Johann Amos (1658) *Orbis Sensualium Pictus*, Nuremberg: Michael Endter.

Damasio, Hanna (2001) "Words and Concepts in the Brain," in Joao Branquinho (ed.) *The Foundations of Cognitive Science*, Oxford: Clarendon Press, 109–120.

Dromi, Esther (1987) *Early Lexical Development*, Cambridge: Cambridge University Press.

Gelman, Susan A. (2006) "Early Conceptual Development," in Kathleen McCartney and Deborah Philipps (eds) *Blackwell Handbook of Early Childhood Development*, Oxford: Blackwell, 149–167.

Gressnich, Eva (2012) "Verbal and Visual Pageturners in Picturebooks," *International Research in Children's Literature* 5.2: 167–183.

Haring, Keith (1998) *Ten*, New York: Hyperion Books.

Hoban, Tana (1986) *Shapes, Shapes, Shapes*, New York: Greenwillow.

Jones, Rhian (1996) *Emergent Patterns of Literacy: A Multidisciplinary Perspective*, London: Routledge.

Kress, Gunther, and van Leeuwen, Theo (1996) *Reading Images: The Grammar of Visual Design*, London: Routledge.

Kümmerling-Meibauer, Bettina (ed.) (2011) *Emergent Literacy: Children's Books from 0 to 3*, Amsterdam: John Benjamins.

Kümmerling-Meibauer, Bettina, and Linsmann, Maria (eds) (2009) *Literatur im Laufstall: Bilderbücher für die ganz Kleinen*, Troisdorf: Bilderbuchmuseum Burg Wissem.

Kümmerling-Meibauer, Bettina, and Meibauer, Jörg (2005) "First Pictures, Early Concepts: Early Concept Books," *The Lion and the Unicorn* 29: 234–347.

Kümmerling-Meibauer, Bettina, and Meibauer, Jörg (2011) "Early-concept Books: Acquiring Nominal and Verbal Concepts," in Bettina Kümmerling-Meibauer (ed.) *Emergent Literacy: Children's Books from 0 to 3*, Amsterdam: John Benjamins, 9–114.

Kümmerling-Meibauer, Bettina, and Meibauer, Jörg (2015) "Picturebooks and Early Literacy. How Do Picturebooks Support Early Conceptual and Narrative Development?" in Bettina Kümmerling-Meibauer, Jörg Meibauer, Kerstin Nachtigäller, and Katharina Rohlfing (eds) *Learning from Picturebooks: Perspectives from Child Development and Literacy Studies*, New York: Routledge, 13–32.

Kümmerling-Meibauer, Bettina, Meibauer, Jörg, Nachtigäller, Kerstin, and Rohlfing, Katharina (eds) (2015) *Learning from Picturebooks: Perspectives from Child Development and Literacy Studies*, New York: Routledge.

Langen, Annette (2012) *Noch mal! Meine ersten Lieblingswörter*, illus. Sabine Kraushaar, Münster: Coppenrath.

Larson, Joanne, and Marsh, Jackie (eds) (2014) *The Sage Handbook of Early Childhood Literacy*, London: Sage.

Lewis, David (2001) *Reading Contemporary Picturebooks: Picturing Text*, London: RoutledgeFalmer.

Meibauer, Jörg (2015) "What the Child Can Learn From Simple Descriptive Picturebooks. An Inquiry Into *Lastwagen/Trucks* by Paul Stickland," in Bettina Kümmerling-Meibauer, Jörg Meibauer, Kerstin Nachtigäller, and Katharina Rohlfing (eds) *Learning from Picturebooks: Perspectives from Child Development and Literacy Studies*, New York: Routledge, 51–70.

Munari, Bruno (1960) *ABC*, San Francisco, CA: Chronicle Books.

Murphy, Gregory L. (2002) *The Big Book of Concepts*, Cambridge, MA: MIT Press.

Nikolajeva, Maria (2003) "Verbal and Visual Literacy. The Role of Picturebooks in the Reading Experience of Young Children," in Nigel Hall, Judith Larson, and Jackie Marsh (eds) *Handbook of Early Childhood Literacy*, London: Sage, 235–248.

Nodelman, Perry (1988) *Words about Pictures: The Narrative Art of Children's Picture Books*, Athens: University of Georgia Press.

Oxenbury, Helen (1981) *Playing*, London: Walker Books.

Oxenbury, Helen (1981) *Working*, London: Walker Books.

Picthall, Chez (2008) *Baby Sees Farm Animals*, Bromley: Picthall & Gunzi.

Radunsky, Vladimir (2002) *square, triangle, round, skinny*, Cambridge, MA: Candlewick Press.

Rakison, Henry, and Oakes, Lisa M. (eds) (2003) *Early Category and Concept Development: Making Sense of the Blooming, Buzzing Confusion*, New York: Oxford University Press.

Rémi, Cornelia (2011) "Reading as Playing: The Cognitive Challenge of the Wimmelbook," in Bettina Kümmerling-Meibauer (ed.) *Emergent Literacy: Children's Books from 0 to 3*, Amsterdam: John Benjamins, 115–140.

Retzlaff, Erich (1949) *Das erste Bilderbuch*, Frankfurt: Wolfgang Metzner Verlag.

Spanner, Helmut (1979) *Mein Spielzeug*, Ravensburg: Otto Maier.

Steichen Calderone, Mary (1930) *The First Picture Book: Everyday Things for Babies*, photos by Edward Steichen, New York: Harcourt, Brace.

Steichen Martin, Mary (1931) *The Second Picture Book*, photos by Edward Steichen, New York: Harcourt, Brace.

Stickland, Paul (1990) *A Child's Book of Things*, Yeovil: Matthew Price.

Taylor, John R. (2004) *Linguistic Categorization: Prototypes in Linguistics*, Oxford: Oxford University Press.

Thomas, Glyn V., Nye, Rebecca, Rowley, Martin, and Robinson, Elisabeth (2001) "What Is a Picture? Children's Conceptions of Pictures," *British Journal of Developmental Psychology* 19: 475–491.

Werner, Annette (2011) "Color Perception in Infants and Young Children: The Significance of Color in Picture-books," in Bettina Kümmerling-Meibauer (ed.) *Emergent Literacy: Children's Books from 0 to 3*, Amsterdam: John Benjamins, 39–53.

16

WIMMELBOOKS

Cornelia Rémi

Terminology

The term 'wimmelbook' is an English adaptation of the German *Wimmelbuch*, which has become a household name for a specific type of non-directive wordless picturebook. It suggests an experience of dynamic wealth and a somewhat messy overabundance of visual material as central features of this book type, since the German verb *wimmeln* translates as 'to teem' or 'to swarm.' In the early 2000s the expression firmly established itself as a generic paratext in book titles, popularized particularly by Rotraut Susanne Berner's wimmelbook series (2003–2008). Before Berner's success it was mostly used as an informal reference in reviews, at bookshops, or at libraries.

However, the book type itself predates this canonization of the generic term by several decades. In 1968 graphic artist and painter Ali Mitgutsch published *Rundherum in meiner Stadt* (All Around My City), which was to become the prototype of the wimmelbook genre (Palluch 1998: 6–8; Schröder and Weber 2005). The book project was initiated by educator Kurt Seelmann, then head of Munich's Department of Youth Services, who had asked Mitgutsch to draw complex scenes from urban life. He hoped that they might prompt children to engage intensely with their baffling visual wealth and – in the spirit of progressive pedagogy – empower them to communicate about their perceptions with equally baffled adult beholders.

The expression *Wimmelbuch* derives from the older term *Wimmelbild* (busy picture), which refers to a single sheet filled with 'teeming' graphics rather than to an entire book. It appears to have been introduced to academic and critical discourse in the 1950s by German art historian Franz Roh, who used it to characterize both contemporary and early modern works of art, such as some paintings of the 'Zen 49' group or the famous painting *The Proverbs* (1559) by Pieter Bruegel the Elder (Roh 1955/56, 1960: 4, 26). A wimmelbook is an (often) uncommented collection of stylistically uniform wimmelpictures united by a specific programmatic idea (Rémi 2011).

Characteristics of the genre prototype

The idea of 'teeming' refers to the visual copiousness of the images in a wimmelbook. Each doublespread presents a detailed panoramic landscape which encloses several minor scenes, richly populated by dozens of characters (sometimes more than a hundred), engaged in simultaneous inter-actions and often subtly connected to each other. Almost no part of the panorama remains free of characters, so that they rather than the landscape or buildings surrounding them draw the eye of the beholder and dominate the visual impression. In addition, recurring objects, such as cars, animals, houses, and trees, attract the attention of children. To give these details enough space to unfold, such books are usually printed in large formats, often on sturdy cardboard, which makes them robust enough to be handled already by very young children. Most wimmelbooks focus on everyday scenes, often familiar and recognizable to young readers from their own immediate experience or as stock scenes from other picturebooks, with characters portrayed large enough to keep their facial expressions clearly visible and legible.

In wimmelbooks of the first generation, each doublespread forms a separate unit with a unique cast of such characters. There are usually no recurring scenes, characters, or overarching story lines, so that the spreads appear only loosely connected through a common topic, usually a certain spatial setting (in the town, in the mountains, at the seaside). Since the beginning of the twenty-first century this basic concept has been varied and expanded in different ways, particularly relating to their spatial and narrative coherence, which demonstrates the impact of postmodern concepts in picturebooks (Allan 2012; Van Meerbergen 2012; Kümmerling-Meibauer 2015).

Wimmelbooks offer a rich amount of material, which their readers can explore in many different ways. Their visual overabundance resembles the graphic style of search, game, or puzzle books, like Martin Handford's *Where's Wally?* series (1987ff.), but unlike these books wimmelbooks most often do not confront their readers with explicit search tasks (Rémi 2011). They actually tend to contain no verbal elements at all inside their covers, apart from a few words on street or shop signs. Occasionally their back cover might highlight a selection of possible focus objects, but it presents them as suggestions for a first exploration of the images rather than as imperative targets, because wimmelbooks lack a clear hierarchy, unlike search books of the *Wally* type. The images in search books are usually designed around the search objects as their hidden centers and are therefore full of somewhat repetitive visual distractors to divert the reader's attention, as in Hans Jürgen Press's *Die Abenteuer der "schwarzen Hand"* (The Adventures of the "Black Hand" 2008), while the characters in wimmelbooks tend to appear all equally interesting.

The typical perspective of wimmelpictures enhances this impression, because it combines elements of both distance and proximity (Palluch 1998: 4). On the one hand, it evokes a bird's-eye view from a highly elevated vantage point, with little or no visible horizon and spatial depth, so that the scenery appears vast and impossible to scrutinize at a glance. On the other hand, the characters are not shown from above, but seen at eye-level from the front or the side. Since the visual elements are arranged in a paratactic pattern and distributed planarly across the page rather than presented in central perspective, all scenes appear to be equally important. This perspective offers a privileged overview, superior to the point of view of any of the characters, and also challenges the viewer to develop a coherent understanding of all the details.

Another characteristic feature that points to such hidden layers of meaning is the occasional use of cross sections, which echoes the aesthetics of an open-front dollhouse and grants the beholder views into the otherwise inaccessible interiors of some houses. Since all or most of the characters appear to be of equal size, wimmelbooks direct the beholder's gaze only little. Their images lack a clearly defined center and indicate next to no visual hierarchy, so that the decision about what to look at and think about poses an essential challenge.

The characteristic combination of visual overabundance on the one hand and a lack of explicit reading instructions on the other relates to the cognitive experience of someone who is faced with the challenge of coping with a new situation. This might happen by breaking the complex whole into manageable subunits, understanding their relations, and developing a language for describing both the observed objects and one's own experiences. For this reason, wimmelbooks demand a particularly high degree of reading activity and support a multitude of possible approaches, which makes them attractive for a broad audience, from small children to primary school children and beyond. Wimmelbooks may therefore serve as a 'bridge genre' with the potential to accompany learners through different stages of their cognitive and linguistic development (Rémi 2011: 116).

Precursors: traditions of busy pictures in Western art

Mitgutsch's concept of teeming pictures is far from unprecedented: there is a long tradition of similar compositions in the history of Western art, which resemble wimmelpictures both in their structure and in the modes of expected response connected with them. Many large-format pictures that show a huge number of characters without a dominant central scene have 'wimmel' qualities, among them representations of battles and religious or secular ceremonies in paintings and illustrated broadsheets. Similar structures occur in intricate altarpieces, which may unite entire sequences of episodes from legends or biblical tales to provide worshippers with a wealth of material for intense pious contemplation. This supports the worshippers in developing vivid mental models to recollect key lessons of their faith (Silver 2006: 122, 81f.). By documenting key moments of elusive historical or mythical events, these ancestors of modern wimmelpictures give their beholders a chance to test and train a prolonged, intense gaze, and to advance their attention and their analytical and empathic skills.

Particularly noteworthy among the precursors of wimmelpictures are some populous paintings by the early modern Dutch artists Hieronymus Bosch and Pieter Bruegel the Elder. Art historians have characterized both these works and the response to them in terms that qualify them as wimmelpictures: they are brimming with clever details, but lack a clear focal point, so that approaching them is bound to challenge the beholder's hermeneutic creativity (Bonn 2006: 35).

Outside the realm of the fine arts proper the tradition of busy pictures in early modern popular prints and illustrated broadsheets continues in the entertaining prints of the Industrial Era, like the Épinal prints or *Bilderbogen* of the nineteenth century. The links between such commercial prints and the traditions of satirical drawing, caricatures, and cartoons remain evident in satirical search books, as in Daniel Lalic's *Where's Bin Laden* (2006); in books with whimsical cartoon-style busy pictures, for instance in Jean-Jacques Loup's *Patatrac* (1975); and even in some recent geographical wimmelbooks, whose illustrators populate the scene with stylized images of local personalities, as in Tora Marie Norberg's *Æ elske Trondhjæm* (I Love Trondheim 2014) (Figure 16.1).

Figure 16.1 Illustration from Marie Norberg's *Æ elske Trondhjæm*. Oslo: Figenschou, 2014.

Reproduced by permission of Figenschou, Oslo.

Related concepts

Wimmelbooks are related to several other types of picturebooks that stimulate children's visual literacy and empower them to 'read' contents before they actually can decode written words (Kümmerling-Meibauer and Meibauer 2013). Unlike wimmelbooks, these other types of picturebooks combine their images with accompanying verbal clues, which facilitate the readers' initial approach to the pictures, but articulate only minor aspects of the visual material. The texts may serve as first access points for the readers, but tend to vanish into insignificance, while the images offer enough material for explorations independent of and far beyond the scope of the printed word.

Prominent examples are Richard Scarry's 'encyclopedic spreads' in *Cars and Trucks and Things That Go* (1974) and search and puzzle books like Sven Nordqvist's *Var är min syster?* (Where Is My Sister? 2007), which rely less on the finding and puzzle-solving than on aesthetic pleasure. In the case of wimmelpictures that have been turned into jigsaw puzzles, the beholder's task of making sense of the picture and finding coherence in it is reflected even in the medium itself, and the solving of the puzzle refers to the entire image rather than to just one of its elements.

The line between wimmelbooks and panoramic books, like Mitsumasa Anno's *Journey* series (1978ff.), is particularly blurry. Both genres share an interest in spatial perception and intricate landscapes, but panoramic books focus on the overall impression and atmosphere of these landscapes rather than on individual characters populating them. Moreover their perspective adds depth to the scenery, so that their panoramas offer a more realistic impression than the usual backdrops of wimmelbooks. However, the recent publishing trend towards geographic wimmelbooks with recognizable real-world settings has begun to narrow the gap between the spatial approach of panoramic books and the character-centered approach of wimmelbooks even further. Tom Schamp's *Otto in de stad* (Otto in the City 2008) for example combines intertextual geography (references to Brussels) and teeming sceneries. Schamp's picturebook actually goes even a step further, as the story unfolds in the right and left margins of the book so that the reader has to turn and twist the doublespreads in different directions in order to reveal the multiple links between the characters and the depicted actions. The term 'loop book' has been coined to describe this new book type (Van Meerbergen 2012, 2013).

Reader response

The unbroken popularity of wimmelbooks is based on the numerous reading approaches they support and the manifold responses they can evoke among their readers (Rémi 2011: 128–130). This versatility connects them to several stages of cognitive and linguistic development (Kümmerling-Meibauer and Meibauer 2015: 28), which makes them attractive for a broader audience than other picturebook types. Due to their wealth of visual elements and their open, non-hierarchical structure they provide a rich reservoir of material for acquiring and training a whole range of literacy skills: perception and attention; patience and persistence; the ability to filter and structure a great amount of visual information, to memorize and combine observations; the analytic competence to question superficial appearance and connect diverse observations; and finally the linguistic and social skills to articulate one's own reading impressions and discuss them with others. The lack of printed text frees the readers from the usual routine of sticking to a default narrative and challenges them to spin the images into tales of their own. Each attempt to understand the visual construction is likely to yield new discoveries, new combinations, and new hermeneutic paths, so that the complex plenitude of the pictures fuels and rewards both persistent contemplation and playful experiments.

Very young children still rely on the prompts of a mature caregiver to guide them through a wimmelbook and encourage active responses from them. Wimmelbooks facilitate these collaborative reading experiences by providing experienced readers with additional incentives, e.g., in the form of visual quotes or allusions to other books (Rémi 2011: 131–133). At the most basic level the reading companions will probably focus on only a few elements in the teeming chaos of the wimmelpicture: child and adult might try to agree upon an object to look at together and establish ways of communicating about it. This may involve identifying and labeling different objects, providing sound effects, or acting out snippets of conversations between the characters.

Such a highly selective approach will gradually broaden when young readers begin to take in more and more details and move from punctual observations to the complex texture and coherence of an entire picture or wimmelbook. Advanced readers will segment the page into single scenes and then speculate about relations within or between them, for instance, by empathizing with different characters or by establishing causes, motivations, and possible outcomes. As soon as they begin considering such causal and temporal relations, they turn the visual cues of the wimmelpicture into stories.

While the concept of wimmelbooks may drive intense collaboration between children and their adult reading companions, it also empowers young readers to emancipate themselves quickly from such guidance, gain full control of the reading situation, and become autonomous authors and storytellers (Berner and Weinkauff 2004: 53; Arizpe 2013: 170), because they do not require a literate reader to grant them access to a printed text. The usual hierarchy between novice and experienced readers may even be leveled or completely reversed, since children often outmatch adults in sifting visual detail (Nikolajeva and Scott 2001: 261).

Variations and developments

Since Ali Mitgutsch published his first wimmelbook in 1968, the genre has expanded and varied its themes, structure, and mediality, with a noticeable increase in significant innovations since the beginning of the twenty-first century. Many of these recent developments can be interpreted as attempts to adjust the structure of wimmelbooks in a way that reflects key responses of their readers, such as the urge to perceive the book as a whole rather than as an arbitrary sequence of separate wimmelpictures, to relate its content to real locations, to spin stories out of the pictures, and to approach them from different characters' points of view. These strategies can be clearly connected to postmodern developments in picturebooks (Allan 2012).

Thematic expansion

While Mitgutsch's early wimmelbooks show predominantly realistic scenes from the world of contemporary Western culture, some recent publications embrace historical locations or introduce characters that expand the fictional setting to the realm of pure fantasy, for instance, anthropomorphic animals in Thé Tjong-Khing's *Waar is de taart?* (Where Is the Cake? 2004) or other fantastic creatures, as they appear in Judith Drews's *Berlin Wimmelbuch* (Berlin Wimmelbook 2010). Visual quotes that evoke well-known myths and legends may even dominate some wimmelbooks to a degree that lends them an encyclopedic character and turns their panoramas into memory palaces. This mnemonic purpose is evident for instance in wimmelbooks compiling biblical stories, as in Stefanie Rausch's *Das Bibel-Wimmelbuch* (The Bible Wimmelbook 2005), or populating specific geographic locations with characters from local folklore, as in Andreas Ganther's *Romantischer Rhein* (Romantic Rhine 2008).

Spatial expansion

A number of authors have varied the spatial structure of wimmelbooks regarding their perspective construction, the connections between the doublespreads, and even their material design. While Mitgutsch's pictures present all objects at an equal distance from the beholder, other artists add depth to their images by lowering their point of view, introducing several layers of foreground and background and scaling their elements accordingly, which is a predominant feature of Berner's Wimmlingen books (2003–2008), or by framing the scene with a prominent layer of objects seen at close range, like the branches of a tree, as done in Oliver Regener's *Wir reisen durch das ganze Land* (We Travel through the Whole Country 2008). The illusion of depth may also be evoked by a book's material design. In *Wo ist die goldene Krone? Mein großes Wimmel-Guckloch-Buch* (Where Is the Golden Crown? My Big Wimmel-Peephole-Book, 2009), Ulla Bartl equips her wimmelbook with peepholes that allow the reader to see objects from the preceding or following doublespread in different contexts and to reframe their meaning.

While this depth draws the beholder into the picture and suggests delving into its riches, another innovation has more far-reaching conceptual consequences: artists affirm the coherence of entire wimmelbooks by furnishing them with continuous backdrops that connect all doublespreads. This turns the book into one giant stage, along which the reader moves horizontally, as in Stephan Baumann's *Das große Wimmelbilderbuch. Durch Stadt und Land* (The Big Wimmelpicturebook. Through Town and Countryside 2000), or vertically, as in Bernd Lehmann's *Von Oben nach Unten Wimmelbuch* (From Top to Bottom Wimmelbook, 2011).

Josh Cochran's *New York* (2014), a hybrid of wimmelbook and panoramic book, further advances this connection between the spatiality of the book's subject on the one hand and its material design on the other hand. Cochran uses the form of a concertina book that unfolds into a seamless panorama and directs the beholder's gaze through the streets of New York in one long pan shot. This visual path, however, is presented in two versions, one on each side of the cardboard chart. Flipping the chart over corresponds to a literal look behind the scenes, since the back version of the panorama peels away the superficial outer layers of the city and presents its buildings, statues, and even some characters in cross section, revealing their hidden interiors.

Factualization and localization

Since Cochran's *New York* focuses on the local identity of one specific city, it represents even another trend: geographic wimmelbooks claim to depict not arbitrary fictitious landscapes, but real locations. While Mitgutsch still embeds such snippets of reality in the texture of an altogether fictional setting – for instance, impressions from Munich's Englischer Garten in Mitgutsch's *Mein Wimmel-Bilderbuch. Frühling, Sommer, Herbst und Winter* (My Wimmelpicturebook. Spring, Summer, Autumn and Winter 2007) (Figure 16.2) – several German and Austrian publishing houses began launching decidedly geographic wimmelbooks from 2007 onwards, a trend that since has spread even to Scandinavia. One of the many examples is Judith Drews's *Stockholm Vimmelboken* (Stockholm Wimmelbook 2013). Bachem's publishing house in Cologne is responsible for the bulk of this output, with dozens of titles dedicated not only to entire cities or areas, but also to more specific locations like different zoological gardens, hospitals, museums, and even theme parks. They are marketed as gifts that represent their subject area, as visual city guides and souvenirs of popular tourist destinations, but may even support children in coping with complex and confusing situations, particularly in the case of the hospital books.

Authors of such geographic wimmelbooks face special challenges: not only do they need to study their subject areas in detail before portraying them, but their artistic freedom is also severely limited, since they need to accommodate a sufficient number of familiar landmarks and keep them recognizable. Since geographic wimmelbooks need to compromise between documentation and artistic invention, they may grant insights into the construction of cultural spaces, identities, and stereotypes. The spaces portrayed in these books can be interpreted as representatives of both their real-world templates and the mental models that govern the perception and cognitive construction of these spaces.

Narrative expansion

The merging of isolated wimmelpictures into a continuous landscape points to a key need of their readers: the need to connect seemingly disparate observations into a coherent whole. Storytelling is one of the most efficient techniques for building such meaningful connections. Several wimmelbook

Figure 16.2 Illustration from Ali Mitgutsch's *Mein Wimmel-Bilderbuch. Frühling, Sommer, Herbst und Winter.* Ravensburg: Ravensburger, 2007.

(c) 2007 by Ravensburger Buchverlag Otto Maier GmbH, Ravensburg.

authors have embraced this by anticipating their readers' narrative activity and designing their doublespreads as a narrative sequence of events, linked by recurring characters and identical locations or a continuous backdrop (Berner and Weinkauff 2004: 52f.; Jacoby 2008). While these spatial markers indicate continuity, the page breaks serve as temporal markers that catapult the action forwards to the following snapshot in the sequence.

In some books the narrative connections may remain loose and discrete, because only few characters or minor visual clues connect the double spreads. Regener's *Wir reisen durch das ganze Land* (We Travel through the Whole Country 2008), for example, has a wedding party release a cluster of balloons early on in the book, which then float through all the following doublespreads. The narrative profile of a wimmelbook emerges more clearly once a larger cast of characters remains present throughout the book, engaged in a series of connected events, which may constitute an entire bundle of multiple, densely connected story lines that intersect and influence each other in an intricate mesh of causal chains (Rémi 2011: 123–128). Since these plot threads can be explored on many different reading paths, narrative wimmelbooks reward multiple rereadings even more than ordinary ones. By leafing back and forth or jumping between subplots and different focus characters, the recipient may even build a rhizomatic reading structure all across a book. Readers face the challenge of filling the temporal gaps between the doublespreads, which becomes particularly demanding in books with a large number of characters that change their positions unpredictably, move from the foreground to the background (or vice versa), and seem to dance across the pages.

Rotraut Susanne Berner has taken the complexity one step further in her five wimmelbooks, published between 2003 and 2008. Each follows the same route through the town of Wimmlingen and chronicles the activities of its inhabitants during one hour (Figure 16.3). Since the sequence

Figure 16.3 Illustration from Rotraut Susanne Berner's *Herbst-Wimmelbuch*. Hildesheim: Gerstenberg, 2008. Reprinted by permission of Gerstenberg.

of locations remains identical throughout the series, Berner's wimmelpictures are connected both horizontally within each book and vertically between the books, so that not only the characters, but even the entire town is provided with a story of its own (Berthold 2014).

While Berner's books move along their scenery in fairly straight lines, as if the beholders were walking along a lengthy stage, Doro Göbel and Peter Knorr's *Unser Zuhause. Eine Wimmelbilder-Geschichte* (Our Home. A Wimmelpicture Story 2015) combines narrative and spatial complexity in their attempt to follow the events in the microcosm of a residential neighborhood. They have the beholder orbiting a group of houses that surrounds a central lawn, with the house in the foreground of each doublespread presented in cross section. Since the vantage point keeps changing from doublespread to doublespread, each of the houses is presented from a multitude of different angles. This elaborate construction demonstrates the value of approaching one world sample in different ways, which helps to understand and appreciate its complexity.

Medial expansions

These transformations of the genre have affected even the medial profile and environment of wimmelbooks. Jan von Holleben's *Konrad Wimmel ist da!* (Konrad Wimmel Is Here 2015) blurs the line between fictional storytelling and reality by using the seemingly realistic medium of photography (Figure 16.4). His wimmelpictures are monumental montages, composed of photos showing children arranged in 'sideways scenes' on the floor. By turning everyday household objects into spectacular props and decorations, von Holleben anticipates how a wimmelbook might inspire children to transform even their real-world experiences by means of their creative imagination: some shoes, chairs, tennis rackets, and coffee mugs may turn into a fire-breathing dragon. Depending on the preferences of the reader, it is therefore perfectly possible to focus on two different levels of reality in von

Figure 16.4 Illustration from Jan von Holleben's *Konrad Wimmel ist da!* Stuttgart: Gabriel, 2015.

Reprinted by permission of Gabriel/Thienemann-Esslinger Verlag, Stuttgart.

Holleben's wimmelbook: either on the illusions evoked by the creative use of props or on the process of playing itself, which creates this make-believe world.

Spin-off products to both Berner's and Thé's wimmelbook series exploit their narrative potential. In each volume of her pocket-sized Wimmlingen chronicles (*Wimmlinger Geschichten*), Berner presents the background story of a character from the main series in rhyming couplets, as in *Petra* (2009). The spin-off to Thé's series even leaves the realm of books completely. In 2012 a Dutch company produced a cross-media adaptation of his second Cake book (*Picknick met taart* 2005), consisting of an animated TV series and an interactive online 'storyworld.' Each episode of the TV series tells the story from a different character's individual point of view, while the website offers the additional option of jumping between focus characters. The spin-off products act out exemplary approaches to the books' storyworlds and provide their audiences with additional information about selected characters, which may enrich individual wimmelbook readings and inspire the readers to grapple with different characters. By imitating reading strategies familiar to experienced book readers, this adaptation of Thé's story may inspire the less experienced to use similar approaches with other books.

Multidisciplinary perspectives

Apart from studies into wordless picturebooks in general (Arizpe 2013), academic research has not discussed wimmelbooks profusely so far, although they might make worthwhile subjects of study for several disciplines. Scholars working in the realm of the humanities might analyze their composition and artistic quality (Rémi 2011; Van Meerbergen 2012), influences, and historical contexts, investigate their epistemic relevance, and ask for possible parallels in other artistic domains. Cognitive scientists and psycholinguists have used busy pictures from search books as stimuli to study how test subjects filter and process visual information (Clarke, Elsner and Rohde 2013). The even more complex texture of wimmelbooks might be used for further research into our strategies for handling clusters of information. Social scientists and educators mention wimmelbooks as training tools in the contexts of linguistic and cognitive development, language acquisition, and literacy promotion (Rau 2007: 176), but also as diagnostic instruments for assessing a child's developmental status (Demirkaya and Gültekin 2008: 70). Their use in language therapy and didactic interventions for children with special needs might reward further studies.

Two complementary attitudes may clash in academic discussions on wimmelbooks: the pragmatic view of educational researchers, who consider them as tools for achieving specific developmental goals, and the aesthetic view of literature scholars, who see them as complex artistic objects, designed to engage their readers and bring them pleasure (Arizpe 2013: 164–168). Both views are not mutually exclusive, however, if one manages to understand the connections between the two aspects. This becomes apparent in critical objections against some recent wimmelbook publications which weaken the free, unregulated, and open gaze that constitutes this book type by toning down wild plenitude in favor of conventional story lines and narrowing search tasks.

While this criticism is obviously directed at search books marketed with wimmelbook titles, its main point remains valid: wimmelbooks *do* help children to learn, but they do this by granting them maximum freedom, not by subjecting themselves to a specific pedagogical agenda. They expose their readers to a challenging model world that imitates our complex reality and offer them the chance to develop their own strategy for coping with this world, fueled by the joy of exploring and playing with it. To interpret the act of reading a wimmelbook as free play or as exploring a "semiotic playground" (Van Meerbergen 2012) reconciles aesthetic and pragmatic aspects, the motivating power of sheer aesthetic pleasure and the didactic benefits of an advanced cognitive training (Rémi 2011: 133f.).

References

Allan, Cherie (2012) *Playing with Picturebooks: Postmodernism and the Postmodernesque*, Basingstoke: Palgrave Macmillan.

Anno, Mitsumasa (1978) *Anno's Journey*, London: Bodley Head.

Arizpe, Evelyn (2013) "Meaning-Making from Wordless (or Nearly Wordless) Picturebooks: What Educational Research Expects and What Readers Have to Say," *Cambridge Journal of Education* 43.2: 163–176.

Bartl, Ulla (2009) *Wo ist die goldene Krone? Mein großes Wimmel-Gucklock-Buch*, Bindlach: Loewe.

Baumann, Stephan (2000) *Das große Wimmelbilderbuch: Durch Stadt und Land*, Würzburg: Arena.

Berner, Rotraut Susanne (2003) *Winter-Wimmelbuch*, Hildesheim: Gerstenberg.

Berner, Rotraut Susanne (2004) *Frühlings-Wimmelbuch*, Hildesheim: Gerstenberg.

Berner, Rotraut Susanne (2005) *Sommer-Wimmelbuch*, Hildesheim: Gerstenberg.

Berner, Rotraut Susanne (2005) *Herbst-Wimmelbuch*, Hildesheim: Gerstenberg [*In the Town All Year 'Round*, New York: Chronicle, 2008 – this book includes all the books by Berner about the four seasons].

Berner, Rotraut Susanne (2008) *Nacht-Wimmelbuch*, Hildesheim: Gerstenberg.

Berner, Rotraut Susanne (2009) *Petra*, Hildesheim: Gerstenberg.

Berner, Rotraut Susanne, and Weinkauff, Gina (2004) "Geheimnisse in Bildern und Texten. Kinderliteratur im Gespräch: Zu Gast: Rotraut Susanne Berner," *Lesezeichen: Mitteilungen des Lesezentrums an der Pädagogischen Hochschule Heidelberg* 15: 25–56.

Berthold, Sabine Maria (2014) "Aesthetics of Childhood: The Visual Art of Rotraut Susanne Berner," *Bookbird* 52.4: 113–116.

Bonn, Robert L. (2006) *Painting Life: The Art of Pieter Bruegel, the Elder*, New York: Chaucer Press.

Clarke, Alasdair D. F., Elsner, Micha, and Rohde, Hanna (2013) "Where's Wally: The Influence of Visual Salience on Referring Expression Generation," *Frontiers in Psychology* 4.329: 1–10.

Cochran, Josh (2014) *New York*, Dorking: Big Picture Press.

Demirkaya, Sevilen, and Gültekin, Nazan (2008) "Die Begleitstudie der Bielefelder vorschulischen Sprachfördermaßnahme," in Chlosta, Christoph, Leder, Gabriela, and Krischer, Barbara (eds) *Auf neuen Wegen: Deutsch als Fremdsprache in Forschung und Praxis*, Göttingen: Universitätsverlag, 65–82.

Drews, Judith (2010) *Berlin Wimmelbuch*, Berlin: Wimmelbuchverlag.

Drews, Judith (2013) *Stockholm Vimmelboken*, Stockholm: Lilla Piratförlaget.

Ganther, Andreas (2008) *Romantischer Rhein: Rhein – Mosel – Lahn – Nahe*, Köln: Bachem.

Göbel, Doro (2015) *Unser Zuhause: Eine Wimmelbilder-Geschichte*, illus. Peter Knorr, Weinheim: Beltz & Gelberg.

Handford, Martin (1987) *Where's Wally?*, London: Walker.

Holleben, Jan von (2015) *Konrad Wimmel ist da!*, Stuttgart: Gabriel.

Jacoby, Edmund (2008) "Geschichten. Die Erzählerin Rotraut Susanne Berner im Spiegel der wissenschaftlichen Literatur," in Armin Abmeier (ed.) *Alphabet und Zeichenstift: Die Bildwelt von Rotraut Susanne Berner*, Munich: Hanser, 40–49.

Kümmerling-Meibauer, Bettina (2015) "From Baby Books to Picturebooks for Adults: European Picturebooks in the New Millennium," *Word & Image* 31.3: 249–264.

Kümmerling-Meibauer, Bettina, and Meibauer, Jörg (2013) "Towards a Cognitive Theory of Picturebooks," *International Research in Children's Literature* 6.2: 143–160.

Kümmerling-Meibauer, Bettina, and Meibauer, Jörg (2015) "Picturebooks and Early Literacy: How Do Picturebooks Support Early Cognitive and Narrative Development?," in Bettina Kümmerling Meibauer, Jörg Meibauer, Kerstin Nachtigäller, and Katharina Rohlfing (eds) *Learning from Picturebooks: Perspectives from Child Development & Literacy Studies*, New York: Routledge, 13–32.

Lalic, Daniel (2006) *Where's Bin Laden?*, illus. Xavier Waterkeyn, Sydney: New Holland.

Lehmann, Bernd (2011) *Von Oben nach Unten Wimmelbuch*, Berlin: Wimmelbuchverlag.

Loup, Jean-Jacques (1975) *Patatrac*, Paris: Hachette.

Mitgutsch, Ali (1968) *Rundherum in meiner Stadt*, Ravensburg: Otto Maier.

Mitgutsch, Ali (2007) *Mein Wimmel-Bilderbuch: Frühling, Sommer, Herbst und Winter*, Ravensburg: Otto Maier.

Nikolajeva, Maria, and Scott, Carole (2001) *How Picturebooks Work*, New York: Garland.

Norberg, Tora Marie (2014) *Æ elske Trondhjæm*, Oslo: Figenschou.

Nordqvist, Sven (2007) *Var är min syster?*, Bromma: Opal.

Palluch, Andrea (1998) "Ali Mitgutsch," in Kurt Franz, Günter Lange and Franz-Josef Payrhuber (eds) *Kinder- und Jugendliteratur: Ein Lexikon. Teil 2: Illustratoren*, 5th suppl. Feb. 1998, Meitingen: Corian, loose-leaf collection.

Press, Hans Jürgen (2008) *Die Abenteuer der "schwarzen Hand": Detektivgeschichten zum Mitraten*, Ravensburg: Otto Maier (first published 1965).

Rau, Marie Luise (2007) *Literacy: Vom ersten Bilderbuch zum Erzählen, Lesen und Schreiben*, Bern: Haupt.

Rausch, Stefanie (2005) *Das Bibel-Wimmelbuch*, Hamburg: Sankt Ansgar.

Regener, Oliver (2008) *Wir reisen durch das ganze Land: Mein Wimmelbilderbuch*, Munich: cbj.

Rémi, Cornelia (2011) "Reading as Playing: The Cognitive Challenge of the Wimmelbook," in Bettina Kümmerling-Meibauer (ed.) *Emergent Literacy: Children's Books from 0 to 3*, Amsterdam: John Benjamins, 115–139.

Roh, Franz (1955/56) "ZEN 49," *Das Kunstwerk* 9.2: 52.

Roh, Franz (1960) *Pieter Bruegel d. Ä.: Die niederländischen Sprichwörter*, Stuttgart: Reclam.

Scarry, Richard (1974) *Cars and Trucks and Things That Go*, New York: Golden.

Schamp, Tom (2008) *Otto in de stad*, Tielt: Lannoo [*Otto in the City*, Mustang, OK: Tate, 2013].

Schröder, Gabriele, and Weber, Jochen (2005) "Auswahlbibliographie," in Maria Linsmann and Barbara Scharioth (eds) *Ali Mitgutsch: Ein Chronist der Welt im Kleinen*, Troisdorf: Burg Wissem, 30–39.

Silver, Larry (2006) *Hieronymus Bosch*, trans. Ingrid Hacker-Klier, Munich: Hirmer.

Thé Tjong-Khing (2004) *Waar is de taart?*, Tielt: Lannoo.

Thé Thong-Khing (2005) *Picknick met taart*, Tielt: Lannoo.

Van Meerbergen, Sara (2012) "Play, Parody, Intertextuality and Interaction: Postmodern Flemish Picture Books as Semiotic Playgrounds," *BLFT: Nordic Journal of ChildLit Aesthetics* 3. Doi: http://dx.doi.org/10.3402/blft.v3i0.20075.

Van Meerbergen, Sara (2013) "Ola Paola en TobleRhône: Een verkenning van het postmoderne landschap van Tom Schamp," *Literatuur zonder leeftijd* 27.90: 87–102.

17

ABC BOOKS

Marie-Pierre Litaudon

Dictionaries define the abecedary as a book for learning the alphabet and the rudiments of reading (the order and written form of the letters, orthography, and syllabification). But the reality is more complex. Over the centuries, the abecedary has been transformed in terms of its contents, its presentation, its target audience, and its methods of use. Originally devoted to the learning of sacred texts, the abecedary for a long time did without any illustrations. While their introduction was earlier in Protestant than in Catholic countries, images began their remarkable rise in the nineteenth century. Their promotion stems as much from the pedagogical reflection that accompanied the development of literacy as from the progress achieved in the reproduction of images. At the beginning of the twentieth century, following educational reforms, the abecedary ceased to be used as a reading manual. Reduced to solely an illustrated alphabet, it has been understood from that time on as a picturebook that plays with the ludic relations between letter and image. It takes a huge variety of forms and addresses itself to a large public.

Origins

The term *abecedarius* is a neologism created by Saint Augustin to describe the alphabetical psalms of the Bible. Rufinus of Aquileia used it as a substantive noun to define the students who were learning their letters. Throughout medieval Christianity, the psalms served as a manual for reading and writing for the students of monks, before being replaced – when education opened up to laypeople in the thirteenth century – by the major prayers (the Lord's Prayer, Hail Mary, the Apostle's Creed), which were placed after the alphabet in psalters or books of hours. In the fifteenth century, these elementary texts were isolated to form a manual, called an 'abcie,' 'absey book,' or else a 'primer,' containing numerous texts. To the prayers could be added the prayers of Grace, the commandments of God and of the church, the psalms of penitence, or even a little catechism or a summary of Genesis (Alexandre-Bidon 1986; Litaudon 2014). Illustrated when they were addressed to princely children, they most often lack any illustrations. In its most popular form, the abecedary was reduced to a wooden tablet furnished with a handle on which was fixed a page of parchment (or of paper). This tablet was protected by a thin layer of horn, from which its name 'hornbook' was derived; it was sometimes also called a 'criss-cross-row,' in reference to the cross that preceded the alphabet, presented in capital letters and in lower case. These were followed by a syllabary (from the sixteenth century on), the Lord's Prayer, and sometimes Roman numerals. In England and the United States, the use of a hornbook remained frequent until the end of the eighteenth century (Tuer 1963; Avery 1995).

From the abecedary to the illustrated abecedary: the rise of empiricist pedagogy from the sixteenth to the eighteenth century

With the printing press, the abecedary was democratized. The literacy campaigns of the Reformation (Protestant), and then of the Counter-Reformation (Catholic), contributed to its development, without establishing the necessity of illustrating the manual. It was considered to be for learning and reciting by heart, under the fear of the rod. Perhaps following the educational treatise of Erasmus, *De pueris instituendis* (The Education of Children 1528), John Hart published in 1570 *A Method or Comfortable Beginning for All Unlearned*. The book was intended to make the learning of letters easier by associating each of them with an illustrated object and with a word corresponding to this object. It was not until the publication of the *Orbis Sensualium Pictus* (The Visible World 1658), a Latin-German illustrated encyclopedia by the Czech Johann Amos Comenius, that the idea of teaching through images developed by Comenius became widespread in England. His encyclopedia, translated into English in 1659, began with an alphabet illustrated with animals. The cry emitted by the animal served to introduce the sound and the written form of the letter being studied. Convinced of the advantages of the image, which held the shifting attention of the child and aided in identifying the phono-orthographic functioning of the language, other authors followed suit. A schoolmaster with the initials T.H. published *A Guyde for the Childe and Youth* (1667) in London. The book included an illustrated alphabet with a couplet that facilitated its memorization. It very quickly became popular, and went through multiple reprints. The alphabet, which opens with an illustration of the biblical original sin, is illustrated with a vignette representing Adam and Eve by the Tree of Knowledge, accompanied by the lines: "In Adam's Fall / We sinned all" (see Zipes 2005). This illustrated alphabet was taken up by the author and editor Benjamin Harris, as he reassembled the elements of his *New England Primer*, published for the first time in London in 1683. This book became the reference manual for Puritans in the New World when Benjamin Harris went to Boston in exile in 1686.

In 1669, *School Pastime for Young Children* was published by the mathematician and astronomer John Newton. The work offered an illustrated alphabet, but without couplets. At the bottom of the title page, the author, an advocate of educational reform, placed a quotation from Erasmus (also used by Comenius): "I cannot tell whether anything be better learn'd, than which is learn'd by play" (Zipes 2005: 2).

This interest in the physical world of the senses, which is offered to our eyes in the form of images and to our ears in the form of sounds, was considerably influenced in Protestant countries, by a moral education that supported learning to write. Contrary to the Catholic tradition, the literary discipline played upon the sensory experience of young children, their pleasures, and their games. The recommendations of the empiricist philosopher John Locke, in *Some Thoughts Concerning Education* (1693), advocated such an approach:

> There may be Dice and Playthings, with the Letters on them, to teach Children the Alphabet by playing; and twenty other ways may be found, suitable to their particular Tempers, to make this kind of Learning a Sport to them.
>
> § 148

Hence, images and rhyming games, originally used in the service of a religious discourse devoted to the mortification of desires, became secularized and aimed towards enjoyment.

In 1702, the alphabetical nursery rhyme "A was an Archer" was printed, followed by an illustrated and rhyming alphabet in *A Little Book for Little Children* by T.W. (aka Thomas White). This idea was taken up in 1764 in an American primer *Tom Thumb's Play-Book. To Teach Children Their Letters as Soon as They Can Speak*, in addition to another nursery rhyme that became popular: *A Apple Pye*. From the middle of the eighteenth century on, the publication of such abecedaries became a trend, notably thanks to the London editor John Newbery, who put into practice John Locke's notion of 'plaything' and published four game-books (Pickering 1978), which were soon copied by his American counterpart Isaiah Thomas. The best known is *The Little Pretty Pocket Book* (1744 UK; 1787 USA) and *A Little Lottery-Book for Children* (1756 UK; 1788 USA), both ascribed to John Newbery. Indeed, the wood-engraved artwork is still crude and clumsy, but this gained in finesse with the developments in wood engraving by Thomas Bewick in the final third of the eighteenth century (Darton 1982).

The book type of battledore also benefited from this development. Appearing around 1750 in England and the United States, it consisted of a printed and folded sheet of cardboard on which elements of a hornbook were drawn, combined with an illustrated alphabet displaying people, objects, or animals from everyday life. This format expanded rapidly; the religious content disappeared and was replaced by thematic illustrations (animals, professions, etc.) in a variety of page layouts.

The idea of visual education steadily won over the enlightened minds of northern Europe. In 1759, Kornelis de Wit published *Een nieuwlyks uitgevonden A.B.C. Boek* (A Newly Invented ABC Book) in Amsterdam, while in 1790, the German Karl Philipp Moritz authored *Neues ABC-Buch* (New ABC Book). The images, accompanied by a simple and rhythmic prose, were intended to develop the elementary bases of reflection through observation.

The Catholic tradition saw nothing of this sort. Until the end of the eighteenth century, illustrated manuals remained exceptions. The celebrated *Rôti-cochon ou Méthode tres-facile pour bien apprendre les enfans a lire en latin & en françois, par des inscriptions moralement expliquées de plusieurs representations figurées de différentes choses de leurs connoissances*, (Roast Pig, or a very simple method for children to learn well to read in Latin and in French, through moral inscriptions explained through several illustrated representations of different things of their knowledge) is an anonymous chapbook edited around 1689, mixing together moral precepts and culinary pleasure. In 1744, Abbot Berthaud published *Le Quadrille des enfans* (Children's Quadrille) for the education of princes by using a method of reading without spelling. It unites a box-game with a manual – following the same rules – of illustrated lessons (the counters in the box-game present a familiar object on one of their faces, and the final sound of the word that designates that object and its written form on the other). However neither the *Rôti-cochon* nor the *Quadrille* is properly speaking an abecedary, since they do not follow the alphabetical order.

For the most part, the manuals in use were the *Croix de par Dieu* (from the name of the cross that preceded the alphabet), which were equivalent to the English religious primers. They only evolved through the development of the syllabary and, in the nineteenth century, through the adoption of the vernacular language rather than the use of Latin (this had been common practice since the sixteenth century in Protestant countries). Equally widespread in France, following the work of Erasmus's *De civilitate morum puerilium* (A Handbook on Good Manners for Children 1530), were the abecedaries of *civilités* (manners), which, in the guise of first exercises in reading, substituted the rules of social conduct for the major prayers. The illustration was restricted to possibly a vignette on the frontispiece or on the title page. Such abecedaries, following the example of the *New England Primer*, were published until the middle of the nineteenth century, with certain adjustments, for use in traditional education situations (families, or rural or religious schools).

From the illustrated abecedary to the picturebook: the nineteenth century

Jean-Jacques Rousseau introduced the ideas of Locke to the French public in his far-reaching educational treatise *Émile ou de l'Éducation* (Emile, or on Education 1762). He emphasized a praxis-oriented and playful education which is respectful of the nature of the child. The repercussions of these ideas could be felt in the wake of the French Revolution. Thus, the *Alphabet républicain orné de gravures* (Republican Alphabet Decorated with Engravings 1793–1794) by Jean-Baptiste Chemin-Dupontes is the first to introduce an illustrated alphabet at the opening of a manual intended for teaching at primary schools and at home. Its tabular structure allowed three elements to be connected in a frame: a letter, a word starting with this same letter, and a visual representation of this word. The National

Assembly, the patriotic army, Jean-Jacques Rousseau, and the lesser trades constituted remarkable *icônes* (symbols) found in the famous allegories of equality and of liberty (Lapacherie 2000). After an illustrated syllabary, the text continued with the alphabet accompanied by comments in the form of informal paternal lessons: "*Regarde, mon enfant*" ("Look, my child"). This conversational model, taken from *Lessons for Children* (1778/79) by Anna Laetitia Barbauld, was widely adopted in the following decades by abecedaries for instructive use (by private tutors). The use of characters of decreasing size, also promoted by Barbauld, became widespread starting from the beginning of the nineteenth century. In turn, pedagogy by image, which allowed students to identify the phonographic function of language, was only established slowly. Until the 1840s, the presence of an illustrated alphabet at the beginning of a manual was rare and always derived from an English influence, for example, *Jeu récréatif de la maison que Pierre le Grand a bâtie* (Recreational Game of the House that Peter the Great Built, ca. 1830) and *Syllabaire des lectures graduées pour les enfans du premier âge* (Syllabary of Gradated Readings for Children from Babyhood 1840) by Louis Gaultier. Images appeared only in collections of fables and short moral stories, or thematic dictionaries, as in *Alphabet des arts et métiers* (Alphabet of Arts and Professions 1826). In the first third of the nineteenth century, meticulous French abecedaries increasingly included extra-textual illustrations. To escape the coarseness of the tradition of the wood engraving, which was typical of abecedaries sold by *colporteurs* (i.e., booksellers that travel around), they had steel engravings (intaglio), thus distinguishing them from those abecedaries that had typographic characters in relief.

This is also the case concerning lithography. This technique, in which the artist designs directly on the stone, allows great liberty of the line and preserves the fine details of shading. Promoted by the Romantic aesthetic, lithography was primarily used for the creation of luxurious keepsakes, that is, collections in quarto, or even in folio, of alphabetical board books, which were considered precious Christmas gifts and were often created by renowned artists. These books mostly contained an illustrated alphabet only or short texts that played a supporting role for the images, for instance, in *Nouvel Abécédaire en énigmes* (New Abecedary in Riddles, ca. 1840) by Victor Adam. These works are regarded as the cradle of modern picturebooks. They were appreciated by children as well as by their parents.

Aimed at a broader audience, lithography was widely used in alphabets *en bandes* (in bands), which were folded into the shape of an accordion, in formats of up to sixteen and sixty-four inches in size, before they were replaced by wood engravings. Introduced to France in 1817 by Thompson, a student of Bewick's, this technique was rapidly honed and met with huge success due to its flexibility. Text and image, both engraved in relief, could be combined on the page in various layouts. Moreover, wood-engraved blocks are more economical than their competitors. They withstand wear and tear better, allow for the modification of details, and facilitate stereotype wood-engraved reproduction in order to promote cheaper resales. Therefore, books with wood-engraved illustrations dominated the market after 1850.

The evolution of the abecedary is as closely tied to the development of popular instruction, encouraged by governmental politics, as it is to progress made in the reproduction possibilities of the images and the mechanization of printing methods. With the decrease in production costs, the illustrated book reached a wider audience. The publications became more diverse in order to adapt to all price categories, which were dependent on the format, paper, number of pages, type of illustration, black-and-white versus full-color illustrations, and binding. The content of these books expanded widely, referring to the sciences and to technology. This phenomenon is more palpable in France than in the Anglo-Saxon countries, where the tradition of nursery rhymes, *Mother Goose* editions, and biblical stories continued to dominate a large part of the book production.

In this regard, English abecedaries were the first to celebrate the development of transport, where, for the letter A (the first postulate), the arch of bridges under which passed steam boats or trains came to replace Noah's Ark or the apple of the temptation of Adam and Eve (for instance, *Cousin Chatterbox's Railway Alphabet* 1854). A new concept emerged in abecedaries, leading to the category of *toybook*. This is a paperback book with few pages, where the image, artistically conceived and printed in color (usually in chromotypography, later in chromolithography), plays a decisive role. These were soon illustrated by artists such as Walter Crane, Randolph Caldecott, and Kate Greenaway. The French writer Huysmans dedicated a praising article to them, in which he concluded:

> One can, boldly, agree that these picturebooks are today, with those of the Japanese, the only works of art worthy of the name that remain for us to contemplate, in Paris, when the Exhibition of the Society of Independent Artists closes.
>
> *Huysmans 1881*

From this time on, these picturebooks, although conceived of in England, were henceforth printed in the Netherlands or in Germany, and saw an international distribution in North America and Europe. The images more than the text were their attraction. In France, for example, the nonsense of nursery rhymes stood in contrast to abecedaries influenced by the pedagogy of the Enlightenment. The editors substituted the nonsense verses with short prosaic and moralizing texts, from which all play with sound and rhyme had disappeared. Nonetheless, these books dominated the market, distributed in numerous collections, until the First World War. Among the many topics, the emphasis on the 'universe of the child' (the objects that surround them, their activities and games) held first place. Children found themselves increasingly placed in the situation of autonomous learning. To this end, indestructible books came into fashion: the illustrations were pasted onto canvas, cardboard, or fabric. Although the abecedary was no longer designed for learning to read, it participated in an initiation to letters and words in the family setting or the American kindergarten since the educational reforms, and benefited from the development of active teaching methods (such as John Dewey's "learning by doing").

ABC books from the twentieth century until the present: playful pedagogy and creation

Liberated from didactic prescriptions, editors started to encourage artists to further develop the pedagogical and ludic potential of the image, not only in connection with the letter, the word, or even a short text, but equally with its material, the paper, and layout. The adopted and often combined strategies can be considered as games, encouraging visual and manual activities. Children are asked to identify an illustrated letter on a single page or a doublespread. This letter is either printed on a white background or inserted into a decoration, which increases the difficulty of its discovery. A precursor is the alphabet designed by Théophile Schuler in *Le Premier Livre des petits enfants* (1868; English transl. *Letters Everywhere* 1869) (see Figure 17.1). The same method applies to Stephen T. Johnston's wordless picturebook *Alphabet City* (1996), where only the title gives a clue as to the book's meaning.

A related 'game' technique consists in providing illustrated acrophonic words, which are either printed on a negative space or inserted into the image. Acrophony is a method of naming the letters of an alphabetic writing system in which a letter's name begins with the letter itself. An acrophonic word for 'A' would be any word that begins with this letter, such as 'apple' or 'ark.' Abecedaries like *A.B.C. de Babar* (Babar's ABC 1934) by Jean de Brunhoff present a series of scenes which abound in items presenting acrophonic words of a specific letter. The recognition of the objects that present the acrophonic words is made more difficult, since they are situated in an authentic context. Such ABC books have existed since the nineteenth century, where they often tend to display *natura morte* scenes with heterogeneous objects, as in *The Pretty Picture A.B.C.* (ca. 1860) (see Figure 17.2).

Figure 17.1 Illustration from *Letters Everywhere: Stories and Rhymes for Children*. London: Seeley, Jackson & Halliday, 1869. Coll. Marie-Pierre Litaudon-Bonnardot, IMEC. The letter 'W' did not appear in the French edition and was specially designed for the English translation.

This visual game can double as a sound game carried by an accompanying text, which is of a poetic (rhymes, assonance, and/or alliteration), and often bizarre, nature. Some texts emphasize a word or several acrophonic words represented in the image, while others form a tautogram which describes the image, as in the tongue-twister *Peter Piper's Alphabet* (1959), which revisits an older version, *Peter Piper's Practical Principles of Plain and Perfect Pronunciation* (1813) by John Harris.

The abecedary pertains to a poetic of the fragment, that is, the letter. Its discontinuous character is spatialized by the page and by the turning of pages. In this regard, the book concept can refer to the

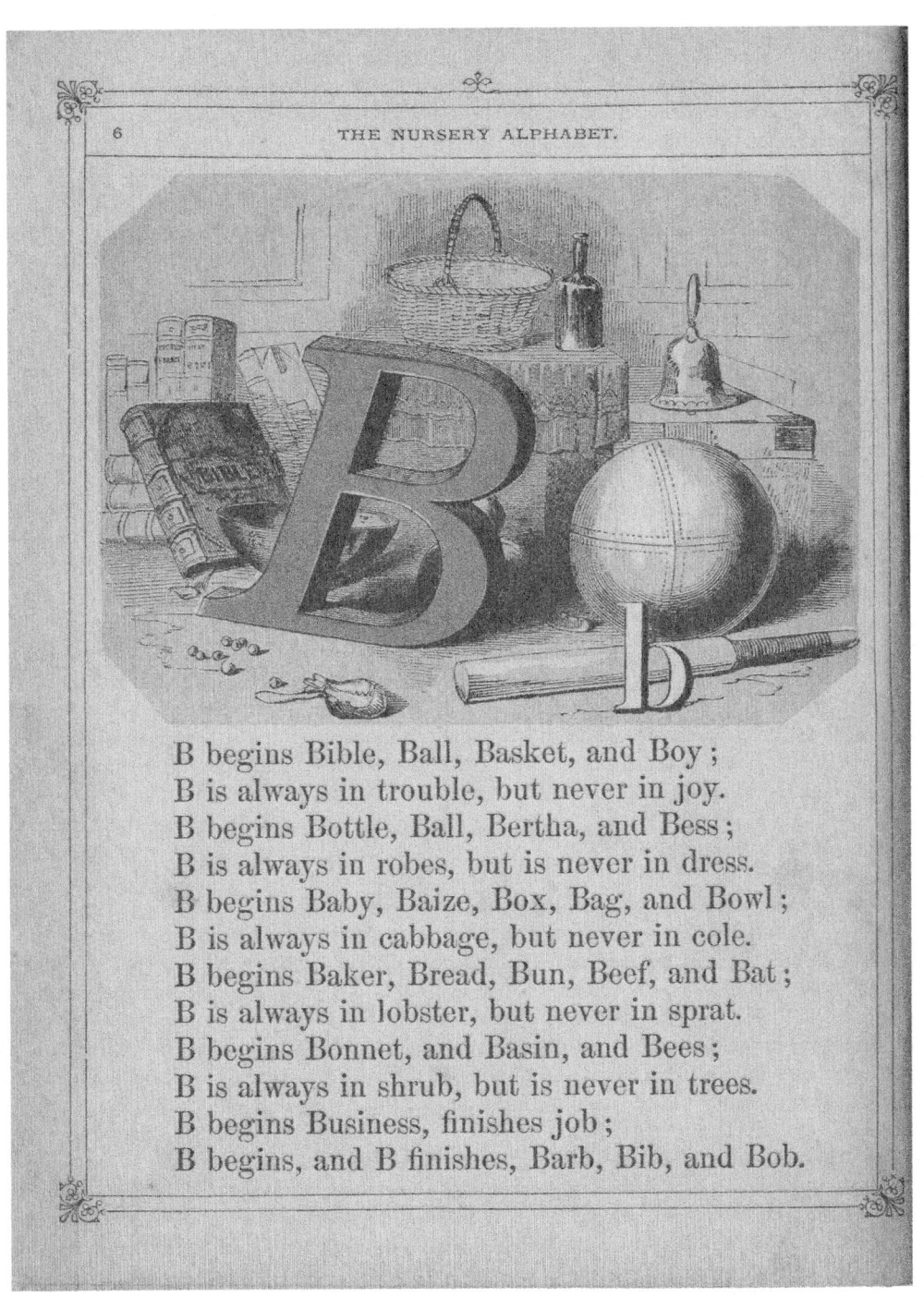

B begins Bible, Ball, Basket, and Boy;
B is always in trouble, but never in joy.
B begins Bottle, Ball, Bertha, and Bess;
B is always in robes, but is never in dress.
B begins Baby, Baize, Box, Bag, and Bowl;
B is always in cabbage, but never in cole.
B begins Baker, Bread, Bun, Beef, and Bat;
B is always in lobster, but never in sprat.
B begins Bonnet, and Basin, and Bees;
B is always in shrub, but is never in trees.
B begins Business, finishes job;
B begins, and B finishes, Barb, Bib, and Bob.

Figure 17.2 Illustration from *The Pretty Picture A.B.C.* Edinburg & London: T. Nelson & Sons, ca. 1860. Coll. Marie-Pierre Litaudon-Bonnardot, IMEC.

arbitrariness of the alphabetic sequence by proceeding in a graphic or narrative succession of letters or of pages, as in *A Mickey Mouse Alphabet Book* (1936) by Walt Disney and in *L'Histoire de Monsieur A* (The Story of Mr. A 2003) by Jean-Pierre Blanpain. Other picturebooks present manual activities developed in the interwar period by the *Éducation nouvelle* (progressive education) movement, which promoted experiential learning. Another case in point is the coloring book abecedary, which is based on an illustrated acrophonic word, thus stimulating the child to color the letters. The objective consists in calling the child's attention to the form of the letter and exercising the child's hand in order to master its movement.

As for the 'connect the dots' abecedaries, the child has to rely on the order of the letters or numbers scattered across the page, which bring out the form of the acrophonic word connected to the letter. Other abecedaries even invite the child to cut or tear out images – placed at the end of the picturebook – to insert them in the section devoted to the alphabet, next to the letter that they illustrate. The silhouette of the object outlined next to the letter aids the child in spotting it.

Rarer are those abecedaries that are to be cut up (in part or totally) in order to create a game of cards or alphabetic lotto, as in *ABC du Père Castor* (The ABC of Father Beaver 1936) by Feodor Rojankovsky. The same applies to abecedaries for construction. These picturebooks have a pocket containing basic shapes, such as bars and curves, which, appropriately laid out, form letters. A prominent example is *The Little Builder's ABC* (1943) by Nell Reppy, in which the illustrated alphabet refers to diverse professions. Contemporary French ABC books in this tradition are *Le Jouet* (The Plaything 2011) and *Machine à lettres* (The Letter Machine 2012) by Julien Magnani.

Another pedagogical strategy focuses on the spectacular character of the image in tight relation with the type of material used for the book. The role of the image is to surprise, fascinate, and stimulate the imagination. The first picturebooks of this type were the alphabets in a strip that are laid out to form a panorama that the child can look at in one glance. During the final third of the nineteenth century, mechanical abecedaries appeared. When playing with a pull-back flap or a shutter, the reader is able to unveil the acrophonic word hidden behind the letter. Particularly after the Second World War, pop-up ABC books became widespread, often in combination with the shutter. This book type is characterized by the principle of a riddle that connects a letter to an acrophonic word, as in *A is for Animals* (1991) by David Pelham. Using such books gives the child the feeling that they can, in naming the object, bring it to life.

With the further development of the picturebook, the abecedary has become the work of an illustrator more than the book of an author. Since childhood and creation are often connected with the idea of experimenting with a new language, the abecedary especially has proved to be an emblematic exercise in artistic styles and new concepts. Sometimes such abecedaries only have limited print runs, such as *Alphabet* (1932) by photographer Emmanuel Sougez or *Abcdefghijklmnopqrstuvwxyz* (1924) by Lucien Laforge. These books are now rare collectibles, which raises the question of the reception and of the audience. In contrast, Sonia Delaunay created *Alphabet* (1972), which was first edited as a bibliophilic edition before it came out as a children's book. Moreover, abecedaries dedicated to art have multiplied since 1990. These books focus on the discovery of renowned national museums/galleries, painters, or the world through art, such as Alain Le Saux and Grégoire Solotareff's *Petit Musée* (Little Museum 1992), recommended by l'Éducation nationale (The National Education Board), or *I Spy, an Alphabet in Art* (1996) by Lucy Micklethwait. The objective is to foster the sensibility of the child, and to initiate them into the plural modalities of modern language and art. Thus, the most successful contemporary abecedaries explore the combined resources of the letter and the image: the enchantment of the naming/appearance connects the pop-up shutter and the mystery of the drawn sign, to which the 'legend' offers a sonorous key, with an alphabetical story, which plays with the materiality of language in order to better reinvent the visible world. In this sense the editor Harlin Quist conceived *Q Is for Crazy* (1977), with a text by Ed Leander and illustrations by Jozef Sumichrast

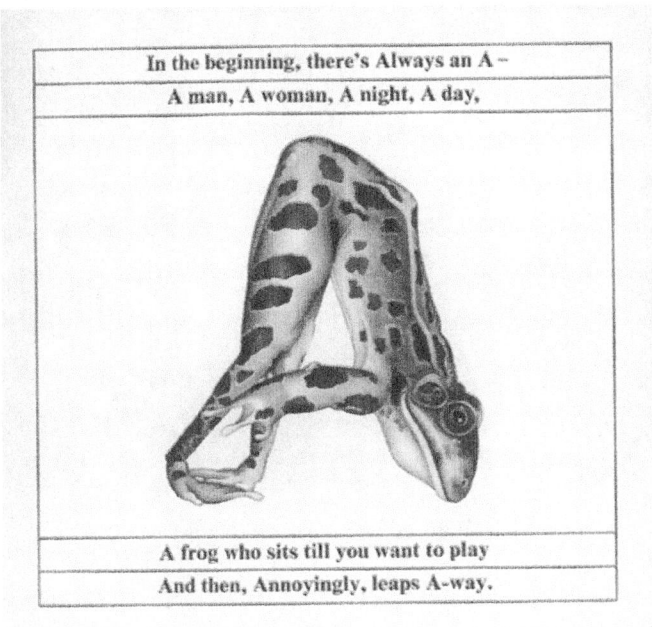

In the beginning, there's Always an A –

A man, A woman, A night, A day,

A frog who sits till you want to play

And then, Annoyingly, leaps A-way.

Figure 17.3 Illustration by Jozef Sumichrast from Ed Leander: *Q is for Crazy*. New York: Harlin Quist, 1977.

(see Figure 17.3), and *Roll Call. The Story of Noah's Ark and the World's First Losers* (1978) by John Goldthwaite and Henri Galeron, the latter being a surreal inventory of impossible animals, born of portmanteaus, that Noah, in his haste, forgot to bring on board. *Alphabet farfelu* (Bizarre Alphabet 2005) by Marie-Pierre Schneegans and Jean Molla plays with the arbitrariness of the alphabet by presenting on one page two letters/words/images that are married graphically or syntactically on the following page: G for *gâteau* (cake) and H for *histoire* (story) form a *gâteau d'histoires* (story cake). With *A Is for Salad* (2000), Mike Lester perverts the phonographic rule upon which the relationship between text and image is classically based. The text gives the wrong designation; it is up to the child to observe the image in order to recognize that "A is for Alligator eating a salad."

In abecedaries created by artists, the letter also finds an expression of its own beauty, without resorting to *realia*. Kveta Pacovska's *Alphabet* (1996) is distinguished by a playful composition of colored rhymes and of simple but suggestive forms, to which are sometimes added effects of relief and of the material. In *ABC3D* (2008), Marion Bataille has created a paper sculpture which surges out of the work, thus creating a letter in movement that renews itself at the turn of the page. Paul Cox goes almost as far as reinventing the letters of the alphabet in *Animaux* (English transl. *Abstract Alphabet: A Book of Animals* 2001) and creates, with shapes and colors, an abstract alphabet landscape that demands to be decrypted. Anne Bertier's *Blanches* (Whites 2009) (see Figure 17.4) and Colleen Ellis's *ABCing: Seeing the Alphabet Differently* (2010) highlight the ludic facets of the principles of design. The latter also has a multimedia numerical adaptation.

Nowadays the ABC book is a genre which is mostly devoted to the celebration of the creative act, of which the child is the first master/mistress. The insertion of the image into the writing has thus, in two centuries, radically transformed the educational principles that underlie the learning of reading: communal and normative targets have been replaced by the appeal to the individual child's imagination and creativity.

Figure 17.4 Illustration by Anne Bertier from *Blanches*. Paris: Éditions MeMo, 2009.
Reprinted by permission of Éditions MeMo, Paris.

References

Adam, Victor (ca. 1840) *Nouvel Abécédaire en énigmes*, Paris: Aubert & Cie.

Alexandre-Bidon, Danièle (1986) "Abécédaires et alphabets éducatifs du XIIIe à la fin du XVe siècle," *Nouvelles de l'estampe* 90: 6–10.

Alphabet des arts et métiers (1826) Paris: J. Brianchon.

Avery, Gillian (1995) "Beginnings of Children's Reading to c. 1700," in Peter Hunt (ed.) *Children's Literature: An Illustrated History*, Oxford and New York: Oxford University Press, 1–25.

Barbauld, Anna Laetitia (1841) *Lessons for Children*, London: Baldwin & Cradock (first published 1778/79).

Bataille, Marion (2008) *ABC3D*, Paris: Albin Michel jeunesse [*ABC3D*, London: Roaring Brook Press, 2008].

Berthaud, Claude-Louis (1744) *Le Quadrille des enfans*, Paris: Jacques Vincent.

Bertier, Anne (2009) *Blanches*, Paris: Éditions MeMo.

Blanpain, Jean-Pierre (2003) *L'Histoire de Monsieur A*, Paris: Thierry Magnier.

Brunhoff, Jean de (1934) *A.B.C. de Babar*, Paris: Editions du Jardin des Modes [*A.B.C. of Babar*. New York: Random House, 1936].

[Chemin-Dupontes, Jean-Baptiste] (1793–1794) *L'Alphabet républicain orné de gravures*, Paris: Imprimerie de l'auteur.

Comenius, Johann Amos (1658) *Orbis Sensualium Pictus*, Nuremberg: Michael and Johannes Friedrich Endter.

Cousin Chatterbox's Railway Alphabet (1854) London: Dean & Sons.

Cox, Paul (1997) *Animaux*, Paris: Seuil jeunesse [*Abstract Alphabet: A Book of Animals*, San Francisco, CA: Chronicle Books, 2001].

Darton, Frederick J.H. (1982) *Children's Books in England: Five Centuries of Social Life*, 3rd ed., Cambridge: Cambridge University Press.

Delaunay, Sonia (1972) *Alphabet*, Paris: L'École des loisirs [*Alphabet*, New York: Thomas Y. Crowell, 1972].

Disney, Walt (1936) *A Mickey Mouse Alphabet Book*, Racine, WI: Whitman.

Ellis, Colleen (2010) *ABCing: Seeing the Alphabet Differently*, New York: Mark Batty.

Erasmus (1528) *De pueris instituendis*, Straßburg: Egenolphus.

Erasmus (1544) *De civilitate morum puerilium*, Ingolstadt: Weissenhorn (first published 1530).

Gaultier, Louis (1840) *Syllabaire des lectures graduées pour les enfans du premier âge*, Paris: Jules Renouard et Cie.

Goldthwaite, John (1978) *Roll Call: The Story of Noah's Ark and the World's First Losers*, illus. Henri Galeron, New York: Harlin Quist Books.

Harris, Benjamin (ca. 1683) *New England Primer*, London: John Gaine.

Harris, John (1813) *Peter Piper's Practical Principles of Plain and Perfect Pronunciation*, London: Griffith and Farran.

Harris, John (1959) *Peter Piper's Alphabet; Peter Piper's Practical Principles of Plain and Perfect Pronunciation: Manifold Manifestations Made by Marcia Brown*, illus. Marcia Brown, New York: Charles Scribner's & Sons.

Hart, John (1570) *A Method or Comfortable Beginning for All Unlearned*, London: Henrie Denham.

Huysmans, Joris-Karl (1881) "Les albums anglais: les albums enfantins illustrés," *Revue Littéraire et Artistique* 16 (August 15).

Jeu récréatif de la maison que Pierre le Grand a bâtie (ca. 1830) Paris: Delarue.

Johnston, Stephen T. (1996) *Alphabet City*, New York: Viking Books.

Laforge, Lucien (1924) *Abcdefghijklmnopqrstuvwxyz*, Paris: Henri Goulet.

Lapacherie, J.-G. (2000) "Apprendre à lire et idéologie politique: L'alphabet républicain du citoyen Chemin," *Tréma* 17: 27–41.

Leander, Ed (1977) *Q is for Crazy*, ill. Jozef Sumichrast, New York: Harlin Quist.

Le Saux, Alain, and Solotareff, Grégoire (1992) *Petit Musée*, Paris: L'École des loisirs.

Lester, Mike (2000) *A is for Salad*, New York: Putnam & Grosset.

Litaudon, Marie-Pierre (2014) *Les Abécédaires de l'enfance: verbe & image*, Rennes: Presses universitaires de Rennes/ IMEC.

Locke, John (1693) *Some Thoughts Concerning Education*, London: A. & J. Churchill.

Macé, Jean, and Stahl, Pierre-Jules (1868) *Le Premier Livre des petits enfants*, illus. Théophile Schuler, Paris: J. Hetzel [*Letters Everywhere: Stories and Rhymes for Children*, London: Seeley, Jackson & Halliday, 1869].

Magnani, Julien (2011) *Le Jouet*, Nantes: MeMo.

Magnani, Julien (2012) *Machine à lettres*, Nantes: MeMo.

Micklethwait, Lucy (1996) *I Spy, an Alphabet in Art*, London: Greenwillow Books.

Moritz, Karl Philipp (1790) *Neues ABC-Buch*, Berlin: Christian Gottfried Schöne.

[Newbery, John] (1744) *The Little Pretty Pocket Book*, London: John Newbery.

[Newbery, John] (1756) *A Little Lottery-Book for Children*, London: John Newbery.

Newton, John (1669) *School Pastime for Young Children: or The Rudiments of Grammar*, London: Robert Walton.

Pacovska, Kveta (1996) *Alphabet*, Paris: Seuil jeunesse.

Pelham, David (1991) *A is for Animals*, New York: Little Simon.

Pickering, Sam (1978) "'Cosen'd into a Knowledge of the Letters': Eighteenth-Century Alphabetic Game Books," *Research Studies* 46.4: 223–236.

The Pretty Picture A.B.C. (ca. 1860) Edinburg and London: T. Nelson & Sons.

Reppy, Nell (1943) *The Little Builder's ABC*, New York: Simon and Schuster.

Rojankovsky, Feodor (1936) *ABC du Père Castor*, Paris: Flammarion-Père Castor.

Rôti-cochon ou Méthode tres-facile pour bien apprendre les enfans a lire en latin & en françois, par des inscriptions moralement expliquées de plusieurs representations figurées de différentes choses de leurs connoissances (ca. 1689) Dijon: Claude Michard.

Rousseau, Jean-Jacques (1762) *Émile ou de l'Éducation*, A La Haye: Jean Néaulme.

Schneegans, Marie-Pierre, and Molla, Jean (2005) *Alphabet farfelu*, illus. Marie-Pierre Schneegans, Paris: Grasset jeunesse.

Sougez, Emmanuel (1932) *Alphabet*, Paris: Antoine Roche.

T. H. [schoolmaster] (ca. 1667) *A Guyde for the Childe and Youth*, London: Wing (2nd ed.).

Tom Thumb's Play-Book: To Teach Children Their Letters as Soon as They Can Speak (1764) Boston, MA: A. Barclay.

Tuer, Andrew W. (1963) *History of the Horn Book*, 2 vols, London: The Horn Book.

T.W. [White, Thomas] (1702) *A Little Book for Little Children: Wherein Are Set Down Several Directions for Little Children*, London: Sold at the Ring in Little Britain.

Wit, Kornelis de (1759) *Een nieuwlyks uitgevonden A.B.C. Boek*, Amsterdam: Kornelis de Wit.

Zipes, Jack (2005) "Alphabets," in Jack Zipes, Lissa Paul, and Lynne Vallone (eds) *The Norton Anthology of Children's Literature*, New York: W.W. Norton, 1–32.

18

POP-UP AND MOVABLE BOOKS

Ann Montanaro Staples

What are movable books?

A movable book, quite simply, is a book that has moving parts within its printed pages. They include illustrations and text that can be rotated, lifted, pushed or pulled from side to side, or in the case of pop-ups, arise from the flat surface in three-dimensional form when a page is turned. (While some digital picturebooks have integrated motion, that action is achieved through animation, not moving paper, and those books are not included in this study.) The ingenious mechanical paper devices in pop-up and movable books are handmade creations designed to amaze, entertain, and educate the reader. It is both surprising and engaging to turn a page and to have an illustration spring up. For more than a thousand years, philosophers, scientists, artists, and designers have added movement to text to increase the readers' understanding, pleasure, and involvement with the words, concepts, and emotions. Pop-ups, tabs, rotating wheels, and lift-the-flaps are just some of the kinds of movable devices that have been used in books to enhance the text.

Movable books have existed for centuries

Pop-up books are often thought of as a fairly recent phenomenon in the history of children's literature, but movable books, of which pop-ups are just one example, have existed for centuries (Evers 1985; Montanaro 1993, 1996; Knipschild 2006; Bluemeland and Harris Taylor 2012). The mechanicals have a long and engaging history that begins before the advent of printed books. To understand the role of pop-up books in contemporary children's literature, it is useful to have an appreciation of the history of movable books (The Renier Collection 1988; Pelachaud 2010).

It is not certain who first added a movable piece to a book, but in the thirteenth century Matthew Paris, a Benedictine monk, included a revolving wheel or volvelle in his *Chronica Majora*. Handwritten abbey manuscripts had drawings of circular tables used to determine holy days. Paris created a volvelle to make it easier to line up the tables by rotating the paper wheel rather than having to move the whole manuscript (DuLong 2004: back cover). The word 'volvelle' is derived from the Latin, meaning 'to turn or roll around.' Some books had two or more volvelles or round paper disks that rotated on a common spindle secured to the page at the center of the circle (Helfand 2002). Volvelles have been used in books throughout history and they continue to be used in books in a variety of ways. A twentieth-century example that includes two volvelles is Alice and Martin Provensen's *Leonardo Da Vinci: The Artist, Inventor, Scientist in Three-Dimensional, Movable Pictures* (1984). Those paper wheels transform one illustration into another showing example of Da Vinci's work.

Another early type of movable book was one with lift-the-flaps. These books had layers of super-imposed plates or flaps that could be lifted one at a time to reveal additional images. In the sixteenth century dissections were banned, but flap books were used as an anatomy teaching aid. Lift-the-flap books, just like their predecessors, are widely used today in books for children.

A popular eighteenth-century movable book was the harlequinade, also called turn-up books or metamorphoses books (Weiss 1932; Brown 2006). While there are some variations, typically harlequinades have one or two printed sheets with the first sheet folded perpendicularly into four sections. A second sheet was cut in half and hinged at the top and bottom edges of the first so that each flap could be lifted separately. There are earlier examples of harlequinades, but English printer Robert Sayer produced the first printed version in the 1760s. These books actively engaged the reader in the text and illustrations. Initially produced as religious narratives, Sayer and others soon turned to moral texts and theatrical topics. These inexpensive books became known as harlequinades because the theatrical character Harlequin became a central figure in many of these books and the word often appeared in the title (Opie 1975: 66).

Peepshow books, alternately called tunnel books, are also movables. The most obvious forerunner of the paper peepshow was the baroque theater with its view through the proscenium arch to the scenery beyond (Hyde 2015: 12). The "sets" evolved into small books and three-dimensional displays and, by the eighteenth century, peepshows were often quite elaborate constructions depicting scenes from distant cities, famous stories, or topical events used by traveling showmen at fairs and festivals. Viewers often paid to view the image. Handheld peepshow books were smaller objects with front and back covers and side panels attached accordion-style on either both sides or the top and bottom. Like the larger versions, illustrations were viewed through a hole in the cover, and, when the book was extended, a three-dimensional effect was achieved (Balzer 1998: 12). Many current children's books include a peepshow. Two notable examples are Edward Gorey's *The Tunnel Calamity* (1984) and *Hidden Flower Fairies: 5 Secret 3D Scenes of Flower Fairyland* (2009) by Cicely Mary Barker.

Yet, while movables had been a part of book design for centuries – they were almost always used in scholarly works and in books for adults – it was not until the nineteenth century that these techniques were applied to books to entertain children (Higonnet 2014). Dean & Son, a publishing firm founded in London before 1800, claimed by the 1860s to be the "originator of children's movable books in which characters can be made to move and act in accordance with the incidents described in each story" (Haining 1979: 21). That was not exactly true, because there were others before them, but Dean had a significant impact on the history of movable books.

To produce these books Dean established a special department of skilled craftsmen who prepared the handmade mechanicals. One of the designs used the peepshow principle of cutout scenes aligned one behind the other to give a three-dimensional effect. In Dean's *Little Red Riding Hood* (1856), each layer was fixed to the next by a ribbon that emerged behind the uppermost portion, and, when pulled, the whole scene sprang up into perspective. Dean also produced books with pull tabs and transformational plates.

London publishers H. Grevel & Co., Ward & Lock, Darton and Co., and Read & Co. all produced movable books in the late nineteenth century. The publishers Ernest Nister and Raphael Tuck were the first to seriously challenge the dominance of Dean & Son. In 1870, Raphael Tuck and his sons founded a publishing business in London that produced luxury paper items, including scrapbook pictures, valentines, puzzles, paper dolls, decorated papers, and books. The publisher produced movable books in varying sizes incorporating many different types of mechanisms: panoramas with loose pieces, pull tabs, peepshow-like illustrations, and stand-up scenes – what would now be called pop-ups.

To produce these books, Tuck, like Dean, formed editorial and design studios in London, where volumes of high pictorial quality were created. The work was then sent to Germany for printing and assembly. The Germans developed a mastery of color printing in the second half of the nineteenth century and their equipment and techniques superbly reproduced the finest chromolithographed artwork. Of Tuck's many books that included movables, three notables are *Fun for Little Folks* (1890), *A Very Good Book* (1897), and *Seaside Pleasures* (1896).

Another nineteenth-century publisher who specialized in movable books was Ernest Nister. He began a printing business in 1877 that was capable of producing works by all of the major processes of the time, but he is best known for his movable books, published from 1890 (Krahé 1988; Hunt and Hunt 2006). Nister's works were similar to those produced by his contemporaries, but in some of his books, like *Model Menagerie* (1895) (Figure 18.1) and *Little Pets* (1896), the illustrations stood up automatically (Figure 18.2). These books had die-cut figures that were mounted within a three-dimensional peepshow framework. The figures were connected by linen or paper guides so that as the pages were turned, the figures lifted away from the adjacent page creating the perspective-like setting. Nister also produced movable books with 'dissolving' and revolving transformational slats. *Here and There* (1894) incorporated this mechanism. As the tab at the bottom of the page was pulled, the divided sections of the first picture slid over the sections of the second picture to display a completely different illustration.

The most original movable picturebooks of the nineteenth century were devised by Lothar Meggendorfer. The Munich artist had a rare comic vision that he was able to transmit both through his art and through ingenious mechanical devices. In contrast to most of his contemporaries, Meggendorfer was not satisfied with only one action on each page. He often had five parts of the illustration move simultaneously and in different directions. Meggendorfer devised intricate levers, hidden between pages that gave his characters enormous possibilities for movement (Krahé 1983; Abate 2012). He used tiny metal rivets, actually tight curls of thin copper wire, to attach the levers, so that a single pull tab could activate all of them, often with several delayed actions as the tab was pulled farther out. Some illustrations used more than a dozen rivets. In *Comic Actors* (1891), Meggendorfer showed how he could take an ordinary situation and find humor in it. In

Figure 18.1 Illustration by L.L. Weedon from *Model Menagerie: With Natural History Stories.* Illus. Evelyn Fletcher. London: Ernest Nister (ca. 1895).

Collection of Ann Montanaro Staples.

Figure 18.2 Illustration from *Little Pets: A Panorama Picture Book of Animals.* London: Ernest Nister (ca. 1896). Collection of Ann Montanaro Staples.

one scene, a man presses a jacket while a cat sits on the ironing board. As the tab is pulled, the iron moves across the fabric and the cat pulls its tail away from the hot iron. Tiny metal rivets attached at the man's shoulder and elbow provide life-like movement (Meggendorfer 1985: inside back cover). Meggendorfer's *International Circus* (1887) is one of his most outstanding panoramas. This six-panel tableau, which extends to a full 133 cm, has pull-down, three-dimensional pictures of circus performers.

The beautifully chromolithographed movable books of the Victorian period were almost all produced in Germany. With the start of the First World War, the manufacture of movable books for the English-language market ceased, and it was many years before books of such high quality again appeared on the market.

In 1929, a new series of movable books was initiated. British book publisher S. Louis Giraud conceived, designed, and produced books with movable illustrations described as "living models." While the term had yet to be used, these were authentic pop-up books. Each title contained at least five doublespreads that erected automatically when the book pages were opened and the illustrations could be viewed from all sides (Dawson 1997: 6). Unlike their German-produced precursors, Giraud's books were moderately priced and lacked the quality of earlier movable books. Printed on coarse, absorbent paper, using inferior printing and color reproduction techniques, and finished with inexpensive covers and bindings, they were low in price and successful.

By the mid-1930s, as the Depression deepened, publishers sought ways to rekindle book buying. Blue Ribbon, an American publishing house founded in 1930, copied the stand-up techniques successful in the earlier British books. They found a combination that proved successful: animating books of Walt Disney characters and classic fairy tales with pop-ups. Blue Ribbon registered the term 'pop-up' to describe movable illustrations and received the trademark for "full legal protection for the exclusive use of this name" ("Biggest Juvenile Book Scoop in Years" 1933: 1532).

In the 1930s, Casa Editrice Hoepli of Milan, Italy, published the first of their "theater books," with six stage sets designed to be displayed in the round when the front and back covers were snapped together. *La Bella Addormentata Nel Bosco* (Sleeping Beauty 1942) was made in this carousel format; the depth created by the three-dimensional illustrations brought the stage to life. Another carousel book from the same decade was the *Cinderella Panorama Book* (1930s), based on Perrault's fairy tale and published in London.

A new group of artists and publishers transformed the movable book market in the 1940s with an increased focus on the youth audience. In 1942 Random House published Walt Disney's *Victory March*, which sold over 50,000 copies. In that book, the reader pulled a tab to see Dumbo fly, then turned a wheel to watch the Disney gang chase the enemy.

The Exciting Adventures of Finnie the Fiddler (1942) was the inaugural book of a series of titles featuring the animations of Julian Wehr (Figure 18.3). His illustrations were printed on lightweight paper and movement was created by tab-operated mechanicals. The pages were slit at various points to permit arms, heads, legs, or other moving parts to protrude. By moving the tab, which extended through the side or lower edge of the illustrated page, the reader put the various parts of the animation into motion. The action was transmitted to as many as five different parts of the picture. Wehr's books were relatively inexpensive and very popular and included depictions of Snow White, Little Black Sambo, Mother Goose, Hansel and Gretel, and many other familiar children's stories.

Geraldine Clyne was the creator of the Jolly Jump-ups series of ten titles published between 1939 and 1954. They conveyed a comforting, idealized view of American life during and after World War II. Geraldine's husband Ben engineered the new process used in their books. Until then, pop-up

Figure 18.3 Illustration from Julian Wehr's *The Exciting Adventures of Finnie the Fiddler*. New York: Cupples and Leon Co., 1942.

books had been made from die-cut sheets which were folded and glued onto flat pages. The Jolly Jump-up illustrations were different because they were printed on a single sheet of paper which was die-cut and folded to form a three-dimensional scene. The flat portions of the illustration were glued to stiff boards so the pop-up would stand as the page opened. The books were formatted horizontally with the text printed parallel to the spine. *The Jolly Jump-ups and Their New House* (1939) featured Mr. and Mrs. Jump-up, their five perfect children, a kitten, and a dog all living together in a modern, stylized house (Figure 18.4). Despite Clyne's patent on the design, many publishers imitated this novel technique and it is still being used.

While there were a few pop-up books produced during the 1940s and 1950s, none was as appealing in both content and illustration as those made by the Czechoslovakian illustrator Vojtěch Kubašta. The artist began with simple v-fold pop-ups in advertising mailers and cards, but he soon expanded to full-length books. Most of his earliest titles, published from the 1950s, were fairy tales featuring Kubašta's bold colors and distinctive graphic style. They all opened sideways with the text printed parallel to the spine (Rubin 2013: 2).

Over the years Kubašta's work evolved and became much more complex, as seen in a series of large format pop-ups published in London by Bancroft between 1960 and 1962, including *The Voyage of Marco Polo, Ricky the Rabbit, The Day of the Bison Hunt, Peter and Sally on the Farm* and more. They had many pages of text followed by a single, voluminous, double-page pop-up (Gubig and Köpcke 2003).

Building on the success of the innovative Czech books, American publishers began to enter the field, publishing a wide range of pop-up books for children. Random House was the first major

Figure 18.4 Illustration by Geraldine Clyne from *The Jolly Jump-ups and Their New House*, Springfield, MA: McLoughlin Bros. Inc., 1939.

Collection of Ann Montanaro Staples.

publisher to begin issuing pop-ups with *Bennett Cerf's Pop-Up Riddles* (1965). It was followed by forty-five other titles in their numbered series. The riddle book, with glossy covers and brightly colored illustrations included pop-ups, flaps, and tabs. This book, like others in the series, had universal appeal addressing familiar themes such as colors, the alphabet, counting, and Old Testament stories; later titles featured comic book characters and super heroes.

Hallmark Cards began producing pop-up books in 1966 and issued about seventy books of uniform dimension and style during the late 1960s and the 1970s. Each of Hallmark's pop-up books was, according to testimony on the back cover, "tested" to insure that they would be a "happy and healthy experience for young people" (Loberg 198-?: back cover).

While Random House and Hallmark continued to produce attractive and interesting pop-ups during the 1960 and 1970s, other publishers also began to enter the movable book marketplace, many with increasingly complex mechanicals. However, the publication explosion of pop-up books that took place in the 1980s was unlike anything seen before: hundreds of extraordinary books were produced with newly developed formats and mechanisms. Pop-up books, which in the past had often been dismissed as toy books or ephemera, began to be accepted and appreciated for their artistry, content, and mechanical ingenuity. Many pop-up titles were printed in multiple languages for distribution throughout the world.

While traditional stories, such as the fables in *Roaring Lion Tales* (1984), continued to be interpreted in pop-up format, many authors began to write original stories to be illustrated with pop-ups. The spare text in *Sophie's Hideaway* (1983) was brought to life with Ray Marshall's expressive pop-ups filling the pages. Similarly, David Carter's illustrative pop-ups in *Ben's Box* (1986) showed parts of the story that did not need to be told in the text.

Pop-ups have also been used to enhance the text. Keith Moseley's luminous watercolors and dramatic pop-ups bring life to *Hiawatha* (1988), the poem by Henry Wadsworth Longfellow. Moseley's planes in *Flight: Great Planes of the Century* (1985) soar off the page and graphically illustrated the detailed text. *The Human Body* (1983) and *Facts of Life* (1984) both explored human organs and anatomy in much the same way as their predecessors in the 1600s. With bright contemporary colors and large, scientifically accurate body parts, David Pelham's movables in both books explain how the body functions in a way that can be easily understood.

Split page, mix-and-match books reappeared as pop-ups. In *Have You Seen a POG?* (1988), wacky animals are created when the pop-up pages are combined: The top of a pig and the bottom of a dog forms a "pog." The minimal text is almost irrelevant as the pictures tell the story. *Don't Go Out Tonight* (ca. 1982) reintroduced another mechanical used in the nineteenth century. Babette Cole's story, illustrated with witty pictures, had six stand-up scenes that became an amusingly scary three-dimensional panorama. Peepshows also made a reappearance in the 1980s. Readers of *Tomie dePaola's Country Farm* (1984) looked through the plastic-covered barn window on the cover to see people and animals on the farm portrayed in a nine-section, three-dimensional display. Edward Gorey's humor was captured in *The Tunnel Calamity* (1984), part of the same Magic Windows peepshow series.

The National Geographic Action Book series began in 1985 and continued through 1994. *Amazing Monkeys* (1985) and *Hide and Seek* (1985) had sophisticated pop-ups, detailed illustrations, and knowledgeable text. These books are excellent examples of how three-dimensional work can enhance an understanding of nature. Other books in the series of twenty titles explored weather, undersea life, and animals from throughout the world.

David Carter began designing pop-up books in the 1980s and achieved acclaim with his Bugs in a Box series of more than a dozen titles including *How Many Bugs in a Box: A Pop-Up Counting Book* (1988). The bright, bold graphics in this book invites children to open boxes on each page and count the pop-up bugs inside. Similarly, his *One Red Dot* (2005), the first of a series of wordless books with pop-up sculptures, challenges the reader to find the hidden red dot in each of the ten spreads and amazes viewers with the unusual designs and movement.

Robert Sabuda's first pop-up book, *The Christmas Alphabet* (1994), is an imaginative holiday alphabet contribution with twenty-six pure white pop-ups encased inside colorful cards. His *Cookie Count* (1997), both a traditional counting book and a masterful paper engineering accomplishment, is complete with twirling pinwheels and a stand-up gingerbread house (Sabuda 2005). Sabuda provides a beautiful introduction to C.S. Lewis's classic *The Chronicles of Narnia* (2007), presenting one large pop-up illustration for each of the seven books including a dramatic pop-up of Narnia's creator, the Great Lion Aslan.

Nature is accurately portrayed in many pop-up books and provides both an entertaining and educational experience for the child. *The Ultimate Bug Book* (1993) has informative text and pop-up spreads that explain how insects live, eat, and defend themselves. The full-size pop-up of the mega moth shows how it could be mistaken for a small bird. The large bumblebee is the only pop-up in *The Bee* (1991), but it shows how effectively a complex mechanism can be used to aid in the understanding of a species.

Most well-known fairy tales and folk tales have been interpreted in pop-up format and are wonderful introductions to these stories. Traditional tales like *Cinderella, Snow White, Beauty and the Beast, Little Red Riding Hood, The Princess and the Pea, The Wizard of Oz, The Three Little Pigs*, and *Aesop's Fables* have been interpreted many times by different illustrators and paper engineers. These are some notable examples. *Cinderella: A Peepshow Book* (1979) is a carousel book with covers that tie together, forming a five-panel, three-dimensional scene: Text printed at the base of each page briefly tells the story. *Pop-up Aesop* (2005) is full of fanciful creatures that help bring the tales to life. Tab-operated mechanicals bring life to the characters in Julian Wehr's interpretation of *Little Red Riding Hood* (1944). Chuck Murphy's *Jack and the Beanstalk* (1998) features "giant" pop-ups and lengthy retelling of the story.

Many classic children's narratives have also been adapted in pop-up form. There are almost two dozen pop-up versions of *Alice in Wonderland* but none has the complete, rich text found in Lewis Carroll's original version. Ludwig Bemelmans's three-dimensional *Madeline* (1987) has all of the charm of the original with the additional surprise of tabs and pop-ups. *The Little Prince* (2009) by Antoine de Saint-Exupéry is unusual among pop-up books because it includes the full text and illustrations by the author.

Matthew Reinhart and Robert Sabuda have collaborated on a number of wonderful books. Their Encyclopedia Prehistorica series explores *Dinosaurs* (2005), *Sharks* and *Other Sea Monsters* (2006), and *Mega-beasts* (2007). Each book is packed with more than thirty-five intricate pop-ups: large ones fill the openings as the pages are turned and smaller ones are tucked inside gatefolds on extended pages. Detailed text accompanies each of illustrations in these books giving children an introduction to prehistoric creatures.

Rudyard Kipling's *The Jungle Book* (2006) was expertly interpreted by Matthew Reinhart with voluminous, complex pop-ups. His beautiful illustrations and exuberant mechanicals draw the reader into the story. Reinhart reached into a different sphere with *Star Wars: A Pop-Up Guide to the Galaxy* (2007). Celebrating the thirtieth anniversary of the classic film, the book is encyclopedic in its review of the people, places, and events that shaped the *Star Wars* universe. The final spread depicts the penultimate light saber duel between Darth Vader and Luke Skywalker, complete with battery-operated lights.

French artists Anouck Boisrobert and Louis Rigaud have created three remarkable pop-up books that have been widely translated into world languages: *Popville* (2010), *Wake Up Sloth* (2011), and *Under the Ocean* (2013). Their ingenious and stylish books present environmental themes through pop-ups.

Sam Ita has re-envisioned four classic books as pop-up graphic novels: *Moby-Dick* (2007), *20,000 Leagues under the Sea* (2008), *Frankenstein* (2010), and *The Odyssey* (2011). They capture the young reader's attention through the presentation of the abridged text in comic book format and detailed illustrations.

Teaching with pop-up books

Because pop-up books are unlike traditional illustrated books, they can engage children differently: they teach in clever ways, making the experience more effective, interactive, and memorable (Van Dyk et al. 2010: 7). As children use them to learn early educational concepts, the book's tactile appeal stimulates the child's curiosity and imagination. Children can actually touch the letters and numbers, feel shapes, and learn about textures through the inclusion of inserts. Classic tales, abridged and retold in pop-up books, can introduce traditional stories to young readers and help them understand the essence of the tale while giving them active engagement in the story through the mechanicals. The reluctant reader may be captivated by the stimulating action of the moving paper and be challenged to follow the story in the text. Beyond reading, pop-up books can be used to inspire art and science projects.

Conclusion

Pop-up books today, like their earliest predecessors, are handmade creations. Each of the paper parts that make up the mechanical are machine die-cut, but all of the folds and glue points are done by hand. The artists who make the paper come to life are the most important individuals in the creation of pop-up books. Yet it was not until the 1960s that recognition was given to those artists and the term "paper engineer" coined to acknowledge their contribution (Phillips and Montanaro 2012).

The popularity and complexity of pop-ups has grown significantly in the last forty years: readers expect to be 'wowed' by every new pop-up book they open. And, for the most part, they are not disappointed. Many wonderful pop-up books are being published for children, and many of them are introducing innovative ways of using paper as mechanical devices to educate and entertain.

Pop-up books are extraordinary creations. They are resilient, handmade paper constructions that can tell stories, communicate ideas, and demonstrate concepts while being fascinating, entertaining, and full of surprises.

References

Abate, Michelle Ann (2012) "When Clothes Don't Make the Man: Sartorial Style, Conspicuous Consumption, and Class Passing in Lothar Meggendorfer's *Scenes in the Life of a Masher*," *Children's Literature Association Quarterly* 37.1: 43–65.

Bader, Barbara (1976) *American Picturebooks from Noah's Ark to the Beast Within*, New York: Palgrave Macmillan.

Balzer, Richard (1998) *Peepshows: A Visual History*, New York: Harry N. Abrams.

Barker, Cicely Mary (2009) *Hidden Flower Fairies: 5 Secret 3D Scenes of Flower Fairyland*, London: Frederick Warne.

Bemelmans, Ludwig (1987) *Madeline: A Pop-up Book Based on the Original by Ludwig Bemelmans*, New York: Viking Kestrel.

"Biggest Juvenile Book Scoop in Years!" (1933), *The Publishers' Weekly* CXXIV: 1532.

Bluemel, Nancy, and Harris Taylor, Rhonda (2012) *Pop-up Books: A Guide for Teachers and Librarians*, Santa Barbara, CA: Libraries Unlimited.

Boisrobert, Anouck, and Rigaud, Louis (2010) *Popville*, New York: Roaring Brook Press.

Boisrobert, Anouck, and Rigaud, Louis (2013) *Under the Ocean*, London: Tate.

Boisrobert, Anouck, and Rigaud, Louis (2011) *Wake Up Sloth*, New York: Roaring Brook Press.

Brown, Gillian (2006) "The Metamorphic Book: Children's Print Culture in the Eighteenth Century," *Eighteenth-Century Studies* 39:3: 351–362.

Carter, David A. (1988) *How Many Bugs in a Box: A Pop-up Counting Book*, New York: Little Simon.

Carter, David A. (2005) *One Red Dot*, New York: Little Simon.

Cerf, Bennett (1965) *Bennett Cerf's Pop-up Riddles*, New York: Random House.

Clyne, Geraldine (1939) *The Jolly Jump-ups and Their New House*, Springfield, MA: McLoughlin Bros.

Cole, Babette (ca. 1982) *Don't Go Out Tonight*, New York: Doubleday.

Dawson, Michael (1997) *A Collector's Guide to the History of Pop-ups, Movables and Children's Novelty Books*, Ludlow: Shropshire.

DePaola, Tomie (1984) *Tomie dePaola's Country Farm*, New York: G.P. Putnam's Sons.

DuLong, Jessica, Sabuda, Robert, Baron, Andrew, The Movable Book Society (2004) *A Celebration of Pop-up and Movable Books, The Movable Book Society* [New Brunswick, New Jersey].

Eugene, Tony (1985) *Hide and Seek*, illus. Barbara Gibson, Washington, DC: National Geographic Society.

Evers, Edwina (1985) "A Historical Survey of Movable Books," *AB Bookman's Weekly* 76: 8–9.

Foreman, Michael (1986) *Ben's Box: A Pop-up Fantasy*, Sevenoaks: Hodder and Stoughton Children's Books.

Fun for Little Folks (1890) London: Raphael Tuck & Sons.

Gorey, Edward (1984) *The Tunnel Calamity*, New York: G.P. Putnam's Sons.

Gubig, Thomas, and Köpcke, Sebastian [2003] *Pop Up: Die dreidimensionalen Bücher des Vojteck Kubašta*, Berlin: Gubig & Köpcke.

Haining, Peter (1979) *Movable Books: An Illustrated History: Pages & Pictures of Folding, Revolving, Dissolving, Mechanical, Scenic, Panoramic, Dimensional, Changing, Pop-up and Other Novelty Books From the Collection of David and Briar Philips*, London: New English Library.

Harris, John (2005) *Pop-up Aesop*, illus. Calef Brown, Los Angeles, CA: Getty.

Helfand, Jessica (2002) *Reinventing the Wheel: Volvelles, Equatoria, Planispheres, Fact-finders, Gestational Charts*, New York: Princeton Architectural Press.

Higonnet, Margaret (2014) "Movable Books: Transnational Publication and Cultural Translation," in Gabriele von Glasenapp, Ute Dettmar, and Bernd Dolle-Weinkauff (eds) *Kinder- und Jugendliteraturforschung international*, Frankfurt: Peter Lang, 405–429.

Homer (2011) *The Odyssey: A Pop-up Book*, illlus. Sam Ita, New York: Sterling.

Hunt, Julia, and Hunt, Frederick [2006] *Peeps Into Nisterland: A Guide to the Children's Books of Ernest Nister*, Chester: Casmelda.

Hyde, Ralph (2015) *Paper Peepshows: The Jacqueline and Jonathan Gestetner Collection*. Suffolk: Antique Collectors' Club.

Kipling, Rudyard (2006) *The Jungle Book: A Pop-up Adventure*, illus. Matthew Reinhart, New York: Little Simon.

Knipschild, Kristen (2006) "Movable Magic," *Friends of the Library Magazine: University of Wisconsin-Madison* 46: 8–11.

Kozikowski, Renate (1983) *Sophie's Hideaway*, New York: Harper and Row.

Krahé, Hildegard E. (1988) "The Importance of Being Ernest Nister," *Phaedrus* 13: 73–90.

Krahé, Hildegard (1983) *Lothar Meggendorfers Spielwelt*, Munich: Hugendubel.

Kubašta, Vojtěch (ca. 1960) *Ricky the Rabbit*, London: Bancroft.

Kubašta, Vojtěch (1962) *The Day of the Bison Hunt*, London: Bancroft.

Kubašta, Vojtěch (1961) *Peter and Sally on the Farm*, London: Bancroft.

Kubašta, Vojtěch (ca. 1962) *The Voyage of Marco Polo*, London: Bancroft.

La Bella Addormentata Nel Bosco (1942) Milan Casa Editrice Hoepli.

Lewis, C. S. (2007) *The Chronicles of Narnia: Pop-ups by Robert Sabuda*, illus. Robert Sabuda, New York: Harper Collins.

Little Pets: A Panorama Picture Book of Animals (ca. 1896) London: Ernest Nister.

Little Red Riding Hood (ca. 1856) London: Dean & Son.

Longfellow, Henry Wadsworth (1988) *Hiawatha*, illus. Keith Moseley, New York: Philomel Books.

Loberg, Mary Alice, and Harrison, David L. (198-?) *The Kingdom of the Sea*, illus. Carl Cassler, Kansas City, MO: Hallmark.

Lopez, Donald S. (1985) *Flight: Great Planes of the Century*, New York: Viking Press.

Meggendorfer, Lothar (1985) *The Genius of Lothar Meggendorfer: A Moveable Toy Book: With an Appreciation by Maurice Sendak*, New York: Random House.

Meggendorfer, Lothar (1891) *Comic Actors: A New Movable Toy Book*, London: H. Grevel.

Meggendorfer, Lothar (ca. 1887) *International Circus*, Esslingen: J.F. Schreiber.

Melville, Herman (2007) *Moby-Dick: A Pop-up Book*, illus. Sam Ita, New York: Sterling.

Miller, Jonathan, and Pelham, David (1984) *Facts of Life: Three-dimensional, Movable Illustrations Show the Development of a Baby From Conception to Birth*, illus. Harry Willock, New York: Viking Press.

Miller, Jonathan, and Pelham, David (1983) *The Human Body*, illus. Harry Willock, New York: Viking Press.

Moerbeek, Kees (1988) *Have You Seen a POG?* Los Angeles, CA: Price Stern Sloan.

Montanaro, Ann R. (1993) *Pop-up and Movable Books: A Bibliography*, Metuchen, NJ: Scarecrow Press.

Montanaro, Ann R. [1996] "A Concise History of Pop-up Books," www.libraries.rutgers.edu/rul/libs/scua/montanar/p-intro.htm.

Murphy, Chuck (1998) *Jack and the Beanstalk: Illustrated in Three Dimensions*, New York: Little Simon.

Norden, Beth B. (1991) *The Bee*, illus. Biruta Akerbergs Hansen, New York: Stewart, Tabori, & Chang.

Opie, Iona, and Opie, Peter (1975) "Books That Come to Life," in John Hadfield (ed.) *The Saturday Book*, London: Hutchinson, 61–79.

Pelachaud, Gaelle (2010) *Livres Animés du Papier au Numérique*, Paris: L'Harmattan.

Perrault, Charles (ca.1930) *Cinderella Panorama Book: Six Magnificent Scenes*, London: Collins.

Phillips, Trish, and Montanaro, Ann R. (2012) *The Practical Step-by-step Guide to Making Pop-ups & Novelty Cards: A How-to Guide to the Art of Paper Engineering*, Wigston, Leicestershire: Lorenz Books.

Presencer, Alain (1984) *Roaring Lion Tales: A Pop-up Book*, illus. Ron Van der Meer, London: Bedrick/Blackie.

Provensen, Alice, and Provensen, Martin (1984) *Leonardo Da Vinci: The Artist, Inventor, Scientist in Three-dimensional, Movable Pictures*, New York: Viking.

Pym, Roland (1979) *Cinderella: A Peepshow Book*, London: Chatto & Windus.

The Renier Collection of Historic and Contemporary Children's Books (1988) *Occasional List no. 3: Moveable Books*, London: Bethnal Green Museum of Childhood.

Reinhart, Matthew (2007) *Star Wars: A Pop-up Guide to the Galaxy*, New York: Orchard Books.

Rinard, Judith E. (1985) *Amazing Monkeys*, illus. Robert Hynes, Washington, DC: National Geographic Society.

Rubin, Ellen G.K. (2013) *Pop-Ups From Prague: A Centennial Celebration of the Graphic Artistry of Vojtěch Kubašta*, New York: The Grolier Club.

Sabuda, Robert (1994) *The Christmas Alphabet*, New York: Orchard Books.

Sabuda, Robert (1997) *Cookie Count*, New York: Little Simon.

Sabuda, Robert (2005) "Making the Paper Listen and Obey," *The Lion and the Unicorn* 29: 9–11.

Sabuda, Robert, and Reinhart, Matthew (2005) *Dinosaurs: Encyclopedia Prehistorica*, Cambridge, MA: Candlewick Press.

Sabuda, Robert, and Reinhart, Matthew (2007) *Mega-beasts: Encyclopedia Prehistorica*, Cambridge, MA: Candlewick Press.

Sabuda, Robert, and Reinhart, Matthew (2005) *Sharks and Other Sea Monsters: Encyclopedia Prehistorica*, Cambridge, MA: Candlewick Press.

Saint-Exupéry, Antoine de (2009) *The Little Prince*, New York: HMH Books.

Seaside Pleasures (1896) London: Raphael Tuck & Sons.

Shelley, Mary Wollstonecraft (2010) *Frankenstein: A Pop Book*, illus. Sam Ita, New York: Sterling.

Van Dyk, Stephen H., Broman, Elizabeth, Rubin, Ellen G.K., and Montanaro, Ann R. (2010) *Paper Engineering: Fold, Pull, Pop & Turn*, [Washington, DC]: Smithsonian Institution Libraries.

Verne, Jules (2008) *20,000 Leagues Under the Sea: A Pop-up Book*, illus. Sam Ita, New York: Sterling.

A Very Good Book (ca. 1897) London: Raphael Tuck & Sons.

Weatherly, F. E. (ca. 1894) *Here and There: A Book of Transformation Pictures*, London: Ernest Nister.

Weedon, L. L. (ca. 1895) *Model Menagerie: With Natural History Stories*, illus. Evelyn Fletcher, London: Ernest Nister.

Wehr, Julian (1942) *The Exciting Adventures of Finnie the Fiddler*, New York: Cupples and Leon Co.

Wehr, Julian (1944) *Little Red Riding Hood*, New York: Dunewald Print Corp.

Weiss, Harry B. (1932) "Metamorphoses and Harlequinades," *The American Book Collector* (August–September): 100–118.

Whitton, Blair (1986) *Paper Toys of the World*, Cumberland, MD: Hobby House Press.

Williams, Chester A. (1942) *Victory March; or, The Mystery of the Treasure Chest*, New York: Random House.

Woelflein, Luise (1993) *The Ultimate Bug Book: A Unique Introduction to the World of Insects in Fabulous, Full-Color Pop-Ups*, illus. Wendy Smith-Griswold, New York: Artists & Writers Guild.

19

WORDLESS PICTUREBOOKS

Emma Bosch

In recent years both the number of wordless picturebooks published and the interest in finding out more about them have increased. There is therefore an urgent need for them to be studied in greater depth. This chapter presents a selection of works which demonstrate that there are so many types of wordless picturebooks that they should not be considered a 'genre.'

Picturebooks: the sum of text and images?

Studies on picturebooks tend to highlight their bipolar nature by pointing out that they are usually formed by a conjunction of text and images (Schulevitz 1980; Arizpe and Styles 2003). Experts therefore mostly concentrate on studying the relationships between the two languages (Doonan 1996; Nikolajeva and Scott 2006). When it comes to defining what a picturebook is, some argue that text and image form a single unit (Lewis 1990), while others maintain that it is much more than the sum of its two components (Kiefer 1985; Nodelman 1988; Arizpe and Styles 2003). At least they unanimously believe that the images in a picturebook have an absolutely essential function and predominate over the text (Schulevitz 1980; Duran 2000; Salisbury 2004). Strangely enough, despite the picturebook being defined on the basis of a conjunction of text and image, picturebook experts sometimes also acknowledge the possibility of wordless picturebooks (Schulevitz 1980; Kiefer 1988).

The fact that wordless picturebooks exist means that the definition of the picturebook should be reformulated and the presence of a written text as a prerequisite be put into perspective. For this reason I suggest that a picturebook should be defined as a "story composed of fixed, printed, sequential images consolidated in a book structure whose unit is the page and in which the illustrations are primordial and the text may be underlying" (Bosch 2012: 75). In wordless picturebooks, "apart from the title, the name(s) of the author(s) and the credits, no other words appear in the pages of the book" (82). By contrast, almost-wordless picturebooks are "those narratives conceived essentially as visual representations that include a number of words on their pages. These could be single words, sentences, paragraphs or even some pages of text" (82). Moreover, one should distinguish between words that form part of the narrative and the intra-iconic text, that is, text and words that form part of the image, for instance those shown on signs and labels (Bosch 2012; 2014).

Wordless picturebooks: a publishing trend

The number of wordless picturebooks has increased noticeably over the last few years. As Sandra Beckett (2012) points out, wordless picturebooks have become a contemporary publishing trend with several newly created wordless picturebook series and some highly acclaimed author-illustrators working exclusively in this genre (83f.). As a result, readers, mediators (librarians and teachers), and researchers have shown an increasing interest in investigating their narrative structure and composition and studying the readers' responses. This is evident from the proliferation of talks and courses on the subject in educational circles, the establishment of international dissemination projects such as *Silent Books: From the World to Lampedusa and Back*, promoted by IBBY-Italia in 2012, and publications in which artists explain the creative processes that determine their work. Prominent examples for the latter are *Sketches from a Nameless Land: The Art of the Arrival* (2010) by Shaun Tan, in which the artist talks about his inspiration sources, the process of documentation, and the construction of characters and settings for his award-winning wordless graphic novel; and *La trilogia del limite* (The Border Trilogy 2012) by Suzy Lee, in which the author reveals how she composed and created *Mirror* (2003), *Wave* (2008), and *Shadow* (2010), which resulted from her experiments with the narrative use of the space between two facing pages.

Sara Dowhower (1997) noted at the end of the twentieth century that the proliferation of wordless picturebooks over the previous thirty years had been astonishing (71). She added that, although these types of books were useful for developing different registers of spoken language and many teachers recommended them, there was still a great deal of research to be done. Twenty years later, despite the fact that the publishing market seems to be growing constantly and ever more people are attending activities revolving around wordless picturebooks, they still only rarely appear in studies.

Evelyn Arizpe (2014) also stresses the lack of theoretical research into the subject, emphasizing that wordless picturebooks still need to be studied in greater depth. She distinguishes studies which carry out detailed analyses of wordless picturebooks (Nières-Chevrel 2010); suggest classifications of wordless picturebooks (Richey and Puckett 1992; Tuten-Puckett and Richey 1993; Rowe 1996; Dowhower 1997; Walker 2006); concentrate on crossover books and artists' books (Beckett 2012); focus on the so-called wordless graphic novels of the last century (Beronä 2008); and investigate the reader's active participation in family and educational environments (Nodelman 1988; Rowe 1996; Nikolajeva and Scott 2006; Bosch and Duran 2009; Nières-Chevrel 2010; Beckett 2012; Ramos and Ramos 2012).

It was in this context and with the aim of contributing to a better knowledge of wordless picturebooks that I analyzed a corpus of 385 wordless or almost-wordless picturebooks in my doctoral thesis, *Estudio del Álbum Sin Palabras* (A Study on Wordless Picturebooks 2015). A crucial issue discussed in this study and which is center stage in this chapter concerns the question whether wordless picturebooks constitute a genre or whether there are different genres sheltering under the 'wordless picturebook' umbrella.

Wordless picturebooks: a genre?

Many scholars categorize wordless picturebooks as a 'genre' (Dowhower 1993: 63; Crawford and Hade 2000; Jalongo et al. 2002: 167). Evelyn Arizpe (2014) calls this view into question by discussing whether wordless picturebooks are a genre or a subgenre of picturebooks (95).

In literary studies, the notion of genre refers to a group of (literary) works that share certain characteristics concerning the story line, the plot construction, the depiction of characters and place, the topic, the narrative devices, and so forth, which are regarded as typical for this specific genre. If one takes these considerations seriously, wordless picturebooks do not constitute a genre. Quite the contrary, wordless picturebooks display an astonishing variety of topics and narrative forms drawn from different genres. Based on the classic distinction between telling (diegesis) and showing (mimesis), which has been transferred by Nikolajeva and Scott (2006) to picturebooks in general, I have developed a classification that shows the great variety of wordless picturebooks (see Table 19.1).

Table 19.1 Classification of wordless picturebooks

WORDLESS PICTUREBOOKS			
Stories focused on TELLING		*Stories focused on SHOWING*	
SOURCE	Adaptation Re-Creation Original Stories	TOPIC	Chronicle Panoramic Explicative/Conceptual

Wordless picturebooks focusing on telling a story

In wordless picturebooks focusing on telling a story, the narrative centers on characters and the actions they are involved in. Depending on the origin of the story, these can be divided into three groups: adaptations, re-creations, and original stories.

Wordless adaptations

Wordless and almost-wordless adaptations are essentially graphic versions of pre-existing fictional stories. Obviously the language is different (now exclusively visual), and there may also be changes in the length of the story, the tone, and the narrative structure. These stories cannot be understood 'optimally' without knowledge of the original text (hypotext) on which they are based. They are therefore 'reminders,' that is, picturebooks where the images invite the reader to remember a story they already know from other sources. Without previous knowledge of the hypotext, the reader is usually not able to understand the story or highly significant information is lost. It is not surprising that the biggest group comprises adaptations based on classic fairy tales. Most of the Design collection from the Hungarian publisher Csimota is made up of wordless or almost-wordless classic and popular fairy tales. The books in this collection have a small, square format, and have been created by different authors with very different graphic styles. So far five adaptations of three fairy tales – *Puss in Boots*, *Three Little Pigs*, and *Little Red Riding Hood* – have been published. *Little Red Riding Hood* is one of the most frequently adapted fairy tales all over the world, and this also holds true concerning almost-wordless and wordless picturebooks, among which Adolfo Serra's (2011) *Caperucita Roja* stands out due to its original handling of graphics. The illustrations are filled with visual metaphors and polysemic plays, as is evident in the following illustration showing the wolf, who is both an animal and a landscape (Figure 19.1). Red Riding Hood strolls through this 'wolf-forest,' which connects the dangers of the wild forest and the savage animal.

Wordless adaptations of fables, myths, and legends are much less frequent. The few that exist include the 2010 winner of the Caldecott Medal, *The Lion and the Mouse* (2009) by Jerry Pinkney, which almost wordlessly narrates one of Aesop's fables. The wordless picturebook *El coratge de Sant Jordi* (The Courage of St. George 2002), by Xavier Blanch and Mikel Valverde, tells the well-known legend of the knight who slayed a dragon to free a princess.

Although readers usually have to be familiar with the hypotext in order to comprehend a wordless adaptation, there are exceptions to this rule, like Ajubel's *Robinson Crusoe: una novela en imágenes inspirada en la obra de Daniel Defoe* (Robinson Crusoe: A Wordless Novel Inspired by the Work of Daniel Defoe 2008), which won the BolognaRagazzi Award in 2009. This is an almost-wordless picturebook whose unusual length (eighty scenes, seventy-six of which are doublespreads) characterizes it as a successor to the so-called illustrated novel. In this case it is indeed possible to figure out the story with no previous knowledge of the original text. In a note at the end of the book, Leonardo Padura mentions that the tools available to a graphic storyteller when adapting a well-known text are "summary, suggestion, and connotation," and that Ajubel has managed to use them magnificently.

Figure 19.1 Illustration by Adolfo Serra from *Caperucita Roja*. Madrid: Narval, 2011.
Reprinted by permission of Narval Editores, Madrid.

Wordless re-creations

In re-creations, the artists use an existing work as the basis for creating a new one with a considerable degree of alteration. Knowing the hypotext enriches the comprehension of these picturebooks, but it is not essential. There are very few re-creations among wordless and almost-wordless picturebooks. The almost-wordless picturebook *Alice in Wonderland* (2002) by Suzy Lee is the author's 'response' as an adult to a re-reading of the novel *Alice's Adventures in Wonderland* (1865) by Lewis Carroll. Lee expresses her intentions in her *Artist's Statement* (2013):

> I tried to produce a book that reflects upon subject matters like constructed illusions and realities and the dream-within-a-dream structure, which contains a circular regression and self-reflexivity [...] I may say that Lewis Carroll's book appealed to me in terms of illuminating the relationship between illusion and reality.
>
> *n. pag.*

A prominent picturebook that re-creates a popular tale is *Le code de la route* (The Highway Code 2010) by Mario Ramos, which describes humorously, by the use of traffic signs, the 'dangerous' ride taken by a girl dressed in red when she cycles through the forest to visit her grandmother. Apart from being based on *Little Red Riding Hood*, this entertaining story makes various references to other popular fairy tales such as *Goldilocks and the Three Bears, The Three Little Pigs*, and *Tom Thumb*. Another example of a re-creation based on a well-known fairy tale is the almost-wordless picturebook *Deep in the Forest* (1976) by Brinton Turkle. Here the characters' roles are reversed, and it is a baby bear that enters Goldilocks's house.

An outstanding re-creation of a classic fairy tale is the almost-wordless picturebook *Der standhafte Zinnsoldat* (The Steadfast Tin Soldier 1996) by Jörg Müller, based on the famous story by Hans Christian Andersen. Müller changed the fairy tale story in order to create a socio-economic critique set in the present. This information and a brief recap of the story are printed on the back cover of the original edition. Moreover, the picturebook is described as "*ein Roman ohne Worte*" (a wordless novel), thus maintaining that each image contains a story and that these stories join together to form a longer story. The text goes on to say that, using the many details to be found in the illustrations, readers can "make up their own story." Nevertheless, this edition provides a loose-leaf with the tale by Andersen. The publishers obviously believed that all this information was essential for the reader in order to understand the wordless story. In contrast to the German edition, the Spanish version, *El soldadito de plomo* (2005), omits the Andersen text and includes only some of the comments from the German edition, thus stressing that Müller's version can be understood perfectly well without knowing the original text.

A very unusual source for wordless and almost-wordless picturebook re-creations is film. One example is *Le Jacquot de Monsieur Hulot* (The Parrot of Monsieur Hulot 2005), in which David Merveille invents an almost-wordless story about the well-known film character created by Jacques Tati. In this new Monsieur Hulot adventure, there are many references to the filmography of this French filmmaker and actor. The book can be interpreted on a number of levels and if the reader acknowledges the references to the films by Tati, the experience is much more satisfying. Recognizing the buildings, cars, and characters is a precondition for the understanding of the allusions, references, hidden messages, and reasons why particular elements appear in the scenes of the book.

Original wordless picturebooks

Original wordless picturebooks are those picturebooks that present stories which are not based on a pre-existing text. They are newly invented, previously unpublished, and generally bundled together under the generic term 'works of fiction.' The stories are either realistic, verisimilar, or fantastic. Most fictional wordless picturebooks are adventure stories. The main characters have to overcome various obstacles to achieve their goals. This is what happens in *The Night Riders* (2012) by Matt Furie, which has a narrative structure very similar to the 'classic' adventure film in which secondary characters are introduced throughout the story to accompany the main character. A renowned example of a story that combines realistic and fantastic elements is the almost-wordless picturebook *Tuesday* (1991) by David Wiesner, winner of the Caldecott Medal in 1992, which tells the story of the strange events that take place at dusk one Tuesday involving flying frogs.

In dramatic picturebooks the characters have to face problems such as loss, loneliness, poverty, and death. These are works that aim to move the viewer by appealing to their sensitivity and feelings, like *A Day, A Dog* (1982) by Gabrielle Vincent, which tells the story of a dog abandoned by its owners by the roadside.

Love stories and comic stories are rare among wordless picturebooks. There are tales based on loving relationships, such as *Pip i el color vermell* (Pip and the Color Red 1987) by Ricardo Alcántara and Gusti, in which a prick from a rose thorn causes Pip to fall in love with his caretaker. The almost-wordless picturebook *Des hauts et des bas* (High and Low 1988) by Christian Bruel and Nicole Claveloux is a comic story distinguished by absurdist humor. In this book, not only the penguins are puzzled and surprised by what they see, but the reader is too (Figure 19.2). Each doublespread shows the interiors of elevators that move up and down in a building. The elevators are crowded with pigs which use them in quite unusual ways: as a living room, wardrobe, or a photo booth. The book seems difficult to understand, set in a fantasy world based on the absurd. It is only when the reader discovers that this is an incongruous universe governed by irrational rules that they begin to enjoy it.

Wordless picturebooks focusing on showing

Wordless picturebooks focusing on showing have a 'documentary' appeal in the sense that they concentrate on the narrative depiction of everyday life situations, landscapes and cityscapes, and the explanation of concepts. In these books the 'showing' is more important than the 'telling.' While the majority of these picturebooks depict real sceneries and events, some even include fantastic elements. The term covers chronicles, panoramic storybooks, and concept-explaining storybooks.

Figure 19.2 Illustration by Nicole Claveloux from Christian Bruel and Nicole Claveloux's *Des hauts et des bas*. Paris: Éditions Être, 2005.

Wordless chronicles

Chronicles are those picturebooks with narrative sequences that describe everyday or general events, that is, stories of everyday life in which no particular incidents occur. A good example is *Tchibum!* (2009) by Gustavo Borges and Daniel Kondo, which received an honorable mention in the New Horizons category at the 2010 Bologna Children's Book Fair. It contains a simple narrative sequence in which a child dives into a swimming pool and swims across it under the watchful eye of an adult. Chronicles can also have animals as their main characters and describe everyday activities in their natural environment. An example of this is the almost-wordless picturebook *Spider* (1979) by Susumu Shingu, which features a spider that spins a web and waits patiently for prey to become trapped.

Panoramic wordless picturebooks

Panoramic picturebooks are more focused on the context than on what happens to the characters. Settings, sceneries, landscapes, cityscapes, and people share the limelight with the main characters, if any. In fact, the main characters' prime function consists in connecting the scenes. An obvious example is the series of almost-wordless picturebooks *Anno's Journey* (1977–2009) by Mitsumasa Anno, in which a horse rider travels silently through different countries. In each volume the main character lands on a beach in a rowboat and buys a horse. Apart from negotiating with a horse dealer, he interacts with nobody else. On only one occasion, in the first volume *Anno's Journey* (1977), does the rider dismount to cheer on the runners in a race. The readers' attention focuses on the context, examining the rural and urban landscapes characteristic of the area and scrutinizing the activities of the inhabitants.

Panoramic picturebooks can sometimes be confused with non-narrative panoramic books or even search-and-find books. For instance, in the picturebook *The City* (1984) by Teresa Ribas and Pilar Casademunt with illustrations by Roser Capdevila, the reader wanders through a port city following a tourist couple. These characters serve as a device for showing the city's squares, streets, buildings, and other attractions. One hardly notices the small couple, which appears on every doublespread, and therefore, on the basis of a rapid and inattentive reading, this picturebook might seem to be a mere picture sequence without any narrative thread.

Panoramic picturebooks can also follow an improbable story line. In the almost-wordless picturebook *Krochnouk Karapatak* (2006) by Julien Martinière, some children cross a surreal landscape aboard bizarre flying machines. But although these children appear on each page, they are not the main characters; they assume the role of observers of the strange settings and the fantastic people living in them.

Another prominent type of panoramic picturebook is the wimmel picturebook, which tells several stories at the same time, as in Rotraut Susanne Berner's series about the fictional city of Wimmlingen (2003, 2004, 2005a, 2005b, 2008), which is depicted in different seasons and at various times of the day. The main characters reappear on each doublespread and throughout the whole series of five volumes, thus constituting a complex narrative universe. Cornelia Rémi (2011) describes the reading habit of these books as "reading as playing" because the pages, teeming with characters, "allow for manifold reading options and encourage a highly active response [. . .] which rightfully might be described as a form of playing" (115). A simpler version of this book type are those wimmelbooks whose narrative microunits are restricted to one doublespread, but do not develop over the course of the book, as in *Mein Wimmel-Bilderbuch: Frühling, Sommer, Herbst und Winter* (My Wimmelbook: Spring, Summer, Autumn and Winter 1968) by Ali Mitgutsch.

Concept-explaining picturebooks

Concept-explaining picturebooks use a narrative to explain concepts. Concept-explaining picturebooks usually include words to explain the different concepts; for this reason there are not many wordless concept-explaining picturebooks. An early example was published in the 1960s, when graphic designers created books aimed at the very young, providing "purposely innovative formal research" (Duran 2010: 17). *L'altalena* (See-Saw 1961) by Enzo Mari has an accordion format and is based on his *Sedici Animali* (Sixteen Animals) puzzle designed in 1957. Mari's picturebook focuses on scales and how they can be perfectly balanced. Another picturebook that uses a narrative to develop a concept is *The Colors* (1991) by Monique Felix. The author illustrates color-mixing theory through the experimentation of the main character, a mouse, which wields tubes of paint and 'by chance' discovers how colors are made. A third example is *L'autre côté* (The Other Side 2006) by Elodie Pasgrimaud, which develops the subject of opposites in a very specific way. Far from explaining the concept didactically, as happens in the previous books, the author approaches the subject by using an enigmatic and poetic language. In this picturebook, the comparison of rural and city life is just an excuse for emphasizing that opposing concepts have more in common than one might usually expect (Figure 19.3).

Wordless picturebooks: a multitude of genres

As this selection of works has shown, wordless and almost-wordless picturebooks reveal an astonishing variety. Adaptations and re-creations, works of fiction, and documentary picturebooks are all too different to be grouped under the same 'genre' label. This variety also applies to other parameters,

Figure 19.3 Illustration from Elodie Pasgrimaud's *L'autre côté*. Champigny sur Marne: Le Textuaire, 2006.
Reprinted by permission of Elodie Pasgrimaud.

such as the age of the reader, the graphic style, and the narrative structure. This high degree of diversity shows that the various types of wordless picturebooks need to be dealt with in different ways. The analysis of the particular features of wordless picturebooks permits us to achieve a better knowledge of the narrative and aesthetic functions of visual narration. What should also be considered are the required competencies of the reader, a target question which concerns educationalists as well as picturebook researchers. In order to enjoy wordless picturebooks, children have to acquire cognitive and narrative abilities that enable them to comprehend the sophisticated visual language in these works. Only by getting to know the diversity and complexity of wordless picturebooks can readers, teachers, and scholars fully appreciate their cognitive, emotional, and aesthetic appeal.

References

Ajubel (2008) *Robinson Crusoe: una novela en imágenes inspirada en la obra de Daniel Defoe*, Valencia: Media Vaca.
Alcántara, Ricardo (1987) *Pip i el color vermell*, ill. Gusti, Barcelona: PAM.
Anno, Mitsumasa (1978) *Anno's Journey*, Cleveland: Collins World (first published 1977 in Japanese).
Arizpe, Evelyn, and Styles, Morag (2003) *Children Reading Pictures: Interpreting Visual Texts*, London and New York: Routledge.
Arizpe, Evelyn (2014) "Wordless Picturebooks. Critical and Educational Perspectives on Meaning-Making," in Bettina Kümmerling-Meibauer (ed.) *Picturebooks: Representation and Narration*, New York: Routledge, 91–106.
Beckett, Sandra L. (2012) *Crossover Picturebooks: A Genre for All Ages*, New York: Routledge.
Berner, Rotraut Susanne (2003) *Winter Wimmelbuch*, Hildesheim: Gerstenberg.
Berner, Rotraut Susanne (2004) *Frühling Wimmelbuch*, Hildesheim: Gerstenberg.
Berner, Rotraut Susanne (2005a) *Sommer Wimmelbuch*, Hildesheim: Gerstenberg.
Berner, Rotraut Susanne (2005b) *Herbst Wimmelbuch*, Hildesheim: Gerstenberg.
Berner, Rotraut Susanne (2008) *Nacht Wimmelbuch*, Hildesheim: Gerstenberg.
Beronä, David A. (2008) *Wordless Books: The Original Graphic Novels*, New York: Abrams.
Blanch, Xavier (2002) *El coratge de Sant Jordi*, ill. Mikel Valverde, Barcelona: La Galera.
Borges, Gustavo (2009) *Tchibum!*, illus. Daniel Kondo, Sao Paulo: Cosac Naify.
Bosch, Emma (2012) "¿Cuántas palabras puede tener un álbum sin palabras?" *Ocnos* 8: 75–88.
Bosch, Emma (2014) "Texts & Peritexts in Wordless and Almost Wordless Picturebooks," in Bettina Kümmerling-Meibauer (ed.) *Picturebooks: Representation and Narration*, New York: Routledge, 71–90.
Bosch, Emma (2015) *Estudio del Álbum Sin Palabras*, Ph D Thesis, Universidad de Barcelona, http://hdl.handle.net/10803/297430.

Bosch, Emma, and Duran, Teresa (2009) "OVNI: un álbum sin palabras que todos leemos de manera diferente," *AILIJ: Anuario de Investigación de Literatura Infantil y Juvenil* 7.2: 39–52.

Bruel, Christian (2005) *Des hauts et des bas*, ill. Nicole Claveloux, Paris: Éditions Être (first published 1988).

Crawford, Patricia A., and Hade, Daniel D. (2000) "Inside the Picture, Outside the Frame: Semiotics and the Reading of Wordless Picture Books," *Journal of Research in Childhood Education* 15.1: 66–80.

Doonan, Jane (1996) "The Modern Picturebook," in Peter Hunt (ed.) *International Companion Encyclopedia of Children's Literature*, London: Routledge, 228–238.

Dowhower, Sarah (1997) "Wordless Books: Promise and Possibilities, a Genre Comes of Age," in Kay Camperell, Bernard L. Hayes, and Richard Telfer (eds) *Promises, Progress and Possibilities: Perspectives of Literacy Education: Year Book of the American Reading Forum* 16: 57–79 (first published 1993).

Duran, Teresa (2000) *¡Hay que ver! Una aproximación al libro ilustrado*, Salamanca: Fundación Germán Sánchez Ruipérez.

Duran, Teresa (2010) "L'àlbum dins la narrativa visual," *Articles de Didàctica de la Llengua i la Literatura* 52: 10–22.

Felix, Monique (1991) *The Colors*, New York: Creative Editions Mankato, Mouse Books (first published 1991 in French).

Furie, Matt (2012) *The Night Riders*, San Francisco, CA: McSweeney's & McMullens.

Jalongo, Mary, Dragich, Danise, Conrad, Natalie K., and Zhang, Ann (2002) "Using Wordless Picture Books to Support Emergent Literacy," *Early Childhood Educational Journal* 29.3: 167–177.

Kiefer, Barbara (1985) "Looking Beyond Picture Book Preferences," *Horn Book* 61.6: 705–713.

Kiefer, Barbara (1988) "Picture Books as Context for Literacy, Aesthetic, and Real World Understandings," *Languages Arts* 65.3: 260–271.

Lee, Suzy (2003) *Mirror*, Mantova: Edizioni Corraini.

Lee, Suzy (2005) *Alice in Wonderland*, Mantova: Edizioni Corraini (first published 2002).

Lee, Suzy (2008) *Wave*, San Francisco, CA: Chronicle Books (first published 2008 in Italian).

Lee, Suzy (2010) *Shadow*, San Francisco, CA: Chronicle Books (first published 2010 in Italian).

Lee, Suzy (2012) *La trilogia del limite*, Mantova: Corraini.

Lee, Suzy (2013) "Artist's Statement: *Alice in Wonderland*," Author's website: www.suzyleebooks.com/books/alice/statement.htm (accessed November 10, 2015).

Lewis, David (1990) "The Constructiveness of Texts: Picture Books and the Metafictive," *Signal* 62: 130–146.

Mari, Enzo (2008) *L'altalena*, Mantova: Edizioni Corraini (first published 1961).

Martinière, Julien (2006) *Krochnouk Karapatak*, Champigny sur Marne: Le Textuaire.

Merveille, David (2005) *Le jacquot de Monsieur Hulot*, Rodez cedex: Éditions du Rouergue.

Mitgutsch, Ali (1968) *Mein Wimmel-Bilderbuch: Frühling, Sommer, Herbst und Winter*, Ravensburg: Ravensburger Buchverlag.

Müller, Jörg (1996) *Der standhafte Zinnsoldat*, Aarau: Sauerländer.

Müller, Jörg (2005) *El soldadito de plomo*, Santa Marta de Tormes: Lóguez.

Nières-Chevrel, Isabelle (2010) "The Narrative Power of Pictures: *L'Orage* (The Thunderstorm) by Anne Brouillard," in Teresa Colomer, Bettina Kümmerling-Meibauer, and Cecilia Silva-Díaz (eds) *New Directions in Picturebook Research*, New York: Routledge, 129–138.

Nikolajeva, Maria, and Scott, Carole (2006) *How Picturebooks Work*. New York: Routledge (first published 2001).

Nodelman, Perry (1988) *Words about Pictures: The Narrative Art of Children's Picture Books*, Athens: University of Georgia Press.

Pasgrimaud, Elodie (2006) *L'autre côté*, Champigny sur Marne: Le Textuaire.

Pinkney, Jerry (2011) *The Lion and the Mouse*, London: Walker Books (first published 2009).

Ramos, Ana Margarida, and Ramos, Rui (2012) "Ecoliteracy Through Imagery: A Close Reading of Two Wordless Picture Books," *Children's Literature in Education* 42: 325–349.

Ramos, Mario (2010) *Le code de la route*, Paris: L'école des loisirs.

Rémi, Cornelia (2011) "Reading as Playing. The Cognitive Challenge of the Wimmelbooks," in Kümmerling-Meibauer, Bettina (ed.) *Emergent Literacy: Children's Books from 0 to 3*, Amsterdam: Benjamins, 115–139.

Ribas, Teresa, and Casademunt, Pilar (1986) *The City*, ill. Roser Capdevila, London: Annick Press (first published 1984 in Catalan).

Richey, Virginia H., and Puckett, Katharyn E. (1992) *Wordless/Almost Wordless Picture Books: A Guide*, Englewood, CO: Libraries Unlimited.

Rowe, Anne (1996) "Voices Off. Reading Wordless Picture Books," in Morag Styles, Eve Bearne, and Victor Watson (eds) *Voices Off: Texts, Contexts and Readers*, London: Cassell, 219–234.

Salisbury, Martin (2004) *Illustrating Children's Books*, London: A&C Black.

Schulevitz, Uri (1980) "What Is a Picture Book?" *Wilson Library Bulletin* 55.2: 99–101.

Serra, Adolfo (2011) *Caperucita roja*, Madrid: Narval.

Shingu, Susumu (1979) *Spider*, Tokyo: Bunka Publishing Bureau.

Tan, Shaun (2010) *Sketches From a Nameless Land: The Art of "The Arrival,"* Sydney: Hachette Australia.

Turkle, Brinton (1976) *Deep in the Forest*, New York: Dutton Children's Books.

Tuten-Puckett, Katharyn, and Richey, Virginia H. (1993) *Using Wordless Picture Books: Authors and Activities*, Englewood, CO: Libraries Unlimited.

Vincent, Gabrielle (1999) *A Day, a Dog*, Asheville: Front Street (first published 1982 in French).

Walker, George A. (2006) *Graphic Witness: Four Wordless Graphic Novels*, Buffalo, NY: Firefly Books.

Wiesner, David (1991) *Tuesday*, New York: Clarion Books.

20

POSTMODERN PICTUREBOOKS

Cherie Allan

The impact of postmodernism was felt in the final decades of the twentieth century, particularly in the Western world, which in turn led to significant changes in the field of literature. As picturebooks have always responded to the various social and cultural milieu in which they are produced, it is hardly surprising that evidence of postmodern influences on picturebooks began to emerge as early as the 1950s and 1960s. Publication of forerunners, perhaps Crockett Johnson's *Harold and the Purple Crayon* (1955) and certainly *Where the Wild Things Are* (1963) by Maurice Sendak heralded the beginning of a movement that would continue until the beginning of the twenty-first century. Picturebooks, with their dual modes of words and pictures, are ideally placed to create playful texts that nevertheless challenge both the narrative strategies and embedded ideologies of conventional picturebooks. Postmodern picturebooks are cultural artifacts that reflect aspects of the prevailing social, cultural, and political conditions of a particular time in literary history.

Postmodernism and its influence on picturebooks

The discipline of literary studies and the production of literature in the second half of the twentieth century have been preoccupied by questions relating to postmodernism. However, the often uncritical use of the term makes any attempt to define it as problematic. Debates still remain over the exact meaning of postmodernism (Hutcheon 1988; Butler 2002) and its relationship to modernism (Lyotard 1984; Jameson 1991; Eagleton 1996). It is regarded as a rejection of many of the cultural certainties on which life in the West had been structured over the previous two hundred years (Sim 2005). The resultant skepticism of this rejection affects all aspects of life and finds expression in architecture, literature, art, music, and more recently law, science, and technology. This postmodern resistance, often expressed through playfulness in postmodern picturebooks, led to the emergence of fictions that questioned the nature of literary representation, blurred the boundaries between high and popular culture, raised notions of difference by destabilizing compulsions towards homogeneity, and promoted uncertainty and indeterminacy rather than certainty and resolution.

The enterprise of postmodernism has always been to challenge, question, and/or subvert *all* totalizing systems that led to literary texts that interrogated established beliefs and understandings about truth, reality, and history, whereby dominant ideologies, rather than being naturalized within the narratives, are 'laid bare.' Postmodern narratives question the mimetic function of realist fiction and argue that no text can fully represent the fragmentation, indeterminacy, and heterogeneity of 'real' life. Eagleton (1996: 201) describes the typical postmodern work of art that results from these impulses as "arbitrary, eclectic, hybrid, decentered, fluid, discontinuous, pastiche-like." He adds that the postmodernist form, including that of narrative, tends to be ironic, indulges in playfulness and pleasure, and points to its status as a construct, its intertextual origins, and its parodic recycling of other works (201). These characteristics are evident in postmodern picturebooks such as Tohby Riddle's *The Great Escape from City Zoo* (1997) and *Das Buch im Buch im Buch* (A Book in a Book in a Book 1990) by Jörg Müller, among many others. Perhaps the most prolific production of the postmodern picturebook was during the 1990s with the publication of a range of titles including *Black and White* (1990) by David Macaulay, *The Stinky Cheese Man and Other Fairly Stupid Tales* (1992) by Jon Scieszka and Lane Smith, and *Voices in the Park* (1998) by Anthony Browne. This impetus continued into the first decade of the new century, with titles such as David Wiesner's *The Three Pigs* (2001), Shaun Tan's *The Lost Thing* (2000), and Lauren Child's *Who's Afraid of the Big Bad Book?* (2003).

The first critical comments on the postmodern picturebook began to emerge in the early 1990s, with David Lewis (1990), Ann Grieves (1993), and Clare Bradford (1993) all noting the utilization of metafictive strategies such as excess, indeterminacy, and boundary-breaking (Lewis), irony and self-reflexivity (Bradford), and questions of originality and ontological plurality (Grieves). More recently, a number of commentators have attempted to offer definitions of exactly what a postmodern picturebook might look like. Lewis (2001), for instance, is not convinced that such an artifact exists, arguing that most so-called postmodern picturebooks are merely metafictive. Lawrence Sipe and Sylvia Pantaleo (2008) grapple with this dilemma by claiming that, not only is it difficult to list the specific characteristics that are necessary for a book to be classified postmodern, but such a list creates a binary of postmodern/not postmodern. Instead, they propose a continuum of postmodern characteristics on which picturebooks are located according to the number of characteristics or qualities of postmodernism they utilize. They then classify picturebooks with many postmodern characteristics as 'truly postmodern,' thereby reinscribing the very binary they were hoping to avoid. This contradiction only highlights the difficulties of definition.

Other critics point to conventional picturebooks' propensity to reinforce cultural norms. Perry Nodelman (2008) claims that while picturebooks labeled postmodern may seem to be open, they inevitably lead towards conventional understandings and assumptions. He argues that they represent a form of postmodernism peculiar to children's literature that is hardly surprising given the format of the picturebook and the nature of its primary audience. Linda Hutcheon's (1988) model of postmodern fiction is perhaps the most complete framework by which to define postmodern literature. Hutcheon argues that postmodern texts are those texts that *both* subvert the strategies and devices of conventional narrative *and* interrogate dominant discourses of liberal humanism. While the presence of these dual characteristics raises the texts above the 'merely metafictive,' it also is necessary to acknowledge that postmodern picturebooks require different considerations and different approaches from, for example, a postmodern novel for adults.

Postmodern picturebooks

While more conventional, Aristotelian narratives adhere to the beginning-middle-end formula, postmodern picturebooks often deviate from this norm. This disruption is achieved largely through the utilization of metafictive strategies such as intertextuality, parody and irony, narrative disruptions and discontinuities (frame-breaking, visual and verbal puns, etc.), multi-stranded and polyphonic narratives, and disruption to conventional spatio-temporalities. Readers of *Black and White* (1990) by David Macaulay, for instance, are confronted by a doublespread over which are four seemingly separate stories each with their own title, a border between them on each page, and the gutter helping to visually frame each as an individual tale. While each of the stories begins in the early morning, by the seventh opening the disjunction between the time frames of these tales is quite pronounced. In addition, at various times throughout the book the spatial borders between the stories are disrupted by elements from one story appearing in another rendering the story lines and storyworlds ambiguous. However, opening 15, the penultimate illustration, reverts to the previous structure of four tales, each with its own media and borders, once again creating a multiplicity of possible worlds. Just when readers might feel they can create a satisfactory resolution to each of the four stories, the final illustration of a child's hand reaching in to pick up the (toy?) railway station from Story 2 violates the already unstable ontology of the narrative and questions the possibility of an achievable conclusion.

Figure 20.1 Illustration from David Macaulay's *Black and White*. Boston: Houghton Mifflin, 1990.

These strategies are not necessarily metafictive in themselves; instead it is how they are used that render them self-reflexive. They foreground the ways in which meaning is constructed, highlight the texts' own processes of production and reception, and disrupt the codes and conventions of realist fiction. The appearance of metafictive strategies in postmodern picturebooks was first documented in the 1960s where, according to Stephens (1992), its progress mirrored that of the mainstream, where resistance gradually turned over time to acceptance and, eventually, celebration. Through these strategies postmodern picturebooks draw attention to their status as texts; they do so in order to reflect upon processes through which narrative fictions are constructed, read and made sense of, while simultaneously posing questions about the relationships between the interpretation and representation of fiction and reality (McCallum 1996). This is evident in the postmodern picturebook *Wait! No Paint!* (2001) by Bruce Whatley, in that the illustrator self-consciously draws readers' attention to the narrative processes by constantly disrupting these very processes by entering the storyworld of The Three Pigs.

Such self-reflexivity is particularly evident through the exploitation of the dual codes of words and pictures. Authors and illustrators of postmodern picturebooks play with the conventional sign systems of both linguistic and visual grammars, particularly by foregrounding the relativity of the sign-thing relationship that in turn interrogates the idea of established 'truths' and ideologies (Stephens 1992). Anthony Browne, for instance, plays with the arbitrary relationship between the signifier and the signified in the picturebook *Willy the Dreamer* (1997), in that he employs a banana motif that at times represents Elvis's microphone, rabbits' ears, the turrets of a castle, and ballet shoes, among many others. Through this playfulness, readers are made aware of the instability of the sign and the impossibility of attributing fixed meanings to textual readings. Not surprisingly, given this playfulness, the acknowledged dual readership of picturebooks (adult and child) is a particular feature of postmodern picturebooks. They often specifically appeal to an older readership, adolescents and adults alike, particularly because of their ironic and parodic nature, and yet young children remain as their primary audience.

Typographic and formatting experimentation, as well as the appropriation of peritextual elements of the text, serve to remind readers of the status of the book as artifact. Many of the picturebooks mentioned in this chapter employ changing font size and color, unusual page layouts, and pages that appear torn, nibbled, or folded. These formatting innovations highlight the normally 'invisible' elements of a work of fiction. The materiality of the book is also made explicit in constructed, interactive, and participatory picturebooks that deliberately draw attention to the book's format as text. Readers are expected to actively engage with the physical aspects of the book as part of the reading process. These texts foreground the nature of the book as an artifact that can be handled and manipulated. *Little Mouse's (Emily Gravett's) Big Book of Fears* (2007) by Emily Gravett, as well as having a self-reflexive title, contains flaps to be lifted and a folded map that has to be removed from its pocket and unfolded in order to be read. Such devices operate metafictively; their very interactivity draws the attention of readers away from the illusion of the fictive world of the narrative to the material substance of the book itself.

Other picturebooks exploit the elements of a literary work (author's name, a title, preface, illustrations, and a dedication) known as the *peritext*. Genette (1980) maintains that while these features remain subordinate to the body of the text, they nevertheless have the ability to create an 'implicit context' that defines or modifies the text's meaning and may affect the reception and consumption of the primary text through the positioning of its readers. When Jack, the narrator of *The Stinky Cheese Man and Other Fairly Stupid Tales*, realizes the dedication page is upside down, he declares "Who reads this stuff anyhow?," and reader's attention is immediately and self-reflexively pointed towards that very 'stuff.' In fact, Jack looks over his shoulder and invites the reader to become an active participant, or playmate, in the text by saying: "If you really want to read it – you can always stand on your head." Postmodern picturebooks delight in these playful games, with play used here in both senses of the word: as a sense of enjoyment as well as the possibilities of interpretation (Geyh 2003). Thus, this postmodern play, through the codes of both written and visual texts, engages readers on two levels: the subversive and the playful. This playfulness, however, has a serious purpose in that it draws attention to its own metafictive constructedness and, importantly, the ideologies of the text.

While conventional picturebooks typically adhere to particular genres and conventions of illustration, postmodern picturebooks dismantle hierarchies and break down boundaries. Postmodernism's insistence on blurring the distinctions between hierarchies, such as 'high and low culture,' is, as Hutcheon (1988: 9) observes, an attempt to transgress "previously accepted limits: those of particular arts, of genres, of art itself" resulting in fluidity between the borders of, for example, literary genres. Hutcheon argues that one of the ways postmodernism achieves a paradoxical popular-academic identity is by installing and then subverting familiar conventions of both kinds of art. This de-differentiation is evident in the picturebook *Willy the Dreamer* (1997), which playfully adapts the surreal artworks of Henri Matisse, Salvador Dalí, and Henri Rousseau to construct narratives about an ordinary character (Willy is an anthropomorphized chimp) who dreams of being extraordinary. This blurring of boundaries extends to genres where the status of serious literary mode is conferred on popular genres. Andrew Hoberek (2007) cites the current elevation of the graphic novel to the status of serious literary mode as an example of postmodernity's openness to popular culture resulting in an expansion of what counts as 'literature.' Another result of this impulse is to draw on a number of genres within a single text. Such hybrid texts might utilize elements of comics, graphic novels, and picturebooks within a single work. These hybrid texts disrupt conventional practices of reading, whereby readers bring to a text certain interests, expectations, and competence. For instance, when a text begins with the words "Once upon a time," readers are, consciously or unconsciously, already positioned by their previous experiences of fairy tale texts, whereas hybrid texts typically employ elements of a number of genres that then often require more complex reading strategies. This is evident in the fiction of Shaun Tan, whose text *The Arrival* (2008) deliberately and self-consciously blurs the boundaries between picturebooks, comics, and graphic novels. Another example of an author-illustrator who employs various degrees of hybridity is David Wiesner in *Tuesday* (1991) and *The Three Pigs* (2001); the former uses a mix of fantasy and realism conveyed through surrealist images, while the latter at times employs speech bubbles and comic-like panels.

A central concern of the postmodern literary undertaking, including the work of authors and illustrators of picturebooks, is the interrogation of the dominant discourses of conventional texts. Children's literature is traditionally seen as a vehicle through which to enculturate children into the social and cultural norms of the prevailing society for which the texts are produced. Following this model of children's literature, most conventional picturebooks present a hierarchy of discourses in which one discourse is privileged over all others (Belsey 2002). This privileging often leads to the representation of a sense of order and certainty that belies the realities of everyday life that, according to postmodernists, do not conform to order and uniformity as implied by realist texts but rather are partial and incomplete. Picturebooks, in particular, are well-placed to disrupt these conventional hierarchies through the utilization of both written and illustrative texts. For instance, rather than achieving a conventional sense of closure where all loose ends are firmly tied up by the story's end, postmodern picturebooks may provide multiple points of view, evident in *Voices in the Park* (1988) by Anthony Browne, or a number of alternative or possible endings, such as in Emily Gravett's *Wolves* (2006), which dismantles any notion of resolution. Other postmodern picturebooks employ a fragmentary style of narrative by exploiting the gaps that logically occur in a narrative. By refusing to disclose aspects of the narrative, texts require readers to work to construct a plausible story line from the often skeletal details available to them or, indeed, resist any such structuring. By drawing readers' attention to these gaps, the texts reinforce the postmodern belief that life, society, and self are not unified wholes, but are fragmentary and, at times, random, as is evident in *Granpa* (1984) by John Burningham.

Conventional texts often reinforce their own metanarratives and children's literature may appear to promote a version of 'real life' in that seemingly inherent 'truths,' such as the notion of a stable identity, are endorsed. Postmodern picturebooks seek to unmask the constructed nature of these 'truths' not by denying the 'truths' of reality and fiction, but by contesting them. A popular strategy employed by postmodern picturebooks for raising awareness of the 'truth' status of various worlds, both fictional and 'real,' is having a character enter, by various means, the projected world of a book. This occurs in Lauren Child's picturebook *Who's Afraid of the Big Bad Book?* (2003). This strategy contrasts the 'real' world of the protagonist, Herb, with that of the fictional world(s) within the book. It also self-consciously exposes the writing process as well as the fictional text as an artifact.

So too, in its examination of history and the past, postmodernism questions the previously accepted view that history has a claim to the truth. It is through the genre of historiographic metafiction that history is shown to be a signifying system constructed from the textual remains of the past. This textualization of the past makes problematic any claims to 'the truth' of, or about, historical events and personages. Historiographic metafiction works to unmask these seemingly 'natural' features of history by disrupting the conventional frames of historiography such as linear, chronological, causal, and teleological relationships between events and people. A number of postmodern picturebooks work to destabilize representations of the past by mixing historical and fictive elements; disruptions to the so-called objective, third person narration of historiography; transgressions of conventions of historiography; challenges to the conventions of narrative; destabilization of notions of continuity; questioning the status of historiography's 'facts'; and the exploitation of intertextuality and anachronism. These metafictive strategies reveal the interpretative nature of historical writing and can be found in a range of postmodern picturebooks, including *A Coyote Columbus Story* (1992) by Thomas King and William Kent Monkton, Raymond Briggs's *The Tin Pot General and the Old Lady* (1984), and *The Discovery of Dragons* (1996) by Graeme Base.

Liberal humanist discourses tend to privilege unity and homogeneity over heterogeneity and often attempt to erase difference. Postmodernism, on the other hand, is committed to difference and works to dismantle any representations of unity or homogeneous identity. See for instance the parade of 'characters' represented in both *Rosie in New York* (2002) by Monika Helfer and Brigitta Heiskel, and *The Stinky Cheese Man and Other Fairly Stupid Tales* (1992) by Jon Scieszka and Lane Smith. Underpinning this attention to difference is a postmodernist tendency to promote the politics and ideologies of the marginalized rather than those of the center. As a result, in the second half of the twentieth century postmodern picturebooks emerged that interrogated notions of difference relating to ethnic, national, class, and gender groups and, more recently, those defined by sexual orientation. Minor marginalized characters appear in a number of postmodern picturebooks, while other texts, such as *The Great Escape from City Zoo* (1997) by Tobhy Riddle and *The Lost Thing* (2000) by Shaun Tan, examine these concerns in detail. These postmodernist impulses have contributed to what is now recognized as a 'politics of identity' under the umbrella of postcolonialism. Note that the use of postcolonialism here is used in its widest possible application to include not only picturebooks that deal with the postcolonial experience of colonized peoples but also peoples colonized by any hegemonic discourse, such as patriarchy, heterogeneity, and so on.

One of the paradoxes of postmodern picturebooks is that children's literature has a tradition of being both compliant and resistant. On the one hand, these texts show signs of postmodernism's opposition to the seemingly fixed notions of liberal humanism and modernism; on the other hand, they are often caught up in promoting aspects of a liberal humanist perspective and adopting modernist strategies. This contradictory position is evident in many so-called postmodern picturebooks. Undoubtedly many of these texts do exhibit both disruption to the narrative strategies and interrogation of dominant discourses (Hutcheon 1988). However, while delighting in transgressive behavior, the texts also attempt to foster socio-cultural values (cooperation, kindness, stable identity) in order to enculturate children into the prevailing ways of the society in which they live. In doing so however, the picturebooks may undermine the postmodernist influences otherwise evident in the texts. *The Three Pigs* (2001), for instance, certainly embraces a number of postmodern influences including breaking of frames, indeterminacy, multiple spatio-temporalities, and ontological layers as well as dismantling hierarchies of power and promoting "ex-centrics" (Hutcheon 1988), such as the cat (marginalized) and the dragon (grotesque). In the end, though, the text appears to privilege the qualities of order, cooperation, compromise, and a stable identity – thereby, at the level of implicit ideology at least, it reinscribes a liberal humanist view. Postmodern picturebooks are caught between the transgressive impulses of postmodernism and the didacticism of traditional (modern) children's literature that reinforces the position discussed earlier, that the postmodernism of children's literature is likely to be a representative type of postmodernism.

Postmodernesque picturebooks

In his essay "Literature of Exhaustion," John Barth (1967) argues that all literary trends or movements follow a cycle of resistance-acceptance-decline and reach a point of exhaustion when the particular strategies and themes of the movement become clichéd. This cycle is evident within the postmodern picturebook that has undergone its own shift, with the emphasis changing from an interrogation of liberal humanist discourses to those of postmodernity, with particular attention on the effects of globalization, media and technology, and consumerism. While a number of postmodern picturebooks written after the turn of this century continue to interrogate both the process of writing and the dominant attitudes and values inherent in many conventional picturebooks, many of those emerging in more recent times have turned to an examination of the effects of the social, political, and economic structures of postmodernity. It seems that postmodern picturebooks, which were the experimental literature of the 1980–2000 years, moved away from challenging the dominant ideologies of liberal humanism to examining those of postmodernity. To paraphrase Wood (1999), these new texts are not so much postmodern picturebooks but rather, picturebooks *about* postmodernity and require a separate designation: postmodernesque (Allan 2012).

The term 'postmodernesque' draws upon the term 'carnivalesque' and is used in a similar manner but with a postmodern inflection. Carnivalesque texts are those that have emerged from carnival literature, as identified by Mikhail Bakhtin (1968) and based on the work of François Rabelais. Just as elements of the carnivalesque were carried over into literature, postmodernesque picturebooks have emerged from the postmodern tradition and yet exhibit a sufficient shift in direction to warrant a new term. These texts draw attention to aspects of postmodernity, including globalization and its attendant components of mass media and consumerism. Such a shift is evident in some of the postmodern picturebooks published in recent years, such as Paul Cox's *Le livre le plus court du monde* (The Shortest Book in the World, 2002), *The Short But Incredibly Happy Life of Riley* (2005) by Colin Thompson and Amy Lissiat, and *Race of the Century* (2008) by Barry Downard.

Conclusion

The postmodern picturebook is a complex and evolving genre that utilizes the visual and verbal dynamic to create a multifaceted text that is playful and has a tendency towards resistance, if not subversion, of both narrative conventions and aspects of society. Postmodern picturebooks employ a pastiche of styles and generally defy categorization. They are playful, parodic, and ironic; they resist closure and offer multiple points of view through exploration of both the verbal and visual texts. Postmodern picturebooks blur boundaries between high and popular culture, promote the position of the marginalized, create uncertainty, and generally provide a space for resistance. They achieve all, or some of this, by utilizing metafictive strategies, such as parody, intertextuality, and polyphony. Further, postmodern picturebooks playfully exploit the interanimation between the visual and verbal codes of the picturebook genre to draw attention to the constructed nature of narrative and the naturalized values and attitudes embedded within these narratives. Postmodern picturebooks are sophisticated artifacts that have challenged and delighted children and adults alike over the past thirty or forty years, and no doubt will continue to do so for future generations.

References

Allan, Cherie (2012) *Playing with Picturebooks: Postmodernism and the Postmodernesque*, Basingstoke: Palgrave Macmillan.

Barth, John (1967) "Literature of Exhaustion," in John Barth, *The Friday Book: Essays and Other Non-Fiction*, Baltimore: Johns Hopkins University Press, 1984, 62–76.

Bakhtin, Mikhail (1968) *Rabelais and His World*, trans. Helene Iswolsky, Bloomington: Indiana University Press.

Base, Graeme (1996) *The Discovery of Dragons*, Melbourne: Penguin Books.

Belsey, Catherine (2002) *Critical Practice*, London: Routledge.

Bradford, Clare (1993) "The Picture Book: Some Postmodern Tensions," *Papers* 4.3: 10–14.

Briggs, Raymond (1984) *The Tin-Pot Foreign General and the Old Iron Woman*, London: Hamish Hamilton.

Browne, Anthony (1997) *Willy the Dreamer*, London: Walker Books.

Browne, Anthony (1998) *Voices in the Park*, London: Double Day.

Burningham, John (1984) *Granpa*, London: Jonathan Cape.

Butler, Christopher (2002) *Postmodernism: A Very Short Introduction*, Oxford: Oxford University Press.

Child, Lauren (2003) *Who's Afraid of the Big Bad Book?*, London: Orchard Books.

Cox, Paul (2002) *Le livre le plus court du monde*, Paris: Editions du Seuil.

Downard, Barry (2008) *The Race of the Century*, New York: Simon & Schuster.

Eagleton, Terry (1996) *Criticism and Ideology: A Study in Marxist Literary Theory*, 2nd ed., London: Humanities Press.

Genette, Gerard (1980) *Narrative Discourse*, Oxford: Blackwell.

Gravett, Emily (2006) *Wolves*, London: MacMillan Children's Books.

Gravett, Emily (2007) *Little Mouse's (Emily Gravett's) Big Book of Fears*, Oxford: MacMillan Children's Books.

Geyh, Paula (2003) "Assembling Postmodernism: Experience, Meaning, and the Space in Between," *College Literature* 30.2: 1–29.

Grieves, Ann (1993) "Postmodernism in Picture Books," *Papers* 4.3: 15–25.

Helfer, Monika (2002) *Rosie in New York*, illus. Brigitta Heiskel, St. Pölten: G & G Kinder- und Jugendbuchverlag.

Hoberek, Andrew (2007) "Introduction: After Postmodernism," *Twentieth Century Literature* 53.3: 233–247.

Hutcheon, Linda (1988) *A Poetics of Postmodernism: History, Theory, Fiction*, New York: Routledge.

Jameson, Fredric (1991) *Postmodernism, or The Logic of Late Capitalism*. London and New York: Verso.

Johnson, Crockett (1955) *Harold and the Purple Crayon*, New York: Harper & Row.

King, Thomas (1992) *A Coyote Columbus Story*, illus. William Kent Monkman, Toronto: Groundwood Books.

Lewis, David (1990) "The Constructedness of Texts: Picture Books and the Metafictive," *Signal* 61–63: 131–146.

Lewis, David (2001) *Reading Contemporary Picturebooks: Picturing Text*, London: RoutledgeFalmer.

Lyotard, Jean-Francois (1984) *The Postmodern Condition: A Report on Knowledge*, Minneapolis: University of Minnesota Press.

Macaulay, David (1990) *Black and White*, Boston, MA: Houghton Mifflin.

McCallum, Robyn (1996) "Metafictions and Experimental Work," in Peter Hunt (ed.) *International Companion Encyclopedia of Children's Literature*, London: Routledge, 397–409.

Müller, Jörg (1990) *Das Buch im Buch im Buch*, Aarau: Sauerländer.

Nodelman, Perry (2008) *The Hidden Adult: Defining Children's Literature*, Baltimore: Johns Hopkins University Press.

Riddle, Tohby (1997) *The Great Escape From City Zoo*, Sydney: Angus & Robertson.

Scieszka, Jon (1992) *The Stinky Cheese Man and Other Fairly Stupid Stories*, illus. Lane Smith, New York: Viking Penguin.

Sendak, Maurice (1963) *Where the Wild Things Are*, New York: Harper & Row.

Sim, Stuart (2005) *The Routledge Companion to Postmodernism*, 2nd ed., London: Routledge.

Sipe, Lawrence R., and Pantaleo, Sylvia (eds) (2008) *Postmodern Picturebooks: Play, Parody, and Self-Referentiality*, New York: Routledge.

Stephens, John (1992) *Language and Ideology in Children's Fiction*, Harlow: Longman.

Tan, Shaun (2000) *The Lost Thing*, Melbourne: Lothian Books.

Tan, Shaun (2006) *The Arrival*, Melbourne: Lothian Books.

Thompson, Colin (2005) *The Short and Incredibly Happy Life of Riley*, illus. Amy Lissiat, Melbourne: Lothian Books.

Whatley, Bruce (2001) *Wait! No Paint!* Sydney: HarperCollins.

Wiesner, David (1991) *Tuesday*, New York: Clarion Books.

Wiesner, David (2001) *The Three Pigs*, New York: Clarion Books.

Wood, Tim (1999) *Beginning Postmodernism*, Manchester and New York: Manchester University Press.

21

CROSSOVER PICTUREBOOKS

Sandra L. Beckett

Picturebooks as a crossover genre

In children's literature scholarship, 'crossover' refers to literature that transcends the traditional boundaries between child and adult readers. Although the term was not adopted until J.K. Rowling's Harry Potter books gave this literature a high profile, crossover literature has existed for centuries. Its long and rich history is perhaps best illustrated by folk and fairy tales. A number of other terms have been adopted to refer to literature involving dual address, notably that of 'crosswriting.' The latter is not synonymous with crossover, however. Crosswriting refers to the phenomenon of writing for both child and adult audiences but in separate works. For example, some primarily adult authors have also written picturebooks for children, as in the case of Umberto Eco's *I tre cosmonauti* (The Three Astronauts 1966). Unlike crosswriters, crossover authors address both audiences in the same work. Furthermore, it is not sufficient to see crossover books in terms of dual address or dual audience. They address a diverse, cross-generational audience that can include readers of all ages: children, adolescents, and adults.

The use of the term 'crossover picturebook' is even more recent than that of 'crossover literature' or 'crossover fiction.' The picturebook genre was largely ignored in the initial years of the crossover phenomenon, which focused on bestselling children's and young adult novels such as Philip Pullman's *Northern Lights* (1995) and J.K. Rowling's *Harry Potter and the Philosopher's Stone* (1997). One of the few critics to evoke picturebooks in this context in the 1990s was Judith Rosen in a 1997 article titled "Breaking the Age Barrier." In a 1993 article devoted to "postmodern tensions" in the picturebook, Clare Bradford points out that "the notion of dual readership" is rarely discussed with regard to the picturebook. Yet, as she rightly maintains, the genre "offers so many possibilities for ironic interplay and multiple construction of meaning that it inevitably crosses boundaries between younger and older readers, between children's fiction and adult fiction" (1993: 13f.). A year later, Jane Doonan noted that certain unconventional modern picturebooks share "the open address" that was formerly reserved for folk and fairy tales (1994: 166). The almost complete lack of attention paid to picturebooks within the discussion of crossover literature prompted my 2012 study *Crossover Picturebooks: A Genre for All Ages*, a follow-up to *Crossover Fiction: Global and Historical Perspectives*, published in 2009. More than any other literary genre, picturebooks can genuinely be books for all ages.

The unique interplay of text and image in the picturebook makes it one of the most exciting and innovative contemporary literary genres. Creative graphics and complex dialogue between the verbal and visual text generate multiple levels of meaning that invite readings on different levels. Carol

Driggs Wolfenbarger and Lawrence Sipe rightly describe picturebooks as "a unique visual and literary art form that engages young readers and older readers in many levels of learning and pleasure" (2007: 273). The authors of *How Picturebooks Work* point to the use of what they call "counterpoint" to address a dual audience of children and adults (Nikolajeva and Scott 2001: 17, 24). Picturebooks offer children and adults a unique opportunity for collaborative reading, since they empower the two audiences more equally than any other narrative form (Beckett 2012: 2; Scott 2005: 12). Crossover picturebooks challenge adults as well as children, promoting decoding skills and encouraging critical thinking in both readerships. Children and adults share a common reading experience but bring to it their own perspectives and interpretations. Crossover picturebooks are multilevel works suitable for all ages because they invite different forms of reading depending on the age and experience of the reader.

Historical perspectives

The picturebook has traditionally been considered a children's genre (Bader 1976: 1; Nodelman 1988: vii). Crossover picturebook artists create works that do not "conform to generic expectations about picturebooks as children's literature only" (Doonan 1994: 166). Today the picturebook is increasingly seen as a narrative form that can address any or all age groups. Authors and illustrators challenge age-specific categories of readers, while publishers create series of books for all ages. Publishers themselves have argued that there is no reason why a thirty-two-page picturebook format should necessarily prescribe a book for children only. Crossover picturebooks are not a recent phenomenon, however. Picturebook artists have been addressing a cross-generational audience for many decades. Maurice Sendak's *Where the Wild Things Are* (1963) and Tomi Ungerer's *The Three Robbers* (1962), "classics" of the genre, were published more than fifty years ago. A few pioneering examples of crossover picturebooks date back to the early twentieth century. The groundbreaking French picturebook *Macao et Cosmage ou L'expérience du bonheur* (Macao and Cosmage or The Experience of Happiness), Edy Legrand's powerful story of the destructive impact of civilization and progress on the idyllic island existence of a black and white couple, appeared almost a century ago in 1919 (Figure 21.1). In the 1920s the Russian avant-garde artist El Lissitzky published his picturebook hommage to Suprematism, *Pro 2 kvadrata: suprematicheskii skaz v shesti postroikakh* (About Two Squares: A Suprematist Tale in Six Constructions 1922), and the German Dada artist Kurt Schwitters released his revolutionary children's book *Die Scheuche Märchen* (The Scarecrow Fairy Tale 1925).

Since the mid-twentieth century, children's publishing houses have been founded with the express goal of producing picturebooks that blur the boundaries between children's literature and adult literature. In 1948, Japanese publisher Yasoo Takeuchi founded the Shiko-sha publishing house with the conviction that a picturebook is not intended only for children. Billed "for children from 0–99 years" (Taniuchi 2003), their books include Kota Taniuchi's *Nichiyobi* (Sunday 1997), an aesthetic, nostalgic reflection on childhood. European pioneers include the visionary French publisher Robert Delpire, who was responsible for a graphic renewal of the picturebook in France from the mid-1950s to the end of the 1960s. The French publishers François Ruy-Vidal and Christian Bruel have been claiming for four decades that there is no such thing as art, literature, or graphics specifically for children; objecting to the idea of 'children's books,' they promote works that touch children as well as adults. The daring innovations introduced by Harlin Quist in the 1960s resulted in quirky crossover picturebooks that remain unique in US children's publishing. Quist's collaboration with Ruy-Vidal led to landmark crossover picturebooks such as Eugène Ionesco's *Conte numéro 1* (Story Number 1 1968), the first of the playwright's experimental "stories for children under the age of three." The 1960s and 1970s saw the creation of a number of French publishing houses determined to challenge the boundaries between children's and adult literature (see Beckett 2015a). Renowned for the exceptional aesthetic quality of its books, Ipomée attempted, from its creation in 1973, to

Figure 21.1 Illustration from Édy Legrand's *Macao et Cosmage ou L'expérience du bonheur*. Paris: La Nouvelle
Revue Française, 1919.

walk the tightrope of the so-called border between child readers and adult readers. Ipomée–Albin
Michel published Frédéric Clément's Premio Grafico winner *Magazin Zinzin: Aux Merveilles d'Alys*
(The Merchant of Marvels and the Peddler of Dreams 1995), a whimsical, charming story whose
poetic text, fantastic images, and unusual typography enchant readers of all ages.

In recent decades, there has been a proliferation of publishing houses specializing in crossover
picturebooks. In Spain, Media Vaca's highly original and challenging "*Libros para niños*" (children's
books) target "children of all ages" and are "NOT ONLY for children," informs the back cover.
Intent upon profoundly revolutionizing the graphics of picturebooks, many of these publishers
turned to artists who were not children's book illustrators. These publishers have been accused of
creating picturebooks for adults rather than children. In fact, they seek to offer picturebooks that
bring the generations together and encourage intergenerational communication. Like the authors
and illustrators they promote, these publishers acknowledge the continuum between children's and
adults' understanding and experience; they celebrate the continuity that connects readers of all ages
(Beckett 2012: 3–7).

In the past, but even still today, crossover picturebooks often provoke controversial discussions regarding their intended audience. When Maurice Sendak's *Outside Over There* (1981) was published for both children and adults in 1981, some critics insisted the author had forgotten the child reader (DeLuca 1984: 4). More than a decade later, *We Are All in the Dumps with Jack and Guy* (1993) provoked an even louder outcry that it was no longer a picturebook for children. When the German edition of David Wiesner's *The Three Pigs* was released in 2002, the public disagreed as to whether it was a book for children or for adults. Sipe's 2008 case study demonstrates clearly that young children can indeed grasp the rather complex ideas about reality and fiction inherent in Wiesner's challenging book. The perception that picturebooks are essentially a genre for children is shifting more rapidly in some countries than others. Vicente Ferrer founded Media Vaca in 1998 to create complex, multi-layered books that would provide a unique alternative to the highly conventional Spanish children's books of the 1990s. During the same period in Norway, adults were already collecting the highly innovative picturebooks of illustrators such as Fam Ekman. Stian Hole (2008) points out that the crossover appeal of *Garmanns Sommer* (Garmann's Summer 2006) is a characteristic trait of modern Scandinavian picturebooks, "which are often labeled 'All-age books'" (Christensen 2014).

Crossover paratexts

Many picturebooks announce their implied crossover audience in the paratextual matter (see also Kümmerling-Meibauer and Meibauer 2013). Paratext has actually been determining a book's crossover audience for more than half a century. The bilingual picturebook *Das Zauberschiff / The Magic Ship*, published in 1947 by the German novelist and graphic artist Hans Leip, bears the subtitle "Ein Bilderbuch nicht nur für Kinder / A Picture Book Not Only for Children." On the dust jacket of Nancy Willard's *A Visit to William Blake's Inn* (1981), whose subtitle "Poems for Innocent and Experienced Travelers" implies a dual audience, the publisher informs readers that this is a book "for readers of all ages." Jon Scieszka and Lane Smith defy the specific age categories of children's books in their groundbreaking *The Stinky Cheese Man and Other Fairly Stupid Tales* (1992) by adding the recommendation "Ages: All" to the dust jacket. The back cover of many books bears a publisher's blurb intended to establish the work's crossover appeal with potential buyers. Readers are informed that Tohby Riddle's Australian picturebook *The Great Escape from City Zoo* (1997) "soars straight and true right across age barriers." Since the 1990s, blurbs claiming crossover status for picturebooks have been on the rise in many countries.

Distinguishing characteristics

It is understandably difficult to establish an exhaustive set of characteristics for a genre that includes picturebooks as diverse as Peter Sís's profound graphic memoir *The Wall: Growing Up Behind the Iron Curtain* (2007) and Werner Hozwarth and Wolf Erlbruch's international bestseller *Von kleinen Maulwurf, der wissen wollte, wer ihm auf den Kopf gemacht hat* (The Story of the Little Mole Who Went in Search of Whodunit 1989), the ultimate bathroom book for all ages. Crossover picturebooks challenge the conventional codes and norms of the picturebook genre. They transcend age boundaries due to the complex nature of the text-image relationship and the innovative narrative and discursive devices. Among the narrative strategies frequently used in crossover picturebooks are generic blending, chronological uncertainty, polyphony, metafiction, mise en abyme, intertextuality, parody, and irony. Picturebook artists are constantly experimenting with form and format, marking new directions for the genre.

Innovative formats

Crossover picturebooks push at generic boundaries, challenging the conventional thirty-two-page format. The remarkable range of formats to be found is indicated by two wordless books published in

2002 by the French illustrator Paul Cox. In visual narratives with spiral bindings, Cox presents two neverending stories: the four-page book *Le livre le plus long du monde* (The Longest Book in the World) was followed by *Cependant* . . . (Meanwhile . . .), a 116-page book bearing the subtitle *le livre le plus court du monde* ("the shortest book in the world"). Innovative formats include a variety of book-objects that completely defy classification. Katy Couprie's *Anima* (1991) unfolds to create a long mural on which a mass of stampeding African animals seems to come to life, while Katsumi Komagata's *Snake* (1995) unfolds to form the shape of the titular snake. Frédéric Clément's *Muséum* (1999) consists of a variety of texts and images presented in an attractive box. Format and design are an integral part of the narrative of many crossover picturebooks (Beckett 2014). These picturebooks share characteristics of the artists' book (Beckett 2012: 19–80). Bruno Munari's *Nella notte buia* (In the Darkness of the Night 1956) and *Nella nebbia di Milano* (The Circus in the Mist 1968), in which the narrative is largely carried by paper and paper cutting, are landmarks in children's publishing, but the Italian designer's experimentations with the book's form fascinate a cultured adult audience as well. The Japanese artist Katsumi Komagata has pursued Munari's innovative experimentations in crossover picturebooks such as *Blue to Blue* (1994), *Namida* (Tears 2000), and *Little Tree* (2008). The latter is an exquisite pop-up picturebook for all ages. These innovative children's books blur the borders between the artists' book and the picturebook.

Wordless narratives

A striking number of crossover picturebooks are wordless, relying entirely on the visual text to tell the story. Artists' books by Bruno Munari, Warja Lavater, and Paul Cox fall into this category. Wordless picturebooks have increased dramatically in number since the late 1990s and they now constitute a very successful and important sub-genre (Beckett 2012: 81–145). However, there are also notable earlier examples of wordless crossover picturebooks. In 1977, Mitsumasa Anno published *Tabi no ehon* (Anno's Journey), the first of his popular Journey picturebooks, intricate and minutely detailed panoramas filled with allusions to Western culture. Sophisticated cultural references are also an essential ingredient of Tord Nygren's Swedish picturebook *Den röda tråden* (The Red Thread 1987), in which readers follow a red thread as it winds its way through the enigmatic visual text. Some picturebook artists specialize in wordless books and devote their career to the art of visual storytelling. The challenging and poetic wordless picturebooks of the Belgian illustrator Anne Brouillard are inspired by her memories and experiences, by trivial everyday events such as the storm in *L'orage* (The Storm 1998) (see Nières-Chevrel 2010). Through her medium of torn paper, the French illustrator Sara is able to reflect on difficult subjects and express subtle feelings and moods in ambiguous, atmospheric picturebooks such as *À quai* (Alongside the Quai 2005). David Wiesner's passion for wordless storytelling has produced award-winning crossover picturebooks such as *Tuesday* (1991) and *Flotsam* (2006), which invite viewers of all ages to see the world through new eyes. Wordless crossover picturebooks are multilayered texts that present a complex and enigmatic form of narration with an endless possibility of meanings. Each reader brings his or her own personal knowledge and experience to the interpretation of the visual images and the construction of the narrative. Wordless crossover picturebooks, which do not disadvantage non-readers, can truly transcend age boundaries.

Genre blending

The dual nature of the picturebook, born of a marriage of text and image, no doubt explains the genre's propensity for hybridization. In 1990, David Lewis saw the picturebook emerging "as a kind of supergenre" absorbing "other, more closed and 'finished' forms" (142). Generic boundaries have become increasingly blurred between the picturebook and the comic book, the artists' book, the graphic novel, and so forth. Yvan Pommaux's picturebooks borrow so heavily from the comic genre (notably the John Chatterton series, for instance, *John Chatterton détective* (1993), and the Corbelle and Corbillo series) that some of them have been designated *albums-bandes dessinées* ('picturebook-comics'). Shaun Tan's wordless *The Arrival* (2006) is a unique blend of picturebook and comic strip. Crossover picturebooks also draw heavily on various media including film, television, and animated cartoons, as in the case of Jörg Müller and Jörg Steiner's *Aufstand der Tiere oder Die neuen Stadtmusikanten* (The Rebellion of the Animals or The New Town Musicians 1989) or Tohby Riddle's *The Great Escape from City Zoo*.

References to fine art

Crossover picturebooks often contain sophisticated intertextual allusions, some of which are inaccessible to children and present only for the enjoyment of adults. Visual allusions to the fine arts and metadiscourse on art are particularly common in today's crossover picturebooks (Beckett 2010: 83–98; Beckett 2014: 147–208). Anthony Browne has made the citation of surrealist art, notably that of Magritte, a signature of his oeuvre. His multilevel picturebooks such as *Willy the Dreamer* (1997) and *Voices in the Park* (1998) are equally popular with children and adults. Both audiences can likewise appreciate the ingenious referencing of art in the Norwegian picturebook *Kattens skrekk* (The Cat's Terror 1992) by Fam Ekman, who reworks the art of Henri Rousseau to create the dreams of a fearful cat (Figure 21.2). A wide range of contemporary picturebook artists, including Mitsumasa Anno,

Figure 21.2 Illustration from Fam Ekman's *Kattens skrekk*. Oslo: Cappelen, 1992.

Reprinted by permission of Fam Ekman.

Nicole Claveloux, Jean Claverie, Piet Grobler, Sören Jessen, Tord Nygren, and Shaun Tan, to name only a few, reference or recreate canonical works of art for the entertainment of young and old alike.

Challenging subject matter

Crossover picturebooks often contain profound or controversial content that may be considered by some to be 'adult' in nature. In fact, they deal with cross-generational topics of interest to young and old alike. Children, like adults, need reading experiences that allow them to explore dark, disturbing, and painful subjects because such subjects can touch them personally and constitute part of their life experience. Since the 1960s, picturebooks have made great strides in freeing themselves from the rigid moral codes and taboos that long prevailed in children's literature. Picturebooks now deal with a wide range of topics that are often quite contentious (Beckett 2012: 209–272).

Many crossover picturebook artists such as Maurice Sendak, Tomi Ungerer, and Wolf Erlbruch continue in the fairy tale tradition, introducing children as well as adults to terrible and disturbing truths (see Beckett 2015b). The dark and unsettling side of childhood emerged in Sendak's *Outside Over There* (1981). In subversive picturebooks such as *Moon Man* (1967), *No Kiss for Mother* (1973), and *Flix* (1998), Ungerer brought chaotic scenes of violence, bloodshed, smoking, and sexuality to children's books. Despite the fairy tale origins of *L'ogresse en pleurs* (The Ogress in Tears 1986), by Valérie Dayre and Wolf Erlbruch, adult mediators objected to the cruelty of a picturebook in which an ogress eats her own son. In many European countries, violence, nudity, and sexuality do not have the taboo status that is attached to them in English-language children's book markets. Anne Ikhlef and Alain Gauthier's daring French picturebook *Mon Chaperon Rouge* (My Red Riding Hood 1998) is an erotic, nocturnal version of the tale, in which readers become complicit spectators during the ritualistic striptease and the intimate bedscene of a naked Little Red Riding Hood lying on top of the wolf. Long a taboo subject in picturebooks, death is now the topic of numerous contemporary titles by picturebook artists cognizant of the fact it can affect readers of all ages. Wolf Erlbruch makes the sensitive topic accessible to children while offering reflection for adults in his highly acclaimed *Ente, Tod und Tulpe* (Duck, Death and the Tulip 2007).

Challenging issues are also found in picturebooks set in a more real, often contemporary urban context. Gro Dahle and Svein Nyhus broach the subject of domestic violence in the poetic but powerful Norwegian picturebook *Sinna Mann* (Angry Man 2003), which has been used as a therapeutic tool for adults as well as children (see Bjorvand 2010). The fear, hatred, and violence engendered by xenophobia are the subject of the somber, haunting picturebook *Die Insel* (The Island 2002) by the Swiss-born illustrator Armin Greder. Shaun Tan's *The Red Tree* (2001) can help readers of all ages cope with the experience of depression and despair. In a sophisticated stream-of-consciousness style, the Swiss author-illustrator Béatrice Poncelet addresses the subject of dementia in the poetic and enigmatic picturebook *Les cubes* (The Cubes 2003). The Danish team Oscar K. and Dorte Karrabæk courageously tackle the controversial issue of euthanasia in *Idiot!* (2009), the story of a mentally challenged boy whose dying mother does not wish to leave him alone.

Deeply philosophic picturebooks, such as Erlbruch's *La grande question* (The Big Question 2003), acknowledge that children also ask those big questions. Crossover picturebooks explore the human condition and deal with the important issues that touch young and old alike. Due to challenging subject matter, crossover picturebooks are often deemed to be inappropriate for children. Many critics felt that was the case for Sendak's *We Are All in the Dumps with Jack and Guy* (1993), which depicts the dire living conditions of homeless children abandoned by an indifferent society. Crossover picturebook artists respect children's ability to deal with difficult and controversial issues. They recognize the necessity of exploring the nightmare side of life, but they also understand the importance of presenting potentially disturbing images and ideas in a manner that is appropriate for their young readers. The nursery rhyme text, the dramatic events, and the cartoon characters of *We Are All in the Dumps* help to mitigate the harshness for young readers. The blackness of the subject matter in Karrebæk's

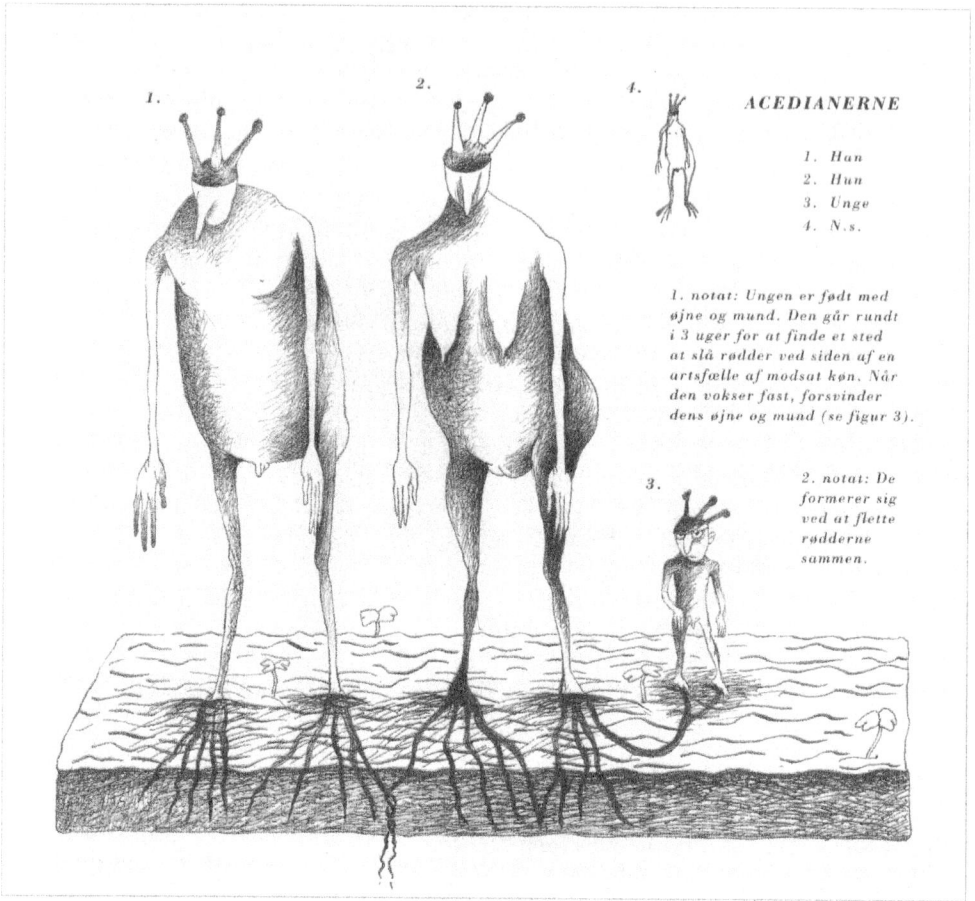

Figure 21.3 Illustration from Dorte Karrebæk's *Den sorte bog om de syv dødssynder*. Hillerød: Alma, 2007. Reprinted by permission of Dorte Karrebæk.

Den sorte bog om de syv dødssynder (The Black Book: On the Seven Deadly Sins 2007), inspired by the famous work of Hieronymous Bosch, is made more palatable by the humor and tenderness with which the stark, distressing facts are presented (Figure 21.3). Crossover picturebook artists soften the impact of painful and disturbing subjects by using a variety of techniques which range from fantasy and lyricism to exaggeration and humor. Carole Scott (2005) argues convincingly that the authors of challenging, so-called inappropriate picturebooks

> must view their texts as appropriate, providing an introduction to our world rather than constructing a cocoon for children to shelter from it ... as artists, they shy away from presenting 'inappropriate' works that are not truthful to the reality they perceive.
>
> 12

Forging new paths

The significance and sophistication of the graphic element in today's picturebooks reflect the prevalence of visual narratives in the new media technologies. Picturebooks have embraced these recent technologies and interacted with them to their mutual benefit (Dresang 1999). The "experiments in form and format" that have resulted from this interplay are "significantly affecting the aesthetics of visual narratives," according to Kimberley Reynolds (2007: 38), who cites the examples of Sara Fanelli's *Dear Diary* (2000) and Lauren Child's *What Planet Are You from, Clarice Bean?* (2001). Some of the most radical innovations in the arts occur in picturebooks, which foster exciting experimentations with the text-image relationship and push technology to new limits. The possibilities of this challenging medium have attracted artists from a wide range of fields to the picturebook. Every medium and mixed media imaginable is used, ranging from engraving and India ink through watercolor and oil to photography and computer graphics. The picturebook genre is an astonishingly fertile and vibrant sphere of literary and artistic creation.

Often the market has not been ready for the avant-garde picturebooks of authors, illustrators, and publishers who defy generic expectations. However, the public is gradually becoming aware of the sophistication and power of a genre that challenges readers of all ages. Crossover picturebook artists have altered expectations about picturebooks, which are increasingly being bought by and for all ages. This is particularly striking in the Scandinavian markets, where picturebooks are often classified as 'all-ages books' and even targeted specifically at adults (Ommundsen 2014). Pioneering experimentation in graphics and content still prevent many crossover picturebooks from penetrating more conservative markets, however. Crossover picturebooks from some European countries are often too unconventional for the Anglo-American markets and do not get translated into English.

Today there is nonetheless a widespread realization that the codes of picturebooks can transcend age boundaries and provide a medium for intergenerational communication. Adults are no longer seen only as co-readers or mediators of picturebooks, but as readers in their own right. Crossover picturebooks challenge current definitions of the picturebook and defy generic expectations about picturebooks as children's literature only. They demonstrate clearly that the picturebook is an art form suitable for all ages and capable of forging new paths for crossover narratives.

References

Anno, Mitsumasa (1977) *Tabi no ehon*, Tokyo: Fukuinkan Shoten [*Anno's Journey*, London: Bodley Head, 1978].

Bader, Barbara (1976) *American Picturebooks from Noah's Ark to the Beast Within*, New York: Macmillan.

Beckett, Sandra L. (2009) *Crossover Fiction: Global and Historical Perspectives*, New York: Routledge.

Beckett, Sandra L. (2010) "Artistic Allusions in Picturebooks," in Teresa Colomer, Bettina Kümmerling-Meibauer, and Cecilia Silva-Díaz (eds) *New Directions in Picturebook Research*, New York: Routledge, 83–98.

Beckett, Sandra L. (2012) *Crossover Picturebooks: A Genre for All Ages*, New York: Routledge.

Beckett, Sandra L. (2014) "The Art of Visual Storytelling: Formal Strategies in Wordless Picturebooks," in Bettina Kümmerling-Meibauer (ed.) *Picturebooks: Representation and Narration*, New York: Routledge, 53–69.

Beckett, Sandra L. (2015a) "Manifestations of the Avant-Garde and Its Legacy in French Children's Literature," in Elina Druker and Bettina Kümmerling-Meibauer (eds) *Children's Literature and the Avant-Garde*, Amsterdam: John Benjamins, 217–239.

Beckett, Sandra L. (2015b) "From Traditional Tales, Fairy Stories and Cautionary Tales to Controversial Visual Texts: Do We Need to Be Fearful?" in Janet Evans (ed.) *Challenging and Controversial Picturebooks: Creative and Critical Responses to Visual Texts*, New York: Routledge, 49–70.

Bjorvand, Agnes-Margrethe (2010) "Do Sons Inherit the Sins of Their Fathers? An Analysis of the Picturebook *Angry Man*," in Teresa Colomer, Bettina Kümmerling-Meibauer, and Cecilia Silva-Díaz (eds) *New Directions in Picturebook Research*, New York: Routledge, 217–231.

Bradford, Clare (1993) "The Picture Book: Some Postmodern Tensions," *Papers* 4.3: 14.

Brouillard, Anne (1998) *L'orage*, Orange: Grandir.

Browne, Anthony (1997) *Willy the Dreamer*, London: Walker.

Browne, Anthony (1998) *Voices in the Park*, London: Walker.

Child, Lauren (2001) *What Planet Are You From, Clarice Bean?* London: Orchard Books.

Christensen, Nina (2014) "'Thought and dream are heavenly vehicles': Character, *Bildung*, and Aesthetics in Stian Hole's Garmann Trilogy (2006–2010)," in Bettina Kümmerling-Meibauer (ed.) *Picturebooks: Representation and Narration*, New York: Routledge, 109–119.

Clément, Frédéric (1995) *Magasin Zinzin, ou, Aux merveilles d'Alys*, Paris: Ipomée-Albin Michel [*The Merchant of Marvels and the Peddler of Dreams*, San Francisco: Chronicle Books, 2001].

Clément, Frédéric (1999) *Muséum*: petite collection d'ailes et d'âmes trouvées sur l'Amazone, Paris: Ipomée-Albin Michel.

Couprie, Katy (1991) *Anima*, Paris: Le Sourire qui mord.

Cox, Paul (2002) *Le livre le plus long* (quadrichonie), Paris: Les Trois Ourses.

Cox, Paul (2002) *Cependant . . .*, Paris: Seuil.

Dahle, Gro (2003) *Sinna Mann*, illus. Svein Nyhus, Oslo: Cappelen.

Dayre, Valérie (1996) *L'ogresse en pleurs*, illus. Wolf Erlbruch, Toulouse: Milan.

DeLuca, Geraldine (1984) "Exploring the Levels of Childhood: The Allegorical Sensibility of Maurice Sendak," *Children's Literature* 12: 3–24.

Doonan, Jane (1994) "Into the Dangerous World: *We Are All in the Dumps with Jack and Guy* by Maurice Sendak," *Signal* 75: 155–171.

Dresang, Eliza T. (1999) *Radical Change: Books for Youth in a Digital Age*, New York: H.W. Wilson.

Eco, Umberto (1966) *I tre cosmonauti*, illus. Eugenio Carmi, Milan: Bompiani [*The Three Astronauts*, London: Secker & Warburg, 1989].

Ekman, Fam (1992) *Kattens skrekk*, Oslo: Cappelen.

Erlbruch, Wolf (2003) *La grande question*, Paris: Éditions Être [*The Big Question*, New York: Europa, 2005].

Erlbruch, Wolf (2007) *Ente, Tod und Tulpe*, Munich: Verlag Antje Kunstmann [*Duck, Death and the Tulip*, Wellington, NZ: Gecko Press, 2008].

Fanelli, Sara (2000) *Dear Diary*, London: Walker Books.

Greder, Armin (2002) *Die Insel*, Aarau and Frankfurt: Sauerländer [*The Island*, Crow's Nest, NSW: Allen & Unwin, 2007].

Hole, Stian (2006) *Garmanns Sommer*, Oslo: Cappelen [*Garmann's Summer*, Grand Rapids, Mich.: Eerdmans Books for Young Readers, 2008].

Hole, Stian (2008) "Interview With Stian Hole, author and illustrator of *Garmann's Summer* (May 2008)," *Eerdmans Books for Young Readers*, www.eerdmans.com/Interviews/holeinterview.htm (accessed June 3, 2010).

Holzwarth, Werner (1989) *Vom kleinen Maulwurf, der wissen wollte, wer ihm auf den Kopf gemacht hat*, illus. Wolf Erlbruch, Wuppertal: Peter Hammer Verlag [*The Story of the Little Mole Who Went in Search of Whodunit*, New York: Stewart, Tabori & Chang, 1993].

Ikhlef, Anne (1998) *Mon Chaperon Rouge, illus.* Alain Gauthier, Paris: Seuil Jeunesse.

Ionesco, Eugène (1968) *Conte numéro 1, pour enfants de moins de trois ans*, illus. Étienne Delessert, Paris: Harlin Quist and François Ruy-Vidal [*Story Number 1, for Children Under Three Years of Age*, New York: Harlin Quist, 1968].

K., Oscar [Ole Dalgaard] (2009) *Idiot!* illus. Dorte Karrebæk, Copenhagen: Høst & Søn.

Karrebæk, Dorte (2007) *Den sorte bog om de syv dødssynder*, Hillerød: Alma.

Komagata, Katsumi (1994) *Blue to Blue*, Tokyo: One Stroke.

Komagata, Katsumi (1995) *Snake*, Tokyo: One Stroke.

Komagata, Katsumi (2000) *Namida*, Tokyo: One Stroke.

Komagata, Katsumi (2008) *Little Tree*, Tokyo: One Stroke.

Kümmerling-Meibauer, Bettina, and Meibauer, Jörg (2013) "On the Strangeness of Pop Art Picturebooks: Pictures, Texts, Paratexts," in Evelyn Arizpe, Maureen Farrell, and Julie McAdam (eds) *Pictures: Beyond the Borders of Art, Narrative and Culture*, New York: Routledge, 23–41.

Legrand, Édy (1919) *Macao et Cosmage ou L'expérience du bonheur*, Paris: Éditions de la Nouvelle Revue Française.

Lewis, David (1990) "The Constructedness of Texts: Picture Books and the Metafictive," *Signal* 62: 131–46.

Leip, Hans (1947) *Das Zauberschiff: Ein Bilderbuch nicht nur für Kinder*, Hamburg: Hammerich & Lesser.

Lissitzky, El [Eliezer Markovich] (1922) *Suprematicheskii skaz pro dva kvadrata v shesti postroikakh*, Berlin: Scythian [*About Two Squares: A Suprematist Tale*. Facsimile reprint. Forest Row: Artists Bookworks, 1990].

Munari, Bruno (1956) *Nella notte buia*, Milan: Muggiani [*In the Darkness of the Night*, Mantova: Corraini, 2000].

Munari, Bruno (1968) *Nella nebbia di Milano*, Milan: Emme Edizioni [*The Circus in the Mist*, New York: World, 1969].

Nières-Chevrel, Isabelle (2010) "The Narrative Power of Pictures: *L'Orage* (The Thunderstorm) by Anne Brouillard," in Teresa Colomer, Bettina Kümmerling-Meibauer, and Cecilia Silva-Díaz (eds) *New Directions in Picturebook Research*, New York: Routledge, 129–137.

Nikolajeva, Maria, and Scott, Carole (2001) *How Picturebooks Work*, London: Garland.

Nodelman, Perry (1988) *Words about Pictures: The Narrative Art of Children's Picture Books*, Athens: University of Georgia Press.

Nygren, Tord (1988) *Den röda tråden*, Stockholm: Raben & Sjögren [*The Red Thread*, Stockholm: R & S Books, 1988].

Ommundsen, Åse Marie (2014) "Picturebooks for Adults," in Bettina Kümmerling-Meibauer (ed.) *Picturebooks: Representation and Narration*, New York: Routledge, 17–35.

· Pommaux, Yvan (1986) *Le théâtre de Corbelle and Corbillo*, Paris: L'École des loisirs.

Pommaux, Yvan (1993) *John Chatterton détective*, Paris: L'École des loisirs.

Poncelet, Béatrice (2003) *Les cubes*, Paris: Seuil Jeunesse.

Pullman, Philip (1995) *Northern Lights*, London: Scholastic.

Reynolds, Kimberley (2007) *Radical Children's Literature: Future Visions and Aesthetic Transformations in Juvenile Fiction*, Basingstoke: Palgrave Macmillan.

Riddle, Tohby (1997) *The Great Escape From City Zoo*, Sydney: HarperCollins.

Rosen, Judith (1997) "Breaking the Age Barrier," *Publishers Weekly* (September 8): 28–31.

Rowling, J(oanne) K. (1997) *Harry Potter and the Philosopher's Stone*, London: Bloomsbury.

Sara (2005) *À quai*, Paris: Seuil Jeunesse.

Schwitters, Kurt, Steinitz, Käte, and van Doesburg, Theo (1925) *Die Scheuche Märchen*, Hannover: Apossverlag.

Scieszka, Jon (1992) *The Stinky Cheese Man and Other Fairly Stupid Tales*, illus. Lane Smith, New York: Viking.

Scott, Carole (2005) "A Challenge to Innocence: 'Inappropriate Picturebooks for Young Readers,'" *Bookbird* 43.1: 5–13.

Sendak, Maurice (1963) *Where the Wild Things Are*, New York: Harper & Row.

Sendak, Maurice (1981) *Outside Over There*, New York: HarperCollins.

Sendak, Maurice (1993) *We Are All in the Dumps with Jack and Guy*, New York: HarperCollins.

Sipe, Lawrence R. (2008) "First Graders Interpret David Wiesner's *The Three Pigs*: A Case Study," in Lawrence R. Sipe and Sylvia Pantaleo (eds) *Postmodern Picturebooks: Play, Parody, and Self-Referentiality*, New York: Routledge, 223–237.

Sís, Peter (2007) *The Wall: Growing Up Behind the Iron Curtain*, New York: Farrar, Straus and Giroux.

Steiner, Jörg (1989) *Aufstand der Tiere oder Die neuen Stadtmusikanten*, illus. Jörg Müller, Aarau: Sauerländer.

Tan, Shaun (2001) *The Red Tree*, South Melbourne: Lothian.

Tan, Shaun (2006) *The Arrival*, South Melbourne: Lothian.

Taniuchi, Kota (1997) *Nichiyobi*, Tokyo: Shiko-sha.

Taniuchi, Kota (2003) "Interview," *Kota Taniuchi* (February 2, 2003), http://kota.taniuchi.free.fr/pages/interview.html (accessed August 31, 2010).

Ungerer, Tomi (1962) *The Three Robbers*, New York: Atheneum.

Ungerer, Tomi (1967) *Moon Man*, New York: Harper & Brothers.

Ungerer, Tomi (1973) *No Kiss for Mother*, New York: Harper & Row.

Ungerer, Tomi (1998) *Flix*, Zurich: Diogenes [*Flix*, Boulder, CO: Roberts Rinehart, 1998].

Wiesner, David (1991) *Tuesday*, New York: Clarion Books.

Wiesner, David (2001) *The Three Pigs*, New York: Clarion Books.

Wiesner, David (2006) *Flotsam*, New York: Clarion Books.

Willard, Nancy (1981) *A Visit to William Blake's Inn: Poems for Innocent and Experienced Travelers*, illus. Alice and Martin Provensen, New York: Harcourt, Brace.

Wolfenbarger, Carol Driggs, and Sipe, Lawrence R. (2007) "A Unique Visual and Literary Art Form: Recent Research on Picturebooks," *Language Arts* 83.3: 273–280.

22

PICTUREBOOKS FOR ADULTS

Åse Marie Ommundsen

Introduction

Picturebooks are a major art form in contemporary society, and many artists who would previously have exhibited their artwork in museums and galleries now exhibit their art in the picturebook format. This may be one of the reasons why not only crossover picturebooks but also picturebooks for adults have been a growing trend in recent decades. Picturebooks for adults represent a new literary trend that emerged in Scandinavia in the early 1990s. The innovative form of these books confused many critics, who were unsure whether to review the books as children's books or adult books. But as the phenomenon became more established, it gave rise to a new literary category called 'picturebooks for adults.' Even though the phenomenon – picturebooks addressing an adult audience – is not new, the recognition of the distinct literary category is indeed recent. Whereas Perry Nodelman describes picturebooks as "books intended for young children" (1988: vii), Sandra Beckett more recently points out:

> In the past, adults were generally seen only as co-readers or mediators of picturebooks, but now they are being recognized as readers in their own right. While this is not an entirely new phenomenon, adults now seem more willing to acknowledge the fact that they buy picturebooks for their own pleasure.
>
> *2012: 13*

Beckett points to Japan, where the Japanese pioneer publisher Yasoo Takeuchi already claimed in 1949 that a picturebook is "a work of art in itself, and is therefore not intended only for children" (10).

The fictional picturebook for adults can be defined as a narrative text addressed to adults, with one or more pictures on each spread. Many of these books are published and marketed exclusively for an adult audience, but quite a few examples were originally marketed as crossover picturebooks. This fact demonstrates the blurred lines between crossover picturebooks and picturebooks for adults. The definition does not include factual works such as cookbooks, travel guides, or coffee-table books, nor the modernist avant-garde tradition, or related variations such as illustrated classics, art books, or phototexts. However, some of these genres, like phototexts, might be considered subgenres of the medium. Other visual expressions have paved the way: artists' books and graphic novels addressed to adults, as well as popular gift books published in mini editions, which replace the greeting card and are easy to put in a handbag. A German example of the latter is Helme Heine's *Freunde* (Friends 2015), a pocketbook about friendship. A Norwegian example is Henrik Hovland and Toril Kove's *Johannes Jensen og kjærligheten* (Johannes Jensen and Love 2004), which is about finding love and is typically sold as a gift on Valentine's Day. The line between picturebooks for adults and crossover picturebooks is constantly challenged, and often blurred; we can see the advanced crossover picturebook as a foundation for the picturebooks for adults.

The picturebook for adults can be published in the standard thirty-two-page picturebook format, a medium that has traditionally been regarded as the exclusive aesthetic expression of children's literature. Picturebooks for adults may also be published in a variety of other formats, as will be shown in the following examples. They may be short or long, in large format or in mini editions, and are also found in hybrid forms as picture novels. Comics and graphic novels for adults are related media in this field, and the boundaries between them are sometimes fuzzy.

Picturebooks targeted at adults demonstrate that adults are interested in visual stories and stories in which the verbal and visual texts constitute a polyphonic play. The illustrations may complement, expand, or even contradict the written narrative (Nikolajeva and Scott 2001). Beckett defines crossover picturebooks as

> multileveled works that are suitable for all ages because they invite different forms of reading, depending on the age and experience of the reader. [. . .] Children, adolescents, and adults read crossover picturebooks from their various perspectives, but they can all take equal pleasure in the reading experience.
>
> *2012: 16*

Typically, crossover picturebooks that win major literature prizes often have strong adult appeal. "Sophisticated intertextual allusions that cannot be decoded by children and seem to be there for the enjoyment of adults are a common trait of crossover picturebooks" (Beckett 2012: 16). In some of these books, the humor is dependent on the complex intertextual references, which are likely to be beyond the horizons of children. Some of these books may have extensive and difficult verbal text, or the topic may be more intriguing for adults than for children – topics like nostalgia, aging, and memories of the past. One example of a picturebook in which the nostalgic appeal and the subtle intertextual allusions may exclude the child reader is the forty-eight-page picturebook *The Last Resort* (2002) by J. Patrick Lewis and illustrator Roberto Innocenti, which has intertextual allusions to *Don Quixote*, *Moby Dick*, *A Face for a Clue*, *Huckleberry Finn*, *Treasure Island*, and *The Little Prince*. In this respect Deborah Dean argues that "without familiarity with those stories and characters, the reader won't understand what's going on. Prior knowledge is an essential element in engaging with Lewis' text" (2010: 14–16). This is clearly a picturebook for adults, as not all readers can take equal pleasure in it; there is no 'dual address.'

According to Barbara Wall (1991), the narrator-narratee relationship defines whether a book is for children or not. Åse Marie Ommundsen defines crossover picturebooks according to Wall's concept of 'dual address': crossover picturebooks have a dual address, being aimed at the child and adult simultaneously, not the one at the expense of the other (2006, 2010b). Picturebooks for adults, on the other hand, have a single address, in which the addressee is an adult (Ommundsen 2010a). Another important aspect is the perspective in the verbal and the visual text. If, like Peter Hollindale (1997), we search for childness in the books, we can search for the child perspective. Most picturebooks for adults do not have a child perspective but an adult perspective. But when it comes to perspective, there may also be exceptions to the rule. Using the notions of 'addressee' (Wall 1991), 'implied reader' (Iser 1978), and 'childness' (Hollindale 1997), we can investigate to whom the book is addressed. Another factor to be taken into consideration is what a book is published and marketed as, even though quite a few picturebooks for adults are published as children's literature. Along with the marketing strategy of picturebooks for adults, also picturebooks targeted at young adults or teenagers have been developed since the turn of the millennium. Three Scandinavian examples of young adults' or teenagers' picturebooks are all about a young female teenager's passage into adulthood. The Norwegian *Skylappjenta* (Little Miss Eyeflap 2009) by Iram Haq and Endre Skandfer is about a young girl's search for her own path and her dramatic detachment from her family. Swedish Anna Höglund's *Om detta talar man endast med kaniner* (This Matter You Only Discuss with Rabbits 2013) is about a 13-year-old girl who feels different, visually pictured as a rabbit among human beings. Norwegian Gro Dahle and Kaja Dahle Nyhus's *Megzilla* (2015) is a picturebook on puberty, ending with the heroine's first sexual intercourse.

The former BolognaRagazzi Award judge, Martin Salisbury, referring to "the exceptional, highly sophisticated visual quality" of picturebooks from Norway wrote:

> Perhaps we can dare to hope that the postmodern picturebook is leading a revival of illustration in books for adults, with growing awareness of the intellectual demands that narrative pictures can make. Adults are increasingly buying picturebooks for their own consumption.
>
> *quoted in Pantaleo and Sipe 2008: 32*

Since the 1990s, picturebooks exlusively for adults have represented a growing trend in Scandinavia, and presuppose an adult reader with visual literacy:

> Picturebooks for adults presuppose a reader with ability and determination to read both words and pictures. The picturebook expands major aspects of literary expression: themes, form, style and address; and the time has come for literature research and literature teaching to recognize this boundary-crossing phenomenon as part of contemporary literature.
>
> *Ommundsen 2014: 32*

Picturebooks for adults are a growing phenomenon and certainly an important issue to study, but there has been little research so far on the topic. It is impossible to give a worldwide overview, or even a European one. So far Scandinavia seems to dominate the European scene in picturebooks for adults, and Japan seems to dominate the Asian scene. It is always possible to find exceptions and examples from other parts of the world, and a few of them will be mentioned in this chapter. The picturebook for adults is a boundary-crossing medium of quality literature deriving from the increasingly advanced picturebooks for children and related phenomena such as art books, graphic novels, and gift books in mini editions, as already mentioned. Studies of picturebooks for adults show that there is great variation (Ommundsen 2014; Kümmerling-Meibauer 2015). The label (as in the subheading 'A picturebook for adults'), the addressee, the perspective, the verbal and/or visual language, or even the topics discussed may all indicate that a picturebook is for adults, like an artwork targeted solely at adults. In what ways does the picturebook for adults differ from the advanced picturebook for children from which it borrows its visual expression?

Label and subheading

Picturebooks for adults are artworks whose target group is adults only, and are often marked as such using labels and/or subheadings. Some countries, like Norway, have established picturebooks for adults as a separate category. Every year a number of picturebooks for adults are bought and financed through the unique Norwegian purchasing system, a generous public funding of quality books to ensure a rich variety of national literature of high artistic quality in the national libraries. In the past, due to the Norwegian purchasing system, several picturebooks clearly not created for children were published for children but read by adults only.

The picturebooks for adults are sometimes, but not always, supplied with the label and subheading 'A picturebook for adults.' One example is Anna Fiske's 40-page-long mini edition *Fra t-bane til lenestol. En bildebok for voksne* (From the Underground to the Armchair. A Picturebook for Adults

2008) (Figure 22.1). The register of the Norwegian national bibliography confirms that this is a picturebook for adults. In the register it is catalogued under a number and the letter S, signifying fiction for adults. Also, even though the format and dictionary style may resemble a typical children's book, the child's perspective is absent. It is a combination of a narrative picturebook and a visual dictionary, in which important words in the story and in Norwegian culture are listed in words and pictures. Every doublespread contains one page with a picture and one spread with the visual dictionary. The visual narrative is a wordless love story about a lonely immigrant man who falls in love with his Norwegian neighbor. Together they do typical things a Norwegian adult couple would do, like making dinner together, walking in the woods, and going to the cinema. As the visual dictionary has words, the book is not wordless. The visual dictionary helps in narrating the story, such as when the words 'sweat,' 'hand,' and 'hands' are placed in a sequence (Figure 22.2). In this way the visual explanation of the words tells the reader that the couple is holding hands (with sweaty hands) for the first time. The book won the picturebook competition *Leser søker bok* ("Reader Seeks Book") in 2007. As the visual story can be read and understood regardless of language and nationality, the book can be seen as a picturebook introducing important Norwegian concepts to new residents in Norway.

Figure 22.1 Illustration from Anna Fiske's *Fra t-bane til lenestol. En bildebok for voksne.* Oslo: No Comprendo Press, 2008.

Reproduced by permission of Anna Fiske/No Comprendo Press.

Figure 22.2 Illustration from Anna Fiske's *Fra t-bane til lenestol. En bildebok for voksne*. Oslo: No Comprendo Press, 2008.

Reproduced by permission of Anna Fiske/No Comprendo Press.

In Germany several picturebooks for adults have been published in recent years. The German picturebook artist Helmut Heine's *Wie der Fußball in die Welt kam. Ein Bilderbuch für Erwachsene* (How the Football Came into the World. A Picturebook for Adults 2012) is a humorous narrative based on the biblical story of Adam and Eve in paradise. In his office, God has a globe made of leather, with black markings for land and white for the ocean. One day the globe falls into the Garden of Eden, and Eve picks it up. She shows it to Adam, who is excited. From now on he is no longer interested in housekeeping chores or pulling weeds. He is only interested in the ball, playing and stroking it so lovingly that Eve is almost jealous. One of the pictures shows that the football has literally come between the two; another illustration shows that Adam sleeps with his football and not with Eve (Figure 22.3). Adam has literally lost his head, wondering whether to replace it with the football, as can be seen in another illustration. The story of Adam and Eve may be well-known to many children, so why is this book labeled a picturebook for adults by the publisher?

What makes this a picturebook for adults, in addition to the publisher's label, is the fact that the humor in the book is dependent on intertextual references not only to the Bible, but also to football and gender issues. The humoristic play with the relationship between the characters and between Adam and the football is mainly funny for adult readers, but may also be recognizable for child readers experienced with football fans. Still, a child and an adult would not enjoy the book on equal terms, as too much of the humor would be beyond the children's grasp. The book ends with the couple opening the gate to paradise, leaving the Garden of Eden for good: "That's it," Adam said to Eve, "this is no longer our world. Let's try our luck elsewhere" (60). When leaving paradise, they take with them their love of football. So that is how football came into the world, and why we no longer live in paradise. The first human beings left paradise because of football. The symbolic meaning of this implied message may be powerful for many couples with only one football addict in the family.

Figure 22.3 Illustration from Helme Heine's *Wie der Fußball in die Welt kam. Ein Bilderbuch für Erwachsene*. Zurich: Kein & Aber, 2014.

The addressee

As said, in most countries, picturebooks for adults are not yet a separate category. Still, picturebooks for adults have been published in several countries. A case in point is the somewhat controversial picturebook on abortion, *De skæve smil* (The Crooked Smiles 2008) by the Danish author Oskar K., with illustrations by Lillian Brøgger. All the main characters are aborted fetuses, "the ones who never were born." The book was published in the middle of a political and ethical debate in Denmark about early ultrasound screening to enable abortion of fetuses with Down syndrome, and has been referred to as a picturebook for adults (Ommundsen 2015), although the concept does not exist in Denmark as yet, and picturebooks are still classified as being solely for children (Christensen 2003). It is worth noting, however, that Danish libraries have put a big stamp on their copies of *The Crooked Smiles* declaring: "Not to be lent to children!" Some of the picturebooks Oskar K. has created with his wife, illustrator Dorte Karrebæk, are clearly picturebooks for adults as well, not least due to the sophisticated intertextual references to political issues and other adult texts. One example is the picturebook *Biblia Pauperum Nova* (2013), about 'the poor in spirit' (Matt. 5:3) in a biblical play performed by mentally handicapped human beings. The humor in the book is dependent on advanced intertextual references to the Bible as well as politics and – for adults – well-known quotes, like letting Joseph use the Lewinski-Clinton affair's "I did not have sexual intercourse with that woman." As one reviewer asks in relation to the book, "Is this really a book for children? Couldn't picturebooks just as well be for adults?" (Straume 2013).

Perspective

A picturebook for adults that resembles children's books in the sense that it is published in the traditional children's book format is not only a Nordic phenomenon. In 2011, the picturebook *Go the*

Fuck to Sleep by American author Adam Mansbach and illustrator Ricardo Cortés topped Amazon .com's bestseller list a month before its release. The book was described as "adult comedy" and "a children's book for adults," and was mentioned in newspapers around the world (for instance, Elmelund 2011). Why did the book arouse such great interest? In the American market, picturebooks for adults were not yet seen as a category, so the book caused some confusion as to which audience it was addressing. The title suggests that it is not a children's book, even though the illustrations might indicate that it is a children's book. The book is an intertextual game with traditional bedtime stories, but seen from the adult perspective of the frustrated parent terrorized by an annoying child that will not fall asleep. This is a well-known scenario for most parents, and thus easy to identify with. *Go the Fuck to Sleep* was later published in an adapted version for children, called *Seriously, Just Go to Sleep* (2012), which in the advertisement is presented as a crossover picturebook. The illustrations in the two editions are the same, but the verbal text is changed. Words like 'fuck' and 'hell' are removed. The reason is probably that they are seen as unsuitable words for children, not that most children would not know these words. The perspective is altered too, from the tired, almost desperate adult trying to get the child to sleep, to a more traditional bedtime story for children with the aim of making the child fall asleep.

Verbal and visual language

The label 'adult literature' is, of course, not only a matter of label and perspective. It is also a question of whether the verbal and visual language makes sense in the world of a child's frame of reference. Sometimes extensive verbal text indicates that it is a book for adults, and even more so if the text is written in difficult, inaccessible language. The 157-page-long French picture novel *Bel Oeil, confessions argentiques d'un gardien de phare* (Beautiful Eye, Silvery Confessions of a Lighthouse Keeper 2004) by Frédéric Clément is published under the heading 'les Beaux-livres-fiction pour adultes' by the publisher Albin Michel. On the back cover it is described as "A beguiling poem-novel, erotic and dark, a disturbing mystery which unveils a fascination for corpses and death." The language is poetic and obscure, both inside and on the back cover:

> In the no-exit room of a lighthouse, near his camellia, Jules Le Guern can't sleep. Paces to and fro. Dies of boredom. Everything is saturated with oil, humidity, cold and salt. As each flower falls off, the desire to write submerges him and Jules covers the pages of his book with rough, poignant language, delicately perverse. Under his eyes, images reveal themselves: Narcisse Belloccio, the blue-gloved dandy, and women with powdery and fragile skin. 9 flowers, 9 young women. Perturbed, the lighthouse warden unleashes his brutal sensuousness.
>
> *n. pag.; translated by the author with the support of Clémentine Beauvais*

The lighthouse keeper Jules Le Guern writes in his diary on January 21, 1887, that it is a calm night with no moon and no sleep. Together with his camellia he watches through the window. Camellias are a type of plant and flower, but here it is also a reference to the famous novel *La Dame aux camélias* (The Lady of the Camellias 1848) by Alexandre Dumas, which was the inspiration for Giuseppe Verdi's opera *La Traviata* (1853). Throughout the dreamlike landscapes in a never-ending stream of consciousness, the lighthouse keeper dreams and writes about flowers and naked, dead women he addresses in terms like *la petite putain* ("the little whore"). The book is difficult to understand, as it is dominated by verbal text written in highly poetic and advanced language. The pictures are dark, as is the text, with challenging illustrations of dead and/or violated women, naked or only partly clothed. Were the women killed? Tortured? An image of a naked woman tied with a rope may suggest a painful, unnatural death. Sandra Beckett writes about Frédéric Clément that "it is impossible to divide the artist's oeuvre into children's books and adult books" (2012: 315). This book, however, is definitely for adults. The verbal text would be too complicated and overwhelming for a child, and the visual text includes challenging photos of naked, dead women, their vulvas exposed in the center of the pictures. The lighthouse keeper's dark and erotic fascination for dead women represents experiences remote from children's worlds.

Topics and frames of reference

What language or words would exclude a child reader because of the life experiences, knowledge, and frame of reference which they render? The Italian picturebook *L'amore t'attende* (Love Awaits You 2009) by the Argentine-Italian author Fabian Negrin has an Italian library stamp stating that it should not be lent out to children under the age of fourteen. The publisher, Orecchio acerbo, has published several crossover picturebooks, but this particular one is not a crossover book for all ages. According to the Italian publisher it was marketed as a Valentine gift meant to target teenagers and young adults, but it can appeal to an adult readership as well. Its perception depends on the cultural approach to art and sexuality in each country. One could call it a picturebook for young adults about love and sexuality, but one could also argue that it is rather a picturebook for adults. Both the verbal text and the pictures are highly erotic.

The text is set up as a poem, with one stanza on every doublespread. The book has an accordion (or concertina fold) format. When folded out it makes a 2-meter-long picture of a naked, loving couple, a man and a woman, shown in a setting with beautiful pastel colors. The full meaning can only be grasped when the whole accordion book is folded out. In contrast, when reading only one doublespread at a time, the book reveals the sensations in one part of the body at a time, while the folded out accordion format gives the perspective of the two bodies linked together as 'one.' The

Figure 22.4 Illustration from Fabian Negrin's *L'amore t'attende*. Rome: Orecchio acerbo, 2009. © 2009, Orecchio acerbo, Rome.

first doublespread begins with a picture of two feet flying in what looks like a clear blue sky. The relationship between verbal text and picture is mutually interdependent and expansive. For instance, in the picture of the man's chest the words imitate the heartbeat. It is a play with rhythm and sound, ending with "I love you":

> tu-tuum
> tu-tum
> tu-tam
> ti-tam
> ti-am
> ti-amo

The stanzas follow the picture's movement from the man's feet and upwards to the mouth and eye, and then downwards along the female body. Little by little the picture unfolds and leads the way, while the stanzas follow the body parts shown in the part of the picture where they occur within each doublespread. For instance, on the spread showing the woman's breasts (Figure 22.4), the verbal text reads:

Around each nipple	Attorno a ogni capezzolo
Halo	un'aureola
but you are not a saint	ma tu non sei una santa
Luckily	per fortuna
you offer me your breasts	mi offri i tuoi seni
the one in shadow the other is moon	l'uno in ombra l'altro è luna
(translation by the author)	

Aureola means halo in Italian, but the similarity to the Latin word *areola* suggests a word play with the medical term for the ring of pigmented skin surrounding the nipple. In the next spread, the first person narrator is searching for the clitoris:

This thing here	Questa cosa qui
is the clitoris?	è la clitoride?
Or is it more down?	O è quella più giù?
right or left?	destra o sinistra?
no?	no?
Then where?	Allora dov'è?

When the whole book is folded out, the picture depicts a loving couple. They are lying down in colorful surroundings that can be interpreted as flowers in various colors. They are floating or flying in a sky of appealing pastel colors, within a pleasing pink dream. The title is "Love awaits you." Throughout the poem there is a movement from 'you' to 'us,' and the story – or poem – ends happily with the conclusion: "Come, love awaits us."

Topics and perspective: two hybrid examples

The Swedish author Joanna Rubin Dranger has published several hybrid picturebooks for adults with a political feminist viewpoint which could be labeled picture novels for adults. Her *Alltid redo att dö för mitt barn* (Always Ready to Die for My Child 2009) is a collection of picturebook stories aimed at new parents. Picturebook narratives seen from the new mother's perspective are quite common, and may suggest that the picturebook medium appeals to young mothers. A Norwegian example is Hilde Hagerup and Kristin Roskifte's fifty-six-page picturebook, *Barnet mitt* (My Child 2015). This is a short picture novel about the ups and downs of motherhood. The main character suffers from sleep deprivation, a bad conscience, and fear that her imperfect behavior will damage her child. There is one picture on every doublespread except for three doublespreads with only verbal text, thus the book could even be called an illustrated short novel. Still, as the pictures bring meaning to the narrative, and are not merely illustrations, it fits better in the picturebook or picture novel category.

Likewise, Dranger's *Always Ready to Die for My Child* touches the borderline of the graphic novel. But as it has very little text and only one picture on every page, which, with few exceptions, are not pictures in panels as in a graphic novel, it is better classified as a hybrid form of picturebook for adults, with the size of a picture novel. In her drawing, Dranger uses several devices from the graphic novel, such as speech bubbles, which is one of the reasons it is a hybrid form. Still, as it is published for adults and has one picture on every page and very little text, it fits the definition of picturebooks for adults. The book starts with a dramatic story about pregnancy and delivery, in which the main character's experiences at the hospital are traumatic. In the following story, breast-feeding is called "the religion for Swedish people in the 2000's," an ideology the main character and her husband refuse to adhere to. Also here the humor is based on intertextual references mainly familiar to adults (parents), like political debates, gender issues, and baby care. The stories cover various themes such as happiness, anxiety, and stories about being the worst mother in the world. The book presents a thoroughly political, feminist view on childrearing and the world, in which boys are given too much latitude, and a section on 'biological evidence' counterpoints another on the question as to whether gender differences are due to being "born that way or brought up that way." The visual episode from "An Ordinary St. Hans" tells a visual story of fathers talking in a relaxed way, seated at table, while the mothers are occupied in taking care of the children. The verbal text contrasts with the visual story with the words "in the world's most equal nation in the world's most equal generation."

Conclusion

Picturebooks for adults are art works whose target group is adults. They can be defined as a narrative text addressed to adults with at least one picture on each spread. As all rules have exceptions, it is possible to find variations within the concept of picturebooks for adults. Picturebooks for adults cross boundaries to other mediums and genres. Some do not have narrative stories, and others are wordless picturebooks. The medium, the picturebook, is old, but as a category, picturebooks published exclusively for an adult audience are new. In Scandinavia there has been a growing tendency to publish picturebooks exclusively for adults since the early 1990s, but as demonstrated in this chapter, picturebooks for adults can also be found in other parts of the world. Alongside books in the traditional thirty-two-page picturebook format there is a great variety of formats, formal and visual elements, and devices and content, and hybrid forms, like picture novels, are common.

The picturebook for adults separates itself from the mentioned definitions of crossover picturebooks. The main difference between the picturebook for adults and the advanced crossover picturebook is the addressee (Wall 1991). As shown in the examples discussed in this chapter, some picturebooks for adults are labeled with their adult target group by the publishing house, for instance, with the subheading, 'Picturebook for adults.' Even in countries where picturebooks for adults are not yet registered as a category, other devices can indicate that a given picturebook is a picturebook for adults: the perspective, the addressee, the verbal and/or visual language, or even the topics dealt with may indicate, singly or together, that a particular book is a picturebook for adults. It is important to note, however, that even if the definition takes the implied adult reader as its point of departure, it does not say anything about the real readers. Research has shown that the dividing line between competent and non-competent readers does not necessarily relate to age, but rather to literacy, experiences with different texts, and means of communication, knowledge, and education. Since the turn of the millennium, a growing number of picturebooks for adults have opened up a new horizon for adults with the ability and determination to read both words and pictures. Picturebooks are gaining increasing prestige as a multimodal art form. This change is mirrored in the emergence of picturebooks for adults.

References

Beckett, Sandra L. (2012) *Crossover Picturebooks: A Genre for All Ages*, New York: Routledge.

Christensen, Nina (2003) *Den danske billedbog 1950–1999*, Copenhagen: Roskilde Universitetsforlag.

Clément, Fréderic (2004) *Bel Œil, confessions argentiques d'un gardien de phare*, Paris: Albin Michel.

Dahle, Gro (2015) *Megzilla*, illus. Kaja Dahle Nyhus, Oslo: Cappelen Damm.

Dean, Deborah (2010) *Book Links* (March 2010): 14–16, www.thecreativecompany.us/news_pdfs/thelastresort_bridgingthegap.pdf (accessed January 15, 2016).

Dranger, Johanna Rubin (2009) *Alltid redo att dö för mitt barn*, Stockholm: Albert Bonniers Förlag.

Elmelund, Rasmus (2011) "Monstre, pot og stædige unger," www.information.dk/print/287293 (accessed October 1, 2014).

Fiske, Anne (2008) *Fra t-bane til lenestol: En bildebok for voksne*, Oslo: No comprendo Press.

Hagerup, Hilde (2015) *Barnet mitt*, illus. Kristin Roskifte, Kolbotn: Magikon forlag.

Haq, Iram (2009) *Skylappjenta*, illus. Endre Skandfer, Oslo: Cappelen Damm.

Heine, Helme (2012) *Wie der Fußball in die Welt kam: Ein Bilderbuch für Erwachsene*, Zurich: Kein & Aber.

Heine, Helme (2015) *Freunde*, Weinheim: Beltz.

Höglund, Anna (2013) *Om dette talar man endast med kaniner*, Stockholm: Lilla piratförlaget.

Hollindale, Peter (1997) *Signs of Childness in Children's Books*, Stroud: The Thimble Press.

Hovland, Henrik (2004) *Johannes Jensen og kjærligheten*, illus. Toril Kove, Oslo: Cappelen Damm.

Iser, Wolfgang (1978) *The Act of Reading. A Theory of Aesthetic Response*, Baltimore: Johns Hopkins University Press.

K., Oskar (2008) *De skæve smil*, illus. Lillian Brøgger, Copenhagen: Klematis.

K., Oskar (2013) *Biblia Pauperum Nova*, illus. Dorte Karrebæk, Copenhagen: Alfa.

Kümmerling-Meibauer, Bettina (2015) "From Baby Books to Picturebooks for Adults: European Picturebooks in the New Millennium," *Word & Image* 31.3: 249–264.

Lewis, J. Patrick (2002) *The Last Resort*, illus. Roberto Innocenti, Mankato: Creative Editions.

Mansbach, Adam (2011) *Go the Fuck to Sleep*, illus. Ricardo Cortés, Brooklyn, NY: Akashic Books.

Mansbach, Adam (2012) *Seriously, Just Go to Sleep*, illus. Ricardo Cortés, Brooklyn, NY: Akashic Books.

Negrin, Fabian (2009) *L'amore t'attende*, Rome: Orrechio acerbo.

Nikolajeva, Maria, and Scott, Carole (2001) *How Picturebooks Work*, New York: Garland.

Nodelman, Perry (1988) *Words about Pictures: The Narrative Art of Children's Picture Books*, Athens: University of Georgia Press.

Ommundsen, Åse Marie (2006) "All-alder-litteratur. Litteratur for alle eller ingen," in Kari Sverdrup and Jon Ewo, (eds) *Kartet og terrenget: Linjer og dykk i barne-og ungdomslitteraturen*, Oslo: Pax, 50–71.

Ommundsen, Åse Marie (2010a) "Bildeboka for voksne," *Norsk Litterær Årbok*, Oslo: Samlaget, 178–210.

Ommundsen, Åse Marie (2010b) *Litterære grenseoverskridelser: Når grensene mellom barne- og voksenlitteraturen viskes ut*, Oslo: Universitetet i Oslo.

Ommundsen, Åse Marie (2014) "Picturebooks for Adults," in Bettina Kümmerling-Meibauer (ed.) *Picturebooks: Representation and Narration*, New York: Routledge, 17–35.

Ommundsen, Åse Marie (2015) "Who Are These Picturebooks for? Controversial Picturebooks and the Question of Audience," in Janet Evans (ed.) *Challenging and Controversial Picturebooks: Creative and Critical Responses to Visual Texts*, New York: Routledge, 71–93.

Pantaleo, Sylvia J. and Sipe, Lawrence R. (eds) (2008) *Postmodern Picturebooks: Play, Parody, and Self-Referentiality*, New York: Routledge.

Straume, Anne Cathrine (2013) "Biblia Pauperum Nova," www.nrk.no/kultur/bok/biblia-pauperum-nova-1.11277706 (accessed June 10, 2015).

Wall, Barbara (1991) *The Narrator's Voice: The Dilemma of Children's Fiction*, Basingstoke: Macmillan.

23

INFORMATIONAL PICTUREBOOKS

Nikola von Merveldt

Recent series names such as *Eye Know* and *Eyewitness* (Dorling Kindersley), *Les yeux de la découverte* (Eyes of Discovery – Gallimard), or *Sehen, Staunen, Wissen* (Seeing, Wondering, Knowing – Gerstenberg) are indicative of a pictorial turn in information literature, which could be observed beginning in the 1990s. Far more than just an increase in visual material on the printed page, this turn marks an epistemic shift in the relationship between text and image, fundamentally changing the way in which knowledge is constituted, understood, and communicated (Dresang 1999; Mitchell 2008; Oetken and Oldenburg 2014).The privileged status of images in knowledge transmission has led to an exciting convergence of informational literature and the picturebook format in the past three decades, resulting in innovative informational picturebooks that more often than not transcend the boundaries of media, genre, gender, and age.

Emphasis on the visual is certainly nothing new in children's literature. Indeed, the first book of its kind, the *Orbis Sensualium Pictus* (1658) by Johann Amos Comenius, presented "the visible world in pictures" because its author, Comenius, was convinced that the eye served as the gateway to learning. Enlightenment pedagogues, inspired by sensualist philosophy, prized images as the most appropriate medium for perception and cognition, especially for children.The nineteenth century proudly documented its technological progress using the newest image printing techniques. The television era inspired book designers to adopt the image-dominated doublespread format. In our present digital age, images have proven to be the ideal medium for experimenting with more interactive, participatory, and inclusive forms of communication that help break down long-standing information barriers (Dresang 1999, 2008). Informational books and picturebooks thus share a long but mostly forgotten history with several pictorial turns, each unique in its complex historical and medial contexts.

In the following sections, I will identify characteristics and parameters that help define informational books in general and informational picturebooks for children specifically, reviewing seminal research to trace lines of inquiry and suggesting promising scholarly perspectives, and drawing on examples from the Anglo-American, French, and German publishing context to reflect on some of the more recent developments.

Beyond fact: defining features and different forms

Defining features

While 'nonfiction' remains the standard label in English (especially in libraries and marketing), authors, illustrators, and critics use it only reluctantly (Fisher 1972; Macaulay 1993): first, because trying to define the genre by what it is not remains largely unproductive; second, because these attempts tend to fall into the trap of the fact/fiction debate, positing an opposition between factual information and fictional devices, apologetically called 'incidental fiction,' which distorts and misinterprets the very mechanisms that constitute the core of the genre. Other terms include the attributes 'expository' or 'descriptive' to differentiate information books from narrative texts, while the term 'literary' or 'creative nonfiction' is being adopted from the realm of adult nonfiction (Kiefer and Wilson 2011) in an effort to accord the same critical attention to a genre only discriminated against in the sector of children's literature.

In the digital age of information society with its increasingly multimodal literacies (Jewitt and Kress 2003), changing understanding of knowledge, Web 2.0, and participatory culture, the terms 'information books' or 'informational literature' have gained critical currency. To exploit the potential of the qualifier 'information,' however, it is vital not to misunderstand information purely as extractable data, as facts and figures (as lamented by Colman 2007). To qualify as information, data have to be organized, structured, interpreted, or presented so they can be perceived to be meaningful (cf. Zins 2007: 480). This is precisely what information books do: they do not merely store data, but select, organize, and interpret facts and figures using verbal and visual codes – drawing on narrative and descriptive forms specific to their historical and cultural context – making information accessible to the interested layperson, engaging readers intellectually and emotionally. While it is widely recognized that texts use rhetoric and narrative techniques to present facts in informational picturebooks, this equally applies to the images: they do not merely represent or illustrate transparent data or facts; rather they render them visible or visualize them, which means they take on an active, interpretative role (Bredekamp, Dünkel and Schneider 2015). Informational books thus go far beyond facts, readily available elsewhere, to awaken curiosity, inspire awe, and nurture community.

Surely, 'information/al book' is a huge umbrella term since information can be conveyed on many levels. Indeed, it is quite impossible to imagine a "non-informational book" (Macaulay 1993), and Hunt reminds us that all books "must teach something" (1994: 3). If one is to read the picturebook *The Cow Who Fell into the Canal* (1957) by Phyllis Krasilovsky on the text level, for example, it is a purely fictional animal story of an anthropomorphized cow longing for adventure. However, Dutch-born Peter Spier's illustrations, which include meticulously researched detail of dress, architecture, and farming, convey a wealth of historical information on the pictorial level, sketching a visual history of the Dutch countryside in the early 1900s. Conversely, it is conceivable to read a fictional book purely for its factual information. Hence, the great British advocate of nonfiction for children, Margaret Mallett, defines an informational book based on its communicative intent or function as one "whose main intention is to impart knowledge and ideas" (2004: 622).

Still true to the Enlightenment motto "instruction and delight," informational books distinguish themselves from textbooks and scholarly books by their desire to amuse, entertain, and inspire their readers – they popularize knowledge to make it accessible. Pictures have always been considered the key medium to achieve this dual goal (Mitchell 2008). Informational literature for children thus tends to rely heavily on graphics and pictures, employing them in different forms and functions, often pushing the limits of printing technology and communicative conventions more radically than adult nonfiction. Overall, it seems that over the last two centuries, the text-image ratio in informational books has continually shifted in favor of images (Unsworth 2001; Norman 2010: 2). These days it is hard to imagine information books without any images at all. Picturebooks thus have become the format of choice to describe, explain, report, instruct, and inspire (Mallett 2010).

For a more nuanced understanding, the quantitative approach needs to be supplemented by a qualitative one, one which assesses the various forms and functions of text and image individually as well as the effects of their intermedial interaction in the series of picture-text combinations. In a strict sense, only those books count as informational picturebooks in which "the visual information is as important as the verbal" (Dresang 2008: 296), and in which pictures do not just document or illustrate facts, but visually organize and interpret them, thereby not merely enhancing and amplifying the text, but at times even reversing the roles between text and image. While traditional books were mostly conceived textually, with the images serving as illustrations, newer books tend to be products of visual thinking, in which images serve as the main communicator of information, and the text is reserved for explanatory functions in the form of labels (Oetken 2014). This pictorial turn is the reason why informational picturebooks are presently among the most innovative and groundbreaking books for children being published.

Spectrum of forms

Browsing library and bookstore shelves, one is stunned by the variety of genres, formats, and media assembled under the classificatory nonfiction rubric. Within this broad spectrum of informational books, one very general overall difference will be readily apparent to the eye. On the one hand, there are series topic books, which typically cover conventional topics (volcanoes, dinosaurs, trucks) according to standard, often formulaic formats, are commissioned, co-authored, and illustrated with copyrighted images from image agencies, and are produced for the global market by large publishing houses such as Dorling Kindersley – in the mind of many, this is the prototype of the informational book. While literary critics generally shun the topic-book series, they deserve critical attention since they do represent the staple of informational literature found in libraries and schools, they play an important role in building information literacy, and, with their emphasis on the visual, they were at the forefront of the pictorial turn (see Dresang 2008: 296). On the other hand, there is a steadily increasing number of more unconventional and very often single-authored books, which tend to take up more unusual topics and to explore them using a whole range of intermedial and narrative devices (Oetken and Oldenburg 2014). Significantly, the creators of the hybrid titles are generally illustrators or graphic artists who approach the topic from the visual angle and add the text at a later stage rather than illustrating a factual text.

Information books cover a broad range of genres and span the spectrum from simple textless concept books, showing infants and toddlers everyday objects or introducing them to basic concepts, all the way to complex science encyclopedias or history books for teenagers and adults. The boundaries of what still qualifies as an informational picturebook are fluid.

On the image side of the spectrum, concept books visualize elementary information, teaching children to name their immediate surroundings and to organize their everyday experience. ABC and number books provide practical packaging to coherently present otherwise loosely linked information. Wimmelbooks, especially the many recent city wimmelbooks, put these isolated concepts into spatial and temporal relationships, opening up nonlinear reading paths, suggesting narrative connections, and providing readers with a wealth of real-world information. Photoessays (Defourny 2001) build on the documentary, narrative, and aesthetic qualities of photographs, which capitalize on their real-world appeal. Paper-engineered books, such as lift-the-flap and pop-up books, explore the materiality of the book to present information in nonlinear, interactive, and palpable ways. So-called educational comics translate information into more focused instructional or narrative iconotext sequences, while graphic novels amplify the narrative dimension and emotional appeal. Traditionally on the text side of the spectrum, biographies and memoirs/autobiographies build on the narrative of an individual life to portray inner ambitions, dreams, or struggles and depict the times. But a recent trend toward the picturebook format – author Nobleman speaks of the "Golden Age of Picture Book Biography" (Noblemania, April 26, 2009) – shows how generic media balances can change over time. Travelogues shift the biographical narrative from time to space, and from inner to outer struggles, often drawing on narrative conventions of journalism or the adventure novel. Travel guides, experiment and activity books provide practical information for real-world orientation and hands-on interaction, inviting readers to observe, experiment, and explore beyond the book. Topic books offer condensed compendiums about one specific theme, such as dinosaurs or volcanoes, most often within the strictly regulated framework of publishing series. Reference books, finally, such as encyclopedias, atlases, or picture dictionaries offer information in highly standardized ways, initiating young readers to the more traditional tools of information literacy.

This vast generic spectrum can be differentiated according to a number of categories, depending on the analytic perspective. Mallett (2010) uses a pragmalinguistic approach to distinguish between informational books that recount, instruct, report, explain, discuss, or persuade. Others have proposed sets of opposing categories, allowing for a more nuanced analysis of individual titles by placing them within a continuum between opposing but by no means exclusive poles. From a cognitive perspective, Jörg Meibauer (2015: 52) bases his analysis on the fundamental opposition of descriptive versus narrative, simple versus complex, and less text versus more text, while nonfiction author Penny Colman (2007) concentrates more on the literary qualities, distinguishing between factual versus fictional, episodic versus encyclopedic, use of more versus fewer literary devices, weaker versus stronger presence of author's voice, and the presence of less versus more visual material (again in Kiefer and Wilson 2011: 296–297). These categories offer heuristic typologies for comparing and classifying the vastly different books of the informational sector as well as for identifying trends. Meibauer rightly admits, however, that his (like any other) "taxonomy is by no means exhaustive and that there are many intermediate or overlapping categories" (2015: 52). Indeed, one of the most striking trends in recent years has been the playful hybridization of forms (Pappas 2006), mainly of the factual and fictional on the one hand (for instance, picturebooks by Peter Sís, François Place, and Torben Kuhlmann) and of descriptive and narrative on the other (for instance, the *Magic Schoolbus* series; Hachette's series *Demi-page*, or books by Anne Möller or Irmgard Lucht).

Trend toward hybridization

The picturebooks of Jason Chin perfectly illustrate this hybridization of forms. In *Redwoods* (2009), he skillfully mixes fantasy, nonfiction, and even meta-fiction (or meta-nonfiction?): When a boy (looking very much like Chin) riding the New York subway picks up an abandoned book about the Californian redwood forests, his urban environment merges with the ancient forest world he is reading about (Figure 23.1). In the end, he forgets the book on a park bench, where it is soon found and picked up by a girl, who plunges into the same world. The text remains purely descriptive, providing facts about the history, flora, and fauna of the redwoods; the images, however, develop a breathtaking narrative of time and space travel, mixing naturalistic with fantasy images of transitional worlds, scientific imagery, and informational comic panels. In the visual narrative, New York is the 'real world' and the Redwoods are fantasy; in the textual description, however, the Redwoods are the real world, and New York remains completely absent – denouncing it to be the incidental fiction in the form of visual fictional framing. This counterpoint, an intermedial reversal between the real and the imagined, is ironically reflected in a clever mise en abyme: the book the boy finds on the subway shows him on the cover and ultimately turns out to be the very book readers are holding in their hands – the fictional frame is visualized in the paratextual frame by the boy's hands holding the title page and the girl's hands opening the book to the informational endmatter. As the real reader's hands are holding the book, the extratextual world and intratextual fictional framing briefly converge and literally come into contact, reminding us of the transporting power of nonfiction (Figure 23.2).

Examples such as these clearly show that informational picturebooks can be just as complex, playful, and innovative – and thus worthy of critical attention – as the narrative picturebooks (cf. also Bamford and Kristo 2003), which have traditionally captured the imagination of literary historians. Exemplary analyses of some of the classics that have shaped the genre (any books by Piero Ventura, David Macaulay, or Stephen Biesty, for example) and of recent titles (by Joelle Jolivet, Brian Floca, or Anke M. Leitzgen, for example) would wipe out prejudice against informational literature once and for all and show that informational picturebooks are worthwhile objects of study.

Styles and media

The range of artistic styles and media in informational picturebooks is equally impressive, leaving the image types (cross-sections, line-drawings, and maps, etc.) and media (pen-and-ink, photos, or computer-aided graphics, etc.) of traditional nonfiction far behind or reinventing them. While Swedish author Pernilla Stalfelt, for example, mixes her quirky comic-like drawings with printed type and hand-lettered text to address questions surrounding the topics of death (1999), violence (2005), or feces (1997), French comic and graphic designer Blexbolex uses experimental screen printing in the *ligne claire* tradition and retro-design to portray the variety of people (2010), seasons (2009), and narrative prototypes (2013) of Western culture. American nonfiction author Steve Jenkins renders his fascination for the natural world in compellingly simple compositions and complex collages (for instance, *Actual Size* 2004), while German photographer Jan von Holleben transcends the photo as a documentary medium to allow for playful metaphorical compositions answering questions surrounding puberty in *Does This Happen to Everyone?* (2014) (Figures 23.3 and 23.4).

While the media and styles are vastly different, there is a general trend from informational graphics to narrative-poetic images, magazine-style graphic design, or hybrid forms. Furthermore, most of the recent informational picturebooks have one thing in common: they are visually conceptualized rather than textually. This medial role reversal is made explicit on the title page of the German original of *Does This Happen to Everyone?*, which reads: "A book by Jan von Holleben – with texts by Antje Helms" (2013). The paratext identifies Jan von Holleben, the photographer, as the main author of the book; the "texts" (note the plural, which changes the one authoritative text to subservient paratexts presenting the images) almost seem like an afterthought – ancillary additions to the prime medium of the image.

Far more than illustrations or scientific visualizations, the images in more recent informational picturebooks often set the tone, or interact with the text to produce a multilayered message open to interpretation instead of telling the one, supposedly objective truth. Three examples from picturebooks about African American history can illustrate this. In *Remember* (2004), Toni Morrison imagines deeply personal, thoughtful interior monologs to accompany archival photographs documenting 'The Journey to School Integration' (subtitle), inviting readers to identify with the children living the historic event. Tom Feelings chooses a very different approach in his monochromatic and large-format visual narrative of the journey of slaves from Africa to America, *The Middle Passage: White Ships, Black Cargo* (1995). In a series of sixty-four textless pen-and-ink and tempera drawings, he recounts the pride and suffering of the deported people in highly symbolic imagery, using "historical narrative pictures," but going beyond mere documentation to portray "the psychological and spiritual journey" of his people (Feelings 1995: preface) (Figure 23.5). *Ellington Was Not a Street* (2004) combines elegiac autobiographical poetry by Ntozake Shange with celebratory, colorful oil paintings and portraits by Kadir Nelson to pay homage to the African American men of the Harlem Renaissance.

Just as the choice of artistic medium, style, and tone is no longer determined by the fact/fiction divide, so the authors are free to select their literary form, devices, and voice. Poetry has become extremely popular in informational books, no matter whether it celebrates nature's wonders or explains the intricate mechanism of steam-engine tanks, such as in Brian Floca's Caldecott Medal winner *Locomotive* (2013). Historical fact, personal memories, technical details, and imagination are not bound to one medium or form, but interact through and across the media, resulting in emotionally powerful, multiperspectival, and historically complex narratives that challenge readers to think for themselves.

Because of the trend toward narrative hybrids, in which image types or literary forms are no longer genre-specific, the boundaries between fact and fiction are less clearly delineated in more recent titles. One of the defining – if not essential – features of the informational picturebook,

Figure 23.1 Illustration from Jason Chin's *Redwoods*. New York: Flashpoint/Roaring Brook Press, 2009.

they are the tallest living
things on the planet. Redwoods
regularly grow to be more
than 200 feet tall.

Figure 23.1 Continued

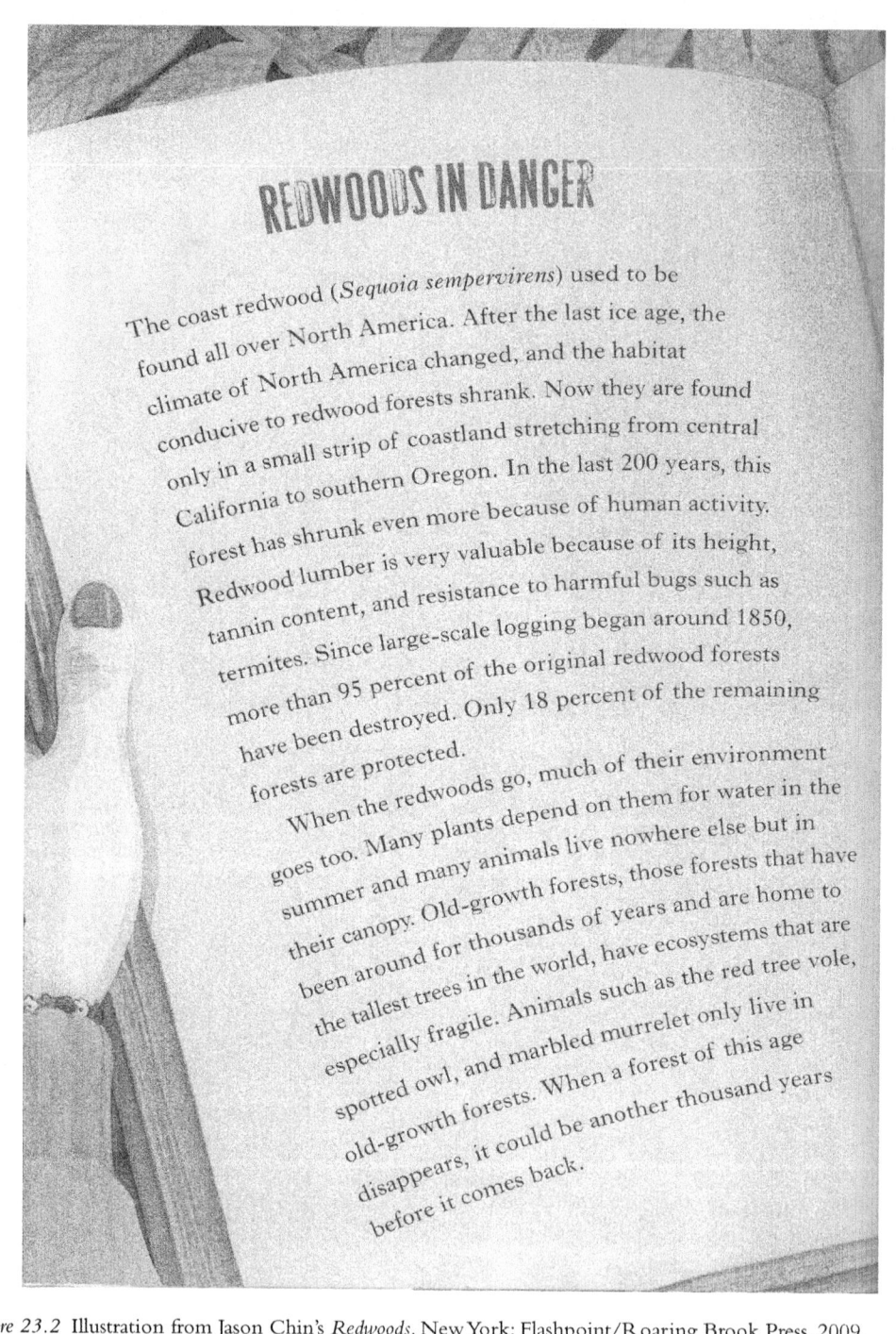

REDWOODS IN DANGER

The coast redwood (*Sequoia sempervirens*) used to be found all over North America. After the last ice age, the climate of North America changed, and the habitat conducive to redwood forests shrank. Now they are found only in a small strip of coastland stretching from central California to southern Oregon. In the last 200 years, this forest has shrunk even more because of human activity. Redwood lumber is very valuable because of its height, tannin content, and resistance to harmful bugs such as termites. Since large-scale logging began around 1850, more than 95 percent of the original redwood forests have been destroyed. Only 18 percent of the remaining forests are protected.

When the redwoods go, much of their environment goes too. Many plants depend on them for water in the summer and many animals live nowhere else but in their canopy. Old-growth forests, those forests that have been around for thousands of years and are home to the tallest trees in the world, have ecosystems that are especially fragile. Animals such as the red tree vole, spotted owl, and marbled murrelet only live in old-growth forests. When a forest of this age disappears, it could be another thousand years before it comes back.

Figure 23.2 Illustration from Jason Chin's *Redwoods*. New York: Flashpoint/Roaring Brook Press, 2009.

330 feet

300 feet

200 feet

100 feet

Redwood needles
(actual size)

Redwood cone
(actual size)

human adult

THE COAST REDWOOD

Sequoia sempervirens

Figure 23.2 Continued

Figure 23.3 Book cover of Jan von Holleben and Antje Helms's *Kriegen das eigentlich alle?* Stuttgart: Gabriel, 2013.

Reprinted by permission of Gabriel/Thienemann-Esslinger Verlag.

Figure 23.4 Photo by Jan von Holleben from Jan von Holleben and Antje Helms's *Kriegen das eigentlich alle?* Stuttgart: Gabriel, 2013.

Reprinted by permission of Gabriel/Thienemann-Esslinger Verlag.

Figure 23.5 Illustration from Tom Feelings's *The Middle Passage*. New York: Dial Books, 1995.
Reprinted by permission of Dial Books/a division of Penguin Books.

however, is the strong presence of paratextual framing of the information presented (see Kerper 2003). In fact, while many picturebook biographies appear indistinguishable from fictive stories both in text and image, author's notes, prefaces by authorities or celebrities, bibliographies, documentary photographs, maps, and timelines identify these stories as factual. The main function of this expanded front- and endmatter is to establish the information character of the book, confirm the factuality and accuracy of the information presented in what seems a fictional guise, and build authorial credibility. Author's bios and notes, forewords by authorities in the field, acknowledgments listing the experts, and bibliographies listing the sources consulted all lend authority to informational titles in a time where digital image processing has led to an erosion of the truth-value of pictures. Timelines and maps organize information visually and situate the information in real time and space, while glossaries, labels, keys, captions, and typographical foregrounding provide readers with basic word knowledge or more advanced terminology. Structural paratexts and reference aids such as a table of contents, page numbers, an index, and appendices allow for easier navigation of the book and for nonlinear ways of reading, which encourage essential information literacy skills (such as skimming, scanning, etc.). Sidebars, text boxes, bubbles, flaps, fold-outs, typographical differences in size and fonts, appendices, and diagrams allow for a layering of the information, leaving it up to the readers how much detail to seek and in which sequence.

Beyond bias: research and criticism

Given the importance of informational books in general and informational picturebooks in particular in publishing, libraries, and schools, it is rather striking that scholarship on the topic is scarce and scattered. There still is a general critical bias in favor of fiction over nonfiction. Partly due to the grand narrative according to which the history of children's literature should be seen as a triumphant emancipation from instruction to delight, scholars of children's literature have considered carefree fictional literature as the more worthy object of study. The romantic prejudice according to which children prefer imaginative fiction to dreary didactic fact is one of the enduring myths that needs to be dispelled (Colman 2007: 258). Indeed, empirical studies have shown that children of both genders actually prefer reading informational books over fiction (Carter and Abrahamson 1990).

Among the many recent guides, handbooks, and companions in the field of children's literature, none mentions informational picturebooks as a specific genre, and only a few devote an entry or chapter to the broader category of informational books (Bush 2002; Mallett 2004; Kiefer and Wilson 2011; Ossowski and Ossowski 2012) – most do not even mention them at all as an object of study or neglected area of interest.

Tellingly enough, Mallett's succinct handbook essay is titled "Informational Texts" (2004), betraying the textual bias still present in most classic scholarship on informational literature, which strives to establish the literary qualities of the genre and focuses on the more narrative sub-genres of biographies or travel writings (Doderer 1961; Fisher 1972; Carr 1982; Ossowski and Ossowski 2012). On the image side, most classic picturebook studies tend to exclude what they (dis)qualify as nonfiction, dismissing the genre as a whole as nonnarrative (Nikolajeva and Scott 2001: 26). To this day, there exists no scholarly study attempting a historical or systematic overview of the genre of informational children's literature – at least for the Anglo-American, German, or French contexts (note, however, the richly illustrated thematically ordered historical survey by Defourny 2013).

While the literary devices and strategies used to bring facts alive on the textual level, often called incidental fiction, have largely been inventoried (Doderer 1961; Carr 1982; Pappas 2006; Kiefer and Wilson 2011: 294–295), there is still little research and a lack of consensual terminology or typology for the analysis of informational imagery and the various forms of text – image interaction. Kiefer and Wilson (2011: 295–296) give a useful summary of the analytic schemes proposed by Pappas (2006) and Unsworth (2001). The special issue of *La revue des livres pour enfants* devoted to "*l'illustration documentaire*" (Ballanger et al. 1997) surveys the various forms, types, functions, and trends of the Francophone informational publishing sector and proposes promising lines of inquiry far beyond the national context.

Library and information studies continue to be the driving discipline in the promotion and study of informational literature. Many inputs to the field come from practitioners – librarians, educators – notably Margery Mallett (2004, 2010). A broader understanding of literacy, traditionally understood as the ability to read and write texts, which includes visual literacy, information literacy, and multimodal literacy, provides promising theoretical frameworks as well as empirical data for the study of informational picturebooks (Dresang and Koh 2009; Norman 2010; Jewitt and Kress 2003). Empirical studies are needed to test the commonly held views – especially in reading promotion programs – that informational literature is best suited for reluctant readers and boys (Moss 2007).

From a scholarly point of view, the most promising recent studies approach the topic of informational picturebooks from a cognitive, socio-semiotic, or historical-cultural perspective, and are interdisciplinary, drawing on insights from developmental psychology, linguistics, sociology, media and communication studies, visual cultural studies, history of science, and book history. Cognitive approaches are beginning to give us a better understanding of how informational picturebooks help children acquire word and world knowledge (Kümmerling-Meibauer and Meibauer 2013; Meibauer 2015; Norman 2010). The emerging interdisciplinary field of multimodal studies combines and develops social and semiotic frameworks, methods, and concepts for describing and analyzing communicative practices, taking into consideration their visual, aural, tactile, and spatial dimensions and how they construct meaning and social identities (Jewitt 2009; Jewitt and Kress 2003). Book historical and cultural studies of the Enlightenment period offer deeper discussion of the verbal and visual strategies deployed in early examples of information literature, but most importantly the discursive contexts that shaped the early informational books (te Heesen 2002; Paul 2011; Chakkalakal 2014). Art history and the history of science are joining forces in the equally young field of *Bildwissenschaft*, the German brand of visual culture studies, which is still waiting to be discovered by children's literature scholarship. The landmark book *The Technical Image. A History of Styles in Scientific Imagery* (Bredekamp, Dünkel and Schneider 2015) provides astute theoretical background, sound methodological tools, and exemplary case studies to inspire historically informed analyses and interpretations of the scientific practices and iconographic traditions within which informational books are produced and read. What all these contributions teach us is that every book must always be judged and analyzed within its specific medial, cultural, and historical context.

Finally, it should be mentioned that some of the most innovative and productive reflections on informational picturebooks are being published by artists, writers, and educators on their blogs, which provide precious resources for scholars. Author Marc Tyler Nobleman, for example, observes current trends and develops useful descriptive tools for biographical picturebooks on his blog "Noblemania." Cruschiform gives insight into the artistic development and intellectual background of her graphic designs; educator Keith Schoch's blog "Teach with Picture Books" not only offers a stunning overview of thematically grouped books but also gives hands-on advice on how to bring the books into the classroom.

Beyond the book?

For the so-called digital natives, who literally have the facts at their fingertips, informational books no longer simply have to provide facts. Instead, they can draw on their media-specific potential to nurture curiosity, teach skills, build community, and generate knowledge. Purely factual information continues to migrate to online platforms, challenging and inviting creators of informational books to explore the innate potential of the picturebook medium to present, share, and question information in familiar and trustworthy formats or in new and unexpected ways.

The doom of the codex has been declared innumerable times, but both the market and unbiased research have proven the resilience, compatibility, and innovative force of the book. While informational books may seem especially threatened in the digital age, in which facts are just a click or touch away and images are easy to come by, publishers, writers, and artists have typically responded in three ways. First, they have adopted and adapted digital aesthetics and strategies by offering information and multiple meanings in nonlinear, nonsequential ways or by incorporating interactive and multimedia elements, such as moving images and audio files. Second, in addition to being multimodal, most informational picturebooks of the digital age are also multiplatform books, meaning the printed book has digital and other extensions, such as audiobook versions, publisher's or author's websites offering video material, 3-D visualizations, course packs for teachers, activities for readers, and participation via social media. As such, the informational book has not only responded to marketing pressure by building consumer fidelity through branding, but it has also created synergies with other media within a constantly evolving media ecology (Dresang 2008; Helm 2014). Third, bold artists and visionary publishing houses have embraced the digital challenge by rethinking the picture part of informational picturebooks. Liberated of the burdens of evidence, objectivity, and truth-telling, characteristic of the age of print and authoritative knowledge, the informational picturebook imagery of the digital age is free to play with iconographic conventions, to deploy sophisticated narrative techniques, to transgress genre boundaries, to ignore hierarchies, and to experiment (Thiele 2004; Dresang 2008; Oetken 2014).

References

Ballanger, Françoise et al. (eds) (1997) "Dossier: L'illustration des documentaires," Special Issue of *La revue des livres pour enfants*: 175–176.

Bamford, Rosemary A. and Kristo, Janice V. (eds) (2003) *Making Facts Come Alive: Choosing & Using Quality Nonfiction Literature K-8*, 2nd ed., Norwood, MA: Christopher-Gordon.

Blexbolex (2009) *Saisons*, Paris: Albin Michel Jeunesse.

Blexbolex (2010) *L'imagier des gens*, Paris: Albin Michel Jeunesse.

Blexbolex (2013) *Romance*, Paris: A. Michel Jeunesse.

Bredekamp, Horst, Dünkel, Vera, and Schneider, Birgit (eds) (2015) *The Technical Image: A History of Styles in Scientific Imagery*, Chicago and London: University of Chicago Press.

Bush, Margaret (2002) "Information Books," in Anita Silvey (ed.) *The Essential Guide to Children's Books and Their Creators*, New York: Houghton Mifflin, 217–221.

Carr, Jo (ed.) (1982) *Beyond Fact: Nonfiction for Children and Young People*, Chicago: American Library Association.

Carter, Betty, and Abrahamson, Richard F. (eds) (1990) *Nonfiction for Young Adults: From Delight to Wisdom*, Phoenix, AZ: Oryx Press.

Chakkalakal, Silvy (2014) *Die Welt in Bildern: Erfahrung und Evidenz in Friedrich J. Bertuchs "Bilderbuch für Kinder" (1790–1830)*, Göttingen: Wallstein.

Chin, Jason (2009) *Redwoods*, New York: Flashpoint/Roaring Brook Press.

Colman, Penny (2007) "A New Way to Look at Literature: A Visual Model for Analyzing Fiction and Nonfiction Texts," *Language Arts* 84.3: 257–268.

Cruschiform (n.d.) blog, http://cruschiform.blogspot.ca/ (Last accessed February 19, 2016).

Defourny, Michel (2001) *Flash sur les livres de photographies pour enfants, des années 1920 à nos jours*, Paris: Fédération française de coopération entre bibliothèques.

Defourny, Michel (2013) *De quelques albums qui ont aidé les enfants à découvrir le monde et à réfléchir*, Paris: L'École Loisirs.

Doderer, Klaus (1961) *Das Sachbuch als literarpädagogisches Problem*, Frankfurt: Diesterweg.

Dresang, Eliza T. (1999) *Radical Change: Books for Youth in a Digital Age*, New York: Wilson.

Dresang, Eliza T. (2008) "Radical Change Revisited: Dynamic Digital Age Books for Youth," *Contemporary Issues in Technology and Teacher Education* 8.3: 294–304.

Dresang, Eliza T., and Koh, Kyungwon (2009) "Radical Change Theory, Youth Information Behavior, and School Libraries," *Library Trends* 58.1: 26–50.

Feelings, Tom (1995) *The Middle Passage: White Ships, Black Cargo*, New York: Dial Books.

Fisher, Margery (1972) *Matters of Fact: Aspects of Non-Fiction for Children*, London: Hodder & Stoughton.

Floca, Brian (2013) *Locomotive*, New York: Atheneum Books.

Helm, Wiebke (2014) "Wissen rundum: Multimedialität in der Kinder- und Jugendsachliteratur," *Interjuli* 2: 42–56.

Holleben, Jan von, and Helms, Antje (2013) *Kriegen das eigentlich alle? Die besten Antworten zum Erwachsenwerden*, Stuttgart: Gabriel.

Holleben, Jan von, and Helms, Antje (2014) *Does This Happen to Everyone? A Budding Adult's Guide to Puberty*, Berlin: Little Gestalten.

Hunt, Peter (1994) *An Introduction to Children's Literature*, Oxford: Oxford University Press.

Jenkins, Steve (2004) *Actual Size*, Boston: Houghton Mifflin.

Jewitt, Carey (ed.) (2009) *The Routledge Handbook of Multimodal Analysis*, London: Routledge.

Jewitt, Carey, and Kress, Gunther R. (eds) (2003) *Multimodal Literacy*, New York: Peter Lang.

Kerper, Richard M. (2003) "Choosing Quality Nonfiction for Children: Examining Access Features and Visual Displays," in Rosemary A. Bamford and Janice V. Kristo (eds) *Making Facts Come Alive: Choosing & Using Quality Nonfiction Literature K–8*, 2nd ed., Norwood, MA: Christopher-Gordon, 41–64.

Kiefer, Barbara, and Wilson, Melissa I. (2011) "Nonfiction Literature for Children: Old Assumptions and New Directions," in Shelby A. Wolf, Karen Coats, Patricia Enciso, and Christine A. Jenkins (eds) *Handbook of Research on Children's and Young Adult Literature*, New York: Routledge, 290–299.

Krasilovsky, Phyllis (1957) *The Cow Who Fell Into the Canal*, illus. Peter Spier, Garden City, NY: Doubleday.

Kümmerling-Meibauer, Bettina, and Meibauer, Jörg (2013) "Towards a Cognitive Theory of Picturebooks," *International Research in Children's Literature* 6.2: 143–160.

Macaulay, David (1993) "The Truth About Nonfiction," in Zena Sutherland and Betsy Hearne (eds) *The Zena Sutherland Lectures, 1983–1992*, New York: Clarion Books, 141–159.

Mallett, Margaret (2004) "Children's Information Texts," in Peter Hunt (ed.) *International Companion Encyclopedia of Children's Literature*, New York: Routledge, 622–631.

Mallett, Margaret (2010) *Choosing and Using Fiction and Non-Fiction 3–11: A Comprehensive Guide for Teachers and Student Teachers*, London: Routledge.

Meibauer, Jörg (2015) "What the Child Can Learn From Simple Descriptive Picturebooks: An Inquiry Into Lastwagen/Trucks by Paul Stickland," in Bettina Kümmerling-Meibauer, Jörg Meibauer, Kerstin Nachtigäller, and Katharina Rohlfing (eds) *Learning from Picturebooks: Perspectives from Child Development and Literacy Studies*, London: Routledge, 51–70.

Mitchell, W.J.T. (2008) "Visual Literacy or Literary Visualcy? Four Fundamental Concepts of Image Science," in James Elkins (ed.) *Visual Literacy*, New York: Routledge, 11–29.

Morrison, Toni (2004) *Remember: The Journey to School Integration*, Boston: Houghton Mifflin.

Moss, Gemma (2007) *Literacy and Gender: Researching Texts, Contexts, and Readers*, London: Routledge.

Nikolajeva, Maria, and Scott, Carole (2001) *How Picturebooks Work*, New York: Garland.

Nobleman, Marc Tyler (2008–present) *Noblemania*, http://noblemania.blogspot.ca/ (last accessed February 19, 2016).

Norman, Rebecca R. (2010) "Picture This: Processes Prompted by Graphics in Informational Text," *Literacy Teaching and Learning* 14.1–2: 1–39.

Oetken, Mareike (2014) "Wo geht's lang? Erzählungen, Bilder und Berichte vom Fremden im Bildersachbuch," in Mareile Oetken and Ines Oldenburg (eds) *Erzählen: Darstellen. Berichten: Interdisziplinäre Perspektiven auf das Sachbuch in der Kinder- und Jugendliteratur*, Baltmannsweiler: Schneider Hohengehren, 27–42.

Oetken, Mareike, and Oldenburg, Ines (eds) (2014) *Erzählen: Darstellen. Berichten: Interdisziplinäre Perspektiven auf das Sachbuch in der Kinder- und Jugendliteratur*, Baltmannsweiler: Schneider Hohengehren.

Ossowski, Ekkehart, and Ossowski, Herbert (2012) "Sachbücher für Kinder und Jugendliche," in Hannelore Daubert and Günter Lange (eds) *Kinder- und Jugendliteratur der Gegenwart: Ein Handbuch*, 2nd ed., Baltmannsweiler: Schneider Hohengehren, 364–388.

Pappas, Christine C. (2006) "The Information Book Genre: Its Role in Integrated Science Literacy Research and Practice," *Reading Research Quarterly* 41: 226–250.

Paul, Lissa (2011) *The Children's Book Business Lessons from the Long Eighteenth Century*, New York: Routledge.

Schoch, Keith (2009) *Teach with Picture Books*, http://teachwithpicturebooks.blogspot.ca/ (Last accessed February 17, 2016).

Shange, Ntozake (2004) *Ellington Was Not a Street*, illus. Kadir Nelson, New York: Simon & Schuster.

Stalfelt, Pernilla (1997) *Bajsboken*, Stockholm: Eriksson & Lindgren.

Stalfelt, Pernilla (1999) *Dödenboken*, Stockholm: Eriksson & Lindgren.

Stalfelt, Pernilla (2005) *Våldboken*, Stockholm: Eriksson & Lindgren.

te Heesen, Anke (2002) *The World in a Box: The Story of an Eighteenth-Century Picture Encyclopedia*, Chicago: University of Chicago Press.

Thiele, Jens (2004) "Die Sache mit dem Sachbild: Neun Spotlights auf das Illustrieren einer Sache," in Petra Josting and Gudrun Stenzel (eds) "Wieso, weshalb, warum . . ." Sachliteratur für Kinder und Jugendliche, special issue *Beiträge Jugendliteratur und Medien*, 44–56.

Unsworth, Len (2001) *Teaching Multiliteracies Across the Curriculum: Changing Contexts of Text and Image in Classroom Practice*, Philadelphia: Open University Press.

Zins, Chaim (2007) "Conceptual Approaches for Defining Data, Information, and Knowledge," *Journal of the American Society for Information Science and Technology* 58.4: 479–493.

Further resources

Awards

Boston Globe-Horn Book Awards (nonfiction category since 1976), www.hbook.com/boston-globe-horn-book-awards/#.

Deutscher Jugendliteraturpreis (nonfiction category since 1964), www.djlp.jugendliteratur.org/.

National Council of Teachers of English Orbis Pictus Award for Outstanding Nonfiction for Children (since 1989), www.ncte.org/awards/orbispictus.

Robert F. Sibert Informational Book Medal (since 2001), www.ala.org/alsc/awardsgrants/bookmedia/sibertmedal.

Annotated selection lists

Andreau, Francoise, and Ballanger, Francoise (eds) (1999) *À la découverte des documentaires pour la jeunesse*, Le Perreux sur Marne: CRDP de l'Acad. de Créteil.

Cianciolo, Patricia J. (2000) *Informational Picture Books for Children*, Chicago: American Library Association.

Isaacs, Kathleen T. (2013) *Picturing the World: Informational Picture Books for Children*, Chicago: American Library Association.

Kobrin, Beverly (1988) *Eyeopeners! How to Choose and Use Children's Books About Real People, Places, and Things*, New York: Penguin Books.

24

POETRY IN PICTUREBOOKS

Donelle Ruwe

Maurice Sendak observed that picturebooks are "a complicated poetic form that requires absolute concentration and control" (1990: 186). And yet, verse picturebooks are rarely the result of a collaborative process between poets and artists. Most illustrators are hired by publishers after a poetic text is already written and have little contact with the poet. For instance, after J. Patrick Lewis (American Children's Poet Laureate, 2011–2013) wrote the verse for his collection *Doodle Dandies: Poems That Take Shape* (2000a), he had no interaction with his book's illustrator Lisa Desimini. In fact, Lewis and Desimini first met months after *Doodle Dandies* was published. As Lewis remarks:

> Generally speaking, artists don't want to be intruded upon in their half of the creative process. They have their own vision. Writers, I think, must respect that. Many people seem to think it's unfair that the author has so little say in how his or her book will actually appear, but you have to trust editors and art directors to do the right thing, choose the right illustrator, design the best book, etc. Alas, sometimes they goof.
>
> *2000b: n. pag.*

However, just because there is no immediate collaboration between poets and illustrators, it does not mean that artists have no influence on the poetry. Illustrators shape a reader's response to a poem. They can elevate the most mundane of verse through their art and revitalize old poems through new illustrations that reflect new socio-cultural environments. Unfortunately, illustration also narrows the multifaceted potential of verse. According to Perry Nodelman, "any specific picture at all, even one we invent for ourselves, is bound to destroy some of the special impossibility, perhaps even unimaginability, of the images evoked by the rhymes themselves" (1987: 199).

Illustrating pre-existing verse

The illustration history of Ann Taylor's sentimental children's poem "My Mother" (1804) demonstrates how artists shape responses to a poem. In "My Mother," one of the most popular British poems of the nineteenth century, a child describes her mother and then contemplates her mother's old age and inevitable death. Two picturebook editions of this poem that straddle the nineteenth century, Peltro Williams Tomkins's 1807 art book and Walter Crane's 1873 toy book, exemplify how illustrations determine a reader's entrance into a poem and participate in an era's ideology.

The language of Taylor's poem is remarkably nondescript. It has no sounds, textures, vivid colors, or unique details, providing no guidance for an illustrator's imagination. "My Mother" consists of eleven three-line stanzas in a gentle iambic tetrameter (the same meter, coincidentally, as her sister Jane Taylor's 1806 "The Star," also known as "Twinkle, Twinkle, Little Star"). Each stanza concludes with the refrain "My Mother." The poem begins as follows:

> Who fed me from her gentle breast,
> And hushed me in her arms to rest,
> And on my cheek sweet kisses prest?
> My Mother.

> Who sat and watched my infant head,
> When sleeping on my cradle bed?
> And tears of sweet affection shed?
> My Mother.
> *1807: n. pag.*

The deliberate neutrality of the poem's bland imagery allowed it to be the empty vessel into which generations of artists poured their particular ideologies of mother and child. For nineteenth-century readers, "My Mother" perfectly straddled two conflicting ideologies of the mother: that of the educating heroine of impeccable character and stern virtue, and that of the sentimentalized, self-sacrificing nurturer. Early illustrators emphasized the poem's educating heroine aspects, depicting the maternal role as a deliberate and carefully scripted act. Later editors were so uneasy with the idea of mothering as a conscious task that they excised parts of the poem, and illustrators emphasized the naturalness of maternal affections (Ruwe 2014: 84–107).

The first picturebook of "My Mother" emphasized motherhood as a staged, public performance as befits an Enlightenment approach to rational motherhood. *My Mother: A Poem Embellished with Designs* (1807) was illustrated by Peltro Williams Tomkins, drawing master to the daughters of George III. Each page of this generously sized art book features elegant engravings of a stylish young matron who is modeled after Lady Emma Hamilton (Figure 24.1). In her heyday Hamilton was celebrated for her 'attitudes,' a type of tableau performance in which she posed as Medea, Circe, or other characters from classical literature. Tomkins's highly stylized engravings emphasize motherhood as an 'attitude' – a conscious, artificial act, neither natural nor instinctive, that is aware of audience and effect. The viewer's eye follows the spiraling lines of the engraving, moving counterclockwise from the mother's knee, to the chair seat, to the curved chair back, to the mother's sloping shoulder, to her dark hair as it frames her face, to the child's head, to the mother's inner arm, to finally end at the focal point of the picture: a suckling infant and the mother's exposed breast.

Tomkins's display of a sensuous dishabille contrasts to later Victorian images in which elaborate layers of corset, crinoline, satins, and lace separate mother and child. When Walter Crane illustrated "My Mother" for Routledge's New Six Penny Toy Book series in 1873, the breastfeeding scene focused on the material goods so typical of Victorian homes with their displays of wealth (Figure 24.2). Crane was the first president of the Arts and Crafts Exhibition Society, and his illustration's emphasis on elegant textiles typifies this movement's credo: that decorative arts (furnishings, wallpapers, fabrics) should rise above the aesthetic poverty of modern industrialized society and mass-produced culture. Crane (with the assistance of his talented printer Edmund Evans) integrated text with "title pages, headers, tailpieces, and full-page pictures," allowing readers to experience all elements of a text as a single effect (Hutton 2010: 28). In the image reproduced here, the green curtains and rug and the orange dress and chair cushion echo the autumn colors of distant trees. The mother is 'naturalized.' She coordinates with her surroundings and surrounds, in turn, the white-clothed infant in the picture's center.

Who fed me from her gentle breast,
And hush'd me in her arms to rest,
And on my cheek sweet kisses prest?
      My Mother.

Figure 24.1 Engraving by Peltro Williams Tomkins from Ann Taylor's *My Mother: A Poem Embellished with Designs*. London: Darton, 1807. Courtesy of the Children's Book Collection, Department of Special Collections, Charles E. Young Research Library, UCLA.

Although Tomkins and Crane work with the same poem, their interpretations reflect different sociocultural trends. Tomkins presents a conscious performance of motherhood, while Crane encapsulates the Victorian ideology of the angel in the house: the purity of mother love is the heart of the home, and women are sheltered within domestic space. In the top right corner of Crane's illustration,

MY MOTHER.

WHO fed me from her gentle breast.
And hush'd me in her arms to rest,
And on my cheek sweet kisses prest?
    My Mother.
When sleep forsook my open eye,
Who was it sung sweet hushaby,
And rock'd me that I should not cry?
    My Mother.

1

Figure 24.2 Illustration by Walter Crane from Ann Taylor's *My Mother*. London: Routledge, 1873. Courtesy of the Baldwin Collection of Historical Children's Literature, George A. Smathers Libraries, University of Florida.

a boy plays outdoors, further emphasizing the ideology of separate spheres in which the public masculine world contrasts to woman's private sphere.

Another important role that illustrators play in shaping readers' responses to pre-existing verse is when they take compilations of miscellaneous poems and, by creating a unified look and feel, turn the compilation into a single whole that is greater than the sum of its parts. For example, when Paul B. Janeczko selected concrete verse (in which meaning is conveyed through the graphic shape of words on the page) to form the collection *A Poke in the I* (2002), illustrator Chris Raschka's inventive artwork pulled it together. Raschka paired torn paper, watercolor, and ink pictures with concrete poems by John Hollander, Mary Ellen Salt, and others. To illustrate Robert Froman's "Easy Diver," Raschka clipped newspaper into the shape of a rectangular apartment building and placed the building side by side with Froman's skinny poem:

Pigeon on the roof.

Dives.

Go-

ing

fa-

st.

GOING TO

HIT HARD!

Opens Wings.

softly, gently

down.

2002: 7

These words, set up literally as a nosedive from the word "Dives" to "down," mimic the flight of a pigeon as it plunges from the roof, picks up speed as the verse narrows into single-letter lines, and abruptly halts when "HITS HARD" is followed by "opens wings" and a soft landing. In a chapter devoted to visual children's poetry in *Poetry's Playground*, Joseph T. Thomas, Jr. notes how Raschka turns even the paratext in Janeczko's collection (book elements beyond the main text such as cover art, blurbs, and title pages) into concrete verse (2007: 103). Raschka typesets the table of contents to shape an elegant console table, and he turns "Notes from the Editor" into a two-page, shaped poem. Raschka places a strange green figure playing a saxophone on the right-hand page, and on the left-hand page fans out the editor's notes like sound waves (literally turning editorial notes into music notes) originating from the saxophone's bell.

Poetry about art

I have focused so far on illustrations of pre-existing poetry. However, one type of poetry, ekphrastic verse, reverses this pattern. In this genre, a poem responds to pre-existing art such as canvases, mobiles, sculptures, and photographs. For example, in the ekphrastic *Heart to Heart: New Poems Inspired by Twentieth-Century American Art* (a 2001 Prinz Honor Book) edited by Jan Greenberg, one finds Lyn Lifshin's poem about a photograph of Martha Graham performing "Letter to the World" and Jane Yolen's eerie response to Grant Wood's *American Gothic*: "Do not dwell on the fork, / the brooch at the throat, / the gothic angel wing / of window" (Yolen 2001: 39). Another ekphrastic picturebook, Anushka Ravishankar's *Excuse Me, Is This India?* (2001), responds to the colorful Indian textiles and scenes that appear in the quilted work of Swiss textile artist Anita Leutwiler. Ravishankar's protagonist is a blue mouse who sets off on a fantastic journey, encountering bandicoots, three-wheeled cars, elephants, and Chennai Airport – all verses accompanied by reproductions of Leutwiler's quilts.

Who Look at Me (1969), a long poem by the Caribbean American poet and civil rights activist June Jordan, demonstrates the complexity of ekphrastic work. Richard Flynn notes that, as a children's poet, Jordan insists "on a poetics that interrogates private notions of childhood through activist, public positions" (2002: 159). Jordan also insists that the full tradition of poetry, its European as well as African American heritage, be available to children: "there really are black children who dream, and who love, and who undertake to master such 'white' things as poetry" (qtd. in Flynn 2002: 159). Jordan's verse responds to twenty-seven pictures of black people (painted by both black and white artists) that were selected by her editor Milton Meltzer. The poetic text and the images are inter-mixed over the course of the book, and the poem title doubles as the opening line of the poem. The rhetorical question "Who look at me?" is not easily answered. It sets off a series of explorations of black identity as when the lines "look close / and see me black man mouth / for breathing" (1969: 25) are followed by four portraits of black men. Sometimes, however, Jordan's verse takes off on its own, leaving the reader to seek out connections between verse and image, and in the act of seeking, to discover new resonance between text and image.

Who Look at Me merges classic European poetic tropes, Black English, and civil rights. For example, Jordan includes an early American painting by an unknown artist, *Enigmatic Foursome*, that depicts an older white man, a young white man, a black man, and a white child – all shown of equal size and importance, although only the black man looks directly at the viewer. Jordan's accompanying verse speaks from the point of view of the painting itself:

I am
impossible to explain
remote from old and new interpretations
and yet
not exactly.

1969: 17

Jordan's biblical opening salvo "I am" – with its echoes of Yahweh ("I Am Who Am"), Coleridge's definition of the primary imagination as the "infinite I AM," and British Romantic John Clare's great poem of despair and isolation, "I Am" – announces that the history of the enslaved African refuses to be forgotten. Simultaneously, "I am" argues for the irreducible persistence of the art object that confronts the viewer and demands to be understood. Jordan's unclassifiable work is a fugue of art and word, perhaps best understood as an iconotext.

William Blake and the poet-artist

For most verse picturebooks, the creation of the poems and the creation of the pictures are separated temporally. Either the artist interprets pre-existing verse, or the poet responds to pre-existing art. Any discussion of the true gestalt of art and verse, of the great artist who is also a great poet and whose art and verse are created in tandem, begins with William Blake.

Before Blake, children's poetry collections were either without illustration or were participating in the tradition of emblem verse, in which an image or emblem is presented, followed by a poetic depiction of the emblem and a moral lesson. Early alphabet verse, such as this one for the letter B from *The New England Primer* – "Thy life to mend / *This* book attend" – was accompanied by a rough woodcut emblem, the image of a book labeled "Bible" (1727: n. pag.). A more sophisticated emblem text, John Huddlestone Wynne's *Choice Emblems* (1772), presents forty-seven emblems, each discussing a vice or virtue. Each chapter includes an image, poetic text, moral, a sermon linking the moral to historical or mythological tales, and an application. Image and text have parallel functions, and the imagery of the woodcuts is obvious. Emblem XL "Of Vain Glory" depicts a peacock, and Emblem XLVII "Of War" shows Mars, the god of war. As Joseph Viscomi notes, by the 1750s emblem books had ceased to offer a viable medium for the combination of text and design and were mainly addressed to children, as Wynne's simplistic linking of stock images to moral texts demonstrates (1993: 72).

Although Blake's engravings in *Songs of Innocence and of Experience* (1789, 1794) are indebted to emblem books, Blake disliked their moralizing attitude and hackneyed imagery. Blake's images are not trite, overused emblems inserted onto the page. Rather, his poems and images are original and fully integrated into the whole. As Heather Glen suggests of the "Holy Thursday" plate from *Songs of Innocence*, the combination of verse and visual elements evoke the image of orphaned children marching to church as well as Blake's cynical take on the hypocrisy underlying Christian charity as practiced (1978):

'Twas on a Holy Thursday, their innocent faces clean,
The children walking two and two, in red and blue and green,
Grey headed beadles walk'd before, with wands as white as snow,
Till into the high dome of Paul's they like Thames' waters flow.
Blake 1988: 13

The rhythm of marching feet is accentuated by long verse lines and short jostling syllables (of the forty-four words in these lines, only eleven have more than one syllable) and by the horizontal lines of children pictured at top and bottom of the plate (Figure 24.3). The unnatural stiffness of children forced into marching lines is interrupted by curling tendrils separating every line, and even between words, to interrupt the reading. Blake uses images from nature, thus, to interrupt the unnatural regimentation of the children as described in his lines of verse. Although Blake's poems such as "The Tyger" have been co-opted into the children's poetry canon, Blake probably intended his work for adults, not children. Blake produced small print runs (sometimes no more than ten copies of a title) at his own press, and he sold his volumes to collectors and artists as high-priced art books.

Despite not being written for the child reader, Blake's visionary poetry inspired numerous children's writers. Nancy Willard's *A Visit to William Blake's Inn* (1981) was the first poetry book to win the Newbery Award, and its gouache illustrations by Alice and Martin Provensen received a Caldecott Honor Award. Willard's poetry is delightful and fantastical:

The driver bowed and took my things.
He wore a mackintosh and wings.

He wore a mackintosh and boots
the tender green of onion shoots,

and on his cap, in dappled green,
was "Blake's Celestial Limousine."
Willard 1981: 16

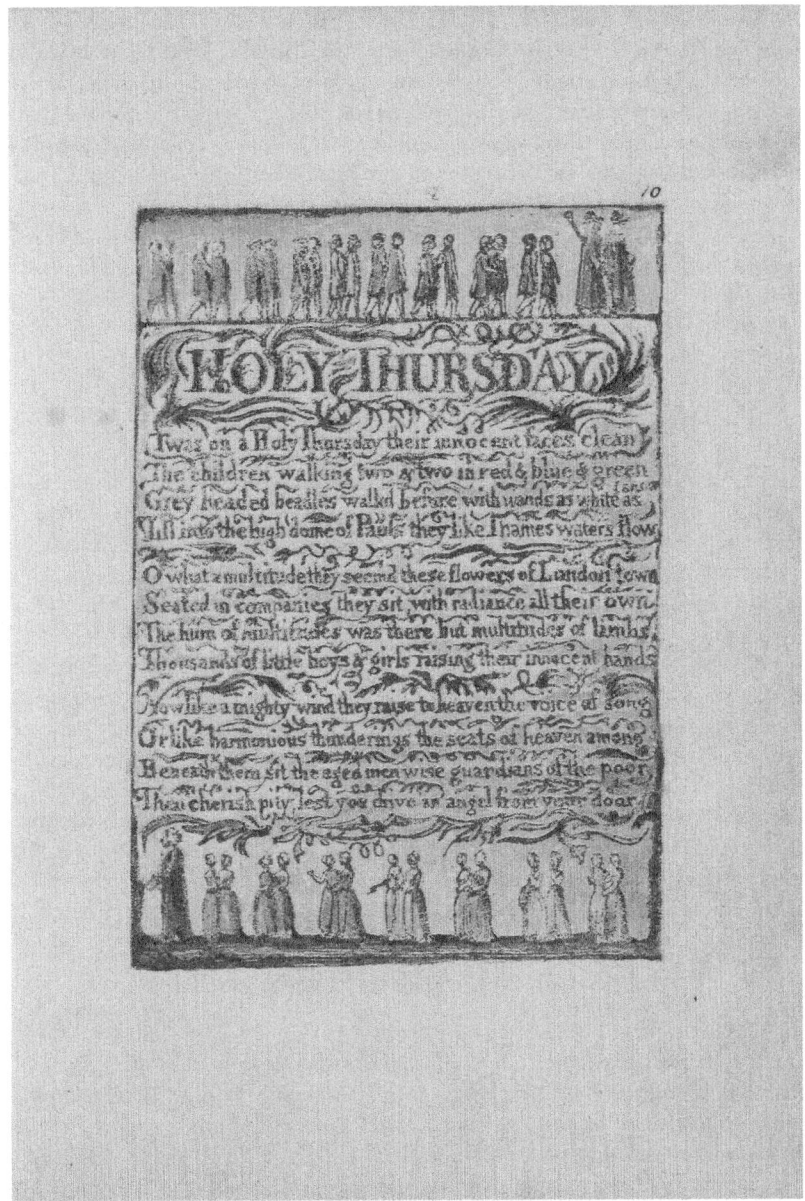

Figure 24.3 Plate 10, "Holy Thursday," illustration from William Blake's *Songs of Innocence and of Experience*. Bentley Copy L. Courtesy of the Yale Center for British Art, Paul Mellon Collection.

Willard, though inspired by Blake, does not aim for his dark irony. Blake emphasizes the archetypal, whereas Willard enjoys playing with topical imagery such as mackintoshes and limousines. This passage also suggests Willard's affinity for Emily Dickinson. These lines allude to Dickinson's famous verse about an otherworldly driver taking a passenger to celestial realms: "Because I could not stop for Death –/ He kindly stopped for me –/ The Carriage held but just Ourselves –/ And Immortality" (1960: 348).

Maurice Sendak's posthumous *My Brother's Book* (2013), a Lion and the Unicorn Award for Excellence in North American Poetry Honor Book, echoes Blake's preoccupation with the pre- and post-lapsarian state of the human soul through his imagery of contraries (ice/heat, earth/sky, passive/ active) and archetypes (stars, brothers, blazing light) (Paul et al. 2014). In this elegiac work of mourning and loss, Sendak's protagonists Jack and Guy (characters first introduced in Sendak's *We Are All in the Dumps with Jack and Guy*) are split apart when a meteor-like star hits the earth. Jack hurtles into a world of ice and Guy into other worlds:

> On a bleak midwinter's night
> The newest star! – blazing light!
> So crystal bright! – eclipsing the moon,
> Scorching the sky,
> Smashed! – and heaved the iron earth in two.
>
> 8

The two brothers in this primal scene recall Adam and Eve's expulsion from the Garden, and as the poem continues, they are eventually reunited in an "ice-ribbed underworld" of "veiled blossoms" that might represent heaven or a post-apocalyptic eternity (26, 28). Sendak's cryptic verbal language is rich with aural poetic effects and literary allusions. His description of "caverns and corridors paved with painted petals / Wound round a wild cherry tree" (26) is lush with alliteration (as in the "c," "p," and "w" repetitions), assonance (the long "a" in "paved" and "painted"), spondees ("Wound round" and "wild cher-"), and inner rhyme ("wound" and "round"). Like his textual imagery, Sendak's visual language is also Blakean, as Mark Crosby notes in "Annotating *My Brother's Book*" (2015). Crosby traces Sendak's elongated figures, fields of stars, uncanny pastoral landscapes, and cruciform poses to Blake's *Milton, The Marriage of Heaven and Hell*, and other texts. Scholars have long admired Sendak's interplay of text and image, although his fine qualities as a poet are less often addressed, perhaps because his picturebooks are classified as prose despite their extraordinary range of poetic techniques. For example, Sendak's *In the Night Kitchen* (1970) manipulates nursery chants, blues rhythms, and rhyme: "Milk in the batter! Milk in the batter! Stir it! Scrape it! Make it! Bake it!" (n. pag.). Lines such as these, notes Joseph T. Thomas, Jr., are "unmistakably poetry" (2015: 1113).

The poet-artist and the light verse tradition

While Blake and Sendak form one tradition of the visionary poet-artist who works with archetypal themes and apocalyptic imagery, the light verse tradition has long been a stronghold of poet-artists such as Shel Silverstein and Ludwig Bemelman (of the Madeline books). This tradition begins with Edward Lear's 1846 *The Book of Nonsense* and reaches a height of artistry with Edward Gorey, Dr. Seuss, and JonArno Lawson.

Nonsense-verse writers have a shared affinity for neologisms, anthropomorphism, and all sorts of word play, but their illustration styles vary widely. Edward Lear's illustrations reflect his early work as an ornithological draftsman for London's Zoological Gardens and as an illustrator cataloguing the twelfth Earl of Derby's menagerie. Lear's streamlined, cartoonlike illustrations diverge completely from typical Victorian illustrations, such as Kate Greenaway's adorable children in nostalgic settings or Randolph Caldecott's fantastic nursery-rhyme books. Lear draws human-sized birds and whimsical human figures with noses that resemble beaks and frock coats that stand out like tails (Figure 24.4). Lear's illustrations, crude in their simplicity, are nonetheless professionally executed and full of movement. Children's book illustrator Quentin Blake likens the economy and "graphic authority" of Lear's drawings to "what many years later became the shorthand language of the cartoonist" (2007: n. pag.).

There was an Old Man with an owl, who continued
to bother and howl;
He sat on a rail and imbibed bitter ale,
Which refreshed that Old Man and his owl.

Figure 24.4 Illustration from Edward Lear's *The Book of Nonsense*. New York: Crowell, n.d. Private collection of Donelle Ruwe.

In trying to make sense of Lear's nonsense, many critics turn to his personal life. For example, Peter Levi links the young ladies in Lear's limericks to his steadfast sister Ann (1995: 60). Mark I. West (1987) suggests that the incredibly eccentric characters of the limericks, such as the Old Person of Putney whose "food was roast spiders and chutney" (Lear 1986: 179), reflect the iconoclast attitudes of a rebellious youth. In particular, Lear's long poem "The Dong with a Luminous Nose," in which the Dong searches endlessly for his lost love the Jumbly girl, has inspired biographical interpretations. As the Dong searches, he weaves a "wondrous Nose" of "vast proportions and painted red" within which he suspends "a luminous Lamp" (1986: 294). According to West, the Dong's distorted body expresses the "sadness of an aging homosexual in a sexually repressed society" (1987: 155); Myra Cohn Livingston attributes the Dong's story to Lear's "acute sensitivity about his unattractive nose" (1990: 47); and Morag Styles links the loneliness of the Dong to Lear's well-known struggles with depression (1998: 136–137). By contrast, Michael Heyman contends that critics who seek out logical meaning in Lear's verse are missing a vital point about the nature of nonsense: it thrives not on meaning-making but on the gap between the 'sensical' and the non-sensical (1999: 190).

The gap between sense and nonsense is exacerbated to an even greater comic effect when the reader is a child. One can see how children might confuse Lear's neologisms with the Latinate adjectives peppering the closing lines of his limericks. The decidedly nonsensical string of adjectives in "He's a Moppsikon, Floppsikon bear!" and the neologism in the line "You abruptious Old Man of Thames Ditton!" are not that dissimilar from Lear's other polysyllabic adjectives such as "propitious," "innocuous," "laconic," "eclectic," and "obsequious." The clever images accompanying each limerick, thus, gain even more importance to the child who revels in the silliness but also grasps at any clue to puzzle out the sense, if there be any, behind the nonsense.

Edward Gorey, like Lear, published illustrated limericks (*The Listing Attic* 1954), and he even re-illustrated several of Lear's works, including a much praised rendering of "The Dong with a Luminous Nose" (1969). In making a case for Gorey as a children's poet, Kevin Shortsleeve notes that Gorey's brooding melancholy, like Lear's, blends the tragic and the comic, with a strong emphasis on the comic, and that of Gorey's fifty-two picturebooks, thirty-nine include children (2002: 29). Gorey produced macabre alphabet-rhyme books such as *The Chinese Obelisks* (1970), which begins with the stereotypical "A was an Author" but soon morphs into a Gorey-esque tale of improbable events, all described in dry couplets: the unnamed author, over the course of the alphabet, is trapped in a thunderstorm that dislodges the Urn that kills him. At his burial, "Y was the Yew beneath which he was laid. / Z was the Zither he left to the maid." In his best known alphabet book, *The Gashleycrumb Tinies* (1963), Gorey offers one-line descriptions of bizarre accidents that befall children, "A is for Amy who fell down the stairs. / B is for Basil assaulted by bears." The prosaic, matter-of-fact language announcing these improbable events contrasts with the rollicking anapestic meter and heightens the poem's ridiculousness while emphasizing the verse's spoofing of baby-book phrasings, "A is an Apple. B is a Ball."

Gorey's work is unmistakable yet hard to define: his detached formal tone and images are too elegant to be traditionally gothic and yet too macabre to be anything but. According to Karen Wilkin, Gorey's books "unfold as a series of laconic declarations, sometimes in rhyme, so pared down that the narrative is carried as much by omission as by description" (2009: 19). His black-and-white images are stylized and elegant with an art nouveau look not unlike the stylized violence of Aubrey Beardsley's illustrations for Oscar Wilde's *Salome*, but without Beardsley's transparent sexual references. Wilkins suggests that the vulnerability of children in contrast to threatening stonework, wallpaper, and paneling (a far cry from the beautifying decorative arts of Crane's picturebooks) is the fundamental dramatic tension of Gorey's work. Gorey's set of stock characters – Edwardian men in smoking jackets, Roaring Twenties vamps with cigarettes, innocents with hair bows, stiff-backed governesses, and callow young men in striped blazers – includes Gorey himself, wearing a long fur coat with sneakers or ballet slippers (Wilkins 2009: 19–20).

For many children, the work of Theodor Geisel, or Dr. Seuss, represents the best that nonsense-verse picturebooks can offer. Seuss began his artistic career as an advertisement writer and political cartoonist. His style is brash, American, slangy, and full of advertising vernacular: "The Circus McGurkus! Colossal! Stupendous! / Astounding! Fantastic! Terrific! Tremendous!" (*If I Ran the Circus* 1956: 7). Seuss's verse features onomatopoeia, syntax reversals, tongue twisters, alliterative names like Bitsy Big-Boy Boomeroo (*The Butter Battle Book* 1984), and syncopated repetitions ("I would not, could not, in a tree. / Not in a car! You let me be," *Green Eggs and Ham* 1960: 30). The anapestic meter of his first published children's book, *And to Think That I Saw It on Mulberry Street* (1937), was inspired by the chugging of an ocean liner. He favors rollicking headless anapests (as in Lear's limericks) to pull readers along: "We'll DRESS you right UP in a FANcier SUIT!" (*Butter Battle* 1984: n. pag.). Seuss's easy readers such as *The Cat in the Hat* (1957) and *One Fish Two Fish Red Fish Blue Fish* (1960) create rhythms and sound patterns using a limited vocabulary. *The Cat in the Hat* was conceived of as an easy reader for Houghton Mifflin, so Seuss's vocabulary was limited to the publisher's beginning-reader word list and uses only 236 different words. Of the sixty-five books associated with Seuss, all but five are in verse.

While the forward momentum and jazzy sound of Seuss's verse reflects America at its best, the content of his verse sometimes reflects America at its worst, as when it participates too uncritically in the Anglo-American habit of downplaying racist traditions while co-opting black performing arts. For example, *The Cat in the Hat*, as Philip Nel (2014) argues, originates in minstrelsy and blackface traditions: a white-faced, grinning cool cat in white gloves, top hat, and bowtie performs juggling tricks, sleight-of-hand magic, and slapstick for his audience.

Seuss's artistic medium is the cartoon – a generally dismissed form that rarely wins awards like the Caldecott. Seuss's "exuberant loopy sense of line" with "Gaudi-esque architecture" creates images with such energy that they look as if they are in the process of being sketched (Nel 2004: 71). By 2001, according to *Publisher's Weekly*, Seuss had sold 71,186,554 hardcover children's books – more than any other author in America including J.K. Rowling.

Of poet-artists writing today, Canadian JonArno Lawson deserves special mention. Like Lear, Gorey, and Seuss, Lawson is inspired by constraint-based "childish" forms such as alphabet books. In *A Voweller's Bestiary: From Aardvark to Guineafowl (and H)* (2008), Lawson established strict rules for his playful riff on traditional alphabet books. Lawson organized the book around the thirty-one vowel combinations (rather than the twenty-six letters) of the English language. The "Deer" poem, for example, uses only the vowel "e":

> Whenever we freeze,
> then flee –
> Whenever we're tender,
> then severe –
> We resemble deer.
> *2008: 10*

Lawson exploits his chosen constraints for full poetic effect. The chiming interplay of short-vowel, rhyming anaphora – "when-," "then," "when-," "then" – leads to the long-vowel "w" word "We." As Lawson notes, since Western culture assumes that "the fascination of secret codes, rhyming, punning, spoonerisms" is "inherently childish," these and other modes of wordplay have not reached their "potential adult stage" in Western poetry (2008: 87).

Lawson's verse is accompanied by rough sketches that, in their very minimalism, paradoxically suggest both movement and contemplation. For the prose poem "The Tailors and the Butcher," which asks uncomfortable questions about Adam and Eve, Lawson's image is a riff on Michelangelo's arm of God from the Sistine Chapel (2013: 99). In the "Shade Garden" sequence from *Enjoy It While It Hurts* (2013), Lawson pairs soundscape verses about the slow, quiet growth of shade plants – "To me it seems the ivy chokes slowly / But to the ivy the pace is perfect / Quick with its tendrils and fast" (18) – with botanical drawings inspired by long-dead designers of bookplates, stone carvings, and ornamental ironwork (2013: 116). The stately iambic cadence of "to ME it SEEMS the Ivy" is broken by back-to-back stressed syllables and long "o" diphthongs that express the act of choking: "CHOKES SLOWly." Lawson emphasizes the ivy's sprightly perspective in the subsequent triple-meter lines by using only short vowels: "QUICK with its TENdrils and FAST." In recognition of his superb prosody, Lawson has won the Lion and the Unicorn Award for Excellence in North American Poetry multiple times.

Conclusion

There is much more to say about poetry in picturebooks than can be covered here. I have barely touched upon the history of illustrated nursery rhymes and rhyming alphabet books, for example, or poetry picturebooks written and illustrated by children themselves. One such book, *I Never Saw Another Butterfly: Children's Drawings and Poems from Terezín Concentration Camp 1942–1944* (published by the State Jewish Museum in Prague, 1959), features poems and artwork created by some of the 15,000 children imprisoned in Terezín. This poetry picturebook is a rarity, a book by children that bears witness to the atrocities suffered by children. Scholarship on poetry and the picturebook is still in its infancy, and as more scholars study the rich history of poetry in picturebooks, it is to be hoped that more work by children will come to light.

References

Blake, Quentin (2007) "Introduction," in Edward Lear, *So Much Nonsense*, Oxford: Bodleian Library. n. pag.

Blake, William (1988) *The Complete Poetry and Prose of William Blake*, ed. David V. Erdman, New York: Anchor.

Crosby, Mark (2015) "Annotating *My Brother's Book*: Some Initial Thoughts on Sendak's Use of Blake's Pictorial Language," *Nine kinds of pie: Phil Nel's Blog*, www.philnel.com/2013/03/09/sendakblake/ (accessed January 1, 2015).

Dickinson, Emily (1960) *The Complete Poems of Emily Dickinson*, ed. Thomas H. Johnson, New York: Little, Brown.

Flynn, Richard (2002) "'Affirmative Acts': Language, Childhood, and Power in June Jordan's Cross-Writing," *Children's Literature* 30: 159–185.

Froman, Robert (2002) "Easy diver," in Paul B. Janeczko (ed.) *A Poke in the Eye: A Collection of Concrete Poems*, illus. Chris Raschka, New York: Scholastic, 7.

Geisel, Theodor Seuss (1937) *And to Think That I Saw It on Mulberry Street*, New York: Vanguard Press.

Geisel, Theodor Seuss (1956) *If I Ran the Circus*, New York: Random.

Geisel, Theodor Seuss (1957) *The Cat in the Hat*, New York: Random.

Geisel, Theodor Seuss (1960) *Green Eggs and Ham*, New York: Random.

Geisel, Theodor Seuss (1960) *One Fish Two Fish Red Fish Blue Fish*. New York: Random.

Geisel, Theodor Seuss (1984) *The Butter Battle Book*, New York: Random.

Glen, Heather (1978) "Blake's Criticism of Moral Thinking in *Songs of Innocence and of Experience*," in Michael Phillips (ed.) *Interpreting Blake*, Cambridge: Cambridge University Press, 32–69.

Gorey, Edward (1954) *The Listing Attic*, New York and Boston: Duelle/Little.

Gorey, Edward (1963) *The Gashleycrumb Tinies; Or, After the Outing*, New York: Simon.

Gorey, Edward (1970) *The Chinese Obelisks, Fourth Alphabet*, New York: Fantod.

Greenberg, Jan (ed.) (2001) *Heart to Heart: New Poems Inspired by Twentieth-century American Art*, New York: Abrams.

Heyman, Michael (1999) "A New Defense of Nonsense; or, Where Then Is His Phallus? And Other Questions Not to Ask," *Children's Literature Association Quarterly* 24.4: 187–194.

Hutton, John (2010) "Walter Crane and the Decorative Illustration of Books," *Children's Literature* 38: 27–43.

I Never Saw Another Butterfly: Children's Drawings and Poems from Terezín Concentration Camp 1942–1944 (1978) ed. Hana Volavková, trans. Jeanne Němcová, New York: Schocken.

Janeczko, Paul B. (ed.) (2002) *A Poke in the Eye: A Collection of Concrete Poems*, ill. Chris Raschka, New York: Scholastic.

Jordan, June (1969) *Who Look at Me*, New York: Crowell.

Lawson, JonArno (2008) *A Voweller's Bestiary, From Aardvark to Guineafowl (and h)*, Erin, Ontario: Porcupine's Quill.

Lawson, JonArno (2013) *Enjoy It While It Hurts*, Hamilton, ON: Wolsak and Wynn.

Lear, Edward (1846) *The Book of Nonsense*, New York: Crowell.

Lear, Edward (1969) *The Dong with the Luminous Nose*, ill. Edward Gorey, New York: Young Scott Books.

Lear, Edward (1986) *Nonsense Omnibus*, Harmondsworth: Penguin.

Levi, Peter (1995) *Edward Lear: A Biography*, New York: Scribner.

Lewis, J. Patrick (ed.) (2000a) *Doodle Dandies: Poems That Take Shape*, illus. Lisa Desimini, New York: Scholastic.

Lewis, J. Patrick (2000b) Interview with Carolyn Brodie. *School Library Media Activities Monthly* (April 2000), www.jpatricklewis.com/teachers_interview1.shtml.

Livingstone, Myra Cohn (1990) *Climbing Into the Bell Tower: Essays on Poetry*, New York: Harper.

Nel, Philip (2004) *Dr. Seuss: American Icon*, New York and London: Continuum.

Nel, Philip (2014) "Was the Cat in the Hat Black? Exploring Dr. Seuss's Racial Imagination," *Children's Literature* 42: 71–98.

The New-England Primer (1727) Boston: Kneeland.

Nodelman, Perry (1987) "The Nursery Rhymes of Mother Goose: A World Without Glasses," in Perry Nodelman (ed.) *Touchstones: Reflections on the Best in Children's Literature*, vol. 2, West Lafayette, IN: Children's Literature Association, 183–201.

Paul, Lissa, Ruwe, Donelle, and Svonkin, Craig (2014) "Old Guard > Avant-Garde > Kindergarde >: The 2013 *Lion and the Unicorn* Award for Excellence in North American Poetry," *The Lion and the Unicorn* 38: 381–400.

Ravishankar, Anushka (2001) *Excuse Me, Is This India?* illus. Anita Leutwiler, Chennai, India: Tara.

Ruwe, Donelle (2014) *British Children's Poetry in the Romantic Era: Verse, Riddle, and Rhyme*, Basingstoke: Palgrave Macmillan.

Sendak, Maurice (1970) *In the Night Kitchen*, New York: HarperCollins.

Sendak, Maurice (1990) *Caldecott & Co.: Notes on Books & Pictures*, New York: Noonday Press.

Sendak, Maurice (1993) *We are All in the Dumps with Jack and Guy*, New York: Harper Collins.

Sendak, Maurice (2013) *My Brother's Book*, New York: HarperCollins.

Shortsleeve, Kevin (2002) "Edward Gorey, Children's Literature, and Nonsense Verse," *Children's Literature Association Quarterly* 27.1: 27–39.

Styles, Morag (1998) *From the Garden to the Street: An Introduction to 300 Years of Poetry for Children*, London: Cassell.

Taylor, Ann (1807) *My Mother, a Poem Embellished with Designs*, illus. William Peltro Tomkins, London: Darton.

Taylor, Ann (1873) *My Mother*, illus. Walter Crane, London: Routledge.

Thomas, Joseph T., Jr. (2007) *Poetry's Playground: the Culture of Contemporary American Children's Poetry*, Detroit: Wayne State University Press.

Thomas, Joseph T., Jr. (2015) "Modern and Contemporary Children's Poetry," in Alfred Bendixen, and Stephen Burt (eds) *The Cambridge History of American Poetry*, Cambridge: Cambridge University Press, 1103–1122.

Viscomi, Joseph (1993) "William Blake, Illuminated Books, and the Concept of Difference," in Karl Kroeber, and Gene W. Ruoff (eds) *Romantic Poetry: Recent Revisionary Criticism*, New Brunswick, NJ: Rutgers University Press, 63–87.

West, Mark I. (1987) "Edward Lear's *Book of Nonsense*: A Scroobious Classic," in Perry Nodelman (ed.) *Touchstones: Reflections on the Best in Children's Literature*, vol. 2, West Lafayette, IN: Children's Literature Association, 150–156.

Wilde, Oscar (1894) *Salome*, illus. Aubrey Beardsley, London: Mathews and Lane.

Wilkin, Karen (2009) *Elegant Enigmas: The Art of Edward Gorey*, Petaluma, CA: Brandy Wine River Museum.

Willard, Nancy (1981) *A Visit to William Blake's Inn: Poems for Innocent and Experienced Travelers*, illus. Alice and Martin Provensen, New York: Harcourt.

Wynne, John Huddlestone (1772) *Choice Emblems, Natural, Historical, Fabulous, Moral and Divine*, London: Riley.

Yolen, Jane (2001) "Grant Wood: American Gothic," in Jan Greenberg (ed.) *Heart to Heart: New Poems Inspired by Twentieth-Century American Art*, New York: Abrams, 39.

25

MULTILINGUAL PICTUREBOOKS

Nancy L. Hadaway and Terrell A. Young

Multilingual children's books can be traced back several hundred years. The first multilingual book considered to be written for children, a type of illustrated encyclopedia, was the Latin-German primer *Orbis Sensualium Pictus* (The World in Pictures) by Johann Amos Comenius, published in 1658 (Vardell 1991). *Orbis Pictus* was translated into other languages and spurred the publication of nonfiction and textbooks for children (Kümmerling-Meibauer 2013b). During the Age of Enlightenment in Europe, classic literary works were translated to help the middle class learn a foreign language. In 1779 Joachim Heinrich Campe published *Robinson der Jüngere* (Robinson the Younger), an adaptation for younger readers of Daniel Defoe's *Robinson Crusoe*; translations and foreign language teaching editions followed (von Merveldt 2013).

The rise of multilingual picturebooks and fiction for children is more recent (Kümmerling-Meibauer 2013b). Beyond foreign language learning, multilingual children's books reflect several needs in our world, including language preservation in indigenous communities, language maintenance in immigrant communities and countries with more than one official language of different status, and additional language learning for newcomers to different geographic and language areas. Recent research has also examined the new wave of sophisticated picturebooks and multilingual picturebooks as well as the "bilingual brain" (Kokkola 2013). This chapter examines the intersection of studies related to picturebooks and multilingual picturebooks with research in linguistics, language/ second language acquisition, and literacy learning.

The potential of multilingual picturebooks

There are various types of picturebooks: nonfiction including picturebook biographies, picture dictionaries, alphabet books, counting books, and concept books (for instance, colors); and fiction in the form of predictable books and picture storybooks, folktales, and poetry. Some picturebooks are multilingual, which extends their potential as they merge the visual with complete text in two or more languages (bilingual) or terms and phrases in two or more languages interspersed throughout the text (interlingual). Translated picturebooks, or separate versions in different languages, may also be considered multilingual picturebooks.

In a study with bilingual learners and two sophisticated picturebooks, the teacher reads aloud Anthony Browne's *The Tunnel* (1989), showing the pictures and drawing the class into a discussion (Coulthard 2003). Mehmet, a Turkish student learning a new language, cannot read the story but listens and participates in the discussion: "The focus on reading the pictures is significant as it removes a barrier in terms of the written text and puts him on a more equal footing with the rest of the group" (168). Coulthard argues that "words may form a barrier but visual image is universal" (184), but not always. In the study, *The Tunnel* is more successful with the bilingual students because the visual and the textual narrative are complementary and the book has universal themes such as love, fear, conflict, and reconciliation. Anthony Browne's *Zoo* (1993) presents challenges as well: first, the written narrative tells one story while a different story unfolds in the pictures; second, the "theme of animal rights is less universal and does not provide the same reference point for those whose cultural experience does not encompass this issue" (184).

Multilingual picturebooks support readers in several ways. First, they allow readers to transfer literacy skills and concepts developed in one language to another (Wang 2011). Next, multilingual picturebooks offer practice in repeated reading, which facilitates comprehension and reinforces the way print works (Sneddon 2008). Multilingual books also encourage readers to compare and contrast texts and develop metalinguistic ability, noticing different features and structures in languages (Sipe 2000). In terms of metalinguistic awareness, comprehending multilingual picturebooks equates with the linguistic model of code-switching. Kümmerling-Meibauer (2013a) notes that code-switching requires "the ability to discern between at least two languages, to understand the meaning of words, grammatical structures, and their pragmatic use, to master underlying codes and conventions" (19), and likewise when reading multilingual picturebooks, "code-switching takes place on several levels, between different languages, between variable visual codes, and between text and pictures" (19). More advanced imaging has also helped researchers examine readers' brain functioning, noting that language functions occur primarily in the left hemisphere, but when code-switching, the right hemisphere also comes into play. So, when thinking in one language, monolinguals and bilinguals have similar left hemisphere brain activity, but "the use of the right hemisphere in language processing is at its height when the individual is code switching" (Kokkola 2013: 33). Moreover, switching between visual images and text processing encourages hemisphere switching (Kokkola 2013; Kümmerling-Meibauer 2013a). Therefore, multilingual picturebooks support language learning and brain development.

Finally, (multilingual) books strengthen the home-school connection as revealed by Fain and Horn (2011). Using bilingual books, teachers first read the books aloud in English in class and then sent the books home with the children. The families read the books in Spanish and reacted in a response journal. Consequently, the children were motivated and affirmed

> to hear a story and discuss it in more than one language. They also had access to family stories that related to the book they read, framing their conversations in two languages. This linguistic and cultural mediation assisted students as they discussed multiple perspectives of the literature and achieved greater comprehension.
>
> *227*

Publication of multilingual picturebooks

Publication of multilingual picturebooks varies from country to country and region to region, and reflects economic, political, and sociocultural issues. Western cultures dominated children's publishing in the past, but this is changing. In Africa, South Africa has an established publishing industry, and some recent books reflect its multilingualism with eleven official languages. Prior to the end of apartheid, only authors writing in Afrikaans or English were published, which limited minority perspectives. In post-apartheid South Africa, there is a focus on including more voices (Stan 2014). While Japan has the largest presence in children's tradebook publishing in Asia, other countries have begun to publish high quality picturebooks, including China and India (Stan 2014). India's Tara Books has produced picturebooks in English (an official language and vestige of colonialization) with translations to Tamil and Hindi, including artwork that often reflects traditional Indian designs. Australia and New Zealand now have a well-developed children's literature scene, although indigenous writers and illustrators and multilingual books have just recently emerged thanks to indigenous presses and concerns about language preservation. In Europe, the UK, Germany, France, Belgium, the Scandinavian countries, and the Netherlands are active in both the publication of children's books, translated works, and multilingual picturebooks, with the UK as the leader (Stan 2014). In the last thirty years in Latin America, children's book publication is emerging. Canada, with two official languages (English and French) and various indigenous languages, is producing multilingual picturebooks, many simultaneously published in the United States. Finally, the United States and its strong children's book industry experienced a rise in publication of multilingual picturebooks beginning in the 1960s (Kümmerling-Meibauer 2013b).

Multilingual picturebook formats

Multilingual picturebooks are published in various formats. Bilingual books with complete text in two languages on the same or opposite pages include:

- Indigenous languages, for instance, *Alego* (2009) by Ningeokuluk Teevee, in Inuktitut and English, published in Canada;
- The languages of growing immigrant groups, as in *Þankaganga = Myślobieg* (Thoughtwalk 2010) by Vala Þórsdóttir and Agnieszka Nowak, in Icelandic and Polish, published in Iceland;
- Official languages in multilingual nations, such as *Let's Play Tucheze Numbody* (2011) by Masayo, in Swahili and English, published in Tanzania;
- Numerous other languages for learning.

A few bilingual picturebooks present the text in one language and then the translation in an appendix which may signal language status or prestige. Hirini Melbourne's *Te Wao Nui a Tāne* (= ancient classical name for the dense forest 1999), a collection of Māori poems that celebrate New Zealand's native forest, privileges the Māori with full-page presentations of twenty-eight poems opposite illustrations, adding English versions in smaller font in ten pages following the Māori. In contrast, Rogé's *Mingan, mon village: poèmes d'écoliers innus* (Mingan, My Village: Poems by Innu Students 2012) presents fifteen portraits of Innu children from northeastern Quebec and their poems, first in French and in the endnotes in Innu.

Bilingual books present some instructional and translation concerns. Usually, children reading the books are either proficient in one language but not the other or semi-proficient in both, so the book must present text in both languages that closely matches (Sneddon 2009: 61). Freeman, Freeman and Ebe (2011) suggest students "can read primarily in one language but use the other language as a resource when comprehension starts to break down. [They] can also compare and contrast the two languages" (227). The need for parallel text, however, may limit translators from capturing the spirit of the original text: "The more literary qualities the original text has, the more challenging the translation task" (Sneddon 2009: 61). Accordingly, publishers may seek specially written or adapted texts without hard to translate stylistic features, thus resulting in a stilted text.

In bilingual picturebook layout, directionality can be an issue. For instance, while the illustrations and character names reflect Arabic culture in Al-Maari's *Jade et l'armée des poules: conte bilingue français-arabe* (Jade and the Army of Hens: Bilingual Story in French and Arab 2007), French is given precedence over Arabic. A more authentic reading experience would have been provided if the book had respected the directionality of Arabic and been bound so the reader would turn pages from left to right (Hélot 2011).

A slightly different bilingual picturebook is the flip book as in the Toon book series, for example, *Jack et la boîte/Jack and the Box* (2009) by Art Spiegelman, published by the Franco-Belgian publisher Casterman. These books feature the text in one language front to back; they can be read in the other language by flipping the book over and reading in the opposite direction (Hélot 2011). While the different language versions are bound into one book, there are *two* books, which can allow more latitude in translation: "This avoids a situation in which students read the text that is in their stronger language and ignore the other language" (Freeman, Freeman and Ebe 2011: 227). *Jack et la boîte/Jack and the Box* offers a sophisticated comic strip design with panels and dialogue bubbles and colorful illustrations. Comics, graphic novels, and manga are popular across cultures, so this highly visual format mirrors recent publishing trends.

Hélot (2011) cites another format using two languages but no translation. The idea behind this type of picturebook is language learning. French publisher Éditions Talents Hauts has two picturebook series in French-English: Oops & Ohlala and Filou & Pixie. In both series, one character speaks French and the other English. Students must 'read' the illustrations as much as they do the text to comprehend both sides of the interaction. Readers with less proficiency in one of the languages may initially capture only the gist of the story.

Beyond two languages, there are books with multiple languages and translation. Juta Gariep's *Khushu Khushu* (2002) was published in South Africa as part of the First Words in Print project and features rhymes in English and Afrikaans and six other South African languages with English translations at the end. Some illustrated poetry books feature multiple languages. Austrian publisher Residenz Verlag offers *Kommt ein Boot* (A Boat is Coming 2012) by Heinz Janisch – one poem translated into eleven languages and interpreted visually by different illustrators. The target language of the poem is identified on each page with five repeating key words embedded within the illustrations and translated into other languages. The book begins with the poem in the source language, German, and five key words in Polish. Twenty-two different languages, including poems written in the Cyrillic alphabet and Perso-Arabic script, are highlighted in this book. Another illustrated multilingual collection is Danielle Wright's *My Village: Rhymes from around the World* (2010). All the poems are translated into English with additional transliterated versions of the Chinese, Japanese, Farsi, and Russian poems. Such books offer opportunities to increase language awareness as both 'dominant/prestige' and 'minority' languages are included.

A common type of multilingual picturebook is the interlingual book, with text in one language interspersed with words/phrases from one or more other languages. Sometimes, not always, a translation or a glossary is provided. Unlike bilingual books, interlingual books are not a complete reading experience in two languages but just a small measure of diversity. Leyla Torres's *Subway Sparrow* (1993), the story of a bird in a New York subway and the English, Polish, and Spanish speakers who help the bird, is an interlingual book with several languages without translation. While the main story line is English, individuals use their own languages to communicate. No translation is provided but the language switching is minimal, and the illustrations provide some support to decipher the gist. In one interaction, the young girl says, "If I go that way maybe he'll fly toward you" (n. pag.). The man responds, "*Sí, corre! corre!*" (n. pag.). The illustration shows the girl move, but there is no indication that she is running or that *corre* means 'run.' Perhaps the reader interprets *sí* as an affirmative response. The intent is a positive portrayal of multilingualism and communication across supposed barriers.

If the purpose of interlingual texts is language awareness, appreciation, learning, and revitalization, then translation helps, as well as the inclusion of glossaries and language information. One interlingual picturebook that provides such support is Agnus Wallam and Suzanne Kelly's *Corroboree* (2004), published in Australia. Some terms in Nyungar are followed by English equivalents, but often the meaning is indicated using appositives, for instance, "Wirring pours gaba (water) into the coota – a bag made from kangaroo skin" (n. pag.). Indigenous terms are reiterated around the page's border, with Nyungar in white font followed by English in black font. The endpapers provide an alphabetized list of the indigenous terms used in the book.

Another format is translation, or separate language versions either published simultaneously in both languages or released sequentially. Different language versions may be written by the same author or by a translator. The English version of Chris Szekely's *Rāhui* (2011), with embedded Māori terms and phrases and a glossary, was simultaneously published in Māori and translated by Brian Morris. In terms of sequential translation, José Manuel Mateo's *Migrant* (2014) was published in Spanish only under the title *Migrar* in Mexico in 2011, and released in the United States in 2014 in a bilingual version translated by Emmy Smith Ready. As an example of same author/translator, Pat Mora authored *Tomás and the Library Lady* (1997a) and translated the Spanish language version *Tomás y la señora de la biblioteca* (1997b), which was released the same year.

Separate language versions seem an ideal solution to the stilted parallel text of some bilingual books. However, the great debate in translation is whether "the translated [work] remains close to its source text or will it get reinterpreted to fit more closely with the target language and culture" (Sneddon 2009: 58). In Virginia Football's *How Fox Saved the People* (2009), the text of an original retelling of the tale by Tłıchǫ elder Harry Mantla is included. A publisher's note states: "We continue to make efforts to maintain the integrity of each legend even as we change its form from the original oral tradition to the written word" (n. pag.).

Illustration in multilingual picturebooks

A significant part of the format of multilingual picturebooks is the visual dimension. If Western cultures dominated children's book publishing in the past, this influence extended to the illustrations as well. This is changing because globalization is changing the status quo: "The Internet has erased national borders for editors, artists, and writers, so that editors are now able to work directly with illustrators around the world" (Stan 2014: 17). As an example, Stan notes that NordSüd Verlag in Switzerland has worked with illustrators and writers across Europe for some time; then, some of their books have been published by their American partner NorthSouth Books. Also, international events such as the Bologna Book Fair allow publishers to share projects across cultures and languages. Finally, many children's book illustrators (and authors) move to other countries to work and bring their international worldview and professional training. An analysis of three multilingual picturebooks (one translated book and two bilingual books) follows to demonstrate some diverse visual codes from more literal image-text relationships to more symbolic ones.

One, Two, Tree! (2003) by Anushka Ravishankar is a concept book that teaches numbers; it was published in India, first in English and then translated to Tamil (Figure 25.1). Durga Bai from Madhya Pradesh is the artist/illustrator. Her illustrations reflect the Gond tradition of visually stunning art in central India usually painted on the floors and walls of homes. Because concept books have a vocabulary and teaching function, the illustrations and the text are generally closely matched as in this book. Each doublespread introduces a number with the numeral, an adjective, and an animal, for example, "1 dizzy ant" (n. pag.) and the illustration. The next doublespread has a brief phrase with the number spelled, for instance, "One dizzy ant totters up the tree" (n. pag.). The corresponding number of animals is added to the branches of a tree which becomes home to the animals and, by extension, the numbers the reader is learning. This seems appropriate because the Gond area is forested, and the tree is often central to their art. When each number is introduced and added to the tree, the animal and the number are in the same color as the numeral name (for example, yellow). As the next number is added, the previous animal decreases in size and fades into black and white, so it is somewhat difficult to distinguish on the background of the tree. This reflects a feature of Gond traditional art, as "objects are depicted as flat rather than three-dimensional and their relative size indicates their importance and not their relationship to one another in real life"

One

dizzy ant totters up
the tree

Figure 25.1 Illustration by Durgai Bai from Anushka Ravishankar's *One, Two, Tree!* New Delhi: Tara Books, 2003. © Tara Books, 2003. Reprinted by permission of Tara Books.

(Stan 2014: 15). The addition of the animals to the tree also provides an engaging hide and seek game for the reader.

The second picturebook is Jorge Argueta's English/Spanish bilingual *Salsa: Un poema para cocinar/A Cooking Poem* (2015). Since the poem functions as a recipe, it is sequential, and the illustrations complement the narrative although there is not the close one-to-one correspondence of concept books as noted earlier (Figure 25.2). Duncan Tonatiuh, a native of Mexico, illustrated *Salsa*. According to the book jacket (n. pag.), Tonatiuh has a keen interest in "honoring the art of the past," and his illustrations reflect pre-Columbian art and the Mixtec codex. This influence is evident in the illustrations which reference Latin American geography (volcanoes), history (Nahua, Aztec, and Maya peoples), and traditional cooking with the *molcajete*. A teaching and vocabulary opportunity is afforded by an illustrated border at the top and bottom of each page which highlights key items (peppers, tomatoes, onions, lime, etc.) referenced in the poem on the opposite page and shown in the main illustration. The vibrant illustrations evoke a cheerful mood as the two young people, who resemble pre-Columbian figures in modern attire, move through the process of making salsa. Because of the Mixtec influence, people are always presented in profile with ears that resemble the numeral 3. The illustrations symbolize cooking as an extension and celebration of culture and history and the many native foods (tomatoes, chili peppers, and corn for the tortillas) that Latin America shared with the world.

Migrant (2014) by José Manuel Mateo is a bilingual English/Spanish picturebook published originally in Spanish only as *Migrar* (2011) by Ediciones Tecolote. The text is written to the left of a vertical, accordion-style frieze patterned after a pre-Columbian codex that spans nine panels (Figure 25.3). The illustrations when unfolded actually constitute one entire work of art (Figure 25.4). The text

Figure 25.2 Illustration by Ducan Tonatiuh from Jorge Argueta's *Salsa: Un poema para cocinar/A Cooking Poem.* Toronto: Groundwood Books 2015.

Figure 25.3 Illustration by Javier Martinez Pedro from José Manuel Mateo's *Migrar*. Mexico, D.F.: Ediciones Tecolote, 2011.

continues vertically from panel to panel rather than on pages from left to right; on one side of the panels is the English text and on the other, Spanish. The remarkably detailed pen and ink illustration was drawn on *amate* paper made from fig bark, as was practiced until the time of Spanish colonization. The illustrator, Javier Martinez Pedro, lives and works in Xalitla, Mexico, where the tradition of making *amate* paper is still practiced. In the narrative, a boy describes the dangers he and his family face as they travel from their Mexican village to the United States. The illustrations complement the text, but they are complex and multilayered, providing details well beyond the boy's narrative. The beginning scenes of rural life resemble Mexican folk art but the later scenes reflect hardship and dangers. The black-and-white palette calls attention to the perilous journey and life situation of migrants.

Figure 25.4 Unfolded pages of José Manuel Mateo's *Migrar*, with illustrations by Javier Martinez Pedro. Mexico, D.F.: Ediciones Tecolote, 2011.

Conclusion

"By providing high quality culturally relevant [multilingual] books to children, teachers are creating a bridge to help students cross the language border" (Freeman, Freeman and Ebe 2011: 225). The language border is not just a barrier for those who need to learn a new language or to preserve an endangered one. As noted earlier, globalization is changing the landscape and as the digital era erases national borders, all learners will need to be more linguistically and culturally aware and proficient. Multilingual picturebooks are an excellent means to encourage intercultural learning. Yet, research shows that they also support language learning and brain development.

Interlingual books are a first step, as they can expose readers to other languages and cultures and validate the many diverse students in classrooms. However, interlingual books often do not provide enough information for the next step, such as language learning or revitalization if additional information is not included in the form of translation, glossaries, and so forth. Bilingual books and translated works, particularly the same book in different language versions, can help students compare and contrast languages and hopefully spark an interest in investigating other languages and cultures and learning another language.

References

Al-Maari, Boutros (2007) *Jade et l'armée des poules: conte bilingue français-arabe*, Clichy: Éd. du Jasmin.
Argueta, Jorge (2015) *Salsa: Un poema para cocinar/A Cooking Poem*, ill. Duncan Tonatiuh, Toronto: Groundwood Books.
Browne, Anthony (1989) *The Tunnel*, London: Walker.
Browne, Anthony (1993) *Zoo*, New York: Knopf.

Campe, Joachim Heinrich (1947) *Robinson der Jüngere*, Stuttgart: Loewes Verlag F. Carl (first published 1779).

Comenius, Johann Amos (1664) *Orbis Sensualium Pictus*, London: J. Kirton (first published 1658).

Coulthard, Kathy (2003) "'The Words to Say It': Young Bilingual Learners Responding to Visual Texts," in Evelyn Arizpe, and Morag Styles (eds) *Children Reading Pictures: Interpreting Visual Texts*, London: RoutledgeFalmer, 164–189.

Fain, Jeanne Gilliam, and Horn, Robin (2011) "Valuing Home Language to Support Young Bilingual Children's Talk About Books," in Richard J. Meyer and Kathryn F. Whitmore (eds) *Reclaiming Reading: Teachers, Students, and Researchers Regaining Spaces for Thinking and Action*, New York: Routledge, 209–218.

Football, Virginia (2009) *Edànì Nogèe done God'edì = How Fox Saved the People*, ill. James Wedzin, Penticton, BC: Theytus Books.

Freeman, Yvonne, Freeman, David, and Ebe, Anne (2011) "Bilingual Books: Bridges to Literacy for Emergent Bilinguals," in Richard J. Meyer and Kathryn F. Whitmore (eds) *Reclaiming Reading: Teachers, Students, and Researchers Regaining Spaces for Thinking and Action*, New York: Routledge, 224–235.

Gariep, Juta (2002) *Khushu Khushu*, Lansdowne, Cape Town: Juta Gariep.

Hélot, Christine (2011) "Children's Literature in the Multilingual Classroom: Developing Multilingual Literacy Acquisition," in Christine Hélot and Muiris ÓLaoire (eds) *Language Policy for the Multilingual Classroom, Pedagogy of the Possible*, Bristol: Multilingual Matters, 42–64.

Janisch, Heinz (2012) *Kommt ein Boot*, various illustrators, St. Pölten: Residenz Verlag.

Kokkola, Lydia (2013) "Reading Multilingual Literature: The Bilingual Brain and Literacy Education," *Bookbird* 51.3: 22–35.

Kümmerling-Meibauer, Bettina (2013a) "Code-Switching in Multilingual Picturebooks," *Bookbird* 51.3: 12–21.

Kümmerling-Meibauer, Bettina (2013b) "Introduction: Multilingualism and Children's Literature," *Bookbird* 51.3: iv–x.

Masayo (2011) *Let's Play Tucheze Numbody*, Dar es Salaam: Mkukina Nyota.

Mateo, José Manuel (2011) *Migrar*, illus. Javier Martinez Pedro, Mexico D.F.: Ediciones Tecolote.

Mateo, José Manuel (2014) *Migrant*, ill. Javier Martinez Pedro, trans. Emmy Smith Ready, New York: Abrams.

Melbourne, Hirini (1999) *Te Wao Nui a Tane*, Te Whanganui-a-Tara: Huia.

Merveldt, Nikola von (2013) "Multilingual Robinson: Imagining Modern Communities for Middle-Class Children," *Bookbird* 51.3: 1–11.

Mora, Pat (1997a) *Tomás and the Library Lady*, ill. Raúl Colón, New York: Knopf.

Mora, Pat (1997b) *Tomás y la señora de la biblioteca*, ill. Raúl Colón, New York: Knopf.

Þórsdóttir, Vala (2010) *Þankaganga = Myślobieg*, illus. Agnieszka Nowak, trans. Jacek Godek, Reykjavik: Iðnu.

Ravishankar, Anushka (2003) *One, Two, Tree!* illus. Durga Bai, New Delhi: Tara Books.

Rogé (2012) *Mingan, mon village: poèmes d'écoliers innus*, Montreal: Éditions de la Bagnole.

Sipe, Lawrence R. (2000) "The Construction of Literacy Understanding by First and Second Graders in Oral Response to Picture Storybook Read-alouds," *Reading Research Quarterly* 35.2: 252–275.

Sneddon, Raymonde (2008) "Young Bilingual Children Learning to Read with Dual Language Books," *English Teaching: Practice and Critique* 7.2: 71–84.

Sneddon, Raymonde (2009) *Bilingual Books: Biliterate Children Learning to Read Through Dual Language Books*, Staffordshire: Trentham.

Spiegelman, Art (2009) *Jack et la boîte/Jack and the Box*, Tournai: Casterman.

Stan, Susan (2014) *Global Voices: Picture Books from Around the World*, Chicago: American Library Association.

Szekely, Chris (2011) *Rāhui*, ill. Malcolm Ross, trans. Brian Morris, Wellington: Huia.

Teevee, Ningeokuluk (2009) *Alego*, Toronto: Groundwood.

Torres, Leyla (1993) *Subway Sparrow*, New York: Farrar, Straus, Giroux.

Vardell, Sylvia (1991) "A New 'Picture of the World': The NCTE Orbis Pictus Award for Outstanding Nonfiction for Children," *Language Arts* 68.6: 474–479.

Wallam, Angus, and Kelly, Suzanne (2004) *Corroboree*, ill. Norman MacDonald, Crawley: Cygnet Books/University of Western Australia.

Wang, Xiao-lei (2011) *Learning to Read in the Multilingual Family*, Bristol: Multilingual Matters.

Wright, Danielle (2010) *My Village: Rhymes From Around the World*, ill. Mique Moriuchi, London: Frances Lincoln Children's.

26

DIGITAL PICTUREBOOKS

Ghada Al-Yagout and Maria Nikolajeva

As a field of academic research, that of digital picturebooks is nascent but rapidly expanding. With the exception of Nixon and Hateley (2013), none of the numerous recently published handbooks of and companions to children's literature offers any information on digital picturebooks. The second edition of the widely acknowledged *Children Reading Picturebooks* (2016), by Evelyn Arizpe and Morag Styles, contains a new chapter on the subject (Mackey 2016). The edited volume *Digital Literature for Children* (Manresa and Real 2015), while focused on digital texts as such, also includes chapters on digital picturebooks. This increasing attention to digitality is understandable, since various digital texts are such a conspicuous presence in today's cultural sphere. Yet the relative paucity of research specifically on digital picturebooks, that is, multimodal narratives delivered on reading devices, is obviously the result of the phenomenon itself being among the most recently emerging types of texts. While digital, or electronic books, including enhanced and interactive books, have been in circulation for a while, the first digital picturebooks appeared in 2010 when the first iPad was launched in the United States. The choice of the earliest digital picturebooks to be produced was by no means accidental. *Goodnight Moon* (1947; digital version 2013), by Margaret Wise Brown and Clement Hurd, and *The Cat in the Hat* (1957; digital version 2014), by Dr. Seuss, are considered indispensable to the North American children's literature canon. The title character of *The Cat in the Hat* is a transgenerational cultural icon and a vast industry, and the bedroom setting of *Goodnight Moon* is easily recognizable. As classics, these picturebooks appeal to the nostalgic feelings of several generations of North American adults who may not know much about recent children's literature. For them, purchasing these familiar texts on what was recently an unfamiliar platform may have seemed less daunting. Since then, the production of digital picturebooks has been increasing exponentially (see, for instance, Turrión 2015; Yokota 2015).

Concepts and definitions

Obviously, since the phenomenon is new, the field of study is just emerging and the metalanguage for it has not yet been properly established. The phenomenon has been referred to as electronic picturebooks, e-picturebooks, digital picturebooks, picturebook apps, and interactive story apps. None of these is wholly satisfactory, and as scholarly terms all are cumbersome. Further, while it is legitimate to borrow terminology from existing picturebook theory, including its central concepts of iconotext, materiality, and sequentiality, some characteristic features of digital picturebooks need definitions and labels, beginning with the object of study itself. The expanded multimodality of digital picturebooks demands paying attention to several additional dimensions. Some terms can be successfully adopted from film and game studies (cut, zoom, hotspot); others need to be invented to label specific features such as the icon or the opening screen (Al-Yagout 2011). Utilizing picturebook theory, Ghada Al-Yagout and Maria Nikolajeva (2015) identify a number of concepts and terms useful in discussing digital picturebook aesthetics, to cover some of their essential formal aspects. Some elements found in printed picturebooks do not translate into their digital equivalents, and others acquire a different meaning, while some, prevalent in digital texts, have so far been irrelevant in picturebook scholarship. As digital texts become more sophisticated and include a wider variety of features, new terminology will doubtless emerge, and some terms need to be urgently devised on the fly. Not least, it is desirable to develop a common metalanguage before international research takes the variety of terms in different directions.

'Digital picturebook' seems to be the most encompassing (and easily understood) phrase that refers to a wide range of texts delivered electronically, from e-picturebooks to texts with a high level of animation and interaction; however, the component 'book' may be misleading, because it excludes texts that approximate or even transgress the boundaries of games and films. Electronic picturebooks, or e-picturebooks, commonly refer to one specific category of digitally delivered texts not significantly different from any other texts digitalized for electronic reading devices, such as Kindle or Nook. E-picturebooks are primarily digitalized existing picturebooks that retain certain features of printed books such as covers, title pages, endpapers, blurbs, and other paratextual features, as well as the conventional doublespread layout. Similarly to other e-texts, both novels and non-fiction, e-picturebooks occasionally add some level of interactivity. For instance, readers can highlight or bookmark, consult dictionaries and encyclopedias, and connect to other readers in real time through the internet. E-picturebooks may offer an audio version, adding music or sound effects of turning pages. Sargeant (2015) differentiates between e-books that are read and apps that are used. While this distinction is far too simple given the broad spectrum of existing digital texts, it captures the main characteristic of e-picturebooks as texts intended for traditional reading, albeit delivered on an electronic device. For mediators, there may be reasons to discuss the practicalities of such texts, but for academic purposes they are of little interest and will not be covered in the present chapter.

An app(lication) is, strictly speaking, any software that runs on an electronic device, such as a smartphone or tablet. A picturebook app is an app that emulates a printed picturebook, in the same way an address book app mimics a physical address book. However, just as an address book app offers more interactivity and connectivity than a conventional address book, so do picturebook apps display features beyond those available in printed picturebooks. It is the extent of interactivity and connectivity that sets apps apart from e-books. Picturebook apps differ from e-picturebooks because they include modes such as written and oral language, sound, music, still images, moving images, and haptic elements. Even though the term 'digital picturebooks' is widely used, there is a strong tendency within children's literature studies to refer to the phenomenon as 'apps,' with or without the descriptor 'picturebook.' Thus contextualized, the term is unambiguous, and since it is short and easy to use, it may eventually become established, although children's literature scholars should be wary that it could be misunderstood outside the field. Confusingly, Mireia Manresa and Neus Real (2015: 10) have chosen to limit the concept of digital picturebooks to digitalized versions of printed picturebooks and refer to other types of digital texts as 'e-lit.' In the present chapter, we have chosen to use 'app' as the term to refer to the phenomenon we are investigating.

The distinction between a book app and a game app is blurred, as Marie-Laure Ryan (2009) points out. Mackey (2016) provides examples of two apps, one of which she suggests leans toward a book, the other toward a game. She uses the concept of 'digital spectrum' to refer to the variety of digital texts that defy classification. Similarly, it is appropriate to refer to a spectrum between apps with a strong element of animation and fully animated films.

The next concept necessary to define is the person interacting with the text. The conventional term for a young person engaging with printed picturebooks is 'reader,' 'listener,' or 'viewer.' To adopt any of these terms in referring to a young person engaging with apps is problematic. Not least, engagement with apps inevitably goes beyond the aspects appearing in picturebook studies. The term 'user' is too closely associated with any digital device consumers, while 'player,' employed in game theory, emphasizes the entertaining element that literary scholars may find undesirable. 'Recipient,' found in reader-oriented semiotics, suggests passive rather than active involvement. In this chapter, we employ the conventional term 'reader' with the understanding that the act of reading an app includes viewing, listening, and, in many cases, playing.

The state of the art

Unlike printed picturebooks, the world of apps is hard to review (see Turrión 2015 for the most comprehensive survey to date). There are no catalogues or databases, no publication statistics, and generally no reliable information. So far, few research libraries have been systematically purchasing picturebooks apps and making them available for scholars and students. Locating apps in a digital store is not straightforward. To find a particular app, you need to know what you are looking for. Browsing categories, which may be 'children's books,' 'kids' books,' or 'education' (the scholarly term 'picturebooks' is not employed by app stores), recalls an array of counting, coloring, and sticker books, as well as crude Disney, Ladybird, or Golden Book imitations. Searching for 'children's apps' in an app store usually returns games. There are few professional reviews, and those existing are frequently focused on education. Hence, finding picturebook apps of academic interest involves searching for authors, titles, and app developers, and depending heavily on colleagues' recommendations. Finding an app is possible by knowing its serial number, when a title is cropped or changed. Virtual libraries or platforms offer a pre-selection of apps that makes it easier to browse. The availability is, however, limited to the selection provided by the platform. Initially it was not possible to browse an app before buying; some platforms now allow customers to test a sample or obtain a free 'light' version. Most recently, app trailers have appeared on YouTube. Certain publishers have their own app stores.

Only the latest version of an app is available for browsing and purchase, and the software periodically prompts the owner to update; therefore, there is no way of retaining an original version, something that is of value with printed picturebooks, as comparison between editions is occasionally illuminating. Early updates of apps only contained technical changes. Recent updates contain new features that add to the aesthetic experience of the narrative, similarly to new book editions. Yet since the earlier digital version cannot be saved, the comparison between versions is hardly possible. It is conceivable that in the future updates will change opening screens and develop new interactive features. Some early apps are by now out of circulation and have not been preserved. Older apps may not work on new devices and vice versa. This undoubtedly affects scholarship, just as scholarship on computer technology becomes obsolete as soon as a newer version of the technology is launched. Thus the material existence of books and apps is radically different.

For a number of reasons, including copyright, the overwhelming majority of apps are based on canonical texts, most often fairy tales, such as countless Red Riding Hoods, Cinderellas, Goldilocks, and Three Little Pigs. Similarly, national picturebook classics are frequently remediated, such as *The Tale of Peter Rabbit, Struwwelpeter, Harold and the Purple Crayon*, and *Goodnight Moon*. App developers clearly utilize existing picturebook canons in their choices and sell the brand. Remediation from book to app is, as a whole, not radically different from other types of adaptation and remediation, and adaptation theory can be fruitfully applied in such studies (see, for instance, Hutcheon 2013). Technically, but also aesthetically, book-to-app remediation is closest to book-to-film remediation, in particular the transformation of a picturebook into an animated film. In remediating existing picturebooks, app developers can either reduce multimediality, omitting significant visual elements, such as page layout, or enlarge it, by adding not only further modalities (sound, touch) but also a whole range of features and functions that the new medium affords. Yet the absence of some remediated texts is conspicuous. Picturebooks by Maurice Sendak, Leo Lionni, Anthony Browne, Mitsumasa Anno, and John Burningham, for instance, are viewed by scholars as canonical, but so far they have not been remediated. Some picturebook creators have openly declared they will never allow their books to be remediated into apps, even though they have been transposed into other media. The significance of statements like this is at the moment impossible to predict, yet it is conceivable that the absence of a digitalized version will be of consequence for the popularity of a printed text. Pirated versions and imitations that circumvent copyright are ubiquitous.

Apps are already creating their own canon, circulated both by word of mouth and in academic publications. Thus *The Heart and the Bottle* (2011), an ingenious remediation of Oliver Jeffers's printed picturebook, has received considerable scholarly attention, published (for instance, Schons 2011; Al-Yagout and Nikolajeva 2015; Manresa 2015), presented at academic conferences, and featured in course syllabi. It can be argued that the digital version is indeed excellent and therefore has quickly become famous and popular, or that Jeffers is a well-known picturebook creator and therefore likely to be perceived as canonical. Another app that has already produced some academic work is *The Fantastic Flying Books of Mr. Morris Lessmore* (2012) by William Joyce (Nixon and Hateley 2013; Schwebs 2014; Sargeant 2015). This text was first released as a short animated film, followed by an app, and finally a printed picturebook. Numerous recent texts exist as a printed book, animated film, and app, and it is often impossible to determine which came first. Just as successful films are frequently followed by novelization, it is conceivable that successful apps will appear in print versions. The ubiquitous transmediality of the contemporary world also encompasses apps.

In addition to apps that have begun to be established as canonical for picturebook studies, to date several developers have gained a reputation, notably Nosy Crow. While early remediated apps were produced by publishers or in collaboration with publishers, today app developers produce apps specifically taking the affordances of the medium into consideration. Potentially, this trend may result in a wholly new artistic form. Borrowing terms from film studies, we can perhaps distinguish between adaptations and original apps (see Yokota 2015). The latter use various artistic devices that would be impossible to remediate into printed form, such as panoramic view, zoom, or action hotspot. Yokota (2015) suggests a number of features that make a successful app, and features of printed books that translate well into apps.

App aesthetics: app-specific formal features

Several studies draw parallels between printed and digital picturebooks, identifying the latter's characteristic features (Yokota 2015; Mackey 2016). While recent picturebook studies emphasize the materiality of the printed book, ascribing aesthetic qualities to its physical features such as size, format, paratexts, and doublespread layout, an app makes materiality ambiguous. The device on which the app is delivered is unequivocally material, while the 'text' itself is purely virtual. Unlike a printed book, the first encounter with which is the cover, the first paratextual constituent in an app is the icon, sometimes accompanied by a shortened or corrupted title, appearing on the home screen of the device. App icons are of the same size and format as other icons on the device. Size and format are important material picturebook features, and the standardized icon format, like the standardized screen, limits the variety and diversity of picturebooks expressed through these material features. Naturally, one can argue that an icon is not really a part of an app; yet if we, with printed picturebooks, take various paratexts into consideration, icons are indeed integral to apps and create a new functional and aesthetic feature. This is especially evident in series apps, where the uniformity of the icon, often accompanied by a sub-icon, emphasizes seriality (Al-Yagout 2011).

In addition to icons, apps have opening screens, another element both similar to and different from book covers. Opening screens provide basic instructions and tips, for obvious reasons redundant on book covers. Back covers are typically omitted. Apps may have mock endpapers and offer some interactivity; for instance, personalizing the app with the photo and name of the owner, emulating a similar element in a printed book. In contrast to still images in books, opening and title screens in apps frequently have moving images. These screens vary in the level of interactivity required of the reader. Sometimes the movement is automatic – that is, tapping, pressing, touching, or tracing produces no effect. Other screens invite swipe if they contain a screenswiper, corresponding to a pageturner in a printed book. The speed of movement is also a relevant element. The back matter of apps can contain back endpapers. Apps may have tabs that work similarly to epitextual blurbs on back covers or flaps of books, providing information about the author, the publisher, or other apps by the same author or in the same series. There are links leading directly to the relevant web page.

Page layout is an important aesthetic feature of printed picturebooks that affects the reader's perception. Apps can both emulate printed doublespreads and add medium-specific traits. App developers are seemingly restrained by the medium, that is, the determined size and format of the screen. Although the device can be rotated to emulate portrait and landscape format, it cannot reflect the wide variety of sizes or formats of printed picturebooks. The variation in page layout, thoroughly examined within picturebook theory, such as balance between verso and recto, multiple panels, framing or full doublespread, cannot be utilized in apps. Instead, apps employ medium-specific features, of which spatiality, temporality, movement, and zoom are the most prominent. Horizontal movement, whether automatic or effected by the reader's action, converts a screen into a scene which can be significantly wider than a printed book doublespread and offer a panoramic view revealing objects and characters that do not appear on the original screen. Movement can cause the scene to change, again with or without the reader's intervention. Vertical movement allows the scene to create a sense of height, for instance, to depict a tree or a tall building. Movement can be accelerated or slowed down; speed and rhythm convey temporality that is merely suggested in printed picturebooks through simultaneous succession or a sequence of panels. A character's movement through the scene, implicit in printed books, again, by simultaneous succession, motion lines, or the character's body posture or position on the page, occurs in an app by actual repositioning and plot progression.

Zoom, whether automatic or effected by the reader, is a powerful device that both expands a screen into a scene and focuses on details. Zooming is either imposed on readers when they read alone or are being read to, or needs interaction. With automatic zoom, the reader has no control over the function. With interactive zoom, the reader needs to find the hotspot that elicits the zoom function. Zooming in and out creates a sense of perspective change and in some cases conveys a character-tied point of view. Unlike printed picturebooks, but similar to film and games, apps allow shifts in point of view from the visual narrator to the characters, as well as between characters within the same scene. All these features allow the app to utilize the spatial potential of the medium without necessarily going beyond the scene into full animation. When partial animation is added, the variety of layout is further enhanced. Most recent apps employ visual effects borrowed from film: fade in/out, dissolve, wipe, morph, and split screen. Transition between screens and scenes, corresponding to pageturning in printed books (or opening flaps in movable books), also evokes cinematic effects such as various cuts.

The combination of still and moving images, oral and written narration and direct speech, the latter often in speech bubbles, sound, and touch provides unlimited variation for app developers and offers the reader a holistic experience of a text (see Turrión 2015). As in printed picturebooks, the relationship between different modes can be balanced and imbalanced; they can duplicate, complement, enhance, or contradict each other (see Nikolajeva and Scott 2001); they may or may not be synchronized; the sound may be diegetic (part of the narrative) or extradiegetic (either merely decorative or to emphasize the mood of the story). Similarly to games, original app music is already becoming an art form in its own right. Some modes may be more important for the overall experience of the text; for instance, switching off extradiegetic music is likely to affect the experience less than failing to discover a hotspot that initiates movement or leads to a new screen. The decisive tactile element of apps places them close to games. Swiping, tapping, touching, thumb-pressing, tracing, dragging, turning, shaking, and even blowing are embodied additions to reading, viewing, and listening, which potentially enhance the reader's affective engagement with the text as more senses are involved. Thus an app is always more dynamic and interactive than a book, less dynamic but also considerably more interactive than a film, and as such perhaps closest to a game. Performativity and engagement, then, become crucial for understanding how apps work and how they affect the reader.

Performativity

Not much research has been done on theorizing the distinction between the reader reading on their own or being read to; nor are there any reliable studies considering the consequences of books read by different voices. Although audiobooks do add a performance aspect, in that you press or tap a device to initiate or stop the performativity element, to rewind or to forward, it has not been considered as a significant dimension of the listener's interaction with the narrative. In an app, performance is decisive, and apps offer a number of performance modes, such as Autoplay, Read to Me, Read Myself, or Play [a game]. Most apps aimed at younger readers have performance modes with detailed instructions for adults. Some performance modes, though, allow child readers to partake of the text without an adult's assistance and thus make texts more accessible to an increasingly younger audience. Interactive elements further add to the attraction of a text in digital format.

In Autoplay and Read to Me modes, the text is narrated, sometimes with printed words highlighted while they are read. In most apps, the difference between Autoplay and Read to Me is that the latter demands swiping between screens while Autoplay moves from screen to screen automatically, limiting interactivity to pressing Play and Exit buttons. Thus the Read to Me mode allows the reader more agency, either to listen to the text and proceed, or to stay on the screen and explore it further by tapping on various objects, causing the words to appear on the screen. Such exploration may reveal elements hidden in Autoplay. The recorded narrator's voice in the Autoplay and Read to Me modes is predetermined, which creates certain worries. Some apps are narrated in childish voices; some have prominent accents, which can be irritating; some imitate characters' voices. Recent apps offer a recording mode where either a parent or the child can record their own voice and replay it afterwards. There is an increasing number of multilingual apps.

Play mode is found in apps that include elements of games in addition to the narrative. This mode may include helping characters to get from one place to another, painting or coloring in, building with blocks, doing math, tracing letters, or playing a matching or memory game. These elements may be diegetic (appearing inside the narrative, as the reader performs actions alongside the character) or extradiegetic (interrupting the flow of the narrative, while the results of the actions do not affect it). Turrión (2014) calls the latter false participation. When a game is offered in the end, it does not interrupt the narrative, but if inserted inside the narrative it may become distracting (cf. Stichnothe 2014). Excessive gamification switches the reader's attention from the narrative to the game, especially for a very young child with a short attention span. Occasionally a Read and Play mode combines the two activities. Some apps offer Rewards, that is, scores and tips for interactivity. Yet while these simple tasks, involving tapping on various objects to make them move, shake, fall, or burst, may seem to be a game, they do exactly what mediators encourage children to do with printed picturebooks: look carefully and explore details. Apps obviously have significantly wider possibilities for such exploration. Yet in many apps, actions are performed regardless of the reader's participation, which in a way negates the purpose of interaction. The Read Myself mode may seem closest to engaging with a printed picturebook. However, already in printed books the reader's perception inevitably alternates between text and image, between the linearity of the verbal and the non-linearity and spatiality of the visual. The expanded multimodality of the app both amplifies linearity and can potentially disrupt it, and the balance of modes is of great consequence. The overall experience of an app, then, irrespective of performance type, is different from that of a book.

Apps can contain several parallel plots or a main plot and subplots; direct speech, often in speech bubbles, appears with or without the reader's participation; a character can ask the reader for assistance; a peripheral character can act as a narrator, comment on the story, and encourage the reader to perform actions. The main plot may still work without these additional elements; however, they certainly enhance the experience. Moreover, depending on the reader's participation, the narrative changes slightly at each repetition, similarly to a game with multiple choices. It is impossible and hardly fruitful to argue at what point a particular app has passed the boundary of a digital picturebook and entered the realm of gaming. Tentatively, it happens when the reader's attention is focused more on accomplishing tasks than on the narrative itself.

Apps are by nature interactive, only realized to their full potential through the reader's participation. With few exceptions, such as movable books, the only physical action expected from a printed picturebook reader is pageturning. Apps contain a wide spectrum of levels and modes of interaction, and some afford and encourage more interactivity than others (see Turrión 2014, 2015). The least imaginative app screens simply show still images and require little of the reader apart from screen-swiping. More often, substantial intervention is required. Swiping screens or tapping on forward/backward arrows is most similar to pageturning. By finding hotspots, with or without hints or prompts, by tapping, pressing, tracing, dragging, or filling in, the reader causes movement and zoom, appearance or disappearance of characters and objects; they affect characters' actions – that is, they contribute to the plot as well as to the narration.

Apps differ in their requirement of reader engagement for the progression of the plot. In some apps, the reader's interaction is essential, and screens will not change without interference. In other apps, the plot progresses without the reader's intervention after a certain time (some apps have a function for scene duration); some offer a prompt when the scene is fully explored; in some, the reader is allowed to make mistakes and remain in a scene until all tasks have been performed. In contrast, some hotspots do not contribute to plot development, but are merely embellishments or gaming elements: puffing clouds, popping balloons, shaking trees to make fruit fall. Yet they certainly contribute to the overall experience. Many apps encourage the reader to draw, the drawing appearing further in the plot, with or without significance.

The visual point of view in an app is predominantly omniscient, as in a printed picturebook or film; but it can also be internal, the app offering the reader an avatar, similar to games. Arguably, in addition to physical interactivity, such texts can also enhance empathic identification. It is perhaps fruitful to make a distinction between interactivity, as a material element of the app, and engagement, similar to cognitive and affective engagement with other works of art.

Critical approaches to picturebook apps

Since it is a dynamic, rapidly changing field, research into apps is developing alongside the phenomenon itself, focusing on apps as both educational tools and aesthetic objects. The former is predominantly the subject of educational discourse aimed at practitioners and is best summarized by the article title "Kids' Book Apps Are Everywhere. But Are They Any Good?" (Bird 2011). As previously with film and television, educators are anxious that apps will replace printed books; there are alarming, mostly speculative reports in the press about the dangers of electronic media for young children's physical and mental health. However, the urge to assist mediators in making informed choices (for instance, Yokota and Teale 2014) has led to discussions on the artistic features of apps, as well as the difference in the aesthetic appeal of apps and printed picturebooks. Seemingly, the most natural way for a children's literature scholar to explore the field is to utilize the existing, well-developed picturebook theory. However, the expanded multimodality of apps and their radically new ways of performance and interactivity render conventional approaches insufficient. Apart from developing a new terminological framework (Al-Yagout and Nikolajeva 2015), scholars have employed semiotics, narrative theory, adaptation theory, film theory, video game studies, performance theory, and hypertext theory, and any attempt to study apps is inevitably interdisciplinary (see, for instance, Schons 2011; Schwebs 2014; Stichnothe 2014; Turrión 2014, 2015; Sargeant 2015; Yokota 2015).

Finally, apps have become the subject of empirical studies focused on young readers' engagement with the new art form (for instance, Mackey 2011, 2016; Merchant 2014; Manresa 2015). These studies differ from research into children's digital skills. Some of them utilize the medium's own features, such as hotspot tracking, to investigate exactly how readers explore the surface of the device, prompted by the verbal, visual, and auditory elements of the text, whether the game elements are distracting, and whether the delivery method, print or digital, affects children's learning and deeper meaning-making.

For the current generation of children in the Western world at least, apps are likely to be the first kind of multimedial text they encounter, and possibly the first kind of any text. Just as there are good and bad printed picturebooks, there are good and bad apps, whether remediated or produced directly for the new medium. Successful apps utilize the affordances of the medium, offering young readers unique educational and aesthetic experiences. Printed picturebooks are likely to continue to coexist with apps, just as they have survived alongside film, audiobooks, television, and video games. In each case, the emergence of a new medium caused alarm among educators who saw the printed book threatened; in each case the new medium proved to have its own aesthetic and educational values. There is no reason to expect apps to be different. Rather, it is necessary for mediators to understand what new skills and pleasures young readers can find in apps.

References

Al-Yaqout, Ghada (2011) "From Slate to Slate: What Does the Future Hold for the Picturebook Series?" *New Review of Children's Literature and Librarianship* 17.1: 57–77.

Al-Yaqout, Ghada, and Nikolajeva, Maria (2015) "Re-Conceptualizing Picturebook Theory in the Digital Age," *Nordic Journal of ChildLit Aesthetics* 6. Doi: http://dx.doi.org/10.3402/blft.v6.26971.

Bird, Elizabeth (2011) "Planet App: Kids' Book Apps Are Everywhere. But Are They Any Good?" *School Library Journal* 57.1: 26–31.

Brown, Margaret Wise (2013) *Goodnight Moon*, illus. Clement Hurd, Version 1.4. Loud Crow Interactive.

Hutcheon, Linda (2013) *A Theory of Adaptation*, London: Routledge.

Jeffers, Oliver (2011) *The Heart and the Bottle*, Version 1.0. Penguin.

Joyce, William (2012) *The Fantastic Flying Books of Mr. Morris Lessmore*, Version 1.4. Moonbot Studios.

Mackey, Margaret (2011) "The Case of the Flat Rectangles: Children's Literature on Page and Screen," *International Research in Children's Literature* 4.1: 99–114.

Mackey, Margaret (2016) "Digital Picturebooks," in Evelyn Arizpe, and Morag Styles, *Children Reading Picturebooks: Interpreting Visual Texts*, 2nd ed., London, Routledge, 169–179.

Manresa, Mireia (2015) "Traditional Readers and Electronic Literature: An Exploration of Perceptions and Readings of Digital Works," in Mireia Manresa and Neus Real (eds) *Digital Literature for Children: Texts, Readers and Educational Practices*, Brussels: Lang, 105–120.

Manresa, Mireia, and Real, Neus (eds) (2015) *Digital Literature for Children: Texts, Readers and Educational Practices*, Brussels: Lang.

Merchant, Guy (2014) "Young Children and Interactive Story-Apps," in Cathy Burnett et al. (eds) *New Literacies Around the Globe: Policy and Pedagogy*, New York: Routledge, 121–138.

Nikolajeva, Maria, and Scott, Carole (2001) *How Picturebooks Work*, New York: Garland.

Nixon, Helen, and Hateley, Erica (2013) "Books, Toys, and Tablets: Playing and Learning in the Age of Digital Media," in Kathy Hall et al. (eds) *International Handbook of Research on Children's Literacy, Learning, and Culture*, Oxford: Wiley, 28–40. Doi: 10.1002/9781118323342.ch3.

Ryan, Marie-Laure (2009) "From Narrative Games to Playable Stories: Toward a Poetics of Interactive Narrative," *StoryWorlds: A Journal of Narrative Studies* 1.1: 43–59. Doi: http://doi.org/10.1353/stw.0.0003.

Sargeant, Betty (2015) "What Is an ebook? What Is a Book App? And Why Should We Care? An Analysis of Contemporary Digital Picture Books," *Children's Literature in Education* 46.4: 454–466. Doi: 10.1007/s10583-015-9243-5.

Schons, Lisa Margarete (2011) "Is the Picture Book Dead? The Rise of the iPad as a Turning Point in Children's Literature," *Journal of Digital Research & Publishing* 2: 120–128, http://hdl.handle.net/2123/8136.

Schwebs, Ture (2014) "Affordances of an App – A Reading of the Fantastic Flying Books of Mr. Morris Less-more," *BLFT: Nordic Journal of ChildLit Aesthetics* 5. Doi: http://dx.doi.org/10.3402/blft.v5.24169.

Seuss, Dr. (2014) *The Cat in the Hat*, Version 2.6.1. Oceanhouse Media.

Stichnothe, Hadassah (2014) "Engineering Stories? A Narratological Approach to Children's Book Apps," *BLFT: Nordic Journal of ChildLit Aesthetics* 5, http://dx.doi.org/10.3402/blft.v5.2360.2.

Turrión, Celia (2014) "Multimedia Book Apps in a Contemporary Culture: Commerce and Innovation, Continuity and Rupture," *BLFT: Nordic Journal of ChildLit Aesthetics* 5, http://dx.doi.org/10.3402/blft.v5.24426.

Turrión, Celia (2015) "Electronic Literature fir Children: Characterising Narrative Apps (2010–2014)," in Mireia Manresa and Neus Real (eds) *Digital Literature for Children: Texts, Readers and Educational Practices*, Brussels: Lang, 87–102.

Yokota, Junko (2015) "The Past, Present and Future of Digital Picturebooks for Children," in Mireia Manresa and Neus Real (eds) *Digital Literature for Children: Texts, Readers and Educational Practices*, Brussels: Lang, 73–86.

Yokota, Junko, and Teale, William H. (2014) "Picture Books and the Digital World: Educators Making Informed Choices," *The Reading Teacher* 67.8: 577–585. Doi: 10.1002/trtr.1262.

PART III

Interfaces

27

PICTUREBOOKS AND ILLUSTRATED BOOKS

Elizabeth Bird and Junko Yokota

Definitions and relationship between picturebooks and illustrated books

Inextricably linked and yet significantly different, the picturebook and the illustrated book are often confused for one another. Although both may be created by the same artists and illustrators, their differences lie primarily in the treatment of the material and the ways in which their pictures inform the reader's interpretation of the overall text.

The picturebook, in its current state, is best described as a work of visual literature. According to Martin Salisbury and Morag Styles in *Children's Picturebooks: The Art of Visual Storytelling* (2012), the contemporary picturebook is "defined by its particular use of sequential imagery, usually in tandem with a small number of words, to convey meaning" (7). Unless they are wordless, picturebooks produce a composite text from words and pictures. A further feature is that picturebooks often contain a low word-to-page ratio.

In contrast, the 'illustrated book' is more broadly defined. Under the heading 'Illustrations' in the *Oxford Encyclopedia of Children's Literature*, Bettina Kümmerling-Meibauer gave the following definition of what best typifies an illustrated book:

> In comparison to 'picture books,' which are characterized by an equal relationship between pictures and words, the broader term 'illustrated children's book' applies to any children's book containing at least one illustration in any artistic medium – woodcut, copperplate.
>
> *2006: 276*

Pictures may enhance, decorate, and amplify the text, but the narrative is not reliant on their presence. The pictures in an illustrated book must have relevance to the text but should one remove the illustrations, the writing would stand alone. As a further difference from picturebooks, illustrated books more typically have a high word-to-page ratio.

Whereas Kümmerling-Meibauer shows a comparative relationship between illustrated books and picturebooks, we propose considering the picturebook (as described previously) as a subset within the broader category of illustrated books. We base this on assertions that illustrated books are any that have at least one illustration. Kümmerling-Meibauer further delineates that the illustration may even be just a decorative element like ornamentation, or inserted to break the monotony of printed page for older children by serving as chapter openers.

Differentiated purpose, function, and pacing

Thus, within the larger field of illustrated books, picturebooks are distinct in purpose, function, and pacing. The *purpose* can be succinctly described as creating a book that is an art form in and of itself, either presenting solely illustration (that is, wordless or silent books), or balancing and intertwining text and illustration to convey something that is more than the sum of these two parts. Those well-defined text-illustration relationships in picturebooks are described by Maria Nikolajeva (2005) as follows: symmetrical, complementary, enhancing, counterpointing, or contradictory. On the other hand, illustrated books that are *not* picturebooks typically have a much looser definition for the role illustrations play within the book.

The *function* of illustrations within illustrated books may be to provide decoration and aesthetic appeal or visual stimulation. While illustrations in the more general realm of illustrated books may also support the comprehension needs of children for whom text is not the primary method of communication, they serve a primary meaning-creating function in picturebooks (Kress and van Leeuwen 1996), from board books to early readers to beginning transition chapter books.

The *pacing* of picturebooks has been defined by parameters influenced by the printing press, which historically limited picturebooks to thirty-two pages, or to multiples of sixteen. This externally forced format created a situation where content had to be tightly controlled – each word, line, and image purposeful and without wasted energy. On the other hand, illustrated books as a whole do not have such limitations; often, books with hundreds of pages may contain lavish or limited numbers of illustrations.

English-speaking countries, as well as many others such as Germany and Japan, have developed a relatively similar sensibility for defining picturebooks and illustrated books. But the same demarcation has not necessarily emerged in other countries; for example, in Portugal and Brazil, *livro illustrado* applies to any book including illustration, and picturebooks are not a separate category. Even in countries where picturebooks exist as a category within illustrated books, the range of understandings across cultures with respect to how to define the concept of picturebook varies significantly. In many countries, the notion of 'visual narrative' is central to what it means to identify a book as a picturebook. In others, the interpretations of what constitutes a picturebook do not contain related, sequential imagery that are illustrative or representational; rather, the pictures serve to be evocative, metaphoric, and even poetic. Images may evoke mood, they may metaphorically allude to a theme, or they may poetically depict the essence of a situation. In other words, their goal is not necessarily to straightforwardly convey character, setting, and plot. One example is the case of children's books from Russia: frequently they contain numerous pages of long text, and then, suddenly – a beautiful painting worthy of hanging on the wall (Lemmens and Stommels 2009).

In many instances in such books, the illustrations reference but do not particularly represent the text, instead often alluding to the subject in evocative ways. Recent winners of the Polish book of the year award for illustration also typically do not fit the definition of picturebook previously described. For example, a recent biography series published by Muchomor Publishing House focuses on how design conveys meaning through visual devices – color, font, shapes, and more. Although these books have many illustrations, the text is the foundational element for readers to understand the intended information. The illustrations in these cases serve as a *visual response* to the text and arise from the illustrator's interpretation of the author's words. But in a way, they create their own, almost parallel, 'story' through what is expressed, as the illustrator conveys her own attitudes and knowledge of the subject, attitudes and knowledge that are not necessarily present in the text. In some senses, the art serves more as the illustrator's impression of the person about whom the biography has been written rather than the author's perspective that is represented in the text. The poster art tradition of Poland can be seen to be referenced in such books by not being overly representational but more thought-provoking in reference (Wincencjusz-Patyna 2016).

Spotlights on historical milestones

Cultures around the world have various roots to which they point when considering the origins of print illustrated books. For example, between the eighth and fourteenth centuries, *emaki* in Japan were scrolls that continuously revealed a visual narrative interwoven by illustrations and by text to reveal a sequential story in print form. However, the focus in this section is on the historical development of illustrated books in Western cultures. In the beginning, the earliest books for children, those published before the Romantic Age, were occasionally illustrated with crude woodcuts. Widely considered to be the first illustrated book for children, the *Orbis Sensualium Pictus* (The World in Pictures) by Johann Amos Comenius, was published in 1658. Though illustrations did occasionally appear in books for the elite, such books were rarities and were generally unavailable to the literate public. Indeed, until the end of the eighteenth century, the idea of producing illustrated books for children was not a widely established concept (Whalley 2004: 319). It was during the nineteenth century that the perception of children's literature as a separate form gained ground, and yet many illustrators continued to be reluctant to put their real names on works produced for the young. When *Kinder- und Hausmärchen* (Children's and Household Tales 1812–1815), the fairy tale collection by the Brothers Grimm, were translated into English in 1823 for the first time and illustrated accordingly, George Cruikshank's illustrations in England accompanied the publication. Today these pictures are considered by some to have been the first to provide amusing illustrations in a work for children (Zipes 2015).

In the 1830s new methods of illustration appeared in works for children, and the sheer number of books published increased accordingly. This trend was followed closely in the 1840s by a marked uptick in nonsense tales and fairy tales as well. For the first time, a great many artists were unafraid to put their real names on books produced for children and youth. Advances in printing techniques in the 1850s accounted for an increase in color illustrations in books, although some artists still preferred to work in black and white well into the 1860s. Patrick Hearn (1996: 10–11) describes how artist Walter Crane was particularly enamored of the range of colors available to illustration artists, and he began designing his art specifically for the color printer Edmund Evans. Crane took care to illustrate book covers, title pages, contents pages, and more. *The Baby's Bouquet* (1878) provided him an opportunity to go so far as to design the endpapers as well, an act that would lead some to declare this is the moment when the modern picturebook was born (Alderson 1986). Others claim that Heinrich Hoffmann's *Der Struwwelpeter* (Slovenly Peter 1845) marked the picturebooks' true inception for its way of relying on visuals to convey much of the message of exaggerated consequences for misbehaviors (Friese and Krämling 1998). Although illustrations convey a large part of what is communicated, it was not developed as a visually revealed story in a narrative sense. Still others contend that Randolph Caldecott holds the true honor of the picturebook's birth, by his elevating of the role of the images in the narrative. Maurice Sendak said as much when he wrote:

> Caldecott's work heralds the beginning of the modern picture book. He devised an ingenious juxtaposition of picture and word, a counterpoint that never happened before. Words are left out – but the picture says it. Pictures are left out – but the word says it. In short, it is the invention of the picture book.
>
> *1988: 21*

At the same time, illustrated books were being created by authors and illustrators in tandem with one another. Lewis Carroll's two Alice books mark one of the first times that an author and an artist would produce an illustrated story in collaboration. It is interesting to note that the original story penned in 1865 was written as a chapter book, but *The Nursery "Alice,"* released twenty-five years later by Charles Dodgson in 1890, was a shortened version that many of us would recognize as more akin to the modern picturebook than the original Alice ever was. The British Library describes the book as being aimed at "under-fives, reflecting the continued expansion of the children's literature market" (The British Library 2015).

The occupation of professional illustrator arose first in Europe and then in America. While the early days of American publishing yielded few illustrators that specialized entirely in children's books, many artists would spend much of their careers illustrating both for adults and children. Designers of adult and juvenile books specialized in different careers only after Reconstruction, and by the early twentieth century the picturebook was recognized as separate from the illustrated book.

In the 1930s, artist Lynd Ward illustrated several renowned picturebooks as well as illustrated books. Working in woodcuts and largely responsible for the emergence of the woodcut novel in American publishing, he disdained the illustrated books that employed, "the stifling practice [. . .] of commissioning a set of pictures to be scattered through the pages of the book in the way they have come into being" (Lewis 2001: xiii). To his mind, an artist whose work is not integral to the function of the book itself is "a mere complementary decorator" (xiii). This opinion is shared among those who believe that in the best books, images are more than mere decorative elements. It is little wonder that his woodcut novels are often regarded as precursors of the graphic novel (Beronä 2008).

Sequential illustrations appear in illustrated novels of the time. Often, artists who had begun their careers working for newspapers, for example, were not opposed to short visual sequences, as found in books like A.A. Milne's *Winnie-the-Pooh* (1926), illustrated by Ernest Shepard. And like Shepard, many of the best artists were plucked from occupations not traditionally associated with children's books, allowing them to the field of illustrated books as new kinds of art. In *Wild Things* (2014), Bird, Danielson and Sieruta reveal many of the stories behind illustrators. Jules Feiffer was a cartoonist with *The Village Voice* before he illustrated Norton Juster's *The Phantom Tollbooth* (1961). In that book, his penchant for panels and sequential storytelling keenly aids Juster's narration. Other artists like Shel Silverstein (who wrote and created art for *Playboy*), Tomi Ungerer (who had no personal difficulty keeping his children's books separate from his pornographic art), and David Small (who reillustrated such classics as Russell Hoban's *The Mouse and His Child* [1967/2001]) included in their books styles honed in cartoons and caricatures. Yet though they brought new artistic sensibilities to sophisticated children's books, their work tended to replicate the same techniques.

Artists today come to children's books from an even wider pool. Whether it is comics, animation, or even greeting cards, the contributions of these new artists are significantly different from illustrated classics of the past. Where once a book told a story where the art was, if not superfluous, at least not integral to the storytelling, we now live in a visual world. In today's books the storytelling is done alternatively by means of picture sequences and text. Now if you cut the images out of the book, part of the narrative has been cut as well.

Additionally, contemporary illustrated books for children have experienced increased attention by the public and scholars alike. As Frank Serafini and James Blasingame put it, "One of the most recognizable changes in the contemporary novel is the inclusion of visual images and elaborate graphic design features in addition to written text" (2012: 146). Publishers, willing to try new and different techniques, have opened the door to innovative visual narratives. Many of the recent developments typify a new comfort with fusion between different visual genres. Few books illustrate this better than Brian Selznick's Caldecott Award–winning title *The Invention of Hugo Cabret* (2007). This book and Selznick's follow-up titles *Wonderstruck* (2011) and *The Marvels* (2015) make a point to alternate between passages of text and extended wordless charcoal sketches. In *Hugo Cabret*, the relationship between image and words is seamless, the pictures continuing the story voiced in the text. *Wonderstruck*, in contrast, tells one story in words and one in pictures, moving back and forth between the two, until the denouement where they come together at last. Finally, *The Marvels* begins with 389 pages of near wordless visual storytelling, followed by 213 pages of text, ending with 44 pages of illustrated closure. These illustrated novels have effectively blurred the lines between the reading public's perception of what is a picturebook and what is an illustrated novel. Serafini and Blasingame state, "When *The Invention of Hugo Cabret* was awarded the Caldecott Medal for outstanding picture book, the boundary between picture book and novel was forever blurred" (2012: 146). As Selznick has said of *Hugo Cabret* on the book's website, "*The Invention of Hugo Cabret* is not exactly a novel, and it's not quite a picture book, and it's not really a graphic novel, or a flip book, or a movie, but a combination of all these things" (Nel 2012: 451).

Around the same time that Selznick released *Hugo Cabret*, Shaun Tan's wordless Australian title, *The Arrival* (2006), presented textless pictures that plunge the reader into the shoes of an immigrant navigating an unfamiliar new country. This textless picturebook is akin to a graphic novel thanks to its unique form of sequential storytelling. And like *Hugo Cabret* and other works of illustrated fiction, it is possible to read the book "in multiple genres at once" (Nel 2012: 451). Though books that incorporate multiple visual genres challenge comfortable picturebook and illustrated book forms, Salisbury and Styles point out that the original picturebook style itself is a "hybrid artform" (2012: 7), and one that is being "stretched and challenged by an increasingly experimental body of 'makers' (a suitable term for the artist-author of the picturebook has yet to be found)" (7).

Illustrated books by classification

As delineated earlier, any book with even a single illustration fits into the description of the umbrella term 'illustrated book.' Illustrated books are themselves not limited by a distinct length. Indeed they may include as many or as few pages as fits their content. Unlike picturebooks, the text's connection to the book's illustrations is far less symbiotic. In the past, traditionally illustrated books were considered different from picturebooks thanks in large part to the fact that one could read the text without the experience changing significantly if the art were removed.

A distinctive feature of picturebooks and illustrated books that highlights their differences (beyond their respective lengths and the ratio of text to art) concerns our conceptualization of the relationship between text and image. Where picturebooks contain words and pictures that complement (or sometimes even contradict) one another, in illustrated books the connection between text and illustrations is far less defined. It is possible to remove the pictures from an illustrated book, though to do so would often make a more significant difference in books like *The Invention of Hugo Cabret* (2007) or journal format tales like in the series created by Jeff Kinney that begins with *Diary of a Wimpy Kid* (2007), where the visuals continue the textual narrative.

In the following, we identify ways to describe the array of books that are illustrated, categorizing them with examples, but knowing full well that a number of books defy single categorization and instead could fit into multiple categories. The following categories are not presented as if hierarchical, but descriptively.

Illustrated books that are picturebooks

As mentioned previously, historically, picturebooks have adhered to a standard thirty-two-page length, determined in large part by the parameters of the printing press and its creation of sixteen-page signatures. Although some books have extended this to forty-eight or even more pages, thirty-two is generally regarded as the optimal number for a given picturebook work. An exception to this can be found in Torben Kuhlmann's *Lindbergh: Die abenteuerliche Geschichte einer fliegenden Maus* (Lindbergh: The Tale of a Flying Mouse 2014), in which ninety-six pages are employed for telling the story of a mouse, yet it retains the picturebook drama of illustration pacing and the power of the page turn. Clearly, Kuhlmann understands why the impact of an entirely illustrated doublespread is necessary for how readers take the emotional journey alongside the mouse. He effectively uses dramatic doublespreads to bookend his story in ways that visually echo the beginning and the ending. In the beginning, the mouse is completely surrounded by mousetraps, and viewers pause and take in the emotion of that moment of fear; in the end, the mouse is again surrounded, but this time by mice who welcome him to his new home and celebrate. In fact, despite its heft, those very wordless doublespread sequences, along with the spot illustrations sprinkled throughout the book make clear that this is indeed, a picturebook – a ninety-six-page picturebook.

Picture-storybooks

Classic definitions of picturebooks typically describe picture-storybooks, although more broadly, the category of picturebooks includes nonfiction, poetry, and other genres that are not centered on story. They are stories in which the visual and the textual parallel, combine, reflect, and extend in how they tell the story together (for instance, Moebius 1986, 2011). Usually, each word is carefully considered, as if the text were poetry. This economy of words echoes the idea that illustrations drive the overall experience and thus, an overabundance of words is avoided to keep the experience primarily, or at least equally visual. Maurice Sendak's world-renowned seminal work, *Where the Wild Things Are* (1963), is credited as an early example of visual narrative where the illustrations and the entire book design reveal the story's pacing. The illustrations occupy space on the doublespreads in ways that echo the story development through text.

Easy readers

On the one hand, these books appear like picture-storybooks, but there are two major differences: they typically have a smaller trim size and, most significantly, they are intended for developing young readers' abilities to practice reading, so the texts in them have controlled numbers of words and types of words that are readily decipherable. In the 1960s, Dr. Seuss (pseudonym for Theodor Geisel) pioneered this type of book for a general market as opposed to the easy readers created for school instruction, authoring and illustrating numerous works including *The Cat in the Hat* (1957). These books relied on language play to convey the rhythmic, rhyming text while often, the story was revealed in the ways those words interplayed with the illustrations (see Johnson and Alderson 2014 on the easy readers in the Ladybird book series).

Illustrated books that are wordless

Wordless books tell stories or convey information visually. Perry Nodelman says that to consider "words [as being] merely lineal and pictures merely spatial is extremely simplistic. We could not read words if we could not interpret the visual symbols that stand for them on paper; reading is itself an act of vision" (1988: 199). They vary from board books for babies with simple concepts to detailed spreads like the wimmelbooks by Rotraut Susanne Berner, to elaborately illustrated pages that convey story with rich complexity like the picturebooks by David Wiesner. His *Mr. Wuffles!* (2013) is an example of a nearly wordless book that relies on text very sparingly to show the interactions between a cat and an alien spaceship and its passengers. In Guojing's *The Only Child* (2015), the 112-page book sequentially paneled illustrations convey the character's emotional journey wordlessly. The 208-page graphic novel *Robot Dreams* (2007) by Sara Varon – wordless except for chapter headings, signs that are part of the artwork, and noises (that is, ring, ring; sniff, sniff; wha-ha-ha) – conveys the story about the friendship between a dog and a robot through illustration without the use of either dialogue or prose text. No matter what the country or linguistic background, the illustrations tell it all; therefore, wordless books have communicative power that transcends language barriers (Beckett 2012).

Illustrated books that are illustrated novels

An example of a novel with illustrations is Cornelia Funke's *Herr der Diebe* (The Thief Lord 2000), in which the author drew small pen and ink line drawings of decorative images of Venice, the setting of the story, as chapter openers. Their function is primarily decorative, and while contributing to the ambience of the setting, the illustrations do not convey the story. On the other hand, a book with spot art has the possibility of carrying many aspects of the story rather than being limited to serving a decorative function. *Seirei no Moribito* (Moribito: Guardian of the Spirit 1996) by Nahoko Uehashi contains illustrations that depict characters in various settings and situations but also includes plot elements as well. A twenty-page chapter may have only one full-page illustration, though by the time you reach the end of a nineteen-chapter book, cumulatively, the illustrations convey many aspects of the story.

In the Moomin books, Tove Jansson treats illustration as "spot art" designed spatially for visual balance, but does not expect readers to interact with the art and text simultaneously. In fact, the illustrations appear more like little sketches to accompany the story for visual décor than to tell any part of the story. For example, in *Kometjakten* (Comet in Moominland 1946), Moomin is shown putting up a swing. If all aspects of illustration are to be interpreted, as in a picturebook, one would assume he is angry because of how his eyebrows are depicted. But instead, the text simply says he was interested in what Snuff was describing. Later, a silk monkey is shown on the top of one page, presumably to balance the spot art at the bottom of the following page on the opposite side of the doublespread. However, the silk monkey is not introduced as a character for another page and a half in the text. Clearly, the intent here is to create visual balance rather than to pace with the text to reveal the story simultaneously.

Illustrated books that are variously illustrated classic novels

Why do so many famous illustrators create their interpretations of famous 'classic stories'? These texts were not written dependent on particular illustrations to co-tell the story. Therefore, the illustrations have been created by various illustrators as *interpretations* of the text. Examples of such works are *Alice's Adventures in Wonderland* (1865) by Lewis Carroll, *The Adventures of Pinocchio* (1883) by Carlo Collodi, *The Wonderful Wizard of Oz* (1900) by L. Frank Baum, *Peter Pan* (1911) by James Matthew Barrie and numerous others. Thus, the art of an illustrated novel can often be replaced or supplanted with art from another artist and, therefore, differs from the symbiotic relationship between text and image typically found intertwined, interdependent, and irreplaceable in illustrated books classified as picturebooks.

Illustrated books that are compilations of picturebooks

Ezra Jack Keats is known for having created thirty-two-page picturebooks with well-paced page turns in which illustration and text work together to reveal and develop story. However, in the anthologized book, *Keats's Neighborhood* (2002), ten of his picturebooks have been combined into one. Thus, each picturebook, which originally had approximately sixteen doublespreads, gets from three to six doublespreads each, and at times another page or half a doublespread. Such a reduction means keeping the entire text, yet reducing the number and size of illustrations, as well as changing the pacing and design in which it is presented.

Illustrated books that are anthologized folklore

The Helen Oxenbury Nursery Collection (2003) is an anthology of poems, nursery rhymes, and stories. The individual stories collected in it are ones that are often illustrated as picturebooks in Western cultures: *Little Red Riding Hood, The Turnip, The Little Red Hen, The Three Billy Goats Gruff, Henny-Penny, Goldilocks and the Three Bears*, and *The Three Little Pigs*. When anthologized, however, such picturebook formats of lavishly illustrated stories have reduced proportions of illustrations to text. For example, the story of *Little Red Riding Hood* has only four illustrations altogether. The first serves as a story opener and is a half-page image of the mother tying the hooded cloak under the girl's chin. The second illustration jumps into the story to show a full page of the wolf pulling on the grandmother's nightdress. The third is a doublespread showing the wolf leaping from the bed towards the little girl who leans back in surprise. The fourth is a small image that closes the story, showing Little Red Riding Hood running. In comparison, picturebook versions of this story vary enormously in how the story is depicted visually; however, what they have in common is that most depict the entire story line through illustration. The character, the setting, and the plot are all revealed through illustration as well as through text. What typically happens in the situation of the anthologized version is that the dramatic power of the page turn in pacing the tension is not a part of the visual story experience.

Illustrated books that are story collections

Shaun Tan's *Tales from Outer Suburbia* (2008) is a collection of short stories told with a sense of wonder about the world. Matter-of-fact textual presentation combines with illustrations that vary across media and styles. Sometimes, the text within the illustration acts as text that conveys story; at other times, surreal illustrations serve to offer metaphors to be pondered. In the end, the reader has been exposed to a range of ways in which stories have been offered, implied, and experienced. Yet this collection, despite its heavy inclusion of numerous illustrations paced throughout the book, serves as illustrated book rather than picturebook.

Illustrated books that are graphic novels

In many countries, recent years have witnessed a marked increase in the number of illustrated books in which the sequential visuals convey as much if not more than the text. Once seen as the purview of comic books, such illustration style is now taken seriously for its content and its development as a validated form of visual expression of story and information in books for children and people of all ages. In Ben Hatke's *Little Robot* (2015), text plays a minimal role in comparison to the illustrations, which readily depict characterization richly, even without dialogue, and theme, through the revelations of thoughts and feelings.

Illustrated books that are books of poetry

Poetry books range from a single poem represented as a picturebook to anthologized poetry representing many poets. Single-poem picturebooks are typically illustrated by one person and the illustrations have visual unity and flow, such as in *Swirl by Swirl: Spirals in Nature* (2011). In Joyce Sidman's spiral-laden text, illustrator Beth Krommes integrates the curls and coils of the natural world into colorful scratchboard art that perfectly complements the poem's swirling imagery. On the other hand, anthologized poetry may have single or multiple illustrators, and often the variation in poetry is reflected in the variation of illustrations. Such books would be more broadly considered illustrated books than picturebooks. One example is the Polish multiple award-winning *Tuwim: Wiersze dla dzieci / Tuwim: Poems for Children* (2013), presenting seven different Tuwim poems, illustrated by seven different illustrators, offering stylistic harmony rather than stylistic singularity. In fact, there are seven different cover versions available: a different one has been created by each of the illustrators.

Illustrated books that are informational books

When considering illustrations in informational books, the need to convey information through a graphic format emphasizes the role of design and graphics as illustration. In addition to drawings, photographs, and other traditionally used aspects of conveying visual story, there are often graphs, charts, infographics, and other forms of visual communication. Since the publication of *Orbis Sensualium Pictus* (1658), nonfiction has often included illustration to convey information. Although line drawings and photographs and charts were standard publishing practice for centuries, the ease of color printing changed the possibilities. In the 1980s, the Dorling Kindersley nonfiction series was noted for its rich, color photographs that appealed across ages and lent support for the decreased amount of text, so information could be visually consumed as well as through text. A shift to a non-representational depiction of information is the innovative example found in the biography series of Polish publisher Muchomor and their use of design as an important aspect of the visual communication. Blocks of color, typography, and layering of images all add up to the totality of the visual experience. But the interpretation of visual cohesion is far from showing a visual narrative; rather, they appeal to the reader through design elements and strong graphic images that draw attention.

Considerations for the future of illustrated books

Indeed, David Lewis alludes to the possibility that any type of illustration may accompany text, but for picturebooks, the two must be "woven together to create a single text composed of two distinct media" (2001: 3). We have made the case in this chapter that the degree to which the two are woven together, the balance of one over the other, the length of the work, and many other factors distinguish picturebooks as a subset of illustrated books. However, it is also clear from our discussion of illustrated books by categories that in order to be successful, the two should have a discernable relationship with one another, even in an illustrated book. The history of illustrated books is rich with examples of the development, the present offers a varied range of interesting productions, and the future promises even more variety as print and digital technologies develop. The arrival of digital formats of illustrated books marks a shift in what has been produced thus far, and the possibilities afforded by such a distinctly different format will be unveiled as the technologies for producing illustration include increased creative control over digital productions utilizing tablets and stylus (Yokota 2015).

References

Alderson, Brian (1986) *Sing a Song for Sixpence: The English Illustrative Tradition and Randolph Caldecott*, Cambridge: Cambridge University Press.

Barrie, James Matthew (1911) *Peter Pan; or, the Boy Who Wouldn't Grow Up*, illus. F.D. Bedford, London: Hodder & Stoughton.

Baum, L. Frank (1900) *The Wonderful Wizard of Oz*, illus. W.W. Denslow, Chicago: George M. Hill Co.

Beckett, Sandra (2012) *Crossover Picturebooks: A Genre for All Ages*, New York: Routledge.

Beronä, David A. (2008) *Wordless Books: The Original Graphic Novels*, New York: Harry N. Abrams.

Bird, Betsy, Danielson, Jules, and Sieruta, Peter (2014) *Wild Things: Acts of Mischief in Children's Literature*, Somerville, MA: Candlewick Press.

British Library (2015) www.bl.uk/collection-items/the-nursery-alice (accessed February 18, 2016).

Carroll, Lewis (1865) *Alice's Adventures in Wonderland*, illus. John Tenniel, London: Macmillan.

Collodi, Carlo, (1883) *Le avventure di Pinocchio*, illus. Enrico Mazzanti, Florence: Bemporad & Figli [*The Adventures of Pinocchio*, trans. Mary Alice Murray, London: T. Fisher Unwin, 1892].

Comenius, Johann Amos (1658) *Orbis Sensualium Pictus*, Nuremburg: Michael Endter.

Dodgson, Charles (1890) *The Nursery Alice*, London: Macmillan.

Friese, Inka, and Krämling, Thomas (1998) "Lustige Geschichten und drollige Bilder," in Otto Brunken, Bettina Hurrelmann, and Ulrich Pech (eds) *Handbuch zur Kinder- und Jugendliteratur: Von 1800 bis 1850*, Stuttgart and Weimar: Metzler, 462–482.

Funke, Cornelia (2000) *Herr der Diebe*, Hamburg: Cecilie Dressler [*The Thief Lord*, trans. Oliver Latsch, New York: Scholastic/The Chicken House, 2002].

Grimm, Jakob, and Wilhelm (1812–1815) *Kinder- und Hausmärchen*, Berlin: Andreas Reimer [*German Popular Stories*, trans. Edgar Taylor, illus. George Cruikshank, London: C. Baldwyn, 1823].

Guojing (2015) *The Only Child*, New York: Schwartz & Wade.

Hatke, Ben (2015) *Little Robot*, New York: Roaring Book Press.

Hearn, Michael Patrick (1996) "Discover, Explore, Enjoy," in Trinkett Clark and Nicholas B. Clark (eds) *Myth, Magic, and Mystery*, Boulder, CO: Roberts Rinehart, 1–44.

Hoban, Russell (2001) *The Mouse and His Child*, illus. David Small, New York: Harper & Row (first published, with illus. by Lillian Hoban, 1967).

Hoffmann, Heinrich (1845) *Der Struwwelpeter*, Frankfurt: Literarische Anstalt.

Jansson, Tove (1946) *Kometjakten*, Stockholm: Söderström [*Comet in Moominland*, trans. Thomas Warburton, New York: Macmillan, 1951].

Johnson, Lorraine, and Alderson, Brian (2014) *The Ladybird Story: Children's Books for Everyone*, London: The British Library.

Juster, Norton (1961) *The Phantom Tollbooth*, illus. Jules Feiffer, New York: Random House.

Keats, Ezra Jack (2002) *Keats's Neighborhood: An Ezra Jack Keats Treasury*, New York: Penguin Putnam/Viking.

Kinney, Jeff (2007) *Diary of a Wimpy Kid*, New York: Abrams.

Kress, Gunther, and van Leeuwen, Theo (1996) *Reading Images: The Grammar of Visual Design*, New York: Routledge.

Kuhlmann, Torben, (2014) *Lindbergh: Die abenteuerliche Geschichte einer fliegenden Maus*, Zurich: NordSüd Verlag [*Lindbergh: The Tale of a Flying Mouse*, trans. Suzanne Levesque, New York: North South, 2014].

Kümmerling-Meibauer, Bettina (2006) "Illustration," in Jack Zipes (ed.) *The Oxford Encyclopedia of Children's Literature*, vol. 2, Oxford: Oxford University Press, 276–281.

Lemmens, Albert, and Stommels, Serge (2009) *Russian Artists and the Children's Books 1890–1992*, Nijmegen: LS.

Lewis, David (2001) *Reading Contemporary Picturebooks: Picturing Text*, London: RoutledgeFalmer.

Milne, A. A. (1926) *Winnie-the-Pooh*, illus. E.H. Shepard, London: Methuen.

Moebius, William (1986) "Introduction to Picturebook Codes," *Word & Image* 2.2: 141–158.

Moebius, William (2011) "Picture Book," in Philip Nel and Lissa Paul (eds) *Keywords in Children's Literature*, New York: New York University Press, 169–173.

Nel, Philip (2012) "Same Genus, Different Species? Comics and Picture Books," *Children's Literature Association Quarterly* 37.4: 445–453.

Nikolajeva, Maria (2005) *Aesthetic Approaches to Children's Literature: An Introduction*, Lanham, MD: Scarecrow Press.

Nodelman, Perry (1988) *Words about Pictures: The Narrative Art of Children's Picture Books*, Athens: University of Georgia Press.

Oxenbuy, Helen (2003) *The Helen Oxenbury Nursery Collection*, London: Egmont.

Salisbury, Martin, and Styles, Morag (2012) *Children's Picturebooks: The Art of Visual Storytelling*, London: Laurence King.

Selznick, Brian (2007) *The Invention of Hugo Cabret*, New York: Scholastic.

Selznick, Brian (2011) *Wonderstruck*, New York: Scholastic.

Selznick, Brian (2015) *The Marvels*, New York: Scholastic.

Sendak, Maurice (1963) *Where the Wild Things Are*, New York: Harper & Row.

Sendak, Maurice (1988) *Caldecott & Co.: Notes on Books & Pictures*, New York: Farrar, Straus & Giroux.

Serafini, Frank, and Blasingame, James (2012) "The Changing Face of the Novel," *The Reading Teacher* 66.2: 145–148.

Seuss, Dr. (1957) *The Cat in the Hat*, New York: Random House.

Sidman, Joyce (2011) *Swirl by Swirl: Spirals in Nature*, illus. Beth Krommes, Boston, MA: Houghton Mifflin Harcourt.

Tan, Shaun (2006) *The Arrival*, London: Hodder & Stoughton.

Tan, Shaun (2008) *Tales from Outer Suburbia*, Sydney: Allen & Unwin.

Tuwim, Julian (2013) *Tuwim: Wiersze dla dzieci / Tuwim: Poems for Children*, illus. Małgorzata Gurowsa, Monika Hanulak, Marta Ignerska, Agnieszka Kucharska-Zajkowska, Anna Niemierko, Gosia Urbańska-Macias, and Justyna Wróblewska, Warsaw: Wytwórnia.

Uehashi, Nahoko (1996) *Seirei no Moribito*, Tokyo: Kaiseisha [*Moribitio: Guardian of the Spirit*, trans. Cathy Hirano, New York: Scholastic/Arthur A. Levine Books, 2009].

Varon, Sara (2007) *Robot Dreams*, New York: Macmillan/First Second.

Wiesner, David (2013) *Mr. Wuffles!* Boston, MA: Houghton Mifflin Harcourt.

Whalley, Joyce Irene (2004) "The Development of Illustrated Texts and Picture Books," in Peter Hunt (ed.) *International Companion Encyclopedia of Children's Literature*, 2nd ed., London: Routledge, 318–327.

Wincencjusz-Patyna, Anita (2016) "Attractive Lives on Attractive Pages: Polish Illustrated Biography Books for Young Readers," *Problemy Wczesnej Edukacji / Issues in Early Education* 34.3: 107–117.

Yokota, Junko (2015) "The Past, Present and Future of Digital Picturebooks for Children," in Mireia Manresa and Neus Real (eds) *Digital Literature for Children: Texts, Readers, and Educational Practices*, Brussels: Peter Lang, 73–86.

Zipes, Jack (2015) *Grimm Legacies: The Magic Spell of the Grimms' Folk and Fairy*, Princeton, NJ: Princeton University Press.

28

ARTISTS' BOOKS AND PICTUREBOOKS

Generative dialogues

Johanna Drucker

Overview

Artists' books and picturebooks spring from different impulses and have very distinct genealogies, conceptual parameters, and audiences. But they share an interest in innovative structures, unusual materials, and imaginative engagement with books as objects. Both forms play with conventions and codes of presentation (format, design, graphics, typography, and so on) and engage with the potential of the codex book as an expressive means of visual communication. At least as far back as the nineteenth century, artists have made works that have become classic children's books, and in more recent times book artists have adopted approaches from picturebooks as part of their inventory of techniques. In the discussion that follows, examples of experimental and often playful approaches will chart some common ground at the intersection of picturebooks and artists' books.

We can begin by noting a few basic principles that describe the overlap between artists' books and picturebooks. Looking at examples made by book artists with children in mind, we can see some of the ways the book format functions as an essential feature of these works, not merely as an incidental part of their making. Next, we can identify a number of artists' books that take their inspiration from picturebooks, and show how influence flows in this direction. We can also point to works not originally intended as children's books that have become classics in part because of their innovative engagement with the book format (Beckett 2014). In conclusion, we can gesture towards the ways technological innovations are extending possibilities of imaginative engagement in the book as a digitally enhanced artifact.

Artists' books: a working definition

The term 'artist's book' is much debated. The simplest definition is "a book created as an original work of art" (Drucker 1995: 2). Characterized in this way, an artist's book can be made of images, texts, prints, photographs, unusual paper, and a wide array of materials. Scrapbooks, albums, and even gift books have some of these properties (Hubert and Hubert 1999; Perrée 2002). Lines among genres blur easily if only formal features, rather than subject matter and context, are taken into account as they share a deliberate, self-conscious, engagement with the features of the bound codex and use these elements as part of an aesthetic project (Chol 2015). When sequence, development, intertextual play, formal elements (such as margins or fore edges), or the physical form of the object are given an expressive role in the production, then the use of physical, material, and graphical effects becomes part of meaning of the work.

Opinions about when artists' books first appeared divide book historians. Some take a very long view and note that artists have contributed images and designs, illuminations and calligraphic decoration, to works in the book format for millennia (in Egyptian papyri, Chinese scrolls, and early illuminated manuscripts) (Lyons 1985). Some advocate beginning with artistic modernism, the coming of art markets, freedom from patronage systems, new forms of publication, and ideas about individual talent and imagination as crucial milestones. They claim early nineteenth-century Romantic, William Blake, as the first book artist (Drucker 1995). Others argue for a more narrowly defined contemporary stance in which artists' books are seen as the invention of mid-twentieth-century conceptual artists, who began making multiples in the 1960s (Moeglin-Delcroix 1997). The field of artists' books is as capacious as that of picturebooks, however, and conceptual work is one small section of a field that includes personal accounts, activist works, projects based on social issues, and works with emotional force and aesthetic range.

As we see from this brief introduction, in the productive dialogue between picturebooks and artists' books, many long historical traditions come into play as part of the imaginative engagement with formal and conceptual features (Khalfa 2001). Each of these many areas of exchange will be addressed in turn.

Movables: harlequinades, flaps, tabs, and wheels

The basic acts of opening a book, turning a page, and reading across a sequence of spreads are already dynamic actions. Books are rarely static objects, but their dynamic potential expands when they make use of extra devices and techniques. One form of movable, interactive book is made by cutting pages. Called harlequinades, these sliced books have their common version in the children's books that allowed segmented bodies – heads, torsos, legs of different figures (for instance, doctor, firefighter, ballerina, queen) to be combined. These playful works, developed in the eighteenth century by Robert Sayer, have been adopted for many purposes – entertainment, moral teachings, and surprise. In the hands of a member of the French experimental literary group, OuLiPo, Raymond Queaneau, the approach was used to make a book titled *Cent Mille Milliard de Poèmes* (A Hundred Million Poems 1961). Sliced through to the spine, this sequence of sonnets is nearly inexhaustible in its combinatoric range, and considered a classic literary artist's book.

Other methods of introducing interactivity with a book include the use of flaps – any piece that can be flipped or lifted. These have their origin in reference books with adult concerns, such as anatomy books and other works of reference (Montanaro 1993). Humphrey Repton, an eighteenth-century landscape architect and designer, used flaps glued onto printed pages to show before and after views of a scene. His *Sketches and Hints on Landscape Gardening* (1795) was used to promote his principles for cultivated transformation of landscapes. Another historical example, *The Toilet* (1822), a book created by Stacey Grimaldi, was actually a didactic work in spite of its suggestive title. Written to instruct children on various aspects of decorum and behavior, the book used flaps to reveal advice and commentary (e.g. a lifted image of a mirror revealed the word "humility"). As early as the sixteenth century, flaps were commonly used in anatomy books to show different views into the body because of their use in exposing cutaways and separating skeletal, circulatory, muscular, and other systems. These techniques have found their way into numerous artists' books. Margot Lovejoy used the flap technique repeatedly, as in her elaborate work *Labyrinth: The Controlling Gaze* (1991). Lovejoy framed her project in terms of the control of a reader subjected to the disciplining regimes of media. This is a far cry from the innovations meant to showcase a designer's art or teach good behavior. Other artists have taken advantage of the surprise, shock, and humorous effects in making use of these basic structures of revelation. Susan Baker's flap book, *How to Humiliate Your Peeping Tom* (1989), is irreverent and pointed, and its surprise effects serve the dark humor of the book.

Volvelles, or turning wheels that engage in combinatoric activity, have also been appropriated for artists' books and picturebooks, though, like other movable features, they had their origins in serious scientific or reference works (Gravelle et al. 2012). Volvelles are found in the work of the astronomer Peter Apianus, whose *Cosmographicus Liber* (Cosmographical Book), published in 1524, was a major reference work in navigation and astronomy and used paper wheels to show movement of the stars, though the device may have appeared in much earlier in other astronomical treatises (Kansas 2005). Medieval manuscripts with leather tabs to turn wheels, pointers, and several rings of texts may have borrowed their technology from Arabic culture. In picturebooks, flaps for creating animation make use of motion to put action into a scene (Lindberg 1979). The early twentieth-century illustrator, Julian Wehr, exploited such techniques in illustrating many popular books, from *The Wizard of Oz* (1944) to *Finnie the Fiddler* (1942) with "Pictures come to life!" Wehr's work is truly graphic, and dynamic, but turning wheels and combinatoric elements can been used in artists' books for conceptual and critical work as well. Dan Mayer's clever *Book Arts Jargonator*, and *Election 2000 Jargonator*, both published in 2000 as phrase generators, repurpose the antique device for contemporary issues.

Pop-ups and dimensional books

The term 'paper engineering' covers some of the devices just described, but also includes the elaborate work of pop-up books, those designs that take advantage of the basic motion of opening a page spread to create a scene in three dimensions. To this day, paper engineering is not mass produced, but hand-assembled. The much-admired work of major figures like the twentieth-century Czech artist, Vojtech Kubasta, or more current, Robert Sabuda, has inspired many book artists through direct imitation or instruction (Schmidt n.d.). Their ingenious feats are based on a few simple principles (and some very complicated ones) of folding and gluing that have been incorporated into artists' books. A useful comparison between this children's genre and that of artists' books can be made by putting Lothar Meggendorfer's *Internationaler Zirkus* (International Circus 1888) into contrast with designer Ron King's *Bluebeard's Castle*, a collaboration with writer Roy Fisher published under King's imprint, Circle Books, in 1973. *Zirkus* contains six openings, each like a small stage set, whose scenes are activated by pulling on flaps. Like the popular *Showman* series issued by the New York based McLoughlin Brothers in the nineteenth century, they use folds and cuts to create a theatrical proscenium within each opening. King and Fisher's *Bluebeard's Castle* elaborates these ideas and works on a much larger scale. The book extends more than a meter and contains drawers, complex scenes, and puppets to be removed and used separately. The imaginative nineteenth-century works provided the precedents and technical foundations for pop-up books as a part of twentieth-century book arts.

Not all paper engineering is mere amusement. Sjoerd Hofstra takes paper engineering into conceptual realms that engage memory, history, and literary topics as well as personal dimensions. Whether revisiting the models of Euclid's *Elements of Geometry*, included in Ernst Ratdolt's fifteenth-century edition of the work, or creating an edition based on a passage from modern American writer John Dos Passos, *They Pair Off Hurriedly* (1992), Hofstra's work uses paper engineering to add critical as well as physical dimensions to his pages. *Poemobiles* (1974), Julio Plaza's design of Brazilian Concrete poet Augusto de Campos's deliberately reductive texts, remains among the most remarkable pop-up books in the literary artists' books canon. A work in which paper engineering has been put completely at the service of language, it is highly graphic, even pictorial, by virtue of the strength of the typographical emphasis, use of color, and ways the dimensionality of the language is emphasized by the design. Finally, Kara Walker's powerful pop-up books, such as *Freedom: A Fable* (1997), use her striking silhouette images to address the history of slavery, racism, and stereotypes in American culture.

Thematic materials and shapes

Materials often reinforce the theme of a book. The Janus Press version of Margaret Kaufmann's *Aunt Sallie's Lament*, first published in 1988, used quilting methods, patterns, and motifs within its elaborately folded and sewn structure to emphasize the sentimental family history. The result is a work whose materials are part of its meaning production. Cloth books have long been popular for children as well, since they are durable and, in some cases, washable, in ways that paper ones are not. Hand-quilted contemporary alphabet books, made in brightly colored cotton, extend the nineteenth-century innovation of printing ABC books on linen to make them last longer under extensive use. Shaped books, die cut and made to resemble an object, are often made for early readers (for example, Frances Brundage's 1932 *The Cat's Pajamas*, one of a series of 'shape books'). The imaginative children's author, Peter Newell, created the *Hole Book* (1908) and *Slant Book* (1910) in the early twentieth century, boring through pages in the first case and cutting the book at an angle to the spine on the other. The subject matter of each book matched its striking physical properties. Gelett Burgess's *Le Petit Journal des Refusées* (The Little Journal of Rejects 1896) was printed on wallpaper and trimmed to trapezoidal shape to emphasize its Bohemian irregularities, and its points and edges are echoed in Phil Zimmermann's *High Tension* (1993), a book with sharp folds expressing a distressed psychic state (Figure 28.1).

Figure 28.1 Illustration from Phil Zimmermann's *High Tension*. Rochester, NY: Visual Studies Workshop Press, 1993.

Materials as well as shapes can be used for parody, citation, or invention, whether in the artists' book or children's genres. *Sassy Baby's First Book* (n.d.) set contains a teething ring among its cloth pages and plastic flaps. In the artists' book world, books take almost any and every possible shape and use materials from found objects, bodily fluids, dirt, recycled materials, and every conceivable natural or cultural object. Joni Mabe's limited edition *Book of Hair* (1982) has paper made with human hair and contains samples of hair donated by living people. The viewing impact of such materials is visceral.

Unusual materials of all kinds have found their way into artists' works. John Latham's chewed remains of Clement Greenberg's *Art and Culture* (a 1966 performance) and Dieter Rot's *Pometrie* from the 1960s (comprised of sealed pages containing body fluids, cheese, and other substances) take the investigations to extremes. Books that grow grass, are placed underground to rot, outside to absorb weathering, are big enough to walk into, or made into new objects also appear among the many other inventions of altered books (Scott 2014). Whether these are picturebooks, sculptures, novelties, or conceptual art objects depends upon one's point of view.

Thematic works also take the shape of objects. Byron Clercx's *Big Stick* (1993) was made from shredding works by Sigmund Freud and casting the paper with resin to make a baseball bat. The entire object resides in a redlined black case turned into an artifact and enshrined. At the point where books really become sculptural objects, they lose most of their connection to the codex, and to the traditions of picturebooks.

Graphical storytelling

The first appearance of printed visual books is in the Far East, and the *Diamond Sutra* (886 CE) is generally cited as the earliest complete block book in existence. In the West, block books were introduced in the fifteenth century at almost the same time as movable type. They often contained moral instruction: *Ars Moriendi*, the art of dying, was a particularly popular topic. The storytelling techniques of these works relied on a series of panels, each a scene in the unfolding action of the narrative depicting a dying person tempted by angels and devils in vivid scenes.

Similarly, graphic novels, developed in the early twentieth century, such as those of the remarkable woodcut artists Frans Masereel and Lynd Ward, were entirely cut from blocks. Masereel's subject matter turned to modern life and alienation. Masereel's *Die Stadt* (The City 1925) deals with the difficulties of urban life, and existential crises. Ward's *God's Man* has remained in print since it was first published in 1929. The graphical power of storytelling in these artists' books is in a direct line from those early block books, even if nearly five hundred years separates them. Ward also produced a book meant for children, *The Silver Pony* (1973), a story about a lonely boy on a farm told in black and white and shades of gray.

In the 1930s, the Surrealist artist Max Ernst invented a very different approach to graphic storytelling. His artists' books, such as *Une Semaine de Bonté* (A Week of Goodness 1934), were made from collages, and like Masereel's they had no texts beyond their titles. Ernst's collages used the engraved prints and illustrations of the late Victorian era, the era of his own childhood, and recombined these in dreamlike and nightmarish sequences of erotic activities, some sadistic and violent, others magical in their combination of elements. While these are not for children, they find their echo in the surrealist-inspired dreamlike picturebooks by Maurice Sendak and Edward Gorey, among others.

Contemporary book artist Eric Drooker and graphic novelist Art Spiegelman cite Ward and Masereel as inspirations for their own graphic novels. Fully pictorial books, or wordless works, are a mainstay of artists' books production and include photographic works, drawn/illustrated works, books that copy or make use of comic book styles, and books whose visual formats play with the book as a space of literal presentation and spatial illusion. These are equally appealing to adults and children, hence the enormous popularity of *Where's Waldo* (originally published in the UK in 1987 as *Where's Wally*) with its absorbing drawings created by Martin Handford. The dense scenes provoke active engagement in seeing and looking, as does the book by Dutch artist Jan Voss, *Detour* (1989), a compelling book that purports to be written entirely as one continuous line (Figure 28.2). The folded sheets used to make the pages of that work provide an extra dimension, since the closed book shows an image on the fore edge.

Not all graphical storytelling is figurative. Sometimes it can be achieved with abstract, or non-representational, forms. Warja Honegger-Lavater, a twentieth-century Swiss book artist, 'translated' fairy tales, such as *Snow White* (1974) into a graphical code. Her notations were generally geometric shapes in bright color that turned the narratives of the stories into graphical patterns. By leaving language behind, they become available to readers across the globe, and make an argument for graphical and visual methods as effective storytelling tools. She turned the work of the Brothers Grimm, Hans Christian Andersen, and Charles Perrault into her own editions. Her formalist impulses combined with a lively sense of color and design, so that what might have been a mechanical exercise was highly engaging. Though children may delight in their bright colors and lively designs, the complexity of these books calls for a sophisticated reader.

Even more abstract, Matt Mullican and Lawrence Weiner's highly esoteric but very beautiful *In the Crack of the Dawn* (1991) uses the tropes and stylistic of devices of a comic book to compose a dreamy hypnotic surreal world in which lines connect rooms and horizons, gaps open in the surface of forms and shapes, and unexpected connections among skies and interiors are all executed with the logic of a simple language that belies the complexity of the form.

Among the many artists and movements involved in graphical storytelling and experiments with the material features of books are part of nearly every movement in modern art, the

Figure 28.2 Illustration from Jan Voss's *Detour*. Amsterdam: Boekie Woekie, and Stuttgart: Staib + Mayer, 1989. Reprinted by permission of Jan Voss.

mid-twentieth-century French Lettrist movement made a particular claim for its pictorial engagement with text. Led by the Romanian artist Isidore Isou, who inaugurated the Lettrist project with his tome, *Introduction à une nouvelle poésie et à une nouvelle musique* (Introduction to a New Poetry and a New Music), published in 1947 by the distinguished French firm, Gallimard, the movement had several additional key figures at its core: Maurice Lemaître and Gabriel Pomerand. Later adherents swelled the group, and extended its activities to production of textiles, wall coverings, film, and all manner of artistic work. But Isou, Lemaître, and Pomerand each made picturebooks in support of the crucial principles of Lettrism: to create a graphical, pictorial system of literature from the atomistic elements of glyphs and scripts. Some of these were invented and some were modified alphabetic or symbol sets. These were used to create what Lemaître termed "hypergraphic" writings – a term that he put into play long before the associations it would carry in the digital writing practices that emerged a decade or so later.

Isou's *Les Journaux des Dieux* (Notebooks of the Gods 1950), Lemaître's Roman Hypergraphique (Hypergraphic Novel 1956), and Pomerand's *Saint Ghetto des Prets* (Saint Ghetto of the Loans 1950) exhibit their individual approaches to Lettrist practice. Isou's book is cartoonlike, almost a graphic novel with its serial panels and captioned images. Though not fully or exclusively pictorial, Isou's work is significant in part because of his hyperbolic rhetoric in support of the force of Lettrism as a literary invention. Isou asserted that Lettrism was a fulcrum point of transformation, and that all literature to that moment had led to the necessity to focus on the letter as the crucial component of innovation. All literature afterwards, he believed, would proceed on the basis of this radical re-focusing on what he considered the basis of language and literary production. Signs without prior meaning could be invented and deployed to create new possibilities freed from the restraints of the past or conventions of composition. Lemaître's short *Roman* consists of five plates (and an explanation) whose variety suggests an inventory of techniques. Rebuses, collage, pastiche, and glyphs drawn, cut, pasted, and collected are all put in the service of a semi-autobiographical (but rather obscure) text. Pomerand's *Saint Ghetto* is a sustained production in which a set of conventions is used to tell a story without words about the urban environment. The impact of Lettrism on literary and artistic production may not have met its founder's expectations, but some of its radical thinking was incorporated into the Situationist movement through personal contacts and artistic exchanges, and the many visual works it spawned in the early 1950s and early 1960s remain striking in their commitment to explore pictorial approaches to literary art.

Book artists creating works for children

A number of classic works made by artists in the book format were not originally intended for children, but have become favorites across generations: William Blake's *Songs of Innocence and Experience* (1794); Christina Rosetti's *Goblin Market* (1862), with illustrations by her brother Dante Gabriel (Darton 1932; Masaki 2006); and Lazar El Lissitzky's *Pro dva kvadrata: suprematicheskii skaz v 6i postroikakh* (About Two Squares 1922), a parable of utopian political struggle (Wye and Rowell 2002). But other book artists have made works with young audiences in mind.

In 1957, the Icelandic artist Dieter Rot created a book titled *Kinderbuch* (Children's Book). Given the conceptual nature of Rot's work, the project can be seen either as an example of a children's book or a commentary upon the genre of books for children (as an object that fulfills expectations by using certain colors, techniques, and formal features). The book is created in three primary colors, a hallmark of pictorial works with children in mind. Red, yellow, and blue pigments combine to make green, and darker shades, and the book has a very simple progression from fewer shapes per page (limited to circles and squares) to a climax showing a crowded scene. While no explicit narrative is suggested, a definite progression engages the fundamental feature of a codex book – the capacity for development of a story or event over the space of the book. A book is a continuous sequence, but the divisions of one spread from another are crucial to its format and operation. The surprise of seeing each opening creates a connection across the gap from one discrete spread to the next.

Rot was a conceptual artist whose book works were each individual investigations of what a codex could do. His work in its entirety is practically a primer on how to understand a book as an object. His *Stupidogramm* (1962) made a comment on the children's game of finding words hidden in a grid and circling them with a boundary. In *Stupidogramm* the only items to circle are commas, and any and each combination is as meaningless/meaningful as the others. For him to take the notion of the children's book as an idea meant executing it as a set of conceptual moves, distilling the basic elements to their essentials: primary color, simple geometric shapes, spiral binding, and sequence. The book certainly works for children as well, its tactile simplicity and ease of handling as well as its bright, vivid, design is immediately engaging – and entirely pictorial (Parsons 2004).

The Italian designer Bruno Munari had a long engagement with making books for children and adult audiences (Maffei 2002). His elegantly designed works use shape, color, pattern, and other fundamental features of graphic design, such as orientation, scale, and position, to engage readers. His work as an illustrator/designer has often focused on young readers, and in 1970s he began working regularly on children's books with an emphasis on visual storytelling. His renowned work in this area, *Nella nebbia di Milano* (The Circus in the Mist 1968) uses bold shapes, strong colors, and die-cut openings to create and reveal its contents. The book is a masterwork of die cutting, shape shifting, and reframing from page to page. Munari's skills show in his use of books as sequential openings, experiences to be orchestrated with color and formal resonances.

In a very different vein, William Wegman, a whimsical postmodern photographer who made a career of picturing his beloved Weimaraner dogs in costumed poses and droll scenes, made a book-length rendition of *Cinderella* (1993) starring his photogenic animals (other fairy tales followed). Unlike Munari, Wegman is not a designer or book artist, and he uses the book simply as a way to present his photographic tableaux.

Book art that mimics children's books

Copying codes of production can produce a parody, critique, or a sly jab at a familiar convention. Dorothy Kunhardt's 1940 classic, *Pat the Bunny*, a perennial of children's literature that may be among the most frequently discussed artifacts in the context of the "is it an artist's book?" discussions, has been parodied repeatedly by various artists. Kate Merrow Nelligan has created *Pat the Daddy* (2010) and other titles, while Aaron Ximm and Kaveh Soofi's *Pat the Zombie* (2011) is unsparing in its offerings of gore and rotting flesh. Margaret Wise's *Goodnight Moon* has been parodied repeatedly, sometimes with children in mind and sometimes not (for instance, Jen Nessel and Lizzie Ratner's *Goodnight Nanny-Cam* 2014). The sacred icons of childhood have such common currency that reworking them has a potent impact in artists' hands.

Parodies and imitations of children's primers sometimes serve to call attention to the biases of race, gender, and hegemony of various kinds that are coded into their texts and images. Clarissa Sligh's *Reading Dick and Jane with Me*, published in 1989, made a pointed intervention by exposing assumptions about race that were present in classic children's readers – with their exclusive focus on white children and conventional nuclear families. These exchanges are characteristic of the dialogue between artists' books and picturebooks.

Ann Tyler's work, *Billy Rabbit* (2007–2008), is a retelling of an English children's story (Figure 28.3). Tyler terms it an "American adaptation" of the work, and it is issued in a limited edition artists' book format, with tipped-in flaps in the form of iconic objects (tools such as a hammer knives, farm implements, etc.), each related to events in the story. The book was hand-set and printed on fine paper in red ink, and at 11 × 15.25 inches, it has the feel and look of a limited edition children's book. The first impression is quickly dispelled as the story is in fact an aggregate of documents of seven different lynchings. Within the visual codes of innocence, the dreadful reality becomes apparent, suggesting the way historical memory is repressed in mainstream culture and the ways that other children's tales contain their own often unacknowledged subtexts beneath their charming surface. Tyler's book is not

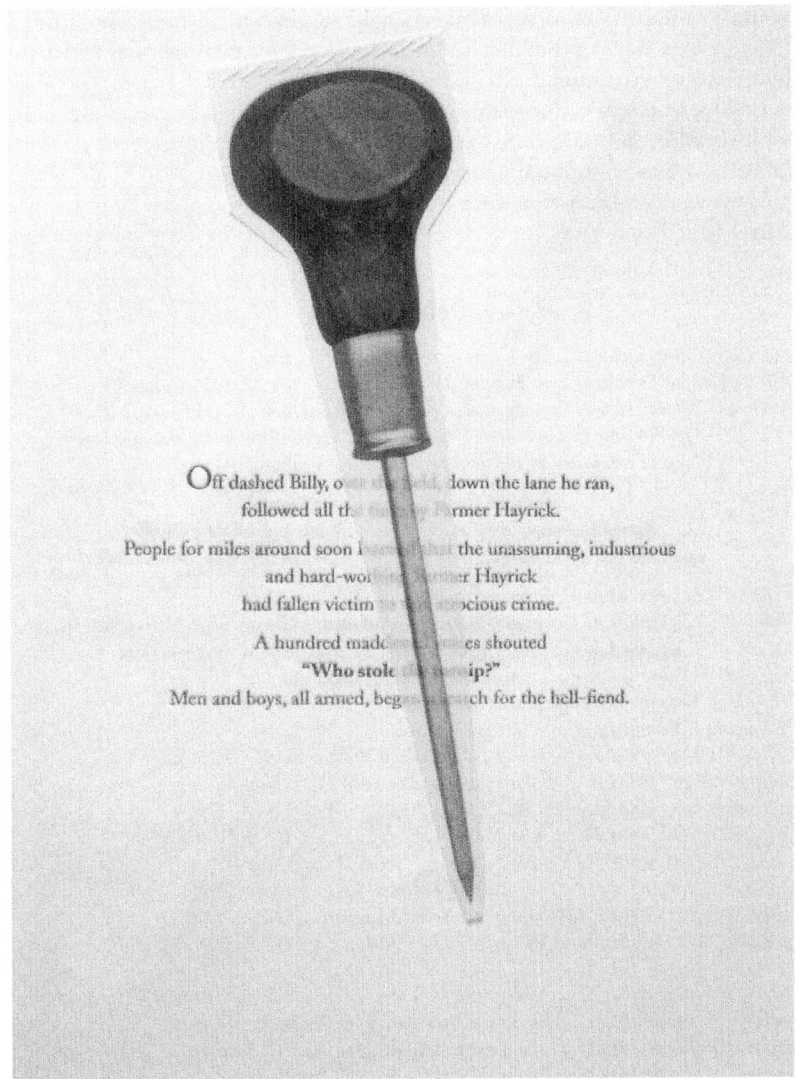

Figure 28.3 Illustration from Anne Tyler's *Billy Rabbit*. Chicago: Ann Tyler Books, 2007–2008.
Reprinted by permission of Anne Tyler.

a parody, but an act of mimicry designed to seduce its readers into viewing the content of the book through a set of assumptions that has to change radically. The cognitive shift is dramatic and reinforces the effect. Graphical codes, as well as textual ones, participate in these conventions and can be used to play with the genre-blurring capacities of artists' books and their sympathetic dialogue with the legacy of picturebooks in all their many identities and dimensions.

Conclusion

This brief survey of crossover influences in picturebooks and artists' books allows us to see how certain principles of engagement with the codex book find expression in both domains. While the physical extension or thematic reinforcement of books through these means is an integral aspect of artist-bookmaking, other ways of thinking about the dialogue of picturebooks and artists' books can be explored by thinking of the intentions with which these books are designed: as children's books, as parodies or imitations, or as works that span audiences and genres. Techniques of digital invention now extend the bookwork beyond the printed page, into augmented reality screens and spaces, and into distributed networks, as well as embodiments in devices and platforms of all kinds. The debates about whether a 'book' that appears on a screen, in a web browser, or as an 'app' can be properly called a book has generated lively discussion in recent decades and likely will do so for quite some time to come.

References

Apianus, Peter (1524) *Cosmographicus Liber*, Landshut: Impensis P. Apiani.
Baker, Susan (1989) *How to Humiliate Your Peeping Tom*, Rochester, NY: Visual Studies Workshop Press.
Baum, L. Frank (1944) *The Wizard of Oz*, animated by Julian Wehr, Akron, OH: Saalfield.
Beckett, Sandra L. (2014) *Crossover Picturebooks: A Genre for All Ages*, New York: Routledge.
Blake, William (1794) *Songs of Innocence and Experience*, London: William Blake.
Brundage, Frances (1932) *The Cat's Pajamas*, Rochester, NY: Stetcher Litho.
Burgess, Gelett (1896) *Le Petit Journal des Refusées*, San Francisco, CA: James Marrion.
Campos, Augusto de (1974) *Poemobiles*, illus. Julio Plaza, São Paulo: edição dos autores.
Chol, Isabel, and Jean Khalfa (eds) (2015) *Les Espaces du Livre / Spaces of the Book*, Oxford: Peter Lang.
Clercx, Byron (1993) *Big Stick*, limited edition artists' book, no publisher.
Darton, F.J. Harvey (1932) *Children's Books in England*, Cambridge: Cambridge University Press.
Diamond Sutra (868).
Drucker, Johanna (1995) *The Century of Artists' Books*, New York: Granary Books.
Ernst, Max (1934) *Une Semaine de Bonté*, Paris: Aux éditions Jeanne Bucher.
Euclid (1482) *Elements of Geometry*, Venice: Ernst Ratdolt.
Fisher, Roy (1972) *Bluebeard's Castle*, designed by Ron King, Guildford: Circle Press.
Gravelle, Michelle, Mustapha, Anah, and Leroux, Coralee (2012) "Volvelles," http://drc.usask.ca/projects/arch-book/volvelles.php (accessed June 18, 2015).
Grimaldi, Stacey (1822) *The Toilet: A Book for Young Ladies*, London: By the author.
Handford, Martin (1987) *Where's Waldo?*, Boston, MA: Little, Brown.
Hofstra, Sjoerd (1992) *John Dos Passos: They Pair off Hurriedly*, Amsterdam: ZET.
Honegger-Lavater, Warja (1974) *Snow White*, New York: Museum of Modern Art.
Hubert, Renée Riese, and Hubert, Judd D. (1999) *The Cutting Edge of Reading: Artists' Books*, New York: Granary Books.
Isou, Isidore (1947) *Introduction à une nouvelle poésie et à une nouvelle musique*, Paris: Gallimard.
Isou, Isidore (1950) *Les Journaux des Dieux*, Paris: Aux Escaliers de Lausanne.
Kansas, Nick (2005) "Volvelles! Early Paper Astronomical Computers," *Mercury* 34.2: 33–39.
Kaufman, Margaret (1988) *Aunt Sallie's Lament*, West Burke, VT: Janus Press.
Khalfa, Jean (2001) *The Dialogue Between Painting and Poetry: Livres d'Artistes 1874–1999*, Cambridge: Black Apollo Press.
King, Ronald, and Fisher, Roy (1972) *Bluebeard's Castle*, Guildford: Circle Press.
Kunhardt, Dorothy (1940) *Pat the Bunny*, New York: Golden Books.
Latham, John (1966–68) *Art and Culture*, unique object, MoMA New York collection.
Lemaître, Maurice (1956) "Roman Hypergraphique," in *La plastique lettriste et hypergraphique*, Paris: Caractères.
Lindberg, Sten G. (1979) "Mobiles in Books: Volvelles, Inserts, Pyramids, Divinations, and Children's Games," trans. William S. Mitchell, *The Private Library*, 3rd series, 2.2, Middlesex: Private Libraries Association.
Lissitzky, Lazar El (1922) *Pro dva kvadrata: suprematicheskii skaz v 6i postroikakh*, Berlin: Skythen-Verlag [*About Two Squares. A Suprematist Tale*, trans. Christiana Van Manen, Forest Row, UK: Artists Bookworks, 1990].
Lovejoy, Margot (1991) *Labyrinth: The Controlling Gaze*, Purchase, NY: Center for Editions.
Lyons, Joan (ed.) (1985) *Artists' Books: A Critical Anthology and Sourcebook*, London: Gibbs Smith.
Mabe, Joni (1982) *The Book of Hair*, Cornelia, GA: Green Street Studio.
Maffei, Giorgio (2002) *Munari. I libri*, Milan: Edizioni Sylvestre Bonnard.
Masaki, Tomoko (2006) *A History of Victorian Popular Picture Books: The Aesthetic, Creative, and Technological Aspects of the Toy Book Through the Publications of the Firm of Routledge, 1852–1893*, 2 vols, Tokyo: Kazamashobo.

Masareel, Frans (1925) *Die Stadt*, Munich: Kurt Wolff Verlag [*The City*, New York: Dover, 1972].

Mayer, Dan (2000) *Book Arts Jargonator* and *Election 2000 Jargonator*, Tempe, AZ: Nomadic Press.

Meggendorfer, Lothar (1889) *Internationaler Zirkus*, London: H. Grevel and J.F. Schreiber (Esslingen bei Stuttgart).

Moeglin-Delcroix, Anne (1997) *L'Esthetique du Livre d'Artiste*, Marseille: Le Mot et le reste.

Montanaro, Ann R. (1993) *Pop-up and Movable Books: A Bibliography*, Metuchen, NJ: Scarecrow Press.

Mullican, Matt, and Weiner, Lawrence (1991) *In the Crack of the Dawn*, Brussels: Mai 36 Galerie, Lucerne and Yves Gevaert.

Munari, Bruno (1968) *Nella nebbia di Milano*, Milan: Emme Edizioni [*The Circus in the Mist*, New York: Putnam, 1969].

Nelligan, Kate Merrow (2010) *Pat the Daddy*, Kennebunkport, ME: Cider Mill Press.

Nessel, Jen, and Ratner, Lizzy (2014) *Good Night Nanny-Cam*, illus. Sara Pinto, New York: Plume.

Newell, Peter (1908) *The Hole Book*, New York: Harper & Brothers.

Newell, Peter (1910) *The Slant Book*, New York: Harper & Brothers.

Parsons, Elisabeth (2004) "Starring in the Intimate Space: Picture Book Narratives and Performance Semiotics," *Image and Narrative 9*, www.image&narrative.be/inarchive/performance/parsons/htm.

Perrée, Rob (2002) *Cover to Cover: The Artists' Book in Perspective*, Rotterdam: N.A.I.

Pomerand, Gabriel (1950), *Saint Ghetto des Prets*, Paris: O.L.B. [*Saint Ghetto of the Loans*, trans. Michael Kaspar and Bhamati Viswanathan, Brooklyn, NY: Ugly Duckling Press, Lost Literature Series, #1, 2006].

"Pop Up and Movable Books. A Tour Through Their History From the Nineteenth Century to the Present. University of North Texas," no year www.library.unt.edu/rarebooks/exhibits/popup2/introduction.htm (accessed February 12, 2015).

Queneau, Raymond (1961) *Cent mille milliards de poèmes*, Paris: Gallimard.

Repton, Humphrey (1795) *Sketches and Hints on Landscape Gardening*, London: W. Bulmer.

Rossetti, Christina (1865) *Goblin Market*, illus. Dante Gabriel Rossetti, London: Macmillan.

Rot, Dieter (1957) *Kinderbuch*, Reykjavik: Forlag Edition.

Rot, Dieter (1968) *Pometrie*, Cologne: Art Intermedia.

Rot, Dieter (1962) *Stupidogramm*, Stuttgart: Edition Hansjörg Mayer.

Sassy Baby's First Book (n.d.) manufactured in China, no publisher.

Schmidt, Suzanne Karr (n.d.) "Constructions Both Sacred and Profane: Serpents, Angels, and Pointing Fingers in Renaissance Books with Moving Parts," *World of Popups!*, www.robertsabuda.com/everythingpopup/suzannekarr.asp (accessed June 21, 2015).

Scott, Carole (2014) "Artists' Books, Altered Books, and Picturebooks," in Bettina Kümmerling-Meibauer (ed.) *Picturebooks: Representation and Narration*, New York: Routledge. 37–51.

Sligh, Clarissa (1989) *Reading Dick and Jane with Me*, Rochester, NY: Visual Studies Workshop Press.

Tyler, Ann (2007) *Billy Rabbit*, Chicago: Ann Tyler Books.

Voss, Jan (1989) *Detour*, Amsterdam: Boekie Woekie, and Stuttgart: Staib + Mayer.

Walker, Kara (1997) *Freedom: A Fable*, Santa Monica, CA: Peter Norton Family.

Ward, Lynd (1929) *God's Man*, New York: J. Cape and H. Smith.

Ward, Lynd (1973) *The Silver Pony*, Boston, MA: Houghton Mifflin.

Wegman, William (1993) *Cinderella*, New York: Hyperion Books.

Wise, Margaret (1991) *Goodnight Moon*, New York: Harper Collins.

Wye, Deborah, and Rowell, Margaret (eds) (2002) *The Russian Avant-Garde Book*, New York: Museum of Modern Art.

Ximm, Aaron (2011) *Pat the Zombie*, illus. Karch Soofi, Berkeley, CA: Ten Speed Press.

Zimmermann, Philip (1993) *High Tension*, Rochester, NY: Visual Studies Workshop Press.

29

PICTUREBOOKS AND PHOTOGRAPHY

Jane Wattenberg

Photography in children's books has a lineage as long as photography itself. Beginning with the invention and launch of photography, this chapter traces the emergence of photographic picture-books into the mainstream of all picturebooks for children. The subjects, themes, and techniques will be addressed while highlighting the creators themselves and recognizing the influence of history and art movements across the decades.

While the majority of picturebooks contain hand-illustrated imagery, photographic picturebooks are replete with photographs or photo-based illustrations. Whether devoid of words or a melding of words and images, a photographic picturebook most often illuminates a sequential narrative and covers a wide spectrum of subjects. Viewed in full color, in partial color, or in basic black-and-white, photographic picturebooks span the gamut from photo-documented real-life scenes to photo fantasy hybrids employing techniques of photomontage and collage. In this chapter, the terms *photographically illustrated picturebook*, *photo-illustrated picturebook*, and *photo picturebook* are interchangeable. The term *photobook* refers to all books containing photography, including picturebooks.

Discourse on photography in books for children is scant and mainly reflects on the last sixty years of children's books. As the new work was built on the old, it is important to view the complete history and revisit the earliest volumes. A large collection of photographic children's books is located in the Cotsen Children's Library at Princeton University. A comprehensive listing of early children's photobooks is found in the bibliography, *From the Mundane to the Magical: Photographically Illustrated Children's Books, 1854–1945 and Beyond* (1999) compiled by Mus White. Katherine Capshaw's *Civil Rights Childhood: Picturing Liberation in African American Photobooks* (2014) contextualizes a profound understanding of the African American experience in photographic picturebooks. Julian Rothenstein and Olga Budashevskaya's *Inside the Rainbow: Russian Children's Literature 1920–1935* (2013) introduces a panoply of Russian photo-illustrated picturebooks, as does the Russian book by Mikhail Karasik, *Udarnaya kniga sovetskoi detvory: Fotoillyustratsiya i fotomontazh v knige dlya detei i yunoshestva 1920–1930* (Soviet Shock Books for Children: Photoillustration and Photomontage in Children's and Youth Books 1920–1930, 2010). The many online independent blog articles as well as essays by Elina Druker, Helene Ehriander, Julia Hirsch, Bettina Kümmerling-Meibauer, and Jörg Meibauer point to a growing interest in this area of research.

Photo-illustrated picturebooks differ from hand-illustrated picturebooks in a photograph's implied associations to authenticity. A photograph mirrors truth – what we see, what we know, how we live. Photographic picturebooks replicate the ordinary and manifest the extraordinary. They inspire social change, provide scientific evidence, offer humor, and evoke emotion. These books range from highly creative to dull and drab. Reality is at the core even as photographs trick the eye, bend truth, and manipulate our assumptions. Even then, the wildly ersatz seems genuine and reliable. With agility, photography in children's books leaps believably from document to dreams.

Early photography

The year 1839 marks the date of the first successful photographs. In the exploratory spirit of the Victorian era, visionary scientists, artists, and lens makers together launched the art of photography; harnessing light and mirroring landscapes. They are the unheralded partners of the most celebrated inventors of photography – Nicéphore Niépce, Henry Fox Talbot, Louis Daguerre, and Hippolyte Bayard, among others. In the remaining decades of the nineteenth century, artists such as Oscar G. Rejlander, Francis Frith, Julia Margaret Cameron, and Lewis Carroll grabbed their large-format cameras and glass negatives, experimented under dark cloths in dark rooms, and made history.

In 1858, the tale of Little Red Riding Hood was the subject of perhaps the first staged photographic fairy tale retelling. Created by the controversial photographer Henry Peach Robinson, four sequential albumen prints spotlight four high points in this well-known drama. All were captioned and exhibited on a wall. The most chilling image shows Red Riding Hood shocked by the sight of dear Granny. The face of Granny among the bedcovers is truly that of a wolf. Although seamless at first glance, these first photographic illustrations of a retold tale combine multiple negatives. Already, photography, proudly proclaiming its ability to mirror nature, experienced manipulation by what were then considered rebel artists. The debate over veracity versus the illustrative dexterity of photography had begun.

Robinson's dramatically staged and darkroom-altered images were melodramas, despised by many and highly prized by others. In his treatise *The Pictorial Effect in Photography* (1869), he expresses his view that "photography is an art *because* it can lie" (cited in Sontag 1973, 127). Opposing Robinson was the naturalist Peter Henry Emerson, a doctor who changed career paths to photograph the grandeur and beauty of nature (Emerson 1889). The Robinson/Emerson controversy, manipulated imagery versus untouched imagery straight from nature, simmers still in photographic circles and in picturebooks for children.

The emergence of photo-illustrated picturebooks

In England, during the latter half of the nineteenth century, Edward Lear, Kate Greenaway, Walter Crane, and Sir John Tenniel were creating a heyday of exemplary picturebooks. Photographers were poised to join this talented and ambitious circle. In 1866, none other than Hans Christian Andersen penned verses for what is considered to be the first bound photographic picturebook, *Fotograferede Bornegrupper* (Photographs of Groups of Children). Danish photographer Harald Paetz posed children playing, praying, and costumed in fantasy garb for this six-page square folio of albumen prints (White 1999).

At the same time as Charles Dickens revealed a chilling portrait of childhood in novels, the earliest photo-illustrated picturebooks for children radiated idyllic leisure and innocence. *Afternoon Tea* (1891), by W.G. Mitchell, contains nine sepia-rich photogravure images printed on delicate tissue, tipped in, and lightly glued down at the corners. A girl, her sibling, and a doll companion delight in a tea party at a child-sized table on a fringe of lawn. Equally idyllic, *Old Friends with New Faces* (1892) and *Mother Goose of '93* (1893), by the American photographer Mrs. N. Gray Bartlett, are perhaps the two earliest photo-illustrated collections of Mother Goose. Costumed children re-enact Georgie Porgie's kiss and Little Miss Muffet's arachnophobia. The deftly placed tissues are printed with exceptional detail and tonal depth.

As glass negatives gave way to film, large, boxy cameras gave way to smaller handheld cameras. In 1890, Kodak's flexible roll film eliminated the need for a personal darkroom. Kodak's advertising slogan promised, "You Press the Button, We Do the Rest." Photographers took to the road with smaller cameras while formal studio settings eased into casual and candid imagery. As this new medium expanded into mainstream children's literature, photobooks rolled off the presses.

Creators of photo-illustrated picturebooks

Many famous photographers took up the challenge of creating books for children. Ansel Adams created only one picturebook, a sedate trip through transcendent landscapes with his children in *Michael and Anne in the Yosemite Valley* (1941). Contemporary photographer Cindy Sherman's *Fitcher's Bird* (1992), an aptly macabre photo re-creation of the German tale, is a variation of *Bluebeard*, involving a serial killer seeking a non-prying wife. Sarah Moon created a dark cityscape, chiaroscuro version of *Little Red Riding Hood* (2002). With emotional depth, *Life* magazine photographer John Shearer speaks of social change in *I Wish I Had an Afro* (1970). In photographer Eikoh Hosoe and author Betty Jean Lifton's book, *A Dog's Guide to Tokyo* (1969), a Tokyo city poodle takes his American poodle cousin on a whimsical, whirlwind tour celebrating the uniqueness of Japanese culture. Fine art and commercial photographers such as Berenice Abbott, Claude Cahun, Robert Doisneau, Gaston Karquel, Ergy Landau, Jan Lukas, Duane Michaels, Pierda, Edward Steichen, and Jean Tourane also illustrated and occasionally authored one or more children's books in their careers.

But ultimately, a picturebook's success does not depend on spectacular photos or a photographer's reputation. Often, it is the lesser-known artists who have produced intriguing books. One such artist was Arthur Ullyett, who posed models in scenes and created photomontage illustrations for George Best's *The Home of Santa Claus* (1900). Minneapolis photographer Paul Skoog, with Frederick Tyner, created the quirky photobook *A Trip to the Man on the Moon* (1939), wherein Jean, Billy, and an old sea captain meet elves, fairies, and angels in this tabletop tableau. Similarly idiosyncratic are the garden dramas of animated vegetables photographed by Louis Wegner in *Tommy Tomato and the Vegets* (1936) by Jane Lansburgh and Scott Wilson. These photographers foreshadow twentieth-century postmodernism in their unselfconscious, handcrafted construction and unpredictable approach to photography.

Techniques and schools of influence

All artists, including photographers of children's books, are of their time. Photo-illustrated picturebooks reflect prevailing historic movements and innovations in art and technology; all trends, techniques, and styles of fine art and commercial photography have been replicated. Lenses attached to nineteenth-century large-format cameras required long shutter speeds, resulting in impressionistic photographs with movement and blur. Photogravure printing lent drama and softness to reproduced photographs on tissue and paper. Sepia tones were fashionable. Faster camera speeds and the invention of offset lithography furthered changes in the industry. Advertising, fashion, and magazine photography soon influenced the content of photo-illustrated picturebooks. Today's crisp digital technology, with its ease of image capture, manipulation, and casual, candid style, is creating its own statement in children's books.

Long before Dada and Surrealism, photomontage and collage embellished Victorian scrapbooks of the 1860s and 1870s (Siegel 2009). This popular pastime involved decorating album pages with cut photos glued onto and entwined with drawings and hand-illustrated backdrops. The kernel of the very first photomontage books for children began here. These techniques were appropriated from the popular arts and reformulated in avant-garde and political art, as well as in book and poster design. In the spirit of artists John Heartfield, Max Ernst, and László Moholy-Nagy, photomontage and found-photography mixed with paintings and drawings illustrate many photo picturebooks. Expropriated photos and anonymous drawings fill the rhyming pages of Robert Dickey's *The Little Crooked Man and His Funny Animals* (1902). Friedrich Böer's *Klaus, der Herr der Eisenbahnen* (Klaus, Master of the Railroad 1933) is possibly the earliest children's book collaging staged photos into illustrations. Soon after, James Riddell, aka Sepp, humorously mixes media in his book *Annabelle's Atlantic Adventure* (1937a) and in *"Rex" the Coronation Lion Comes to Town* (1937b), an oversized fictional romp through London. Disarming photomontage scenes illustrate *Peter and the Twin Giants of Umptyville* (1954) by Carol Brown and Beverly Clark Roman. Hannah Höch's surreal, avant-garde *Bilderbuch* (Picture Book 1945) mystifies with mythical creatures. A poetic, contemporary melding of mediums is lyrically presented in Lisa Desimini's *My House* (1994).

The technique of photograms has existed since the invention of photo-emulsion. Actual objects are placed on photo paper and exposed to the sun, resulting in images detailed as an X-ray, or enigmatically shadowy. The camera is not involved. In 1843, Anna Atkins used this technique with cyanotype emulsion to create the first known photographically bound book. Revived as a Surrealist tool, artists Christian Schad and Man Ray, eponymously called the process Schadographs and Rayographs, respectively. In children's books, photogram techniques have been used by Anthony Denny (Uncle Anty's Album 1941), Paul Henning (*ABC Picture Book*, 1947) (see Figure 29.1), and decades later by Tana Hoban.

When not on location documenting the real world, many photographers create tabletop sets, or tableaux, in which to photograph their narratives of props, dolls, and puppets. Magical realism and haunting pathos are palpable in the fabricated photos by French photographer, L. Zuzine, in Vera Arnold's drama *La Peine de Philomène* (The Torment of Philomène 1947). Feeling neglected and abused, Philomène's dishes, pots, and pans flee from her. With remorse, the old woman retrieves her errant possessions. Paul Henning's stuffed birds illustrate an unforgettable *Who Killed Cock Robin?* (1945), while wooden dolls cleverly stage Mother Goose and other rhymes in Louis Robbins's early *Dutch Doll Ditties* (1904).

X- RAY

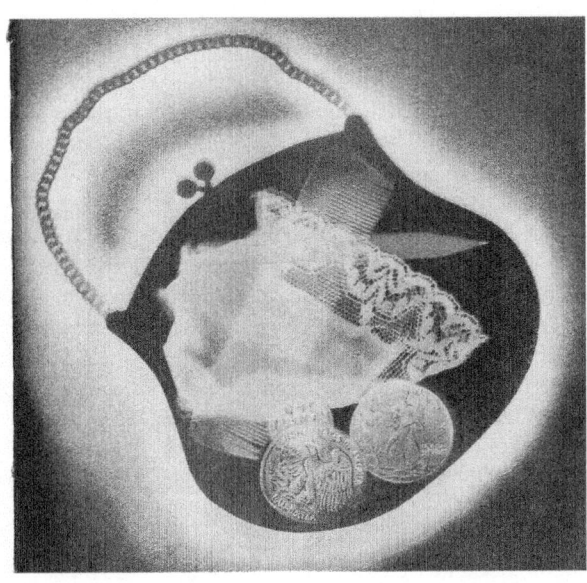

Figure 29.1 Photo by Paul Henning from George Adams's *ABC Picture Book*. London: Collins, 1947.

Styles of art and design are most often traced to the influences of the period. The lingering nostalgia of Pre-Raphaelite drama left its mark on the first wave of photo-illustrated picturebooks. In the early decades of the twentieth century, a surge of creative ferment spread through Europe and Russia. The influence of Bauhaus, Dada, Surrealism, Dutch De Stijl, and Russian Constructivism are clearly visible in photobooks of that time. Equally effecting are the influential schools of thought and educational philosophies of the day. Social Realism fueled 'decisive moments' in documentary photography. The American 'cultural gifts' movement, in celebrating diversity, attempted to subdue racism and anti-immigrant sentiment (Capshaw 2014: 36–37). The impact of book editors, designers, and publishers cannot be overlooked, nor can the stylistic differences from country to country. Photobooks from 1900 have a distinctly different look from books in the 1930s; books from the 1950s differ from those of the 1970s, and so on. Ever influential are trends in child development, vocal educators, and librarians, those who interact with children and those who distribute awards.

Subjects, themes, topics, and issues

The subjects, themes, and topics of photo-illustrated picturebooks are frequently similar to those found in all picturebooks for children. The iconic Mother Goose is infinitely photogenic. Along with Mary Bartlett's *Mother Goose of '93*, Edith R. Wilson and photographer Carolyn Wells produced the photo-illustrated collection *Everychild's Mother Goose* (1918). Dolls and figurines curiously illustrate handwritten rhymes – some rowdy, some bawdy. Two surprisingly sly photo-illustrations reinterpret the rhyme "Peter, Peter, Pumpkin Eater." Magazine photographer Toni Frissell gives a distinctly different interpretation in her *Mother Goose* collection (1948). Children act out rhymes in quiet, lyrical, full-page black-and-white photos. Frissell presents an idealized, homogeneous world, although historically we know she was fresh from photographing military women, African American airmen, and the strife of World War II. Crossing oceans and cultures, Isaac Taylor Headland's book, *Chinese Mother Goose Rhymes* (1900), takes us into rural China. The bilingual text, often laced with antipathy towards girls, sets Chinese nursery ditties alongside documentary snapshots of rural China at the turn of the century.

Photography is well suited to the didactic and educational. Alphabets, numbers, and useful concepts flood the picturebook market. Sontag speaks of "the plurality of meanings that every photograph carries" (1973: 108). This is especially true in baby books – books with few words or with no words at all for the youngest readers. For comparison we look at three such books. *The First Picture Book: Everyday Things for Babies* (1930) by Mary Steichen (Martin) Calderone with her celebrated father, photographer Edward Steichen, fomented an international wave of edifying books for babies and young children, a wave still cresting today (Kümmerling-Meibauer and Meibauer 2005). In the truest form of flattery, the images and title were copied almost verbatim in two subsequent photo picturebooks: *Baby's First Book* (1932) and George Adams's *First Things: A Picture Book in Colour Photography* (1943).

Steichen's photographs present objects formally with no text. Under the spell of the educational theory of the time, Mary Steichen Martin decried fantasy for little children; therefore, true-to-life, luminous images of balls, bread, cup, and crib appear new and untouched by smudgy child hands. Conversely, in the anonymously photographed *Baby's First Book*, a bib is frayed, the bread shows crumbs, toys are dented, and the wagon is worn. Floral wallpaper evokes old-fashioned, income-challenged Midwestern hospitality. A decade later, English photographer Paul Henning's version *First Things* surprises us with delicate color, strong shadows and yet, the very same baby objects. The two American books are almost identical in the placement of a brush quite close to a comb – "almost kissing," says John Updike in his foreword to the re-issue of *The First Picture Book* (1990). In the British book, *First Things*, the comb has jumped into the brush.

ABCs and counting books offer artists full freedom to create. These concept books encourage all ideologies and welcome all styles of art. *The Animal Alphabet* (1900), by Henry Morrow Hyde, with "photographs from real life" by Charles C. Cook, is one of the earliest photo ABCs. Robert Moss's *A.B.C. in Real-Life Pictures* (ca. 1960) brims with humor and sentiment (Figure 29.2). John

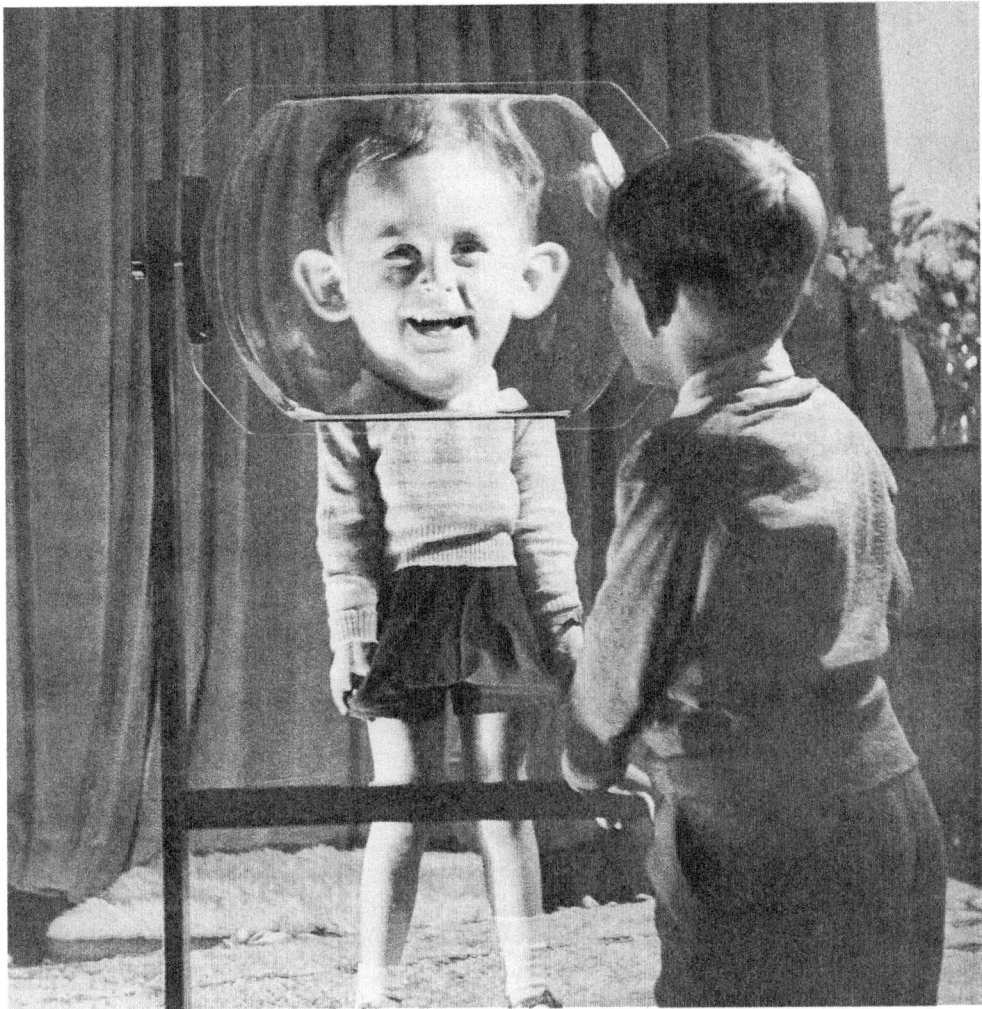

Figure 29.2 Photo from Robert Moss's *A.B.C. in Real-Life Pictures.* London: Juvenile Productions, ca. 1960.

Markham's *Bird ABC* (1950) displays colorful, real birds in their environment. Dexter and Patricia Oliver's *I Want to Be . . .* (1974), uses alphabet letters to highlight professions: "Z, I want to be a Zoologist"; "E, I want to be an Engineer." A documentary photo-illustrated alphabet book for older children is unusual, and *I Want to Be . . .* shows African American children engaged in empowering roles, promoting achievement and potential in a year poised between Martin Luther King Jr.'s assassination and the Soweto uprisings of South Africa.

Dutch photographer Piet Marée's *Van 1 tot 10* (From 1 to 10, 1920) uses toys and dolls in an early counting book, while French photographer Robert Doisneau captures images from nature in his counting book *1, 2, 3, 4, 5* (1955), with a text by Arthur Gregor. In dramatic black-and-white tones, the number 4 presents four white rabbits popping through the slats of a dark diagonal fence, carrots scattered willy-nilly.

Intriguing photographic puzzle books challenge readers. Vladimir Griuntal and G. Yablonsky photo-illustrated the 1932 Russian puzzle book, *Chto eto takoe?* (What Is This?). Containing what Griuntal called "snap-shot puzzles" or in Russian, *snimki-zagadki* (Bird 2011), a magnified photo asks the reader to guess the origin of the image, such as a close-up of keys on a piano. Paul Henning's books *Black and White Lies* (1946) and *What's Inside* (1946) offer textural variations of these visual riddles. Photographers Tana Hoban (*Look Again* 1971) and Henry Horenstein (*A is for . . . ?* 1999) created similarly participatory books decades later. A clever contemporary version encouraging sophisticated visual leaps is Jason Fulford and Tamara Shopsin's *This Equals That* (2014).

The factual reality of photographs is well served in how-to, documentary, science, and travel books. Photo-illustrated picturebooks provide what Julia Hirsch calls "instruction in viewing" (1983–1984: 148). The bold 1930 trademark of the Orthovis Publishing Company reads, "Truth in Pictures." Promising 3-D authenticity with 3-D viewing glasses, Orthovis published informational photo-novelty picturebooks on such incongruent topics as geometry, Native Americans, algebra, and strange animals. Baseball legend Babe Ruth, ever the showman, took "instruction in viewing" to new heights in his eponymous picturebook for young readers, *Babe Ruth's Baseball Advice* (1936). A multitude of theatrically illustrated science books also rely on photographs for authenticity. With high-contrast black-and-white photos, photographer Berenice Abbott dramatically illuminates *Magnet* (1964) and *Motion* (1965) by E. G. Valens. Perhaps intended to alleviate anxiety in children, Roger Russell's simple and comforting black-and-white photos explain a child's tonsillectomy in Ellen Paullin's *No More Tonsils!* (1947).

Children of other lands

It has been suggested that photobooks about 'Children of Other Lands' had origins in response to the horrors of World War II (Ehriander 2011: 155). Although a new urgency created a flood of significant books at that time, there was an earlier passion for cultural exchange at the turn of the twentieth century, when immigrations flowed and travel had become more accessible. Many of these early photo-illustrated travel books were longer in length, as were most books for children of those decades. They were nonetheless replete with photos and are the precursors to mid-twentieth-century photo picturebooks. Josephine Diebitsch Peary, wife of Admiral Peary, documented her Alaskan adventure with baby Marie, her child, in *The Snow Baby* (1901). The same year welcomed a lengthy, round-the-world travel fiction, *The Six Inch Admiral* (1901) by George A. Best. Photo-illustrated with dolls by C. H. Park, the themes of this book range from humane treatment of animals to provocative cultural differences. Photographer and ethnographer Edward Curtis portrayed Native American life and lore in his book, *Indian Days of the Long Ago* (1914), while intrepid photographer Madeline Brandeis travelled the globe with her camera and young daughter formulating her successful Children of All Lands series from 1922–1938, including *Shaun O'Day of Ireland* (1929) and *Carmen of the Gold Coast* (1933).

World traveler Dominique Darbois produced an expansive book series, Les Enfants du Monde (Marchant 2015). Her books *Hassan, l'enfant du desert* (Hassan, Child of the Desert 1960) and *Achouna le petit esquimau* (Achouna the Little Eskimo 1958) show vitality in design unusual for documentary photobooks. Sonia and Tim Gidal made their extensive photo picturebook travel series My Village in the 1950s and 1960s. Documentary photographer Anna Riwkin-Brick enhanced this oeuvre with photo stories from Israel to Ethiopia. The success of her first photobook, *Elle-Kari*, written by Elly Jannes in 1951, portrayed the life of a Sami girl from Lapland. A series of nine books with author Astrid Lindgren followed. Astrid Bergman and Robert Vavra are among a host of others who crafted their stories and focused their cameras internationally.

Travel photobooks transported the world to a child's lap, promoting global friendship and commonality in cultural diversity. With an eye to the unusual, they searched for a shared humanity. Yet questions persist as to whether these books were "promoting tolerance and understanding" or idealizing with an "interest in the exotic" (Druker 2011: 176). Are "primitive aspects of culture [. . .] romanticized," and was their perspective "ethnocentrically Western [. . .] even colonial and imperialistic"? (Ehriander 2011: 155f.). And if so, what are the implications? This is a topic for further discussion.

Harmony and discord

Children's books are not immune to stereotypes, gender and ethnic assumptions, religious prejudice, racism, and xenophobia. Photographs have the power to spur social change as well as inflict damage. For example, a bold sans-serif font lends a modern look to the 1932 *Alphabet* by Emmanuel Sougez. In a global embrace, each word representing a letter is printed in three languages. An unfortunate choice is the letter *C*. At the blackboard, a Caucasian boy draws a dehumanizing stick figure of a Chinese man in 'coolie' attire. The photograph etches the artist's prejudice deeper into the meaning of the text, and deeper still into the heart of the reader.

Hallerloogy's Ride with Santa Claus by Bernie Babcock (1943) is a pernicious photo picturebook in the guise of playful black dolls on a Santa Claus adventure. In contrast, poet Langston Hughes, in his 1932 essay "Books and the Negro Child," wrote, "[f]aced too often by the segregation and scorn of a surrounding white world, America's Negro children are in pressing need of books that will give them back their souls. They do not know the beauty they possess" (cited in Capshaw 2014: 28). The "beauty they possess" comes clear in *My Dog Rinty*, by Ellen Tarry with photographs by Alexander and Alexandra Alland (1946). It tells the story of a young boy coping with his mischievous dog. As they run hither and yon, we delve into the 1940s community of New York's Harlem. The dog is the story's vehicle, but the young boy becomes the power of change. The photos show real children reaching beyond assumed limitations of size and race.

In picturebooks, harmony often gives way to discord as violence is conveniently displaced on animals, dolls, and toys. Dolls are smacked about, dolls run away, spankings abound, teddy bears carry knives, dolls hate, and animal kingdoms make war.

In the 1916 photo picturebook *Pussycat Princess*, by Harry Whittier Frees, Tabbyland is in a messy war with King Fido's Dogland (Anthony 1922). The disquieting black-and-white photos of wooden dolls in Harry Golding and Albert Friend's *War in Dollyland* (1915) reenact war in all its battles, glories and ghastly dismembering. In a tongue-in-cheek, hyperbolic narrative, the Flat Heads battle the Wooden Heads, a doll stands before a firing squad, soldiers fall like dominoes, and a ship is named Terror (Figure 29.3). It was 1915 and the Great War had begun. With wit, Golding illustrates the folly of war.

The humane treatment of animals is another reoccurring theme in photographic picturebooks, especially in the late nineteenth and early twentieth centuries as the message of the newly formed Society for the Prevention of Cruelty to Animals spread internationally. Elizabeth Gordon's *The Mighty Hunter of Toyland* (1908) weaves politics, animal cruelty, and girl power into a story about runaway pet bears. The doll protagonist resembles the big-game hunter, President Theodore Roosevelt, for whom the Teddy Bear was named. The hunt ends with rifles lowered, bears saved, and life celebrated.

Characters

Substituting for the child, dolls and animals often dramatize the rebellion, existential loneliness, and kaleidoscope of emotion children experience. No one expresses loneliness as profoundly as Dare Wright in her series of books posing dolls fashioned in her own image. *The Lonely Doll* (1957) and *Lona, A Fairy Tale* (1963) are just two of her transparently revealing stories.

Crafting handmade dolls and photographing them in natural settings of woodlands and streams, Swedish artist Karin Fryxell portrays the mysterious world of fairies and trolls in her photo-illustrated picturebooks – among them *Luddkolts Aventyr* (Luddkolts Adventure 1945) and *Sotlugg och Linlugg* (Sotlugg and Linlugg 1941). Themes of mischief, willfulness, and doll abuse come to the fore in Carine and Will Cadby's *A Dolls Day* (1915) where dolls rise up, protest, and run away. Similarly, in Edna Billings's *Buttons and Bo* (1940), paper dolls engage in midnight shenanigans. Most often, the aftermath of such rebellion is remorse, contrition, and a welcome return to the child-parent.

Prolific photographer Harry Whittier Frees immortalized dressed-up kittens, puppies, piglets, and bunnies early in the twentieth century. His illustrations for *Bunnies of Bunnyboro* (1916) and *Animals*

Figure 29.3 Photo by Albert Friend from Harry Golding's *War in Dollyland*. London: Ward, Lock & Co, 1915.

in *Land and Sea* (1915) are but a sliver of his prodigious output, still popular today. Animal photographer Ylla, née Camilla Koffler, collaborated with writers Margaret Wise Brown and Crosby Bonsall to produce many animal dramas such as *They All Saw It* (1944) and *Look Who's Talking* (1962). Hyperreal, stroboscopic photos by *Life* magazine photographer Frank Scherschel tell the story of a very real bear in Robert Doyle's *Tuffy* (1942), while Jean Tourane's *Firmin* (1952) is the fanciful story of a pig, like Wilbur of *Charlotte's Web*, escaping the butcher's knife. Contemporary photobooks by William Wegman and his costumed Weimaraner dogs apply sly wit to original and retold tales in which dogs deliver pizza, reenact Mother Goose, partake in farm chores, and pose for ABCs. Photographers Milada Einhornova, Henry B. Kane, and others offer equally riveting picturebooks with live animals as lead characters.

Dressed-up fruits and vegetables also enliven photobooks. In Henry Rox's photo-illustrated picturebook *Banana Circus* (1940), sculpted bananas perform dazzling circus acts. Saxton Freymann and Joost Elffers create a believable universe transforming vegetables and fruit in popular books such as *How Are You Peeling?* (2004) and *Gus and Button* (2001).

Photo picturebooks also revel in retellings of favorite folk and fairy tales. In Bertha Parker Hall's *Ducky Daddles and the Three Bears* (1921), a toy duck and three doll friends reenact the story of *Goldilocks and the Three Bears*. *The Three Koala Bears and Little Goldilocks* (1935) offers an Australian twist. Other tales retold with cameras are *Cinderella* (William Wegman (1993), Paul Henning with Amalia Serkin (Adams 1942)), Jane Wattenberg's *Henny-Penny* (2000) and *Never Cry Woof!* (2005), and Graham Rawles's vibrant version of *The Wizard of Oz* (2008). A comparative study of photographic and hand-illustrated picturebook retellings would be compelling.

Transformations: up- and downsizing

Ever popular shape-shifting transformations stretch our imaginations. Jonathan Swift published his satirical tale *Gulliver's Travels* in 1726. Gulliver was a giant in a miniature land and miniature in a land of giants. Elsewhere, Alice in Wonderland followed the directive on a bottle that read, "Drink Me." From tiny, she stretched tall. Both tales of transformation have been recreated in photobooks several times over. The shrinking metaphor in *Jaunts of Junior* (1911) showcases Arthur Phelan's meticulous darkroom and retouching skills in a photomontage fantasy created long before digital technology (Figure 29.4).

Two Russian photobooks brilliantly transport miniature children into altered landscapes. In *Neobyknovennye Priklyuchenija Karika i Vali* (The Remarkable Adventures of Karik and Valya 1937) by Jan Larry, photo-illustrated by S. Petrovich, children riding a dragonfly soar into realms of fantasy in a photo-narrative based in reality. The study of electricity is dangerous and exhilarating in *Puteshestvie po Elektrolampe* (The Journey Inside the Electric Lamp 1937), by Nikolai Bulatov and Pavel Lopatin with seamless photomontage by M. Makhalov. In Hans Malmberg and Gunnel Linde's *The Enchanted Forest* (1966), three siblings on a mission shrink to the size of frogs, skunks, and hedgehogs. By popping a pill, South African author and entomologist Sydney Harold Skaife shrinks two children in the service of a scientific adventure in *The Strange Old Man* (1930). The inherent authenticity of a photograph amps up the drama as we give credence to these psychedelic projections of children riding snails and hiding from insects.

Conclusion

Photobooks are time capsules. For well over a century, the camera's lens has sharpened and blurred our preoccupations. From a bird's-eye view we witness the sociology, design movements, political, scientific, and artistic ferment of the decades in just this slim slice of illustration, the photo-illustrated picturebook.

Many topics yet to be explored include questions of authenticity in documentaries, inherent bias, and misinformation. The expression of humor and the role of nostalgia, as well as attitudes of children and on child-rearing itself might be traced. An exploration of the artists themselves, the countries who vigorously published photobooks and the advocacy of certain publishers who gave photobooks momentum would be welcome.

In assessing the sum of picturebooks, the rich variety and extent of photographic children's books may be surprising to many. While photography's appeal in the children's realm is continually debated, there is no clear use – or, as has been suggested, misuse (Bader 1976: 100) – of photography in picturebooks. A camera, much like a paintbrush or a stylus, is but a tool. And yet, the ability of the camera to record the world accurately sets it apart. A conundrum and continual fascination rises from the notion that although photography presents factual information, photo fictions run rampant in the picturebook. The tension between the assumed expectation of genuine information and the

Figure 29.4 Photomontage by Arthur Phelan from Lillian Hunt's *Jaunts of Junior*. New York: Harper & Brothers, 1911.

frequent fictional application gives the photo-illustrated picturebook a unique quality distinguishing it from all others.

References

Adams, George A. (1943) *First Things: A Picture Book in Colour Photography*, photos by Paul Henning, London: Collins.

Adams, George A. (1942) *The Story of Cinderella – A Fairy Tale in Colour Photography*, photos by Paul Henning, dolls by Amalia Serkin, London: Collins.

Adams, George A. (1947) *ABC Picture Book*, photos by Paul Henning, New York: Platt and Munk.

Adams, Virginia Best (1941) *Michael and Anne in the Yosemite Valley*, photos by Ansel Adams, New York: Studio.

Andersen, Hans Christian (1866) *Fotograferede Børnegrupper af Harald Paetz; med tildigtede Riim af H.C. Andersen*, photos by Harald Paetz, Copenhagen.

Anthony, Edward (1922) *Pussycat Princess*, photos by Harry Whittier Frees, New York: The Century Co.

Arnold, Véra (1947) *La Peine de Philomène, adapté du Conte russe de K. Tchoukovski*, par Alice Orane, photos by L. Zuzine, Paris: Éditions Albin Michel.

Babcock, Bernie (1943) *Hallerloogy's Ride with Santa Claus*, Arkansas: B. Babcock.

Baby's First Book (1932) New York: Saalfield.

Bader, Barbara (1976) *American Picturebooks from Noah's Ark to the Beast Within*, New York: Macmillan.

Bartlett, Mrs. (1892) *Old Friends with New Faces*, New York: American Photographic.

Bartlett, Mrs. N. Gray (1893) *Mother Goose of '93*, Boston, MA: Joseph Knight Co.

Best, George A. (1900) *The Home of Santa Claus*, photos by Arthur Ullyett, London: T. Fisher Unwin.

Best, George A. (1901) *The Six Inch Admiral*, photos by C.H. Park, London: Grant Richards.

Billings, Edna (1940) *Buttons and Bo*, New York: Random House.

Bird, Robert, ed. (2011) *Adventures in the Soviet Imaginary: Children's Books and Graphic Art*, Chicago: University of Chicago Library.

Böer, Friedrich (1933) *Klaus, der Herr der Eisenbahnen*, Baden-Baden: Stuffer.

Bonsall, Crosby (1962) *Look Who's Talking*, photos by Ylla, New York: Harper & Brothers.

Brandeis, Madeline (1929) *Shaun O'Day of Ireland*, New York: Grosset and Dunlap.

Brandeis, Madeline (1933) *Carmen of the Gold Coast*, New York: Grosset and Dunlap.

Brown, Carol (1954) *Peter and the Twin Giants of Umptyville*, photos by Beverly Clark Roman, New York: Scylla.

Brown, Margaret Wise (1944) *They All Saw It*, photos by Ylla, New York: Harper & Brothers.

Cadby, Carine (1915) *A Dolls Day*, photos by Will Cadby, London: Mills & Boon.

Calderone, Mary Steichen (1930) *The First Picture Book: Everyday Things for Babies*, photos by Edward Steichen, New York: Harcourt, Brace (reprinted in 1991 with a foreword by John Updike, New York: Fotofolio-Whitney).

Capshaw Smith, Katherine (2014) *Civil Rights Childhood: Picturing Liberation in African American Photobooks*, Minneapolis: University of Minnesota Press.

Curtis, Edward (1914) *Indian Days of the Long Ago*, New York: World Book Company.

Darbois, Dominique (1960) *Hassan, l'enfant du desert*, Paris: Fernand Nathan.

Darbois, Dominique (1958) *Achouna le petit esquimau*, Paris: Fernand Nathan.

Desimini, Lisa (1994) *My House*, New York: Henry Holt.

Dickey, Robert L. (1902) *Little Crooked Man and His Funny Animals*, Henry Neil: Chicago.

Doyle, Robert (1942) *Tuffy*, photos by Frank Scherschel, New York: Simon and Schuster.

Druker, Elina (2011) "To Mirror the Real: Ideology and Aesthetics in Photographic Picturebooks," in Bettina Kümmerling-Meibauer and Astrid Surmatz (eds) *Beyond Pippi Longstocking. Intermedial and International Aspects of Astrid Lindgren's Works*, New York: Routledge, 173–183.

Ehriander, Helene (2011) "Everyday and Exotic: Astrid Lindgren's Co-Operation With Anna Riwkin-Brick," in Bettina Kümmerling-Meibauer and Astrid Surmatz (eds) *Beyond Pippi Longstocking. Intermedial and International Aspects of Astrid Lindgren's Works*, New York: Routledge, 155–172.

Emerson, Peter Henry (1889) *Naturalistic Photography for Students of the Art*, New York: Scholar's Choice (reprinted in 2015).

Freyman, Saxton (2001) *Gus and Button*, photos by Joost Elffers, New York: Arthur A. Levine/Scholastic.

Freyman, Saxton (2004) *How Are You Peeling?*, photos by Joost Elffers, New York: Arthur A. Levine/Scholastic.

Frees, Harry Whittier (1915) *Animals in Land and Sea*, Boston, MA: Lothrop, Lee & Shepard Co.

Frissell, Toni (1948) *Mother Goose*, New York: Harper & Brothers.

Fryxell, Karin (1941) *Sotlugg och Linlugg: En saga om smatroll*, Stockholm: Nordisk Rotogravyr.

Fryxell, Karin (1945) *Luddkolts Aventyr*, Stockholm: Nordisk Rotogravyr.

Fulford, Jason (2014) *This Equals That*, photos by Tamara Shopsin, New York: Aperture.

Golding, Harry (1915) *War in Dollyland*, photos by Albert Friend, London: Ward, Lock.

Gordon, Elizabeth (1908) *The Mighty Hunter of Toyland*, New York: Dodd, Mead.

Gregor, Arthur (1955) *1, 2, 3, 4, 5*, photos by Robert Doisneau, Philadelphia: J.B. Lippincott.

Griuntal, Vladimir (1932) *Chto eto takoe?*, photos by G. Yablonsky, Moscow: OGIZ, Molodaia gvardija.

Hall, Bertha Parker (1921) *Ducky Daddles and the Three Bears*, New York: E.P. Dutton.

Headland, Isaac Taylor (1900) *Chinese Mother Goose Rhymes*, New York: Fleming H. Revell.

Henning, Paul (1945) *Who Killed Cock Robin?*, London: Methuen & Co.

Henning, Paul (1946) *Black and White Lies*, London: Guilford Press.

Henning, Paul (1946) *What's Inside*, London: Methuen.

Hirsh, Julia (1983–84) "Photography in Children's Books: A Generic Approach," *The Lion and the Unicorn* 7/8: 140–155.

Hoban, Tana (1971) *Look Again*, New York: Simon and Schuster.

Höch, Hannah (2010) *Bilderbuch*, Berlin: The Green Box.

Horenstein, Henry (1999) *A is for . . . ?: A Photographer's Alphabet of Animals*, New York: HMH Books for Young Readers.

Hunt, Lillian B. (1911) *Jaunts of Junior*, photos by Arthur Phelan, New York: Harper & Brothers.

Hyde, Henry Morrow (1900) *The Animal Alphabet*, photos by Charles C. Cook, New York: George M. Hill.

Jannes, Elly (1951) *Elle-Kari*, photos by Anna Riwkin-Brick, Stockholm: Raben & Sjögren.

Karasik, Mikhail (2010) *Udarnaya kniga sovetskoi detvory: Fotoillyustratsiya i fotomontazh v knige dlya detei i yunoshestva 1920–1930*, Moscow: Kontakt-Kultura.

The Three Koala Bears and Little Goldilocks (1935) Australia: Cinesound Productions.

Kümmerling-Meibauer, Bettina, and Meibauer, Jörg (2005) "First Picture Books, Early Concepts: Early Concept Books," *The Lion and the Unicorn* 3: 324–347.

Lansburgh, Jane, and Wilson, Scott (1936) *Tommy Tomato and the Vegets*, photos by Louis Wegner, New York: Oquaga Press.

Larry, Jan (1937) *Neobyknovennye Priklyuchenija Karika i Vali*, photos by S. Petrovich, Moscow.

Lifton, Betty Jean (1969) *A Dog's Guide to Tokyo*, photos by Eikoh Hosoe, New York: W.W. Norton.

Linde, Gunnel (1966) *The Enchanted Forest*, photos by Hans Malmberg, Manchester: World Distributors.

Lopatin, Pavel, and Bulatov, Nikolai (1937) *Puteshestvie po Elektrolampe*, photomontage by M. Makalov, Moscow.

Marchant, Frédérique (2015) "Dominique Darbois et la collection 'Enfants du monde,'" *Strenæ* 8: 2–15.

Marée, Piet (1930) *Van 1 tot 10*, Den Haag: G.B. Van Goor Zonens.

Markham, John (1950) *Bird ABC*, London: Collins.

Mitchell, W.G. (1891) *Afternoon Tea*, Boston, MA: Nims & J. Knight.

Moon, Sarah (2002) *Little Red Riding Hood*, Mankato, MN: Creative Editions.

Moss, Robert (ca. 1960) *A.B.C. in Real-Life Pictures*, London: Juvenile Productions.

Oliver, Dexter (1974) *I Want to Be . . .* , photos by Patricia Oliver, Chicago: Third World Press.

Orville, Florence (1916) *Bunnies of Bunnyboro*, photos by Harry Whittier Frees, New York: Simmons-Peckham.

Paullin, Ellen (1947) *No More Tonsils!*, photos by Roger Russell, New York: Island Press Cooperative.

Peary, Josephine Diebitsch (1901) *The Snow Baby*, New York: Frederick A. Stokes.

Rawle, Graham (2008) *The Wizard of Oz*, Berkeley, CA: Counterpoint Press.

Riddell, James (1937a) *Annabelle's Atlantic Adventure*, London: Hutchinson.

Riddell, James (1937b) *"Rex" the Coronation Lion Comes to Town*, London: Hutchinson.

Robbins, Louis (1904) *Dutch Doll Ditties*, New York: Longmans, Green.

Robinson, Henry Peach (1869) *The Pictorial Effect in Photography*, London: The British Library (reprinted in 2010).

Rothenstein, Julian, and Budashevskaya, Olga (eds) (2013) *Inside the Rainbow: Russian Children's Literature 1920–1935: Beautiful Books, Terrible Times*, London: Redstone Press.

Rox, Henry (1940) *Banana Circus*, New York: G.P. Putnam's Sons.

Ruth, Babe (1936) *Babe Ruth's Baseball Advice*, New York: Rand McNally.

Shearer, John (1970) *I Wish I Had an Afro*, New York: Cowles Book Co.

Sherman, Cindy (1992) *Fitcher's Bird*, New York: Rizzoli.

Siegel, Elizabeth (2009) *Playing with Pictures: The Art of Victorian Photocollage*, Chicago: Art Institute of Chicago in association with Yale University Press.

Skaife, Sydney Harold (1930) *The Strange Old Man*, London: Longmans, Green.

Sontag, Susan (1973) *On Photography*, New York: Farrar, Straus and Giroux.

Sougez, Emmanuel (1932) *Alphabet*, Paris: Antoine Roche.

Tarry, Ellen (1946) *My Dog Rinty*, photos by Alexandra and Alexander Alland, New York: Viking Press.

Tourane, Jean (1952) *Firmin*, Paris: Ides et Calendes.

Tyner, Frederick (1939) *A Trip to the Man on the Moon*, photos by Paul Skoog, Minneapolis, MN: Skoog-Smith Printing Co.

Valens, E.G. (1964) *Magnet*, photos by Berenice Abbott, New York: World.

Valens, E.G. (1965) *Motion*, photos by Berenice Abbott, New York: World.

Wattenberg, Jane (2000) *Henny-Penny*, New York: Scholastic Press.

Wattenberg, Jane (2005) *Never Cry Woof!*, New York: Scholastic Press.

Wilson, Edith R. (1918) *Everychild's Mother Goose*, photos by Carolyn Wells, New York: Macmillan.

Wegman, William (1993) *Cinderella*, New York: Hyperion.

White, Mus (1999) *From the Mundane to the Magical: Photographically Illustrated Children's Books, 1854–1945 and Beyond*, Los Angeles, CA: Dawson's Book Shop.

Wright, Dare (1957) *The Lonely Doll*, New York: Doubleday.

Wright, Dare (1963) *Lona*, New York: Random House.

30
PICTUREBOOKS AND COMICS

Lara Saguisag

Although major picturebook studies have briefly noted the connections between picturebooks and comics (Nodelman 1988; Nikolajeva and Scott 2001; op de Beeck 2010), the emergence of in-depth comparative studies of the two genres is a relatively new development. Such recent work tends to emphasize that distinguishing between the two forms is no easy task. Rather than shoring up the line between picturebooks and comics, scholarship points to the permeability of this boundary. The 2012 symposium "Why Comics Are and Are Not Picture Books," edited by Charles Hatfield and Craig Svonkin, emphasizes the broad intersections between the two genres. As Philip Nel, one of the featured essayists, puts it, picturebooks and comics "are not fundamentally different genres [. . .] [they] differ in degree, rather than in kind" (2012: 445).

The symposium, however, also proposes that picturebooks and comics ultimately differ in ideological framework rather than form. While both are visual-verbal narratives that frequently appropriate formal elements from one another, each maintains different assumptions about childhood and presumed (child) readers. Ideological contexts, specifically the ways each genre is shaped by and participates in contemporary cultural constructions of childhood, have been explored by other scholars (Gibson 2010; Beaty 2012: 40; Sanders 2013). In "Watch This Space: Childhood, Picturebooks and Comics," a special issue of *The Journal of Comics and Graphic Novels*, edited by Mel Gibson, Golnar Nabizadeh, and Kay Sambell (2014), several articles demonstrate how ideological as well as historical and cultural contexts are vital to comparative studies of picturebooks and comics.

This chapter seeks to contribute to this ongoing, lively discussion of picturebook-comic relationships. It reviews existing studies that compare and contrast the formal elements of the two genres, and proposes that rather than maintaining a focus on identifying formal overlaps, scholarship should also examine the purpose of appropriation of narrative techniques and devices. The chapter also argues that a deeper and deliberate consideration of the histories of comics is necessary to arrive at a more comprehensive understanding of how picturebooks and comics converge and diverge. As comics' status has changed across time, the notion that the genre is necessarily subversive needs to be interrogated. Moreover, as comics have branched out into various formats, styles, and systems across time and geography, the diversity of comics in Western and global contexts needs to be acknowledged when comparing and contrasting picturebooks and comics.

A focus on form

Picturebooks and comics are generally understood as two distinct genres, and scholars have carefully parsed texts and contexts in attempts to identify exactly how the two differ from one another. Critics concede that delineating between picturebooks and comics is not without its challenges. As Joe Sutliff Sanders reminds us, definitions of picturebooks and comics are virtually interchangeable: both tell narratives by placing images in sequence, creating interplay between verbal and visual modalities, and utilizing the page turn (2013: 57). Hybrid texts further confound efforts to distinguish between the two. Maurice Sendak's *In the Night Kitchen* (1970), Raymond Briggs's *The Snowman* (1978), Jan Ormerod's *Sunshine* (1981), Peter Sís's *The Wall: Growing Up Behind the Iron Curtain* (2007), and Shaun Tan's *The Arrival* (2007) are just a few of the many titles that straddle – and trouble – the boundary between picturebooks and comics. Furthermore, artists such as Crockett Johnson, Dave McKean, David Small, and Art Spiegelman have published both picturebooks and comics, an indication that practitioners themselves recognize the fluidity between the two genres.

Still, efforts to distinguish between picturebooks and comics persist, especially when those that consider formal elements. One aspect that is often identified as key to differentiating between the two is the use of panels. In comics, each page is typically divided into multiple panels, while in a picturebook, a page or spread is often occupied by a single panel. Although comics narratives sometimes use a "splash page" – a panel that takes up a single page or spread – this device means to provide emphasis. Juxtaposed with smaller panels that precede and proceed it, the splash page serves to capture the reader's attention or create a sense of surprise, awe, or climax. Panels also shape a reader's sense of time. As each panel represents what Hillary Chute calls a "[box] of time" (2010: 9), the number of panels helps pace the narrative. Hence, in comics, multiple panels create a sense of time passing in a single page, while in picturebooks time "tends to unfold over many pages" (Nel 2012: 445).

Another aspect that is frequently used to differentiate between picturebooks and comics is the types of connections between visual and verbal modalities. Scott McCloud proposes that in comics, words and pictures combine in seven ways: (1) word specific, in which pictures illustrate, but do not elaborate on words; (2) picture specific, in which words primarily serve as auditory accompaniment to pictures; (3) duo specific, in which both text and image communicate the same idea; (4) additive, in which one modality elaborates the other; (5) parallel, in which words and pictures do not appear to follow the same narrative line; (6) montage, in which the words are integrated into the fictive visual world; and (7) interdependent, in which both modalities work together to arrive at a meaning that neither the visual nor the verbal could express independently (1993: 153–155). For Hatfield, comics depend on a "tension" between text and image: verbal and visual codes work "to gloss, to illustrate, to contradict or complicate or ironize the other" (2005: 133). But neither McCloud's nor Hatfield's discussions of the relationships of words and pictures seem exclusive to comics. In fact, picturebook terminology used to describe the interplay of words and pictures, such as congruency, symmetry, complementation, elaboration, amplification, extension, contradiction, deviation, and counterpointing (see Schwarcz 1982; Doonan 1993; Nikolajeva and Scott 2001), echo the descriptions offered by McCloud and Hatfield.

A clearer difference emerges when considering how each genre defines spatial relationships between words and pictures. Often, text and image are more closely integrated in comics than in picturebooks. As Neil Cohn (2013) puts it, visual and verbal modalities are linked in comics in three ways: in inherent relationships, words exist as part of the visual world; in emergent relationships, words are not "embedded" in the visual world but are implied as originating from a "root" visual source, as in speech balloons and sound effects emanating from a character or object; in adjoined relationships, words are not directly attached to the pictures, although there is an implied connection between the two modalities, as in images accompanied by narrative captions. Thus comics employ multiple kinds of text-image relationships. Although Cohn does not consider picturebooks, his description of adjoined relationships is most fitting when thinking about the spatial relationship of visual and verbal modalities in the genre. Additionally, there is less proximity between words and pictures in picturebooks than in comics. While narrative captions in comics are often overlaid on an image, the verbal text in picturebooks frequently appears above or below the image, or on the opposite page.

Breaking formal boundaries: not only how, but also why

Of course, one does not have to look far to find titles that disregard the formal conventions discussed earlier. Lat's *Kampung Boy* (1979) and Renee French's *h day* (2010), marketed as graphic novels, feature single-panel pages and spreads. Pascal Doury's comics narrative *Paul* (1989) not only uses single panels per page but also relies on adjoined relationships between words and pictures, with narrative captions appearing outside and below the panels. Conversely, picturebooks also borrow formal devices associated with comics. Barbara Lehman's *The Red Book* (2004) and David Wiesner's *Flotsam* (2006) include pages that are divided into multiple panels. Mini Grey's *Traction Man Is Here!* (2005) uses inherent, emergent, and adjoined word-picture relationships, with words appearing in speech balloons, sound effect bubbles, and caption boxes, as well as in the world inhabited by the characters.

These hybrid titles remind us that the border between picturebooks and comics are permeable, even artificial. It may dissatisfy some to think that distinguishing between the two genres is a problem without a clear solution. But as Nel suggests, this predicament also reminds us that "genre itself is multiple, unstable, and always evolving" (2012: 453). In other words, the tricky issue of differentiating picturebooks and comics enables us to question the assumption that establishing rigid categories is necessary to the scholarly enterprise.

Another vein worth exploring is *why* artists co-opt tropes and conventions often associated with another genre. What narrative purpose does such formal appropriation serve? Such a question could perhaps add nuance to studies of hybrid books like *The Wall: Growing Up Behind the Iron Curtain* (2007), Peter Sís's account of his boyhood in Communist Czechoslovakia. As *Booklist* puts it, the book is "a powerful combination of graphic novel and picture book" (Mattson 2007). As with many picturebooks, the illustrations in *The Wall* are accompanied by narrative captions at the bottom of the page. Occasionally, text also appears along the margins. Written in a documentary-like tone, these marginal notes describe the rules imposed upon Czech citizens. The book also recalls comics, as it occasionally features balloons and multi-panel pages. *The Wall*'s blending of different genre conventions can be understood as necessary to its effort to comment on political ideology. By splitting some pages into several panels, Sís emphasizes how the government sowed social division among its citizenry. The multiple, separate panels also serve as a graphic representation of how, in an atmosphere of suspicion and surveillance, Czechs resorted to isolating themselves from one another in order to avoid the prying eyes of relatives, neighbors, and the secret police.

The physical separation of text and image in *The Wall* also creates a sense of social estrangement and fragmentation. Text and image occupy different spatial planes, and the limited interaction between the two narrative modes expresses Sís's struggle with confronting his childhood memories. In order to tell his story, he uses a collage of texts and images, pasting together short narrative captions, marginal annotations, journal excerpts, black-and-white illustrations, photographs, paintings, and sketches. His reliance on multiple types of verbal and visual texts implies that as an adult artist, he recalls the traumas of his past in a disjointed rather than a cohesive manner (Saguisag 2012).

While the comics elements in *The Wall* are used to explore themes of suffering and alienation, Mo Willems's picturebook *Don't Let the Pigeon Drive the Bus!* (2003) uses comics devices to create humor and a sense of immediacy. Willems sets the stage for comedy through the use of a cartoonish style commonly found in humorous comics strips and cartoons. The book's protagonist, an anthropomorphized pigeon, is also reminiscent of characters in 'funny animal' comic books. Meanwhile, word balloons help build intimacy between the characters and the reader. The use of balloons 'attaches' speech to the characters and sustains the illusion that the driver and the pigeon are speaking directly to the reader. While Sanders asserts that comics are typically difficult to read aloud (2013: 74), *Don't Let the Pigeon* arguably uses word balloons to imply an 'audible' dialogue between character and reader; the reader is encouraged not only to read aloud the pigeon's lines but also to respond to him. Willems also uses multiple panels to establish plot and characterization. Most of the pages feature a single panel, but Willems builds toward the climax by suddenly dividing a spread into several panels (Figure 30.1). These multiple panels also characterize the pigeon as persistent and manipulative, showing how he employs several strategies to convince the reader to let him drive the bus.

Comics narratives also borrow picturebook conventions. Jenny Allen's *The Long Chalkboard and Other Stories* (2006), a collection of three short stories illustrated by Jules Feiffer, is marketed as a graphic novel, yet its format recalls that of a picturebook. Most of its pages contain a single discrete image with narrative captions appearing above or below it. Allen's straightforward, 'simple' prose may also remind readers of the 'easy' language of picturebooks. Especially notable is "What Happened," the second entry in *The Long Chalkboard*, as it is a picturebook-like narrative *about* making picturebooks. "What Happened" tells the story of Audrey, a children's book author who enters into a professional and romantic partnership with another author whom she previously viewed as a rival. The story

Figure 30.1 Spread from Mo Willems's *Don't Let the Pigeon Drive the Bus!* New York: Hyperion, 2003.

also references activities that have become institutionalized in the world of picturebook publishing, including editorial meetings, book signings, promotional events, and awards banquets.

Ultimately, "What Happened" presents a reductive view of picturebooks. Allen's story characterizes picturebooks as clichéd narratives that contain "Valuable Lessons." It also implies that adults involved in the children's publishing industry tend to act juvenile: Audrey is deeply insecure and "thin-skinned," and the "coveted Kenny Award" is named after a man who is "forty-three years old [and] still lived with his parents." That *The Long Chalkboard* is classified as a graphic novel rather than, say, a picturebook for adults, is clearly an effort to disassociate the book from a so-called childish genre.

Reconsidering the conservatism of picturebooks and the radicalism of comics

While "What Happened" implicitly criticizes picturebooks as formulaic and didactic, many adults hold a positive view of picturebooks precisely because these texts are assumed to be safe, predictable, and effective in teaching literacy and morals. Comics, on the other hand, have been historically viewed as crude, anti-intellectual, and even dangerous materials. Reformers in early twentieth-century America denounced newspaper comic strips for supposedly encouraging bad behavior in children (Saguisag 2015). In the mid-twentieth century, campaigns against so-called vulgar comic books emerged in countries in Asia, Europe, and North America (Lent 2009). The most widely documented of these attacks on comic books was led by psychiatrist Fredric Wertham, whose book *Seduction of the Innocent: The Influence of Comic Books on Today's Youth* (1954) and testimony before the US Senate Subcommittee on Juvenile Delinquency helped popularize the view that comic books cause juvenile delinquency and sexual deviance.

As some scholars suggest, the contrast between the ways picturebooks and comics are valued is what ultimately solidifies the boundary between the two genres. While picturebooks are generally embraced as socializing, edifying texts that "commemorate childhood and grant knowledge in culturally sanctioned ways" (op de Beeck 2012: 475), comics are weighed down by the connotation that they miseducate the young or prematurely introduce children to themes that 'naturally' belong in the sphere of adulthood. Picturebooks and comics are also shaped by different assumptions about their readerships. As Sanders states, picturebook reading is typically mediated by adults and "anticipate being read aloud by a proficient reader/viewer to a preliterate reader/viewer" (2013: 74). Comics, however, are not "chaperoned" by adults and instead assume a solitary, independent child reader (Sanders 2013: 74). For Sanders, the removal of adult mediation in comics reading is what makes the genre suspect in the eyes of adults (2013: 75–76).

Scholars seem to find the anti-authoritarian aura of comics to be particularly appealing. Op de Beeck, for example, implies that comics are more empowering and liberating for child readers when she states that the genre "retains its 'seduction of the innocent' status, whereas well-behaved picture books participate in the socially acceptable indoctrination of the innocent" (2012: 476). But the claim that picturebooks tend to be conservative and comics tend to be subversive limits our understanding of both genres. Kimberley Reynolds reminds us that despite being "highly regulated" and "orthodox," children's literature (including picturebooks) can be and has been a "breeding ground and an incubator for innovation" (2007: 15). She not only illustrates how such innovation can be seen in terms of formal experimentation, but also points to Julia Mickenberg's research on how children's literature introduces young readers to "visionary thinking and [. . .] political engagement" (16). Reynolds specifically cites the juxtaposition of verbal and visual modalities as key to radicalism in children's literature. While she identifies comics as distinct from children's literature, we can infer that picturebooks and comics, both being visual-verbal narratives, are cut from the same subversive cloth.

As we consider the radical promise of picturebooks, we also need to reexamine the assumption that comics inherently have what op de Beeck refers to as a "countercultural function" (2012: 476). Bart Beaty cautions against the "essentialism" of equating comics with subversion:

> [t]he idea that comics are subversive [...] seems to be little more than a defence mechanism. Condemned for much of their history by proponents of legitimated cultures, participants in the comics world have themselves adopted a rhetoric that purports to make a virtue of their marginalized social position.
>
> *46–47*

To insist that comics are fundamentally countercultural glosses over the fact that these texts have been deployed to reproduce and perpetuate the values and prejudices of dominant cultural groups. American comic books, for example, have reinforced patriarchal, Anglo-Saxon, and imperialist ideologies through sexist, racist, and jingoistic images. Hergé's *The Adventures of Tintin* series (1930–1976) is a global phenomenon that still confounds critics because of its racist typographies of Chinese, Congolese, Arabs, and other non-white peoples. Moreover, mass-market comics arguably induct young readers into the culture of capitalist consumerism. While comics allow children to exercise purchasing power, agency, and independence (Kline 1993), they are also commercial products that define children's public participation as consumerist.

Moreover, it is important to note that in the twenty-first century, so-called subversive comics have become mainstream (see Saguisag 2017). From the 1970s to the 1990s, underground comix artists such as Robert Crumb, Justin Green, and Trina Robbins and alternative comics pioneers such as Françoise Mouly and Art Spiegelman rallied to demonstrate the artistic, social, and political significance of what was then a peripheral genre (Mouly and Spiegelman 2016). Their efforts have not been in vain: today, comics, especially in the graphic novel format, are now upheld as an important literary and artistic form. It was the critical and commercial success of comics among adult readers that motivated gatekeepers of children's literature to reexamine and eventually elevate the status of comics for children (Hamer 2013: 167–168). Comics are now promoted as appealing materials for emerging and reluctant readers. The genre is also seen as effective in developing visual-verbal literacy, a skill that is perceived to be essential for young people growing up in the digital age (see Jaffe 2014). But the comics endorsed by today's teachers, librarians, and industry leaders no longer resemble the ten-cent magazines that children purchased in drugstores and newspaper stands in mid-twentieth-century America. As comics have become reconfigured as educational tools, they now resemble picturebooks more than 'forbidden' comic books. It is quite telling that the children's comics imprint TOON Books, founded by comics 'rebels' Mouly and Spiegelman, unabashedly declare that "[e]ach TOON Book has been vetted by educators to ensure that the language and the narratives will nurture young minds" (Mouly and Spiegelman). Thus children's comics in the twenty-first century are being tamed to resemble well-mannered picturebooks.

This domestication of comics has also redefined children's interactions with the genre. While earlier forms of children's comics enabled young people to engage in a private peer culture that was largely insulated from adults, they also empowered children by inviting them to participate in public culture. Certainly, the comics industry encouraged children to take part in economic culture through the act of consumption. But comics producers also coaxed young readers to play a role in cultural production. In the United States, creators and publishers of comic strips and comic books frequently entered into dialogue with their young audiences, soliciting ideas through contests and letters columns and encouraging readers to co-opt characters and narratives by including "From Our Readers" pages, in which readers' drawings and stories were published (Pustz 1999, Saguisag 2015: 117–120). So while it is commonly held that comics remove adults from the equation, history shows that producers turned comics into spaces in which children and adults could communicate and collaborate.

At first glance, it seems the collaborative aspect of comics is a feature that sets apart comics from picturebooks: while picturebooks imagine children to be relatively passive receptors of culture, comics address children as active producers and creative partners. In the graphic novel *The Adventures of Super Diaper Baby* (2002), author-artist Dav Pilkey relishes in highlighting children's roles in comics-making. The cover of the graphic novel declares that authorship belongs to two young boys, George Beard and Harold Hutchins (Figure 30.2). The book also begins with an "origin story" that explains

Figure 30.2 Cover of Dav Pilkey's *The Adventures of Super Diaper Baby*. New York: Scholastic, 2002.

how the young author-illustrator team came to "write a comic about [a new super hero]," exemplifying young people's ability and desire to produce narratives. *Super Diaper Baby*'s unabashedly 'vulgar' content and celebration of scatological humor also implies that comics is a medium in which children can freely express their tastes and values. Furthermore, the final pages include instructions on how to draw the characters, thus encouraging child readers to appropriate the characters and create new narratives. Yet even as *Super Diaper Baby* champions the image of the child as comics creator and makes a case for comics' capacity to subvert adult authority, the book is, of course, authored by the adult Pilkey. In other words, the figure of the creative, subversive child in *Super Diaper Baby* is a fiction imagined by an adult. It seems that as today's children's comics become increasingly adult-mediated texts, they shed the collaborative aspects that marked earlier forms of comics (see Saguisag 2017).

Paying attention to the pluralities of comics

The preceding sections emphasize why it is crucial to historicize comics when comparing them to picturebooks. Comics (and picturebooks, for that matter) are dynamic rather than static, and their cultural status and relationship with child readers are not the only aspects that have undergone change. Across time and geography, comics have appeared in diverse formats and styles. In the American context, for example, comics have been published in the form of newspaper comic strips (in single tier and multiple tiers), magazine cartoons, mainstream comic book magazines, small-press and self-published comic books, graphic novels, and webcomics, with each form bearing particular connotations. Various types of comics have emerged all over the world, including Franco-Belgian *bande dessinée*, Italian *fumetti*, Spanish *historieta*, Japanese *manga*, Korean *manhwa* (see Mazur and Danner 2014), and comics in the African diaspora (see Repetti 2007).

Thus, when comparing picturebooks to comics, we need to begin identifying the specific type of comics we are referring to. Although panels and word balloons are often considered to be standard elements of the language of comics, there are actually multiple, unique comics language systems. In his study of American comic books and Japanese manga, Cohn acknowledges "language contact" in comics, in which one comics system appropriates techniques and signs from another system (2013: 170). However, he also carefully outlines the different grammars and morphologies of American and Japanese comics, and highlights how each language system has different "dialects" (137–171). For his part, Thierry Groensteen, who primarily studies Franco-Belgian comics, states that the assumption that comics has a universal system can be "reductive or problematic" (2011: 5).

Comparative studies of picturebooks and comics have largely ignored the multiplicity of comics languages. Future scholarship can perhaps examine more closely how and why particular comics systems are included or excluded in picturebook practices. It is likely that the enduring notion that picturebooks are 'innocent' texts determines why certain comic styles and techniques are resisted by picturebook practicioners. Perhaps the hypermasculine and hypersexual bodies that dominate American superhero comic books are perhaps too sexual (and sexist) to reproduce in 'wholesome' picturebooks.

Cultural bias could also be at play. Despite the popularity of manga among young readers, picturebook artists in the West have yet to embrace the aesthetics of Japanese comics. While there are examples of picturebooks that have adapted manga techniques (see Kümmerling-Meibauer 2013: 107–111), they appear to be exceptions. Adult gatekeepers may still perceive manga as dubious texts whose language is too difficult to police. For example, a common manga technique is to draw a character with animal ears and whiskers as a means of characterizing her as a mischief-maker (Cohn 2013: 157). It may be that such manga morphology is too 'strange,' 'unsettling,' and 'foreign' to include in the purportedly comfortable, familiar realm of the picturebook.

More focused attention on picturebooks and comics in non-Western contexts can also enrich current research. For example, one can look at the unique developments of these cultural forms in the Philippines. Both genres are heavily influenced by trends in American publishing: as in the United States, picturebooks are generally embraced as educational, innocuous texts while Philippine *komiks* connote crude art, slapstick humor, and cliché adventure stories. Moreover, picturebooks are more likely to be purchased by middle class families while mass-market komiks are typically purchased (and rented) by working class and poor readers. Yet komiks have also been used as a platform for political protest while picturebooks – often funded or purchased by Philippine government agencies – typically avoid questioning the political status quo. Such openness to the specific histories and contexts of picturebooks and comics outside of the global North is necessary to add nuance to scholarship. If picturebook studies and comics studies mean to rescue texts from the periphery, they need to be more purposeful in putting an end to the persistent marginalization of texts produced in the global South.

Conclusion

Comparative studies of picturebooks and comics have made significant contributions to our understanding of both genres. Some may say that scholarship is close to exhausting all possible avenues of identifying the similarities and differences between the two. Current research, however, tends to be hindered by a dehistoricized view of comics. In order to complicate and deepen our analyses of picturebooks-comics relationships, we need to put more effort in recognizing the pluralities of comics. Paying more attention to the development and diversity of comics across history and culture will allow us to generate new perspectives in picturebook and comics research.

References

Allen, Jenny, and Feiffer, Jules (2006) *The Long Chalkboard and Other Stories*, New York: Pantheon.

Beaty, Bart (2012) *Comics Versus Art*, Toronto: University of Toronto Press.

Briggs, Raymond (1978) *The Snowman*, New York: Random House.

Chute, Hillary (2010) *Graphic Women: Life Narrative and Contemporary Comics*, New York: Columbia University Press.

Cohn, Neil (2013) "Beyond Speech Balloons and Thought Bubbles: The Integration of Text and Image," *Semiotica* 197: 35–63.

Cohn, Neil (2013) *The Visual Language of Comics: Introduction to the Structure and Cognition of Sequential Images*, London: Bloomsbury.

Doonan, Jane (1993) *Looking at Pictures in Picture Books*, Stroud: Thimble Press.

Doury, Pascal (1989) "Paul," in Art Spiegelman and Francoise Mouly (eds) *Raw: Open Wounds From the Cutting Edge of Commix*, New York: Penguin Books, 87–114.

French, Renee (2010) *h day*, Brooklyn, NY: PictureBox.

Gibson, Mel (2010) "Graphic Novels, Comics and Picture Books," in David Rudd (ed.) *The Routledge Companion to Children's Literature*, London: Routledge, 100–111.

Gibson, Mel, Nabizadeh, Golnar, and Sambell, Kay (2014) "Watch This Space: Childhood, Picturebooks and Comics," Special issue of *Journal of Graphic Novels and Comics* 5.3.

Grey, Mini (2005) *Traction Man Is Here!*, New York: Random House.

Groensteen, Thierry (2011) *Comics and Narration*, trans. Ann Miller, Jackson: University Press of Mississippi.

Hamer, Naomi (2013) "Jumping on the 'Comics for Kids' Bandwagon," *Jeunesse: Young People, Texts, Cultures* 5.2: 165–187.

Hatfield, Charles (2005) *Alternative Comics: An Emerging Literature*, Jackson: University Press of Misssissippi.

Hatfield, Charles, and Svonkin, Craig (eds) (2012) "Why Comics Are and Are Not Picture Books," *Children's Literature Association Quarterly* 37.4: 429–497.

Hergé (1930–1976) *The Adventures of Tintin* series (23 vols), 22 vols reprinted by New York: Little Brown (first French ed. 1929–1976).

Jaffe, Meryl (2014) *Raising a Reader! How Comics and Graphic Novels Can Help Your Kids Love to Read!*, New York: Comic Book Legal Defense Fund.

Kline, Stephen (1993) *Out of the Garden: Toys and Children's Culture in the Age of TV Marketing*, London: Verso.

Kümmerling-Meibauer, Bettina (2013) "Manga/Comics Hybrids in Picturebooks," in Jaqueline Berndt and Bettina Kümmerling-Meibauer (eds) *Manga's Cultural Crossroads*, New York: Routledge, 100–120.

Lat (2006) *Kampung Boy*, New York: First Second (first published 1979).

Lehman, Barbara (2004) *The Red Book*, New York: HMH Books for Young Readers.

Lent, John A. (2009) "The Comics Debate Internationally," in Jeet Heer and Kent Worcester (eds) *A Comics Studies Reader*, Jackson: University Press of Mississippi, 69–76.

Mattson, Jennifer (2007) "The Wall: Growing Up Behind the Iron Curtain," *Booklist*, www.booklistonline.com/The-Wall-Growing-Up-behind-the-Iron-Curtain-Peter-Sís/pid=1929463 (accessed February 20, 2016).

Mazur, Dan, and Danner, Alexander (2014) *Comics: A Global History, 1968 to the Present*, London: Thames and Hudson.

McCloud, Scott (1993) *Understanding Comics*, New York: HarperPerennial.

Mouly, Françoise, and Spiegelman, Art, "Our TOON Books Mission," *TOON Books*, www.toon-books.com/our-mission.html (accessed February 20, 2016).

Nel, Philip (2012) "Same Genus, Different Species? Comics and Picture Books," *Children's Literature Association Quarterly* 37.4: 445–453.

Nikolajeva, Maria, and Scott, Carole (2001) *How Picturebooks Work*, New York: Garland.

Nodelman, Perry (1988) *Words about Pictures: The Narrative Art of Children's Picture Books*, Athens: University of Georgia Press.

op de Beeck, Nathalie (2010) *Suspended Animation: Children's Picture Books and the Fairy Tale of Modernity*, Minneapolis: University of Minnesota Press.

op de Beeck, Nathalie (2012) "On Comics-style Picture Books and Picture-Bookish Comics," *Children's Literature Association Quarterly* 37.4: 468–476.

Ormerod, Jan (2009) *Sunshine*, London: Frances Lincoln (first published 1981).

Pilkey, Dav (2002) *The Adventures of Super Diaper Baby*, New York: Scholastic.

Pustz, Matthew (1999) *Comic Book Culture: Fanboys and True Believers*, Jackson: University Press of Mississippi.

Repetti, Massimo (2007) "African Wave: Specificity and Cosmopolitanism in African Comics," *African Arts* 40.2: 16–35.

Reynolds, Kim (2007) *Radical Children's Literature: Future Visions and Aesthetic Transformations in Juvenile Fiction*, New York: Palgrave Macmillan.

Saguisag, Lara (2012) "The Wall: Growing Up Behind the Iron Curtain [Peter Sís]," in Beaty, Bart and Weiner, Stephen (eds) *Critical Survey of Graphic Novels: Independents and Underground Classics*, Pasadena, CA: Salem Press, 863–866.

Saguisag, Lara (2015) "Family Amusements: *Buster Brown* and the Place of Humor in the Early Twentieth-Century Home," *Children's Literature Association Quarterly* 40.2: 103–125.

Saguisag, Lara (2017) "RAW and Little Lit: Resisting and Redefining Children's Comics," in Mark Heimermann and Brittany Tullis (eds) *Picturing Childhood: Youth in Transnational Comics*, Austin: University of Texas Press, 128–147.

Sanders, Joe Sutliff (2013) "Chaperoning Words: Meaning-Making in Comics and Picture Books," *Children's Literature* 41: 57–90.

Schwarcz, Joseph (1982) *Ways of the Illustrator: Visual Communication in Children's Literature*, Chicago: American Library Association.

Sendak, Maurice (1970) *In the Night Kitchen*, New York: Harper.

Sís, Peter (2007) *The Wall: Growing Up Behind the Iron Curtain*, New York: Farrar, Straus, and Giroux.

Tan, Shaun (2007) *The Arrival*, New York: Scholastic/Arthur A. Levine (first published 2006).

Wertham, Fredric (1954) *Seduction of the Innocent: The Influence of Comic Books on Today's Youth*, New York: Rinehart.

Wiesner, David (2006) *Flotsam*, New York: Houghton Mifflin.

Willems, Mo (2003) *Don't Let the Pigeon Drive the Bus!*, New York: Hyperion.

31

PICTUREBOOKS AND MOVIES

Tobias Kurwinkel

Film and literature share a special relationship: soon after cinema was born at the end of the nineteenth century, with the public screening held by the Lumière Brothers at Salon Indien du Grand Café in Paris, film turned to literary sources of all kinds. Literature provided an abundance of ready-made material, as Timothy Corrigan points out, that could easily be transposed to film (2012: 13). Early filmmakers adapted fairy tales like *Cinderella* or popular novels, among them *Robinson Crusoe, Gulliver's Travels* or *Uncle Tom's Cabin*. Later they turned to less canonized literature like bourgeois melodramas, middle class fiction or folkloristic tales (Corrigan 2012: 13) and also to children's literature. The famous French illusionist and filmmaker Georges Méliès's *Le Voyage dans la lune* (A Trip to the Moon 1902) was inspired by Jules Verne, a writer whose books were read by children (Wojcik-Andrews 2000: 55).

Today, literature is the main source for fiction films: approximately 50 percent of all these films are based on novels, short stories, and other literary sources. This percentage is much higher for children's films and other films made for, or primarily marketed to, children – roughly 80 percent are based on a literary source (Kurwinkel and Schmerheim 2013: 66). Interestingly, however, very few of these films are based on picturebooks.

Literature as a supplier for all sorts of narratives and ways of telling a story has had and still has a tremendous influence on film, as already Sergei Eisenstein showed in his comparison of Charles Dickens and D.W. Griffith in 1944 (Eisenstein 1949). But the same applies vice versa: after the rise of film at the beginning of the twentieth century, it quickly left its marks on literature. Accordingly, Leo Tolstoy admitted in an interview in 1908 that he would like to write like a film camera:

> You will see that this little clicking contraption with the revolving handle will make a revolution in our life – in the life of writers. It is a direct attack on the old methods of literary art. We shall have to adapt ourselves to the shadowy screen and to the cold machine. I have thought of that and I feel what is coming.
>
> But I rather like it. This swift change of scene, this blending of emotion and experience – it is much better than the heavy, long-drawn-out kind of writing to which we are accustomed. It is closer to life. In life, too, changes and transitions flash before our eyes, and emotions of the soul are like a hurricane. The cinema has divined the mystery of motion.
>
> *Leda 1960: 410*

Tolstoy's "swift change of scene" and divinization of "the mystery of motion" found its quintessential literary expression in the so-called *Reihungsstil*, one of the defining literary devices of the German

Expressionism Movement. The *Reihungsstil* – lining up style or simultaneous technology – can be understood as the *mimesis* of a continuously changing or changed reality, expressed by lining up divergent, seemingly disconnected impressions. Ever since, the employment of *Reihungsstil* and other cinematic techniques has been called 'filmic writing.'

A well-known example of the latter is Alfred Döblin's novel *Berlin Alexanderplatz* published in 1929. Here, Döblin's writing style mimics camera techniques such as zooms in order to, for example, illustrate protagonist Franz Biberkopf's isolation from society. However, the novel's distinguishing filmic feature is the aesthetic method of montage, as Walter Benjamin wrote in his essay "The Crisis of the Novel" from 1930:

> Petit-bourgeois publications, scandal sheets, tales of misfortune, sensations of '28, folk songs, advertisements throng through this text. Montage explodes the novel, explodes its foundations, its style and opens up new, epic possibilities. Above all in terms of form.
>
> *1999: 301*

According to Benjamin, montage is realized as collage in *Berlin Alexanderplatz*, as an assemblage of different textual and pictorial objects.

But filmic writing does not only encompass transformations of cinematic techniques in literature, such as montage or zoom, filmic writing also includes allusions to the medium of film as such, to its cultural, institutional, and productional background, to its language and style (which imitate the dreamlike nature and stream of consciousness movement of screen images), or it simply refers to a narrative's ready-madeness for adaptation.

There has been a lot of research into the relation between film and literature, even though few studies focus on filmic writing as such. Two research paradigms have been particularly influential: Alexandre Astruc's *caméra stylo* (1992) and Christian Metz's film semiology (1974). In 1948, Astruc coined the term *caméra stylo*, contending that filmmakers should use the camera as a means of expressing their personal point of view as if they were writers, effectively becoming film authors. While this reformed notion of the author attempts to grant directors an own kind of poetic signature, Christian Metz rather develops a typology of the language of film, breaking it up into semiotic parts.

In the last twenty years, the concept of intermediality opened up new perspectives on the relationship between film and literature, and thereby on filmic writing.

On that basis, this chapter aims to contribute to a hitherto neglected aspect of research on filmic writing: the use and transformation of cinematic techniques in picturebooks. Among the few scholars to write on such aspects are Sandra Beckett, Perry Nodelman, Amy E. Spaulding, and Jens Thiele, all of whom repeatedly pointed out similarities between film and picturebooks and the influence of filmic narration and writing on the latter (Beckett 2012; Nodelman 1986; Spaulding 1995; Thiele 2000).

While the first section of this chapter discusses the methodical background by introducing a concept of intermediality, the second section develops a typology of filmic writing in picturebooks, whereupon the third section examines selected examples of picturebooks: David Wiesner's *Flotsam* (2006), Istvan Banyai's *Zoom* (1995) and *Re-Zoom* (1995), and Chris Van Allsburg's *Zathura* (2002).

Methodical background: intermediality and the 'as if' character of intermedial references

Film and picturebooks are two different media, each of them being constituted by different semiotic systems. In this regard, filmic writing in picturebooks could be understood as an intermedial phenomenon that in some way takes place between media. The term "intermedial," as Irina O. Rajewsky states, designates

> those configurations which have to do with a crossing of borders between media, and which thereby can be differentiated from *intra*medial phenomena as well as from *trans*medial

phenomena (i.e., the appearance of a certain motif, aesthetic, or discourse across a variety of different media).

2005: 46

Rajewsky distinguishes three subcategories of this broad concept of intermediality: medial transposition (that is film adaption), media combination (that is opera or film as a combination of at least two distinct media), and intermedial references. These references are understood as

> meaning-constitutional strategies that contribute to the media product's overall signification: the media product uses its own media-specific means, either to refer to a specific, individual work produced in another medium [. . .], or to refer to a specific medial subsystem or to another medium qua system. The given product thus constitutes itself partly or wholly in relation to the work, system, or subsystem to which it refers.

2005: 52

Thus, filmic writing in picturebooks can be described in terms of intermedial references, that is, as references to another medium qua system. In such cases, picturebooks evocate or imitate cinematic techniques by relying on their own means of expression.

The difference between the referred and the referring medium gives rise to the so-called as-if character of intermedial references and its specific illusion-forming quality. A picturebook author (including the illustrator) writes as if he were a director, as if he had the instruments of film at his disposal. Using the picturebook-specific means available to him, the author cannot zoom, cannot make use of actual cinematic techniques; by necessity he remains within the specific medial limits of the picturebook. As Rajewsky points out, this inability to pass beyond a single medium reveals a medial difference, an 'intermedial gap' explicitly displayed or concealed by a given medium, a gap that in any case can only ever be bridged in the figurative mode of "as if" (2005: 54).

An intermedial reference only generates an illusion of another medium's specific techniques. Applied to the topic of this chapter, it is this illusion that solicits a sense of filmic quality in the recipient of a picturebook, and this 'as-if' character has given rise to the metaphorical phrase "filmic writing" (54).

The approach presented here is based on Werner Wolf's definition of media. He understands media as

> conventionally distinct means of communicating cultural contents. Media in this sense are specified principally by the nature of their underlying semiotic systems (involving verbal language, pictorial signs, music, etc., or, in cases of 'composite media' such as film, a combination of several semiotic system), and only in the second place by technical or institutional channels.

2005: 253

Consequently, a picturebook can be understood as one specific conventionally distinct means of communicating, as one specific medium – but also as a combination of different semiotic systems, of text and images. In this context, cinematic techniques in picturebooks are intermedial references to film, evocated or imitated by textual, pictorial, or both means.

A typology of cinematic techniques in picturebooks

These cinematic techniques are shown in the following structured chart (Figure 31.1), grouped into two main categories: filmic techniques and narrative techniques. The first category involves three subcategories: image, sound, and editing. The image category is further divided into camera work

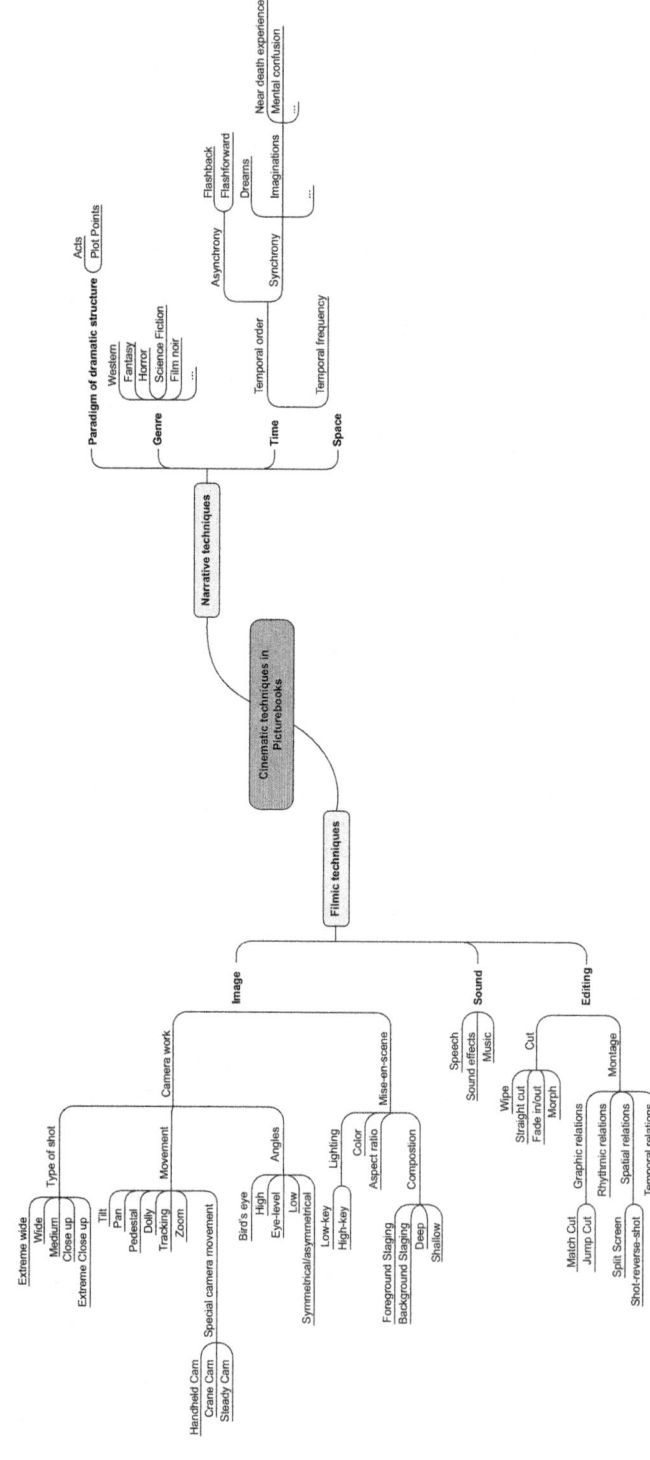

Figure 31.1 Mindmap: Cinematic techniques.

and mise-en-scène (understood as the arrangement of the objects to be filmed). While the first subcategory is aimed at camera techniques that, for instance, can be represented in picturebooks in the form of filmic types of shots, the second subcategory describes elements such as aspect ratio, which picturebooks can represent via the choice of a specific book format. Sound as subcategory is divided into speech, effects, and music, and it refers to the filmic use of sound as a synthesis of image and sound. Something like that can be found in picturebooks that use their text for evoking rhythms or sounds, for instance in *I Got the Rhythm* (2014) by Connie Schofield-Morrison and Frank Morrison. The subcategory of editing is divided into cut and montage; examples for cuts are transitions between scenes via fade-in or fade-out; examples for montage are split screens that correlate two different scenes on a spatial level.

The second category lists narrative techniques of filmic structure: Syd Field's paradigm of dramatic structure, genre conventions, and time and space. The dramaturgy of some picturebooks imitates the film-narrational model developed by Field since they are structured into exposition, confrontation, and resolution accordingly, and sometimes they also imitate the conventions of film genres such as the Western. An example of this is Hildegard Müller's *The Cowboy* (2015), in which a little boy uses his lasso to rescue the female protagonist's toy dog from the sea – thus explicitly paraphrasing the conventional representations of cowboys in classical Western films.

Without any claim to comprehensiveness, this chart provides an overview of cinematic techniques in picturebooks. It is built on traditional analytic categories of literature and film studies. However, one should be aware that, on their own, subcategories such as type of shot or angle do not necessarily indicate an instance of filmic writing in a given picturebook, since they can be – or are – used as analytic categories in other disciplines as well.

More fundamentally, one should be able to describe the mode of presentation of a given picturebook *as a whole* as filmic, and that implies that it responds to several of the categories of the mindmap. For instance, if a picturebook tells a story in which narrative linearity is interrupted by *analepsis*, additionally distinguished from the rest of the story by black-and-white coloring, this can indicate filmic writing. On their own, these two factors do not necessarily imply that the picturebook uses filmic writing. But one can talk of filmic writing, or intermedial references to film, if they are supplemented by a sepia-graded color code, by a grainy impression of the images, or by scratches and artifacts (such as numbers, which were imprinted on the credit rolls of old celluloid films).

Case study: David Wiesner's *Flotsam*

David Wiesner's *Flotsam* (2006), the winner of the Caldecott Medal 2007, serves as a concise example of filmic writing in picturebooks. Wiesner's books have often been described as cinematic, particularly because he tends to use cinematic techniques in order "to draw viewers into the story" (Beckett 2012: 113). This became obvious in 2006, when Houghton Mifflin/Clarion Books participated in the first Picture Book Video Awards. In this program, students and graduates from various US film and animation schools competed to create a trailer for Wiesner's book.

Flotsam begins with a boy playing at the seaside when he finds an old underwater camera that has been washed ashore. He takes its roll of film to a photo lab to get it developed, and finally sees photos of fantastical underwater life: an octopus reading a book while sitting in an armchair in its living room, a marine turtle with a city made of sea shells on its back, or gigantic starfishes wading through the water, whales between their feet. But the most interesting photo is the last one. It contains a girl, holding a photo of a boy, who is again holding a photo of another child, and so forth. After examining the photo with a magnifying glass and a microscope thoroughly, he realizes that he is one in a long line of photographers who have found this camera. Finally he takes a picture of himself, holding the photo with his countless predecessors on it. Then he throws the camera back into the sea. After a long journey through the cold water of the ice-bound South Pole and warm tropical seas, the camera washes up again and is found by another child.

Even though the book contains a plethora of intermedial references to film, such as the filmic techniques of zoom or low-angle shots (Beckett 2012: 114), I want to focus on the montage of and the temporal relations between the images in particular. The book's peculiar way of dealing with these two dimensions can be highlighted with the following example: while the boy is impatiently waiting for the developed photographs, sitting on a bench in front of the photo lab, the passing time is depicted as shown in Figures 31.2–31.8:

Here, the flow of time is not represented via a monoscenic image (as often done in picturebooks), that is, a kind of image that only depicts how things look during one specific moment separated from the flow of time, a kind of image that depends on a text in order to "add time to that frozen instant" (Nodelman 1986: 159). Instead, a wordless sequence or array of seven images conveys a temporal succession, more specifically:

> The sequence of pictures offers enough repetition – images of the same characters in different postures or of the same settings under different conditions – to convey a sense of continuing action.

159

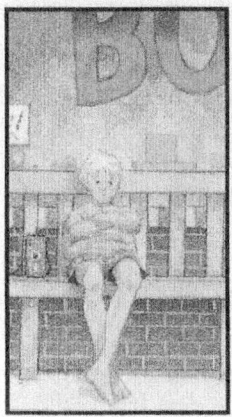 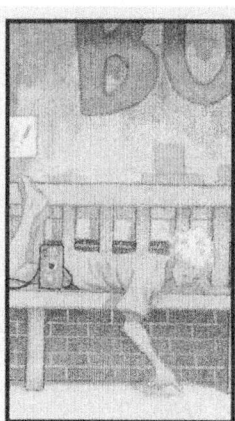  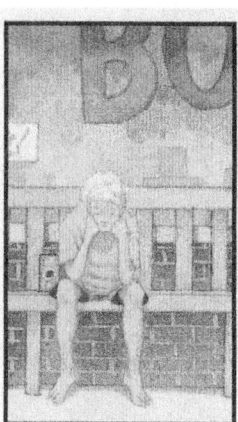

Figures 31.2–31.8 Illustrations from David Wiesner's *Flotsam*. New York: Clarion/Houghton Mifflin, 2006.

This sense is effected not only via the principle of succession, which brings temporal succession into present/presence by relying on repetition, but also via intermediate images, that is, thought-of, imagined association images in between the actual images. Such a process of mentally constructing "a continuous, unified reality" is called 'closure' by Scott McCloud (1993: 67).

This kind of visual narration has been particularly shaped by film montage, which is as much a dissociative as a consolidating principle, that is, "the creation of a sense of meaning not proper to the images themselves but derived exclusively from their juxtaposition" (Bazin 1974: 90). Stephen Roxburgh explicitly refers to this juxtaposition in writing that "[j]ust as the images on a strip of motion-picture film have a 'dynamic sequential existence,' so do the images in a picture book" (1984: 20).

But montage is not the only device that evokes intermedial references to film. In addition, the type of shot of the single pictures corresponds to an eye-level medium shot, thereby representing the inner, child-like perspective of the protagonist while simultaneously allowing the viewer an external perspective that is on a par with the character.

Furthermore, filmic writing here becomes an allusion to the production process, more specifically, to the storyboard as a "tool used in planning film production, consisting of comic-strip-like drawings of individual shots or phases of shots" (Bordwell and Thompson 2013: 505). The partitioning and framing of the panels reminds of the comic, even though two peculiarities of comic narration are missing – apart from the "presentation of the text through balloons, Captions or Narratory Blocks" (Dolle-Weinkauf 2007: 312, my translation): first, the depiction of sounds through onomatopoietic signs and other devices, second, the depiction of motion within panels via speed or action lines that compensate the medial limits of the static image (McCloud 1993: 116).

Case study: Istvan Banyai's *Zoom* and *Re-Zoom*

Another picturebook artist known for his use of cinematic techniques is Istvan Banyai. In the 1980s, Banyai had his breakthrough as a commercial illustrator and animator, and this work has tremendously influenced his children books.

For instance, his wordless picturebooks *Zoom* and *Re-Zoom*, both published in 1995, are homages to the film camera and its ability to zoom. In these works, the zoom is not only a filmic effect (in the sense of an intermedial reference) but also an underlying narrative principle, "gradually zooming out, frame by frame, with each page turn" (Beckett 2012: 108). Banyai combines this very principle with his visual art, which he describes as "an organic combination of turn-of-the-century Viennese Retro, interjected with American pop, some European absurdity added for flavor, served on a cartoon-style color palette" (Banyai 2012).

Zoom begins with an extreme close up of a part of an initially unknown, stellar object (Figure 31.9), which on the next page is revealed as being a rooster's comb (Figure 31.10). The corresponding animal is shown in close up, while on the subsequent page the rooster becomes part of the background of the image (Figure 31.11), sitting on a fence while being observed by two children in the foreground of the panel, hardly reaching the lower frame of the window with their heads. The next image, playing with fore-, middle- and background, shows the room surrounding the children (Figure 31.12), depicting a boy and a girl standing on a bench while looking outside of a window at the rooster in the garden. This narrative pattern is continued until the earth is shown as a small marble in the middle of the dark, black space of the universe (Figure 31.13).

Re-Zoom takes up this narrative pattern, beginning with a prehistoric hunting scene which is shown on the display of a wristwatch, leading to impressions of other cultures and eventually into a New York subway train vanishing into a dark tunnel. While *Zoom* surprised the viewer with a visual journey to different places, such as the rooster's farm or a desert island, in *Re-Zoom* the viewer also travels through time, through historically different epochs and cultures, from the Stone Age and Ancient Egypt to Revolutionary France and, finally, contemporary New York.

Figures 31.9–31.13 Illustrations from Istvan Banyai's *Zoom*. New York: Viking, 1995.

Figures 31.9–31.13 Continued

As in *Zoom*, this tour de force through the history of mankind is realized not only by using the zoom as the underlying narrative pattern, but also with the help of shot perspectives and other filmic techniques. There are also other typical types of shot that repeatedly can be found here, such as wide, medium, and close-up.

In *Re-Zoom*, Banyai also reflects the use of cinematic techniques when he, for instance, paints a film camera whose preview monitor shows the image of the preceding page as a miniature, or when he pays homage to Alfred Hitchcock, sitting on an Indian elephant. The latter is known for popularizing the *Vertigo effect*, a combination of zoom and tracking shot techniques.

Case study: Chris Van Allsburg's *Zathura*

Chris Van Allsburg is another picturebook author who heavily relies on cinematic techniques, especially by evoking the structure and dramaturgy of film as narrative techniques. Van Allsburg is not only known for his books such as *Jumanji* (1981) and *The Polar Express* (1985) (which won the

Caldecott Medal in 1982 and 1986, respectively). He also co-authored the screenplays of the corresponding film adaptations by Joe Johnston (*Jumanji* 1995) and Robert Zemeckis (*The Polar Express* 2004). In 2005, Jon Favreau directed *Zathura: A Space Adventure*, the adaptation of Van Allburg's picturebook of the same name, a sequel to *Jumanji* that, naturally, also features a number of visual as well as textual references to *Jumanji*.

This picturebook exemplifies the use of narrative techniques in picturebooks, even though it also features a number of filmic techniques, for instance, strange asymmetrical camera angles. The following paragraphs will show how *Zathura* corresponds to Syd Field's paradigm of dramatic structure both structurally as well as dramaturgically, and thereby functions like a blueprint for the later film adaptation.

Children's films usually follow a simple narrative pattern:

> At the beginning, there usually is a kind of danger to a pre-existing order – a threatening situation the protagonists have to face in the course of the story in order to restore order without the help of adults. The solution of the conflict, which often is presented as a clear good vs. evil constellation, in most cases leads to a happy ending.
>
> *Heinke and Rabe 2011: 422, my translation*

This delineation of three functionally and content-wise different parts – exposition, confrontation, resolution – represents the "canonic format" (Bordwell 1985: 157) of storytelling. Its earliest expression can be found in Aristotle's *Poetics*, developed around 335 BC (Halliwell 1987).

In the 1920s, Hollywood popularized a specific variant of this pattern that determines the dramaturgy of many films ever since. The screenwriter and screenwriting theorist Syd Field expanded on this paradigm of dramatic structure in the 1980s and started teaching it at the School of Cinematic Arts of the University of California, Los Angeles. Field's basic paradigm, known to everyone in the film business, is used or slightly varied by many other screen writers and theorists (Fuxjäger 1999: 152).

Syd Field directly relies on Aristotle's *Poetics* when he declares that a film has "a definitive beginning, middle, and end" (Field 2005: 30). Assuming an average film length of 120 minutes, Field calculates that one page of the screenplay corresponds to one minute of the film. The three acts of a film are roughly quantified as thirty minutes for the exposition, sixty minutes for the confrontation, and thirty minutes for the resolution.

Zathura corresponds to this format, qualitatively (content and function of the acts) as well as quantitatively (the length of the dramatic units is roughly 1:2:1, in terms of the amount of pages).

The beginning of the picturebook introduces the Budwing family. The parents of Walter and Danny leave their two boys at home alone – this establishes the characters and the set-up, that is, "the circumstances surrounding the action" (Field 2005: 23). The two brothers do not get along well and constantly argue with each other: while the older brother Walter wants to watch TV, Danny insists on playing catch with him. Their confrontation gets out of hand, and they end up in the park across the street of their house, where by accident they find a board game called "Jumanji: A Jungle Adventure." When they explore the game at home, they discover another game called "Zathura" underneath. Danny starts playing Zathura until he comes across a card that says "Meteor shower, take evasive action." Immediately afterwards, it starts raining meteors inside of the boys' home. Danny and Walter soon realize that the game sent them into outer space and that they have to play the entire game in order to be able to return home. This sets up the story, establishes the main character constellation, and launches the "dramatic premise" (Field 2005: 23).

Zathura is narrated on fourteen doublespreads. Corresponding to Field's paradigm, the seven pages of the first act constitute one-fourth of the text. In the second act (Field's "confrontation"; Field 2005: 24), the main characters encounter a number of obstacles that keep them from achieving their dramatic need, defined "as what the character[s] want to win, gain, get, or achieve during the course of the screenplay" (Field 2005: 24). In the case of *Zathura*, the main characters' objective is obvious: Walter and Danny want to complete the board game in order to return home. This external need is correlated with their internal need for a harmonic sibling relation without rivalry, a mutual recognition of the other's value. This applies to Walter in particular: the brothers can only finish the game and return home if they learn to act together instead of against each other.

Their encounters with obstacles such as zero gravity, a destructive robot, or a Zorgon pirate help them in learning to fight for their goal together. Walter in particular learns to value his little brother. This second act, making up roughly half of the entire text, is followed by the resolution of the third act, "that unit of action that resolves the story" (Field 2005: 26). The end of Van Allsburg's picturebook is initiated by one last move in the Zathura game. Walter, throwing the dice, draws a playing card according to which he has reached a black hole, forcing him to go two hours back in time. Walter vanishes into darkness, and finds himself in the park again, arguing with Danny. When Danny discovers the Jumanji board game (again), Walter throws it away. The story ends with Walter inviting Danny to play catch with him – just as Danny wished for.

Apart from the three-act structure, the narrative techniques of *Zathura* also correspond to Field's paradigm in other respects: the two most important plot points are located at the end of the first and second act. A plot point

> is defined as any incident, episode, or event that hooks into the action and spins it around in another direction – Plot Point I moves the action forward into Act II and Plot Point II moves the action into Act III.
>
> *Field 2005: 26*

Accordingly, Plot Point I is the moment in which the brothers realize that *Zathura* is not merely a normal game since they find themselves floating in outer space, forced to finish the game in order to return home. Plot Point II begins with Walter reading out the last card, and it ends when he opens his eyes, lying in the park again.

Coda

Cinematic techniques in picturebooks do not merely evoke filmic effects. They can also function as a narrative principle that, in a philosophical manner, establishes a view of the bigger picture by rendering possible visual journeys through time and space (Banyai's *Zoom, Re-Zoom*), by representing temporal structures in a filmic manner (Wiesner's *Flotsam*), or by using the structure and dramaturgy of film as a narrative technique (Van Allsburg's *Zathura*).

These techniques, understood as expressions of filmic writing in picturebooks, are characteristic for the contemporary picturebook. Consequently, one cannot merely understand it as a medium that is constituted by different semiotic systems, by text and images. It is rather determined by its medial delimitations and ensuing intermedial references: "[N]o medium has its meaning or existence alone, but only in constant interplay with other media" (McLuhan 1964: 39), as Marshall McLuhan already wrote in 1964 in *Understanding Media*.

Acknowledgment

I would like to thank Philipp Schmerheim for his useful suggestions as well as his great help translating this chapter into English.

References

Astruc, Alexandre (1992) *Du stylo à la caméra et de la caméra au stylo: Écrits (1942–1984)*, Paris: L'Archipel.
Banyai, Istvan (1995) *Zoom*, New York: Viking.
Banyai, Istvan (1995) *Re-Zoom*, New York: Viking.

Banyai, Istvan (2012) *About*, www.ist-one.com/about.php (accessed March, 31, 2015).

Bazin, André (1974) "What Is Cinema?," in Gerald Mast and Marshall Cohen (eds) *Film Theory and Criticism: Introductory Readings*, New York: Oxford University Press, 90–102.

Beckett, Sandra L. (2012) *Crossover Picturebooks: A Genre for All Ages*. New York: Routledge.

Benjamin, Walter (1999) "The Crisis of the Novel," in Michael W. Jennigs, Howar Eiland, and Gary Smith (eds) *Walter Benjamin: Selected Writing*, volume 2, part 1: 1927–1930, Cambridge, MA: Harvard University Press, 299–304.

Bordwell, David (1985) *Narration in the Fiction Film*, Madison: University of Wisconsin Press.

Bordwell, David, and Thompson, Kristin (2013) *Film Art: An Introduction*, New York: McGraw-Hill.

Corrigan, Timothy (2012) *Film and Literature: An Introduction and Reader*, New York: Routledge.

Döblin, Alfred (2004) *Berlin Alexanderplatz*, Frankfurt: S. Fischer (first published 1929).

Dolle-Weinkauff, Bernd (2007) "Comic," in Harald Fricke, Klaus Grubmüller, Jan-Dirk Müller et al. (eds) *Reallexikon der deutschen Literaturwissenschaft*, vol. 1, Berlin: Walter de Gruyter, 312–315.

Eisenstein, Sergei (1949) "Dickens, Griffith, and the Film Today," in Jay Leda (ed.) *Film Form: Essays in Film Theory*, New York: Harcourt, Brace, 195–255.

Field, Syd (2005) *Screenplay: The Foundations of Screenwriting*, New York: Bantam/Dell Random House.

Fuxjäger, Anton (1999) "Was zum Teufel ist ein 'Plot Point'? Zur filmwissenschaftlichen Anwendbarkeit eines Begriffs von Syd Field," *Maske und Kothurn* 1.3: 149–162.

Halliwell, Stephen (1987) *The Poetics of Aristotle*, translation and commentary, London: Duckworth.

Heinke, Susanne, and Rabe, Beate (2011) "Kinderfilm," in Günter Lange (ed.) *Kinder- und Jugendliteratur der Gegenwart: Ein Handbuch*, Baltmannsweiler: Schneider Verlag Hohengehren, 421–446.

Jumanji (1995) film, dir. Joe Johnston. USA: Interscope Communications.

Kurwinkel, Tobias, and Schmerheim, Philipp (2013) *Kinder- und Jugendfilmanalyse*, Konstanz: UVK.

Leda, Jay (1960) *Kino. A History of the Russian and Soviet Film*, New York: Macmillan.

MacLuhan, Marshall (1964) *Understanding Media: The Extensions of Man*, New York: McGraw-Hill.

McCloud, Scott (1993) *Understanding Comics: The Invisible Art*, Northampton: Kitchen Sink Press.

Metz, Christian (1974) *Film Language: A Semiotics of the Cinema*, Chicago: University of Chicago Press.

Müller, Hildegard (2015) *The Cowboy*, New York: Holiday House.

Nodelman, Perry (1986) *Words about Pictures: The Narrative Art of Children's Picture Books*, Athens: University of Georgia Press.

The Polar Express (2004) film, dir. Robert Zemeckis, USA: Castle Rock Entertainment, Shangri-La Entertainment, ImageMovers Playtone.

Rajewsky, Irina O. (2005) "Intermediality, Intertextuality, and Remediation: A Literary Perspective on Intermediality," *intermédialités* 6: 43–64.

Roxburgh, Stephen (1984) "A Picture Equals How Many Words? Narrative Theory and Picture Books for Children," *The Lion and the Unicorn* 7/8: 20–33.

Schofield-Morrison, Connie (2014) *I Got the Rhythm*, illus. Frank Morrison, New York: Bloomsbury.

Spaulding, Amy E. (1995) *The Page as a Stage Set: Storyboard Picture Books*, Metuchen, NJ: Scarecrow Press.

Thiele, Jens (2000) *Das Bilderbuch: Ästhetik, Theorie, Analyse, Didaktik, Rezeption*, Oldenburg: Isensee.

Van Allsburg, Chris (1981) *Jumanji*, Boston, MA: Houghton Mifflin.

Van Allsburg, Chris (1985) *The Polar Express*, Boston, MA: Houghton Mifflin.

Van Allsburg, Chris (2002) *Zathura. A Space Adventure*, Boston, MA: Houghton Mifflin.

Le Voyage dans la lune (1902) film, dir. Georges Méliès, France.

Wiesner, David (2006) *Flotsam*, New York: Clarion/Houghton Mifflin.

Wojcik-Andrews, Ian (2000) *Children's Films: History, Ideology, Pedagogy, Theory*, New York: Garland.

Wolf, Werner (2005) "Intermediality," in Marie-Laure Ryan and David Herman (eds) *The Routledge Encyclopedia of Narrative Theory*, London: Routledge, 252–256.

Zathura: A Space Adventure (2005) film, dir. Jon Favreau, USA: Columbia Pictures.

PART IV

Domains

32

THE EDUCATION OF A PICTUREBOOK-MAKER

Martin Salisbury

The term 'illustrator' now seems somehow inadequate or even redundant in the context of the picturebook as we know it today. As this art form evolves in its unique way, requiring total synthesis of word, image, and design, it is becoming less and less common for the word-maker and picture-maker to be separate individuals. The French term 'auteur,' which is most commonly used in relation to film directors who exert total artistic and creative control, may perhaps be the most appropriate term for picturebook-makers such as Beatrice Alemagna, Oliver Jeffers, Jon Klassen, and Shaun Tan, who have redefined the picturebook in recent years, pushing at and testing its boundaries and creating a new kind of visual authorship or origination of graphic literature.

Most research into the picturebook has hitherto tended to focus on the published outcome. This research has been situated predominantly within the fields of children's literature and education. Yet the making of picturebooks is an activity that emerges primarily from the field of art and design, most picturebook-makers having graduated from art schools, or in the case of the younger generation of practitioners, from what are now faculties and departments of art and design within universities. This situation has led to a body of theory that could be said to come largely 'from the outside, looking in.' While much of the research has been extremely useful to art students, it could be argued that such a situation is comparable to artists researching into medical practice, or geologists developing theory about icebergs by drilling into the top few centimeters. In this chapter I shall be examining the relationship between practice and theory in the education of the picturebook-maker, at undergraduate, postgraduate, and PhD level. In doing so, I shall be drawing on my own experiences as a teacher of illustration at each of those levels and equally importantly, my own experiences as an art student and then as a professional illustrator. I shall be looking at the tensions between *making stuff* and *making theory*. And I shall be examining the meaning of the term *research* with a small 'r' and big 'R,' that is the research that the practitioner undertakes as part of the creative process as compared to the academic, practice-led research increasingly undertaken by practitioners, employing experiential knowledge. In order to do this, I shall first of all take a tour through the general history of art and design education, and its complex relationship with traditional academic disciplines.

Art school

As I briefly touched upon earlier, the world of higher art education has undergone seismic change over the last twenty years or so. In the United Kingdom, specialized art institutions or 'art schools' have all but disappeared, having been absorbed into polytechnics, which then became universities. This has caused a clash of cultures, particularly in the area of research (and what that means), which has yet to be fully resolved. The clash centers on the nature of knowledge, the relationship between traditional scholarly/academic study, and learning through making or *experiential* knowledge.

Many of the art schools in the United Kingdom (including my own institution, Cambridge School of Art, now part of Anglia Ruskin University) were originally set up in the mid-nineteenth century to foster stronger links between the so-called fine arts and industry. After the Great Exhibition of 1851, a number of provincial art schools were formed for this purpose. Cambridge School of Art, formed in 1858 and opened by the great Victorian artist and critic John Ruskin, was one such establishment. Ruskin's name has since been adopted by the university within which the school now sits, and it is fitting that he oversees our toils. Ruskin's strong commitment to the importance of drawing from observation is still upheld in our teaching today. He felt that the activity of learning to draw from observation was key to understanding, to *knowing* the visual world. Among his many pronouncements in *The Elements of Drawing* (here quoted from my battered 1907 copy, given to me by the late head of school, John Bolam), Ruskin outlined his thoughts on learning to truly *see* through drawing:

> For I am nearly convinced, that when once we see keenly enough, there is very little diffi-culty in drawing what we see; but, even supposing that this difficulty be still great, I believe that the sight is a more important thing than the drawing; and I would rather teach drawing that my pupils may learn to love Nature, than teach the looking at Nature that they may learn to draw.
>
> *1907: xv*

In other words, Ruskin was explaining that the ability to draw is a means to an end. It is a way of knowing, a facilitator. Had the term been current at the time, he might have suggested that drawing was a route to *visual literacy*. It is a term that appears to be increasingly used, but with little consensus as to its meaning. For many years, drawing from observation was the primary or even sole activity for art students. Now, however, it is rarely taught formally in the UK, least of all on fine art courses, where conceptual art has become the leading form of expression. Illustration courses are perhaps the last bastion of drawing as a fundamental language.

Little has been written about the history of art education as a whole, even less about the educa-tion of the illustrator (with the notable exception of Heller and Arisman 2000). Richard Carline's excellent work *Draw They Must: A History of the Teaching and Examining of Art* (1968) picks up on Her-bert Read's (1943) belief that art should be the basis of education and traces this rather ad hoc and unstructured history over the last few centuries. The writer's embattled tone and evident exaspera-tion over the way the subject of art has been treated over the years at all levels of education may well strike a chord with many practicing artists. Carline was a talented artist himself and senior examiner in schools in the 1960s and 1970s and had a lifelong interest in the teaching of art at all levels. He echoes Ruskin's assertions as he discusses one of the most fundamental misconceptions about draw-ing – what drawing *is*, what drawing is *for*:

> The main goal of art teaching is not technical efficiency or skill, as usually assumed, but the development of the visual perceptions. Perhaps the art class might gain in status by a change in name, with 'art' discarded in favour of 'vision.'
>
> *1968: preface*

Here the writer is referring to knowing-through-drawing and is pre-empting the previously men-tioned contentious term, *visual literacy*, or rather he is pre-empting the term as some might say it should be more correctly used. Carline goes on to lament the way that art practice was only deemed important to those who would go on to study at art school:

> Thus it is evident that pupils are not expected to remain in the art class unless they have already decided on a career in art or are backward in other subjects . . . To enlarge the community of artists while ignoring the general public's ability to appreciate their work, which is how we tend to proceed at present, can only end disastrously for art.
>
> *1968: 5*

Carline argued strongly that the practical study of art is about much more than 'becoming an artist.' It should inform and underpin the understanding of many other areas of learning. He goes on to trace the evolution and development of art schools in Britain, the drawing class at Christ's Hospital in London in the seventeenth century, through the Society of Arts and the Royal Academy, the Government School of Design, and the subsequent appearance of the schools of art.

Bruce Archer was Professor of Design Research at the Royal College of Art in the 1970s and 1980s. He did more than anyone to push research *through* design and worked hard to break down the misperception that *thinking/intellect* and *making/designing/drawing* exist in separate universes. He too bemoaned the separation of these activities at an early stage at school, and its consequences:

> It is really rather an alarming thought that most of those who make the most far-reaching decisions on matters affecting the material culture, such as businessmen, senior civil servants, local government officers, members of councils and public committees, not to mention members of parliament, had an education in which contact with the most relevant disciplines ceased at the age of thirteen.
>
> *1979: 18*

Archer set up the Design Research Department at the RCA and was a champion of design as not 'just' a craft skill but a knowledge-based discipline such as any other. But the situation that he outlined has only become worse, as successive governments have marginalized the teaching of art. So the gap between the artist-maker and the decision-maker/observer/researcher/critic grows ever larger.

The perception that the ability to draw, make or design is a kind of innate gift or 'trick' is becoming increasingly common. Yet the practical study or *making* of art is now undertaken within the university structure at undergraduate, postgraduate, and doctorate level. This square peg–round hole transition has not been an easy one. As long ago as 1957, the great American artist-illustrator Ben Shahn mused on the 'fit' of the artist in the academy in his Charles Eliot Norton lectures:

> there is always the possibility that art may be utterly stifled within the university atmosphere, that the creative impulse may be wholly obliterated by the pre-eminence of criticism and scholarship. Nor is there perfect unanimity on the part of the university itself as to whether the presence of artists will be salutary within its community, or whether indeed art itself is a good solid intellectual pursuit and therefore a proper university study.
>
> *Shahn 1957: 2*

Sir Christopher Frayling was rector of London's Royal College of Art from 1996 to 2009. He has been an important voice in the debate about the relationship between traditional notions of scholarship and the teaching of art and design. In the introduction to his Henry Sidgwick Memorial Lecture at Newnham College, Cambridge in April 2015, "The Head the Heart and the Hand," he writes:

> The Government School of Design was founded in London in 1837, in an attempt by the government of the day to grow designers for a range of manufacturing industries – and to

compete with continental designers (especially in France and Prussia) who seemed to be becoming more effective. There followed a series of lively – and sometimes angry – debates about the nature and purposes of design education – involving artists, designers, officials and educationalists. Should it be a matter of 'the head' (learning a visual language), 'the hand' (learning a craft) – or 'the heart' (engaging the whole person)? And how could the education system actively engage with industry while still remaining educational?

2015: n. pag.

The picturebook-maker in the academy

Where does all this leave the education of the picturebook-maker? Like film, the picturebook falls within the visual arts. It has probably been seen as an area of children's literature primarily because its final form resides stubbornly within the physical form of *the book* – a number of paper pages, commonly thirty-two but always in multiples of eight, bound in sections and attached to cover boards. Yet that is where the resemblance to the traditional book (illustrated or not) now ends. Graphic literature delivers meaning through a language that is primarily visual and is in many ways more closely related to the *livre d'artiste* than to traditional notions of literature.

In the first half of the twentieth century, when illustration was not considered to be a discrete subject, many illustrators emerged from fine art courses, where they had studied painting. Often, the activity was seen as a prostitution of the hallowed skills. It was a way of earning a living, using painting skills for visual representation in the context of advertising, design, and the book. Among those who challenged such prejudices was a particular group of students at the influential Royal College of Art in the early 1920s. At this time, one of the teachers at the Design School at the RCA was the painter Paul Nash. In 1922, he had under his tutelage a group of students who he was later to refer to as "an outbreak of talent." These included Edward Bawden (who had gained a scholarship from Cambridge School of Art), Eric Ravilious, and Douglas Percy Bliss. Also studying there at the time was Enid Marx, who became a leading designer for industry and creator of several splendidly eccentric picturebooks. But Marx was in the painting school because, like many at the time, she fell victim to the perceptions of design or 'commercial art' as a lesser, more modest activity. But Bawden and Ravilious saw no conflict and went on to happily traverse gallery art, book illustration, ceramic design, wallpaper design, and much more. Both were appointed as official war artists during the Second World War. Bawden, by all accounts a taciturn individual, was not given to speaking or writing about his work but did point out that "drawing is another way of thinking" (Feaver 1987: 3). The influence and pioneering absence of prejudice of these artists is still felt today. And there is a sense that the prejudices are beginning to be loosened as an increasing number of critics and scholars begin to take the art of the picturebook more seriously within the field of art and design. Nevertheless, it is still relatively common to read reviews of picturebooks from those untrained in the visual arts that address the primary content of the book with a footnote along the lines of 'nicely/attractively illustrated.' In fact of course, the picturebook is not strictly speaking 'illustrated' according to traditional definitions of the term, with the visual text often being the primary conveyor of narrative or meaning.

Illustration in its broader sense is often described as a 'hybrid' art. It straddles the applied and 'fine' arts. It functions within a design context and is normally commissioned. Yet it can be expressive and personal. In the institutional context, the discipline has in recent years been variously aligned with graphic design, visual communication, communication design, and other essentially functional sounding subject titles. But illustration education is now finding itself needing to keep up with the emergence and evolution of the authorial picturebook-maker or creator of graphic literature.

Things were very different when I first contributed to the teaching of undergraduate illustration students in the early 1990s. I was joining a long-standing tradition as a busy working illustrator, giving up a day or so a week to teach. Art and design has traditionally been taught by artists and designers. In other words, students learn from practitioners, who are contracted to do a few hours of teaching a week. Full-time tutors (not until recently referred to as 'academics') would also be practitioners. Each artist-tutor works in a different way, with his particular personal approaches, methods, and philosophies. Students navigate a route through sometimes confusingly varied and even conflicting advice. A fundamental difference between teaching and learning in the visual arts and teaching and learning in other, more traditionally academic disciplines is that the outcomes or embodiments of that learning are emerging visibly in a shared studio space in an atmosphere of group support and criticism, using 'the head, the heart, and the hand.' Students learn as much from each other as they do from the teaching.

The picturebook in my early days of teaching, indeed children's book illustration in general, was very much a minority interest among students. It was seen as a less than cool area with which to engage and had an image problem as a backwater of bunny drawing for girls. This was even more the case during my own years of study at art school. At this time, in the late 1970s, art school life involved immersion in a culture of making and freewheeling experimentation. There was little in the way of formal curriculum. We worked on our various projects alongside graphic design students, painters, sculptors, printmakers, fashion designers, and more. We watched films and trooped into the auditorium to listen to lectures from, for instance, Brian Eno (then of Roxy Music) and to watch 'performance art' that might involve a person sitting motionless on an armchair on stage for an hour or so. Our illustration course leader was Gerald Rose, a wonderful children's book illustrator who with his wife Elizabeth had won the 1960 Greenaway Medal for his book, *Old Winkle and the Seagulls*, and who is still illustrating today. Somewhere in the upper reaches of the building, the principal of the school, William Stobbs, had his office. Stobbs was also an important illustrator, highly prolific through the 1960s, 1970s, and 1980s. But we never saw him. Judging by the amount of published work that he produced during his tenure as principal, I can only assume that his office was also his studio and that occasionally someone would bring him some paperwork to sign. Despite, or perhaps because of, this 'other world' of apparently unstructured creative experiment, many of us went on to work successfully within the field. Illustration students alongside me at the time who went on to become particularly significant practitioners included Angela Barrett, Paul Slater, and Russell Mills. But the emphasis was very much on editorial and design illustration. When I recently met up with my old tutor, Gerald Rose, I asked him why he was so reluctant to show us his work at the time. Sadly he explained that the overwhelming leaning at the time toward heavily political, 'issue-based' illustration made him feel that his own work as a children's book illustrator was too out of step to be of use.

Our grounding and experimentation in drawing, printmaking (particularly useful in developing an understanding of the print processes by which our work would be brought to the page), photography and typography would stand us in good stead. Finding myself invited to run occasional projects as a 'guest illustrator' teaching undergraduate students alongside my commissioned work, I found the absence of attention to children's book illustration at the time perverse. It seemed to me that, despite the fact that illustration for children constituted such a huge proportion of the illustration landscape as a whole, the entire emphasis in teaching was on the visual interpretation of text for newspaper and magazine editorial illustration. Those few students who were engaged with the children's book often tended to have been pushed in that direction because they were perceived to be less creatively ambitious. Despite this, the occasional student with a real flair for picturebook-making would emerge. Among my students who achieved professional success in the area in these early days were Alison Bartlett, Ailie Busby, and the late Selina Young. The emergence of the Macmillan Prize for Children's Picturebook Illustration had a significant impact, tempting more students to experiment in this field. The competition was set up by Macmillan Children's Books, at this time led by Kate Wilson (now heading up the influential independent children's publishing house, Nosy Crow), who had the foresight to seek out new talent through this national award. Selina Young was an early winner and was soon followed by another of our students, Jane Simmons, who went on to achieve great commercial success with her Daisy Duck books (Orchard Books).

But in discussing these successes I am already getting ahead of myself. One of the key common factors in the success of these students and others is the period of education that long precedes any attempts at picturebook-making. And here we return to Ruskin, Carline, Bawden et al.

Drawing

The activity of drawing from observation is, for most illustrators, a fundamental building block in the development of a personal visual vocabulary. As I found myself committing more time to teaching alongside my illustration work (I eventually accepted a 0.5 permanent fractional post), I became increasingly interested in this key underpinning aspect of illustration education (Salisbury 2004). With drawing having historically featured so strongly in the educational ethos of Cambridge School of Art I was keen to examine and utilize its role and relevance in relation to the student illustrator. The group drawing trip is something that many graduates recall as instrumental in the development of their work. After an early experience of contributing to the teaching of a student drawing trip to Paris, I began to arrange annual trips to Porto and the Douro valley in northern Portugal, where I had drawn regularly myself. Here undergraduate students would be immersed in an alien visual culture for a week or so and would work in the sketchbook for up to nine hours a day, returning with a massive body of anecdotal, narrative documentary drawing. This experience would invariably have a fundamental impact on the student illustrators' development and creative direction. This process is part learning to see – understanding form, space, light, and tone – but perhaps equally importantly for the illustrator, part learning about human behavior in the visual narrative sense-gesture, body language, relationship of figure to environment. This is what Edward Ardizzone referred to as the 'minor dramas of everyday life.' Perhaps the greatest and most prolific of twentieth-century book illustrators, Ardizzone found little time to pontificate on the art of illustration, but he did speak about the illustrator's need to regularly return to observational drawing to avoid cliché:

> the illustrator, having learnt to draw the symbols for things, must still have recourse to life using his eye and his memory to augment and sweeten his knowledge. Life gives him his pictorial ideas. It increases his repertoire and raises it above a repetition of old work carefully learned.

1957: 4

On returning to their studio-based studies in Cambridge, the undergraduates would use this experience to inform their imaginative, interpretative drawing. Some were perhaps even inculcated with a lifelong attachment to the sketchbook as a suitcase of visual ideas.

Masters-level study

It was on one of these drawing trips, while toiling in the sketchbook myself, that I had the idea to design an MA program in children's book illustration. This would be a postgraduate course that would facilitate a deeper, more specialized study in this field of illustration. After the usual laborious process of preparing documents and presenting the proposal to a team of internal and external reviewers, the program was duly validated. Even at this level of specialization, the emphasis in the early stages of the course is on drawing from observation. With students arriving from a range of undergraduate art and design programs as well as illustration, the return to drawing is particularly important as an open-ended period of visual thinking. Students then move on to a period of studying the sequential image, exploring and testing the making and reading of sequential art. In practice, this means a lot of storyboarding and dummy book making ('writing with pictures') and in particular, learning about how the 'reader' fills in the gaps between pictures – what McCloud refers to as 'closure' (McCloud 2001) – and presenting and discussing these outcomes to staff and peers. Finally, all students work increasingly independently on self-proposed project work, all the while working with a team of internationally renowned artist-authors. As with most art school courses, the study ratio is around 75 percent studio based to 25 percent lecture/theory based. Theory and practice are closely integrated. From the first cohort of nine part-time students, the course has grown in number to around 150 full- and part-time students from twenty-nine countries. Graduates of the course have been shortlisted for most of the major picturebook awards around the world, winning prizes at Bologna and selling hundreds of thousands of books for international publishing houses.

A common misconception about such study is that students are taught 'how to draw for children.' In fact we teach that there is no particular 'way' of drawing for children. The ethos of the course is one of developing as an artist first and as a children's book illustrator second. Much of this development happens in the context of pure problem solving, for example trying to understand through drawing how something works. Masters student Ellie Snowden's long road to final illustrations for Edward Lear's "The Owl and the Pussycat" for her as yet unpublished Masters Stage Project (see Figures 32.1–32.2) involved observing human dancers in complex sequences of motion before projecting these movements onto completely anatomically different creatures.

For the authorial picturebook maker, an excessive consciousness of audience can be a danger and can lead to imitative work. Most leading artists in the field – Shaun Tan is a good example – will explain that the primary objective in picturebook making is to 'make it work for me' first. If the outcome is good, and is an honest attempt to convey a concept, it will find its audience. Of course, in the marketplace, the outcome is subject to the influence of editors and sales departments. But at the masters level, it is creative ambition that must come first.

Practice-based doctoral research

The PhD in art practice subjects has been a thorny issue for many years. While many argue that an original contribution to knowledge can only be disseminated in the form of words, others (including myself) are firmly of the view that, in the creative arts, there other ways of knowing and 'telling,' just as a picturebook shows and tells. A minority of art faculties has accepted PhDs that are submitted entirely in the form of exhibition or artifact. More commonly, the submission will be a mixture of visual/creative output and reflective commentary/literature review/critical writing. What is essential though, is that the outcome is explored and articulated through the kind of knowing-through-making that can only come from creative practice at the highest level. A recent example of progress in this direction can be seen in the form of the doctoral dissertation of Nick Sousanis (Teachers College, Columbia University), which was executed entirely in graphic novel form and which has subsequently been published by Harvard University Press. Sousanis's *Unflattening* (2015), in the words of the publishers,

> defies conventional forms of scholarly discourse to offer readers both a stunning work of graphic art and a serious inquiry into the ways humans construct knowledge.
>
> *2015: cover*

The work of Sousanis and others is crucial, both in terms of the generation of new knowledge and in addressing the anomaly of the increasing insistence on a PhD qualification for new appointments in the university art school (though I understand that in the United States, the use of the phrase "terminal degree or professional experience equivalent" in university job descriptions allows for committees to work around this situation). Illustration students (and prospective students) quite naturally expect their teachers to be leading practitioners in the field. It is extremely difficult to be both

Figures 32.1–32.2 Ellie Snowden's developmental work for a project to create a picturebook version of *The Owl and the Pussycat* involved many hours of research to understand human movement, followed by further work to adapt this to the very different anatomies of the animals.

a career academic and a high-profile working illustrator. It would be unfortunate and quite simply wrong if this gap between the makers and the scholars were to be widened by creating a two-tier structure of academic scholars and 'technical instructors.' Research that is rooted in reflective practice helps to bridge this gap, bringing new knowledge and insight into the processes that underpin the art of the picturebook maker.

At the Centre for Children's Book studies we enrolled the first PhD students in 2007. Research methods are focused on practice as a tool for enquiry. Recent doctoral research topics that have been undertaken by leading practitioners have included investigations into animal character design, an exploration of the possibilities of visual interpretation of the Book of Ecclesiastes in non-representational form, and an examination of the boundaries between the picturebook and the graphic novel. Often, the thesis as a whole includes picturebooks or graphic novels that have emerged over the course of the research and gone on to be published. Examples include Katherina Manolessou's *Zoom, Zoom, Zoom* (2014) and Becky Palmer's *La Soupière Magique* (The Magic Toureen 2014). But there can be conflicts for many artists undertaking research of this kind, conflicts that highlight the complex and varying nature of creative practice. One of the commonest problems is the clash between speculative, intuitive creative enquiry and excessive self-analysis. PhD students sometimes initially find themselves questioning and analyzing every mark that they make on paper, thereby paralyzing the intuitive 'flow' of the creative process. So each researcher has to find a personal method and chronology of reflection and analysis that does not inhibit process. Of course, much of the process of picturebook making is recorded through storyboards and dummies. Notwithstanding the cliché, 'a picture paints a thousand words,' effective visual communication can convey concepts and meanings that cannot be decoded into words and that even the best writers would struggle to express. But the ability to 'read' pictures is becoming scarcer as education through art becomes marginalized. In the UK, the marginalization of art in schools, as lamented by Richard Carline earlier, has increased recently, with universities tending not to regard an art A-Level qualification as relevant to university application, a situation which leads to most pupils giving the subject up early in their education unless already set on a career in art. One consequence of this extreme division between practice and theory is the difficulty of finding appropriately qualified examiners for practice led PhDs in the subject. Early experiences of examiners from the field of children's literature studies rather than art practice revealed a tendency to completely ignore the candidate's visual research and to focus on a line of questioning based solely on the written element, while unable to 'read' answers that were readily available in the visual work. Some time later, I recall asking one such academic whether our knowledge of impressionist painting came primarily from impressionist painting or from what has been written about impressionist painting. The answer was instant and unequivocal: "from what has been written, of course!"

Such alarming experiences have not deterred us. Despite the depressing apparent decline in visual perception, that peculiar species, the picturebook-maker, does not seem to be in danger of extinction. Neither does the picturebook itself, which seems to be leading the charge in rejuvenating the book publishing industry (sales of physical picturebooks in the UK have now increased by over 5 percent for each of the last two years, while sales of children's and young adult non-fiction books have rocketed by over 30 percent). And of course we are currently awash with coloring books for adults, which are selling in colossal quantities. It is easy to be cynical about this particular phenomenon but it clearly reflects a need that has arisen as a result of the growing amount of time that is spent in front of a screen. We are bombarded with an ever-increasing amount of imagery via this medium, but inevitably spending less and less time on each image. Consequently, we are becoming less rather than more 'visually literate.' We are seeing more images but, in Ruskin's terminology, we are perhaps becoming less able to 'see keenly.'

The graphic artist Saul Steinberg, one of the greatest of visual thinkers, put it succinctly. "Drawing," he said, "is a way of reasoning on paper."

Figures 32.3–32.4 When designing a page in framed, sequential form, the distribution of tonal weight across the whole page has to be considered, as well as the need to drive the narrative from left to right and top to bottom. This page from Becky Palmer's *Le Soupiere Magique* (Sarbacane 2014) is shown in its initial linear form to the left and fully realized to the right.

Figures 32.3–32.4 Continued

References

Archer, Bruce (1979) "Design as a Discipline," *Design Studies* 1.1 (June 1979): 17–20.

Ardizzone, Edward (1957) *On the Illustrating of Books*, London: The Private Libraries Association Quarterly (Vol. 1, no. 3, July 1957). Reprinted in book form, *On the Illustration of Books* (1986), Fullbrook: The Weather Bird Press.

Carline, Richard (1968) *Draw They Must: A History of the Teaching and Examining of Art*, London: Edward Arnold.

Feaver, William (1987) "Drawing His Own Conclusion," *The Observer Magazine*, 8 March, 3.

Frayling, Christopher (2015) *The Head, the Hand and the Heart: The Surprising Story of English Design Education*, Cambridge: Henry Sidgwick Memorial Lecture.

Heller, Steven, and Arisman, Marshall (2000) *The Education of an Illustrator*, New York: Allworth Press.

McCloud, Scott (2001) *Understanding Comics*, New York: William Morrow/ Harpercollins.

Manolessou, Katherina (2014) *Zoom Zoom Zoom*, London: MacMillan Children's Books.

Palmer, Becky (2014) *La Soupière Magique*, Paris: Editions Sarbacane.

Read, Herbert (1943) *Education Through Art*, London: Faber & Faber.

Rose, Elizabeth (1960) *Old Winkle and the Seagulls*, illus. Gerald Rose, London: Faber and Faber.

Ruskin, John (1907) *The Elements of Drawing in Three Letters to Beginners*, London: Smith Elder (originally published 1857).

Salisbury, Martin (2004) *Illustrating Children's Books: Creating Pictures for Publication*, London: A & C Black.

Shahn, Ben (1957) *The Shape of Content*, Cambridge, MA: Harvard University Press.

Sousanis, Nick (2015) *Unflattening*, Cambridge, MA: Harvard University Press.

Further reading

Arnheim, Rudolf (1969) *Visual Thinking*, Berkeley: University of California Press.

Backemeyer, Sylvia (2005) *Picture This: The Artist as Illustrator*, London: The Herbert Press.

Frayling, Christopher (1987) *The Royal College of Art: One Hundred & Fifty Years of Art & Design*, London: Barrie & Jenkins.

Munari, Bruno (2008), *Design as Art*, London: Penguin Edition (first published 1966).

Salisbury, Martin (2015) *100 Great Children's Picturebooks*, London: Laurence King.

Salisbury, Martin, and Styles, Morag (2012) *Children's Picture Books: The Art of Visual Storytelling*, London: Laurence King.

Schön, Donald A. (1984) *The Reflective Practitioner*, New York: Basic Books.

33

RESEARCH IN PICTUREBOOKS

The wider path

William Moebius

No field of study or discipline can count itself healthy if it does not continually evolve, nor can it thrive without surveillance over an ever-growing corpus of objects of study. Such a field of study today is that of the picturebook for children. Once upon a time, research in the picturebook, not to mention the field of children's literature, had no place in literary studies, and unless conducted under the flag of library science or of childhood education, it had no place. Research in the broader field of children's literature and in the picturebook now comes under many flags, not a few of which wave over literary studies, but there is room for other approaches as well. As picturebooks themselves find new spaces for their reception in cinema and television, and even in electronic games, as they have for years found spaces in the realm of collectibles, dolls, toys as souvenirs, or reenactments of a reading or viewing experience, these transformed 'picturebooks' generate new insights, new readings, new translations, and they pass into new fields of inquiry. Neither children's literature nor the picturebook have ever been exclusively a child's privilege, as both have always depended on a partnership with adult readers and book-makers, a literature authors can bank on, but also a realm open to explorers from philosophy and education, genre studies, social justice, race and gender studies, immigration and international studies, memory studies, and ecocriticism.

Genetics

With what some have called the 'golden age of children's literature' upon us, the children's picturebook may play a fundamental role in the shaping of not only child understanding but of popular culture for all ages and in many languages. In this chapter, I attempt to sort out how research in children's literature and research in the picturebook cross paths or go their separate ways. Some research protocols embrace both, for example: the genetics of the book; genetic epistemology, or how the way we know things changes over time and how that is reflected in the experience of particular characters in a novel or a picturebook; and human cognitive development from pre-literacy to literacy, where we consider how both characters and readers may construct the world at different stages of development. But even in the first of this triad, the genetics of the book, we may find fewer opportunities in exploring the history of the making of a chapter book with lots of print and few images than we do in learning about the development of a particular picturebook, which can involve more stakeholders and more media. Lengthy monographs on the work of picturebook makers such as Margaret Wise Brown, Claude Ponti, Maurice Sendak, or William Steig form an important part of the system of scholarly response to the picturebook just as do monographs about children's book writers from Charles Dodgson to Erich Kästner (see Van der Linden 2000; Steig 2011).

Classifications: the archive

At least three fields, information science (once library science), systems theory, and literary studies invite critics to classify and in some ways to design archival 'systems' of the book, where a given picturebook may not be as predictable as one might think. Consider the status of a picturebook, *Pisim Finds Her Miskanow* (2013) by William Dumas, recently published in Winnipeg and based on the discovery of the body of a seventeenth-century First Nations woman, narrated and illustrated by First Nations people. Or consider the picturebook from Mexico *La Muerte pies ligeros* (Death with Silent Feet 2005), with text in both Nuatl and Spanish, produced by a prominent Mexican painter, Francisco Toledo, and his partner, Natalia Toledo, featuring a figure of Death extinguishing the life of one creature after another for all but the last opening. To what categories might these picturebooks belong? Where would they fit if we decide that their habitat is 'children's literature?' Where will they belong, if we choose instead to fit them into the habitat of 'picturebook?' I would suggest that this problematic is more likely to occur in the domain of the picturebook than in that of the book for children, especially when the picturebook takes on the role of documentary.

Academic disciplines, the library, and the museum

Research perspectives that favor the study of language, such as spoken language development or language pedagogy, discourse analysis or poetics, may thrive in the world of children's literature, but need special adaptation to the realm of picturebooks. Many research perspectives will prosper in both environments, yet if a veritable library of academic disciplines lies before us when we say 'children's literature,' that library itself may need a separate wing, or a world-class museum of its own for the 'children's picturebook.' Perhaps neither library nor museum would be needed, were we to embrace the concept of the online university, scrap the book, and turn to digital media and the international viewing audiences that depend on them; in a research environment in which images travel as quickly as words, the picturebook would already have served as a storyboard for worldwide children's television (*Curious George, Where the Wild Things Are, Madeline, The Lost Thing*, the Reverend W. Awdry's *Thomas & Friends*, Joceline Sanschagrin's *Caillou*, Vicky Wong and Michael C. Murphy's *The Octonauts*), and many other picturebooks find a kind of immortality in world circulation on stage or screen.

Research on the picturebook may and often must exceed the boundaries of children's book research. The picturebook is not always a writing, not always a fixture of language. It is inevitably a kind of 'drawing,' sometimes with titles and captions, but sometimes a depiction of a fable with no more than a few noises. Take *The Lion and the Mouse* (2009) by the African American author/illustrator Jerry Pinkney, in which the only letters (in an opening near the middle of the book) appear in sound-effect clusters not found in the dictionary, yet recognizable as sounds of pain and frustration. In a wordless picturebook such as *The Lion and the Mouse*, the sudden emergence of letters paradoxically takes the place of a modest illustration in the midst of a fable told in words.

While children's literature will usually be found in a library, the picturebook can also be found on the walls of a museum, joining such visual experiences as the Bayeux tapestry or ancient Greek red or black figure vases. The Eric Carle Museum of the Picturebook may serve as a testimony to such 'apartness.' The picturebook evokes an alternative space, and requires more than a passing acquaintance with the rules and generative practices that govern that space.

The culture of the mural and of the museum permeates the history of the picturebook up to this day, with a whole strand of picturebooks thematizing the visit to the museum, the injunction to 'look closer,' to ascertain what the picture is 'telling' us. Museums of art themselves these days not only sell such picturebooks, but at least one has invited a picturebook maker, Quentin Blake, to remake the visitors' experience of a special exhibition of traditional 'easel' art in gilded frames by drawing caricatures of typically skeptical family viewers on the walls of the Grand Palais in Paris, and adapting these caricatures to his picturebook *Tell Me a Picture* (2001) as a somewhat irreverent stroll with mock viewers through a special exhibition at the National Gallery in London.

Such irreverence of a Quentin Blake is not unknown in nursery rhymes and fables, nor is it foreign to children's literature from Lewis Carroll's *Alice's Adventures in Wonderland* (1865) to Salman Rushdie's *Haroun and the Sea of Stories* (1990). Going 'meta' with language opens the door to critical literacy; playing with homonyms raises eyebrows and begs scrutiny. The contesting of meaning can be very much a fixture of the children's book without any reliance on visual aids. Nonetheless, the picturebook, as a joint venture between word and image, disguises in some ways a contest between the world of commercial art and the world of 'fine art,' made explicit in the distinction between schools of design and schools of fine art, underlining the apartness of art for the printed word and art for the wall. Picturebook makers like Dr. Seuss (aka Ted Geisel) or Leo Lionni would start their careers in the realm of publicity and advertisement, the graphic arts of persuasion, while most painters, at least in the art schools of the nineteenth and early twentieth centuries, would have been trained in the 'beautiful' or the 'sublime,' disregarding the primacy of the word. We may not need to be reminded of the debate, joined by the likes of Leonardo da Vinci, between promoters of the word (as poets) and promoters of the image (as painters), but this debate fostered an academic parting of the ways, a "disaggregation of the faculties" as Stephen Owen (2016) has put it, which is perpetuated in the division of academic pursuits surrounding criticism developed for children's literature, and criticism of the picturebook today. In the early stages of this debate, both parties would likely have agreed that the picturebook is an illegitimate child for both sides, neither literature nor art, but today in the picturebook world we celebrate this hybrid, which can be exploited quite delightfully in picturebooks that take their cue from the writing of famous poets, works such as Philippe Dumas's *Victor Hugo s'est égaré* (Victor Hugo Got Lost 2002), or those that spoof the fine arts, such as in Posy Simmons's *Lulu and the Flying Babies* (1991). A playful spirit of betrayal, abnormality, and caricature has haunted the picturebook, from the days of Heinrich Hoffmann's *Der Struwwelpeter* (Slovenly Peter 1845) to the postmodern twists of David Wiesner's *The Three Little Pigs* (2001) or Françoise Boucher's *Le livre qui t'explique enfin tout sur les parents* (The Book That Explains Everything about Parents, 2012). Some readers, exhausted by the transgressive elements of this kind of picturebook, may turn for solace or modest relief to another kind of picturebook that offers moments of quiet in an artist's studio, once captured again and again by Carl Larsson in his many paintings of children caught up in the enchantment of the book. We may describe this other kind of picturebook as more contemplative, more reflective, exemplified in the work of Allen Say, with his tribute to the Kamashibai or "paper-theater" man (*The Kamishibai Man* 2005), or the gifts and perils of a child artist like Emma, who lives for her art (*Emma's Rug* 1996).

Textuality and the materiality of the book

In this brief chapter, we remain in the world of printed books, mortal, in or out of print, awaiting readers who can handle them, discover meaning, reread and discover more meaning, books that captivate and liberate the reader all at the same time. Such a predilection for the hard copy of the picturebook need not be considered a rite of nostalgia. Recent research indicates that in early childhood, language acquisition through the parent-infant dyad benefits from the experience of wooden puzzles and the (picture)book more than from any electronic toys or media (Sosa 2016). If pictures are needed to tell the story, they cannot be ignored or relegated to an auxiliary position. The specialist in the picturebook must reckon with the history of reading itself, but especially with the special difference of the picturebook in the very "turning of the page," a key factor acknowledged by the choreographer/picturebook maker Remy Charlip and his many admirers (Bader 1976).

Doing justice to the picturebook

Criticism of the picturebook needs a certain mindfulness of the eye, one usually developed in the world of the visual arts. A critical literature on how we may read the picturebook and its tensions between word and image has emerged over the past several decades, thanks to the contributions of Perry Nodelman (1988), Jean Perrot (1991), Jane Doonan (1993), Maria Nikolajeva and Carole Scott (2001), Martin Salisbury (2004), Nathalie op de Beeck (2010), and Sandra Beckett (2012). The picturebook, like William Blake's visual setting of his poems, makes demands on the critic that may not be encountered in the study of nursery rhymes, adaptations of traditional or folk narratives, and chapter books that conform to the dictates of the unadorned page. The picturebook knows no margin on the page and comes in many different kinds, as different as kinds of poetry and music. For those who care about the footnote and line spacing, who prefer to follow the path of a sentence one horizontal queue of letters after another, margins count, but they represent but one option for the maker of a picturebook. 'To get the picture' in the picturebook depends not only on the content of the image but of its size, place, vectors, colors, ornamentation, and placement within a set of pages. Even the lettering must be grasped as a token of the history and symbolic status of particular fonts, or even of ornamented initial letters. Those many rows of letters that adult readers scan for meaning every day, like the ones on this page, have left the biosphere of lettering, but in the picturebook these letters can join the vines and flowers, as they do in the work of Ivan Yakovlevich Bilibin in his treatment of Russian fairy tales, or as happens in the comic strip, become sound effects, as they do in Ziraldo Pinto's *El Menino Quadradinho* (The Panel Boy 1989), a picturebook/comic book that transgresses its own generic limitations at its midpoint by suddenly becoming a strictly ordered series of pages limited to the printed word, a margined sequence marking a shift in genre and in readership.

Exclusion and inclusion: the body, spectatorship, witness

Children's literature, but in particular, the picturebook have long known mechanisms of both exclusion and inclusion. Roald Dahl's books for children could never manage to win an American Library Association award, and Maurice Sendak's *In the Night Kitchen* (1970) rated no. 24 on the American Library Association's list of frequently banned books over the period 2000–2009. What a children's book author can say and what a picturebook maker can show are both at stake, but the modernist injunction to 'show' may breed more controversy and resistance. The study of spectatorship, of peeking, of ogling, of the male gaze, or the animal's gaze on the human, or even on the reader's obsession with particular images, must be a factor in the study of the picturebook, but may not have much to do with the reading of a chapter book. Picturebooks like Frank Tashlin's 1946 *The Bear That Wasn't* (1946) lend themselves to such study, as does Syd Hoff's *Grizzwold* (1963). Both stories position the bear as the disenfranchised, the outsider, and to some extent, the spectacle.

While bodily nudity is still relatively rare in the American picturebook (Sendak's *In the Night Kitchen*, or *Pocahontas* [1946] by the D'Aulaires), battle scenes, street violence, violent death, torture, oppressed mothers, belligerent or dismissive fathers, Holocaust victims, and homeless children all figure in the world of the contemporary picturebook and draw the reader's attention to worlds of poverty, slavery, and brutality, the immediacy of which remains otherwise unspeakable. Here the work of Shoshana Felman and Dory Laub (1992), or more recently of Marianne Hirsch (2012), is highly relevant as both address the phenomenon of witnessing and facing the past.

Picturebooks by such twentieth-century masters as Elzbieta, Tomi Ungerer, and Maurice Sendak and a host of African American picturebook makers lend themselves to such witnessing. Studies of picturebooks depicting slavery and the Civil War in the United States join Michelle H. Martin's classic work *Brown Gold: Milestones of African-American Children's Picture Books, 1845–2002* (2004) in identifying and reflecting on key factors in such a critical approach. Although stereotypes and legacies of physiognomy still play a role in the figuring of bodies in the picturebook, historical scholarship cannot overlook the semblances of the human as constructed in the past, cannot exclude this sensitive topic of how the 'other' is made to look. German historian Andrew Donson addresses an assemblage of picturebooks as instruments of accommodation to the call to war in his *Youth in the Fatherless Land: War Pedagogy, Nationalism, and Authority in Germany, 1914–1918* (2010), exploring a world in which 'critical literacy' was losing ground. Much work remains to be done in the analysis of albums such as the *Bécassine* series (1913–1950) by Jacqueline Rivière and Joseph Pinchon. The firsthand experiences of Tomi Ungerer, as reflected in his *Tomi: A Childhood under the Nazis* (1998), or of Elzbieta, related in her *L'Enfance de l'Art* (1997), fill important gaps.

Cultural criticism

Books for children have long disguised cultural criticism through the focalizing gaze of the child. What is wrong with the world can be seen through the secret agency of the spying child. While children's literature research generally can rely on subtly written descriptions of what is going on in the mind's eye of the protagonist, the researcher of the picturebook can call on both a presented world and a presentational process quite distinct from the words on the page, if any. The image can ironize the text, as well as second it. The image can diffuse and render more fluid what is written down beside or beneath it. None of these cues is available to the reader/researcher of a book for children anchored entirely in a stream of words. Both reader and child detective can lend themselves to the vexations of the curious, and the rewards of the perceptive. The feral child knows things inapprehensible to the cultivated adult: from Curious George to Willy the Wimp, the lead character has a nose for the pretentious, fraudulent, cruel, and staidly 'civilized.' There is room here for research that contextualizes such social commentary, or that links traditional folkloric figures to their latest postmodern manifestations. It is not unrelated to research in cultural imaginaries, such as that of a global South imagined as the birthplace of a Curious George or a simian like Willy the Wimp. Stereotypes of place, race, and gender abound in many traditions of children's literature, but the specialist in the picturebook must have an eye for visual motifs that have a history independent of the story line in a given picturebook. Children's literature scholarship has never failed to flow like a disinfectant or even an inoculation against the threat of the stereotype, but one can also find resistance to such stereotypes in the picturebook itself, the long history of *Bécassine*, for example, mocking stereotypes of the African American and Native American, and even undermining the pretenses of the science of phrenology.

Cultural imaginaries

Without a keen understanding of the cultural imaginary of a given picturebook, let us say one devoted to the representation of an immigrant experience such as *Halmoni and the Picnic* (1993) by Sook Nyul Choi, one cannot produce a rich critical response. A text-based version of the story of Halmoni, a Korean grandmother (*halmoni* means 'grandmother'), who finds herself in New York city walking her granddaughter to her school bus stop, would be utterly impoverished without the signals to be read in the images. Most readers of this book ignore a gesture featured on the book jacket and on the title page where the grandmother, wrapped in a floor-length gown, stands beside her granddaughter, who wears typical American street clothes: both at the bus stop on the cover and in a vignette of a bedroom, Halmoni is holding her hand up to her mouth. Nowhere in the picturebook is this gesture mentioned or explained. One can read it out loud and never ponder this cue. Cultural values imparted visually are inextricable from the meanings that accumulate in a picturebook. The gesture unnoticed might as well be that of a reader who cannot read. In this case, Halmoni, speechless, covers her mouth as she struggles to speak English, but also not to show her teeth or her smile.

Identity, gender, queer studies, and the picturebook

Post-colonial and empire studies as well as gender and queer studies have all staked out territory in the land of children's literature, and continue to make room for more. Even without their impetus, listservs such as the UK-based Picturebook Research Digest open new windows of opportunity for the transnational scholar embedded in sites once orientalized or othered, where one might find *O Menino Quadradinho* (1989) by the Brazilian artist Ziraldo Pinto, *Thambaya Takes a Ride* (2009) by Sybil Wettasinghe from Sri Lanka, or *La Muerte pies ligeros* (2005) by the Mexican team Natalia and Francisco Toledo, each of whose work may rise to the top worldwide.

When we ask ourselves what critical approaches to take towards a picturebook, approaches perhaps not needed for text-centered works for children, we are asking ourselves how to do justice to the picturebook, and how the picturebook itself does justice to the world it creates. Is the picturebook an invitation to understanding or, as some would fear, a vehicle for spectatorship? Such a conundrum emerges in a rather simple poem about the picturebook featured in an 1895 English-language periodical for children. The poem tells us just how useful the picturebook might or might not be for the child to gain insight into the world, especially as concerns 'representation.' This Edwardian-era poem appearing at the height of empire seems to be about difference and otherness, about a child's recognizing the global in the local beckoning to be understood, a meeting for which the spectatorship encouraged by the picturebook is well suited.

Little Paul's Picture-Book

In little Paul's "Instructive Illustrated Picture-Book"
There are scenes in foreign countries, showing
how the people look.
There's a "Scene among the Africans",
In colors gay and bright;
A scene called "Chinese People" –
An interesting sight.
There's a picture named "Among the Turks,"
Where turbaned men go by;
And some "Italian Natives"
Beneath an azure sky.
But strange to say, when Paul walks out and
Sees about the town
Turks, colored men, Italians, too,
with skins of olive-brown
And even placid Chinamen, –
these people never look
As they do in his "Instructive Illustrated Picture-Book."
Opper 1895: 230

The poem gently problematizes picturebook representation in a world increasingly complicated by the business of empire, the traffic of immigration, and the breakdown of terminologies for gendered subjects. It highlights ways in which the picturebook acts as a tool of surveillance, enabling the reader to assign a national or racial identity to otherwise neutral figures: Italians, Chinese, Africans, and Turks. Here, as noted earlier, the picturebook is seen as a disclosure of the physiognomic taxonomies that flourished in the nineteenth century as tacit codes of empire or nationality.

Doing justice to the picturebook requires a close examination of the powers it represents. The picturebook has the power to instruct and entertain, calm and assure, enchant and frighten in ways we associate with television and film. We might ask how the picturebook performs wisdom or pain or caring in ways that no other medium can do, including long and short chapter books that keep the reader engaged for weeks on end or serialized telenovelas that cultivate the viewer's addiction. Some picturebooks have proven to be a treasure trove for scholars in fields such as social justice, gender or race studies, or in ecocriticism, fields which intersect with activist agendas in colleges of education or in literature departments (Dobrin and Kidd 2004; Botelho and Rudman 2009; Bird and Sieruta 2014). In other words, for some scholars, picturebooks may be easy samples or evidence for social and cultural studies, but such studies may be indifferent to pictorial ironies and paradoxes.

Picturebook and book arts

As suggested at the outset of this chapter, the picturebook invites research across a cluster of disciplines related to the book arts, starting in the European medieval period, including paper making, print technologies, woodcuts, engraving, lettering, and typeface, the composition of the page, the recycling of engraved images, the iconography of printed images, and the relation of art intended for the book and art intended for the wall as painting, mural, or backdrop. It needs to be said that the picturebook opens up scholarly conversations that might at times seem out of place in the world of children's literature, as it invites a historical perspective that goes beyond the usual parameters of children's literature studies with their strong focus on the modern and postmodern. Heinrich Steinhöwel's illustrated edition of Aesop's Fables, *Esopus* (1476–1480) or Raoul Lefèvre's *L'Histoire de Jason* (History of Jason, 1460) or his *Recuyell des histoires de Troyes* (Compilation of Histories about Troy, 1464), translated and published respectively by William Caxton ca. 1477 and 1473, help usher in the European world of graphic design in the printed book and set precedents that can be found in picturebooks for children published almost two hundred years later, such as Johann Amos Comenius's *Orbis Sensualium Pictus* of 1658 (Thompson 2004). Lest there be any doubt about the intended readership of Caxton's *History of Jason*, we need only be reminded that the dedicatee, Edward, Prince of Wales, was not more than five years old at the time of publication, and that the book itself is intended to help him learn to read English, "not for ony beaute or good Endyting of our Englissh tonge that is therein. But for the nouelte of the histories whiche as I suppose hath not be had befor the translacion herof" (1913: 2).

There is no ignoring the primary function of the translator to render intelligible a text so that it might be accessible to children, and thus takes its place in the realm of children's literature. But Caxton's prologue also provides a direct link to the visual arts: in an anecdote in the preface, the translator offers a brief account of a visit to a special room in the castle of "Hesdyn" of his patron, Philippe, Duc of Burgundy, "where in was craftily and curiously depeynted the conquest of the Golden Flese by the sayd Iason/in which chamber I haue ben and seen the sayde historie so depeynted" (2). The castle of Hesdin was widely known as a kind of amusement park, a proto–Disney World, furnished with all kinds of deceptive devices visually alluring and at the same time potentially punitive. If we take steps backward in time such as this, we are not only inviting ourselves to the playground of a family once rich and famous, but we are witnessing the gestation of a mixed medium, as neither text nor image by itself will suffice. The calculus of the picturebook critic must factor in developments in pictorialism for which the philologist takes no responsibility.

The picturebook as world traveler and the role of translation

It is not difficult to plot the successes of the twentieth- and twenty-first-century picturebook as a genre well suited for travel beyond the borders of nation and language (Kümmerling-Meibauer 2015). Ever since the end of World War I travel and the once obligatory lessons in geography have been themes in children's books, but especially in picturebooks. A number of illustrated books for children enjoy a worldwide readership, and, for those interested might arguably belong to the category of 'world literature,' or to the 'canonical' along with other gems of literary creativity intended for adults. A short list might include works by Carlo Collodi, Erich Kästner, Astrid Lindgren, Antoine de Saint-Exupéry, Robert Louis Stevenson, and Jules Verne, but the place of the picturebook on such a short list remains problematic, as long as the criteria of such a list circle around the 'art of the word.' The picturebook author/illustrator cannot be a candidate for the Nobel Prize for Literature, but the picturebook author/illustrator in the United States can win the Randolph Caldecott Medal for the most distinguished American picturebook, a medal not meant for 'other kinds' of children's literature. The politics of the word tend to marginalize those of the image, and at their cruelest relegate the picturebook to the status of a sub-genre of children's literature. Yet the award-winning picturebook is more likely to travel far and wide, and to contribute to a shared perspective profoundly rooted in adult memory (Kümmerling-Meibauer 2010).

To help the picturebook on its way around the world requires the intervention of the translator. The role of the translator is crucial to the diffusion of a picturebook, but without an understanding of the gap between the unadorned text and the one with pictures called a picturebook, the translator must learn to do justice to both the images and the text (Oittinen 2000; O'Sullivan 2006). The front cover of Maurice Sendak's *Where the Wild Things Are* (1963) pictures a landscape, with tall trees, both deciduous and tropical, in a straight line in the background of a straight waterway, a sailboat with pennant flying in the opposite direction as the wind blowing the sails, a partially human creature in the academic pose of the thinker, and other paradoxical signs which answer to the broad label of 'wild things.' That the title of this canonical picturebook could be translated as *Max et le Maximonstres* or *Nel paese di monstri selvaggi* should not go unnoticed, as both translations particularize and limit the broader implications of the original, steering the reader down a narrower path with limited possibilities. The multiple opportunities for picturebook research that I have outlined here portend a wider path.

References

Bader, Barbara (1976) *American Picturebooks from Noah's Ark to the Beast Within*, New York: Palgrave Macmillan.

Beckett, Sandra L. (2012) *Crossover Picturebooks: A Genre for All Ages*, New York: Routledge.

Bird, Betsy, Danielson, Julie, and Sieruta, Peter D. (2014) *Wild Things! Acts of Mischief in Children's Literature*, Somerville, MA: Candlewick Press.

Blake, Quentin (2001) *Tell Me a Picture*, London: National Gallery.

Botelho, Maria José, and Rudman, Masha Kabakow (2009) *Critical Multicultural Analysis of Children's Literature: Mirrors, Windows, and Doors*, New York: Routledge.

Boucher, Françoise (2012) *Le livre qui t'explique enfin tout sur les parents*, Paris: Nathan.

Browne, Anthony (1984) *Willy the Wimp*, London: Julia MacRae Books.

Carroll, Lewis (1865) *Alice's Adventures in Wonderland*, London: Macmillan.

Choi, Sook Nyul (1993) *Halmoni and the Picnic*, illus. Karen M. Dugan, Boston, MA: Houghton Mifflin.

Comenius, Johann Amos (1658) *Orbis Sensualium Pictus*, Nuremberg: Michael Endter.

D'Aulaire, Ingri, and D'Aulaire, Edgar Parin (1946) *Pocahontas*, New York: Doubleday.

Doonan, Jane (1993) *Looking at Pictures in Picture Books*, Stroud: Thimble Press.

Dumas, Philippe (2002) *Victor Hugo s'est égaré*, Paris: L'École des loisirs.

Dumas, William (2013) *Pisim Finds Her Miskanow* (English and Cree edition), illus. Leonard Paul, Winnipeg: Portage and Main Press.

Dobrin, Sydney I., and Kidd, Kenneth B. (2004) *Wild Things: Children's Culture and Ecocriticism*, Detroit: Wayne State University Press.

Donson, Andrew (2010) *Youth in the Fatherless Land: War Pedagogy, Nationalism, and Authority in Germany, 1914–1918*, Cambridge, MA: Harvard University Press.

Elzbieta (1997) *L'Enfance de l'Art*, Rodez: Éditions du Rouergue.

Felman, Shoshana, and Laub, Dory (1992) *Testimony: Crises of Witnessing in Literature*. New York: Routledge.

Hirsch, Marianne (2012) *The Generation of Postmemory: Writing and Visual Culture After the Holocaust*, New York: Columbia University Press.

Hoff, Syd (1963) *Grizzwold*, New York: Harper Collins.

Hoffmann, Heinrich (1845) *Der Struwwelpeter*, Frankfurt: Literarische Anstalt.

Kümmerling-Meibauer, Bettina (2010) "Remembering the Past in Words and Pictures: How Autobiographical Stories Become Picturebooks," in Teresa Colomer, Bettina Kümmerling-Meibauer, and Cecilia Silva-Díaz (eds) *New Directions in Picturebook Research*, New York: Routledge, 205–215.

Kümmerling-Meibauer, Bettina (2015) "From Baby Books to Picturebooks for Adults: European Picturebooks in the New Millennium," *Word & Image* 31.3: 249–264.

Lefèvre, Raoul (1913) *The History of Jason*, trans. William Caxton, ed. John James Munro, pub. for the Early English Text Society, by K. Paul, Trench, Trübner, and by H. Milford, London: Oxford University Press (first published 1460).

Lefèvre, Raoul (1894) *The Recuyell des historyes de Troye*, trans. William Caxton, ed. H. Oskar Sommer, London: David Nutt, Ballantyne, Hanson (first published 1464).

Martin, Michelle H. (2004) *Brown Gold: Milestones of African-American Children's Picture Books, 1845–2002*, New York: Routledge.

Nikolajeva, Maria, and Scott, Carole (2001) *How Picturebooks Work*, New York: Garland.

Nodelman, Perry (1988) *Words about Pictures: The Narrative Art of Children's Picture Books*, Athens: University of Georgia Press.

Oittinen, Riitta (2000) *Translating for Children*, London: Garland.

op de Beeck, Nathalie (2010) *Suspended Animation: Children's Picture Books and the Fairy Tale of Modernity*, Minneapolis: University of Minnesota Press.

Opper, Frederick B. (1895) "Little Paul's Picture-Book," *St. Nicolas Illustrated*, Volume XXII, Part 1, New York: The Century Co, 230.

O'Sullivan, Emer (2006) "Translating Pictures," in Gillian Lathey (ed.) *The Translation of Children's Literature: A Reader*, Clevendon: Multilingual Matters, 113–121.

Owen, Stephen (2016) "Don't Look Back," plenary panel, March 19, 2016, annual meeting of the American Comparative Literature Association, Harvard University, Cambridge, MA.

Perrot, Jean (1991) *L'art baroque, l'art d'enfance*, Nancy: Presses Universitaires de Nancy.

Pinkney, Jerry (2009) *The Lion and the Mouse*, New York: Little Brown Books.

Pinto, Ziraldo Alves (1989) *O Menino Quadradinho*, Sao Paulo: Editora Melhoramentos.

Rivière, Jacqueline (1913–1950) *Bécassine*, illus. Joseph Pinchon, Paris: Gautier (27 vols).

Rushdie, Salman (1990) *Haroun and the Sea of Stories*, London: Granta.

Salisbury, Martin (2004) *Illustrating Children's Books: Creating Pictures for Publication*, London: Quarto.

Say, Allen (1996) *Emma's Rug*, New York: Houghton Mifflin.

Say, Allen (2005) *The Kamishibai Man*, New York: Houghton Mifflin.

Sendak, Maurice (1963) *Where the Wild Things Are*, New York: Harper & Row.

Sendak, Maurice (1970) *In the Night Kitchen*, New York: Harper & Row.

Simmons, Posy (1991) *Lulu and the Flying Babies*, London: Puffin.

Sosa, Anna V. (2016) "Association of the Type of Toy Used During Play with the Quantity and Quality of Parent-Infant Communication," https://jamanetwork.com/journals/jamapediatrics/fullarticle/2478386 (accessed October 10, 2017).

Steig, Jeanne (2011) *Cats, Dogs, Men, Women, Ninnies & Clowns: The Lost Art of William Steig*, New York: ABRAMS Comicarts.

Steinhöwel, Heinrich (1477–1478) *Esopus*, Augsburg: Günther Zainer, (reprinted in *Die Inkunabel in ihren Hauptwerken*, vol. 1, Potsdam: Müller, 1922).

Tashlin, Frank (1946) *The Bear That Wasn't*, New York: E.P. Dutton.

Thompson, Wendy (2004) "Woodcut Book Illustration in Renaissance Italy: The First Illustrated Book," Heilbrunn Timeline of Art History, New York: Metropolitan Museum.

Toledo, Natalia (2005) *La Muerte pies ligeros/ Guendaguti ñee sisi*, illus. Francisco Toledo, México: FCE, IEEPO.

Ungerer, Tomi (1998) *Tomi: A Childhood Under the Nazis*, New York: Roberts Rinehart.

Van der Linden, Sophie (2000) *Claude Ponti*, Paris: Éditions Être.

Wettesinghe, Sybil (2009) *Thambaya Takes a Ride*, Maharagama, Sri Lanka: Tharanjee Prints.

Wiesner, David (2001) *The Three Little Pigs*, New York: Houghton Mifflin.

34

PICTUREBOOKS AND REPRESENTATIONS OF CHILDHOOD

Nina Christensen

Picturebooks portray children. If you randomly pick up a couple of picturebooks in a library, a bookshop, or a nursery, the majority of them depict a child or a childlike character as a central element on the cover, and very often the name of the character is part of the title of the book. From small books for the very young to picturebooks for young adults, the actions and behavior of child characters, the choices of these fictive children, and the interaction among them play a central part in the narratives. Furthermore, text and images represent a certain idea of the abilities and qualities of a potential reader (Wall 1991; Weinreich 2000). Portraits, narratives, and implied readers are expressions of certain perceptions of childhood. Paratexts point to specific ideas of what a child is, and ought to read, in the form of recommendations or blurbs, quotes from reviews, or the specification of a certain age group on the cover or dust jacket. Implicitly or explicitly, critical texts and discussions among educators, librarians, editors, researchers, reviewers, and in public media integrate perspectives on children and childhood. These discussions are also a means of including or excluding books from the category of children's books.

Critical approaches to representations of childhood

A critical approach to representations of different ethnic groups and minorities, gender, and sexuality has been part of literary and cultural studies in recent decades. Representations of childhood in children's literature have been debated, especially since the publication of Jacqueline Rose's *The Case of Peter Pan, or, The Impossibility of Children's Fiction* (1984), in which she famously wrote that "[t]here is no child behind the category of 'children's fiction,' other than the one which the category itself sets in place, the one which it needs to believe is there for its own purposes" (10). This was stated from Rose's poststructuralist position, where, among other things, a natural relationship between sign and content, language and object, was problematized. Rose points out that discourses surrounding children's literature must be seen as representations of ideas of childhood in a specific culture, at a specific point in history. In this view, the word 'child' does not denote a transhistorical content of essential qualities, such as innocence or fancifulness. The publication of Jacqueline Rose's book had a tremendous impact on children's literature studies, and led to influential critical investigations by Karín Lesnik-Oberstein, among others (Lesnik-Oberstein 1994, 1998, 2011).

The history of childhood published by the historian Philippe Ariès (1960) and the work by Michel Foucault are preconditions for Rose's attention to the need for a critical approach to images of childhood. Ariès's history of childhood arose from what has been termed *histoire des mentalités*, which paid special attention to the history of concepts or ideas. Contemporary childhood historians, such as Colin Heywood and Hugh Cunningham, use children's literature, among many other sources, in their more recent histories of childhood (Cunningham 1995; Heywood 2001).

Today, the concept of 'agency' has become very important to researchers of childhood and children's literature studies. The study of the relationship between structure (the organization and regulation of society) and agency (the individual's right to, and possibility of, acting independently) has been central to social sciences in general, and to childhood studies in particular (James and James 2008). Childhood sociologist David Oswell writes: "For the sociologists of childhood, it has been important to disclose 'children' as social agents and not simply to see 'childhood' as constructed by adults alone" (2013: 16). Recently, within children's literature studies, David Rudd and Marah Gubar have addressed the complexities surrounding childhood in children's literature studies. Gubar proposes three models of, or discourses concerning, childhood: the deficit model, the difference model, and the kinship model. Whereas the deficit model perceives children as individuals who lack something (abilities, skills, power) in relation to the adult, and the difference model sees the child as an unknown and unknowable 'other' in relation to the adult, Gubar prefers and suggests the kinship model, which is "premised on the idea that children and adults are akin to one another, which means they are neither exactly the same nor radically dissimilar. The concept of kinship indicates relatedness, connection, and similarity without implying homogeneity, uniformity, and equality" (2013: 453). According to Gubar, the infant is in need of care, and thus dependent on the adult, but the difference must be regarded as a "difference of degree, not of kind," since growth must be considered a continuum, not a row of stages to pass through in an orderly sequence. In his attempt to establish a possible position between essentialism and (de)constructivism, Rudd criticizes Rose's idea of the impossibility of children's fiction as being based on a romantic view of childhood, according to which children are conceived of as "distinct from adults, standing outside society and language, rather than being actively involved in negotiating meaning" (2010: 291). Inspired by Mikhail Bakhtin, Rudd perceives children's literature as expressions of a multiplicity of voices, heteroglossia, not as a monological, unequivocal statement. Furthermore, a child reader will engage in a dialogue with a text from his or her specific point of view, and in that process interact with multiple, even contradictory, voices and discourses present in a literary text. Thus, the child reader cannot be regarded as a passive recipient of norms or values: "The child, then, has both a sociocultural and an embodied sense of its location in society, from which vantage point it will respond, dialogically, to the various fictions proffered: liking some and rejecting others" (299). Rudd and Gubar may be regarded as scholars who perceive children's literature as one of the means of expression through which the relationship between dependence and agency is uttered, staged, discussed, and negotiated. This is one of the arguments for an analysis of representations of childhood in picturebooks.

Although meta-critical studies of childhood in children's literature are abundant, specific discussions of approaches to the analysis of representations of childhood in picturebooks have been scarce. An early exception is John Stephens, who includes a chapter on picturebooks in *Language and Ideology in Children's Fiction* (1992). In keeping with discourse analysis as his theoretical framework, Stephens's basic assumption is that ideology is implicitly and explicitly present in all utterances, including children's literature. Stephens writes of picturebooks: "Picture books can, of course, exist for fun, but they can never be said to exist without either a socializing or educational intention, or else without a specific orientation towards the reality constructed by the society that produces them" (158). For a while, now, viewing picturebooks as one of the many ways in which childhood, the education of children, and the relationship between children and adults are represented has been a basic tenet (Christensen 2004), but only recently have analyses of larger corpuses of picturebooks appeared in scholarly publications. Picturebook studies is a fairly new research field, and therefore the first books on picturebook analysis were general introductions aimed at covering a number of aspects (Nodelman 1988; Nikolajeva and Scott 2001; Christensen 2003). Elements from narratology, semiotics, and New Criticism are central elements of the first academic analyses of picturebooks, and very generally speaking, these three approaches share a lack of interest in the historical and cultural context of the work. The inclination to use these approaches may also be seen as part of the attempt to legitimize the study of picturebooks within academia by approaching them with the scrutiny which complex works invite. Today, articles in anthologies of picturebook studies, such as *New Directions in Picturebook Research* (Colomer, Kümmerling-Meibauer and Silva-Díaz 2010) and *Picturebooks. Representation and Narration* (Kümmerling-Meibauer 2014) present a variety of approaches, including some that combine a view of picturebooks as aesthetic expressions in their own right, as well as sources of culturally specific images of childhood and education. In "Picturebooks and Changing Values at the Turn of the Century," Teresa Colomer presents the results of a comparison of the values in picturebooks published between the mid-1970s to 2000 with those in picturebooks from around 2010, and points out various educational goals in different types of society (2010: 48). Using the term "educational goals" in relation to picturebooks, Colomer, like John Stephens, focuses on the socializing function of picturebooks. As Colomer emphasizes, one of the socializing functions of picturebooks may be to introduce the child to means of artistic expression. Similarly, Elina Druker (2014) discusses the works of Swedish author, illustrator, and book designer Eva Billow, both as works of art and as representations of a specific view of childhood in Sweden around 1950. Some picturebooks are indisputably made with an aesthetic intention, but an image of a child, including its sentiments, qualities, actions, and relations, also suggests certain ideas of education. An analysis of representations of childhood may include both elements.

Analysis of childhood in picturebooks

As mentioned in the introduction to this chapter, all aspects of picturebooks contribute in some way to the depiction of an image of childhood in relation to specific works. In the first two analyses I focus on what I consider the most important aspects: visual and verbal depiction of the character, the representation of his or her qualities through actions and choices, and his or her relationships with peers and adults. The third analysis adds analytical questions inspired by the theoretical approach to childhood suggested by Gubar. The examples traverse history in order to identify the multiplicity of images of childhood, from both a diachronic and a synchronic perspective.

When Johann Amos Comenius published *Orbis Sensualium Pictus* in 1658, the first picturebook for children, the example to follow was a young boy (Figure 34.1). The viewer's attention is drawn to the boy, since he is placed in the foreground on the left side of the image. Like most characters represented in the first doublespread in a picturebook, we see him from some distance, so that we get an idea of him as a complete human being, but not so far away that we cannot decode his facial expression. The boy is depicted a little from above, from the point of view of an adult, and one of the ways we know he is a child is by comparison with the person standing next to him, who is almost twice his height. Both individuals have their bodies turned slightly towards each other, so that they are making eye contact. The boy is raising his right arm as a possible sign of eagerness or desire to engage in the conversation, and his head is tilted, as if to pay more attention to what the adult is saying. With his left hand raised and a pointing finger, the adult is signaling "listen to me," or "pay attention." The adult has a serious but not threatening look on his face, and the boy's mouth suggests a little smile. Thus, their postures, gestures, and facial expressions show they are related through mutual interest, but that the adult has a superior position. The difference between child and adult is also represented through their clothes: the boy is wearing knee-length trousers and a jacket, whereas the hat, cloak, and stick of the adult indicate the difference in his age and status compared to the child. The two of them are standing in a rural setting, not in the presence of other adults and children: the focus is on two individuals paying close attention to each other. From the upper right, sunbeams pass behind the head of the adult and straight in the direction of the head of the child, a very explicit indication of light, enlightenment, and knowledge coming from heaven and entering the mind of the child via the teachings of the adult. The heading of the Latin text is *Invitatio*. The scene intends to represent

Figure 34.1 The first image in Johann Amos Comenius's *Orbis Sensualium Pictus*, reprinted from the first Danish edition (Comenius 1672).

an invitation, not an order, but in the accompanying dialogue, the teacher addresses the child in the imperative, saying: "Come boy, learn to be wise." The boy asks who will teach him that; the adult replies that he will, and when asked how, the teacher answers: "I will guide you through all, I will show you all, I will name you all." The boy solemnly responds: "See, here I am; lead me in the name of God" (Comenius 1672: 3; my translation). The short dialogue depicts the relationship between the two of them as based on authority: the adult has the power to tell the child what to do, but he is also dominant owing to his will and ability to guide the child, and his superior knowledge. In this relationship, the child is the passive recipient who will be led, not only because of the authority of the teacher, but also because it is the will of God. This text is represented in three different languages, and thus the child is not primarily characterized based on his relation to a specific mother tongue, but as an individual in a patriarchal society where God reigns. As a visual and verbal sign, the boy is to be read as an example to follow. Comenius's book was translated into a number of languages, and a young child in Europe with access to education around 1700 would also learn to read by saying "lead me." Thereby, he or she would implicitly be encouraged to incorporate the obedient and slightly submissive attitude of the child character. Thus information on what childhood is is given through a number of elements, among others, the composition of the image, depiction of the characters and their relationship, motifs, setting, tone of voice, and the content of the written text.

Points of view and representations of childhood

The example from *Orbis Sensualium Pictus* shows that text and image interact to create a specific depiction of a child character and an implied child reader. When analyzing the representations of childhood in more recently published picturebooks, the use of distance, angle, and height in images participates in creating more varied and detailed depictions of children and child-adult relationships. In Northern European picturebooks, children were rarely portrayed at a very close range until the 1970s, when attention to the young child as an individual with a rich emotional life and a complex psychology increased. From this period onwards, picturebooks include portraits of children showing a variety of feelings, including some that were considered negative and inappropriate in earlier eras, such as anger, aggression, despair, or sorrow. The angle and height from which a child is represented is often significant, since the actual perspective on the world of a young child differs significantly from that of an adult. In *Reading Images* (1996), Gunther Kress and Theo van Leeuwen describe how different points of view instill feelings of distance, proximity, inclusion and exclusion, and power or submission in the viewer. Three scenes in the last part of Bo R. Holmberg's *En dag med Johnny* (A Day with Dad 2002) exemplify how an illustrator uses different heights, angles, and distances to depict the feelings of a child character, and the relationship between child and adult. *A Day with Dad* tells the story of Tim, a young boy whose father comes by train to spend a day in his son's company, since the mother and father are divorced. The relationship between father and son is depicted as close, and during the day Tim expresses his joy at being in his father's company by telling everybody they meet that he is in the company of his father. In the evening, at the train station, just before they are about to part again, the father suddenly carries Tim on his arm into the train car filled with passengers and proudly announces to everybody that the boy on his arm is his beloved son, named Tim (Figure 34.2).

Figure 34.2 Illustration by Eva Eriksson from Bo R. Holmberg's *En dag med Johnny*. Illus. Eva Eriksson. Stockholm: Alfabeta, 2002.

Reprinted by permission of Eva Eriksson and Alfabeta, Stockholm.

The readers view this scene from the height of an adult positioned close to father and son. The fact that the father is holding Tim in his arms, and looking directly at him with a big smile on his face reflects a relationship based on intimacy and love. The point of view makes it possible to see the faces of the other passengers, who confirm the strong father-son relationship with their attention and smiles, and the father's attempt to further reassure the child by means of the gazes of others seems successful. In contrast, the next image shows father and son on the platform, depicted from a point of view of the eye height of Tim, and from some distance. They are looking each other directly in the eye, but without smiles, with the eyebrows a little bit lifted, to express serious attention to the departure that follows. When the father has left, the last image shows mother and son standing at the end of the platform, seen from some distance, as Tim looks at the track, in the direction in which his father has departed. The darkness, their standing there alone, the mother's head bowed towards her son, and her comforting hand around his shoulder create a scene that communicates strong feelings of loss and longing to the reader. The images direct the attention to the feelings of the boy, how very strong his feelings are, and how important it is for him to have the attention and care of his father. Thus the images – and the book in general – represent the child as a sensitive individual, who is different in size than the adult, but equal to the adult in relation to the strength and importance of love. This represented child is dependent on his father's explicitly expressing his feelings, and on his mother's care in a situation of recurrent loss. In the first part of the narrative, the implied child reader meets a character who is able to talk about his need for confirmation of his identity as a child who has a father, that is, a child with a voice. The book may be read as an incitement to a child reader to be explicit about feelings, and engage in a dialogue with others with regard to things that matter. Without a doubt, the adult reader is also encouraged to take the father and mother as examples, to think of a child as an individual with a right to be heard, and to be met with empathy, love, and care. On the one hand, this book portrays elements of an ideal childhood, where love and care are present, and on the other hand, it depicts a less ideal, but quite realistic one, where child life is also characterized by experiences of loss and sorrow.

Prospective, retrospective, and parodic childhoods

The extract from *Orbis Sensualium Pictus* displays a prescriptive and affirmative discourse in relation to childhood: apparently, the intention of text and image is to show how the relationship between child and adult ought to be, and how a learning child should behave. Such a prescriptive approach to representations of childhood in picturebooks has consistently been part of their production, not only in those with an implicit or explicit ideological or religious agenda. A prescriptive approach depicts childhood as it ought to be, and is also present when authors and illustrators push the boundaries of the form or content of picturebooks. The implicit statement behind such publications seems to be that even though the form, content, or image of the child is not mainstream or typical, it should be possible to show it within the picturebook format. Picturebooks have also functioned as a way to promote 'progressive' ideals concerning children and society, and thus have participated in the transformations over time of ideals concerning childhood.

Furthermore, child readers of today are confronted with what could be called a 'retrospective' approach to representations of childhood. A retrospective approach is present in the picturebook market in at least two ways: first, in contemporary fiction, through the representation of characters portrayed in ways that indicate an archaic or deliberately timeless setting, which means that, for example, electronic devices such as cell phones, tablets, or computers are absent. In these books, contemporary child life is depicted as pre-modern. A second variation of a retrospective approach to childhood in picturebooks is to be seen in the very strong canon of picturebooks that confront today's children with a vast variety of representations of childhoods published during their parents or their grandparents' childhoods, or even before. In an English-speaking context, the picturebooks of Beatrix Potter and Randolph Caldecott could be said to belong to the latter canon; in a Nordic context, the picturebooks by Elsa Beskow and some illustrated versions of Astrid Lindgren's books form part of the continuous representation – and perhaps promotion – of childhood as a period of life related to fantasy, nature, and innocence. This idea of childhood as a stage in life that is secluded, natural, and protected is related to the romantic period (Kümmerling-Meibauer 2007), and was precisely the image of childhood that Rose questioned in 1984. Nevertheless, the ongoing reproduction of older picturebooks indicates that adults still find this depiction of childhood, and the narratives linked to it, relevant to contemporary children.

Finally, representations of childhood have been subject to humorous, parodic, and grotesque depictions from the beginning of picturebook production. In 1845, the German doctor Heinrich Hoffmann wrote *Der Struwwelpeter* (Slovenly Peter), a collection of verses that pushed the cautionary tale to its boundaries. In these narratives, a child character was warned, he or she chose to disregard the warning, and was subsequently punished. In Hoffmann's verses, grotesque consequences of misbehavior arise: Kaspar, who will not eat his soup, is first depicted as a chubby boy, then as a grotesque matchstick man, and later dies of starvation. Another boy's thumb is cut off because he will not stop sucking it. No doubt this book is linked to the tradition of using children's stories as a means of character development in children (Christensen 2012), but at the same time, the exaggerations and grotesque elements have strong associations with satire and nonsense. More recent examples are the collections of post–World War II nonsense poetry, for example by Danish author Halfdan Rasmussen, collected in *Børnerim* (Children's Poems 1964), and by Swedish author Lennart Hellsing, for instance *Summa Summarum* (1950). One may also find a number of very recent examples, but as Maria Nikolajeva (2006) has pointed out, there is also an aspect of the confirmation of power in such descriptions of the world turned upside down, or *mundus inversus*. The power that children gain in such instances is given on certain conditions, and is limited by time.

Socratic dialogues between equals

Introducing the 'kinship model,' Gubar (2013) proposes a focus on similarities rather than on deficit or difference when analyzing the relationship between children and adults. The term 'agency' draws attention to the child as a subject with a right to influence his or her own situation, and as an active participant in the creation of his or her own identity. In continuation of this, it is relevant to ask the following questions in an analysis of specific picturebooks: "Which emotions and experiences are shared by fictive adult and child characters?" "What characterizes the interaction between children and adults?" "Is the child character depicted as having an influence on his or her own situation?"

In *Annas himmel* (Anna's Heaven 2013) by Norwegian author and illustrator Stian Hole, the first image depicts the main character Anna on a swing with her head upside down, while she looks the viewer directly in the eye (Figure 34.3). The swing seems to be soaring in the air without any support. A man in a black suit is looking in the direction of the girl from a distance with a rather skeptical gaze: there is neither eye contact between them nor any physical contact. The text starts with Anna's statement that some words can be read both forwards and backwards, such as the word "Anna." The father is nervous, and the flowers in his hand, the church in the background, as well as *vanitas* symbols such as the seeds of a dandelion give rise to associations with transience and loss (Christensen 2014: 118). The picture forms the impression of two lonely individuals in a no-man's land, and Anna's posture suggests her world is turned upside down or out of order.

Like a kind of visual palindrome, the last image in the book mirrors this first one. Here the father is hanging from the swing in the same position as Anna, but he is smiling and Anna is standing on the ground in front of the image, gently caressing his cheek with a feather in an expression of love and care (Figure 34.4). A small rowing boat on the edge of the lake and Anna's statement in the text that "Now I am ready. Hurry up, dad, we've got to go or we'll be late" suggest that in due time father and daughter can move on.

Figure 34.3 First illustration from Stian Hole's *Annas himmel*. Oslo: Cappelen Damm, 2013.
Reprinted by permission of Stian Hole.

Between the sorrowful, almost *unheimlich* first image and the comforting last scene, a child's perspective on death, loss, and love is presented in a very gentle manner. The illustrations shift between
depicting the girl's imagination in beautiful collages that combine heterogeneous material from natural histories, art, and popular culture, with a realistic scene (for instance, of the mother's wardrobe).

Figure 34.4 Last illustration from Stian Hole's *Annas himmel*. Oslo: Cappelen Damm, 2013.
Reprinted by permission of Stian Hole.

The reader learns about the death of the mother by indirect references, for instance when she is referred to in the past tense or appears as a shadow in the sky in one of the images. Halfway through the book father and daughter sit by the lake, still with their bodies turned away from each other, and talk about how they wish the mother could come back. In the lake the mirror image of the father is transformed into a rabbit, which gives rise to associations with *Alice's Adventures in Wonderland* (1865), or even with Salvador Dali's painting *Swans Reflecting Elephants* (1937), again accentuating the theme of the world being full of inexplicable paradoxes. "Do you think there is anything on the other side of the mirror?," Anna asks her father, and he lets her lead him on an imaginary journey through the sea, the sky, and a heavenly garden, while they discuss, among other things, the existence of God and where the mother might be now. Finally, the father asks Anna how they will get home, and she replies that they will "do what cats do when they fall from the ninth floor – twirl around and land on our feet!"

In this picturebook, child and adult characters share the experience of having lost someone they care for, and they are both in a stage of grief where communication and interaction with other human beings, even close ones, is complicated. The world is turned upside down for both of them, and the father does not inhabit the role of a more mature, secure, or knowing individual in this situation. The interaction between the two is reestablished only when the father joins the child on a journey to a surreal world of beautiful sounds, forms, and colors where they can talk about difficult questions and invent imaginary answers. It is remarkable that it is the child who leads the adult through a process of reconciliation, and it is the child who comforts the father in the end.

Some would interpret this as a representation of irresponsible, self-absorbed parenthood. Others might read the narrative as a homage to a romantic childhood, including praise of imagination, beauty, and the connection between the child and the divine. I interpret Anna as a modern child in the sense that she is sensitive and sensible as well as able to find her own way out of a difficult emotional situation. Her father is more a fellow human being than an authority figure, and the child is neither less insightful nor someone who carries a lighter burden.

Through older picturebooks, child and adult readers are exposed to representations of childhood from very different historical periods, and rather different cultural contexts. Thereby they meet a multiplicity of depictions and verbalizations of what it means to be a child. Retrospective, prescriptive, and allegedly realistic or descriptive approaches coexist in picturebooks on the market today, but also intermingle in single picturebooks, as the story about Anna shows. The simultaneous existence of a variety of interpretations encourages picturebook researchers (1) to analyze representations of childhood in picturebooks, based on their knowledge of changing concepts of childhood from a historical perspective; (2) to develop more refined analytical tools; and (3) to execute such analyses with the awareness that different approaches to childhood coexist, blend, and contradict one another to a degree that calls for scrutiny and attention.

References

Ariès, Philippe (1960) *L'enfant et la vie familiale sous l'ancien régime*, Paris: Plon [*Centuries of Childhood: A Social History of Family Life*, trans. Robert Baldick, New York: Random House, 1965].

Christensen, Nina (2003) *Den danske billedbog: Teori, analyse, historie*, Frederiksberg: Roskilde Universitetsforlag.

Christensen, Nina (2004) "Childhood Revisited: On the Relationship Between Childhood Studies and Children's Literature," *Children's Literature Association Quarterly* 28.4: 230–239.

Christensen, Nina (2012) *Videbegær: Oplysning, børnelitteratur, dannelse*, Aarhus: Aarhus Universitetsforlag.

Christensen, Nina (2014) "'Thoughts and dream are heavenly vehicles.' Character, Bildung and Aesthetics in Stian Hole's Garmann Trilogy (2006–2010)," in Bettina Kümmerling-Meibauer (ed.) *Picturebooks: Representation and Narration*, New York: Routledge, 109–120.

Colomer, Teresa (2010) "Picturebooks and Changing Values at the Turn of the Century," in Teresa Colomer, Teresa, Bettina Kümmerling-Meibauer, and Cecilia Silva-Díaz (eds) *New Directions in Picturebook Research*, New York: Routledge, 41–54.

Colomer, Teresa, Kümmerling-Meibauer, Bettina and Silva-Díaz, Cecilia (eds) (2010) *New Directions in Picturebook Research*, New York: Routledge.

Comenius, Johann Amos (1672) *Orbis Sensualium Pictus* [*Dend gandske Verden fuld af de Ting som kan sees och sandses afmaled*], Copenhagen: Daniel Paulii.

Cunningham, Hugh (1995) *Children and Childhood in Western Society Since 1500*, London and New York: Longman.

Druker, Elina (2014) *Eva Billow: Bilderbokskonstnär och författare*, Stockholm: Makadam.

Gubar, Marah (2013) "Risky Business. Talking About Children in Children's Literature Criticism," *Children's Literature Association Quarterly* 38.4: 450–557.

Hellsing, Lennart (1950) *Summa Summarum*, illus. Poul Strøyer, Stockholm: Rabén & Sjögren.

Heywood, Colin (2001) *A History of Childhood: Children and Childhood in the West From Medieval to Modern Times*, Cambridge: Polity.

Hoffmann, Heinrich (1845) *Der Struwwelpeter oder lustige Geschichten und drollige Bilder für Kinder von 3–6 Jahren*, Frankfurt: Literarische Anstalt.

Hole, Stian (2013) *Annas himmel*, Oslo: Cappelen Damm [*Anna's Heaven*, trans. Don Bartlett, Cambridge, MA: Eerdman, 2014].

Holmberg, Bo R. (2002) *En dag med Johnny*, illus. Eva Eriksson, Stockholm: Alfabeta [*A Day With Dad*, Somerville, MA: Candlewick, 2008].

James, Alison, and James, Adrian L. (2008) *Key Concepts in Childhood Studies*, Los Angeles, CA: SAGE.

Kress, Gunther, and van Leeuwen, Theo (1996) *Reading Images: The Grammar of Visual Design*, London: Routledge.

Kümmerling-Meibauer, Bettina (2007) "Images of Childhood in Romantic Children's Literature," in Gerald Gillespie, Manfred Engel, and Bernard Dieterle (eds) *Romantic Prose Fiction*, Amsterdam: John Benjamins, 183–203.

Kümmerling-Meibauer, Bettina (ed.) (2014) *Picturebooks: Representation and Narration*, New York: Routledge.

Lesnik-Oberstein, Karín (1994) *Children's Literature: Criticism and the Fictional Child*, Oxford: Clarendon Press.

Lesnik-Oberstein, Karín (1998) *Children in Culture: Approaches to Childhood*, Basingstoke: Palgrave Macmillan.

Lesnik-Oberstein, Karín (2011) *Children in Culture, Revisited: Further Approaches to Childhood*, Basingstoke: Palgrave Macmillan.

Nikolajeva, Maria (2006) "Børnelitteratur: Kunst, pædagogik og magt," in Nina Christensen and Anna Karlskov Skyggebjerg (eds) *På opdagelse i børnelitteraturen*, Copenhagen: Høst & Søn, 29–45.

Nikolajeva, Maria, and Scott, Carole (2001) *How Picturebooks Work*, New York: Garland.

Nodelman, Perry (1988) *Words about Pictures: The Narrative Art of Children's Picture Books*, Athens: University of Georgia Press.

Oswell, David (2013) *The Agency of Children: From Family to Global Human Rights*, New York: Cambridge University Press.

Rasmussen, Halfdan (1964) *Børnerim*, Copenhagen: Schønberg.

Rose, Jacqueline (1984) *The Case of Peter Pan, or, The Impossibility of Children's Fiction*, London: Macmillan.

Rudd, David (2010) "Children's Literature and the Return to Rose," *Children's Literature Association Quarterly* 35.3: 290–310.

Stephens, John (1992) *Language and Ideology in Children's Fiction*, London and New York: Longman.

Wall, Barbara (1991) *The Narrator's Voice: The Dilemma of Children's Fiction*, New York: St. Martin's Press.

Weinreich, Torben (2000) *Children's Literature: Art or Pedagogy?*, Frederiksberg: Roskilde University Press.

35

PICTUREBOOKS AND LITERACY STUDIES

Evelyn Arizpe, Jennifer Farrar, and Julie McAdam

This chapter gives an overview of the relationship between literacy studies and picturebook studies: two distinct, increasingly well-established fields that have much in common and a great deal to offer one another. The two fields have built on each other since the 1970s and are so closely interlinked that it is difficult to determine exact boundaries or to separate the influence of one on the other. We suggest that the relationship between them can be thought of as reciprocal or symbiotic, a status that is, in part, enhanced by the nature and affordances of contemporary picturebooks, which can offer readers access to the multiple literacies now demanded by modes of communication in the twenty-first century (Serafini 2008; Arizpe and Styles 2016).

We assume readers are familiar with picturebook studies in general, but for the purposes of this chapter, we draw attention to the fact that the core of the picturebook is composed of two main modes, words and images that together produce meaning and tell a story. Given that literacy studies look at all cultural and social artifacts which produce meaning, research that focuses on the picture-book itself has contributed to broader understandings of literacy's cognitive and social aspects. In turn, picturebook studies have benefited from the ways in which literacy studies support an under-standing of how readers make sense of text and the role of texts in children's development.

We begin by offering a broad overview of literacy studies, drawing on existing and emerging research trends in order to sketch out how literacy is conceptualized. We then divide literacy into a series of broad 'subtypes,' for which we provide working definitions and examples, and describe how they can be connected to picturebook studies. However, this conceptualization of literacy studies comes with a series of caveats and we emphasize that these categories are not fixed, exhaustive, or prescriptive but that the strands often overlap. As we illustrate below, the initial descriptive term in the compound nouns normally used to label the literacy subtypes – 'visual,' 'digital,' 'emergent,' 'critical,' and so on – are not equivalent because some pertain to a mode (visual, digital) and some pertain to a process (emergent, critical). In fact, Gunther Kress (2003) argues that that literacy should only refer to print and the skills of decoding and encoding and that we need a new meta-language for other modes of communication.

Despite these conceptual difficulties, it is equally important to recognize that literacy exists within more formal structures that are shaped and strictured by policy and practice. This is especially true within educational settings, where literacy sub-types have gained a life of their own in the literature and can be regarded as representing separate sets of skills. With this in mind, it may be helpful for readers new to the field to visualize literacy as an 'ensemble of communicative practices' (Rowsell and Pahl 2015: 14) in order to emphasize the collective and diverse nature of the practices in this vast field which is being constantly transformed.

Literacy studies: an overview

Literacy has traditionally been associated with the 'basic' skills of decoding and writing printed script, often learned within the limits of a schooled context. Under this view, literacy was seen as largely individual and psychological, a discrete set of skills that, once mastered, could enable individuals to crack codes, access meanings, and gain entry to privileged worlds of work, knowledge, and personal development (Lankshear 1999: 3). At the same time, these worlds influence the shape of literacy practices by determining what 'counts' as literacy. From this perspective, the field of literacy studies encompasses anything related to the reading and writing of printed texts (Beard 1990; Goodman 1996).

Yet, from the early 1970s, the emergence of several distinctive social, cultural, and linguistic theories impacted on this traditional understanding of literacy, causing what James Gee described as 'the social turn' (1998), and challenging the 'schooled' approaches that dominated the literacy landscape at the time. Stemming from developments in fields such as sociology, ethnography, and sociolinguistics, this multidisciplinary 'turn' involved a shift away from a focus on behaviorism and cognitivism, towards a new interest in the importance of social and cultural interaction (Gee 1998).

Social-constructivist learning theories, particularly those of Lev Vygotsky (1962) and Jerome Bruner (1990), stressed the social formation of meaning and the importance of reading and narrative for human development and higher order thinking skills. The recognition of reading as a social practice by Brian Street, Shirley Brice Heath, and Gee, among others, raised questions about what was meant by literacy (Street 1984; Gee 2004) and alerted educators to the socially and culturally constructed nature of the processes used to select and value particular texts and language practices above others (Heath 1983). From underneath the banner of the 'new' literacy studies, research in this field begins from the premise that literacy is an inherently social phenomenon, a standpoint that requires literacy practices to be understood from within the historical, political, social, and cultural context in which they have occurred (Lankshear 1999: 14).

As alluded to earlier, the concept of 'literacy' as a narrow, singular entity has now expanded to 'literacies' (although in this chapter, we will continue to use 'literacy studies' and understand it as encompassing these pluralities). For many theorists today, literacy studies is about wider considerations of the literacies that are embedded and embodied in everyday practices, including responses to different modes such as images, design, and performance. From these new understandings, literacy is reframed as an active process to which "the concept of fixity is no longer tenable" (Rowsell and Pahl 2015: 2), due to the multimodal nature of most practices and the context-specific sets of sociocultural norms and expectations that shape them. Digital technologies enable the mixing of modes to create texts with even more modalities. While there are skills and competencies common to all modes, each of them also demand a specific set of these which allow deeper layers of meaning and a more analytical and critical interpretation to emerge. Therefore, in this age of rapidly diversifying communicative technologies, where practices 'old' and 'new' coexist, overlap, and blend, the concept of literacies has become plural, fluid, and hybrid – in other words, difficult to categorize, yet still prone to structuralist and potentially reductive definitions.

Just as literacy has come to be understood as a social practice embedded in a cultural context rather than an autonomous set of skills, the theory of picturebooks has also moved on from a consideration of the texts as an autonomous object unrelated to the circumstances of its production and reception. While theories of art and design continue to be fundamental to analysis of images, they have now been joined by semiotics and other theoretical approaches such as feminist, multicultural, and eco-critical theories. In addition, new attention to the materiality of the picturebook and the physical gestures involved in reading (for example, the act of turning pages) is also increasingly linked to cognitive theories that shed new light on visual perception and also affective engagement through discoveries in neuroscience (Mackey 2003; Nikolajeva 2014; Kümmerling-Meibauer and Meibauer 2013, 2015). All of these seek to explain how picturebooks work, as aesthetic objects and as artifacts that are part of everyday literacy interactions in a variety of spaces, including as vehicles for teaching and learning.

The connections between literacy studies and picturebooks

In the following section, we briefly define and identify the main ideas behind each of the literacy subtypes included here, and show how they are particularly connected to picturebooks, mapping current research trends in literacy onto contemporary research into picturebooks.

Emergent literacy

Perspectives of literacy learning in young children have developed over time, with work by researchers such as Marie Clay, Frank Smith, and Kenneth Goodman in the 1970s laying the foundations for what is known as emergent literacy theory. Their work suggested that children are active participants in their own learning (Barratt-Pugh and Rohl 2000) that starts at birth when they engage socially and culturally with the world that surrounds them, including artifacts and conventions of reading and writing. Emergent literacy can be defined as the knowledge of these conventions acquired before children receive formal reading instruction, usually in the context of the home or preschool educational establishments (Mason and Allen 1986; Sulzby and Teale 1991; Kümmerling-Meibauer 2011). Since the 1980s there has also been a recognition of the importance of the experiences that construct the knowledge that inducts children into the world of print and provides them with an initial sense of literacy. Researchers in this area agree that later levels of competence and achievement in schooled literacy are the result of a greater or lesser exposure to books and stories in preschool years and of an understanding of the purpose and function of the spoken and written word (Holdaway 1979; Ferreiro and Teberosky 1982; Snow and Ninio 1986).

Some scholars such as Marsh (2004) have critiqued the concept of literacy as 'emergent' arguing that children are already engaging in literacy practices in their own right, emphasizing the social processes that surround each literacy act. Also, there is an increasing recognition that 'emergent literacy' applies to all the different subtypes of literacy we mention here, given that many children now learn a wide range of conventions from a young age, from turning the pages of a book to making sense of sequential pictures and tapping and swiping a screen.

Given that picturebooks are generally the focus of children's first encounter with narrative and textual artifact, these have a significant impact on the way in which a child learns not only about the world and story but also about books and reading. Concept and alphabet books provide information and as narrative strategies gradually become more complex, the child is also introduced to literary fiction, adding to their overall literacy competences (Sulzby 1985; Kümmerling-Meibauer and Meibauer 2011). The induction into the world of images through picturebooks is also now recognized as significant not only for visual literacy (see next section) but for other types of literacy as well, given that pictures stimulate emotional responses and verbal interaction. Most studies tend to look at the connection between emergent literacy and picturebooks for children over three years old, but Kümmerling-Meibauer (2011) has argued that it is necessary to look at this connection earlier, at ten to twelve months, given that even during the first months of life a seminal relationship develops between picturebooks and cognitive, linguistic, and psychological growth. While there has been some research into visual features of early picturebooks (e.g., Werner 2011), there is still more work to be done in understanding how the images support emergent *visual* literacy in very young children.

A substantial group of studies have looked at the different ways in which interaction with picturebooks sheds light on cognitive, linguistic, and aesthetic development (e.g., Snow and Goldfield 1983; Meibauer 2006; Marsh and Hallet 2008), while picturebook studies have contributed by showing how they help develop literate behavior and an understanding of literacy itself in young children (Snow and Goldfield 1983; Meek 1988; Nikolajeva 2003; Kümmerling-Meibauer et al.

2015). Closely connected to this idea of an emerging awareness of literacy, language, and literature is the idea of *linguistic literacy*, which, according to Ravid and Tolchinsky, refers to "the ability to consciously access one's own linguistic knowledge and to view language from various perspectives" (2002: 419–420). This means it is a meta-linguistic skill through which children are able to understand how language works and therefore control and produce language according to purpose and audience. While this type of linguistic ability may begin in early childhood, it must be noted that it continues through and beyond adolescence.

Linguistic literacy can be linked to the reading of picturebooks because of the way in which the child is encouraged to think about how language works and the impact it has on the reader or listener. This can be seen in the particular case of wordless picturebooks, where absence highlights the usual role of words in a narrative and the need for retelling based on images. There is also evidence that reading picturebooks aids in learning a new language (Bland 2013) but also in recognizing and valuing diverse linguistic and cultural resources (Arizpe and Blatt 2011; Zapata 2014). Interactions with picturebooks allow children to understand how language works and gain pleasure from the ways in which it can be structured into story (Wells 1985). Cognitive science confirms the connections between the way the brain processes symbolic representation and the way language develops, but it also confirms the need for "socially interactive situations" if the visual experience is to lead to deeper understanding and empathy for the perspectives of others (Heath 2000). Knowledge about picturebooks can therefore contribute to providing learning experiences that develop emerging literacy skills.

Visual literacy

For several decades, studies of visual images have been part of a wide range of disciplines such as media studies, information technology, cultural studies, and visual arts education. Visual literacy has therefore been defined in many ways, but fundamentally, it can be summarized as an active process that can lead from an awareness of the codes of visual communication to more analytical, critical reading of visual texts (Crouch 2008). New knowledge about visual cognition based on findings from neurobiology has also been linked to cognitive and affective response to art which Heath (2000) argues is deepened through play and work that demands sharing and talking. This means that, as well as being an active process, visual literacy is a social process because it comprises a set of practices that take place within, and are determined by, a particular cultural context. Therefore, the analysis of visual images must consider how they form part of the societies and cultures which created them. In order to do this, Kress and van Leeuwen (1996) provide a theoretical framework for discussing how visual forms of representation communicate through a grammar and vocabulary of design.

Drawing on art history and education (Clark 1960; Perkins 1994), visual culture studies (Mitchell 1994; Mirzoef 2009, 2015), and semiotics and visual design studies (Kress and van Leeuwen 1996; Painter, Martin and Unsworth 2013), visual literacy helps interpret the visual text, looking at, among other aesthetic features, the type of media and techniques used to create a particular mood or feeling and how they convey meaning. Visual literacy also supports the evaluation and critique of images by placing images in context, in relation to the words, to other visuals and texts (intertextuality) and understanding how they are produced; in other words, a "critical visual analysis" (Albers 2008). Without this type of visual knowledge, it is impossible to understand how a picturebook works from an aesthetic point of view and what type of impact it may have on the reader (Serafini 2014).

Many scholars in the area have pushed for the teaching of visual literacy alongside other literacy skills, arguing that it is indispensable to thinking but that most of us only have a superficial comprehension of what we view and that "higher order visual literacy skills do not develop unless they are identified and 'taught'" (Avgerinou and Ericson 1997: 280). Therefore, in order to deepen engagement with a picturebook (or graphic novel, comic, or any other visual art form, for that matter), it is necessary to have some knowledge of terminology, of how visuals work (and how they work together with the words, in some cases), and of the processes of reading an image. Picturebook studies have shown that even young readers can gain a knowledge of art and design and how symbols and other visual codes work through reading picturebooks, especially with a trained mediator (for example, Pantaleo's work in classrooms on color (2012a), typography (2012b), and paneling (2013)). In turn, this knowledge contributes to enriching the reading experience both cognitively and affectively, which is one of the aims in the case of reading picturebooks with young children. Finally, both interpretation and critique can support the creative process, for example, when children are asked to produce their own picturebooks.

New technologies and their impact on literacy

The rapidity of technological change has given rise to a variety of terms to describe the impact of digital devices on literacy, learning, and pedagogy, such as 'digital literacy' (Gilster 1997); 'new literacies' (Lankshear and Knobel 2003), 'multiliteracies' (New London Group 1996), and 'moving image literacy' (Burn and Parker 2003). They all examine similar issues, namely the ability to decode, encode, and make meaning using a range of modes (print, image [still and moving], sound, gesture), mediated through new mediums which only become available through technology.

The work emerging from the New London Group was seminal in that it asked us to consider three fundamental premises: (1) literacy in the plural form encompassing the multimodal and multilingual (Cope and Kalantzis 2009: 165); (2) meaning-making as a process of design; and (3) human communication as the active transformation of the social world that surrounds us and is experienced through multimodal forms. Despite these reframed understandings of how 'literacies' transform and develop, school-based understandings of literacy continue to emphasize print-based decoding and encoding. The resulting gap between home and school multiliteracies has provided the impetus for much of the research in this field, with a clear focus on multimodality.

The concept of multimodality has been examined through two lenses; the first looks at the *sum of its parts* (Serafini 2011) and draws upon knowledge of how each mode functions individually, for instance, the linguistic mode (Halliday 1975) and the visual mode (Kress and van Leeuwen 1996). The second examines *the complex ways in which the modes mesh* to make new meaning (Jewitt 2008; Cope and Kalantzis 2009). Both approaches have led to debates about the necessity of developing new meta-languages to discuss the modes (Anstey and Bull 2006; Serafini 2011) alongside warnings that such a technical approach to something so complex and fluid could be reductive (Jewitt 2008: 252) when used to inform pedagogy. Picturebook studies have drawn upon these developed meta-languages to analyze the ways in which the print and visuals make meaning, and in turn create new roles for readers and teachers (Hassett and Curwood 2009). Teachers have focused their 'text deconstruction' on the language of art and artists (Callow 2008; Hassett and Curwood 2009; Martens et al. 2012) to discuss the ways in which the images and typesetting make visual meaning. Knowledge of the multimodal nature of picturebooks is of fundamental importance, particularly when considering the impact of the technical world on picturebooks as they move from paper to the screen (Yokota and Teale 2014). These books can open up multilingual, personalized, and motivating spaces for young readers, but parents and teachers need to apply selection criteria to ensure they are still quality texts with well-told stories and quality language (585).

In several picturebooks studies (Hassett and Curwood 2009; Martens et al. 2012), the creation of multimodal texts is viewed as a process of design, while authors are emphasized as creators and child readers as active meaning makers. Children arrive in school settings with ample "funds of knowledge" (Gonzales et al. 2005) drawn from the range of print, digital, and multimodal texts consumed within the home. These home techno-literacy practices are where children engage with television, games, mobile phones, and tablets, and incorporate these mediums into their creative play and understandings of narrative (Marsh 2004: 59). This gap between home and school can lead to dissonance, disengagement, and disaffection – a gap the multimodal world of quality picturebooks can bridge by providing complex texts for today's multiliterate children (Serafini 2011).

Media literacy and critical literacy

Media literacy can be defined as the ability to access, understand, create, and critically evaluate different types of media (European Commission 2007; see also Reedy and UKLA 2010). Like the field of literacy studies, media literacy is interdisciplinary, drawing on a diverse range of subjects for its methods and tools (Koltay 2011). Its core aim is for individuals to cultivate a relationship of critical autonomy with diverse media texts, enabling 'intelligent' practices to develop via analysis, critique, and interpretation in the interests of critical solidarity (Kellner and Share 2005: 372).

To a large extent, media literacy shares its key concepts with critical literacy, a broader, equally multi-disciplinary approach that embraces all text types – not simply those produced by forms of electronic and digital media. Rooted in critical theory, critical literacy is an overtly political approach that "melds social, political and cultural debate and discussion with the analysis of how texts and discourses work, where, with what consequences and in whose interests" (Luke 2012: 5). For issues of fluency, we refer here to critical literacy as a broader term that also encompasses media literacy understandings.

In recognition of its growing theoretical and pedagogic significance, the critical dimension has now achieved parity with cognitive and affective aspects of literacy in several literacy frameworks (for instance, New London Group 1996; Luke and Freebody 1999; Serafini 2012). Despite this emphasis, researchers have found that the critical focus is often absent, especially from approaches to reading employed with younger children (Comber 2001). To tackle this imbalance, picturebooks are increasingly used to support the development of a more critical stance in readers of different ages. Picturebooks that deal with complex, taboo, or 'sad' topics can disrupt pupils' and teachers' expectations about what books for young readers *should* contain (McClay 2000; Marshall 2015), while prompting conversations about controversial social issues that might otherwise remain invisible (Leland et al. 2005). Exploration of the interaction between words and images in picturebooks can provide readers with understandings that can be applied to other text types and contexts, such as print journalism (Crafton et al. 2007) and graphic novels (Pantaleo 2011).

In addition, readers' recognition of the contesting discourses at work in picturebooks can create opportunities for critical engagement by encouraging readers to scrutinize texts as deliberately constructed (and de-constructable) objects and to consider the 'trustworthiness' of the different modes they rely on (Souto-Manning 2009; Farrar 2016). As several picturebook scholars have noted, the complex interplay between different modes can force the critical practice of reading between the lines, leaving readers with a heightened sense of how texts are structured and function. Indeed, the game-like process of detangling stories that are multi-layered and multi-voiced can give readers greater agency (Pantaleo 2014), demand increased engagement, and stimulate conversations about "how texts work and how they work in the world" (Comber 2001: 178).

While, of course, it is possible to read contemporary picturebooks uncritically, by critically engaging with the "special structures" at work in this genre (Goldstone 2004: 203), readers can deepen their meta-level understandings of language in use (Lankshear 1999) while enhancing their enjoyment of these highly pleasurable texts.

Mutual benefits

As we have shown in this chapter, the relationship between literacy studies and picturebook studies is mutually beneficial. However, while the contribution is reciprocal, tensions exist, and the place where they tend to come to the fore is in the move from theory to practice. Despite the attempts of Meek (1988) and the advocates of 'balanced literacy' approaches, there continues to be some opposition between the view of picturebooks as either useful resources for developing literacy, or art objects that should offer aesthetic pleasure rather than any sort of 'lesson.' At the same time, families, communities, and educators are encouraged to provide the type of print-rich environments and authentic experiences that picturebooks can offer. Working through the different levels of meaning afforded by the picturebook can allow for further understanding of how words and images can communicate and illustrators consciously or unconsciously guide readers through the more complex 'lessons' that texts such as picturebooks can teach (Meek 1988). In other words, literacy and picturebooks should be seen as intertwined in a positive relationship that is constantly enriched by new studies and research.

As our initial caveats indicate, we encourage readers to conceptualize the field of literacy studies as fluid, interdisciplinary, and connected to a wealth of linguistic, artistic, and social practices. Moving forward, we suggest it may be helpful for scholars working in and across these fields to draw on the concept of transliteracy (Thomas et al. 2007), a perspective that eschews the polarizing of literacies by offering an umbrella term to contain "all communication types, across time and culture" without privileging any one form above the other (3) and which includes a forward look to future modalities. Schools need to underpin decisions about literacy instruction with an understanding of the "epistemological and ontological changes" (Lankshear and Knobel 2003) brought about by shifts in technology (without forgetting social, economic, and political shifts) and its impact on literacy practice, and transliteracy offers a framework to support this understanding.

In relation to picturebook and literacy studies, the concept of transliteracy and the idea of picturebooks as 'transliterate spaces' where all types of modes and forms intersect, may prove fruitful by enacting a shift away from considerations of print as the dominant mode to an intentional focus on the range of modes at work, as well as the impact (and affordances of) the synergies between them all (Thomas et al. 2007: 5). Indeed, the notion of transliteracy may offer ways for scholars to re-articulate understandings about categories that already exist, such as emergent literacy, without creating yet more binaries or obstacles.

This notion may also help teachers avoid taking the usual approach that considers picturebooks (and other forms of children's literature) as merely tools to teach reading or as a way to fill any leisure moments in the curriculum (NCTE 2006; Arizpe et al. 2013). Along with the respect due to the picturebook as an aesthetic and cultural object, teachers can encourage students to consider the relationship between words, images, and other modes, promoting a critical reflection on literature, language, and related social literacy practices. The structure of this chapter shows how the sum of the parts facilitates the ways in which whole meaning can be derived. The central purpose of educators should be to help develop an understanding of the central tenets of how to decode, encode, and make meaning across a range of modes. Knowing how picturebooks work and how to make multimodal meaning will lead to confident educators, mediators and other professionals who can critically select texts that develop 'literacies' required for twenty-first-century life.

References

Albers, Peggy (2008) "Theorizing Visual Representation in Children's Literature," *Journal of Literacy Research* 40.2: 163–200.

Anstey, Michelle, and Bull, Geoff (2006) *Teaching and Learning Multiliteracies: Changing Times, Changing Literacies*, Newark, DE: International Reading Association.

Arizpe, Evelyn, and Blatt, Jane (2011) "How Responses to Picturebooks Reflect and Support the Emotional Development of Young Bilingual Children," in Bettina Kümmerling-Meibauer (ed.) *Emergent Literacy: Children's Books from 0 to 3*, Amsterdam: John Benjamins, 245–264.

Arizpe, Evelyn, McAdam, Julie, and Farrell, Maureen (2013) "Opening the Classroom Door to Children's Literature: A Review of Research," in Kathy Hall, Teresa Cremin, Barbara Comber, and Luis Moll (eds) *International Handbook of Research in Children's Literacy, Learning and Culture*, Chichester: Wiley Blackwell, 241–225.

Arizpe, Evelyn, and Styles, Morag (2016) *Children Reading Picturebooks: Interpreting Visual Texts*, London: Routledge (first published 2003).

Avgerinou, Maria, and Ericson, John (1997) "A Review of the Concept of Visual Literacy," *British Journal of Educational Technology* 28.4: 280–291.

Barratt-Pugh, Caroline, and Rohl, Mary (eds) (2000) *Literacy Learning in the Early Years*, Buckingham: Open University Press.

Beard, Roger (1990) *Developing Reading 3–13*, London: Hodder.

Bland, Janice (2013) *Children's Literature and Learner Empowerment: Children and Teenagers in English Language Education*, London: Bloomsbury.

Bruner, Jerome (1990) *Acts of Meaning*, Cambridge, MA: Harvard University Press.

Burn, Andrew, and Parker, David (2003) *Analysing Media Texts*, London: Continuum.

Callow, Jon (2008) "Show Me: Principles for Assessing Students' Visual Literacy," *The Reading Teacher* 61.8: 616–626.

Clark, Kenneth (1960) *Looking at Pictures*, London: John Murray.

Comber, Barbara (2001) "Critical Literacy: Power and Pleasure with Language in the Early Years," *Australian Journal of Language and Literacy* 24.3: 168–181.

Cope, Bill, and Kalantzis, Mary (2009) "Multiliteracies: New Literacies, New Learning," *Pedagogies: An International Journal* 4: 164–195.

Crafton, Linda, Brennan, Mary, and Silvers, Penny (2007) "Critical Inquiry and Multiliteracies in a First-Grade Classroom," *Language Arts* 84.6: 510–518.

Crouch, Christopher (2008) "Afterword," in James Elkins (ed.) *Visual Literacy*, London: Routledge, 195–199.

European Commission (2007) "Media Literacy," http://ec.europa.eu/culture/policy/audiovisual-policies/literacy_en.htm (accessed January 19, 2016).

Farrar, Jennifer (2016) "Case 3," in Evelyn Arizpe and Morag Styles, *Children Reading Picturebooks: Interpreting Visual Texts*, 2nd ed., London: Routledge, 159–168.

Ferreiro, Emilia, and Teberosky, Ana (1982) *Literacy Before Schooling*, New Hampshire, UK: Heinemann.

Gee, James P. (1998) "The New Literacy Studies: From 'Socially Situated' to the Work of the Social," http://jamespaulgee.com/pdfs/The%20New%20Literacy%20Studies%20and%20the%20Social%20Turn.pdf (accessed January 19, 2016).

Gee, James P. (2004) *Situated Language and Learning: A Critique of Traditional Schooling*, New York: Routledge.

Gilster, Paul (1997) *Digital Literacy*, New York: John Wiley and Sons.

Goldstone, Bette P. (2004) "The Postmodern Picture Book: A New Subgenre," *Language Arts* 81.3: 196–204.

González, Norma, Moll, Luis C., and Amanti, Cathy (eds) (2005) *Funds of Knowledge: Theorizing Practices in Households, Communities, and Classrooms*, Mahwah, NJ: Lawrence Erlbaum.

Goodman, Kenneth (1996) *On Reading*, Portsmouth, NJ: Heinemann.

Halliday, Michael A. K. (1975) *Learning How to Mean: Explorations in the Development of Language*, London: Edward Arnold.

Hassett, Dawnene D., and Curwood, Jen S. (2009) "Theories and Practices of Multimodal Education: The Instructional Dynamics of Picture Books and Primary Classrooms," *The Reading Teacher* 63.4: 270–282.

Heath, Shirley B. (1983) *Ways with Words*, Cambridge: Cambridge University Press.

Heath, Shirley B. (2000) "Seeing Our Way Into Learning," *Cambridge Journal of Education* 30.1: 121–132.

Holdaway, Don (1979) *The Foundations of Literacy*, New York: Ashton Scholastic.

Jewitt, Carey (2008) "Multimodality and Literacy in School Classrooms," *Review of Research in Education* 32.1: 241–267.

Kellner, Douglas, and Share, Jeff (2005) "Toward Critical Media Literacy: Core Concepts, Debates, Organisations and Policy," *Discourse: Studies in the Cultural Policy of Education* 26.3: 369–386.

Koltay, Tibor (2011) "The Media and the Literacies: Media Literacy, Information Literacy, Digital Literacy," *Media Culture and Society* 33.2: 211–221.

Kress, Gunther (2003) *Literacy in the New Media Age*, London: Routledge.

Kress, Gunther, and van Leeuwen, Theo (1996) *Reading Images: The Grammar of Visual Design*, London: Routledge.

Kümmerling-Meibauer, Bettina (2011) "Emergent Literacy and Children's Literature," in Bettina Kümmerling-Meibauer (ed.) *Emergent Literacy: Children's Books from 0 to 3*, Amsterdam: John Benjamins, 1–14.

Kümmerling-Meibauer, Bettina, and Meibauer, Jörg (2011) "Early-Concept Books: Acquiring Nominal and Verbal Concepts," in Bettina Kümmerling-Meibauer (ed.) *Emergent Literacy: Children's Books from 0 to 3*, Amsterdam: John Benjamins, 91–114.

Kümmerling-Meibauer, Bettina, and Meibauer, Jörg (2013) "Towards a Cognitive Theory of Picturebooks," *International Research in Children's Literature* 6.2: 143–160.

Kümmerling-Meibauer, Bettina, and Meibauer, Jörg (2015) "Maps in Picturebooks: Cognitive Status and Narrative Functions," *BFLT: Nordic Journal of Childlit Aesthetics* 6, www.childlitaesthetics.net/index.php/blft/article/view/26970%20-%20article (accessed April 24, 2015).

Kümmerling-Meibauer, Bettina, Meibauer, Jörg, Nachtigäller, Kerstin, and Rohlfing, Katharina J. (eds) (2015) *Learning from Picturebooks: Perspectives from Child Development and Literacy Studies*, New York: Routledge.

Lankshear, Colin (1999) "Literacy Studies in Education: Disciplined Developments in the Post-Disciplinary Age," http://everydayliteracies.net/files/literacystudies.html (accessed January 19, 2016).

Lankshear, Colin and Knobel, Michele (2003) *New Literacies: Changing Knowledge and Classroom Practice*, Buckingham, UK: Open University Press.

Leland, Christine H., Harste, Jerome C., and Huber, Kimberley R. (2005) "Out of the Box: Critical Literacy in a First-Grade Classroom," *Language Arts* 82.5: 257–268.

Luke, Allan (2012) "Critical Literacy: Foundational Notes," *Theory Into Practice* 51.1: 4–11.

Luke, Allan, and Freebody, Peter (1999) "Further Notes on the Four Resources Model," *Reading Online*, http:www.readingonline.org/research/lukefreebody.html (accessed January 19, 2016).

McClay, Jill K. (2000) "'Wait a second . . .': Negotiating Complex Narratives in *Black and White*," *Children's Literature in Education* 31.2: 91–106.

Mackey, Margaret (2003) "Researching New Forms of Literacy," *Reading Research Quarterly* 38.3: 403–407.

Marsh, Jackie (2004) "The Techno-Literacy Practices of Young Children," *Journal of Early Childhood Research* 2.1: 51–66.

Marsh, Jackie, and Hallet, Elaine (2008) *Desirable Literacies: Approaches to Language and Literacy in the Early Years*, 2nd ed., London: Sage.

Marshall, Beth (2015) "Fear and Strangeness in Picturebooks: Fractured Fairy Tales, Graphic Knowledge, and Teachers' Concerns," in Janet Evans (ed.) *Challenging and Controversial Picturebooks: Creative and Critical Responses to Visual Texts*, London: Routledge, 160–177.

Martens, Prisca, Martens, Ray, Hassay Doyle, Michelle, Loomis, Jenna, and Aghdarov, Stacy (2012) "Learning from Picturebooks: Reading and Writing Multimodally in First Grade," *The Reading Teacher* 66.4: 285–294.

Mason, Jana, and Allen, JoBeth (1986) "A Review of Emergent Literacy With Implications for Research and Practice in Reading," *Review of Research in Education* 13.1: 3–47.

Meek, Margaret (1988) *How Texts Teach What Readers Learn*, Stroud: Thimble Press.

Meibauer, Jörg (2006) "Language Acquisition and Children's Literature," in Jack Zipes et al. (eds) *The Oxford Encyclopedia of Children's Literature*, vol. 2, Oxford: Oxford University Press, 400–401.

Mirzoeff, Nicholas (2009) *An Introduction to Visual Culture*, London: Routledge (first published 2000).

Mirzoeff, Nicholas (2015) *How to See the World*, London: Pelican.

Mitchell, W.J. Thomas (1994) *Picture Theory: Essays on Verbal and Visual Representation*, Chicago: University of Chicago Press.

NCTEI (2006)" Resolution on the Essential Roles and Value of Literature in the Curriculum," www.ncte.org/positions/statements/valueofliterature (accessed January 19, 2016).

New London Group (1996) "A Pedagogy of Multiliteracies: Designing Social Futures," *Harvard Educational Review* 66.1: 60–92.

Nikolajeva, Maria (2003) "Verbal and Visual Literacy: The Role of Picturebooks in the Reading Experience of Young Children," in Nigel Hall, Joanne Larson, and Jackie Marsh (eds) *Handbook of Early Childhood Literacy*, London: Sage, 235–248.

Nikolajeva, Maria (2014) *Reading for Learning: Cognitive Approaches to Children's Literature*, Amsterdam: John Benjamins.

Painter, Clare, Martin, James R., and Unsworth, Len (2013) *Reading Visual Narratives*, Sheffield: Equinox.

Pantaleo, Sylvia (2011) "Warning: A Grade 7 Student Disrupts Narrative Boundaries," *Journal of Literacy Research* 43.1: 39–67.

Pantaleo, Sylvia (2012a) "Meaning-Making with Colour in Multimodal Texts: One 11-Year-Old Student's Purposeful 'doing'," *Literacy* 46.3: 147–155.

Pantaleo, Sylvia (2012b) "Middle Years Students Thinking with and About Typography in Multimodal Texts," *Literacy Learning: The Middle Years* 20.1: 37–50.

Pantaleo, Sylvia (2013) "Paneling 'Matters' in Elementary Students' Graphic Narratives," *Literacy Research and Instruction* 52.2: 150–171.

Pantaleo, Sylvia (2014) "The Metafictive Nature of Postmodern Picturebooks," *The Reading Teacher* 67.5: 324–332.

Perkins, David (1994) *The Intelligent Eye: Learning to Think by Looking at Art*, Cambridge, MA: Harvard Graduate School of Education.

Ravid, Dorit D., and Tolchinsky, Liliana (2002) "Developing Linguistic Literacy: A Comprehensive Model," *Journal of Child Language* 29: 419–448.

Reedy, David, and UKLA (2010) "Agenda for Action: UKLA's Vision for Future Literacy Education," *English Four to Eleven* 38: 13.

Rowsell, Jennifer, and Pahl, Kate (eds) (2015) *The Routledge Handbook of Literacy Studies*, London: Routledge.

Serafini, Frank (2008) "The Pedagogical Possibilities of Postmodern Picturebooks," *Journal of Reading, Writing and Literacy* 2.3: 23–41.

Serafini, Frank (2011) "Expanding Perspectives for Comprehending Multimodal Texts," *Journal of Adolescent and Adult Literacy* 54.5: 342–350.

Serafini, Frank (2012) "Expanding the Four Resources Model: Reading Visual and Multi-Modal Texts," *Pedagogies: An International Journal* 7.2: 150–164.

Serafini, Frank (2014) *Reading the Visual: An Introduction to Teaching Multimodal Literacy*, New York: Teachers College Press.

Snow, Catherine E., and Goldfield, Beverley A. (1983) "Turn the Page Please: Situation-Specific Language Acquisition," *Journal of Child Language* 10: 551–569.

Snow, Catherine, and Ninio, Anat (1986) "The Contracts of Literacy: What We Learn From Learning to Read Books," in William Teale and Elizabeth Sulzby (eds) *Emergent Literacy: Writing and Reading*, Norwood, NJ: Ablex, 116–138.

Souto-Manning, Mariana (2009) "Negotiating Culturally Responsive Pedagogy Through Multicultural Children's Literature: Towards Critical Democratic Literacy Practices in a First Grade Classroom," *Journal of Early Childhood Literacy* 9.1: 50–74.

Street, Brian V. (1984) *Literacy in Theory and Practice*, Cambridge: Cambridge University Press.

Sulzby, Elizabeth (1985) "Children's Emergent Reading of Favourite Storybooks: A Developmental Study," *Reading Research Quarterly* 20: 458–481.

Sulzby, Elizabeth, and Teale, William (1991) "Emergent Literacy," in Rebecca Barr, Michael Kamil, Peter Mosenthal, and P. David Pearson (eds) *Handbook of Reading Research*, vol. 2, New York: Longman, 727–757.

Thomas, Sue, Joseph, Chris, Laccetti, Jess, Mason, Bruce, Mills, Simon, Perril, Simon, and Pullinger, Kate (2007) "Transliteracy: Crossing Divides," *First Monday* 12: 12.

Vygotsky, Lev S. (1962) *Thought and Language*, Cambridge, MA: MIT Press.

Wells, Gordon (1985) *Language Development in the Pre-school Years*, Cambridge: Cambridge University Press.

Werner, Annette (2011) "Color Perception in Infants and Young Children: The Significance of Color in Picturebooks," in Bettina Kümmerling-Meibauer (ed.) *Emergent Literacy: Children's Books from 0 to 3*, Amsterdam: John Benjamins, 39–54.

Yokota, Junko, and Teale, William H. (2014) "Picturebooks and the Digital World: Educators Making Informed Choices," *The Reading Teacher* 67.8: 577–585.

Zapata, Angie (2014) "Examining the Multimodal and Multilingual Composition Resources of Young Latino Picturebook Makers," in Pamela J. Dunston, Susan King Fullerton, C. C. Bates, Kathy Headley, and Pamela M. Stecker (eds) *63rd Yearbook of the Literacy Research Association*, Florida: Literacy Research Association, 104–121.

36

PICTUREBOOKS AND DEVELOPMENTAL PSYCHOLOGY

Elaine Reese and Jessica Riordan

Our main aim in this chapter is to provide an up-to-date, critical account of what we know about young children's learning from picturebooks from a psychological perspective. Specifically, our focus will be on the role of picturebooks for children's oral language and print skills, as well as on the critical role of adult conversation for children's learning from picturebooks. We will also present the history of this body of research, along with some of the research methods used, to further aid understanding of the present state of the field. We will conclude by discussing the strengths and limitations of a psychological perspective on picturebook reading, and future directions for this field.

Before presenting our review, we would like to distinguish a psychological perspective from the other perspectives in this volume. We define a psychological perspective as one that adopts an empirical approach to children's thinking and learning as a result of their interactions with both the books themselves and with adults. An empirical approach involves the systematic observation of children's interactions during picturebook reading, combined with the rigorous measurement of children's skills before, during, and after these interactions. Therefore, a psychological perspective can focus on both process (How are children interacting with picturebooks?) as well as product (What are the outcomes of those interactions for children's development?).

A brief history of psychological perspectives on picturebook reading

Research on picturebook reading from a psychological perspective arguably began over forty years ago as an offshoot of the psychological study of children's language (Snow 1972; Brown 1973). Child language researchers began conducting fine-grained longitudinal case studies of children's syntax acquisition and lexical development alongside experimental studies of speech directed to young children. Snow (1972) noted that mothers simplified their speech to young children – later termed 'motherese' – a practice that she theorized facilitated children's language development. Picturebook reading quickly emerged as an especially facilitative context for parent-child interactions that supported children's language learning. In one early case study, Ninio and Bruner (1978) claimed that they chose to study one child's noun learning during picturebook reading "since it appeared to be the major activity in which labelling occurred" (3). From another case study, Snow (1983) identified book-reading interactions as containing many question-response-evaluation sequences (Mother: *What's this?*; Nathaniel (32 months): *Wha deh?* Mother: *I think that's lollipop*; 183). Snow argued that these language routines in the context of picturebook reading served to scaffold children's learning of language, story structure, and print.

At around the same time, clinical psychologists working with children with language delays had also discovered that interactive picturebook reading was a way to advance children's language development (that is, *dialogic reading*; Whitehurst et al. 1988). These studies were all *experimental* from the outset, in that the researchers tested new ways of reading picturebooks with young children (compared to existing ways, or to other activities) to isolate the effectiveness of picturebook reading for children's language skills. Thus, the question motivating this body of research was, "How can we craft book-reading interactions that maximize language benefits for very young children and those with language delays?"

Finally, a third thread of investigation originated with educational researchers, who had long observed that some children arrived at school already reading. These researchers sought to discover what kinds of interactions in the home supported precocious reading, with picturebook reading emerging as a prime candidate (Durkin 1966). Contemporary educational researchers conduct observational studies of picturebook reading in early childhood and primary school classrooms (Dickinson and Smith 1994; Dickinson and Porche 2011). Because of the close interplay in focus and methods between educational and psychological researchers, we also draw from this literature for this review.

Thus, from the outset, the psychological perspective on picturebook reading has embraced both observational and experimental/intervention approaches. From the observational approach, early case studies have blossomed into larger longitudinal studies documenting the way that parents and teachers *naturally* read books with young children as they grow, and as a function of the type of book, characteristics of the child, and the parent's cultural background. From the experimental/intervention approach, the early work with language-delayed children has evolved into large-scale intervention studies with low-income children and others who are academically at risk. These studies aim to discover which styles of book-reading in the home and in the preschool help at-risk children gain a boost at school entry (Sonnenschein and Munstermann 2002). Finally, alongside these observational and experimental methods, new eye-tracking techniques allow us to know precisely where children are looking during picturebook reading (Evans and Saint-Aubin 2005), and brain imaging techniques allow us to examine children's patterns of neural activation during picturebook reading (Ohgi, Loo and Mizuike 2010; see Hutton et al. 2015). The aim of the brain imaging studies is to map the areas of neural activation during the act of picturebook reading, and to understand how activation changes as a function of different books and interaction styles. We predict that we will soon know much more about the neural processes underlying children's learning from picturebook reading. But first, what *do* we know from the psychological research on picturebook reading?

How does picturebook reading help children's oral language skills?

The early observational work from a psychological perspective identified picturebook reading interactions between parent and child as an especially rich context for children's oral language development. We define oral language skills as those that do not require an understanding of print. Thus, children's ability to understand and produce words (*receptive* and *expressive vocabulary*), sentences (*syntax*), and stories (*narrative comprehension* and *production*), as well as their awareness of the sounds of spoken words (*phonological awareness*), are all oral language skills. For instance, Hoff-Ginsberg (1991) confirmed that in comparison to other naturally occurring speech contexts, such as feeding, playing, or bathing, picturebook reading interactions contained speech that was syntactically more complex and used more diverse vocabulary. Indeed, subsequent research documented that parents who read picturebooks more often to their children had children with more advanced oral language skills (particularly in terms of vocabulary size; see Bus, van IJzendoorn and Pellegrini 1995; Scarborough and Dobrich 1994 for reviews). Critically, all of these oral language skills are vital for children's later reading skill and their academic achievement (Scarborough, Neuman and Dickinson 2009; Shanahan and Lonigan 2010).

These studies, however, were all *correlational*, in that the researchers simply observed naturally occurring interactions, with no attempt to change the way parents and children were reading picturebooks. Thus, it is possible that parents and children who read picturebooks more often differ in some other critical way that helps children's oral language skills beyond picturebook reading per se. Further, the frequency of picturebook reading in these studies was typically based on parental report of how often they read to their children, which may have resulted in *social desirability bias*, in which parents report more frequent book-reading than actually occurs. To remedy this bias, later studies have used clever title recognition formats with foil items of fake books included to gain a more valid measure of how often parents share books with their children (see Sénéchal and LeFevre 2002). Further correlational studies have attempted to control for additional variables, such as maternal education and children's nonverbal intelligence. Yet, the results of these studies, somewhat reassuringly, continue to show that children whose parents read to them more often in early childhood have better vocabulary skills (Sénéchal and LeFevre 2002).

A limitation of many of these studies is their focus on vocabulary as the sole measure of children's oral language, to the exclusion of syntax, narrative, or phonological awareness skill. Only a few studies incorporate a broader view of oral language; those studies do find a role of picturebook reading for children's syntax and narrative, but typically not for children's phonological awareness (see Sénéchal and Lefevre 2002; Kümmerling-Meibauer et al. 2015; Reese 2015 for reviews). Children are being exposed to complex sentence and narrative structures when they hear picturebooks. One reason that picturebook reading does not figure prominently in children's phonological awareness could be because most studies do not discriminate between prose and rhyming picturebooks (but see Read et al. 2014). We suggest that rhyming picturebooks, because of their focus on the sounds of words, may be especially supportive of children's phonological awareness. E-books may be another engaging new way for children to learn about the sounds of words through interacting with the text or pictures (Korat, Shamir and Heibal 2013). Thus, traditional picturebook reading clearly helps children to learn new vocabulary and to better understand story and sentence structure. With further research, we may find that certain genres of picturebooks also help children to learn more about the sounds of words. This boost in oral language development bodes well for children's later reading comprehension (Dickinson and Tabors 2001; Sénéchal and LeFevre 2002).

The research we have presented so far has focused primarily on how often children experience picturebooks – a matter of quantity. These conclusions are supported by a host of studies that have examined how parents and teachers are actually reading picturebooks with young children – a matter of quality. In these studies, the researchers recorded the picturebook reading interactions and then laboriously transcribed and classified the interactions word by word, sentence by sentence, for the content and structure of the interactions. These studies focus only on the 'extra' words that parents and children use about the book, not on the text of the picturebook. These studies identify individual differences in the way parents and teachers share picturebooks with young children. For example, some parents and teachers interact extensively, whereas others stick mostly to reading the text. When parents and teachers do talk about the book, some invite the child to participate by asking questions, whereas others mainly issue statements. Some of their interactions focus mostly on the pictures, whereas other interactions go beyond the pictures to talk about the story line and about emotions and other mental states of the characters. This body of research consistently shows that when parents and teachers have longer interactions containing questions that focus on higher-level aspects of the book (the story line, new words, and mental states), children have more advanced vocabulary, abstract language, and narrative skills, even after controlling for key confounding variables such as children's initial language skill and maternal education levels (see Dickinson et al. 1994; Haden, Reese and Fivush 1996; van Kleeck et al. 1997; Hindman et al. 2014).

Again, these studies of book-reading quality are all correlational. Fortunately, a vast body of experimental research supports these basic findings. Much of this experimental research has been conducted on *dialogic reading*, which was the version of picturebook reading that Grover Whitehurst developed through working with language-delayed children (Whitehurst et al. 1988; Whitehurst and Fischel 1994).

Dialogic reading is a highly interactive form of picturebook reading in which the adult reader asks questions on nearly every page, and then subsequently praises and expands upon the child's utterance. Another key component of dialogic reading is repeated readings of the same picturebook over time, with more demanding questions asked of the child with each reading, particularly with older children. For older preschoolers, the goal is to encourage the child to eventually tell the story to the adult. Research consistently shows that dialogic reading advances children's expressive vocabulary and, to some extent, their narrative skills (Whitehurst et al. 1988; Zevenbergen, Whitehurst and Zevenbergen 2003; Lever and Sénéchal 2011). When preschool teachers are trained in dialogic or other methods of interactive reading, children in their classrooms demonstrate gains in oral language (Whitehurst, Arnold et al. 1994; Wasik and Bond 2001). Preschool teachers reported, however, that they found it difficult to maintain over time the small-group readings required for true dialogic reading (Whitehurst, Arnold et al. 1994). In contrast, when parents read dialogically, the gains are larger for middle class and younger children than for low-income and older children (Mol et al. 2008).

Dialogic reading comprises a host of techniques, each of which could be helpful for children's learning. Yet dialogic reading always interrupts the text. Other experimental studies have explored higher-level reading styles in which the reader does not interrupt the text during the reading, but instead prefaces the reading and asks high-level questions after the reading. This higher-level, *performance-oriented* style may advance vocabulary for older preschoolers more effectively than does an interrupting style (Reese and Cox 1999; Wasik, Bond and Hindman 2006). Interestingly, one of the early case studies noted this phenomenon in which a precocious middle class child resisted conversations *during* the reading of the text from about age three and a half (Snow 1983).

Other fine-grained experimental studies have investigated precisely how children learn new words from picturebooks. This body of research sometimes uses experimentally prepared texts, not commercially available picturebooks, in order to control the manner and the frequency with which new words are introduced. These experiments employ carefully designed control conditions in which other groups of children are read the same books, but the new words are not asked about or explained. These studies show that children learn new words from picturebooks best when adults ask questions about those new words, and in which the demand level of the questions gets harder on subsequent readings of the book (Blewitt et al. 2009). Multiple exposures to the new words on repeated readings of the same book also benefit children's word learning (Horst, Parsons and Bryan 2011). Finally, using this focused experimental method, Ganea and colleagues have established that for very young children, pop-out books are distracting for their word learning (Tare et al. 2010). For toddlers and younger preschoolers, picturebooks with simple, realistic illustrations are best for developing their oral language skills (Ganea, Pickard and DeLoache 2008).

When research from all these different perspectives is knitted together, it is clear that traditional picturebook reading benefits children's expressive vocabulary and narrative skills, with potential but under-researched benefits for children's phonological awareness. It is not just how often adults read that matters for children's oral language development; it's also *how* they are sharing the picturebook that matters for children's language learning. These oral language skills in early childhood are critical for children's eventual reading comprehension skills by the mid-primary school years (Dickinson and Tabors 2001). Oral language skills are also crucial for children's socio-emotional development. Children with better oral language skills have fewer behavior problems (Zadeh, Im-Bolter and Cohen 2007), perhaps because they are more advanced in their understanding of emotions (Martin et al. 2015).

How does picturebook reading help children's written language skills?

For children's eventual reading skills, it is also vital for young children to develop print-related literacy skills such as knowing the concepts of words and sentences (*print conventions*), letter names (*alphabet knowledge*), letter sounds (*phonemic awareness*), how to read words (*decoding ability* and *fluency*), and how to construct meaning from print (*reading comprehension*). Studies reveal that preschool-aged children who score higher on measures assessing print conventions, alphabet knowledge, and phonemic awareness go on to become better readers, and better reading in turn predicts greater school achievement (Scarborough 1998; National Reading Panel 2000). These relations hold even after controlling for children's nonverbal intelligence, vocabulary, short-term memory, and phonological awareness (Torgesen et al. 1997; Burgess and Lonigan 1998; Parrila, Kirby and McQuarrie 2004; Evans et al. 2006; Verhagen, Aarnoutse and van Leeuwe 2009). However, as the alphabet is just a collection of symbols with what may seem arbitrarily assigned sounds, young children first need to be both implicitly and explicitly taught how to 'crack the code.' Therefore, many researchers recommend that parents share print-rich picturebooks with their children (Snow, Burns and Griffin 1998; Justice and Ezell 2000).

At first glance, this recommendation appears sound. After all, children can see their parents interacting with the text and follow along, potentially internalizing the respective reading strategies. Nevertheless, when psychologists in the 1980s and 1990s investigated the link between picturebook sharing and children's print skills, the results were mixed at best. Bus, van IJzendoorn and Pellegrini (1995) found in a meta-analysis that the frequency of early parent-child reading accounted for only 8 percent of children's later print-related literacy skills. Even research into the quality of picturebook sharing has produced mixed results. For instance, although some studies demonstrate positive correlations between the quantity and quality of parental extra-textual talk during picturebook reading and children's decoding skills (Haden, Reese and Fivush 1996; Leseman and deJong 1998) and other early print-related literacy skills (Beals and DeTemple 1993; DeTemple 2001), other studies report no relationship at all (Hindman, Skibbe and Foster 2014; Roberts, Jurgens and Burchinal 2005; Anderson et al. 2012). Therefore, mere exposure to picturebooks alone may not be "the literacy event par excellence" (Pellegrini 1991: 380) as once thought.

One reason for these weak links could again have to do with the quality of picturebook reading interactions. When parents' talk during book-reading is analyzed, it is apparent that parents refer to print only rarely during typical picturebook reading (Bus and van IJzendoorn 1988; Justice and Ezell 2000; Hindman et al. 2014), constituting only 6 percent of parents' total extratextual talk (Price, van Kleeck and Huberty 2009). Furthermore, eye-gaze studies show that preschool children barely even look at the text in picturebooks during typical parent-child interactions, at only 4 percent of the time (Roy-Charland, Saint-Aubin and Evans 2007; Evans, Williamson and Pursoo 2008; Justice, Pullen and Pence 2008). Consequently, when Hindman et al. (2014) coded seven hundred videos of mothers sharing a prose picturebook (*Corduroy* [1968] by Don Freeman) with their preschoolers, it was not surprising that their references to print were not linked with any variation in children's print skills. Young children are simply more interested in the pictures than in the text of picturebooks, and parents correspondingly talk little about print during everyday picturebook sharing.

Researchers investigating other genres, however, have uncovered an encouraging pattern – when reading an alphabet book, parents and children are more likely to label letters, find words that start with individual letters on a page, sound out words, and discuss general print-related concepts (Bus and van IJzendoorn 1988; Smolkin and Yaden 1992; Johnson et al. 1996; Van Kleeck 1998; Stadler and McEvoy 2003). Therefore, Hindman et al. (2008) set out to discover if the higher frequency of parental print talk afforded by alphabet books could help to explain the aforementioned relationship between frequency of picturebook reading and children's later print skills. Indeed, the frequency of parents' print talk in alphabet books was more than double the amount elicited by traditional narratives (15 percent versus 6 percent in Price et al. 2009), yet there was still no link between this type of talk and children's print skills. Consequently, naturally occurring print talk during picturebook reading may not be the primary vehicle for fostering children's print skills.

When adults are *taught* in experimental studies to make the text in picturebooks more explicit, however, dramatic increases occur in both parent and child print talk (Ezell and Justice 2000) and in preschool children's short- and long-term print skills (Justice and Ezell 2000; Justice et al. 2002, 2009). For instance, after Justice and Ezell (2000) taught a group of parents to refer to print more often, and provided them with children's books to read over four weeks, post-testing indicated that parents made significantly more verbal and nonverbal prompts about print. Furthermore, children in this group made significant gains in their print skills over this period compared to children of parents who were not taught these techniques, yet were provided the same books. To conclude, picturebooks *can* support children's print skills, but adults first need to be guided to actively and purposefully engage with the text.

Conclusions

From this review, it is clear that frequent and interactive picturebook reading is important for children's oral language and, under certain conditions, for children's early print skills. Fostering children's oral language skill is vital given its role in later reading skill, particularly reading comprehension by the mid-primary school years (de Jong and Leseman 2001; Sénéchal and LeFevre 2002) and in socioemotional development (Zadeh, Im-Bolter and Cohen 2007). Thus, interactions between adults and children during picturebook reading are paramount for children's learning and development. These findings are underscored by brain imaging research that shows that children exhibit greater neural activation (specifically in the frontal lobes, which are responsible for higher-level thinking) when they are interacting with a parent during picturebook reading compared to viewing the same picturebook being read on a video (Ohgi et al. 2010). Conversations are indeed useful when reading picturebooks with young children.

Yet, it is also important to note that the amount and type of interaction that is optimal depends upon the child's age and developmental level. Whether the focus is on the meaning of a story, a word, or on print, questions that are pitched too far below or beyond the child's level are not as effective in advancing their learning. Older and more advanced children, for instance, may be more interested in and responsive to interactions about print (Snow 1983). Furthermore, there are strong hints in the literature showing that older and more advanced children require less extra-textual interaction than younger and less advanced children to stay engaged, yet they still benefit from story discussion before and after reading (Reese and Cox 1999; Wasik et al. 2006).

Another clear pattern in the literature is that the benefits gained from interactive picturebook sharing are, not surprisingly, tied to the focus of that interaction and to the genre of picturebook. For example, children learn new words from picturebooks when adults question them about those new words in context, and when children are not distracted by other features of the book (Blewitt et al. 2009; Tare et al. 2010).

Children's narrative skills, in contrast, are fostered in the context of storybooks when adults ask questions about the plot of the story and emphasize connections between events (Lever and Sénéchal 2011). Conversely, alphabet books are more effective in eliciting adults' and children's print-based interactions than are prose picturebooks (Price et al. 2009). Finally, children can and do acquire print skills through picturebook reading when adults bring children's attention to the text more explicitly (Justice and Ezell 2000; Justice and Kadaverek 2002).

Despite these robust patterns across a range of methods, we still have much to learn from a psychological perspective to picturebook reading. We are on the cusp of learning a great deal about the benefits of picturebook reading for children's phonological awareness (Johnston et al. 2014), their conceptual development (Ganea et al. 2008), and their socioemotional development (Adrián et al. 2007). We are also on the brink of learning more about the delivery system of picturebook reading for children's learning: Will traditional books prevail, or are e-books capable of producing similar benefits? How well do young children understand the visual codes of picturebooks – for instance, the use of speech bubbles, or speed lines? Furthermore, are picturebooks related to children's expressive writing skills and their STEM learning in the early years of schooling? To answer these questions, we will continue to benefit from adopting both correlational and experimental methods. An especially promising direction is the use of intervention designs in which researchers partner with parents and teachers to create new ways of engaging children with picturebooks. Moreover, we are watching the burgeoning brain imaging research with interest as it will complement our behavioral work, helping us to understand the degree and location of neural activation that children exhibit when viewing different types of picturebooks and when engaging in different types of interactions.

As exciting as we find these new directions, we are also aware of the limitations of a psychological perspective on picturebook reading. For example, this literature has not addressed in any thorough way the impact of literary or aesthetic qualities of picturebooks on children and their families, or of connections between the visual and textual aspects of picturebooks (see Nikolajeva and Scott 2001). Moreover, the psychological literature on picturebooks can be fairly accused of being WEIRD science (conducted primarily with families from White, Educated, Industrialized, Rich, and Democratic samples; Henrich, Heine, and Noranzayan 2010; but see Hindman et al. 2014). We add that the focus has been primarily with mothers, yet we know that fathers and other adults are frequent partners in picturebook reading (see Robertson and Reese 2015). Therefore, one must look to the other chapters in this volume for a more complete view of the role of picturebooks in children's lives. What we *do* know from a psychological perspective, however, is that picturebook reading, especially when it is interactive and sensitively pitched to a child's level, helps young children to learn language skills that are crucial for their performance in school and for their communication with others.

References

Adrián, Juan E., Clemente, Rosa Ana, and Villanueva, Lidón (2007) "Mothers' Use of Cognitive State Verbs in Picture-Book Reading and the Development of Children's Understanding of Mind: A Longitudinal Study," *Child Development* 78.4: 1052–1067.

Anderson, Ann, Anderson, Jim, Lynch, Jacqueline, Shapiro, Jon, and Kim, Ji Eun (2012) "Extra-Textual Talk in Shared Book Reading: A Focus on Questioning," *Early Child Development and Care* 182.9: 1139–1154.

Beals, Diane E., and De Temple, Jeanne M. (1993) "Home Contributions to Early Language and Literacy Development," *National Reading Conference Yearbook* 42: 207–215.

Blewitt, Pamela, Rump, Keiran M., Shealy, Stephanie E., and Cook, Samantha A. (2009) "Shared Book Reading: When and How Questions Affect Young Children's Word Learning," *Journal of Educational Psychology* 101:2: 294–304.

Brown, Roger (1973) *A First Language: The Early Stages*, Cambridge. MA: Harvard University Press.

Burgess, Stephen R., and Lonigan, Christopher J. (1998) "Bidirectional Relations of Phonological Sensitivity and Prereading Abilities: Evidence from a Preschool Sample," *Journal of Educational Psychology* 91: 402–414.

Bus, Adriana G., and van IJzendoorn, Marinus H. (1988) "Mother-Child Interactions, Attachment, and Emergent Literacy: A Cross-Sectional Study," *Child Development* 59: 1262–1272.

Bus, Adriana G., van IJzendoorn, Marinus H., and Pellegrini, Anthony D. (1995) "Joint Book Reading Makes for Success in Learning to Read: A Meta-Analysis on Intergenerational Transmission of Literacy," *Review of Educational Research* 65.1: 1–22.

deJong, Peter F., and Leseman, Paul P.M. (2001) "Lasting Effects of Home Literacy on Reading Achievement in School," *Journal of School Psychology* 39.5: 389–414.

De Temple, Jeanne M. (2001) "Parents and Children Reading Books Together," in David K. Dickinson and Patton O. Tabors (eds) *Beginning Literacy With Language*, Baltimore: Paul H. Brookes, 33–51.

Dickinson, David K., and Porche, Michelle V. (2011) "Relation Between Language Experiences in Preschool Classrooms and Children's Kindergarten and Fourth-Grade Language and Reading Abilities," *Child Development* 82.3: 870–886.

Dickinson, David K., and Tabors, Patton O. (eds) (2001) *Beginning Literacy with Language*, Baltimore: Paul H. Brookes.

Dickinson, David K., and Smith, Miriam W. (1994) "Long-Term Effects of Preschool Teachers' Book Readings on Low-Income Children's Vocabulary and Story Comprehension," *Reading Research Quarterly* 29: 105–122.

Durkin, Delores (1966) *Children Who Read Early*, New York: Teachers College Press.

Evans, Mary Ann, Bell, Michelle, Shaw, Deborah, Moretti, Shelley, and Page, Jodi (2006) "Letter Names, Letters Sounds, and Phonological Awareness: An Examination of Kindergarten Children Across Letters and of Letters Across Children," *Reading and Writing: An Interdisciplinary Journal* 19: 959–989.

Evans, Mary Ann, and Saint-Aubin, Jean (2005) "What Children Are Looking at During Shared Storybook Reading: Evidence From Eye Movement Monitoring," *Psychological Science* 16: 913–920.

Evans, Mary Ann, Karen Williamson, and Pursoo, Tiffany (2008) "Pre-Schoolers' Attention to Print During Shared Book Reading," *Scientific Studies of Reading* 12: 106–129.

Ezell, Helen K., and Justice, Laura M. (2000) "Increasing the Print Focus of Adult-Child Shared Book Reading Through Observational Learning," *American Journal of Speech-Language Pathology* 9: 36–47.

Freeman, Don (1968) *Corduroy*, New York: Puffin.

Ganea, Patricia A., Bloom Pickard, Megan, and DeLoache, Judy S. (2008) "Transfer Between Picture Books and the Real World by Very Young Children," *Journal of Cognition and Development* 9:1: 46–66.

Haden, Catherine A., Reese, Elaine, and Fivush, Robyn (1996) "Mothers' Extratextual Comments During Storybook Reading: Stylistic Differences Over Time and Across Texts," *Discourse Processes* 21: 135–169.

Henrich, Joseph, Heine, Steven J., and Norenzayan, Ara (2010) "Most People Are Not WEIRD," *Nature* 466: 7302: 29.

Hindman, Annemarie H., Connor, Carol M., Jewkes, Abigail M., and Morrison, Frederick J. (2008) "Untangling the Effects of Shared Book Reading: Multiple Factors and Their Associations with Preschool Literacy Outcomes," *Early Childhood Research Quarterly* 23: 330–350.

Hindman, Annemarie H., Skibbe, Lori E., and Foster, Tricia D. (2014) "Exploring the Variety of Parental Talk During Book Reading and Its Contributions to Preschool Children's Language and Literacy: Evidence from the Early Childhood Longitudinal Study – Birth Cohort," *Reading and Writing* 27: 287–313.

Hoff-Ginsberg, Erika (1991) "Mother-Child Conversation in Different Social Classes and Communicative Settings," *Child Development* 62.4: 782–796.

Horst, Jessica S., Parsons, Kelly L., and Bryan Natasha M. (2011) "Get the Story Straight: Contextual Repetition Promotes Word Learning from Storybooks," *Frontiers in Psychology* 2. Doi:http://dx.doi.org/10.3389/fpsyg.2011.00017 (accessed November 11, 2015).

Hutton, John S., Horowitz-Kraus, Tzipi, Mendelsohn, Alan L., DeWitt, Tom, Holland, Scott K., and the C-MIND Authorship Consortium (2015) "Home Reading Environment and Brain Activation in Preschool Children Listening to Stories," *Pediatrics* 136.3: 466–478.

Johnson, Rhona S., Anderson, Marjorie, and Holligan, Christopher (1996) "Knowledge of the Alphabet and Explicit Awareness of Phonemes in Pre-readers: The Nature of the Relationship," *Reading and Writing: An Interdisciplinary Journal* 8: 217–234.

Johnston, Jessica, Reese, Elaine, Schaughency, Elizsabeth, and Das, Shika (2014) "A Time to Talk: A Conversational Intervention for Children's Language Learning," Paper presented at the International Association for Child Language, Amsterdam.

Justice, Laura M., and Ezell, Helen K. (2000) "Enhancing Children's Print and Word Awareness Through Home-Based Parent Intervention," *American Journal of Speech-Language Pathology* 9: 257–269.

Justice, Laura M., and Kadaverek, Joan N. (2002) "Using Shared Storybook Reading to Promote Emergent Literacy," *Teaching Exceptional Children* 34: 8–13.

Justice, Laura M., Kaderavek, Joan N., Fan, Xitao, Sofka, Amy, and Hunt, Aileen (2009) "Accelerating Preschoolers' Early Literacy Development Through Classroom-Based Teacher-Child Storybook Reading and Explicit Print Referencing," *Language, Speech, and Hearing Services in Schools* 40: 67–85.

Justice, Laura M., Pullen, Paige C., and Pence, Khara (2008) "Influence of Verbal and Nonverbal References to Print on Preschoolers' Visual Attention to Print During Storybook Reading," *Developmental Psychology* 44: 855–866.

Justice, Laura M., Weber, Sarah E., Ezell, Helen K., and Bakeman, Roger (2002) "A Sequential Analysis of Children's Responsiveness to Parental Print References During Shared Book-Reading Interactions," *American Journal of Speech-Language Pathology* 11.1: 30–40.

Korat, Ofra, Shamir, Adina, and Heibal, Shani (2013) "Expanding the Boundaries of Shared Book Reading: E-books and Printed Books in Parent – Child Reading as Support for Children's Language," *First Language* 33.5: 504–523.

Kümmerling-Meibauer, Bettina, Jörg Meibauer, Kerstin Nachtigäller, and Katharina Rohlfing (eds) (2015) *Learning from Picturebooks: Perspectives from Child Development and Literacy Studies*, New York: Routledge.

Leseman, Paul P.M., and de Jong, Peter F. (1998) "Home Literacy: Opportunity, Instruction, Cooperation, and Social-Emotional Quality Predicting Early Reading Achievement," *Reading Research Quarterly* 33: 294–318.

Lever, Rosemary, and Sénéchal, Monique (2011) "Discussing Stories: On How a Dialogic Reading Intervention Improves Kindergartners' Oral Narrative Construction," *Journal of Experimental Child Psychology* 108.1: 1–24.

Martin, Sarah E., Williamson, Lauren R., Kurtz-Nelson, Evangeline C., and Boekamp, John R. (2015) "Emotion Understanding (and Misunderstanding) in Clinically Referred Preschoolers: The Role of Child Language and Maternal Depressive Symptoms," *Journal of Child and Family Studies* 24: 24–37.

Mol, Suzanne E., et al. (2008) "Added Value of Dialogic Parent – Child Book Readings: A Meta-Analysis," *Early Education and Development* 19.1: 7–26.

National Reading Panel (2000) "Teaching Children to Read: An Evidence-Based Assessment of the Scientific Research Literature on Reading and Its Implication for Reading Instruction," www.dys-add.com/resources/SpecialEd/TeachingChildrenToRead.pdf (accessed April 23, 2015).

Nikolajeva, Maria, and Scott, Carole (2001) *How Picturebooks Work*, New York: Garland.

Ninio, Anat, and Bruner, Jerome (1978) "The Achievement and Antecedents of Labeling," *Journal of Child Language* 5.01: 1–15.

Ohgi, Shohei, Loo, Kek Khee, and Mizuike, Chihiro (2010) "Frontal Brain Activation in Young Children During Picture Book Reading with Their Mothers," *Acta Paediatrica* 99.2: 225–229.

Parrila, Rauno, Kirby, John, and McQuarrie, Lynn (2004) "Articulation Rate, Naming Speed, Verbal Short-Term Memory and Phonological Awareness: Longitudinal Predictors of Early Reading Development," *Scientific Studies of Reading* 8: 3–26.

Pellegrini, Anthony (1991) "A Critique of the Concept of At-Risk as Applied to Emergent Literacy," *Language Arts* 68: 380–385.

Price, Lisa H., van Kleeck, Anne, and Huberty, Carl J. (2009) "Talk During Book Sharing Between Parents and Preschool Children: A Comparison Between Storybook and Expository Book Conditions," *Reading Research Quarterly* 44: 171–194.

Read, Kirsten, Macauley, Megan, and Furay, Erin (2014) "The Seuss Boost: Rhyme Helps Children Retain Words from Shared Storybook Reading," *First Language* 34: 354–371.

Reese, Elaine (2015) "What Good Is a Picturebook? Developing Children's Oral Language and Literacy Through Shared Picturebook Reading," in Bettina Kümmerling-Meibauer, Jörg Meibauer, Kerstin Nachtigäller, and Katharina Rohlfing (eds) *Learning from Picturebooks: Perspectives from Child Development and Literacy Studies* New York: Routledge, 194–207.

Reese, Elaine, and Cox, Adell (1999) "Quality of Adult Book-Reading Style Affects Children's Emergent Literacy," *Developmental Psychology* 35: 20–28.

Roberts, Joanne, Jurgens, Julia, and Burchinal, Margaret (2005) "The Role of Home Literacy Practices in Preschool Children's Language and Emergent Literacy Skills," *Journal of Speech, Language, and Hearing Research* 48: 345–359.

Robertson, Sarah-Jane, and Reese, Elaine (2015) "The Very Hungry Caterpillar Turned Into a Beautiful Butterfly: Children's and Parents' Enjoyment of Different Book Genres," *Journal of Early Childhood Literacy* 15: 1–23.

Roy-Charland, Annie, Saint-Aubin, Jean, and Evans, Mary Ann (2007) "Eye Movements in Shared Book Reading with Children from Kindergarten to Grade 4," *Reading and Writing* 20: 909–931.

Scarborough, Hollis S. (1998) "Early Identification of Children at Risk of Reading Difficulties: Phonological Awareness and Some Other Promising Predictors," in Bruce K. Shapiro, Pasquale J. Accardo, and Arnold J. Capute (eds) *Specific Reading Disability: A View of the Spectrum*, Timonium, MD: York Press, 75–120.

Scarborough, Hollis S., and Dobrich, Wanda (1994) "On the Efficacy of Reading to Preschoolers," *Developmental Review* 14.3: 245–302.

Scarborough, Hollis S., Neuman, Susan, and Dickinson, David (2009) "Connecting Early Language and Literacy to Later Reading (Dis)Abilities: Evidence, Theory, and Practice," in Felicity Fletcher-Campbell, Janet Soler, and Gavin Reid (eds) *Approaching Difficulties in Literacy Development: Assessment, Pedagogy, and Programmes*, New York: Sage, 23–39.

Sénéchal, Monique, and LeFevre, Jo-Anne (2002) "Parental Involvement in the Development of Children's Reading Skill: A Five-Year Longitudinal Study," *Child Development* 73.2: 445–460.

Shanahan, Timothy, and Lonigan, Christopher J. (2010) "The National Early Literacy Panel: A Summary of the Process and the Report," *Educational Researcher* 39.4: 279–285.

Smolkin, Laura B., and Yaden, David B. (1992) "O Is for Mouse: First Encounters with the Alphabet Book," *Language Arts* 69: 432–443.

Snow, Catherine E. (1972) "Mothers' Speech to Children Learning Language," *Child Development* 43.2: 549–565.

Snow, Catherine E. (1983) "Literacy and Language: Relationships During the Preschool Years," *Harvard Educational Review* 53.2: 165–189.

Snow, Catherine E., Burns, M. Susan, and Griffin, Peg (1998) *Preventing Reading Difficulties in Young Children*, Washington, DC: Committee on the Prevention of Reading Difficulties in Young Children, National Research Council, National Academy Press.

Sonnenschein, Susan, and Munsterman, Kimberly (2002) "The Influence of Home-Based Reading Interactions on 5-Year-Olds' Reading Motivations and Early Literacy Development," *Early Childhood Research Quarterly* 17: 318–337.

Stadler, Marie A., and McEvoy, Mary A. (2003) "The Effect of Text Genre on Parent Use of Joint Book Reading Strategies to Promote Phonological Awareness," *Early Childhood Research Quarterly* 18.4: 502–512.

Tare, Medha, Chiong, Cynthia, Ganea, Patricia, and DeLoache, Judy (2010) "Less Is More: How Manipulative Features Affect Children's Learning from Picture Books," *Journal of Applied Developmental Psychology* 31.5: 395–400.

Torgesen, Joseph K., Wagner, Richard K., Rashotte, Carol A., Burgess, Stephen, and Hecht, Stephen (1997) "Contributions of Phonological Awareness and Rapid Automatic Naming Ability to the Growth of Word-Reading Skills in Second-to Fifth-Grade Children," *Scientific Studies of Reading* 1.2: 161–185.

van Kleeck, Anne (1998) "Pre-Literacy Domains and Stages: Laying the Foundations for Beginning Reading," *Journal of Children's Communication Development* 20: 33–51.

van Kleeck, Anne, Gillam, Ronald B., Hamilton, Lori, and McGrath, Cassandra (1997) "The Relationship Between Middle-Class Parents' Book-Reading Discussion and Their Preschoolers' Abstract Language Development," *Journal of Speech and Language Hearing Research* 40: 1261–1271.

Verhagen, Wim G.M., Aarnoutse, Cor A.J., and van Leeuwe, Jan F.J. (2009) "The Predictive Power of Phonemic Awareness and Naming Speed for Early Dutch Word Recognition," *Educational Research and Evaluation*, 15.1: 93–116.

Wasik, Barbara A., and Bond, Mary Alice (2001) "Beyond the Pages of a Book: Interactive Book Reading and Language Development in Preschool Classrooms," *Journal of Educational Psychology* 93.2: 243–250.

Wasik, Barbara A., Bond, Mary Alice, and Hindman, Annemarie (2006) "The Effects of a Language and Literacy Intervention on Head Start Children and Teachers," *Journal of Educational Psychology* 98.1: 63–74.

Whitehurst, Grover J., et al. (1988) "Accelerating Language Development Through Picture Book Reading," *Developmental Psychology* 24.4: 552–559.

Whitehurst, Grover J., Arnold, David S., Epstein, Jeffery N., Angell, Andrea L., Smith, Megan, and Fischel, Janet E. (1994) "A Picture Book Reading Intervention in Day Care and Home for Children from Low-Income Families," *Developmental Psychology* 30.5: 679–689.

Whitehurst, Grover J., and Fischel, Janet E. (1994) "Practitioner Review: Early Developmental Language Delay: What, If Anything, Should the Clinician Do About It?" *Journal of Child Psychology and Psychiatry* 35.4: 613–648.

Zadeh, Zohreh Y., Im-Bolter, Nancie, and Cohen, Nancy J. (2007) "Social Cognition and Eexternalizing Psychopathology: An Investigation of the Mediating Role of Language," *Journal of Abnormal Child Psychology* 35.2: 141–152.

Zevenbergen, Andrea A., Whitehurst, Grover J., and Zevenbergen, Jason A. (2003) "Effects of a Shared-Reading Intervention on the Inclusion of Evaluative Devices in Narratives of Children from Low-Income Families," *Journal of Applied Developmental Psychology* 24.1: 1–15.

37

PICTUREBOOKS AND COGNITIVE STUDIES

Bettina Kümmerling-Meibauer and Jörg Meibauer

Introduction

Picturebooks have mainly been studied as didactic instruments, as objects of art, or as a special book type (a set of picture-text relations). These academic perspectives focus on the view of adults, namely, how picturebooks can be used in education, how picturebooks are created, or how we can analyze the special contributions of pictures and texts to a narrative. Sometimes, a historical perspective is added to these questions. What has been widely neglected, however, is the perspective of the child reader. How can children make sense of a picturebook? What can they learn from it? To answer these questions, the study of picturebooks must take the developmental stages of children into account. And it entails that picturebooks are studied as objects that are (a) accommodated to children's abilities and interests and (b) a specific input to their overall development.

Let us take an example: when children look at the pictures in *The Little House* (1942) by Virginia Lee Burton, they will realize that the main protagonist – the Little House – has a face: the two windows with the curtains and open window frames represent the eyes, while the door stands for the nose and the curbed doorstep for a smiling mouth. By listening to the story, children will also experience that the Little House has feelings, similar to those expressed by humans. As for (a), we may assume that children know a great deal about human faces from early on (Taylor, Batty and Itier 2004), and that they can use this knowledge in the interpretation of pictures. Yet, it is not part of their general knowledge that houses have faces, let alone express emotions. Thus, with respect to (b), they may learn that there are exceptions in fictional storyworlds.

To accept this exception is by all means not a simple task, since it requires that children are able to understand that houses may share some human features. The animation of things marks a radical shift from an object to a subject which holds the position of a character. Imputing animacy and agency to things like houses, toys, and vehicles is a quite common practice in children's literature, which leads to a process commonly known as *anthropomorphization*, that is, the attribution of human properties and habits to animals, vehicles, and natural forces. How this process of understanding actually happens is an important research question at the interfaces of picturebook theory and cognitive studies.

What do we understand by 'cognitive studies'? *Cognitive studies* is an umbrella term for all the disciplines that study (human) cognition. In general, cognition includes such phenomena as language and communication, knowledge and memory, thinking and problem-solving, and the related processes of production and comprehension. These cognitive processes are subject to constant changes, starting in infancy and continuing in childhood, adolescence, and even beyond. Children's development is on the agenda of developmental psychology, but interfaces with other disciplines, such as *linguistics* (e.g., language acquisition; O'Grady 2011), *literacy studies* (e.g., the acquisition of reading and writing; Larson and Marsh 2012), *epistemology* (e.g., knowledge acquisition; Pinkham, Kaefer and Neuman 2012), and *perception theory* (e.g., the acquisition of picture understanding; Elkins 2007). Beyond these disciplines, there are theories of the child's moral, social-cultural, and emotional development (Killen and Smetana 2006; McCarthy and Philipps 2006), which are also important with respect to cognitive studies in general and picturebook theory in particular.

Considering the broad topic and the comprehensive research, this chapter first explains how a cognitive approach to picturebooks might look. A brief report on the actual state of the art follows in relation to cognitive investigations of picturebooks. The chapter then hones in on the crucial concept of theory of mind and its tight connection with the depiction of characters in picturebooks as well as the related ability of perspective-taking.

A cognitive approach to picturebooks

Many 'cognitive' aspects of picturebooks have been discussed with respect to so-called *literacy*. One way of sorting out the field is to distinguish several subfields of literacy, for example, *linguistic literacy* (learning to read and write), *visual literacy* (learning to produce and interpret pictures), and *literary literacy* (learning to tell and interpret narratives). Since picturebooks are essentially text-picture combinations, all of these 'literacies' matter: the child's ability to understand and to produce language, the ability to understand and produce the visual codes of pictures, and the ability to produce and comprehend the specific narrative qualities of literary texts. How these abilities are acquired and how they interact when a child looks at a picturebook cannot be fully grasped without considering the child's overall cognitive development.

There are several frameworks on the market, such as *cognitive criticism, cognitive poetics*, and *cognitive stylistics*, which apply principles of cognitive studies to the interpretation of literary texts and other medial forms by considering the context-related basis of artistic works. Topics addressed in cognitive studies of literature are, for instance, deixis (indexicality), schemata, scripts, foregrounding, conceptual metaphors, prototypes, and more broadly, *cognitive narratology* (Stockwell 2002). A further development is the focus on personal and emotional investment in literary narratives, in the forms of projection, emotional response, and development of empathy (Zunshine 2006; Hogan 2011).

However, what those scholars working in the realm of cognitive poetics usually do not take into consideration is the developmental dimension, that is, how humans acquire the specific cognitive abilities that are necessary for a full understanding of literary works. Since they focus on highly sophisticated literary texts and media to a greater or lesser extent, they completely disregard the significance of children's literature, let alone picturebooks.

Yet there is much to gain from a cognitive approach to picturebooks: For instance, with respect to *The Little House*, children have to understand that the alternations of the rural setting surrounding the Little House are caused by the seasonal changes as well as the increasing intrusion of people who want to live in the countryside. While this refers to the child's world knowledge about the seasons and the effects of construction sites and road building, the specific representation of the space also demands that children have already mastered an understanding of central perspective and the rather abstractly drawn entities, which stand for trees, animals, and fences (Liben 1997; Newcombe and Huttenlocher 2000; Uttal and Tan 2000).

In sum, a cognitive study of picturebooks has to consider children's cognitive development in order to comprehend the multifarious challenges children face when they read picturebooks. In this regard, particularly picturebooks are objects well-suited to the overall purpose of studying the relation between general cognitive development, linguistic literacy, visual literacy, and literary literacy, since they are usually the first books young children are familiar with – at least in Western societies.

The state of the art

Despite a wealth of empirical studies in these fields (Goswami 2008; Suggate and Reese 2012; Hall, Cremin and Comber 2013), we do not know in detail how their findings can explain children's understanding of visuals and texts, let alone the complex text-picture relationship in picturebooks. A prominent method in this regard is to interview children about their interpretations (see, for instance, Arizpe and Styles 2003 [rev. 2016]; Evans 2009). This *reader-response methodology*, however, is not sufficient to gain satisfactory insight into ongoing cognitive processes, since it is not empirically validated.

In contrast, cognitive studies of picturebooks revolve around the crucial question of what children can learn from attentively looking at picturebooks (Kümmerling-Meibauer 2011; Kümmerling-Meibauer et al. 2015; Meibauer 2015). In terms of the complex relationship between pictures and texts three aspects are relevant: (a) on the pictorial level, the relationship between the pictures, and (b) on the textual level, the relationship between the texts presented on each page (Kress and Van Leeuwen 1996; Thomas et al. 2001). In a next step, (c) the close connection between the pictures and the text has to be considered (Bateman 2014). While each picture refers to the text printed on the same or the opposite page and vice versa, thus building a thoroughly constructed picture-text relationship, the sequence of these picture-text levels creates a *narrative*, whose structure is dominated by the juxtaposition of verbal and visual information (Jones 1996; Nikolajeva 2003; Torr 2008). It should be noted here that wordless picturebooks also constitute narratives, which rely primarily on the picture sequence. The affordances of such a sophisticated work of art cannot be fully acknowledged without a consideration of children's *pragmatic abilities*, that is, investigating the ways in which a context (e.g., the reading situation) contributes to meaning (Meibauer 2017). Pragmatics as "the study of the use of language use in all its aspects" (Huang 2012: 9) refers, inter alia, to metalinguistic devices, such as metaphor and irony (Winner 1988; Creusere 2007; Pouscoulous 2014). Without a basic knowledge of metaphors, children may have problems understanding that the Little House in Burton's picturebook metaphorically represents a person, since the little house is able to show emotions as well as inner thoughts.

So far just a few articles by picturebook researchers have delineated the cognitive underpinning of children's picturebook experience. Topics addressed are, among others, young children's conceptual development (Kümmerling-Meibauer and Meibauer 2005, 2011, 2015c), the challenge of wimmelbooks (Rémi 2011); the depiction of emotions (Nikolajeva 2012, 2014; Kümmerling-Meibauer and Meibauer 2015b); the representation of lying in picturebooks (Kümmerling-Meibauer and Meibauer 2013; Silva-Díaz 2015); the understanding of metaphor and irony (Kümmerling-Meibauer 1999; Kümmerling-Meibauer and Meibauer 2017); and the significance of maps for the mental representation of space and time (Kümmerling-Meibauer and Meibauer 2015a, 2017).

There are innumerable cognitive issues that are closely connected to a fully fledged comprehension of picturebooks. In general, children have to master a couple of fundamental concepts in order to make sense of their environment, such as character, emotion, perspective, and space. To begin with, they have to learn the distinction between reality and fiction (Ganea, Pickard and DeLoache 2008), and in the case of picturebooks, the distinction between pictures and texts. This enumeration is far from complete, but it already illustrates the numerous aspects that have to be considered to gain insight into the cognitive dimensions of the picturebook. In this light, a future cognitive theory of the picturebook is interested in two complementary issues. First, given that the creative use of language and pictures results in the intricacies and complexities of picturebooks, what are the unique cognitive processes which this complex use of language and pictures requires? Second, given the fact that despite its complexity, the text and the pictures are in principle interpretable, what are the general cognitive constraints, the adherence to which guarantees the understanding of picturebooks (Kümmerling-Meibauer and Meibauer 2013)? In order to illustrate the significance of a cognitive approach to the investigation of picturebooks, the following sections focus on *theory of mind*, whose acquisition is vital for the understanding of characters and perspective-taking, which are two important narrative concepts (Eder, Jannidis and Schneider 2010; Herman 2013). In this way, we aim to connect developmental aspects with narratological aspects (for emotions in picturebooks, see Chapter 11 in this volume).

Picturebooks and theory of mind

Theory of mind – also coined 'mind-reading' – is the ability to attribute mental states, such as feelings, desires, knowledge, and thoughts, to others and to understand that other people may have beliefs, intentions, and feelings different to one's own (Doherty 2009; Marraffa 2011). Theory of mind appears to be a potential ability that develops over childhood up to adolescence and beyond. Precursors of the theory of mind are the imitation of intended actions at eighteen months of age, the distinction between one's own and another's feelings or goals, and the onset of symbolic and fictional play (Legerstee 2005). By age two, the ability to ascribe feelings and wishes to others (independently of one's own feelings and wishes) has developed. A crucial watershed is the age of four, when children usually acquire a basic understanding of theory of mind, as has been shown by innumerable experimental studies and tests, whose design more or less goes back to the so-called false belief task, developed by Heinz Wimmer and Josef Perner (1983). The basic idea of the false belief task, which is considered a litmus test of theory of mind, consists in testing whether preschool children are able to distinguish between the different perspectives of two persons. The results show that children typically master this test at about four years. Usually a distinction between first-order beliefs and second-order beliefs is made. First-order belief is related to the understanding that one can have a false belief about reality (appearance-reality distinction) (at about three and a half to four years of age), while second-order belief is connected to the understanding that one can have a false belief about the belief of another person (by age six). The insight that different perspectives about a belief of another person are possible is a late achievement in the development of children and young adults (between ages twelve and seventeen).

This advanced form of theory of mind is related to the development of cognitive as well as social abilities. If the focus shifts to older ages, the possibility – indeed the necessity – for integration is essential, as it is evident that theory of mind cannot be strictly separated from other cognitive and social concepts (Miller 2012). For instance, the cognitive and social concept of empathy is tightly connected with theory of mind (Thompson and Lagattuta 2006). As the "ability to understand another's perspective and to have a visceral or emotional reaction" (Hastings et al. 2006: 484), empathy refers not only to the ability to understand other people's feelings and emotions, but also to the aspect of one's own emotional reaction. Consequently, empathy connects affective, cognitive, and physiological processes. An affective reaction usually elicits sympathy, while the possibility of undertaking a change of perspective and understanding another's feelings and thoughts belongs to the cognitive realm (Frijda 2007). Physiological processes are autonomous neural activities, such as empathizing with another's pain, anxiety, and joy, which might even influence one's own bodily perception. The concept of empathy plays an important role, since it influences the acquisition of emotional competence, which encompasses four developmental stages, the two last being "empathy for another's feelings" – often equated with theory of mind – and "empathy for another's life condition," which is typically acquired at the age of eleven or twelve. Case studies in the realm of cognitive psychology have shown that children at four years of age develop "empathy for another's feelings" (Hastings et al. 2006: 487). These studies also provide evidence that mastering of different aspects of emotion is spread across several years. Empathy and theory of mind go hand in hand when it comes to the comprehension that different people may have different opinions and feelings about the same thing (Pessoa 2008). Conceptual role-taking as the ability to understand multiple perspectives as well as to imagine alternatives is a challenge children cannot cope with before the age of nine or ten (Bosacki and Astington 1999). Consequently, theory of mind is key to a comprehensive understanding of picturebook stories, which usually display the interaction of characters whose emotions, desires, beliefs, and intentions propel the narrative both on the textual and the visual level.

Characters in picturebooks

Picturebooks are teeming with characters, whether humans, animals, fantastic creatures, or animated objects and vehicles, not to mention abstract entities such as colors and letters (Nikolajeva and Scott 2001; Nikolajeva 2002; Kümmerling-Meibauer and Meibauer 2014). These characters play a significant role, as they drive the plot of the picturebook story and invite the child to identify or at least feel empathy with them. Many scholars have laid the groundwork for an exploration of literary characters and techniques of characterization. Understanding literary characters requires the ability to attribute motivations and dispositions to them. This procedure encourages readers to form expectations about what these characters will do next and why they react in a specific manner, and, in a next step, to emotionally react to them. This happens through a complex interaction of what the text discloses about the characters and what the reader knows about the world in general, particularly about people. On the visual as well as textual side, several sources of characterizing information are discernible: (a) presentations of a character's features, verbal and nonverbal behavior, physiognomy, and body language; (b) presentation of the character's mental and emotional state; (c) inferred character traits mapped from the presentation of the fictional space to the character; and (d) presentation of characters from different angles (Schneider 2001; Jannidis 2009). Children's engagement with literary characters demands that they are able to transfer their prior knowledge about real people to fictional beings and this cannot be taken for granted. What children first have to learn is the difference between a person and a (literary) character. While the notion of 'person' usually refers to real people, the notion of 'character' is allocated to fictional figures that appear in literature and other art forms (Frow 2016). Yet, when reading a story about a character, children may accept that the character represents a person, although the latter has a right of existence independently of the literary text, while the former does not. Seen in this light, the crucial question then arises regarding in which manner children may learn to "care about literary characters" (Vermeule 2010). This process is highly relevant for an appreciation of literature per se, and it is evident that picturebooks play a significant role in this respect.

Actual studies in (cognitive) narratology investigate in which way readers may feel empathy and even identify with certain characters (Keen 2007; Izard 2009). Identification itself is a complex cognitive notion, yet there appear to be textual clues that support identification, for instance: (a) "sympathy with a character who is similar to the reader"; (b) "empathy for a character who is in a particular situation"; and (c) "attraction to a character who is a role model for the reader" (Jannidis 2009: 24). The degree to which a child reader may identify or feel empathy with a literary character depends on multiple conditions, such as the ability to take the character's perspective, to build up an affective relation to the character, and to understand the societal, moral, and cultural reasons for a character's specific behavior and thoughts (25). In this respect, characters whose appearance and demeanor deviates from common expectations represent a particular cognitive challenge, since they demand that the reader bear in mind social, cultural, and moral values, as well as consider the specific character's point of view.

Moreover, if a character in a picturebook is not a human, but a house – as in Burton's picturebook – children may be confused in terms of their cognitive mapping. Houses usually do not fall under the category of 'character'; they are commonly categorized as 'buildings' or 'dwellings.' Since houses are inanimate and conceived rather as objects than as individual beings, the ascription of emotions and thoughts to a house potentially contradicts children's already acquired categorization schemata (Rakison and Oakes 2003; Cohen and Lefebvre 2017). The switching from a house considered an inanimate building to an animate picturebook character, however, is close to the child's ability of pretend or imaginative play, which is regarded as a precursor to theory of mind. According to studies in developmental psychology, pretend play starts anytime from eleven to eighteen months. It becomes very noticeable when children are three or four years old, because at this age children are able to play out a play scene over a longer time period. Pretend play is a cognitive skill as it demands the ability to (a) use objects and pretend that they are something else (for instance, a shoebox as a bed for a doll), (b) attribute properties to objects (by pretending that a stuffed bear is sleeping), and (c) refer to invisible objects (for example, an invisible dog as a companion) (Carlson and White 2013). Under the condition that children have been schooled in pretend play they might be able to comprehend that a house has something like a face and has humanlike properties. Given this observation, it is only another small step to accord feelings to the Little House as the main character in Burton's picturebook. The changing appearance of the front of the house, whose door, windows, and door-steps represent facial features, perfectly matches with the house's alternating emotions, ranging from happiness to astonishment, curiosity, and sadness. Hence, in accordance with the visuals, the story invites the child to empathize with the Little House as the main character by recognizing certain similarities that the house – due to its smallness and helplessness – shares with children. These aspects are far from complete, but may suggest that the analysis of characters in picturebooks presents an auspicious approach to analyzing children's developing appreciation of the cognitive and narrative functions of characters in fictional texts.

Perspective-taking

Character, understood as a cognitive and narrative notion, also has to do with the perspectives that matter in a story. In *The Little House*, the story is presented by a heterodiegetic narrator, who conveys the feelings of the Little House: "The Little House was curious about the city and wondered what it would be like to live there" (n. pag.). The story proceeds by showing rapid changes in the Little House's surroundings. While the reader becomes aware that the Little House's curiosity is changing to anxiety, there is no dialogue between the Little House and other characters. Yet there is speech representation (McHale 2014), which establishes a frame for the story: "The man who built her so well said, 'This Little House shall never be sold for gold or for silver and she will live to see our great-great-grandchildren's great-great-grandchildren living in her.'" (n. pag.). But no addressee is mentioned. Later, the "great-great-granddaughter of the man who built the Little House" says to her husband: "That Little House looks just like the Little House my grandmother lived in when she was a little girl, only *that* Little House was way out in the country on a hill covered with daisies and apple trees growing around." (n. pag.). When the house is moved again to the countryside and an appropriate place is found, the great-great-granddaughter speaks again: "'There,' said the great-great-granddaughter, 'that's just the place.' 'Yes, it is,' said the Little House to herself" (n. pag.).

While this is not a dialogue, children here realize for the first time that the Little House can speak. It remains a flat character, but what is important from the perspective of the child reader is that direct quotation is used to represent thoughts and attitudes of characters. While the verb *say* is the typical verb of saying here, and direct speech is the first pattern of speech representation that children usually acquire (Köder 2013), it is obvious that the embedding of these speech representations significantly contributes to the story. Hence, even a seemingly quite simple picturebook like *The Little House* asks the child readers to take different perspectives, so that they gain access to the beliefs, thoughts, and desires of fictional characters. They may also ascertain that these perspectives may vary depending on the characters' world knowledge and their social and cultural positions. These complex processes cannot be accessed without the acquisition of theory of mind as a precondition for the understanding of other people's or fictional characters' states of mind. Considering this, a cognitive approach to the investigation of picturebooks might enhance our understanding of how picturebooks work.

Conclusion: developing a cognitive theory of the picturebook

A cognitive theory of picturebooks should address the question of how language acquisition, visual literacy, and literary literacy interact, and how these interactions may be related to other cognitive processes, such as theory of mind or emotional and social development. It goes without saying that this is a big task, demanding interdisciplinary cooperation and work for many years to come.

A first key issue is how best to foster genuine dialogue or interaction between scholarship on narrative and the sciences of mind – as opposed to a unidirectional borrowing, by narrative scholars, of ideas from the cognitive sciences. To this end, Herman (2013) proposes a "transdisciplinary" approach to studying stories vis-à-vis the cognitive sciences. The argument is that the mind-narrative relationship cannot be exhaustively characterized by the arts and humanities, by the social sciences, or by the natural sciences taken alone; hence genuine dialogue and exchange across these fields of endeavor, rather than unidirectional borrowing from a particular field that thereby becomes dominant, will be required to address how mental states, capacities, and dispositions provide the foundation for or, conversely, are grounded in narrative experiences. In reality, a cognitive study of picturebooks has to address the mental processes involved in children's experience of multimodal art forms such as the picturebook. The picturebook, which encapsulates the interface between the verbal and the visual, does indeed pose a challenge to cognitive studies and may subsequently play a significant role in its advancement.

The foremost goal of such an interdisciplinary critical synthesis of cognitive studies and picturebook research consists in gaining a better awareness of what children may learn by looking at picturebooks. Such a theoretical merger is, of course, exploratory and ambitious. At the heart of all the disciplines involved are two shared goals: to uncover the structures of making sense within picturebooks and to reveal their relationship to children's cognitive development. Crucially, this approach primarily aims to explore multimodality in picturebooks from a cognitive-narratological perspective, leading to greater understanding of the way in which children see, read, and make sense of picturebook narratives. This approach may be regarded as a new gateway opening up the study of the picturebook to the study of cognition and vice versa.

References

Arizpe, Evelyn, and Styles, Morag (2003 [rev. 2016]) *Children Reading Pictures: Interpreting Visual Texts*, London: Routledge.

Bateman, John A. (2014) *Text and Image. A Critical Introduction to the Visual/Verbal Divide*, London: Routledge.

Bosacki, Sandra L., and Astington, Jane Wild (1999) "Theory of Mind in Preadolescence: Relations Between Social Understanding and Social Competence," *Social Development* 17: 399–416.

Burton, Virginia Lee (1942) *The Little House*, Boston: Houghton Mifflin.

Carlson, Stephanie M., and White, Rachel E. (2013) "Executive Functioning, Pretend Play, and Imagination," in Marjorie Taylor (ed.) *The Oxford Handbook of the Development of Imagination*, Oxford: Oxford University Press, 161–174.

Cohen, Henri, and Lefebvre, Claire (eds) (2017) *Handbook of Categorization in Cognitive Science*, 2nd ed., Amsterdam: Elsevier.

Creusere, Marlena A. (2007) "A Developmental Test of Theoretical Perspectives on the Understanding of Verbal Irony: Children's Recognition of Allusion and Pragmatic Insincerity," in Raymond W. Gibbs and Herbert L. Lang (eds) *Irony in Language and Thought: A Cognitive Science Reader*, New York: Erlbaum, 409–424.

Doherty, Martin J. (2009) *Theory of Mind: How Children Understand Others' Thoughts and Feelings*, Hove: Psychology Press.

Eder, Jens, Jannidis, Fotis, and Schneider, Ralf (eds) (2010) *Characters in Fictional Worlds: Understanding Imaginary Beings in Literature, Film, and Other Media*, Berlin and New York: de Gruyter.

Elkins, James (2007) *Visual Literacy*, New York: Routledge.

Evans, Janet (ed.) (2009) *Talking Beyond the Page: Reading and Responding to Picturebooks*, London: Routledge.

Frijda, Nico H. (2007) *The Laws of Emotion*, London: Erlbaum.

Frow, John (2016) *Character & Person*, Oxford: Oxford University Press.

Ganea, Patricia, Pickard, Megan, and DeLoache, Judy S. (2008) "Transfer Between Picture Books and the Real World by Very Young Children," *Journal of Cognition and Development* 9: 46–66.

Goswami, Usha (2008) *Cognitive Development: The Learning Brain*, Hove: Psychology Press.

Hall, Kathy, Cremin, Teresa, and Comber, Barbara (eds) (2013) *International Handbook of Research on Children's Literacy, Learning and Culture*, Oxford: Blackwell.

Hastings, Paul D., Zahn-Waxler, Carolyn, and McShane, Keely (2006) "We Are, by Nature, Moral Creatures: Biological Bases of Concern for Others," in Melanie Killen and Judith G. Smetana (eds) *Handbook of Moral Development*, Mahwah, NJ: Lawrence Erlbaum, 483–516.

Herman, David (2013) *Storytelling and the Sciences of Mind*, Cambridge, MA: MIT Press.

Hogan, Patrick Colm (2011) *Affective Narratology: The Emotional Structure of Stories*, Lincoln: University of Nebraska Press.

Huang, Yan (2012) "Introduction: What Is Pragmatics?" in Yan Huang (ed.) *The Oxford Dictionary of Pragmatics*, Oxford: Oxford University Press, 1–19.

Izard, Carroll E. (2009) "Emotion Theory and Research: Highlights, Unanswered Questions, and Emerging Issues," *Annual Review of Psychology* 60: 1–25.

Jannidis, Fotis (2009) "Character," in Peter Hühn, John Pier, Wolf Schmid, and Jörg Schönert (eds) *Handbook of Narratology*, Berlin: de Gruyter, 14–29.

Jones, Rhian (1996) *Emerging Patterns of Literacy: A Multidisciplinary Perspective*, London: Routledge.

Keen, Suzanne (2007) *Empathy and the Novel*, Oxford: Oxford University Press.

Killen, Melanie, and Smetana, Judith G. (eds) (2006) *Handbook of Moral Development*, Mahwah, NJ: Lawrence Erlbaum.

Köder, Franziska (2013) "How Children Acquire Reported Speech in German and Dutch: A Corpus Study," *Perspektiven: Diskussionsforum Linguistik in Bayern/Bavarian Working Papers in Linguistics* 2: 15–28, http://epub.ub.uni-muenchen.de/14616/1/Diskussionsforum_Perspektiven_neu.pdf (last accessed June 25, 2017).

Kress, Gunther, and van Leeuwen, Theo (1996) *Reading Images: The Grammar of Visual Design*, London: Routledge.

Kümmerling-Meibauer, Bettina (1999) "Metalinguistic Awareness and the Child's Developing Sense of Irony: The Relationship Between Pictures and Text in Ironic Picturebooks," *The Lion and the Unicorn* 23: 157–183.

Kümmerling-Meibauer, Bettina (ed.) (2011) *Emergent Literacy: Children's Books from 0 to 3*, Amsterdam: John Benjamins.

Kümmerling-Meibauer, Bettina, and Meibauer, Jörg (2005) "First Pictures, Early Concepts: Early Concepts Books," *The Lion and the Unicorn* 29.3: 324–347.

Kümmerling-Meibauer, Bettina, and Meibauer, Jörg (2011) "Early-Concept Books: Acquiring Nominal and Verbal Concepts," in Bettina Kümmerling-Meibauer (ed.) *Emergent Literacy: Children's Books from 0 to 3*, Amsterdam: John Benjamins, 91–114.

Kümmerling-Meibauer, Bettina, and Meibauer, Jörg (2013) "Towards a Cognitive Theory of Picturebooks," *International Research in Children's Literature* 6.2: 143–160.

Kümmerling-Meibauer, Bettina, and Meibauer, Jörg (2014) "Understanding the Matchstick Man: Aesthetic and Narrative Properties of a Hybrid Picturebook Character," in Bettina Kümmerling-Meibauer (ed.) *Picturebooks: Representation and Narration*, New York: Routledge, 139–161.

Kümmerling-Meibauer, Bettina, and Meibauer, Jörg (2015a) "Maps in Picturebooks: Cognitive Status and Narrative Functions," *BLFT: Nordic Journal of Childlit Aesthetics* 6. Doi: http://dx.doi.org/10.3402/blft.v5.26970.

Kümmerling-Meibauer, Bettina, and Meibauer, Jörg (2015b) "Beware of the Fox! Emotion and Deception in *Fox* by Margaret Wild and Ron Brooks," in Janet Evans (ed.) *Challenging and Controversial Picturebooks: Creative and Critical Responses to Visual Texts*, London: Routledge, 144–159.

Kümmerling-Meibauer, Bettina, and Meibauer, Jörg (2015c) "Picturebooks and Early Literacy. How Do Picturebooks Support Early Conceptual and Narrative Development?," in Bettina Kümmerling-Meibauer, Jörg Meibauer, Kerstin Nachtigäller, and Katharina Rohlfing (eds) *Learning from Picturebooks: Perspectives from Child Development and Literacy Studies*, New York: Routledge, 13–32.

Kümmerling-Meibauer, Bettina, and Meibauer, Jörg (2017) "Metaphorical Maps in Picturebooks," in Nina Goga and Bettina Kümmerling-Meibauer (eds) *Maps and Mapping in Children's Literature: Landscapes, Seascapes, and Cityscapes*, Amsterdam: John Benjamins, 75–91.

Kümmerling-Meibauer, Bettina, Meibauer, Jörg, Nachtigäller, Kerstin, and Rohlfing, Katharina (eds) (2015) *Learning from Picturebooks: Perspectives from Child Development and Literacy Studies*, New York: Routledge.

Larson, Joanne, and Marsh, Jackie (eds) (2012) *The Sage Handbook of Early Childhood Literacy*, London: Sage.

Legerstee, Maria (2005) *Infants' Sense of People: Precursors to a Theory of Mind*, Cambridge: Cambridge University Press.

Liben, Lynn S. (1997) "Children's Understanding of Spatial Representations of Place: Mapping the Methodological Landscape," in Nigel Foreman and Raphael Gillet (eds) *A Handbook of Spatial Research Paradigms and Methodologies*, East Sussex, UK: Psychology Press, 41–83.

Marraffa, Massimo (2011) "Theory of Mind," *Internet Encyclopedia of Philosophy* (November 11, 2011), www.iep. utm.edu/theomind (accessed January 30, 2017).

McCarthy, Kathleen, and Philipps, Deborah (eds) (2006) *Blackwell Handbook of Early Childhood Development*, Oxford: Blackwell.

McHale, Brian (2014) "Speech Representation," in Peter Hühn, Jan-Christoph Meister, John Pier, and Wolf Schmid (eds) *The Living Handbook of Narratology*, Hamburg: Hamburg University, www.lhn.uni-hamburg.de/article/speech-representation (last accessed June 25, 2017).

Meibauer, Jörg (2015) "What the Child Can Learn From Simple Descriptive Picturebooks: An Inquiry into *Lastwagen/Trucks* by Paul Stickland," in Bettina Kümmerling-Meibauer, Jörg Meibauer, Kerstin Nachtigäller, and Katharina Rohlfing (eds) *Learning from Picturebooks: Perspectives from Child Development and Literacy Studies*, New York: Routledge, 51–70.

Meibauer, Jörg (2017) "Pragmatics and Children's Literature," in Rachel Giora and Michael Haugh (eds) *Doing Intercultural Pragmatics: Cognitive, Linguistic and Sociopragmatic Perspectives on Language Use*, Berlin, Munich, and Boston: De Gruyter Mouton, 371–387.

Miller, Scott A. (2012) *Theory of Mind: Beyond the Preschool Years*, New York: Psychology Press.

Newcombe, Nora, and Huttenlocher, Janellen (2000) *Making Space*, Cambridge, MA: MIT Press.

Nikolajeva, Maria (2002) *The Rhetoric of Character in Children's Literature*, Lanham, MD: Scarecrow.

Nikolajeva, Maria (2003) "Verbal and Visual Literacy: The Role of Picturebooks in the Reading Experience of Young Children," in Nigel Hall, Joanne Larson, and Jackie Marsh (eds) *Handbook of Early Childhood Literacy*, London: Sage, 235–248.

Nikolajeva, Maria (2012) "Reading Other People's Minds Through Words and Images," *Children's Literature in Education* 43.3: 273–291. Doi: 10.1007/s10583-012-9163-6.

Nikolajeva, Maria (2014) *Reading for Learning: Cognitive Approaches to Children's Literature*, Amsterdam: John Benjamins.

Nikolajeva, Maria, and Scott, Carole (2001) *How Picturebooks Work*, New York: Garland.

O'Grady, William (2011) *How Children Learn Language*, Cambridge: Cambridge University Press.

Pessoa, Luiz (2008) "On the Relationship Between Emotion and Cognition," *Nature Reviews Neuroscience* 9: 148–158.

Pinkham, Ashley M., Kaefer, Tanya, and Neuman, Susan B. (eds) (2012) *Knowledge Development in Early Childhood: Sources of Learning and Classroom Implications*, New York: Guilford Press.

Pouscoulous, Nausicaa (2014) "'The Elevator's Buttocks': Metaphorical Abilities in Children," in Danielle Matthews (ed.) *Pragmatic Development in First Language Acquisition*, Amsterdam: John Benjamins, 239–260.

Rakison, David H., and Oakes, Lisa M. (eds) (2003) *Early Category and Concept Development: Making Sense of the Blooming, Buzzing Confusion*, New York: Oxford University Press.

Rémi, Cornelia (2011) "Reading as Playing: The Cognitive Challenge of the Wimmelbook," in Bettina Kümmerling-Meibauer (ed.) *Emergent Literacy: Children's Books from 0 to 3*, Amsterdam: John Benjamins, 115–140.

Schneider, Ralf (2001) "Toward a Cognitive Theory of Literary Character: The Dynamics of Mental-Model Construction," *Style* 35.4: 607–640.

Silva-Díaz, Maria Cecilia (2015) "Picturebooks, Lies and Mindreading," *BLFT: Nordic Journal of ChildLit Aesthetics* 6. Doi: http://dx.doi.org/10.3402/blft.v6.2697.2.

Stockwell, Peter (2002) *Cognitive Poetics: An Introduction*, London: Routledge.

Suggate, Sebastian, and Reese, Elaine (eds) (2012) *Contemporary Debates in Childhood Education and Development*, London: Routledge.

Taylor, Margot, Batty, Magali, and Itier, Roxanne (2004) "The Faces of Development: A Review of Early Face Processing Over Childhood," *Journal of Cognitive Neuroscience* 16.8: 1426–1442.

Thomas, Glyn V., Nye, Rebecca, Rowley, Martin G., and Robinson, Elizabeth J. (2001) "What Is a Picture? Children's Conceptions of Pictures," *British Journal of Developmental Psychology* 19: 475–491.

Thompson, Ross A., and Lagattuta, Kristin (2006) "Feeling and Understanding: Early Emotional Development," in Kathleen McCartney and Deborah Philipps (eds) *Blackwell Handbook of Early Childhood Development*, Oxford: Blackwell, 317–337.

Torr, Jane (2008) "Multimodal Texts and Emergent Literacy," in Len Unsworth (ed.) *New Literacies and the English Curriculum*, London and New York: Continuum, 47–66.

Uttal, David, and Tan, Lisa (2000) "Cognitive Mapping in Childhood," in Rob Kitchin and Scott Freundschuh (eds) *Cognitive Mapping: Past, Present and Future*, New York: Routledge, 147–165.

Vermeule, Blakey (2010) *Why Do We Care About Literary Characters?* Baltimore: Johns Hopkins University Press.

Wimmer, Heinz, and Perner, Josef (1983) "Beliefs About Beliefs: Representation and Constraining Function of Wrong Beliefs in Young Children's Understanding of Deception," *Cognition* 13: 102–128.

Winner, Ellen (1988) *The Points of Words: Children's Understanding of Metaphor and Irony*, Cambridge, MA: MIT Press.

Zunshine, Lisa (2006) *Why We Read Fiction: Theory of Mind and the Novel*, Columbus: Ohio State University Press.

38

PICTUREBOOKS AND LINGUISTICS

Eva Gressnich

Picturebook texts seem simple at first glance. They are rather short and, after all, they are usually written for children who are at the beginning of literature acquisition. Thus, one would not expect notable complexity in picturebook language. Yet that is exactly what is to be found when taking a close look. The complexity in picturebook texts shows itself on every level of language and in the form of intricate phenomena. Exploring picturebooks linguistically allows a precise analysis of their verbal qualities.

The benefits of a linguistic perspective actually go beyond a clear grasp of picturebook language. In addition, narrative phenomena occurring in picturebooks as well as the interaction between the verbal and the visual levels can only be fully captured by examining verbal details. A linguistic view of picturebooks is especially necessary when it comes to investigating the complex relation between picturebooks, the joint reading of picturebooks, and language acquisition. Reading picturebooks to and together with children is apprehended as an ideal setting for improving children's verbal skills. Children's literature in general is defined by being suitable for children. Yet we do not know much about the details of this suitability, especially with regard to linguistic qualities. In exploring picturebooks linguistically and linking the results to data from research on language development, we might gain insight into reasons why picturebook language is designed the way it is. A similar perspective could also pay off for researchers interested in language development, as the possibly fine-tuned input children get from picturebooks might play a crucial role in children's acquisition of verbal competencies.

This chapter first outlines the research field of a linguistic approach to picturebooks by elaborating on aspects of the medium picturebook itself, joint reading, and the connection between language acquisition and picturebooks. It then sketches out the results of an exemplary analysis of the use of speech acts in picturebooks.

Picturebooks from a linguistic point of view

Linguistic analyses of picturebook texts can be pursued on every level of language. Regarding *morphological* properties, it is insightful to investigate aspects of both word inflection (e.g., the use of verb tenses) and types of word formation. The latter is particularly interesting with regard to neologisms invented by authors. Exploring *phonological* qualities such as types of rhyme and meter is relevant for picturebooks containing lyrical texts. A *syntactic* approach to picturebook language may cover different parts of sentence analysis. For example, texts in general differ with respect to syntactic complexity.

When focusing on *semantic* aspects, that is, aspects concerning the meaning of verbal items, one important topic is reference, defined as the relation a speaker establishes between a linguistic expression and a referent in the real world or a fictional world. Reference within fictional texts is a complex phenomenon as it does not relate to the real world, but to a world invented by the author of the text. Reference within picturebooks is even more intriguing because it entails the additional option of verbally pointing (that is referring deictically) to elements depicted in the pictures. Besides this, there are numerous referential relations between the utterances of a text, oftentimes leading to complicated referential networks, even in short picturebook texts.

A *pragmatic* approach to picturebooks might focus on the use of speech acts (cf. the exemplary analysis later in this chapter). Furthermore, an inquiry into reported speech and thought is of interest when it comes to communication within and with the help of texts. Other major pragmatic phenomena include irony and metaphor, two important examples of implicature. They not only occur on a micro-level, but can be applied to texts as a whole. This holds true for picturebooks as well (Kümmerling-Meibauer 1999; Rau 2011).

There is a lack of empirical studies on the wide range of text types occurring in picturebooks. For this, a *text-linguistic perspective* is required that not only grasps literary genres, but subtle differences between all kinds of texts as well as important distinctions like the one between descriptive and narrative picturebooks (Kümmerling-Meibauer and Meibauer 2015).

No matter which aspects of a picturebook text are the focus of analysis, there is a necessity for also taking into account the visual level when investigating picturebooks linguistically. A holistic view is imperative for whatever approach to picturebooks one chooses, as has been emphasized in seminal works on picturebooks. A text-picture-oriented analysis based on linguistics probably yields valuable insights that can be utilized for the definition of categories describing the interaction between the verbal and the visual levels in picturebooks. In the introduction to *How Picturebooks Work*, Nikolajeva and Scott (2001) suggest that categories such as symmetry, complementarity, and counterpoint may only be applied to individual qualities of picturebooks (for instance, perspective). In order to attain a precise comparison between verbal reference to and visual depiction of single elements, it seems promising to combine methods of semantics and text linguistics with approaches focusing on the visual level of picturebooks, for example, the comprehensive model presented in Painter, Martin and Unsworth (2013).

One of the major future tasks of a text- and picture-oriented and equally *cognitive linguistic* approach to picturebooks consists of research on how readers, particularly child readers, succeed in establishing a mental model of the content conveyed by a book. One essential quality of mental discourse representations is that they do not simply mirror information provided by the text base, but are substantially enriched by the reader. Readers take information from the text and simultaneously add to it by drawing on context information, linguistic knowledge, and knowledge about the world. They do so in order to establish coherence, and are forced to do so because, generally, texts are informationally underspecified. Hardly anything is known about how discourse representations arise in readers of picturebooks, let alone about how they arise when picturebooks are read in collaboration between a child reader and an adult mediator, which represents the prototypical format of picturebook reading. The visual level in picturebooks constitutes an important source of information and serves as a context for the verbal level (Moerk 1985: 550), which we can or, in most cases, rather must use to achieve coherence.

It is well known that a linguistic approach can offer helpful instruments for research on literature in general. By now, scholars know quite a lot about how literature works. Yet there are still many aspects of literature and the processing of literature that have just been scratched on the surface. Not only in cases of intriguing narrative matters such as free indirect discourse (Canisius 2002) is it necessary to look at linguistic details in order to really understand the ways in which the use of language can result in cognitively demanding phenomena. If we aim to explain how readers process literary texts of different types, it is wise to consult findings about how people process language in general. For quite some time, there have been attempts to intertwine literary studies and linguistics

(Jakobson 1987; Fabb 1997; Mey 2000), partly resulting in well-recognized theories and disciplines such as *cognitive poetics* (Stockwell 2002) and *psychonarratology* (Bortolussi and Dixon 2003). Findings of these approaches are pivotal for picturebook research that is based on cognitive linguistics, because picturebooks contain a wide range of complex phenomena that are the focus of interest in these realms (cf. the seminal interdisciplinary investigation of picturebooks in Stephens 1992). But again, when it comes to the question how these phenomena are processed by readers, one has to account for the special way in which picturebooks are usually read, namely in situations of joint attention between a child and an interlocutor.

Joint reading of picturebooks

There is relatively broad research available on various aspects of joint picturebook reading (Fletcher and Reese 2005). Most studies have been conducted by developmental and cognitive psychologists as well as researchers interested in early literacy development. Depending on what is in focus, linguistic insights and thoughts are taken into account.

One topic of research on joint reading is the verbal behavior of the adult reader, who is usually a parent, caregiver, or teacher. It has mainly been monitored if and how adult interlocutors deviate from the text base, for example, in order to reduce complexity or to enrich the information provided by the book (Martin and Reutzel 1999; Evans et al. 2011). In some cases, scholars have investigated the child's verbal behavior as well (McDonnell, Friel-Patti and Rosenthal Rollins 2003; Fletcher and Finch 2014). Different formats of child-adult interaction during picturebook reading have been identified (Sénéchal, Cornell and Broda 1995; Jones 1996). These collaborative formats emerge as a function of various factors, including the age of the child reader, her literary knowledge and previous experiences with books, the type of picturebook that is being read, and both readers' familiarity with it.

A lot of studies have examined whether and how joint reading affects language acquisition during the early years. Here too, most research comes from psychologists. Although the interplay between joint reading, picturebook input, and children's growing verbal skills is supposed to be of great interest to linguists engaged in studying language acquisition, there has as yet been a major lack of genuinely linguistic research. There are numerous findings proving the positive effect of joint reading on word learning (Ninio 1983; Sénéchal et al. 2008; Blewitt 2015; Horst 2015). In addition, studies have explored if children benefit from joint reading when it comes to the development of morphological and syntactical knowledge (Sénéchal et al. 2008), conversational competencies (Morrow 1988), literacy (Deckner, Adamson and Bakeman 2006), and narrative skills (Reese 2015). Joint reading affects language development in two ways. First, the text base of a picturebook offers model constructions to the child reader which she can incorporate into her language. In addition, paying attention to picturebooks usually induces a conversation between the child and the interlocutor, at least in dialogical, interactive formats of joint reading.

What is often missing in psychological studies on joint reading is an adequate allowance for characteristics of the picturebook being read by the interactants. Researchers tend to abstract away from individual books. In future studies, there needs to be a stronger appreciation of the book as an influential element in contexts of joint reading. For example, one of the key questions in this field is the question how different kinds of interaction between the child and the adult reader are triggered by certain qualities of picturebooks (including linguistic qualities). It is equally important to consider the books that are read in studies examining how joint reading influences language acquisition. It is reasonable to assume that picturebooks differ in their potential of fostering the development of verbal competencies. Furthermore, a picturebook might be suitable for promoting a skill during a certain stage of language acquisition while it might have no affect at all at a different point in time. All of this needs to be factored in when exploring the interplay between joint reading and language development.

Language acquisition and picturebook input

All the aforementioned (and not mentioned) levels and phenomena of language must be acquired. Language acquisition is the lifelong process of learning words, grammar, and pragmatic skills. It is reasonable to believe that children who regularly encounter picturebooks and other works of children's literature are affected by the input they get from them on several levels, including developmental processes such as language acquisition. There certainly is a special effect on language acquisition when children acquire linguistic forms from children's books that are specific to written language, that is, constructions that barely occur in everyday spoken language. However, from a language acquisition perspective, it is wise to presume that children benefit from literary input in many ways and that it helps them to improve their verbal skills in general.

It is also reasonable to expect that producers of children's literature are aware of this possibly strong relation and take it into account when creating literary works. Kümmerling-Meibauer and Meibauer (2013: 148) address this aspect in *assumption 3* (A3) of their seminal framework on the interplay between acquisitional tasks and children's literature. The picturebook analysis below serves as an exemplary contribution to testing this assumption. A3 claims that children's literature is fine-tuned to children's cognitive and verbal skills. This is an assumption shared by many people, but, in fact, very little is known about how exactly books are adapted to the needs of early readers. Verifying A3 requires a special approach to children's literature that links the characteristics of books to findings of studies investigating child development. A3 is similar to what scholars studying language acquisition call *child-directed speech* (Snow 1996). There has been input-oriented research aiming to find out if and how parents and older siblings adapt their language to children's verbal skills in everyday conversations. The key finding has been that interlocutors flexibly adjust themselves to the child's current developmental stage. A3 assumes the same behavior for producers of children's literature by presupposing the existence of child-directed speech in works addressed to young readers. Available research on A3 mainly consists of picturebook analyses (Kümmerling-Meibauer 1999; Gressnich and Meibauer 2010; Rau 2011; Kümmerling-Meibauer and Meibauer 2013, 2015; Stark 2015).

An exemplary analysis of speech acts in picturebooks

The analysis that follows is concerned with the use of speech acts in picturebooks. Characteristics of speech act usage in three picturebooks are correlated with findings from research on language acquisition. Thus, the inquiry may be conceived as a (small-scale) contribution to verifying A3. This means, in turn, that it is only of interest whether the books in focus offer some kind of fine-tuned base for joint reading situations. Empirical investigation of child-adult interaction is necessary in order to find out how readers handle, play with, and deviate from what they encounter in books and in order to estimate whether child readers actually receive input that is adapted to their skills.

The basic insight of speech act theory is that uttering a sentence is equal to performing an intentional communicative act. Examples of speech acts are assertions, promises, questions, requests, greetings, threats, bets, warnings, and prohibitions. A speech act can be neither true nor false, but it can either succeed or not. Utterances in literary texts must be viewed as speech acts, too. Depending on the type of text, they can be performed by different actants: the author (expository texts), the narrator (narrative texts), a character belonging to the plot (narrative, dramatic, and also lyrical texts), or the lyrical self (lyrical texts). They can further be directed to different individuals, the default cases being the reader or a character.

Several aspects of speech act use in picturebooks are worth being studied. This inquiry focuses on the following ones: (a) How many different and which kinds of speech acts are performed? (b) Do single speech acts or sequences of speech acts, such as question-and-answer, occur as a recurring pattern? (c) By whom are the speech acts performed, and who is addressed by them? The small picturebook corpus comprises three works that at first glance seem to differ in speech act usage: *Do*

You Want to Be My Friend? (1988) by Eric Carle, *Bear Hunt* (1994) by Anthony Browne, and *Don't Let the Pigeon Drive the Bus!* (2004) by Mo Willems. Interestingly, two of the three titles contain speech acts; however, it initially remains unclear by whom they are performed and to whom they are directed.

In Carle's picturebook, there is a very limited range of different types of speech acts. Almost all there is a recurring pattern of a question-and-answer sequence, or rather a sequence of offer and refusal, most often framed by the same simple statement and inquit formula: "So the mouse ran on. 'Do you want to be my friend?' 'No,' said the peacock with a crown on his head" (n. pag.). *Bear Hunt* contains slightly more types of speech acts than Carle's book. Besides statements, there are requests, warnings, compliments, and a cry for help. Like in Carle's book, a sequence of speech acts, namely the combination statement(s)-warning-statement(s)-compliment, occurs repeatedly, although not as schematically as in Carle's book. Furthermore, it is realized by different linguistic forms: "Two hunters were hunting. They saw Bear. Look out! Look out, Bear! Quickly Bear began to draw. Well done, Bear!" (n. pag.). Willems's picturebook *Don't Let the Pigeon Drive the Bus!* encompasses instances of request, greeting, introduction, statement, question, acknowledgment, affirmation, lie, expression of joy, complaint, offer, bribery, bet, farewell, and claim. Unlike in the two other picturebooks, speech acts are not repeated in a pattern-like way.

Regarding question (c), the three books differ substantially in complexity. This question is about identifying *communicative constellations*, which indicate who is performing an individual speech act and who is addressed by it. The two communicative constellations in *Do You Want to Be My Friend?* are standard cases of performing speech acts within literary texts. Either the heterodiegetic narrator (that is, a narrator not taking part in the plot) performs a speech act directed to the reader or a character belonging to the plot performs a speech act addressed to another character.

The constellation (heterodiegetic) narrator/reader is also to be found in *Bear Hunt*, but there are several instances of an unusual communicative constellation as well. Among others, the utterances "Look out! Look out, Bear!" and "Well done, Bear!" are the bases of speech acts that are performed by the narrator and directed to a character taking part in the plot. The narrator continuously warns the protagonist of the hunters and commends him every time he succeeds in escaping them. There are several possible explanations for this unusual communicative constellation, one of them being that the narrator is in fact not heterodiegetic, but a person belonging to the plot, who, however, remains highly unspecified (e.g., she does not appear in the pictures).

Willems's comic-like picturebook does not contain any narrative text, and accordingly, the communicative constellation narrator/reader is not possible. Instead, the only one present is the constellation character/reader and vice versa. There is supposed to be a conversation between the reader and the bus driver (who is requesting that the reader prevents the pigeon from driving the bus) as well as a conversation between the reader and the pigeon (who is trying to get permission to drive the bus). This type of communication is anything but a standard case and is highly metafictive as it transcends the boundaries of fictionality. The pictures, of course, play an important role here, providing the reader with depictions of her interlocutors, thereby fostering the simulation of a real conversation.

Knowledge about how to use and how to identify different types of speech acts is an essential part of pragmatic competence. When a child acquires a language, she not only has to learn words and grammar, but also the ability to use and understand language appropriately in various situations. What do the preceding findings tell us about an existing or non-existing fine-tunedness of picturebooks? First, all three picturebooks together provide children with a wide range of speech acts. Of course, the diversity especially applies to *Don't Let the Pigeon Drive the Bus!* and to a lesser extent to the other two books. However, it is legitimate to assume that, by generally being exposed to picturebooks, children encounter a wealthy input of different kinds of speech acts.

The types of speech acts occurring in Carle's picturebook are acquired at a very young age. Pragmatic development and the acquisition of speech acts start early. Already during the first year, even before they are able to produce words, children use gesture, intonation, and phonemes to communicate intentions nonverbally, such as requests, refusals, and calls for attention (Ninio and Snow 1996; Becker Bryant 2009). The range of speech acts increases considerably alongside vocabulary acquisition. However, acquiring certain speech acts like promises takes a long time (Bernicot and Laval 2004), and does not seem to be fully completed until the end of primary school. Having said this, some of the speech acts in *Bear Hunt* and, particularly, in *Don't Let the Pigeon Drive the Bus!* are very complex. Grasping the communicative intents behind speech acts like warning, lie, bribery, or bet as well as their role within a fictional plot is a demanding task, even for children who are not so young anymore.

The sequential repetitions of selected speech acts in the picturebooks by Carle and Browne provide the child reader with a high frequency input. The intention underlying this procedure is probably to give the child the chance to get familiar with and explore these speech acts on multiple occasions. Providing a high frequency input of a linguistic phenomenon (often achieved by means of a pattern-like repetition) is not an unusual practice in the context of picturebooks.

Nothing is known about how and when children acquire types of communicative constellations in the course of literature acquisition. Presumably, this is anything but an easy task. It is important to realize how demanding a seemingly simple picturebook like *Bear Hunt* is in this respect. For one, the child reader has to deal with a constant change of communicative constellations. In addition, she needs to understand the boundary crossing between narrative and plot. Perhaps Anthony Browne was aiming for the readers to be the performers of the warnings and compliments directed to the bear. Then, the interlocutor would have to recognize this and moderate these instances accordingly – for instance, with child-directed utterances like *Shall we warn the bear of the hunters?* And even if this is so, it still holds true that the picturebook is challenging with respect to speech acts. The same applies to Willems's picturebook. Here, however, the consistent use of the interactive communicative pattern between reader and character may also foster language acquisition in a special way, as the child reader is constantly forced to act verbally herself in order to ensure that the plot unfolds.

By taking into account additional qualities of the books such as topic and content as well as complexity of plot, complexity of pictures, and number of complex sentences, it is possible to assess whether the picturebooks are fine-tuned to the capacities of child readers. Carle's picturebook is overall addressed to children of a very young age. It is about making friends, and it deals with this topic on a level that is accessible early in childhood. The plot is rather simple, comprising a chain of homogeneous episodes. Eventually, it holds a small complication and resolution when the mice just manage to escape from the snake. Visual complexity appears low as well, although a reliable judgment remains difficult, as too little is known about children's growing visual literacy. In addition, the book contains numerous visual pageturners (Gressnich 2012), which consist of incomplete depictions of animals and add some intricacy to the visual level. The picturebook text comprises one complex sentence out of forty-five. The total number of sentences appears high in comparison to the numbers of sentences in Browne's and Willems's picturebooks (twenty-one and thirty-six, respectively). However, most linguistic forms in *Do You Want to Be My Friend?* occur as an iterative pattern (which is why, at least here, the number of sentences does not serve as a helpful reference value).

Bear Hunt is more complex as a whole. It shows how one can rescue oneself by being inventive and ingenious. The plot is more intricate than the plot in Carle's book. It contains a chain of episodes, but they vary in content and they all include a complication and resolution. As is standard in Anthony Browne's picturebooks, the visual level is demanding. The pictures include countless details and interpictorial references, although visual perspective and distance mostly remain constant throughout the book. As in Carle's picturebook, there is only one complex sentence (out of twenty-one).

Don't Let the Pigeon Drive the Bus! is probably the most complex, and is directed to children who are advanced in terms of both language acquisition and literature acquisition. The plot is ambitious, resulting from the interactive nature of the book, which intends that the child reader participate in the unfolding of the story by negotiating with the protagonist of the book. Visual complexity is high, but for reasons other than in Browne's book. The pictures are rather minimalistic, having a low density of detail. They are also nearly invariant in distance and perspective. However, something which adds a great deal of intricacy to them is the fact that entities are repeatedly depicted multiple times on a page or doublespread, oftentimes even within one picture. In comparison to Carle's and Browne's books, *Don't Let the Pigeon Drive the Bus!* contains the most complex sentences (four out of thirty-six).

In sum, then, the different uses of speech acts tend to match the overall degrees of complexity, and it is legitimate to conceive of this as an instance of fine-tunedness, thus as evidence for the validity of A3. However, picturebook artists obviously follow other motives too when designing their books, one of which definitively is artistic aspiration, which is evident in all three books that have been in focus. It is most distinct in Anthony Browne's pictures, which ultimately causes them to be somewhat more complex than Willems's pictures (at least from an adult perspective). *Don't Let the Pigeon Drive the Bus!*, in contrast, is clearly more ambitious than *Bear Hunt* when it comes to the use of speech acts. Finally, it goes without saying that in order to thoroughly evaluate the fine-tunedness of a book as a whole it would be necessary to take into account every single characteristic that the book entails.

Conclusion

A linguistic analysis of literature in general is worthwhile because it helps us to fully understand how literature (perceived as a particular use of language) works. A linguistic analysis of picturebooks is especially worthwhile, not only because it helps us to fully understand how picturebooks work. Most of all, it is one of the essential contributions, if not *the* essential contribution, to an approach to picturebooks that is devoted to the intriguing connection between picturebook input and developmental processes in childhood, especially language acquisition. It has become clear that the research field is wide and challenging and that it can only be mastered by means of interdisciplinary collaboration. One of the main goals of this chapter has been to point out opportunities and topics for future linguistic picturebook analyses, studies on joint reading with emphasis on linguistic aspects, and approaches investigating the interplay between picturebooks and language development.

References

Becker Bryant, Judith (2009) "Pragmatic Development," in Edith L. Bavon (ed.) *The Cambridge Handbook of Child Language*, Cambridge: Cambridge University Press, 339–354.

Bernicot, Josie, and Laval, Virginie (2004) "Speech Acts in Children: The Example of Promises," in Ira A. Noveck and Dan Sperber (eds) *Experimental Pragmatics*, Basingstoke and New York: Palgrave Macmillan, 207–227.

Blewitt, Pamela (2015) "Growing Vocabulary in the Context of Shared Book Reading," in Bettina Kümmerling-Meibauer, Jörg Meibauer, Kerstin Nachtigäller, and Katharina Rohlfing (eds) *Learning from Picturebooks: Perspectives from Child Development and Literacy Studies*, New York: Routledge, 117–136.

Bortolussi, Maria, and Dixon, Peter (2003) *Psychonarratology*, Cambridge: Cambridge University Press.

Browne, Anthony (1994) *Bear Hunt*, London: Penguin Books (first published 1979).

Canisius, Peter (2002) "Point of View, Narrative Mode and the Constitution of Narrative Texts," in: Carl F. Graumann and Werner Kallmeyer (eds) *Perspective and Perspectivation in Discourse*, Amsterdam: John Benjamins, 307–322.

Carle, Eric (1988) *Do You Want to Be My Friend?*, New York: Philomel Books.

Deckner, Deborah F., Adamson, Lauren B., and Bakeman, Roger (2006) "Child and Maternal Contributions to Shared Reading: Effects on Language and Literacy Development," *Applied Developmental Psychology* 27: 31–41.

Evans, Mary Ann, Reynolds, Kailey, Shaw, Deborah, and Pursoo, Tiffany (2011) "Parental Explanations of Vocabulary During Shared Reading: A Missed Opportunity," *First Language* 31: 195–213.

Fabb, Nigel (1997) *Linguistics and Literature: Language in the Verbal Arts of the World*, Oxford: Blackwell.

Fletcher, Kathryn L., and Finch, W. Holmes (2014) "The Role of Book Familiarity and Book Type on Mothers' Reading Strategies and Toddlers' Responsiveness," *Journal of Early Childhood Literacy*. Doi: 10.1177/1468798414523026 (last accessed March 12, 2016).

Fletcher, Kathryn L., and Reese, Elaine (2005) "Picture Book Reading with Young Children: A Conceptual Framework," *Developmental Review* 25: 64–103.

Gressnich, Eva (2012) "Verbal and Visual Pageturners in Picturebooks," *International Research in Children's Literature* 5.2: 167–183.

Gressnich, Eva, and Meibauer, Jörg (2010) "First-Person Narratives in Picturebooks: An Inquiry Into the Acquisition of Picturebook Competence," in Teresa Colomer, Bettina Kümmerling-Meibauer, and Cecilia Silva-Díaz (eds) *New Directions in Picturebook Research*, New York: Routledge, 191–203.

Horst, Jessica S. (2015) "World Learning via Shared Storybook Reading," in Bettina Kümmerling-Meibauer, Jörg Meibauer, Kerstin Nachtigäller, and Katharina Rohlfing (eds) *Learning from Picturebooks: Perspectives from Child Development and Literacy Studies*, New York: Routledge, 181–193.

Jakobson, Roman (1987) "Linguistics and Poetics," in Jakobson, Roman *Language in Literature*, Cambridge, MA: Harvard University Press, 62–94.

Jones, Rhian (1996) *Emerging Patterns of Literacy: A Multidisciplinary Perspective*, New York: Routledge.

Kümmerling-Meibauer, Bettina (1999) "Metalinguistic Awareness and the Child's Developing Concept of Irony: The Relationship Between Pictures and Text in Ironic Picture Books," *The Lion and the Unicorn* 23: 157–183.

Kümmerling-Meibauer, Bettina, and Meibauer, Jörg (2013) "Towards a Cognitive Theory of Picturebooks," *International Research in Children's Literature* 6.2: 143–160.

Kümmerling-Meibauer, Bettina, and Meibauer, Jörg (2015) "Picturebooks and Early Literacy. How Do Picturebooks Support Early Conceptual and Narrative Development?," in Bettina Kümmerling-Meibauer, Jörg Meibauer, Kerstin Nachtigäller, and Katharina Rohlfing (eds) *Learning from Picturebooks: Perspectives from Child Development and Literacy Studies*. New York: Routledge, 13–32.

Martin, Linda E., and Reutzel, D. Ray (1999) "Sharing Books: Examining How and Why Mothers Deviate from the Print," *Reading Research and Instruction* 39.1: 39–70.

McDonnell, Susan A., Friel-Patti, Sandy, and Rosenthal Rollins, Pamela (2003) "Patterns of Change in Maternal-Child Discourse Behaviors Across Repeated Storybook Readings," *Applied Psycholinguistics* 24: 323–341.

Mey, Jakob L. (2000) *When Voices Clash: A Study in Literary Pragmatics*, Berlin: de Gruyter.

Moerk, Ernst L. (1985) "Picture-Book Reading by Mothers and Young Children and Its Impact Upon Language Development," *Journal of Pragmatics* 9: 547–566.

Morrow, Lesley Mandel (1988) "Young Children's Responses to One-to-One Readings in School Settings," *Reading Research Quarterly* 23: 89–107.

Nikolajeva, Maria, and Scott, Carole (2001) *How Picturebooks Work*, New York: Garland.

Ninio, Anat (1983) "Joint Book Reading as a Multiple Vocabulary Acquisition Device," *Developmental Psychology* 19: 445–451.

Ninio, Anat, and Snow, Catherine E. (1996) *Pragmatic Development*, Boulder, CO: Westview Press.

Painter, Clare, Martin, James R., and Unsworth, Len (2013) *Reading Visual Narratives: Image Analysis of Children's Picture Books*, Sheffield: Equinox.

Rau, Marie Luise (2011) "Metaphors in Picturebooks from 0 to 3," in Bettina Kümmerling-Meibauer (ed.) *Emergent Literacy: Children's Books from 0 to 3*, Amsterdam: Benjamins.

Reese, Elaine (2015) "What Good Is a Picturebook? Developing Children's Oral Language and Literacy Through Shared Picturebook Reading," in Bettina Kümmerling-Meibauer, Jörg Meibauer, Kerstin Nachtigäller, and Katharina Rohlfing (eds) *Learning from Picturebooks: Perspectives from Child Development and Literacy Studies*, New York: Routledge, 194–208.

Sénéchal, Monique, Cornell, Edward H., and Broda, Lorri S. (1995) "Age-Related Differences in the Organization of Parent-Infant Interactions During Picture-Book Reading," *Early Childhood Research Quarterly* 10: 317–337.

Sénéchal, Monique, Pagan, Stephanie, Lever, Rosemary, and Ouellette, Gene P. (2008) "Relations Among the Frequency of Shared Reading and 4-Year-Old Children's Vocabulary, Morphological and Syntax Comprehension, and Narrative Skills," *Early Education & Development* 19.1: 27–44.

Snow, Catherine E. (1996) "Issues in the Study of Input: Finetuning, Universality, Individual and Developmental Differences, and Necessary Causes," in Paul Fletcher and Brian MacWhinney (eds) *The Handbook of Child Language*, Oxford: Blackwell, 180–193.

Stark, Linda (2015) "Tense Acquisition with Picturebooks," in Bettina Kümmerling-Meibauer, Jörg Meibauer, Kerstin Nachtigäller, and Katharina Rohlfing (eds) *Learning from Picturebooks: Perspectives from Child Development and Literacy Studies*, New York: Routledge, 209–227.

Stephens, John (1992) *Language and Ideology in Children's Fiction*, London: Longman.

Stockwell, Peter (2002) *Cognitive Poetics: An Introduction*, London: Routledge.

Willems, Mo (2004) *Don't Let the Pigeon Drive the Bus!*, London: Walker Books.

39

PICTUREBOOKS
AND NARRATOLOGY

Smiljana Narančić Kovač

Narratology is concerned with the narrative picturebook. Nonnarrative picturebooks are beyond its interest, although narratology offers insights which can be applied to various kinds of picturebooks.

Picturebook research benefits from narratological investigation because it is well-suited to clarifying specific multimodal configurations of the picturebook and offers a theoretical frame which explains its unique and manifold structure, its potentials, and its relationships with other kinds of narratives.

Narratology, or the theory of narrative, explores how a narrative is structured and how meaning-making functions. Its foundations are formalist and structuralist. Narratology is a semiotic-based discipline because it is based on the notion of sign. It describes medium-specific strategies used to convey meanings, the narrative communication, and "how the narrative is manipulated through an interaction of the author's, the narrator's, the character's and the reader's points of view" (Nikolajeva 2003: 10).

Starting points

The term 'narratology,' coined by Tzvetan Todorov in 1969, did not catch on immediately, but the 'narrative,' or 'narrative text,' was extensively discussed by 'classical narratologists' (see Scholes, Phelan and Kellogg 2006 [1996]; Genette 1980, 1988; Chatman 1978, 1990). They differ slightly in their understanding of this concept.

Gérard Genette's French term *récit* corresponds to 'narrative.' In his *Narrative Discourse*, it stands for the signifier, manifested as discourse or narrative text, as distinguished from story (*histoire*), which stands for the signified or narrative content, and from narrating, that is, the very act of producing a narrative (Genette 1980: 27). Genette focuses on literature and language as its medium of expression, but he does acknowledge other forms of narrative expression, such as cinematic narrative, oral narrative, or the comic strip (1980: 33f.). Robert E. Scholes and Robert Kellogg extend the term to film, in contrast to drama, because it presents a story through the controlled point of view of "the eye of the camera" (Scholes, Phelan and Kellogg 2006: 280). Roland Barthes claims that narratives are numberless, and that they include a variety of genres, conveyed by all kinds of substances or materials (1977: 80). Many agree, including Seymour Chatman, who disapproves of literary critics who think "too exclusively of the verbal medium, even though they consume stories daily through films, comic strips, paintings, sculptures, dance movements and music" (1978: 9). The concept of narrative "across media" (Ryan 2004) is widely accepted. Mieke Bal defines a narrative text as "a text in which an agent relates ('tells') a story in a particular medium" (1997: 3). Narratives share a basic structure, but they differ in how they convey narrative meanings. In other words, narratives make use of common design principles, but exploit them in different, media-specific ways (Herman 2004: 51).

The semiotic model of narrative

Explicitly following Barthes, Todorov, and Genette, Seymour Chatman established a semiotic model of the narrative structure. He stated: "I posit a *what* and a *way*. The what of narrative I call its 'story'; the way I call its 'discourse'" (1978: 9). Chatman adopted the model of the sign of Louis Hjelmslev, who elaborated de Saussure's distinction of signifier (form) and signified (substance) and added the levels of expression and content, each comprising form and substance. Thus he developed a four-part scheme of sign. Chatman applied this in his model of narrative, where story (content) has two aspects: form of content (events and existents – characters and settings) and substance of content (specific entities), as does discourse (expression): form of expression (structure of transmission) and substance of expression (medium-dependent manifestation) (26). The form of content and the form of expression are common to all narratives, while the substance of content and the substance of expression differ in each narrative. For example, both Lewis Carroll's *Alice's Adventures in Wonderland* (1865) and the animated film *Finding Nemo* (directed by Andrew Stanton 2003) are narratives; they communicate (narrative) meanings and comprise events, characters, and settings, that is, the form of content. They share the structure of narrative transmission, that is, the form of expression. However, they differ in the substance of content, as the protagonist of the former is a girl called Alice, and the protagonist of the latter is a clownfish called Nemo; the settings are different (underground vs. ocean), as well as events. They also differ in substance of expression, their respective manifestations being verbal discourse (a novel) and animated cinematic discourse (an animated film). However, the same stories can be presented in different media. *Alice's Adventures in Wonderland* also appears as a musical film directed by William Sterling (1972). It shares the story with the book, but not the medium. Similarly, *Findet Nemo*, an illustrated book (Disney 2014), relates the same story as the animated feature, but by means of illustrations and text, and in a different language.

Chatman's model can be presented as a diagram, where the components of the narrative are rearranged to make the common core of all the narratives visible: the form of content and the form of expression (Figure 39.1). Together, they represent a narrative even-weave, or canvas, which

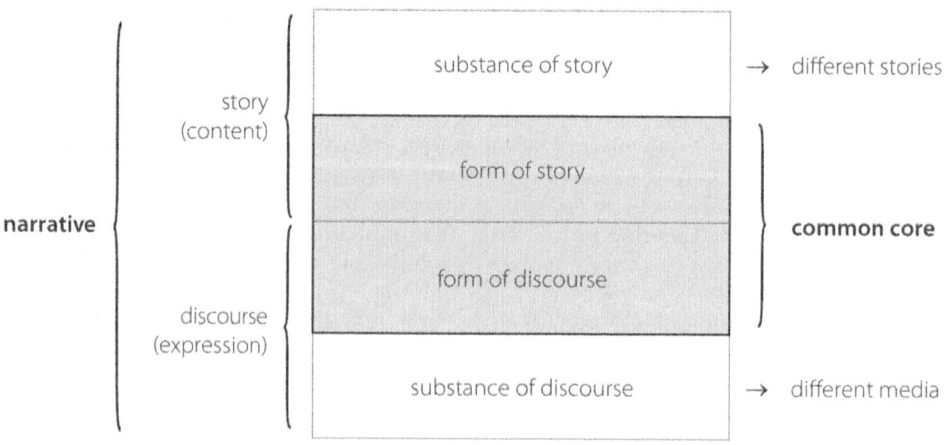

Figure 39.1 General model of the narrative developed from Chatman's model (Narančić Kovač 2015: 100).

receives various patterns provided by the substance of content and the substance of form of individual narratives.

Breaking paths: picturebook research

Turning to the picturebook as a specific kind of narrative, it is obvious that it uses two 'ways' of conveying narrative information. When Barbara Bader claimed that the picturebook as an art form "hinges on the interdependence of pictures and words" (1976: 1), she addressed an issue that is now commonplace in picturebook research. At the time, Kenneth Marantz needed to raise his voice against the widespread treatment of picturebooks as literary pieces with illustrations (1977: 149), explaining that the picturebook is a "visual-verbal entity" (150), different from an illustrated book. Marantz compares the pictures in picturebooks to those in a motion picture, emphasizing their narrativity (148–149).

Margaret Meek soon brought to light the necessity to bridge the gap between literary critics, who ignored narratives such as picturebooks, which would in her opinion "extend their awareness," and children's book specialists, who ignored the new theory of the narrative, which was clearly relevant for children's literature (1982/1990: 173).

The call was soon answered. The narrative turn in picturebook research took place in the 1980s. Stephen Roxburgh, in a special double issue of *The Lion and the Unicorn*, complained about the lack of theoretical consideration of the narrative function of illustrations, and emphasized its centrality for the understanding of the semantic structure of picturebooks (1983–1984: 21). Joseph Schwarcz set an example by exploring pictures as "a means of symbolic communication" (1982: 4). The complexity of visual meanings and sophisticated narrative strategies in comparison to verbal discourse was recognized (Moss 1992: 56; Nodelman 1988; 2010: 17). Leonard S. Marcus joined in by introducing the term "picture narrative" (1983–1984: 41) to describe Mitsumasa Anno's *Anno's Journey* (1977). Further studies about communicating meanings by the picturebook pictorial layer (Shulevitz 1985; Doonan 1986; 1993) include William Moebius's contribution on picturebook codes (1986/1990) and the seminal study *Words about Pictures* (1988) by Perry Nodelman. John Stephens followed Chatman in interpreting the word-picture relationship as "one between differently constructed discourses giving different kinds of information, if not different messages" (1992: 164), and the picturebook as "a duple discourse" (198). Stephens also combined narratology with critical linguistics and extended his research to ideology and subjectivity. Maria Nikolajeva and Carol Scott defined the picturebook as a "combination of two levels of communication, the visual and the verbal," and accentuated their semiotic nature as iconic versus conventional sets of signs (2001: 1).

The relationship between pictures and words is a *topos* of picturebook research. Schwarcz described the picturebook as a composite text; pictures and words are interdependent and their combination is similar to a musical score (1982: 14). Moebius used a geological metaphor, describing words and pictures as plates and their relationship as "semic slippage" (1990: 135). Nodelman discovered an "ironic relationship between the sequential storytelling of words and the series of stopped moments we see in a sequence of pictures" (1988: 239). David Lewis used the term polysystemy to describe the picturebook, and explained that words and pictures "*speak to each other* across the gap between them" (1996: 109, emphasis in original).

The semiotic model of the picturebook

What does this all mean for a narrative model of the picturebook, and how is it related to the general model? The picturebook stands out because it comprises one story conveyed by two distinct narrative voices within two distinct discourses (Narančić Kovač 2015). In contrast to certain other narratives, such as film, with a combined discourse, the picturebook maintains a distinction of the verbal and the visual discourse and of their respective narrators, who mediate the same story (Figure 39.2).

411

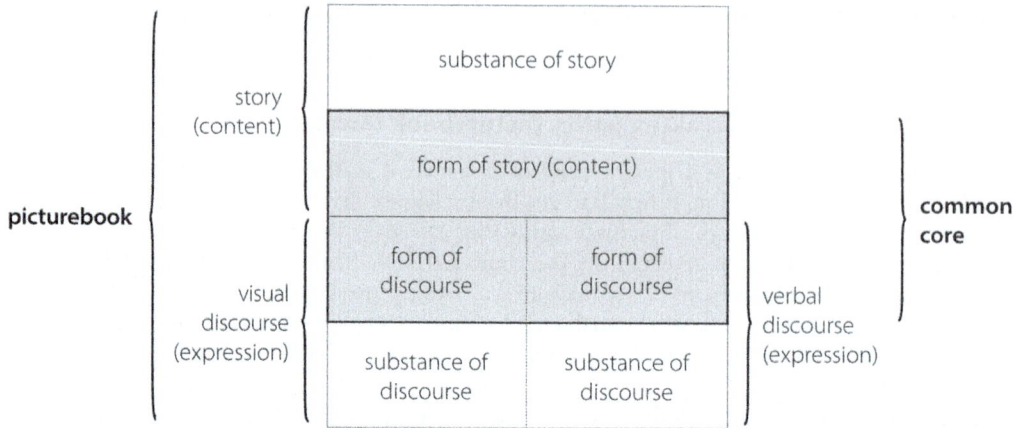

Figure 39.2 Model of the picturebook as a narrative (Narančić Kovač 2015: 101).

This basic model may be extended to represent formal variations of individual picturebooks, which demonstrates the flexibility of the form.

While characters, settings, and events are the elements of the (form of) story, narrator, and plot (the way in which the events are arranged), as well as the possibility to choose the medium of expression, belong to the (form of) discourse. In Chatman's words, the narrator "must stay within the bounds of discourse space" (1990: 123). Thus each discourse necessarily embraces its own narrator. In the picturebook, its two narrators establish a dynamic conversation, a dialogue in which they confront different perspectives, contribute specific items of narrative information, and together tell the same story.

Wordless picturebooks put this model to the test, as they seem to be reduced to the visual discourse. However, picturebook scholars claim that it is the readers that give the story the missing "voice" (Bosch 2014: 79) and provide necessary story lines as active storytellers (Beckett 2012: 144). The readers become verbal narrators, creating verbal signs in response to pictorial signs (Trites 1994: 232). This is supported by empirical findings showing that child readers employ similar sense-making processes when reading wordless picturebooks and verbal texts (Crawford and Hade 2000: 66). In addition, picturebook titles can only belong to the verbal narrator, and visual discourses often incorporate a few words, which turn wordless picturebooks into "almost wordless picturebooks" (Bosch 2014: 74). The visual narrator may be silent, but it is inscribed in the visual narrative, waiting to be activated.

Picturebook narrators

Stephens turns to the narrative voice, exploring its effect both on the presentation of the story and on the significance of the narrative whole, along with ideological assumptions and practices (1992: 200). He relies on Genette's notion of narrator (cf. 1988: 128), just as Nodelman, who studies picturebooks that confront "the subjectivity of a first-person narrator and the distanced objectivity of third-person pictures in a decidedly ironic way" (Nodelman 1991: 29). However, both Stephens and Nodelman connect the narrator with words only, and pictures are somehow considered to narrate themselves. Nikolajeva and Scott join them in ascribing the narrative function to words, not pictures: "The function of pictures is to describe or represent. The function of words [. . .] is primarily to narrate" (2001: 1).

While the 'duple' nature of picturebooks has been widely adopted, the notion of narrative voice remains too often connected with either the verbal layer or the picturebook as a whole. Pictures are assigned the narrating role, but the narrator is not detected. Even when pictures are recognized as a separate discourse, it does not lead to the recognition of two narrators, but rather of two stories, or even two narratives. There are exceptions, though. Claire Bradford clearly states that "both verbal and visual text have narrator and narratee" (1998: 87), but she is followed by only a few (Nières-Chevrel 2010; Yannicopoulou 2010; Narančić Kovač 2015). Similar ideas appeared, albeit sporadically, in early picturebook research. Marantz and Marantz noted: "the illustrator replaces the speaker and the pictures become, symbolically, the voice that conveys some of the special qualities of meaning that language frequently cannot" (1988: xii). Charlotte F. Otten and Gary D. Schmidt also ascribe to "the visual narrator" a distinct voice, separate from the voice of "the textual narrator" (1989: xii, 3).

Narrative strategies

A visual narrator may convey narrative meanings equivalent to those conveyed by a verbal narrator, and may do this by means of narrative techniques implicit to narrative pictures as a medium. Temporality is often accomplished by such strategies as the positioning of depicted objects, repetition, rhythm, and the choice and sequencing of presented events, which give special significance to pageturning. Thus picturebook discourses employ the book itself as a means of meaning-making (see Nodelman 1988: 41; Doonan 1996: 231;). Lawrence R. Sipe emphasizes that each part of the picturebook functions as a sign and has the potential of contributing meaning (2001: 24).

Gunther Kress and Theo van Leeuwen's work on the grammar of visual design (2006) brought new insights. In earlier studies, pictures were often analyzed using tools of art theory, and position, color, line, linear perspective, and so forth were in focus (Nodelman 1988; Moebius 1990). New methodology raised the debate to another level, where pictures lend themselves more easily to a semiotic analysis resembling the semantic structure of language. A depicted object or character can be seen as the equivalent of a word, and a visually presented action functions as a visual sentence, while picturebook codes are equivalent to phonemes, as they produce narrative meanings only when combined. Pictures are also capable of expressing figurative meanings (see Schwarcz 1982: 34). Such devices as first person narration and visual 'reported speech' can be conveyed by pictures by means of medium-specific strategies, as Nodelman (1991) has also shown.

Both picturebook discourses are specific. Schwarcz (1982) describes visual elements of the written word, including such functions as 'visual sound.' Visual discourse is manifold, multi-stranded, polyphonic (likely to embrace parallel points of view), exceptionally interactive, and challenging for the reader. The picturebook discourses exchange their features, and thus become intermedial. Eliza T. Dresang asserts that "words become pictures and pictures become words" (2008: 46). Rosemary Ross Johnston explains the "reversed imagery" of pictures, showing that not only words can provoke imagery, but also pictures, which produce mental images that carry words, that is, "unleash ideas that are articulated in the mind in words" (2012: 422). Research on the visual discourse in picturebooks continues with Painter et al., who extend the social semiotics view of the visual modality and consider it in relation to verbal meanings (2013: 3).

Nikolajeva and Scott blaze a trail in many aspects of picturebook research, and discuss setting and characterization, mimetic and nonmimetic representation and modality, time and movement, intertextuality, metafiction, and paratexts. They study the dynamics of the word-image relationship, in a way somewhat reminiscent of Nodelman (1988), especially in their presentation of different perspectives in and ironic interplay between text and pictures (Nikolajeva and Scott 2001: 259). They offer an elaborated typology of word-picture relationships (symmetrical, complementary, expanding or enhancing, counterpointing, and sylleptic) (12), which is slightly modified later (Nikolajeva 2002a: 88).

Conveying elements of the story

Investigating the construction of the elements of the story in picturebooks, Nikolajeva and Scott (2001) explain that the setting is conveyed by words that describe space, and pictures that make the setting "nonnarrated" (2001: 62). They distinguish among minimal or reduced, symmetrical and duplicative, enhanced and expanded, and complex settings (63–80). They also single out the intraiconic text, that is, words in pictures, as typical of the representation of picturebook settings (73–75).

Further, Nikolajeva and Scott analyze the characterization techniques available to picturebooks (80–115). Several categories span from minimal characterization, which hardly reveals emotions, through psychological, to complex characterization through dialogue and action. Typical picturebook characters comprise animal characters, human beings in disguise, and objects, including abstract images. Picturebooks provide a wide scope of artistic devices for characterization, often showing "a remarkable level of sophistication" (82). Nikolajeva's study on character in children's fiction (2002b), which brings a wider typology of characters and a thorough exploration of character ontology and epistemology, offers groundbreaking insights and establishes a theory that is also relevant for an analysis of picturebook characters. Following this frame, Bettina Kümmerling-Meibauer and Jörg Meibauer (2014) analyze the matchstick man as a picturebook character. They elaborate on its hybridity and make inferences about the child-reader's cognitive processes leading towards a mental model stimulated by its picturebook representation, offering an example of a new direction in picturebook research.

The potential of the visual discourse to multiply narrative information allows for multiple strands of narrative events, running stories, parallel plots, and embedding, which creates additional narrative levels. Supplementary characters follow their own agendas, regardless of the main plot. Additional story lines are neatly incorporated into the fictional world presented by both discourses. Such structures can also be found in other narrative forms, especially novels. This also remains one of the characteristic features of the picturebook as a form and does not jeopardize its basic semantic model. Another phenomenon that belongs to its repertoire is the multiplication of individual discourses, when one verbal discourse refers to two visual discourses, or the other way around, which can be described as a syllepsis.

Visually presented settings can be particularly rich in detail, offering so much information that it becomes difficult to find a character or follow a strand of events. This happens in teeming picturebooks or wimmelbooks, a kind of wordless picturebook that invites readers to find their own paths in a presented scene or a street view (see Rémi 2010). Such pictures turn reading into interactive play. They also exemplify a visual narrator's strategy of introducing external focalization.

Perspective

Narrative perspective or point of view is a prime topic of narratological research focusing on discourse-related narrative strategies and their combinations. Distance and perspective play a crucial role in the regulation of narrative information (Genette 1980: 162), and the temporal perspective, the time of narrating (215), is equally important. Genette distinguished among three types of focalization: zero, internal, and external (210). Modifying his theory, Bal (1997) introduced the term 'focalizer' to denote the character whose perspective is dominant, but Genette never accepted it. Although Bal's term has been widely adopted, Genette's concept of focalization has proved more efficient in the analysis of the complex polyphonic structure of the picturebook.

Nikolajeva and Scott combine Chatman's distinction of perceptual, conceptual, and interest point of view (1978: 151f.) with Genette's distinction of narrative voice (*who speaks?*) and narrative perspective (*who sees?*) (1980: 186). Nevertheless, they claim that "in a picturebook we should probably treat the words as primarily conveying the narrative voice, and pictures as primarily conveying the point of view" (2001: 117). Nodelman generalizes about "the relative objectivity of pictures and the relative subjectivity of words" (1988: 229). These fallacies appeared in consequence of the previously mentioned belief, widespread in the world of narratological research, that only some texts have narrators, and others, including pictures in picturebooks, do not (cf. Nodelman 1991). Being an understandable phase in picturebook research, it led to confusing interpretations of the point of view in picturebooks, which were resolved by accepting the idea of two narrators and a thorough analysis of the medium-specific narrative techniques of picturebook discourses.

The narratological approach to picturebooks asks questions about the specific contributions of verbal and visual information to the narrative meaning (cf. Kümmerling-Meibauer 2014: 4f.). All aspects of these contributions are assembled in the notion of narrative voice, that is, the narrator, or the narrative instance, understood as a technical term comprising "the entire set of conditions [. . .] out of which a narrative statement is produced" (Genette 1980: 31, 212ff.). The narrator is thus a theoretical construct, but inevitable in a narrative discourse.

Acknowledging the existence of the visual narrator as a construct belonging to its discourse in accordance with the model of the narrative picturebook (Figure 39.2), the contrasted perspectives in *Rosie's Walk* (Hutchins 1968), which have been interpreted many times in different ways, can now be explained in consistence with Genette's model. Both narrators establish a heterodiegetic relation to the story (cf. Genette 1980: 244f.). The verbal narrator focalizes narration through the character of Rosie (who does not see that a fox is following her), and the visual narrator offers zero focalization, presenting the whole situation and showing both characters. In order to understand that the narration of the verbal narrator is unreliable, the reader relies on the information offered by the visual narrator. Thus the contradiction in perspective, realized through two narrative voices, is revealed in their combination, that is, in their dialogue. This is where Mikhail Bakhtin's (1981) concept of dialogism steps in. Kümmerling-Meibauer declares that the relationship between the verbal and the visual is "always to some extent dialogical" (1999: 163). In addition, according to Robyn McCallum, narrating events "from the viewpoints of two or more narrators or character focalisers" creates polyphonic narratives (2004: 595). The picturebook is therefore a polyphonic and dialogic narrative by definition. Cherie Allan contributes the insight that such narratives "invite readers to view the text from a range of positions, offering a number of, often competing, discourses" (2012: 35).

Reading picturebooks

There is general agreement that the polyphony and the multimodality of the picturebook make the reader active. Reading a picturebook is an interactive, and an intermittent procedure. The reader chooses his/her trajectory and shifts from one discourse to another. In the process, he/she reconstructs the story. Manifold narratives "foreground the reader's agency" and "subvert traditional linear readings" (Trites 1994: 239–240). Further, the picturebook invites re-readings. This necessity is often discussed (Meek 1988: 13; Nodelman 1988: 179; Kiefer 1995: 6), and Angela Yannicopoulou describes the process as "a round trip" (2010: 72). In every subsequent reading, additional meanings are discovered. Re-reading is at the basis of Sipe's theory of transmediation of verbal and visual meanings, and the total effect depends "not only on the union of the text and illustrations but also on the perceived interactions or transactions between these two parts" (1998: 98–99).

Narrative communication

The reading process brings about another aspect: narrative is understood as communication (Chatman 1978: 28). Chatman presents the process as a sequence: Real author > [Implied author > Narrator > Narratee > Implied reader] > Real reader. The real author and the real reader are placed outside the narrative, and the remaining two pairs of participants are embraced by the narrative itself (1978: 151; 1990: 76). The pairs of real author and reader, and of narrator and narratee, are placed on their respective diegetic levels (Genette 1980: 227ff.). Genette and Chatman generally agree about

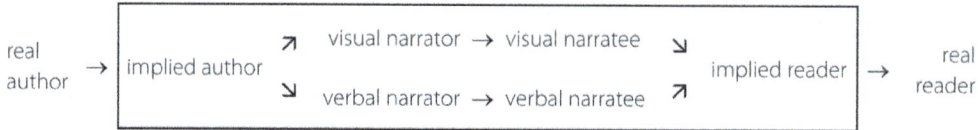

Figure 39.3 Model of narrative communication in the narrative picturebook (Narančić Kovač 2015: 377).

the model of narrative communication and its participants, but Genette accepts the notion of implied author as the principle of the unity of a narrative only in "works written in collaboration" where a reader "would spontaneously construct the image of a single author" (1988: 148).

The model of narrative communication in the picturebook (Figure 39.3) is founded on the general model just described. This model may give rise to contention, because narratologists are not unanimous, especially not in their understanding of the implied reader. Wolfgang Iser, who introduced the term, defines the implied reader as a construct which should not be identified with any real reader but "incorporates both the prestructuring of the potential meaning by the text, and the reader's actualization of this potential through the reading process" (1974: xii). Chatman adopts the idea from Wayne Booth, and defines the implied reader as "the audience presupposed by the narrative itself" (1978: 150). This definition guided scholars in assigning to the term the meaning of an intended or potential reader at which a particular narrative is aimed. In children's literature research the implied reader is usually understood either as a child, as a dual or double audience (Wall 1991), or as crossover audience of adults and children (see Beckett 2012: 17).

Scholars sometimes divide picturebook discourses between adults (words) and children (pictures), as if there were any reader who does not actively read both discourses. In fact, real readers may adopt the roles of the narratees and reconstruct the story, establishing a dialogue between sets of narrative information received by two distinct narratees and offered by two distinct narrators. The implied reader is then understood as the dialogic principle of the picturebook as a whole. An adult or a child may read a picturebook, or it can be read in cooperation, but this does not change its narrative structure or the structure of its narrative communication. However, in order to establish a dialogic relationship, a real reader often assumes the role(s) of the narratee(s) and blends with the narratee(s), especially in metafictive picturebooks, where a character or a narrator may directly address the real reader and thus cross the borderline between fiction and reality. Genette describes the syncretism of participants of narrative communication as another narrative phenomenon, acknowledging that the narratee is in principle distinguishable from the reader, but that they often merge (1988: 132).

Narrativity and storyworld

Picturebook research benefits from the redefined field of interest of narratology now denoted as "transmedial narratology" (Herman 2004) and "media-conscious narratology" (Ryan and Thon 2014). It focuses both on medium-free aspects of narratives and on medium-specific features of various narrative forms. This direction of research puts in the forefront the medium-free notion of "narrativity," as a common center shared by all narratives, and relies on the idea of "storyworld," a mental representation of a virtual world a text must evoke in order to qualify as narrative (3). This approach adds the cultural dimension to the semiotic and technical dimensions of mediality (Ryan 2014: 30). The medium-related concept of storyworld is founded on the idea of possible worlds from analytic philosophy and in cognitive approaches, but it also acknowledges the tradition of semiotic-based classical narratology. The components of storyworlds include existents (characters and objects), the setting, physical laws, social rules and values, events (in a time-span frame), and mental events (34–37). A storyworld often migrates from medium to medium (Ryan and Thon 2014: 19), just as in the examples of Nemo's and Alice's stories (and storyworlds).

The future

It is not possible to cover all the aspects of contemporary research on narrative picturebooks here, but hopefully it has become clear that it combines previous picturebook scholarship with developments in the theory of the narrative, adopting its analytical instruments, and fine tuning them for the study of picturebooks. This only seemingly simple narrative form constantly tests its own conventions and challenges its researchers.

References

Alice's Adventures in Wonderland (1972) musical film, directed by William Sterling, UK, Fox-Rank.

Allan, Cherie (2012) *Playing with Picturebooks: Postmodernism and the Postmodernesque*, Basingstoke: Palgrave Macmillan.

Anno, Mitsumasa (1977) *Anno's Journey*, New York: Philomel.

Bader, Barbara (1976) *American Picturebooks from Noah's Ark to the Beast Within*, New York: Macmillan.

Bakhtin, Mikhail (1981) *The Dialogic Imagination*, Austin: University of Texas Press.

Bal, Mieke (1997) *Narratology: Introduction to the Theory of Narrative*, Toronto: University of Toronto (first published 1985).

Barthes, Roland (1977) "Introduction to the Structural Analysis of Narratives," in Roland Barthes, *Image – Music – Text*, New York: Hill and Wang, 79–124 (first published 1966).

Beckett, Sandra L. (2012) *Crossover Picturebooks: A Genre for All Ages*, New York: Routledge.

Bosch, Emma (2014) "Texts and Peritexts in Wordless and Almost Wordless Picturebooks," in Bettina Kümmerling-Meibauer (ed.) *Picturebooks: Representation and Narration*, New York: Routledge, 71–90.

Bradford, Clare (1998) "Playing with Father: Anthony Browne's Picture Books and the Masculine," *Children's Literature in Education* 29.2: 79–96.

Carroll, Lewis (1865) *Alice's Adventures in Wonderland*, London: Macmillan.

Chatman, Seymour (1978) *Story and Discourse: Narrative Structure in Fiction and Film*, Ithaca, NY: Cornell University Press.

Chatman, Seymour (1990) *Coming to Terms*, Ithaca, NY: Cornell University Press.

Crawford, Patricia A., and Hade, Daniel D. (2000) "Inside the Picture, Outside the Frame: Semiotics and the Reading of Wordless Picture Books," *Journal of Research in Childhood Education* 15.1: 66–80.

Disney (2014) *Findet Nemo*, Bath: Parragon Books.

Doonan, Jane (1986) "Outside Over There: A Journey in Style," *Signal* 50: 92–103, 51: 172–187.

Doonan, Jane (1993) *Looking at Pictures in Picture Books*, Stroud: Thimble Press.

Doonan, Jane (1996) "The Modern Picture Book," in Peter Hunt (ed.) *International Companion Encyclopedia of Children's Literature*, London: Routledge, 231–241.

Dresang, Eliza T. (2008) "Radical Change Theory, Postmodernism and Contemporary Picturebooks," in Lawrence R. Sipe and Sylvia Pantaleo (eds) *Postmodern Picturebooks*, New York: Routledge, 41–54.

Finding Nemo (2003) film, directed by Andrew Stanton, USA, Pixar Animation Studios.

Genette, Gérard (1980) *Narrative Discourse: An Essay in Method*, Ithaca, NY: Cornell University Press (first published 1972).

Genette, Gérard (1988) *Narrative Discourse Revisited*, Ithaca, NY: Cornell University Press (first published 1983).

Herman, David (2004) "Toward a Transmedial Narratology," in Marie-Laure Ryan (ed.) *Narrative Across Media*, Lincoln: University of Nebraska Press, 47–75.

Hutchins, Pat (1968) *Rosie's Walk*, New York: Simon and Schuster.

Iser, Wolfgang (1974) *The Implied Reader*, Baltimore: Johns Hopkins University Press (first published 1972).

Johnston, Rosemary Ross (2012) "Graphic Trinities: Languages, Literature, and Words-in-Pictures in Shaun Tan's *The Arrival*," *Visual Communication* 11.4: 421–441.

Kiefer, Barbara (1995) *The Potential of Picturebooks*, Englewood Cliffs, NJ: Prentice Hall.

Kress, Gunther, and van Leeuwen, Theo (2006) *Reading Images: The Grammar of Visual Design*, London: Routledge (first published 1996).

Kümmerling-Meibauer, Bettina (1999) "Metalinguistic Awareness and the Child's Developing Concept of Irony: The Relationship Between Pictures and Text in Ironic Picture Books," *The Lion and the Unicorn* 23.2: 157–183.

Kümmerling-Meibauer, Bettina (2014) "Introduction: Picturebooks Between Representation and Narration," in Bettina Kümmerling-Meibauer (ed.) *Picturebooks: Representation and Narration*, New York: Routledge, 1–14.

Kümmerling-Meibauer, Bettina, and Meibauer, Jörg (2014) "Understanding the Matchstick Man. Aesthetic and Narrative Properties of a Hybrid Picturebook Character," in Bettina Kümmerling-Meibauer (ed.) *Picturebooks: Representation and Narration*, New York: Routledge, 139–161.

Lewis, David (1996) "Going Along with Mr. Gumpy: Polysystemy and Play in the Modern Picturebook," *Signal* 80: 105–119.

Marantz, Kenneth (1977) "The Picture Book as Art Object: A Call for Balanced Reviewing," *Wilson Library Bulletin* 52: 148–151.

Marantz, Sylvia, and Marantz, Kenneth (1988) *The Art of Children's Picture Books*, New York: Garland.

Marcus, Leonard S. (1983–1984) "Mitsumasa Anno," *The Lion and the Unicorn* 7/8: 34–46.

McCallum, Robyn (2004) "Metafictions and Experimental Work," in Peter Hunt (ed.) *International Companion Encyclopedia of Children's Literature*, 2nd ed., vol 1, London: Routledge, 587–598 (first published 1996).

Meek, Margaret (1990) "What Counts as Evidence in Theories of Children's Literature?," in Peter Hunt (ed.) *Children's Literature: The Development of Criticism*, London: Routledge, 166–182 (first published 1982).

Meek, Margaret (1988) *How Texts Teach What Readers Learn*, Stroud: Thimble Press.

Moebius, William (1990) "Introduction to Picturebook Codes," in Peter Hunt (ed.) *Children's Literature: The Development of Criticism*, London: Routledge, 131–148 (first published 1986).

Moss, Geoff (1992) "Metafiction, Illustration and the Poetics of Children's Literature," in Peter Hunt (ed.) *Literature for Children: Contemporary Criticism*, London: Routledge, 44–66.

Narančić Kovač, Smiljana (2015) *Jedna priča – dva pripovjedača: slikovnica kao pripovijed*, Zagreb: ArTresor.

Nières-Chevrel, Isabelle (2010) "The Narrative Power of Pictures: *L'Orage* (The Thunderstorm) by Anne Brouillard," in Teresa Colomer, Bettina Kümmerling-Meibauer, and Cecilia Silva-Díaz (eds) *New Directions in Picturebook Research*, New York: Routledge, 129–138.

Nikolajeva, Maria (2002a) "The Verbal and the Visual: The Picturebook as a Medium," in Roger D. Sell (ed.) *Children's Literature as Communication*, Amsterdam: John Benjamins, 85–110.

Nikolajeva, Maria (2002b) *The Rhetoric of Character in Children's Literature*, Lanham, MD: Scarecrow Press.

Nikolajeva, Maria (2003) "Beyond the Grammar of the Story, or How Can Children's Literature Criticism Benefit From Narrative Theory," *Children's Literature Association Quarterly* 28.1: 5–16.

Nikolajeva, Maria, and Scott, Carole (2001) *How Picturebooks Work*, New York: Garland.

Nodelman, Perry (1988) *Words about Pictures: The Narrative Art of Children's Picture Books*, Athens: University of Georgia Press.

Nodelman, Perry (1991) "The Eye and the I: Identification and First-Person Narratives in Picture Books," *Children's Literature* 19: 1–31.

Nodelman, Perry (2010) "Words Claimed: Picturebook Narratives and the Project of Children's Literature," in Teresa Colomer, Bettina Kümmerling-Meibauer, and Cecilia Silva-Díaz (eds) *New Directions in Picturebook Research*, New York: Routledge, 11–26.

Otten, Charlotte F., and Schmidt, Gary D. (1989) *The Voice of the Narrator in Children's Literature*, New York: Greenwood Press.

Painter, Clare, Martin, J.R., and Unsworth, Len (2013) *Reading Visual Narratives: Image Analysis of Children's Picture Books*, Sheffield: Equinox.

Rémi, Cornelia (2010) "Reading as Playing: The Cognitive Challenge of the Wimmelbook," in Bettina Kümmerling-Meibauer (ed.) *Emergent Literacy: Children's Books from 0 to 3*, Amsterdam: John Benjamins, 115–139.

Roxburgh, Stephen (1983–1984) "A Picture Equals How Many Words? Narrative Theory and Picture Books for Children," *The Lion and the Unicorn* 7/8: 20–33.

Ryan, Marie-Laure (ed.) (2004) *Narrative Across Media: The Languages of Storytelling*, Lincoln and London: University of Nebraska Press.

Ryan, Marie-Laure (2014) "Story/Worlds/Media: Tuning the Instruments of a Media-Conscious Narratology," in Marie-Laure Ryan and Jan-Noel Thon (eds) *Storyworlds Across Media*, Lincoln: University of Nebraska Press, 25–49.

Ryan, Marie-Laure, and Thon, Jan-Noel (eds) (2014) *Storyworlds Across Media: Towards a Media-conscious Narratology*, Lincoln: University of Nebraska Press.

Scholes, Robert E., Phelan, James, and Kellogg, Robert (2006) *The Nature of Narrative*, New York: Oxford University Press (first published 1966).

Schwarcz, Joseph (1982) *Ways of the Illustrator: Visual Communication in Children's Literature*, Chicago: American Library Association.

Shulevitz, Uri (1985) *Writing With Pictures*, New York: Watson-Guptill.

Sipe, Lawrence R. (2001) "Picturebooks as Aesthetic Objects," *Literacy Teaching and Learning* 6.1: 23–42.

Sipe, Lawrence R. (1998) "How Picture Books Work: A Semiotically Framed Theory of Text-Picture Relation-ships," *Children's Literature in Education* 29.2: 97–108.

Stephens, John (1992) *Language and Ideology in Children's Fiction*, London: Longman.

Trites, Roberta Seelinger (1994) "Manifold Narratives: Metafiction and Ideology in Picture Books," *Children's Literature in Education* 25.4: 225–242.

Wall, Barbara (1991) *The Narrator's Voice: The Dilemma of Children's Fiction*, New York: St. Martin's Press.

Yannicopoulou, Angela (2010) "Focalization in Children's Picture Books: Who Sees in Words and Pictures?," in Mike Cadden (ed.) *Telling Children's Stories: Narrative Theory and Children's Literature*, Lincoln: University of Nebraska Press, 65–85.

40

MULTIMODAL ANALYSIS OF PICTUREBOOKS

Clare Painter

Printed picturebook stories have always been a significant resource both for the socialization of young children and for introducing them to the principles and pleasures of literacy and literature. In recent years there has been an increasing recognition that the best examples of apparently simple materials warrant serious scholarly attention for the ways images are used and combined with words to achieve their goals. The major approaches to examining the interaction of word and image within picturebooks have been usefully summarized by David Lewis (2001) and by John Bateman (2014), both of whom make clear the potential complexity of picturebooks and the fact that visual-verbal analysis is a still developing area of research. In this chapter I will discuss a form of 'multimodal' discourse analysis that can be used to examine how picturebooks make meaning in both visual and verbal modes. Such analysis derives from a 'social semiotic' perspective on meaning exemplified by systemic-functional linguistics (SFL). To explain how this approach can be used in the analysis and interpretation of picturebook narratives, I will first consider the way visual and verbal meaning can be analyzed in comparable ways and then outline a framework for considering the 'synergy' (Sipe 2010) between the two.

Systemic-functional framework for analyzing images

Where the visual mode is concerned, a social semiotic approach differs from the application of fine arts theory, as has been done for Caldecott winners by Peggy Albers (2008) or for Anthony Browne's picturebooks by Jane Doonan (1993, 1999). It draws instead on the 'visual grammar' articulated by Gunther Kress and Theo van Leeuwen (2006), which was developed for the analysis of images of any kind, including advertisements, cartoon strips, news stories, webpages, and diagrams. Their approach derives from an SFL tradition of discourse analysis with a long history in the exploration of purely verbal texts, oral and written, everyday and literary (see for example, Halliday 2002; Martin 2009).

One fundamental tenet of this tradition is that every text embodies three kinds of meaning simultaneously, since every text fulfills a threefold purpose. First, every text is about something: it has some content; in the case of a story, it has characters, actions, and settings. This kind of meaning is referred to in SFL theory as the 'ideational' function or 'metafunction.' Second, every text enters into communicative interaction since the ideational content needs to be asserted, questioned, hedged, imbued with feelings, and so on – this is the 'interpersonal' metafunction. In a narrative, of course, it is not only the affiliations and feelings of the writer that are relevant but also those between the characters in a story. Finally, every text needs to be coherently organized – a story into its stages or phases, for example – with links made between parts and different elements brought into and out of prominence: this is the role of the 'textual' metafunction.

SF linguistics has developed a rich account of the resources of English, as well as other languages, in terms of these three kinds of meanings (Halliday and Matthiessen 2004; Martin and Rose 2007), and this description has been used in the stylistic and ideological analysis of various forms of verbal text. At the same time, Kress and van Leeuwen (2006) offer a comparable description of the visual semiotic – comparable, that is, in allowing any image to be considered from three different metafunctional perspectives, as in the following analysis of the opening image of Anthony Browne's *Voices in the Park* (1998). As shown in Figure 40.1, the first page of this book is dominated by a color image of a grand, imposing two-story house on a slight rise, set in manicured lawns with a screen of trees behind. There is a well-defined fence in the foreground separating the house from a narrow strip of pavement at the bottom edge of the picture. Here, in the lower right corner, taking up a tiny fraction of the whole, we can see a well-dressed woman in a red hat walking a golden labrador. She is accompanied by a small boy whose body is largely obscured behind hers. As in many of Browne's picturebooks the people are presented 'zoomorphically' with animal faces.

In terms of ideational meaning, the image foregrounds the setting in time and place over any action by the participants in the story, which is predictable in a story opening. The blue sky and golden trees depicted indicate a sunny autumn day, and the massive house set apart from any neighbors suggests the wealth and class of the owner. The careful viewer may also observe that one of the finials atop a supporting fence post is in the exact shape of the woman's hat. Such a 'noticeable' or 'out of place' visual element constitutes a 'symbolic attribute' according to Kress and van Leeuwen (2006: 105) – in this case, the attribute of being possessed by the hat-owner. Browne uses such symbolic attributes in many of his books and in this way teaches young readers to read stories for symbolic rather than merely literal meaning. Kress and van Leeuwen also argue that diagonal lines, or 'vectors,' are the visual means of indicating action, being the equivalent of action verbs in language. The only trace of action in this image is provided by the legs of the walking trio and the woman's outstretched arm holding the lead attached to the dog's collar.

Interpersonally, there are a number of meaningful choices actualized in this image. We see the characters full length, rather than in any kind of close-up, which discourages any sense of intimacy with the viewer. This is a choice of public, as opposed to social or personal, 'social distance' in Kress and van Leeuwen's analysis. Moreover, we view them from the side rather than head-on, and the house, too, is set at an oblique angle facing away from us. Only the fence in the lower foreground, providing a barrier between the reader and the depicted residence, faces us directly. These choices in the horizontal angle are explained by Kress and van Leeuwen as carrying the meanings of relative viewer involvement. What is depicted from the side is something 'other,' something not of our world, while what we look at head-on involves us more directly: in this case, only the fence – a symbol of exclusion – faces us directly. When the social distance between the characters is considered by examining their depicted proximity, the adult and child are seen as close, but the way the adult obscures the child hints at the overbearing nature of the adult in the relationship. The vertical angle of viewing is also relevant, with depicted elements that we see from a lower vantage point representing more powerful elements, as is the case with the mansion here. A further interpersonal choice is that of 'ambience' (Painter 2008; Painter et al. 2013), which refers to the use of color to convey a mood to the viewer, with the predominant palette of blue, white, and green in this image creating emotional coolness, leavened by splashes of warmth within the windows and from the leaves in the background.

For the textual metafunction, the framing and layout of different pictorial elements is relevant. This page is one where the picture is framed off by the substantial white margins surrounding it.

Figure 40.1 Illustration from Anthony Browne's *Voices in the Park*. London: Doubleday.
Reprinted by permission of Anthony Browne.

Such a choice renders the image as a discrete 'sight' for the viewer to consider, rather than presenting what is depicted as an integral part of the viewer's immersive world, which would be the case if the image bled to the bottom of the page. The house is centrally positioned and thus of central importance in orienting us, while the splash of red provided by the woman's hat draws the eye from the setting to the characters so that we expect the page turn to reveal more about them.

Overall, the ideational choices in the image tell us that the main character depicted is wealthy, owning a grand mansion isolated from the neighboring community. The ensuing story takes place in a 'nice' neighborhood on a brisk autumn morning and the 'movement' in the bottom right corner

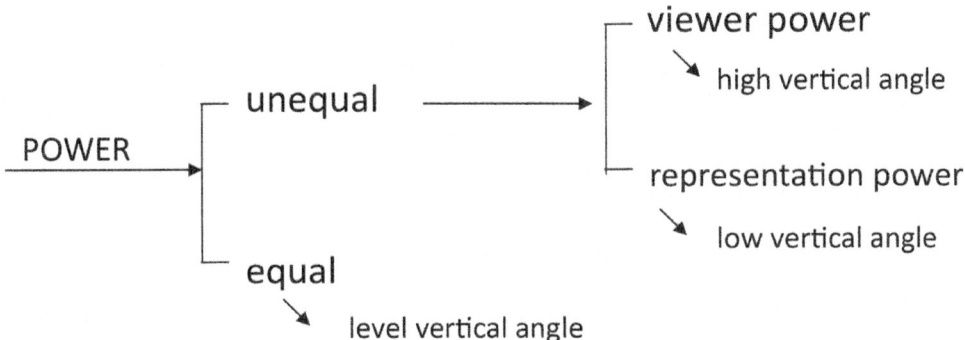

Figure 40.2 Choices in visual power.

encourages us to turn the page and read on. Interpersonal choices create a certain distance, coolness, and detachment on the part of the viewer, while obliging us to 'look up to' the house. At the same time, the boy is shown as closely connected to the adult. Finally, the textual choices emphasize the interpersonal meanings through framing choices: the garden fence that constitutes a partial frame within the picture, the thin line frame around the image, and the wider frame of the white margins all serve to keep us out of the depicted scene.

This brief discussion of one image illustrates two key features of the SFL discourse analytic approach. One is what is known as the 'metafunctional principle' – the fact that any text in any mode embodies simultaneously three strands of meaning: ideational, interpersonal, and textual. The other is that within each metafunction, any text in any mode is to be analyzed as embodying identifiable choices from a 'meaning potential.' This meaning potential is specified in terms of sets of options, known as 'systems' with names such as 'power,' 'social distance,' 'ambience,' 'framing,' and so on. A system is thus a set of possibilities for meaning with specifiable realizations. For example, Figure 40.2 diagrams Kress and van Leeuwen's system of 'power' and is to be read from left to right. It shows three choices – equality, viewer power, and representation power – the realization for each choice being specified beneath the sloping arrow.

Relating the meaning potential of image and language

Over the past fifteen years, this approach to the understanding of visual meaning has borne fruit in picturebook analysis, as evidenced in Lewis (2001), Painter (2007; 2008), Serafini (2010), Unsworth and Ortigas (2008), and Moya-Guijarro (2014). However, to enable multimodal discourse analysis, it is necessary to bring this kind of visual analysis into a systematic relation with verbal analysis. A way to do this has recently been suggested in Painter et al. (2013) and will be briefly presented in what follows. As a first step, it involves lining up the meaning potential of verbal systems with those of visual ones, while recognizing that the different nature of the two modes means that correspondences are between comparable areas of meaning rather than identical sets of choices. Tables 40.1–40.3 present some key areas of meaning to be found in the two modes, metafunction by metafunction, lining up systems where comparable meanings can be realized. It must be emphasized that the names for areas of meaning potential, such as 'action,' 'ambience,' 'social distance,' 'framing,' or 'focus' are simply shorthand for defined sets of options in each mode with associated realizations, such as that shown in Figure 40.2 for visual power. To simplify here, a general statement about realizations in each mode has been provided as a guide in the tables.

Table 40.1 Complementary ideational meaning systems across image and language

ideational metafunction

meaning potential	visual realization	verbal realization
Action		
action	depicted action with vectors	clause structures with action verbs
perception	gaze vectors between characters	clause structures with verbs of perception
cognition	thought bubbles, face/hand gestures	clause structures with verbs of thinking
talking	speech bubbles, face/hand gestures	clause structures with verbs of speaking
inter-event relations	juxtaposition of images (+/− change of setting or character)	conjunctive links; reported and direct speech
Character		
character attribution	depiction of character	identification, classification and description of characters through relational clauses, noun groups, etc.
Setting		
circumstantiation	depiction of place, time, manner	specification of place, time, extent, cause, condition, manner, etc., using prepositional phrases, adverbs, etc.

Table 40.2 Complementary interpersonal meaning systems across image and language

interpersonal metafunction

meaning potential	visual realization	Verbal realization
Affiliation		
focalization	character gaze and alignment (or not) with reader's gaze	focalization via sourcing of perceptions and thoughts
power	vertical angle of viewing	reciprocity vs. inequality of linguistic choices between characters
social distance	shot size	nature of naming choices, endearments, etc. by narrator
proximity	relative proximity/touch of depicted characters	nature of naming choices, endearments, etc. between characters
involvement	horizontal viewing angle of reader	solidarity via specialized vocabulary, slang, range of topic choice by narrator
orientation	horizontal angle between characters	solidarity via specialized vocab, slang, range of topic choice between characters
Feeling		
ambience	color choices of relative, warmth, vibrancy, etc.	atmosphere created through tone and elaboration of circumstantiation
affect	emotion on depicted faces, + body stance	attitude via evaluative language
force	'exaggerated' size or angle, repetitions, proportion of frame filled, etc.	intensification, repetition, etc.

Table 40.3 Complementary textual meaning systems across image and language

textual metafunction		
meaning potential	*visual realization*	*verbal realization*
framing	binding of visual elements into units; separation of units via frames, margins, page edges	chunking of verbiage via tone groups per clause
intermodal integration	image and verbiage placement within layout	
focus	compositional arrangement	information flow via tonic prominence, 'word order,' etc.
genre stages and phases	visual dis/continuity	staging created via internal conjunction, text reference, thematic progression, etc.

Using the framework to analyze picturebooks

Once areas of meaning potential have been lined up in this way, the text analyst can investigate how meaning is either shared out or doubled up between the two modes in any particular text. While a system, such as that of visual power shown in Figure 40.2, displays every possible meaning option and how to recognize it, an individual text, whether it be a single page or a complete story, must instantiate particular choices and realizations from the meaning potential. One way to consider a bi-modal text such as a picturebook, then, is in terms of which meanings are actualized, or 'committed,' in which mode. This allows us to see whether different modes instantiate different areas of meaning, sharing out the semantic work, or whether emphasis is created by a double commitment through both visual and verbal resources, or indeed whether there is some contradiction or counterpointing between the meanings committed in one mode compared with the other.

A famous example of differential commitment is Pat Hutchins's *Rosie's Walk* (1968), where the verbal mode tells a simple recount of Rosie the hen walking through the farmyard, while the visual mode commits an entire additional narrative, where a fox stalks Rosie and comes repeatedly to grief. Both stories are easily 'read' simply through the visual mode, and the slapstick misadventures of the fox are humorous in their own right, but the fact that the narrative voice ignores the entire drama of the hunt increases the humor, adds a layer of irony (Kümmerling-Meibauer 1999) and, as Margaret Meek (1988) points out, encourages an agentive role for young readers who find they know more than the narrator.

In another example, that of Anthony Browne's *Gorilla* (1983), a notable difference in commit-ment between visual and verbal ideational meaning occurs only at one particular point in the story. The narrative concerns a lonely little girl's passion for gorillas and her desire for more attention from her father. In a central sequence in the book, the verbiage states "In the night something amazing happened," committing only a very general meaning in terms of the action. A series of accompany-ing images, however, specifies that the amazing thing is that her new toy gorilla gradually grows and grows to life size, and becomes alive, until it stands looming over the foot of Hannah's bed. By choosing to leave this part of the story uncommitted in the verbal story, the child reader is free to interpret what follows – the little girl's perfect night out with the gorilla – as a dream, the result of a magic toy, or simply as what actually happened in the world of the story.

The examples given so far relate broadly to ideational meaning: to characters and actions present in one mode but absent in the other. But the advantage of a framework of meaning potential laid out according to the three metafunctions is that a much finer grained analysis is possible. First, this means noticing the degree to which any particular area of the ideational, interpersonal or textual meaning potential is differentially committed. For example, much of the humor of David McKee's *Not Now, Bernard* (1980) derives from the visual depiction of affect on the adult characters' faces, while what they say and do in the accompanying deadpan verbal text includes no attitudinal language at all. Since affect can be depicted and verbalized with equal facility, the choice to restrict commitment of this particular area of meaning potential to one mode constitutes a considered and significant choice. And it is only in respect of this particular interpersonal semantic domain that there is this glaring difference in commitment. The various interpersonal systems that constitute 'affiliation' (see Table 40.2) are by contrast fully committed both visually and verbally, ramping up the significance of this area of meaning, which is entirely relevant to the theme of this story, which implicitly comments on dysfunctional parent-child relationships.

As well as in comparing visual and verbal commitment, the framework provided in Tables 40.1 to 40.3 can be used to consider the 'couplings' between visual and verbal choices in every case where a comparable area of meaning potential is instantiated in both modes. There have been a number of very useful taxonomies of word/image relations in picturebooks posited in the literature over the years – for example, by Schwarcz (1982), Agosto (1999), and Nikolajeva and Scott (2001), all of which consider the sharing, doubling or contrasting of meanings in the two modes. These are evaluated in some detail by Batemon (2014), along with other approaches to visual/verbal analysis outside the picturebook sphere. The distinctive feature of the SFL multimodal discourse analysis outlined here is that it enables a close, stylistic examination of a text, where multiple comparisons and contrasts can be made across all the meaning systems identified in Tables 40.1–40.3. That is, rather than supposing that a single relation of likeness or difference in visual and verbal meanings will hold for any page or even the entire book, this approach readily allows for 'convergence' in couplings across modes within one metafunction but 'divergence' in another. Further than this, it allows for convergence in couplings across one pair of complementary systems (such as visual and verbal affect) and divergence in another (such as visual and verbal power or visual and verbal action). Multimodal discourse analysis thus requires a careful consideration both of commitment (Which mode is responsible for which areas of meaning?) and of coupling (Where both modalities commit meaning from corresponding systems, are the meanings more or less convergent or divergent?).

Since the image has already been discussed, the first page of *Voices in the Park* can be used as a quick example to illustrate. The verbal component, which will be referred to as 'verbiage,' comprises two parts: a heading "First Voice" above the image, and a single sentence below: "It was time to take Victoria, our pedigree labrador, and Charles, our son, for a walk." A multimodal analysis would note that the heading commits a textual meaning that is absent from the image – a prospective reference that indicates that what ensues is only one perspective on the story. The story is in fact re-told four times in the book from different points of view, each headed with the number of the 'voice.' And although the prospective and retrospective linking provided by the words *first, second, third*, and *fourth* is a meaning available solely through the verbiage, the staging of the overall story accomplished in this way is entirely convergent with the staging provided visually through different ambience and typography choices for each of the four sections of the book. In terms of story staging, then, there is a convergence of textual meaning. Similarly, on this first page there is convergence in textual couplings: the adult's red hat in the bottom right-hand corner is a textual use of color to draw attention to the character's action just as the verbiage commits the meaning of "take . . . for a walk" as the salient 'new information' in the clause (Halliday and Matthiessen 2004: 89). In this respect there is textual convergence between the modes on the opening page.

Turning to ideational meaning, it is only the image that commits meaning relating to setting and to the appearance of the characters. The verbal text does not mention the house or its grounds, nor the time of year, nor time of day, nor what the characters are wearing. Given that the visual mode is so well able to present such details of appearance and setting 'at a glance,' this is predictable in terms of each mode being used for what it does best. What the rest of the verbiage commits ideationally is an explicit identification of the characters, through their names and familial relationships – something not possible to inscribe explicitly in the visual mode. For the most part then, there is a variation in ideational commitment so as to share the semantic work between the two modalities. The one point where a visual ideational meaning is also found in the verbiage is that of the action of "taking [. . .] for a walk"; this is very understated visually, but prominent in the verbiage to balance out. This convergence is therefore one that facilitates access to meaning but does not greatly amplify the particular meaning. Overall, the sharing out of ideational work between image and verbiage renders the text very economical and accessible and might be predicted from the textual layout of the page, where the verbiage is framed off from the image (that is, in its own defined space outside the frame) rather than being 'integrated' (appearing on the image itself). Such a non-integrated layout in the textual function suggests that image and verbiage each plays a distinct role in the storytelling (Painter et al. 2013: 93).

Interpersonally we have an interesting contrast in focalization. Visually the storyworld is presented from outside the story, realized by the lack of a direct gaze between character and viewer and the lack of a shared visual perspective between them. The verbiage in the first person, however, gives us 'character focalization' from the depicted adult's point of view. This contrast is fundamental to the story, in which the subjectivity of experience is foregrounded, encouraging us to notice occasions where what we see, presented by the author-artist, varies from what we are told in the character's voice, allowing us to make judgements about that character. In this way the interplay of the two modes multiplies meaning and encourages a critical stance, which at various points in the book amusingly alerts the reader to the literary concept of the 'unreliable narrator.' As well as this divergence in terms of focalization, there is also interpersonal convergence on this page in the area of 'force': verbally the repetition of "our" hints at the self-importance of the narrator, just as the way the residence taking up so much space in the image frame emphasizes its grandeur.

It is of course important to consider patterns in commitment and coupling over the course of an entire story and to note points where such patterns are broken for particular effect, since discourse analysis is not an end in itself but has the goal of throwing light on how an author creates significance, positions us to accept values, and leads young readers to appreciate a story's 'themes.' In *Voices in the Park*, the features that discourage too close an identification with the storyworld on the first page – use of framing, long shots, and oblique angles – continue throughout the four stories, encouraging an observant, reflective stance from the viewer. Similarly, the divergence in focalization choices together with the divergence in ideational commitment found on the opening page proves to be a general pattern which brings to the fore the thematic motif of the subjectivity of point of view, and teaches young readers, humorously and non-didactically, to read symbols to provide cues to character. Patterns are also broken at key moments: in particular, in the final story of the quartet, voiced by the optimistic and less constrained child, there is an early moment where interpersonal patterns in the book are disrupted. Instead of obliquely angled ('detached') long shots, the reader gets a face-to-face ('involved') view in close-up, and the pattern of divergence in focalization is broken as the depicted adult gazes directly down at the reader, putting us visually in the shoes of the child narrator. Readers are set up in this way to accept the first-person voice of the final story, the 'fourth voice' of the optimistic, self-confident, and generous child, as the one whose values we are to align with.

Conclusion

Picturebook narratives are bi-modal texts which ideally function to entertain their readers, inculcate in them social values, and introduce them to literary ways of taking meaning. To understand better how this is achieved in any particular case, this chapter has outlined a discourse-analytic framework in which both visual and verbal meaning systems are seen in metafunctional terms. That is, each semiotic is viewed in terms of three domains of meaning: the ideational (relating to action, character, and setting), the interpersonal (relating to reader-author and character-character affiliations and feelings), and textual (relating to the staging and organization of all the meanings). Within each of these domains, a number of specific individual visual and verbal systems can be identified. Using the concepts of commitment and coupling then allows us to consider in a very systematic way the contributions of each semiotic to the construction of any story and the potentially varied nature of the interplay between them.

References

Agosto, Denise E. (1999) "One and Inseparable: Interdependent Storytelling in Picture Storybooks," *Children's Literature in Education* 30.4: 267–80.

Albers, Peggy (2008) "Theorising Visual Representation in Children's Literature," *Journal of Literacy Research* 40.2: 163–200.

Bateman, John A. (2014) *A Critical Introduction to the Visual/Verbal Divide*, London: Routledge.

Browne, Anthony (1983) *Gorilla*, London: Walker.

Browne, Anthony (1998) *Voices in the Park*, London: Doubleday.

Doonan, Jane (1993) *Looking at Pictures in Picture Books*, Stroud: Thimble Press.

Doonan, Jane (1999) "Drawing Out Ideas: A Second Decade of the Work of Anthony Browne," *The Lion and the Unicorn* 23: 30–56.

Halliday, M.A.K. (2002) *Linguistic Studies of Text and Discourse, vol. 2, The Collected Works*, ed. Jonathan J. Webster, London and New York: Continuum.

Halliday, M.A.K., and Matthiessen, Christian M.I.M. (2004) *Introduction to Functional Grammar*, 3rd ed., London: Arnold.

Hutchins, Pat (1968) *Rosie's Walk*, London: Bodley Head.

Kress, Gunther, and van Leeuwen, Theo (2006) *Reading Images: The Grammar of Visual Design*, 2nd ed., London: Routledge.

Kümmerling-Meibauer, Bettina (1999) "Metalinguistic Awareness and the Child's Developing Concept of Irony: The Relationship Between Pictures and Text in Ironic Picture Books," *The Lion and the Unicorn* 23.2: 157–183.

Lewis, David (2001) *Reading Contemporary Picturebooks: Picturing Text*, London: RoutledgeFalmer.

McKee, David (2004) *Not Now Bernard*, London: Andersen Press (first published 1980).

Martin, J. R. (2009) "Boomer Dreaming: The Texture of Re-colonisation in a Lifestyle Magazine," in Gail Forey and Geoff Thompson (eds) *Text-Type and Texture*, London: Equinox, 252–284.

Martin, J. R., and Rose, David (2007) *Working with Discourse: Meaning Beyond the Clause*, London and New York: Continuum.

Meek, Margaret (1988) *How Texts Teach What Readers Learn*, South Woodchester: Thimble Press.

Moya-Guijarro, A. Jesús (2014) *A Multimodal Analysis of Picture Books for Children. A Systemic Functional Approach*, Sheffield: Equinox.

Nikolajeva, Maria, and Scott, Carole (2001) *How Picturebooks Work*, New York: Garland.

Painter, Clare (2007) "Children's Picture Book Narratives: Reading Sequences of Images," in Anne McCabe, Mick O'Donnell, and Rachel Whittaker (eds) *Advances in Language and Education*, London and New York: Continuum, 40–59.

Painter, Clare (2008) "The Role of Colour in Children's Picture Books: Choices in AMBIENCE," in Len Unsworth (ed.) *New Literacies and the English Curriculum: Multimodal Perspectives*, London and New York: Continuum, 89–111.

Painter, Clare, Martin, J. R., and Unsworth, Len (2013) *Reading Visual Narratives: Image Analysis of Children's Picture Books*, Sheffield: Equinox.

Schwarcz, Joseph H. (1982) *Ways of the Illustrator: Visual Communication in Children's Literature*, Chicago: American Library Association.

Serafini, Frank (2010) "Reading Multimodal Texts: Perceptual, Structural and Ideological Perspectives," *Children's Literature in Education* 41: 85–104.

Sipe, Lawrence (2010) "The Art of the Picturebook," in Shelby A. Wolf, Karen Coats, Patricia Enciso, and Christine Jenkins (eds) *Handbook of Research in Children's and Young Adult Literature*, New York: Routledge, 238–251.

Unsworth, Len, and Ortigas, Olondriz (2008) "Exploring the Narrative Art of David Wiesner: Using a Grammar of Visual Design and Learning Experiences on the World Wide Web," *L1 Educational Studies of Language and Literature* 8.3: 1–21.

41

ART HISTORY AND THE PICTUREBOOK

Marilynn Olson

In her study *American Picturebooks from Noah's Ark to the Beast Within* (1976), Barbara Bader says of the late nineteenth century that suddenly picturebooks "became artistic" (3). The technological improvements that made possible mass distribution of good quality color illustrations for children's books, as well as fine art and natural science reproductions, created a milestone. Thus, although art and narrative have been put together since ancient times, the nineteenth century is an expedient moment to begin a brief discussion of the relation of the picturebook to art history. Picturebook illustration is inevitably influenced by the fashion or movements in art of the time in which it is executed (de Bodt 2010: 19). As part of the field of illustration and graphic arts, it shares a similar though not identical relation to art history. Picturebooks continue to be influenced by the artistic mode of caricature, which historically unites them with modernist trends in art; they also visually quote from, as well as parody, art works of the past and present. The relation of picturebooks to art, a varied and layered connection, suggests that the study of the picturebook should interest art historians and that the barriers between the forms of art purveyed to the public in this visual century should be questioned.

Picturebook art reflects dominant art movements of its time

At the turn of the century, the popularity of the "total design" movements such as Arts and Crafts and Art Nouveau, which emphasized the unification of the fonts, borders, and images of a page into a balanced composition, heightened the sophistication of the illustrated book and led to Art Nouveau being a style of choice in early twentieth-century children's books. The internationalization of art at the end of the nineteenth century meant improvements in book design from one country were influential in another. Albert Lemmens and Serge Stommels mention, for example, the influence of the German magazines *Pan* and *Jugend* (Youth) and the Russian journal *Mir iskusstva* (World of Art) on this generation (2009: 24; see also Petrov 1998). The picturebooks published by Edmund Evans in England, featuring Randolph Caldecott, Kate Greenaway, and Walter Crane, were widely known (Engen 1976; Lundin 2001; Lemmens and Stommels 2009). Lothar Meggendorfer, whose books with moving pieces were published in Germany but also distributed in England and America, was an influence on the revival of the artists' book in the late twentieth century (Sendak 1988: 51–60).

The French painter Maurice Boutet de Monvel, who also designed his own pages and lettering and experimented with lithography methods, revolutionized American ideas about graphic design as well as initiating serious discussion of how color may emotionally enhance a text; this influence was conveyed, as other innovations in picturebook design would be, with the help of international traveling museum exhibitions (Bader 1976: 4; see also Brooklyn exhibition catalogue). Examples of artistic experimentation with mutually influential combinations of words and text should also include the experiments of Édouard Manet and Dante Gabriel Rossetti, who variously combined poetry with pictures in an attempt to communicate to more than one sense at once (Olson 2012: 73; Olson 2015: 36–40). Rossetti's work (which was related to his editing of the work of William Blake) contributed to the Arts and Crafts movement's interest in fine art printing, and Manet's to the conception of the artists' book.

The presence of profusely illustrated nursery books starting at the end of the nineteenth century influenced the artists who grew up within the period, in much the same way that we see the illustrated newspapers and mass market Japanese prints influencing the Parisian avant-garde. Victoria Ford Smith explains that such a result was expected by late nineteenth-century art critics, who recognized the potential effect of the wide dissemination among children of good printing and talented illustration (2015: 161).

The end of the nineteenth century, as represented, for example, at the 1900 Paris Exposition, also included a large number of realistic paintings from many countries involving peasant life and national themes. Some of these were influenced by Romantic ideas of the purity of rural life, some influenced by a socialist desire to portray the oppressed, others to support political identity (Dumas in Rosenblum et al. 2000: 282); their influence was felt in the new century. Lemmens and Stommels point to the influence of the artists of the Wanderer group on socialist realism in the thirties and the seminal contribution of the neo-Russian Viktor Vasnetsou, who brought Russian folklore into modern graphic design (2009: 40–45). The Nordic National Romantic Movement was active at the turn of the century, and elements of that ideology, which covered a broad range of styles and subject matter, might be found in the familiar early twentieth-century picturebooks by Elsa Beskow and Maj Lindman. Indeed, in children's picturebooks the use of folkloric motifs, stereotypically regional landscapes, simple life, and national costumes are a recurrent phenomenon. The Romantic association of childhood with nature and rural environments, and the pedagogic intention to teach geography or to convey culture through traditional tales underlies its enduring popularity. Roger Mello's *Carvoeirinhos* (The Little Charcoal Maker 2009) and Kent Monkman's illustrations to *A Coyote Columbus Story* (2002) by Thomas King point to the innovation still possible within this form.

Caricature

The work of English painter and engraver William Hogarth is important both for its movement (via sequential images) in the direction of the later picturebook ideal and because his satiric sequences, arguably the first English popular art, set the tone and form for nineteenth-century illustration (Alderson 1986: 39–45; Johnson 2003: 434–437). Although the satiric thrust of children's book illustrations is milder than Hogarth's, they frequently share the intention to produce reformative results through vigorous and humorous line drawing. His later admirer James Gillray contributed parody of Academic paintings to the form (Varnedoe and Gopnik 1990: 110), a mode popularized again in late twentieth-century children's books.

In many cases, prominent caricaturists and children's illustrators were the same people. J.J. Grandville and George Cruikshank created both political and social satire as well as books for children, a combination that was usual throughout the century, as Wilhelm Busch (*Max and Moritz* 1865), Randolph Caldecott, Walter Crane, Richard Doyle, Eduard Ile, Lothar Meggendorfer, John Tenniel (Lewis Carroll's *Alice* books 1865, 1871), and Florence Upton (the Golliwogg books 1895–1909) drew caricatures for an adult audience as well as creating notable children's book illustrations (Olson 2015: 31–35). Painters of this generation submitted canvasses to Academy showings while contributing to *Punch* (de Bodt 2010: 29). Randolph Caldecott's toybook *The Great Panjandrum Himself* (1885), shows an appeal to both audiences by interpreting the nonsensical panjandrum as a satirically conceived academic (Figure 41.1). Beatrix Potter's masterful watercolors of little animals were influenced by natural science reproductions and nature, but she was also influenced by Caldecott and *Punch* cartoons (Taylor et al. 1995: 45–46).

In art history, caricatures conveyed in line drawings can be seen as harbingers of modernism (Varnedoe and Gopnik 1990: 113–150). Although the figures and settings are often naturalistic, though distorted, the artist's hand makes them unmistakably subjective. There is no effort to maintain illusion of reality on the page, and they are an obvious personal and partial version of whatever truth is being conveyed, simplified to its salient features. As a mode of art common to picturebooks, it points up artificial barriers between scholarly fields of study.

The connection of political satirists and caricaturists with children's picturebooks is a notable feature of twentieth-century publishing. Internationally known picturebooks by Tove Jansson, Dr. Seuss, Peter Sís, Walter Trier, and Tomi Ungerer, for example, were the work of author/illustrators who brought their (different) satiric stances and caricature into mainstream work for young children, which if not specifically attacking the high art of the Academy or oppressive government regimes, was, at least, the enemy of the pompous, the conformist, and the authoritarian (see Nel 2004: 39–88 for Seuss; Neuner-Warthorst 2014 for Trier). Walt Disney, whose first art education involved copying political cartoons from a rural newspaper and who later also contributed propaganda to the war

Figure 41.1 Cover of Randolph Caldecott's *The Great Panjandrum Himself*. London: George Routledge & Sons, n.d. [1885].

Private collection of Marilynn Olson.

effort, became arguably the most recognizable artist of the twentieth century, with many ties to the high art world (Johnson 2003: 741–742; Girveau 2007).

In fact, a work such as Wilhelm Busch's *Max und Moritz* (1865), an ancestor of some distinguished children's books of the twentieth century, is also discussed as a forerunner of the comic strip, a sequential form that is infrequently paired with children's literature in the West, although more often blended in Japan (Varnedoe and Gopnik 1990: 154). The mixture of high and low forms is one of the qualities fundamental to modernism (and later art), and one subject to adverse criticism in children's literature of the early twentieth century. As Bader (1976) and others note, the flat, poster-like look of the W.W. Denslow illustrations to the original Oz books (1900–1920) by L. Frank Baum were one of the reasons that the popular series was not admitted to American libraries, although many later critics value them. Bader identifies this as the result of "the sway of the naturalistic aesthetic" (7). A separation between graphic novels and picturebooks (which is bridged in the works of Neil Gaiman and Dave McKean, for example), as well as comics and picturebook illustration, has been encouraged by gatekeepers of culture on either side of the divides: critics, prize committees, readers, and librarians (McCloud 1994: 201). The commonalties between the various art forms have yet to be generally recognized among scholars.

Art history and graphic or illustrative art

Saskia de Bodt, in her study *Van Poe tot Pooh* (2010), laments the lack of consideration given to illustration in art history scholarship. The reason, she states, is that illustration is tied to the text, and the ideal in art is autonomy. This standard applies to many other uses of art in everyday life. And yet to some extent this argument is one that varies from generation to generation. For example, artistic philosophy enjoining the inter-connection of art and craft encouraged the late nineteenth-century artist to feel that the arts should make all elements of daily life more beautiful and that craftwork would, in turn, enrich the art itself. The Arts and Crafts movement, the Vienna Workshops, the Constructivists, and Bauhaus directly influenced children's book illustration. For example, Holger Fischer and Gudrun Stenzel note that Hilde Krüger, who illustrated *Der Widiwondelwald* (The Widi-wondel Forest 1924), Lily Hildebrandt, and Tom Seidmann-Freud, all avant-garde picturebook creators, were also designers trained in arts and crafts (Fischer and Stenzel 1986: 96; Brooklyn Museum 1926). However, the idea that commercial posters, children's books, and theater designs might be seriously undertaken by artists also means that the connection of the fine arts with commercial art is increasingly complex in the following century. From the first, there were a number of highly valued twentieth-century children's books created by painters who were also producers of graphic work for advertising agencies, government propaganda, or both. El Lissitzky, Fernand Léger (who taught the American illustrator Clement Hurd), Leo Lionni, Kurt Schwitters, Sándor Bortnyik, and Bruno Munari were associated, to some extent, with the first or second Futurist movements, and all produced both advertising designs and children's book illustrations (Varnedoe and Gopnik 1990: 231–268; Albert 2015). William Nicholson, a just-modern English painter whose work in the 1920s was important to the evolution of picturebooks, also was part of the fin-de-siècle poster craze. Although avant-garde experimentation with words had begun earlier, exhibitions of constructivist posters from Russia in the 1920s influenced both children's books *and* advertising (Varnedoe and Gopnik 1990: 54–58; Steiner 1999; Lemmens and Stommels 2009: 166–118; Bader 1976: 355–356).

Bruno Munari, whose estimable career embraced many forms of artistic endeavor, discussed the designer as an artist who wants to have an audience: "The artist has to regain the modesty he had when art was just a trade, and instead of despising the very public he is trying to interest he must discover its needs and make contact with it again" (1966: 13). It is also possible for an artist, such as Kurt Schwitters, to embody ambivalence toward commercial culture as an integral part of his artistic vision. To be both appalled by and have a kind of affection for popular culture is a possibility (Varnedoe and Gopnik 1990: 63–67).

The interest in illustration as an art historical study, however, appears more difficult to engage when the work is for children. If art historians approach sequential art, they are almost entirely interested in work for adult audiences rather than for children, in spite of the substantial links between picturebooks and other high art forms. Martin Roman Deppner, for example, draws important parallels between abstract art, minimal art, conceptual art, and Pop Art and the conceptual processes necessary to present everyday objects abstractly in picturebooks for the youngest child: "there is a close link between the basic design presented in modern art on the one hand, and the educational issues raised by Fröbel and Piaget on the other" (2011: 67). This relation was evidently recognized by Schwitters when he borrowed a picturebook image in his "Cherry" montage of 1921 (68).

Jens Thiele attributes some of the neglect of or disdain for picturebooks as an area of art historical study to the perception that a picturebook illustrator is burdened with expectations about his/her audience (2013: 39). If appropriate childhood reading is defined as gentle and safe, for example, there is a predisposition on the part of many scholars to go instead to edgier venues. This expectation may be the result of ignorance of the range of art possible within the genre, or a questionable prejudice against simplicity. Then, too, actual art training may exaggerate the difference between images intended for adult and child audiences. The cultural context of children's stories may be imparted in such a way that students learn to produce only pictures in a simple, naïve, and cheerful style, with fantastic imagery and funny animals (39). Some of the most critically esteemed work in children's literature required a period of time (or a culture) in which the rules for the picturebook were relatively free and welcoming of innovation, childhood was interpreted in a way that opened picturebooks to a wide variety of content, or there was a publisher willing to encourage avant-garde experimentation, perhaps for a crossover adult/child audience.

For some revolutionary artists, however, it was the educative function of children's books that made it possible for this crossover to occur without compromising ideals. Children could be seen as a force to destroy the mistakes of the past and as a fundamental link in establishing a new world order (Higonnet 2009: 86–87, 91–92). Children also could be perceived as receptive to the dynamism and promise of new technology and new creative ways of thinking. Munari's and Lissitzky's interest in pedagogical approaches led to experiments with the form of interactive and readerly books. Both had messages that could benefit from the techniques of making a strong, direct impression on the viewer that they had developed in other fields.

The license to make the picturebook a vehicle for artistic innovation, such as we see in Russia, and in France and the United States after the First World War, was the result of unprecedented editorial control over children's materials at a time when the picturebook genre was being introduced. Editors such as May Massee, who published Mary Liddell's Russian-influenced *Little Machinery* in 1926, for example, were part of a group of American women librarians, publishers, and booksellers who were inventing a form and looking abroad to encourage the highest standards of art in works for children (Eddy 2006: 101–105; Marcus 2008: 94–96; Steiner 2015: 199; for Sweden, see Druker 2008; for the Netherlands, see de Bodt 2015). The French publisher, NRL, which opened a children's department in 1919, was reflecting the avant-garde milieu represented on its adult list (Beckett 2015: 218). A Russian editor, such as editor/illustrator Vladimir Lebedev, was able to encourage the avant-garde spirit of his own work in the Constructivist/Art Deco images that made the late twenties the golden age of illustration (Lemmens and Stommels 2009: 112–115). This brief burst of freedom before the repression of the 1930s was made possible because Lenin and the Russian government believed in and supported the art; Arkady Ippolitov notes that the "phenomenon [. . .] combined both ideological and artistic renewal" (in Rothenstein and Budashevskaya 2013: 20). Illustrators draw upon the successful innovations and styles of previous work, and the picturebooks of the twenties shared this quality. The Russian style was, for example, a nosegay of earlier styles: Futurism, Dada, Suprematism, Constructivism/Art Deco. But the overall impression, the innovative page layouts and flat spaces with simplified modern fonts, set a standard that was both recognized as innovative at the time and, in its turn, derided as other expectations replaced it.

It is the nature of illustration to call on varying artistic styles for varying purposes (Nodelman 1988: 78–79). The ability to view fine art from any era and images from earlier picturebooks has given the illustrators who grew up with personal computers a great variety of resources. Contemporary illustrators typically list many artistic influences and many image sources for specific books, as well as such things as story movement associated with film-making. The work of American illustrator Maurice Sendak, whose early work predated the computer, contains style elements from Randolph Caldecott, Samuel Palmer, Marc Chagall, Henri Rousseau, William Blake, William Nicholson, Philipp Otto Runge, Wilhelm Busch, and comic artist Winsor McKay, as well as other artists used less frequently (Bader 1976: 498; Maguire 2009: 13–63; Deppner 2011: 58). Contemporary Australian illustrator Shaun Tan's list is perhaps twice as long. Both illustrators have been widely praised and studied because of their complexity and their innovation; the quotation of historic and contemporary artistic styles has been valued as part of that complexity. This art historical borrowing, however, does not always win approval.

In a conservative view, popular art is often accused of trivializing the "true culture" it draws on (Varnedoe and Gopnik 1990: 17). Children's picturebook illustration is a context within which the language of many artistic styles is utilized, and often for a purpose different from that intended by the original art movement. As Nodelman points out, we might be reminded of the experimental nature of impressionism when we see it quoted within a picturebook, but we might also see it as a safe and comforting place quite different from our own (1988: 88–90). Sometimes such utilization is trivial. But sometimes the intention of the illustrator may appear to approximate that of the original style. For example, when artists use newspaper collage in children's book illustration, they might be relishing the scroungy look that opens up the often conservative world of children's literature, enjoying both the high and low art involved in roughly the way the Cubists did. Ezra Jack Keats, whose picturebooks were both innovative in the use of collage, as well as innovative in featuring African American children on city streets, might reasonably fall within this category. Wolf Erlbruch, whose work for children sometimes takes on edgy subject matter, might also be seen as within this spirit (Thiele 2013: 40). The welcoming of pastiche in children's picturebooks and the introduction of quotation from a distinct set of artistic styles in the late twentieth and early twenty-first centuries is linked to a second historic art revolution in the genre.

The 1960s and 1970s

The social and educational revolutions of the 1960s and 1970s changed the picturebook in ways that are still evident. An allied art form, the artists' book, was reintroduced in the early 1960s (Beckett 2012: 19–80). Artists' books usually are intended for an adult audience, but in their twentieth-century iteration they also were concerned with educating children (Dehò 2007; de Bodt 2015; Masaki 2010; Scott 2014). The experiments of Bruno Munari and (later) his admirer Katsumi Komagata with texture, translucent paper, differing page sizes, and paper-cutting of the pages, for example, were meant to change the way children learn about art and the world, as well as narrative (Beckett 2012: 53).

The reassessment of the capabilities of children suggested by the artists' book experiments was reflected in other changes in picturebook publishing in the 1960s. For example, Mabel George, editor at Oxford University Press, pioneered improved color printing processes that could convey brushwork like that of abstract expressionist Brian Wildsmith, whose *ABC* (1962) both startled and was a critical success (Salisbury and Styles 2012: 32). French publisher Robert Delpire, rejecting contemporary children's books, initiated a renewal of the form, which was followed by the better known innovations of publishers Harlin Quist and François Ruy-Vidal, marketed in France and the United States (Beckett 2015: 226–232). The strange and mysterious pictures by Swiss artist Étienne Delessert, who illustrated Eugène Ionesco's unconventional *Conte no. 1* (Story Number 1 1968) and *Conte no. 2* (Story Number 2 1970) for Harlin Quist, assumed that children were able to deal with artistic experiments, pioneering greater freedom for the illustrators that followed him. As Nicholas

Day points out, the books "busted the child-lock off the picture book genre" (2012). The subsequent editorial decision to work only with avant-garde artists who had not previously illustrated children's books made the elements of Surrealism, Dada, and Pop Art familiar to this audience. The use of these forms of figurative art in adult artistic circles can be seen as a reaction to the varieties of abstract art present in mid-century (Kümmerling-Meibauer 2015: 243). In picturebook illustration, which had witnessed little abstraction, it was practical for narratives, since the illustrations were recognizable, as well as introducing a fantastic, dreamlike way of looking at reality. The use of quotations from the works of these painters, as well as mass market comics, ushered in an era of postmodern pastiche and parody.

Pop Art, as Kümmerling-Meibauer and Jörg Meibauer define it,

> is characterized by a permanent transgression of boundaries, for example (1) the shift between fine art and popular art/culture, (2) the contrast between original artwork and reproduction; (3) the revitalization of the European avant-garde, such as Surrealism and Dada, on the one hand, and (4) the indebtedness to the codes and technical processes of mass media on the other hand.
>
> *2013: 23–24*

They point to its use of already existing material, evoking "innovative matters of perception" and "criticism of modern society, politics, and culture" (2013: 24). Although the content of the Pop Art picturebooks was censored, particularly in the United States, the agenda of Pop Art in several ways appears to be similar in intent to the work being carried out by illustrators of picturebooks, who already borrowed the fine art styles of the past, although the mid-century comics or other mass culture elements were new. Caricature, present since the early nineteenth century, provided a humorous outlook on institutions and life, sometimes with defiance. The distinctive fonts, layouts, and page movement of fine quality picturebooks often had the sophistication familiar in mass culture advertisements (being parodied in Pop Art) because they were sometimes designed by the same artists. Two aspects of picturebook art that distinctively changed because of the influence of the Pop Art movement, however, are the abundance of picturebooks that parodied and quoted humorously from iconic artwork and the enthusiastic use of Surrealism and Dada in picturebook illustration (Kümmerling-Meibauer 2015: 263; Kümmerling-Meibauer and Meibauer 2013: 40).

As Beckett and others have noted, highly esteemed picturebook illustrators such as Mitsumasa Anno, Anthony Browne, Etienne Delessert, Leo and Diane Dillon, Fam Ekman, Piet Grobler, Susan Guevara, Dav Pilkey, Yvan Pommaux, and Chris Van Allsburg, among many others, have used iconic works, many of them from the Parisian avant-garde of the fin-de-siècle, in playful and parodic ways (for example, Rosenberg 1999; Beckett 2001: 175–195, 2010: 83–100, 2012: 147–208; Olson 2012: 54–56, 150–153). Beckett makes the point that children who first read these books in the 1990s were comfortable with parody as a form (2001: 176). Moreover, the mass culture/advertising world around them had made some paintings, such as the *Mona Lisa*, the *Scream*, and *American Gothic*, into icons familiar to everyone, usually in playful ways. What might in the Pop Art movement have been taken as a rebellion, however, is usually quoted affectionately in children's picturebooks.

The use of the surreal in contemporary children's picturebooks is a yet more widespread phenomenon, and its definition and intention are much looser than the art movement that inspired it, as well as familiar from advertising and other mass culture uses. Johnson, by noting that René Magritte (and Hieronymus Bosch, whom he admired) both produced images that had to be explained, may give insight into their attractiveness to artists actively involved in telling stories (Johnson 2003: 670). The use of images from Marc Chagall and Henri Rousseau (who were not Surrealists but whose work is often described in that way), however, also may be a reflection of the popular affection for the *Douanier*'s jungles or the celebratory mood of many later Chagalls. Because of the alignment of picturebook surrealism with very conventional ideas about childhood being an entirely different world from adulthood, Surrealism is popular rather than radical in children's picturebooks. In practice, as Phil Nel (2015) has suggested, it may be experienced quite differently by children than by adults.

Critical acceptance of wordless or nearly wordless picturebooks in the twenty-first century seems to indicate that the relation of the visual to literary narrative can change. The pleasure of designing a picturebook may be increased by the ability to use it for self-expression, although the reluctance of some artists to admit that children constitute a large part of their audience suggests that the art historians, too, may continue to shy away from this aspect of the genre (Salisbury 2008: 36–38). It may be that the computer age has increased the value of artwork that shows evidence of a complex drawing process, an echo of a similar cachet given to traditional crafts in the late nineteenth century, and an encouragement to art education for children (Salisbury (2008: 35–36). The works of Brian Selznick, Raul Colón, or Shaun Tan, for example, emphasize laborious handwork as well as highly sophisticated technique. That is, there is currently reason to suppose that artists can find the medium a "testing ground for new visual forms and altered narrative style," in the way that Thiele suggests (2013: 39). Paul Johnson has noted that the twentieth century, although it did not provide young people with as much instruction in drawing as the previous one, provided an unprecedented amount of instruction in art history (2003: 747). Children's picturebooks give children familiarity with artists and artistic language. Since many will find that gallery art reminds them of their picturebooks, a rapprochement between picturebooks and art historians may yet occur.

References

Albert, Samuel (2015) "Sándor Bortnyik and an Interwar Hungarian Children's Book," in Elina Druker and Bettina Kümmerling-Meibauer (eds) *Children's Literature and the Avant-Garde*, Amsterdam: John Benjamins, 65–88.

Alderson, Brian (1986) *Sing a Song for Sixpence: the English Picture-Book Tradition and Randolph Caldecott*, Cambridge: Cambridge University Press and the British Library Board.

Bader, Barbara (1976) *American Picturebooks from Noah's Ark to The Beast Within*, New York: Macmillan.

Baum, L. Frank (1900) *The Wonderful Wizard of Oz*, illus. W.W. Denslow, Chicago: Rand McNally.

Beckett, Sandra L. (2001) "Parodic Play with Paintings in Picture Books," *Children's Literature* 29: 175–195.

Beckett, Sandra L. (2010) "Artistic Allusions in Picturebooks," in Teresa Colomer, Bettina Kümmerling-Meibauer, and Cecilia Silva-Díaz (eds) *New Directions in Picturebook Research*, New York: Routledge, 83–98.

Beckett, Sandra L. (2012) *Crossover Picturebooks: A Genre for All Ages*, New York: Routledge.

Beckett, Sandra L. (2015) "Manifestations of the Avant-Garde and its Legacy in French Children's Literature," in Elina Druker and Bettina Kümmerling-Meibauer (eds) *Children's Literature and the Avant-Garde*, Amsterdam: John Benjamins, 215–240.

Brooklyn Museum (1926) *Exhibit of Art for Children From European Children's Books*, www.artic.edu/sites/default/files/libraries/pubs/1926/AIC1926ArtForChildren_comb.pdf (accessed January 7, 2016).

Busch, Wilhelm (1865) *Max und Moritz*, Munich: Braun & Schneider, www.childrens-booksonline.org/max_undmoritz/index.htm (accessed March 29, 2016).

Caldecott, Randolph (1885) *The Great Panjandrum Himself*, London: George Routledge & Sons, n.d.

Carroll, Lewis (1946) *Alice's Adventures in Wonderland*, illus. John Tenniel, New York: Random House (first published 1865).

Carroll, Lewis (1946) *Through the Looking-Glass and What Alice Found There*, illus. John Tenniel, New York: Random House (first published 1871).

Day, Nicholas (2012) "The Cow Jumped Over the Moon?! Why Children Love Absurdism," www.slate.com/articles/arts/family/2012/12/eugene_ionesco_and_other_absurdist_children_s_loose March 29, 2016).

de Bodt, Saskia (2010) *Van Poe tot Pooh*, Zwolle: Uitgeverij d'jonge Hond.

de Bodt, Saskia (2015) *De verbeelders: Nederlandse boekillustratie in de twintigste eeuw*, Nijmegen: Vantilt.

Dehò, Valerio et al. (2007) *Children's Corner: Artists' Books for Children*, Milan: Edizione Corraini.

Deppner, Roman Martin (2011) "Parallel Reception of the Fundamental: Basic Design in Picturebooks and Modern Art," in Bettina Kümmerling-Meibauer (ed.) *Emergent Literacy: Children's Books from 0 to 3*, Amsterdam: John Benjamins, 55–74.

Druker, Elina (2008) *Modernismens billeder: Den moderna bilderboken i Norden*, Stockholm: Makadam.

Eddy, Jacalyn (2006) *Bookwomen: Creating an Empire in Children's Book Publishing 1919–1939*, Madison: University of Wisconsin Press.

Engen, Rodney K. (1976) *Randolph Caldecott: Lord of the Nursery*, London: Oresko.

Fischer, Holger, and Stenzel, Gudrun (1986) "Von suprematischen Erzählungen zum Widiwondelwald. Bilderbücher im Spiegel künstlerischer Strömungen der 20er Jahre," in Dieter Hoffmann and Jens Thiele (eds) *Künstler illustrierten Bilderbücher*, Oldenburg: BIS, 86–97.

Girveau, Bruno (2007) *Once Upon a Time – Walt Disney: the Sources of Inspiration for the Disney Studios*, Munich: Prestel.

Higonnet, Margaret (2009) "Modernism and Childhood: Violence and Renovation," *Comparatist* 33: 86–108.

Hoffmann, Heinrich (1845) *Der Struwwelpeter*, Frankfurt: Literarische Verlagsanstalt.

Ionesco, Eugène (1968) *Conte numéro 1, pour enfants de moins trois ans*, illus. Étienne Delessert, Paris: Harlin Quist [*Story Number 1, for Children Under Three Years of Age*, New York: Harlin Quist, 1968].

Ionesco, Eugène (1970) *Conte numéro 2*, illus. Étienne Delessert, Paris: Harlin Qvist and François Ruy-Vidal [*Story Number 2*, New York: Harlin Quist, 1970].

Johnson, Paul (2003) *Art: A New History*, New York: HarperCollins.

King, Thomas (2002) *A Coyote Columbus Story*, illus. William Kent Monkman, Toronto: Groundwood.

Krüger, Hilde (1924) *Der Widiwondelwald*, Berlin: J.H.W. Dietz Verlag.

Kümmerling-Meibauer, Bettina (2015) "Just What Is It That Makes Pop Art Picturebooks So Different, So Appealing," in Elina Druker and Bettina Kümmerling-Meibauer (eds) *Children's Literature and the Avant-Garde*, Amsterdam: John Benjamins, 241–265.

Kümmerling-Meibauer, Bettina, and Meibauer, Jörg (2013) "On the Strangeness of Pop Art Picturebooks: Pictures, Texts, Paratexts," in Evelyn Arizpe, Maureen Farrell, and Julie McAdam (eds) *Picturebooks: Beyond the Borders of Art, Narrative and Culture*, New York: Routledge, 23–41.

Lemmens, Albert, and Stommels, Serge (2009) *Russian Artists and the Children's Book, 1890–1992*, Nijmegen: LS.

Liddell, Mary (1926) *Little Machinery*, Garden City, NY: Doubleday, Page.

Lundin, Anne (2001) *Victorian Horizons: The Reception of the Picture Books of Walter Crane, Randolph Caldecott, and Kate Greenaway*, Lanham, MD: Children's Literature Association and Scarecrow.

Maguire, Gregory (2009) *Making Mischief*, New York: HarperCollins.

McCloud, Scott (1994) *Understanding Comics: The Invisible Art*, New York: HarperPerennial.

Marcus, Leonard (2008) *Minders of Make-Believe: Idealists, Entrepreneurs, and the Shaping of American Children's Literature*, New York: Houghton Mifflin.

Masaki, Tomoko (2010) "A Strawberry? Or the Planet? Children's Aesthetic Response to the Picturebook *Strawberries* by Susumi Shingu, Moving Art Sculptor," in Teresa Colomer, Bettina Kümmerling-Meibauer, and Cecilia Silva-Díaz (eds) *New Directions in Picturebook Research*, New York: Routledge, 151–163.

Mello, Roger (2009) *Carvoeirinhos*, Sao Paulo: Companhia dos Letrinhas.

Munari, Bruno (1966) *Design as Art*, trans. Patrick Creagh, London: Penguin.

Nel, Philip (2004) *Dr. Seuss: American Icon*, New York: Continuum.

Nel, Philip (2015) "Surrealism for Children: Paradoxes and Possibilities," in Elina Druker and Bettina Kümmerling-Meibauer (eds) *Children's Literature and the European Avant-Garde*, Amsterdam: John Benjamins, 267–284.

Neuner-Warthorst, Antje (2014) *Walter Trier: Eine Bilderbuchkarriere*, Berlin: Nicolai.

Nodelman, Perry (1988) *Words about Pictures: The Narrative Art of Children's Picture Books*, Athens: University of Georgia Press.

Olson, Marilynn (2012) *Children's Culture and the Avant-Garde: Painting in Paris 1890–1915*, New York: Routledge.

Olson, Marilynn (2015) "John Ruskin and the Mutual Influences of Children's Literature and the Avant-Garde," in Elina Druker and Bettina Kümmerling-Meibauer (eds) *Children's Literature and the Avant-Garde*, Amsterdam: John Benjamins, 19–44.

Petrov, Vsevolod (1998) *Russian Art Nouveau: The World of Art and Diaghilev's Painters*, ed. Irina Kharitonova, trans. Arthur Shkarovsky-Raffe, Bournemouth, UK: Parkstone.

Rosenberg, Teya (1999) "The Inspirations and Resonances of Art and Art History in *Pish Posh, Said Hieronymus Bosch* and *When Cats Dream*," *Language and Literacy* 1.2 ejournals.library.ualberta.ca/index.php/langandlit/search (accessed March 29, 2016).

Rosenblum, Robert, Stevens, Maryanne, and Dumas, Ann (eds) (2000) *1900: Art at the Crossroads*, London and New York: Abrams.

Rothenstein, Julian, and Budashevskaya, Olga (2013) *Inside the Rainbow: Russian Children's Literature 1920–1935: Beautiful Books, Terrible Times*, London: Redstone.

Salisbury, Martin (2008) "The Artist and the Postmodern Picturebook," in Lawrence R. Sipe and Sylvia Pantaleo (eds) *Postmodern Picturebooks: Play, Parody, and Self-Referentiality*, New York and London: Routledge, 22–40.

Salisbury, Martin, and Styles, Morag (2012) *Children's Picturebooks: The Art of Visual Storytelling*, London: Lawrence King.

Scott, Carole (2014) "Artists' Books, Altered Books, and Picturebooks," in Bettina Kümmerling-Meibauer (ed.) *Picturebooks: Representation and Narration*, New York: Routledge, 37–52.

Sendak, Maurice (1988) *Caldecott & Co.: Notes on Books & Pictures*, New York: Farrar, Straus and Giroux.

Smith, Virginia Ford (2015) "Art Critics in the Cradle: Fin-de-Siècle Painting Books and the Move to Modernism," *Children's Literature* 43: 161–181.

Steiner, Evgeny (1999) *Stories for Little Comrades: Revolutionary Artists and the Making of Early Soviet Children's Books*, trans. Jane Ann Miller, Seattle: University of Washington Press.

Steiner, Evgeny (2015) "Mirror Images: On Soviet-Western Reflections in Children's Books of the 1920s and 1930s," in Elina Druker and Bettina Kümmerling-Meibauer (eds) *Children's Literature and the Avant-Garde*, Amsterdam: John Benjamins, 189–213.

Taylor, Judy, Whalley, Joyce Irene, Stevenson Hobbs, Anne, and Battrick, Elizabeth M. (1995) *Beatrix Potter 1866–1943: The Artist and Her World*, London: Warne and The National Trust (first published 1987).

Thiele, Jens (2013) "Zwischen Bilderbuch und Kunst: Überlegungen zu dem schwierigen Verhältnis von Kind und Kunst im Medium Buch" in Iris Kruse and Andrea Sabisch (eds) *Fragwürdiges Bilderbuch*, Munich: kopaed, 35–51.

Upton, Bertha (1895) *The Adventures of Two Dutch Dolls and a "Golliwogg,"* illus. Florence K. Upton, London: Longmans, Green (the series ended in 1909).

Varnedoe, Kirk, and Gopnik, Adam (1990) *High & Low: Modern Art and Popular Culture*, New York: Museum of Modern Art.

Wildsmith, Brian (1962) *ABC*, Oxford: Oxford University Press.

42

PICTURE THEORY AND PICTUREBOOKS

Nicolas Potysch and Lukas R. A. Wilde

Introduction

The consideration of picturebooks might occupy an awkward space somewhere between the domains of the currently developing Picture Theories, which are "not all theories in the same sense" (Sachs-Hombach 2011a: 229). While the term 'picture theory' itself is closely connected to William J.T. Mitchell (1995), his understanding of pictoriality is somewhat special, including all kinds of ambiguous (meta-)'images,' be they moving, mental, or conceptual. For the purposes of this investigation, we will limit our understanding of pictoriality to prototypical representational pictures. The three most prominent approaches treat those as part of the domains of semiotics, anthropology, or perception theory, respectively (Bonnemann 2014). Differing from the recently emerged visual culture studies, which consider visual phenomena mainly with a critical stance towards their relation to social power (see Elkins 2003; 2011; Stocchetti 2011), picture theory and image science(s) share a theoretical and systematic interest in pictorial works, led by philosophical or anthropological questions (see Pichler and Ubl 2014): "The immediate focus of interest is indeed not on single pictures at all, but on the faculty to use (i.e., produce and visually explore) pictures" (Sachs-Hombach and Schirra 2007: 37). With reference to Klaus Sachs-Hombach and Jörg R.J. Schirra, picture theory might then primarily be conceived as a general (and mostly inclusive) theoretical framework. One suggestion for this would be to regard pictures prototypically as "perceptoid signs" – signs close to perception (40). Taking something as a 'sign,' in this sense, implies nothing more but that we are aware of some communicative situation: we recognize some kind of agent who wants to bring something to our attention; in the special case of pictorial signs, this agent aims "to represent – quite literally: to bring into presence – for a receiver something else that is usually not present" (41). A detailed account of such a Griceian/Sperber-Wilson-like understanding of pictorial communication (the ostentation of pictorial objects) is given by Börries Blanke (2003; see also Forceville 2014). The perceptoid component of the definition acknowledges that seeing something 'in' a picture (see Wollheim 1998) involves certain perceptual competences that are – up to a point – likewise employed in the interaction with 'regular' kinds of objects or scenes: "A red balloon is perceived as red in hue and round in shape whether we see the material balloon or a picture of it" (Painter, Martin and Unsworth 2014: 53). This fundamental base level of pictorial comprehension was addressed as the "pre-iconographic level" by Erwin Panofsky (1955: 26) and simply as "denotation" by Roland Barthes (1977: 42) – something they both took as a given, since they saw as it as more or less universal to human perception. One of the most prominent features of images is thus described as the capacity to provoke the imagining of absent objects by visual sensory stimulation ("surrogate stimuli," Eco 2000: 353; see also Sonesson 1989: 250ff.). While it might remain a debatable issue how exactly pictures gain such 'meaning,' it still ought to be fairly uncontroversial that we often use and presuppose these pictorial competences in communicative situations:

> Visual communication is communication by proxy. The sender and the receiver do not have a direct, reciprocal relationship. Images are the proxies through which communication takes place in media discourse. They are the point of contact between sender and receiver, and they are usually the only element in which the sender's intention is manifested for the recipients.
>
> *Kukkonen 2011: 57*

We have to 'learn' how to understand those objects or scenes being depicted in the image and to interact with them and we have to practice word-picture/picture-word relationships as well (see Heffernan 2006: 11–24). The interaction of words and pictures has been approached from a variety of methods and disciplinary backgrounds, such as the multimodal discourse analysis promoted by Gunther Kress and Theo van Leeuwen (1996; see also Painter, Martin and Unsworth 2014). Picture theory (in contrast to art history or visual culture studies) has been strongly influenced by analytical philosophy and the philosophy of language – especially with the consideration of fundamental *differences* between language and pictures. With regard to picturebooks, picture theory would primarily ask whether there is a rather small set of functions and structural properties of pictoriality general enough to be observed in all works, while still serving as a basis for fruitful analysis of specific ones.

In this chapter, we aim to show the relevance of this approach for picturebook analysis on the basis of Dan Santat's *The Adventure of Beekle: The Unimaginary Friend* (2014). This picturebook won the Caldecott Medal of the year 2015 for "mak[ing] the unimaginable, imaginable" (ALSC 2015: n. pag.). We chose the Caldecott Medal as a benchmark for pointing to an exemplary picturebook, because in contrast to other prizes it is awarded "for distinguished illustrations in a picture book and for excellence of pictorial presentation for children. The award is not for didactic intent or for popularity" (ALSC 2008: n. pag.). Santat's work recounts the story of one special creature who is "born on an island far away where imaginary friends were created" (Santat 2014: n.pag.). From this magical realm, beings who are "imagined by a real child" (n.pag.) can cross over into the 'real world'; only by this rite of passage, we learn, do the 'imaginary friends' gain their proper names, devised by their respective 'creators.' Our protagonist's turn, however, does not seem to come; so, one day, he decides to do "the unimaginable" (10): embark on a journey to reality into a bustling city all on his own. In the end, he will meet the young girl, Alice, his 'perfect match,' who will finally grant him his 'special name': "Beekle" (n.pag.). This journey, as well as Beekle's 'ontological condition' throughout, is cleverly linked to the affordances of pictorial representations. In order to illustrate the relation of Beekle and his 'world' to these elemental functions of pictoriality, we would like to elaborate on the concepts of pictorial predication on the one hand and visual context building on the other, to show how *The Adventure of Beekle: The Unimaginary Friend* not only essentially rests on these functions, but also reflects upon them in a playful and inventive way.

With reference to John R. Searle's speech act theory (1986), it is possible to ask whether pictorially represented scenes can also be decomposed into propositional content and illocutionary function, similar to language: "We *warn* or *promise, ask* or *demand, assert* or *doubt*, to name just a few examples of illocutionary functions" (Sachs-Hombach and Schirra 2007: 44 – emphasis in original). While it is altogether common to do the same with pictures, it seems safe to assert that their illocutionary function (much more so than in verbal language) is defined by the pragmatic context of their usage alone: there are no purely pictorial means to indicate a warning, for instance (see Kjørup 1974; 1989; as well as Novitz 1977: 67ff.; Scholz 2004: 162ff.). It is precisely this illocutionary ambivalence that holds a great attraction, though: with equal right, we might assume that the first doublespread (see fig. 42.1) *elaborates* on the appearance of the various creatures, that it *insinuates* a hidden danger within the gloomy forest, or even that it *invites* us to feel reminded of our own holiday recollections at the seaside. Whatever the recipient decides (perhaps unknowingly), the standard and possibly even primal illocutionary function within the picturebook story will always be to show what Beekle, his peers, and their fantastic island look like: it *depicts* the things represented (see Kjørup 1978: 60; Sachs-Hombach 2001; Krebs 2015; Schöttler 2015).

Narrativity and representational affordances

Starting from the observation that picturebooks simultaneously employ the capacities to master language, to use pictures, to combine those two, and to somehow 'understand' the results, we might ask for the possible conceptual relations between telling and showing. Picturebooks are generally considered as a "bisemiotic" (Painter, Martin and Unsworth 2014: 2) or "bimodal form of text" (2), where the concept of intersemiotic meaning is central for representation (see Guijarro 2014: 61–87), because "pictures and texts in a picturebook usually complement each other" (Kümmerling-Meibauer 2014: 4).

However, the reference to the bisemiotic form is unsuitable as a differentiator distinguishing picturebooks from other 'related' literary forms as illustrated books, comics, or graphic novels (see Gibson 2010; Foster 2011; Evans 2013; Palmer 2014). The frequent emphasis that pictures play a 'significant role' for interpretation and that they are of particular 'narrative importance' (see Bader 1976; Kiefer 1995) is correct (and often nonetheless disregarded by analytical approaches). It is not a sufficient criterion to identify a bisemiotic literary text as a picturebook, though, if not already established by "separate areas of publishing" (Gibson 2010: 100). Without going further into depth, there are several examples of illustrated novels and graphic novels where "the visual and the written narratives contribute different layers of meaning to the story, without the implication of a hierarchy between the two" (Dalmaso 2015: 29–30). In our opinion, a prototypical picturebook can only be defined by means of the combination of aspects: Unlike many graphic novels and comics, and nearly all illustrated novels, picturebooks are characterized by a "narrative incompleteness" (Kümmerling-Meibauer 2014: 5). That means that they "are often highly elliptic in their representation of causal, local, and temporal relations" (5) which in turn involves a higher "gap-filling-activity of the reader/viewer" (5). In contrast to comics, that tend to refer to other comics quite frequently, seriality is a rather rare phenomenon in picturebooks (see Gibson 2010: 100ff.). Picturebooks can be distinguished from illustrated books, as "in the picturebook the visual text will often carry much of the narrative responsibility. In most cases, the meaning emerges through the interplay of word and image, neither of which would make sense when experienced independently of the other" (Salisbury and Styles 2012: 7). It is worth mentioning that not only do (especially contemporary) examples exist that are contrary to one or several of these aspects, but there are also many examples of "fusion texts" (Evans 2013: 239ff.) within picturebooks that "include many features from the strip cartoon genre, to include speech bubbles and text incorporated into series of repetitive images" (241) – Beekle, too, clearly draws upon these conventions (see Santat 2014: n.pag.). Such a blurring of forms and formats and a synthesis of styles notwithstanding, it has been mentioned that "they are all 'visual narratives'" (Evans 2013: 245).

Without going into detail on narratological questions (see Stephens 2010), one traditional misunderstanding has to be addressed at the outset. Bettina Kümmerling-Meibauer points to the prevalent notion that "since Antiquity [. . .] the juxtaposition of representation and narration marked an important distinction" (2014: 1) – a distinction roughly equivalent to a division between visual forms of art (which are supposed to show something) and verbal forms of art (distinguished by the alleged capacity to tell). In contrast, the emerging field of a transmedial narratology engages narratives in genres and media, where words are no longer central to narration (see Page 2010) and where readers become viewers and even active participants (see Ryan 2004; 2006; Ryan and Thon 2014; Thon 2016). Scholars tend to agree with Marie-Laure Ryan that 'narrativity' must then be understood as an umbrella term for the "outcome of many different mental processes that operate both inside and outside of stories" (Ryan 2007: 28). According to what is now referred to as a 'cognitive narratology' (Herman 2002: 5ff., 2003), these processes ultimately serve to construct a more or less coherent storyworld, with spatial as well as with temporal and (as far as protagonists are concerned) interpersonal, social, and psychological features and structures (see Herman 2002: 331; Klastrup and Tosca 2004; Ryan 2014: 31ff.; Thon 2015). Any given storyworld – as a cognitive construct, a mental representation – is by definition a transmedial phenomenon which can, in theory, be represented by a lot of different forms of media or art. Words and pictures, however (understood now as different *semiotic resources*, see Kress 2010; van Leeuwen 2004; or *modes* of representation, see Kress 2005), have very different affordances and constraints. These characteristics define their abilities to represent properties and to evoke (and expand) our mental model of these worlds (see Ryan 2006: 26, 2014: 25). Although the concept of character, for instance, is certainly a valid one in most if not all forms of narration, the modal affordances can be influential in the constitution of very unique types of characters, for instance, such that are probably only to be found in picturebooks.

The predicative function of picture usage

We take the doublespread as the starting point of any analysis of picturebooks, because it constitutes the surface that is relevant for the reception (in contrast for instance to Painter, Martin and Unsworth 2014: 11, who start their analysis on the level of the single image). If we look at the very first doublespread in Santat's book (Beekle's 'awakening' on the island of imaginary beings, see Figure 42.1), the verbal text provides an exposition about what is going on: "He was born on an island

Figure 42.1 Illustration from Dan Santat's *The Adventure of Beekle: The Unimaginary Friend*. New York: Little, Brown Books for Young Readers, 2014.

far away where imaginary friends were created." The verbal text refers to the protagonist only by pronoun until 'he' gets his name by Alice much later (see Santat 2014: n.pag.). In written texts the linguistic means employed for designating a character are usually proper names (see Margolin 2007: 66; Winko 2010: 214; Painter, Martin and Unsworth 2014: 59). Nonetheless, we have no problem inferring the protagonist of our story by his visual appearance alone (see Painter, Martin and Unsworth 2014: 58): The composition of the image/text-structure enables us to identify Beekle at first glance. His depiction is placed close to the center of the doublespread, right above the corresponding sentence, highlighted by a radial color contrast. Furthermore, while his peers can easily be described by verbal references to their 'compounds' – a cloud, a drum, a 'cardboard-box panda bear,' or an octopus with sand shovels – Beekle's physical complexion is strangely resistant to any attempt at a verbal transcription that retains a lot of information value or specificity: his 'body' resembles only a very general anthropomorphic configuration (a certain relation of extremities and the schema of a 'face'). "Children's literature is special in that it displays a range of characters that are usually not found in literature written for adults" Kümmerling-Meibauer and Meibauer observed (2014: 140). With reference to Maria Nikolajeva and Carole Scott's (2001: 81–115) and Nikolajeva's (2002: 125–127) taxonomy of picturebook-characters, they not only raised the question "why picturebooks apparently show more nonhuman characters than children's novels" (Kümmerling-Meibauer and Meibauer 2014: 153), but also highlighted the importance of odd "hybrid characters" (152): Beekle, somewhat similar to the recurrent picturebook protagonist of the 'matchstick man,' cannot even be placed clearly within any one of Nikolajeva's and Scott's categories, not human, animal, supernatural creature, object, or abstract entity.

While a systematic account of how such 'hybrid characters' are understood, how they invite identification and achieve narrative relevance has not been given (see Wilde 2017c), we might presuppose that they, too, (a) "are first and foremost elements of the constructed narrative world" (Eder, Jannidis and Schneider 2010: 9; see also Margolin 1983: 7; 2007; Jannidis 2014) and that (b) the minimal condition for recipients to differentiate characters from other parts of the fictional storyworld is to "have acquired a concept of person, which is mostly characterized by ideas of agency, identity, and mental life" (Kümmerling-Meibauer and Meibauer 2014: 152). The recipient is then able to 'enrich' his mental model of the character by the clues and information provided through the 'text' (see Eder, Jannidis and Schneider 2010: 14). The elliptic storytelling of picturebooks relies primarily on pictorial affordances, not only to provide most of such clues, but also to establish any stable identity from one page to the next: "The viewer thus has to infer that multiple depictions of a character or object signify a single constant identity" (Painter, Martin and Unsworth 2014: 58; see also Pichler and Ubl 2014: 50ff.). Allowing only for a pictorial classification as some kind of living being, Beekle is nevertheless easily identified on all the following pages: simultaneously, a wide range of variations is employed which function as representations of different gestures, expressions and 'moods,' each as unique as the next. The reason for such a concurrence of generality and distinctness can be found in the plethora of predications that pictorial representations such as Beekle's enfold.

The utterances of single words are only considered to perform communicative acts in certain defined contexts (outside of which they are, in Gottlob Frege's terms, 'unsaturated'; see Frege 1948) – precisely because isolated single words, as in a dictionary, do not claim any state of affairs. In contrast, any drawing of Beekle is by itself 'saturated': due to its elemental function of predication, the picture can always be understood to make countless 'claims' about Beekle's visual appearance (see Sachs-Hombach 2001; Krebs 2015; Wilde 2017b): the relation of extremities to 'head,' the constellation his 'eyes' and 'mouth' can form, the shape and contours of his 'torso,' as well as color and shading, his complexion, even about his 'body' posture, facial expressions, and his presumed 'mood.' Consider, then, the number of variations of all those within the whole work. Even the slightest modifications are in a 'continuous correlation' to what we see 'in' Beekle's representation (see Scholz 2004: 135ff.). This causes a specific semiotic paradox that has been referred to as the 'semantic paradox' or the 'semantic anomaly' of pictoriality (see Fellmann 2000: 25; Sachs-Hombach 2011b: 77). On the one hand, the references of pictorial signs (typically individuated objects, persons, or events, whether existing, fictional or mytho-logical) can be determined by pragmatic accounts only. Such a reference is thus highly contingent. On the other hand, each represented object or scene in a picture seems to possess an intensional identity of a particular – and specific – individual (see McDonell 1983; Blanke 2003: 80). Kress called this the "*epistemological commitment*" of a picture (Kress 2010: 16 – emphasis in original): it is not possible to draw just 'any circle'; it will always be a specific one (see in detail Sonesson 1989: 299ff.).

The formation of visual contexts

We might go on to ask why we are interested in strange, amorphous Beekle and how he is charac-terized visually in the first place. In order to avoid the textual bias to assign a supplementary role to the picture from the start, we might look for other objects, characters, or aspects of a scene, offered by the pictorial content alone. In fact, we might even be surprised why the text does not mention all the other interesting and fantastic figures at all.

Verbal nomination (the designation of objects or scenes we want to apply a set of predications to) is bound to grammatical rules. Aspects of perceptoid signs, however, are correlated to and interpreted with another logic altogether: either as part of a figure (and given more attention subsequently), or as part of the ground into which it is embedded by necessity. While this distinction has been discussed with reference to picture puzzles or reversible pictures most prominently (see Arnheim 1969: 92; Sonesson 1989: 247ff.; Eco 2000: 391; Blanke 2003: 90ff.), in another sense it is crucial already in most (if not all) cases of picture comprehension. Just the same as 'ordinary' situations of perceptions, no picture can be comprehended 'completely.' Its reception is always negotiation of relevance or, as James Elkins put it in his critical review: a negotiation of "attention and inattention" (1998: 122).

> [O]ur perceptual attention is not focused on all the surrounding objects but moves from one to the other so that something being figure at one moment may become the back-ground of another figure in the next instant.
>
> *Sachs-Hombach and Schirra 2007: 48*

In other words, the differentiation between participants (who or what is depicted) and circumstances (where, when, how, with what), a very central distinction for Kress and van Leeuwen in both verbal texts and pictures (see Kress and van Leeuwen 1996: 43ff.; Painter, Martin and Unsworth 2014: 55), might already be the result of an initial process of picture interpretation and comprehension ('hybrid characters,' such as animated objects, complicate the issue further). The picture nevertheless holds a potential for almost unlimited figure/ground differentiations, wherein the former can function as the subject for subsequent predications: we can talk about the panda-creature apparently being the biggest of the bunch, about the ability of the cat to fly, or about the octopus that seems to like build-ing sandcastles. Since no finite set of assertions will be equivalent (due to the semantic paradox of pictoriality), the doublespread is only restricting, but in no way specifying or determining any or all such potentials. This predicative 'wealth' results in an elemental function of pictoriality, namely their special way to build up perceptual contexts.

> The expression 'context' is used here [. . .] for indicating any finite and structured set of intentional sortal objects, i.e., a couple of individual things standing in relations with each other as far as somebody knows about them (or perceives them).
>
> *Sachs-Hombach and Schirra 2007: 50; see also Sachs-Hombach and Schirra 2013: 135*

As one can see, this understanding is very close to the definition of a diegesis or a storyworld as "some kind of container for individual existents, or [. . .] a system of relationships between individual existents" (Ryan 2014: 32; see Wilde 2017a; 2018). Context building in general is understood as our capacity to focus on things that are not currently present: acts of verbal context building that indicate different locations or times transform the current situational context into the context meant for anchoring the propositional content of the utterance (see Schirra 2005: 48ff.). The interlocutors thus become able to jointly refer to the objects within that context, be it a (allegedly) shared recollection or a fictional context altogether.

The crucial difference between representational pictures and language, in that respect, is that verbal utterances (references to absent contexts) offer no way to perceptually verify the corresponding assertions: we have to rely on deductive means alone in order to question the text on its accuracy or possible inconsistencies. In contrast, the organization of pictorial compositions offers a continuum of representation, from which a vast array of inferences can be drawn and, up to a point, intersubjectively tested: "The essential difference between 'to say' and 'to show' is thus, for short, that verbal context building can re-present facts merely logically, while pictorial context building can re-present facts empirically as well" (Sachs-Hombach and Schirra 2007: 56). Thorough observers might take some effort to scrutinize every little detail in the book, trying not to 'miss' anything. Some might not have noticed the two gloomy imps in the right-hand corner that are never mentioned anywhere in the textual narration (see Figure 42.1); although they are 'there' all the time, their 'reality' is utterly dependent on active recipients who visually explore the many figure/ground-differentiations and predications offered.

It is exactly on that pictorial continuum that Santat builds on later in the story, when Beekle finally meets Alice. Our protagonist has traveled into the 'real world,' looking for a child who might like to 'imagine' him, to bring him to life within his or her imagination (see Figure 42.2). When he climbs a tree for a better look, a girl (Alice) appears, asking him for help: he hands her back a sheet of paper, which had apparently been blown out of Alice's hand to end up in Beekle's tree. At this point, the recipient might notice that the sheet had already been present in the depiction of both the two scenes before, initially just as a minor detail easily overlooked, but gradually sliding into the center

Figure 42.2 Illustration from Dan Santat's *The Adventure of Beekle: The Unimaginary Friend*. New York: Little, Brown Books for Young Readers, 2014.

of attention. The white lines indicating a strong wind (see Figure 42.2) must be understood as a conventionalized diagrammatic sign representing the directionality of the wind: by itself, an invisible phenomenon (see Pombo and Gerner 2010; Wilde 2017b). Without those lines indicating wind, the white space in the sun is much harder to identify as a paper. Some recipients might have noticed the sheet; others might have overlooked it as a mere background feature.

Conclusions

What is fascinating about Beekle's story is how it reflects upon its joint modes of textual and pictorial representation thematically: Beekle and his peers are all "waiting to be imagined" (Santat 2014: n.pag.), so to speak: to become 'real' – but only as objects of imagination. Our role as recipients is reflected by that of the 'real children.' As recipients, we do not need an act of naming *or* even a verbal descriptiveness of Beekle's strange, amorphous appearance to identify or refer to him, since we can experience 'him' within our field of vision. Entirely unlike the most discussed birds of Zeuxis, we nevertheless do not mistake Beekle for more than a skillfully painted assemblage of lines and colors (see Mitchell 1995: 329–338): 'he' is entirely imaginary as well (even though neither any explicit 'code' nor a grasp of communicative intentions is necessary for our experience of recognizing his 'presence'). The default case of picture reception – the core of perceptoid signs – would thus be what Sachs-Hombach and Schirra call the immersive mode: experiencing a represented object within our field of perception while knowing simultaneously about the communicative function of its materiality. This concept of "twofoldness" (Wollheim 1987: 46), which has been very influential in contemporary picture theory (see Lopes 2005: 40ff.), is connected to acts of imagination even more directly in the final passage of the book. After Beekle and Alice meet, we get a glimpse of all the sketches she created. Despite her crude drawing skills, the scenes and situations look familiar, indeed: they seem to represent the very story we have been following so far, until the actual point of encounter with her new friend (see Figure 42.3).

Figure 42.3 Illustration from Dan Santat's *The Adventure of Beekle: The Unimaginary Friend*. New York: Little, Brown Books for Young Readers, 2014.

The story thus resolves Beekle's 'iconic shortcomings' with a charming explanation: since Beekle will be the result of the imagination of a child, his appearance is intrinsically linked to a little girl's drawing skills. More than a mere punchline, this witty commentary must not be overlooked lightly. With regard to the 'matchstick man,' Kümmerling-Meibauer and Meibauer analyzed a recurring trope: his 'coming to life' from a second-order representation ("drawings of matchstick men on depicted walls, blackboards, papers etc."; Kümmerling-Meibauer and Meibauer 2014: 145) into full-fledged, first-order protagonists: characters within the actual story-world. Children are considered to be already acquainted with the matchstick man as he 'occurs' as drawings in their early artistic development. Therefore "illustrators seem to acknowledge the young child's imaginative and creative activity by introducing a character that emanates from the child's imagination" (144). Beekle's story can be read as a smart 'reversion' of that trope: in the end, Santat seems to suggest, all of the story was merely a colorful imagination, brought to life by the interplay of lines, colors, shapes, and – not least – our (that means, Alice and the reader's) shared perceptional competences.

From an anthropological point of view, researchers assume that the faculty of human beings to refer to absent things and facts by linguistic means could be intrinsically linked to our faculty to use pictures, to re-present empirically non-present situations and to specify them in certain predicative ways. If picture theory has an intensified interest in a pictorial logic of representation that is mainly independent from language, it puts all the more emphasis on a mutual interdependence of language and pictures in usage. Picturebooks and their employment could be of special importance to these questions, and not only for didactic and educational purposes. Beekle's journey through the affordances of picture and verbal text can be seen as a site of aesthetic and conceptual experiments.

References

ALSC Association for Library Service to Children (2008) *Caldecott Medal: Terms and Criteria*, www.ala.org/alsc/awardsgrants/bookmedia/caldecottmedal/caldecottterms/caldecottterms (accessed September 30, 2017).

ALSC Association for Library Service to Children (2015) *Welcome to the Caldecott Medal Home Page*, www.ala.org/alsc/awardsgrants/bookmedia/caldecottmedal/caldecottmedal (accessed September 30, 2017).

Arnheim, Rudolf (1969) *Visual Thinking*, Berkeley: University of California Press.

Bader, Barbara (1976) *American Picturebooks from Noah's Ark to the Beast Within*, New York: Macmillan.

Barthes, Roland (1977) "Rhetoric of the Image," in *Image, Music, Text*, trans. Stephen Heath, London: Fontana, 32–51.

Blanke, Börries (2003) *Vom Bild zum Sinn: Das ikonische Zeichen zwischen Semiotik und analytischer Philosophie*, Wiesbaden: Deutscher Universitäts-Verlag.

Bonnemann, Jens (2014) "Bildphilosophie – Bildtheorie – Bildwissenschaften," in Stephan Günzel and Dieter Mersch (eds) *Bild: Ein interdisziplinäres Handbuch*, Stuttgart and Weimar: Metzler, 16–20.

Dalmaso, Renata L. (2015) "Towards a Feminist Reading of Gaiman's Picture Books," in Tara Prescott (ed.) *Neil Gaiman in the 21st Century: Essays on the Novels, Children's Stories, Online Writings, Comics and Other Works*, Jefferson: McFarland, 29–38.

Eco, Umberto (2000) *Kant and the Platypus: Essays on Language and Cognition*, London: Vintage.

Eder, Jens, Jannidis, Fotis, and Schneider, Ralf (2010) "Fictional Characters in Literary and Media Studies. A Survey of the Research," in Jens Eder, Fotis Jannidis, and Ralf Schneider (eds) *Characters in Fictional Worlds: Understanding Imaginary Beings in Literature, Film, and Other Media*, Berlin: de Gruyter, 3–66.

Elkins, James (1998) *On Pictures and the Words that Fail Them*, New York and Cambridge: Cambridge University Press.

Elkins, James (2003) *Visual Studies. A Skeptical Introduction*, New York and London: Routledge.

Elkins, James (2011) "Introduction," in James Elkins and Maja Naef (eds) *What Is an Image?* The Stone Art Theory Institutes Vol. 2, University Park: Penn State University Press, 1–12.

Evans, Janet (2013) "From Comics, Graphic Novels and Picturebooks to Fusion Texts: A New Kid on the Block," *Education 3–13* 41.2: 233–248.

Fellmann, Ferdinand (2000) "Bedeutung als Formproblem," in: Klaus Sachs-Hombach and Klaus Rehkämper (eds.) *Vom Realismus der Bilder: interdisziplinäre Forschungen zur Semantik bildhafter Darstellungsformen*, Magdeburg: Scriptum, 17–40.

Forceville, Charles (2014) "Relevance Theory as Model for Analysing Visual and Multimodal Communication," in David Machin (ed.) *Visual Communication*, Berlin and Boston: de Gruyter, 51–70.

Foster, John (2011) "Picture Books as Graphic Novels and Vice Versa: The Australian Experience," *Bookbird* 49.4: 68–75.

Frege, Gottlob (1948) "Sense and Reference: Translated by Max Black," *The Philosophical Review* 57.3: 209–230.

Gibson, Mel (2010) "Graphic Novels, Comics and Picturebooks," in David Rudd (ed.) *Routledge Companion to Children's Literature*, London and New York: Routledge, 100–111.

Guijarro, Arsenio J.M. (2014) *A Multimodal Analysis of Picture Books for Children. A Systemic Functional Approach*, Sheffield and Bristol: Equinox.

Heffernan, James A.W. (2006) *Cultivating Picturacy: Visual Art and Verbal Interventions*, Waco, TX: Baylor University Press.

Herman, David (2002) *Story Logic: Problems and Possibilities of Narrative*, Lincoln and London: University of Nebraska Press.

Herman, David (2003) "Introduction," in David Herman (ed.) *Narrative Theory and the Cognitive Sciences*, Stanford, CA: CSLI, 1–32.

Jannidis, Fotis (2014) "Character," in: Peter Hühn, Jan C. Meister, John Pier, and Wolf Schmid (eds) *Handbook of Narratology*. Volume 1, 2nd ed., Berlin: de Gruyter, 30–45.

Kiefer, Barbara (1995) *The Potential of Picturebooks: From Visual Literacy to Aesthetic Understanding*, Englewood Cliffs, NJ: Merrill, Prentice Hall.

Kjørup, Søren (1974) "George Inness and the Battle at Hastings, or Doing Things with Pictures," *The Monist* 58.2: 216–235.

Kjørup, Søren (1978) "Pictorial Speech Acts," *Erkenntnis* 12: 55–71.

Kjørup, Søren (1989) "Die sprachliche Verankerung des Bildes," *Semiotik* 11.4: 305–317.

Klastrup, Lisbeth, and Tosca, Susana (2004) "Transmedial Worlds. Rethinking Cyberworld Design," *IT University of Copenhagen*, www.cs.uu.nl/docs/vakken/vw/literature/04.klastruptosca_transworlds.pdf (accessed September 30, 2017).

Krebs, Jakob (2015) "Visual, Pictorial, and Information Literacy," *IMAGE: Zeitschrift für interdisziplinäre Bildwissenschaft* 22: 7–25, www.gib.uni-tuebingen.de/image/ausgaben-3?function=fnArticle&showArticle=375 (accessed September 30, 2017).

Kress, Gunther (2005) "Gains and Losses: New Forms of Texts, Knowledge and Learning," *Computers and Composition* 22.1: 5–22.

Kress, Gunther (2010) *Multimodality. A Social Semiotic Approach to Contemporary Communication*, London: Routledge.

Kress, Gunther, and van Leeuwen, Theo (1996) *Reading Images: The Grammar of Visual Design*, New York: Routledge.

Kümmerling-Meibauer, Bettina (2014) "Introduction. Picturebooks Between Representation and Narration," in Bettina Kümmerling-Meibauer (ed.) *Picturebooks: Representation and Narration*, New York and London: Routledge, 1–14.

Kümmerling-Meibauer, Bettina, and Meibauer, Jörg (2014) "Understanding the Matchstick Man. Aesthetic and Narrative Properties of a Hybrid Picturebook Character," in Bettina Kümmerling-Meibauer (ed.) *Picturebooks: Representation and Narration*, New York and London: Routledge, 139–161.

Kukkonen, Karin (2011) "The Map, the Mirror and the Simulacrum. Visual Communication and the Question of Power," in Matteo Stocchetti and Karin Kukkonen (eds) *Images in Use: Towards the Critical Analysis of Visual Communication*, Amsterdam: Benjamins, 55–67.

van Leeuwen, Theo (2004) *Introducing Social Semiotics: An Introductory Textbook*, London: Routledge.

Lopes, Dominic M. (2005) *Sight and Sensibility: Evaluating Pictures*, Oxford: Clarendon Press.

Margolin, Uri (1983) "Characterization in Narrative: Representation and Signification," *Neophilologus* 67: 1–14.

Margolin, Uri (2007) "Character," in David Herman (ed.) *The Cambridge Companion to Narrative*, Cambridge: Cambridge University Press, 66–79.

McDonell, Neil (1983) "Are Pictures Unavoidably Specific?" *Synthese* 57.1: 83–98.

Mitchell, William J.T. (1995) *Picture Theory: Essays on Verbal and Visual Representation*, Chicago and London: University of Chicago Press.

Nikolajeva, Maria (2002) *The Rhetoric of Character in Children's Literature*, Lanham, MD: Scarecrow.

Nikolajeva, Maria, and Scott, Carole (2001) *How Picturebooks Work*, New York: Garland.

Novitz, David (1977) *Pictures and Their Use in Communication. A Philosophical Essay*, The Hague: Nijhoff.
Page, Ruth (2010) "Introduction," in Ruth Page (ed.) *New Perspectives on Narrative and Multimodality*, New York: Routledge, 1–13.
Painter, Clare, Martin, J. R., and Unsworth, Len (2014) *Reading Visual Narratives: Image Analysis of Children's Picture Books*, Bristol: Equinox.
Palmer, Rebecca (2014) "Combining the Rhythms of Comics and Picturebooks: Thoughts and Experiments," *Journal of Graphic Novels and Comics* 5.3: 297–310.
Panofsky, Erwin (1955) *Meaning in the Visual Arts: Papers in and on Art History*, Garden City: Doubleday.
Pichler, Wolfram, and Ubl, Ralph (2014) *Bildtheorie: Zur Einführung*, Hamburg: Junius.
Pombo, Olga, and Gerner, Alexander (eds) (2010) *Studies in Diagrammatology and Diagram Praxis*, London: College.
Ryan, Marie-Laure (ed.) (2004) *Narrative Across Media: The Languages of Storytelling*, Lincoln: University of Nebraska Press.
Ryan, Marie-Laure (2006) *Avatars of Story*, Minneapolis: University of Minnesota Press.
Ryan, Marie-Laure (2007) "Toward a Definition of Narrative," in David Herman (ed.) *The Cambridge Companion to Narrative*, Cambridge: Cambridge University Press, 22–38.
Ryan, Marie-Laure, (2014) "Toward a Definition of Narrative," in Marie-Laure Ryan and Jan-Noël Thon (eds) *Storyworlds Across Media: Toward a Media-Conscious Narratology*, Lincoln: University of Nebraska Press, 24–49.
Ryan, Marie-Laure, and Thon, Jan-Noël (eds) (2014) *Storyworlds Across Media: Toward a Media-Conscious Narratology*, Lincoln: University of Nebraska Press.
Sachs-Hombach, Klaus (2001) "Bild und Prädikation," in Klaus Sachs-Hombach (ed.) *Bildhandeln: Interdisziplinäre Forschungen zur Pragmatik bildhafter Darstellungsformen*, Magdeburg: Scriptum, 55–76.
Sachs-Hombach, Klaus (2011a) "Theories of Image. Five Tentative Theses," in James Elkins and Maja Naef (eds) *What is an Image?* The Stone Art Theory Institutes Vol. 2, University Park: Penn State University Press, 229–232.
Sachs-Hombach, Klaus (2011b) "Bildakttheorie. Antworten auf die Differenz von Präsenz und Entzug," in Philipp Stoellger, and Thomas Klie (eds) *Präsenz im Entzug: Ambivalenzen des Bildes*, Tübingen: Mohr Siebeck, 57–82.
Sachs-Hombach, Klaus, and Schirra, Jörg R.J. (2007) "To Show and to Say: Comparing the Uses of Pictures and Language," *Studies in Communication Sciences* 7.2: 35–62.
Sachs-Hombach, Klaus, and Schirra, Jörg R.J. (2013) "The Anthropological Function of Pictures," in Klaus Sachs-Hombach and Jörg R.J. Schirra (eds) *Origins of Pictures: Anthropological Discourses in Image Science*, Köln: van Halem, 132–159.
Salisbury, Martin, and Styles, Morag (2012) *Children's Picturebooks: The Art of Visual Storytelling*, London: Laurence King.
Santat, Dan (2014) *The Adventure of Beekle: The Unimaginary Friend*, New York: Hachette Book Group.
Schirra, Jörg R.J. (2005) *Foundation of Computational Visualistics*, Wiesbaden: Deutscher Universitätsverlag.
Scholz, Oliver R. (2004) *Bild, Darstellung, Zeichen: Philosophische Theorien bildlicher Darstellung*, 2nd ed., Frankfurt: Klostermann.
Schöttler, Tobias (2015) "Das bildphilosophische Stichwort 4: Bildhandeln," *IMAGE: Zeitschrift für interdisziplinäre Bildwissenschaft* 22: 155–163, www.gib.uni-tuebingen.de/image?function=fnArticle&showArticle=391 (accessed September 30, 2017).
Searle, John R. (1986) "Meaning, Communication, and Representation," in Richard E. Grandy, and Richard Warner (eds) *Philosophical Grounds of Rationality: Intentions, Categories, Ends*, Oxford: Clarendon Press, 209–226.
Sonesson, Göran (1989) *Pictorial Concepts: Inquiries into the Semiotic Heritage and its Relevance to the Interpretation of the Visual World*, Lund: Lund University Press.
Stephens, John (2010) "Narratology," in David Rudd (ed.) *Routledge Companion to Children's Literature*, London and New York: Routledge, 51–62.
Stocchetti, Matteo (2011) "Images: Who Gets What, When and How?" in Matteo Stocchetti and Karin Kukkonen (eds) *Images in Use: Towards the Critical Analysis of Visual Communication*, Amsterdam and Philadelphia: John Benjamins, 11–37.
Thon, Jan-Noël (2015) "Converging Worlds: From Transmedial Storyworlds to Transmedial Universes" *StoryWorlds: A Journal of Narrative Studies* 7.2: 21–53.
Thon, Jan-Noël (2016) *Transmedial Narratology and Contemporary Media Culture*, Lincoln and London: University of Nebraska Press.

Wilde, Lukas R.A. (2017a) "Comics | Piktogramme: Mediale Transformationen in der 'Sprache' des Comics," in: Matthias Harbeck, Marie Schröer, and Linda Heyden (eds) *Comics an der Grenze: Sub/Versionen von Form und Inhalt*, Berlin: Bachmann, 97–118.

Wilde, Lukas R.A. (2017b) "The Epistemologies of the Drawn Line: Abstract Dimensions of Narrative Comics," in Aarnoud Rommens, Björn-Olav Dozo, Pablo Turnes, and Erwin Dejasse (eds) *Abstraction and Comics/La BD et l'abstraction*, Liège: Liège University Press/Presses Universitaires de Liège, 423–447.

Wilde, Lukas R.A. (2018) *Im Reich der Figuren: Meta-narrative Kommunikationsfiguren und die 'Mangaisierung' des japanischen Alltags*, Köln: van Halem.

Winko, Simone (2010) "On the Constitution of Characters in Poetry," in Jens Eder, Fotis Jannidis, and Ralf Schneider (eds) *Characters in Fictional Worlds: Understanding Imaginary Beings in Literature, Film, and Other Media*, Berlin: de Gruyter, 208–231.

Wollheim, Richard (1987) *Painting as an Art*, London: Thames and Hudson.

Wollheim, Richard (1998) "On Pictorial Representation," *Journal of Aesthetics and Art Criticism* 56.3: 217–226.

43

PICTUREBOOKS AND MEDIA STUDIES

Margaret Mackey

Picturebooks inhabit a complex social, cultural, and intellectual ecology. Many are designed for a young audience, but increasingly few contemporary children approach a picturebook with no prior experience of other media. As in any ecology, changes at one level affect the whole system. The seismic shifts in our textual world have a profound impact on even very young media users.

The academic discipline of media studies provides relevant tools for exploring the significance of how picturebooks relate to a larger and more complex textual universe. This chapter explores the interconnections between picturebook studies and the larger world of media studies.

Many picturebook users are extremely young, yet often sophisticated media consumers. For example, Grover of *Sesame Street* stars in picturebooks, television programs, YouTube videos, and smartphone apps. Grover may participate in children's daily lives as a stuffed toy (and appear in home videos). He may feature on permanent household accessories, and/or come and go in assorted textual ephemera: sticker books, coloring books, and so forth. The Amazon site contains over 5,000 entries, and Google turned up more than half a million hits for "Grover Sesame Street."

Academic study of picturebooks must pay appropriate attention to the textual ecology that Grover embodies and that many contemporary children enfold into their developing textual awareness. A generation of young readers now approaches picturebooks with new understanding that must be appreciated and respected.

Many children move seamlessly between formats; we know far too little about how their literary understanding of characters like Grover is affected by his textual mutability. For example, numerous children will mentally vivify the silence of a picturebook page in Jon Stone's *There's a Monster at the End of this Book* (1999) with Grover's definitive voice as experienced on screen, rather than with a parental tone or their own internal expression. Their internal animation of this fiction is thus more *specified* than is usual with book reading because of cross-media experience.

Scholars interested in picturebooks and in young children's developing literacy must acknowledge the highly intertextual and intermedial nature of contemporary children's literary attention. As picturebooks are reworked into other media forms, taking greater account of the broader media world, the scope of the reading experience shifts. Reading often represents just one entry point into a narrative expressed through a variety of formats, and print literacy and media literacy substantially inflect each other. Picturebooks now often exist as one element in a spectrum of alternatives. Sometimes the book is the originating text, sometimes a later variant (see Dresang 1999, for a discussion of how books themselves are also changing in the face of these developments). Some picturebooks reappear as different picturebooks in a dynamic process of change and reiteration. A media studies approach addresses such textual clusters with due awareness of the conditions that led to their creation and distribution.

Media studies: a complex theoretical framework

According to Cary Bazalgette and David Buckingham, a media studies approach "require[s] us to analyse not only the text itself but also its *production* (working practices, institutional contexts, commercial strategies and so on), and the ways in which it is used and interpreted by different *audiences*" (2013: 99, emphasis in original). The complexity of this approach is compounded when the picturebook itself is embedded in the media ecology just outlined.

A media studies framework will do more than simply look at questions of production and audiences in relation to picturebooks. It will investigate the networks of associations between picturebooks and other related texts. This chapter will address issues arising from four categories of mass media that are agreed upon by many scholars, although their labels sometimes differ: print, recording, broadcasting, and new media (Cubitt 2013; Ott and Mack 2014). To explore how picturebooks relate to this complex matrix, the following theoretical perspectives and terminology may prove useful.

Adaptation

Linda Hutcheon describes adaptations as "deliberate, announced, and extended revisitations of prior works" (2006: xiv). Audiences of a specific text may vary in their prior awareness of the originating text; Hutcheon says they become more or less knowing as a result. Regardless of whether contemporary child readers are aware of a particular adaptation's original source, they do have a large sense that stories can move across media platforms.

Remediation

Jay Bolter and Richard Grusin define remediation as "the representation of one medium in another" (1999: 45). Such re-incorporation, they contend, invites interpreters to oscillate between "immediacy" and "hypermediacy." Immediacy entails immersion in the world created by the text; hypermediacy involves attention to the surface of the text and the dynamics of its manifestations in conditions of change. There has long been an assumption, perhaps overly romantic, that children specialize in immediacy, plunging uncritically and wholeheartedly into their fictions. Children certainly learn the delights of immediacy, but the world of plural versions they inhabit from their earliest awareness onwards must strengthen their sense of hypermediacy.

Convergence

The idea of media convergence has multiple meanings; Henry Jenkins (2008) explores different aspects of this term. Issues of ownership loom large in media studies. As fewer and fewer companies own more and more publishing outlets, the economic forces driving corporate convergence are strengthened, and commercial pressure often emphasizes the virtues of adaptations and sequels. On a different level, technological breakthroughs permit us to experience many different media formats (including picturebooks) on a single platform, say a tablet, with consequences for how children's media literacies develop. Convergence also involves cultural practices: "consumers are encouraged to seek out new information and make connections among dispersed media content" (Jenkins 2008: 3). Young children are often eager to engage in exactly such behavior – spotting Grover, for example, in every available venue.

Transmedia

"Transmedia storytelling represents a process where integral elements of a fiction get dispersed systematically across multiple delivery channels for the purpose of creating a unified and coordinated entertainment experience" (Jenkins 2007: n. pag.) Users must track distributed elements of a text to experience the complete story. Some users will assiduously collect the full set; those of a less completist disposition may experience their story in fragments.

A sample set

What are the implications of this contemporary ecology both for young readers and for adult scholars and professionals? Seven titles help explore this complex territory, offering different manifestations of some of the elements outlined earlier.

My primary case study includes a continuum of three titles by David Wiesner: *The Three Pigs* (2001), *Flotsam* (2006), and *Spot* (2015). Only two of these titles are picturebooks; *Spot* is Wiesner's first app-only text. The section of this chapter that investigates his work is followed by shorter explorations of *The Snowman* (1978) by Raymond Briggs, *The Hockey Sweater* (2014/1984) by Roch Carrier and Sheldon Cohen, *Where the Wild Things Are* (2013/1963) by Maurice Sendak, and *The Fantastic Flying Books of Mr. Morris Lessmore* (2012) by William Joyce and Joe Bluhm. Together, these aesthetically important books and their assorted reworkings demonstrate how picturebooks function variously in a complex web of inter-related media texts. Their participation in cycles of reworking tells us much about the positioning of contemporary picturebooks in our current textual ecology.

Collectively, this sample set represents the main media categories outlined earlier:

- Print: by stipulation, for every title except Wiesner's *Spot*;
- Recording: animations of several of the stories, and the conventionally distributed feature-length movie of *Where the Wild Things Are*;
- Broadcasting: the initial and repeated showings of *The Snowman*;
- New media: *Flotsam, Spot*, and the two apps of *The Fantastic Flying Books of Mr. Morris Lessmore*.

This set also supplies a live action option, with opera and ballet versions of *Where the Wild Things Are*, some of which have also been recorded and converted into new media via YouTube.

With the partial exception of Wiesner's texts, these well-known titles now present themselves to our attention as text clusters rather than singular picturebooks. They participate in a media spectrum in their own right, and young readers bring to them a repertoire of media literacies developed, at least in part, by following their favorite titles and characters through a range of instantiations. Any scholarship concerning the production and reception histories of these titles must necessarily include their place in this dynamic world of remediation and adaptation. Sealing off the print version as some pristine object of study severely limits the value and interest of the scholarly project; few young readers today encounter their picturebooks in such a purist, vacuum-sealed environment.

At the same time, it is also important to note what distinguishes a picturebook from other manifestations of the same story. de Kerckhove points out that paper provides

> a resting place for words. It sounds trite, but in fact the printed page is the only place where words do have a rest. Everywhere else, they are moving: when you speak, when you see them on a screen, when you see them on the Net, words are moving. But a book is a restful place. The printed word is, and always was, still.
>
> *1997: 107*

How much does this stillness matter in a dynamic textual world? Different answers to this question may be supplied by different titles on our list.

Exploring the sampler

The first three examples come from David Wiesner. These stories all play visual tricks, but they occupy different positions on the media continuum.

The Three Pigs

Wiesner won his second Caldecott Medal in 2002 for *The Three Pigs*, published the previous year. This foolishly surreal story tells how the three pigs make a getaway from the inevitable fate inscribed in their story by blowing right out of the page. Turning the panels of their own images into paper planes, they fly off into other fairy tales and nursery rhymes.

Perhaps because of the extreme bookishness of the conceit that supplies the plot engine, *The Three Pigs* is relatively close to being a stand-alone picturebook. A couple of YouTube animations are no longer available, and there appear to be no formal plans to adapt this story into other media. Yet, even if it represents the "singular" end of the spectrum, its links to a media studies framework are robust. Wiesner, in his Caldecott acceptance speech, talks about the genesis of the book in his childhood fascination with a Bugs Bunny animation. In this cartoon, Bugs and Elmer Fudd run "right out of the cartoon. We see the frames of the filmstrip flicker by, as well as the sprocket holes at the edge of the film." Soon they find themselves in a blank white space. They return to the cartoon; it flickers and then runs normally. "Even more than all the reality manipulation that was happening in the cartoon, I was fascinated by the idea that behind the 'normal' reality lay this endless, empty, white nothingness" (Wiesner 2002: n. pag.).

It is tempting to read *The Three Pigs* as a commentary on the nature of the book as object, even as the overwhelming cultural domination of this particular object shows signs of waning. Wiesner's intermedial reference to Bugs Bunny reminds us that such metafiction is not new, nor is it necessarily an offspring of the digital revolution. He also wryly challenges de Kerckhove's assertions about the stillness of the page, when the stability of the drawn images enables the pigs to convert them into paper planes.

In his Caldecott speech, Wiesner also addresses some of the kinds of questions about production, distribution, and audience that Bazalgette and Buckingham claim for the purview of media studies. He describes running his artistic concepts past the production department before he begins work, to make sure that his ideas can be realized. He pays tribute to the contributions of his art director, his editor, his agent, and his readers. The speech does not delve into the economics of publishing picture-books, but it serves as a primer for many of the production concerns that support such work. It also assures us that the kinds of questions raised by media studies can apply directly to the infrastructure that supports the production of picturebooks.

Flotsam

The wordless, Caldecott-winning *Flotsam* (2006) explores the qualities and capacities of the camera, rather than the book: a beachcombing boy discovers a barnacle-encrusted camera and looks at the images it supplies.

Flotsam is currently being 'extended' through a significant transmedia exercise, described by Herr-Stephenson and Alper with Reilly (2013):

> Over the course of 2011–2013, an interdisciplinary team of researchers and designers has worked to develop transmedia extensions to *Flotsam*. . . . As a wordless book, *Flotsam* encourages readers to tell their own story of what they see in its pages. The transmedia extensions were designed to scaffold and enhance these opportunities for storytelling.

Further, the transmedia experience was intended to build upon the book's ocean setting and depiction of marine life by incorporating an age-appropriate life science curriculum.

43

Johanna Holm, a marine biologist working on the digital transformation of this title, describes the project as "something akin to a comic strip, one displayed on the screen of an iPad instead of printed on newsprint and illustrated with images that are animated instead of static" (qtd. in Hoops 2013: n. pag.).

Although involving a very new art form, this account describes a very conventional case of adaptation. The elements of the app are outlined in relation to print on paper. Holm is describing a classic form of remediation. It seems as if comprehending the app with skills developed through picture-book reading (perhaps augmented by experience of watching animations) would be a straightforward exercise. Herr-Stephenson and Alper with Reilly confirm this perspective, commenting "the team thought it would be interesting to use new media to help tell the story about old media" (2013: 44).

But a 2012 description of the project includes a participatory component to the proposed app, an element that lands it squarely in the territory of new media:

> The 'mother narrative' of the *Flotsam* Transmedia Play Experience will be six story chapters delivered in the form of DIY 'explorer kits' that encourage creative remix through the use of a camera that will come as part of the initial kit. These six chapters will extend the digitally dynamic book that we will design for participatory retelling of *Flotsam; user generated retelling* can be shared as gifts with family members and peers, as well as shared into the *Flotsam* community.
>
> *Reilly 2012: n. pag., emphasis added*

The transmedia *Flotsam* thus preserves and remediates many of the qualities of the original book while experimenting with new participatory possibilities opened up by digital affordances. The media literacy skills required to make best use of this new material include the capacity to re-mix elements already provided, to produce new contributions. Children have performed such acts in their private play for centuries, but now their creations will be published and distributed – another territory where a media studies approach can illuminate their understanding of the innovative forces at work.

Spot

As Wiesner continues to explore the potential of digital forms of expression, the transfer between the world of picturebooks and his newest app, *Spot*, is not so straightforward. With this work, Wiesner has abandoned the stability of the paper page completely. *Spot*, so far purely an app, employs fingers pinching and expanding on an iPad screen to create a zoom effect (Figure 43.1). Here is Wiesner on the effect of *Spot*:

> The premise is that there are a series of worlds, all contained within the spot on the back of a bug. As you pinch and enlarge the bug, the tiny spot is revealed to be an island. Zooming in further, are mountains, then a lake in the mountains and another island in the lake and finally, a house on that island. The last pinch takes you into another world.
>
> There are transitions like this between each of the worlds. What was intriguing to me was basing the transitions on graphic ideas like shape, color, and positive/negative space – not just making a small thing larger.
>
> *Wiesner, qtd. in Grabarek 2015: n. pag.*

Figure 43.1 Illustration from David Wiesner's *Spot*. New York: Houghton Mifflin Harcourt, 2015.

Wiesner says he tried to create the world of *Spot* in a book but he could not make his idea operational in this format. The app is not an adaptation, nor does it remediate a previous format, yet it does convey a form of "sequential art" (Eisner 2008) that connects it to the narrative forms of picturebook and film. Its relationship to more traditional formats will undoubtedly be debated for some time. In *Spot*, all connection with the wordless fictional worlds depicted is managed by the reader's hand on the glass of the screen. Just as *The Three Pigs* investigates the limits of what a book page can do, and *Flotsam* plays with the powers of the camera, so *Spot* explores the affordances of the app. Is it the power of literacy that permits us to explore its wordless universes? *Flotsam* and *The Snowman* are equally wordless, but we generally refer to them as being 'read.' *Spot* in some ways resembles the 'sequential art' of an animated film more than a book, but the interpreter's ability to stop and go invokes the literacy of the book. It is an intriguing hybrid.

The Snowman

The Snowman initially appeared as a wordless picturebook by Raymond Briggs. A snowman comes to life for a night, engages in adventures (including flying), and melts by morning. Famously, it was later animated (Raymond Briggs's *The Snowman* 1993/1982), first airing on British television during Christmas 1982. The story remained wordless, except for a hit song, "Walking in the Air"; it also acquired an orchestral soundtrack. Following its TV success (repeated every Christmas), *The Snowman* engendered a variety of commodities, including a range of spin-off picturebooks that reduced the subtlety of the story's original presentation to something much more conventional. A print-on-demand sequel, *The Snowman and the Snowdog*, can be now ordered with personalized content: "bespoke names, hairstyles, skin tones and pyjama colours" (www.thesnowman.com/book/snowman-snowdog-customisable-penwizard/, accessed November 1, 2015).

The adaptation of one highly successful artistic achievement (the book) into another (the animation) raises many interesting questions. For example, Geoff Moss suggests that the film's use of music "actually disguises the fact that there is no language" (1991: 201). Music also establishes a more controlling relationship with the viewer than the book requires of its reader: "The music in the film establishes, through its rhythms, a temporal dimension from which we cannot escape, while the picture book places no such demands on us" (201).

Of all my samples, *The Snowman* follows the most recognizable commercial trajectory. Not only did the broadcast animation lead to the production of spin-off picturebooks, all much less interesting than the original, it also spawned a deluge of *Snowman*-related commodities. Moss suggests that this commodity relationship is built into the animation from the outset, incorporated with a Christmas theme that the film adds to the book story:

> [T]he film … seeks to become a 'natural' element of the Christmas tradition, represented as it is on Christmas cards, wrapping paper, and gifts. … The gift that Father Christmas gives is a scarf, and the scarf is decorated with small snowmen in the film. Thus, the film becomes an advertisement of its own products.

> *1991: 199–200*

Children are consumers too, and many are very familiar with the idea of commodities arising from favorite stories. The story's charm provides a potent opening to the associated sales pitch. A filmed story is much more expensive to produce than a book, and it is no coincidence that commodification often comes in the wake of the movie version. Children would greatly benefit from the kind of sharper awareness of these links that a media studies approach would supply.

The Snowman and the Snowdog takes advantage of digital affordances to personalize a special purchase, but it does not elicit any other kind of participation. The emphasis remains on consumption, as it does for so many *Snowman* products. And yet the initial book and the animation both retain their original appeal for many readers and viewers.

The Hockey Sweater

The classic Canadian title, *The Hockey Sweater* by Roch Carrier, first appeared as a short story in French. The story was translated into English, then animated (in both languages) by Canada's National Film Board. Later it became a picturebook, in French and English versions. Sheldon Cohen provided the images for both film and picturebook (Figure 43.2). The story attained such stature in Canada that a quotation featured on the five-dollar bill.

This iconic text incorporates markers of national identity in all versions: a mythic world of ice hockey played on outdoor rinks, and a nostalgic and unthreatening view of the provincial culture of French Quebec, manifested in the English-language film version, *The Sweater* (1980), through lively folk music and through the delightfully accented English of author/narrator Roch Carrier (www. nfb.ca/film/sweater/). The animation was produced by Canada's National Film Board, which provides its own cultural imprimatur of acknowledged excellence – and government funding reduces the pressure to develop associated commodity lines. The picturebook version (1984) came late in the sequence, appearing after the words-only story had been published in both languages, and after the ten-minute animation won Canadian hearts.

The picturebook version of *The Hockey Sweater* represents De Kerckhove's point about the stillness of the printed page in very specific ways. Following rather than preceding the animation, it pins down the poignancy of the hero's horror at receiving a Toronto Maple Leafs sweater by mail order, rather than the beloved jersey of the Montreal Canadiens. Whereas music and sound were added to *The Snowman* as it was adapted into film, in this case a dynamic soundtrack was subtracted (and readers lost the music, Carrier's inimitable narrative cadences, and an evocative snatch of a French-language radio broadcast of "Hockey Night in Canada"). The brevity of the ten-minute animation means there is an unusual agreement of scale between the storyworlds of film and book. Illustrator Cohen and the page designers of the book distilled the liveliness of the animation into a singular,

Figure 43.2 Front cover by Sheldon Cohen from Roch Carrier's *The Hockey Sweater*, Anniversary Edition. Toronto: Tundra Books, 2014.

stable version. Despite (or because of) these restrictions, the picturebook holds its own secure place in the national psyche of Canada; the fixity of paper means that readers can insert themselves into the story in ways not available through viewing alone.

Where the Wild Things Are

Maurice Sendak's acclaimed *Where the Wild Things Are* has been transformed into an opera, a ballet, and a full-length, live-action movie. The feature-film version inspired a few fan fictions (see, for example, www.fanfiction.net/movie/Where-the-Wild-Things-Are/), and YouTube offers a variety of animated versions. There is also a movie website featuring some simple digital games (http://wherethewildthingsare.warnerbros.com/dvd/#/Splash).

Sendak's original story about Max, sent to his room for misbehaving and escaping to rule the land of the Wild Things, is famous for many reasons, including the American artist's masterful control of page design and his aesthetic reticence. The shrinking and expanding white space of this book plays a cogent narrative role, one difficult to reproduce through the conventions of certain other media. The movie images, not surprisingly, bleed off the screen in all directions; in the book version, only the Wild Rumpus features full bleeding, conveying a sense of excess that all the choreography and lush soundtrack of the movie version cannot fully communicate.

Where the Wild Things Are also exists as opera and ballet. A live story does make room for some equivalence to white space; the mise-en-scène can be shrunk and expanded more eloquently by means of staging and lighting than is often achieved with the fixed rectangle of the movie screen. In YouTube recordings of the opera, the fidelity of the scenery – complete with distinctive crosshatching – and costumes (all created by Sendak) is simultaneously startling and comforting: visual remediation. The music, however, is demanding and less inviting (www.youtube.com/watch?v=TyU9E6hbsf4).

The artistic director of the ballet provides cogent commentary on adaptation to a different art form:

> One of the challenges was that Maurice's drawings *and* his illustrations are so distinct and vibrant, the physicality of the dancers had to equal that vibrancy. You know there was a kind of a battle between his designs and décor and the choreography initially. We had to make them have the same kind of energy and that's why it's a very athletic production.
>
> *Maurice Sendak and Septime Webre's Where the Wild Things Are 2008: n. pag.*

Bodmer suggests, however, that "in bringing them to the stage, the power of these works has been reduced" (1992: 174). The movie version, similarly, in expanding the story to feature-film dimensions, paradoxically diminishes its potency. With a novel, the film version is usually shorter than the book; in a picturebook adaptation, by contrast, the need to infill narrative details to extend the movie story to conventional feature length incurs the risk of padding. The power-punch packed by Sendak's book resides more completely in its austerity, its compactness, and its stillness than may be the case with other stories.

The Fantastic Flying Books of Mr. Morris Lessmore

The Fantastic Flying Books of Mr. Morris Lessmore by William Joyce and Joe Bluhm first appeared as an Oscar-winning animation (The Fantastic Flying Books 2011), followed by an iPad app version (Fantastic 2012). The picturebook followed (Joyce 2012), and a second app from MoonBot introduced a revolutionary element of Augmented Reality (IMAG-N-O-TRON 2012).

All these versions tell roughly the same story, with some shifting details. What changes is the audience relationship to that story. The animation recounts the saga of Morris Lessmore, blown away in a hurricane, who relocates to a library where he spends a happy lifetime caring for books – books that fly, dance, and applaud each other – and writing his own story. When his book is complete and he finally grows old, he departs/dies and a new booklover/caretaker arrives.

Again, the book provides the shortest telling. With Sendak, the short version is distilled and the longer versions are diluted. With *Morris Lessmore*, the case is not so straightforward. The film includes delightful vignettes absent from the picturebook: a book dancing out the tune of "Pop Goes the Weasel" on a piano keyboard, Morris mending a dilapidated book but restoring it to full life only by reading it. The first app retains such scenes and permits user interaction, so that the player is the one who picks out the melody on the keyboard. The book simply eliminates these and other details.

All versions of the story contain a rich intertext that draws on many well-known movies, a set of allusions helpfully elucidated by Schwebs (2014). Such cross-fertilization demonstrates another role for media studies of picturebooks.

The second app breaks new ground by using IMAG-N-O-TRON Augmented Reality to allow readers to overlay scenes from the book on top of live screen images of their own environment. This Moonbot production starts conservatively enough, with readers viewing pages of the paper book through the iPad camera, but certain openings order readers to "look up." When this instruction appears, readers must lift the tablet on which they are reading and point its camera at their surroundings (Figure 43.3). The image from the page survives this transition and is altered by the tablet's movement through space. Sometimes the camera image of the user's own personal environment

Figure 43.3 The Fantastic Flying Books of Mr. Morris Lessmore. Los Angeles, CA: Moonbot Studios, 2012. IMAG-N-O-TRON version.

Image credit: Moonbot Studios.

mingles with images from the book. In one surreal effect, the hurricane blows books and people across the reader's local scenery. On other occasions, the page image becomes animated; readers on a camera-led circuit of the library hear the 'voices' of the books murmuring their famous quotations as the camera eye passes over them. This phenomenon provides a vivid new metaphor for the way in which the reading process mingles textual information with readers' grounded understanding of their own world. It also presents a new and provocative version of remediation, in which the paper book simultaneously lies still under the focus of the camera and is digitally altered on the screen.

Morris Lessmore is conservative in its book-loving message, yet intriguing because the book itself is the least of the messengers. The special effects of its assorted variations are spectacularly rather than narratively radical, but they portend a future in which media effects are much more tightly interconnected with book pages.

Conclusions

These seven examples demonstrate how picturebooks may interconnect with media reworkings. What is more important is that even very young picturebook readers are multimodally alert. They oscillate between immediacy and hypermediacy from their earliest experience, are knowing consumers of adaptations, and intuit the complexities of convergence and transmedia through multiple encounters with different instantiations of the same story. Commercial considerations frame these interactions and also merit close attention. Scholarly work with picturebooks is enhanced by accounting for the insights promoted through media studies – which, in turn, is improved by an awareness of the ongoing potency of the still page. "Converging" and interdisciplinary scholarly approaches will sharpen our textual insights and promote a better understanding of the new skills and awareness that today's child readers bring to the challenge of interpreting their picturebooks (see, for example, Drotner and Livingstone 2008; Calvert and Wilson 2008; Mackey 2011; Lemish 2013).

Similarly, young readers of picturebooks will benefit from a more substantial understanding of the ways in which their text clusters are produced, financed, and converted into new forms. An age-appropriate media studies approach, presenting ideas about production and audience as well as exploring the contents of the book, will equip them to be better readers and more aware consumers.

Picturebooks and their readers inhabit a new and exciting media ecology; expanding and refining our understanding of this world is a necessary and fascinating project.

References

Bazalgette, Cary, and Buckingham, David (2013) "Literacy, Media and Multimodality: A Critical Response," *Literacy* 47.2: 95–102.

Bodmer, George R. (1992) "Sendak Into Opera: Wild Things and Higglety Pigglety Pop!" *The Lion and the Unicorn* 16.2: 167–175.

Bolter, Jay David, and Grusin, Richard (1999) *Remediation: Understanding New Media*, Cambridge, MA: MIT Press.

Briggs, Raymond (1978) *The Snowman*, London: Hamish Hamilton.

Calvert, Sandra L., and Wilson, Barbara L. (eds) (2008) *The Blackwell Handbook of Children, Media and Development*, Hoboken, NJ: John Wiley.

Carrier, Roch (2014/1984) *The Hockey Sweater*, 30th Anniversary Edition, illus. Sheldon Cohen, trans. Sheila Fischman, Toronto: Tundra Books.

Cubitt, Sean (2013) "Media Studies and New Media Studies," in John Burgess, Jean Hartley, and Axel Bruns (eds) *A Companion to New Media Dynamics*, Chichester: Wiley-Blackwell, 15–32.

de Kerckhove, Derrick (1997) *Connected Intelligence: The Arrival of the Web Society*, Toronto: Somerville House.

Dresang, Eliza T. (1999) *Radical Change: Books for Youth in a Digital Age*, New York: H.W. Wilson.

Drotner, Kirsten, and Livingstone, Sonia M. (eds) (2008) *The International Handbook of Children, Media and Culture*, New York: Sage.

Eisner, Will (2008) *Comics and Sequential Art*, New York: W.W. Norton.

The Fantastic Flying Books of Mr. Morris Lessmore (2011) film, dir. William Joyce and Brandon Oldenberg, Los Angeles: Moonbot Studios.

The Fantastic Flying Books of Mr. Morris Lessmore (2012) Los Angeles, CA: Moonbot Studios. App.

Grabarek, Daryl (2015, February 5) "David Wiesner's Spot-On App," *School Library Journal*, www.slj.com/2015/02/industry-news/david-wiesners-spot-on-app-touch-and-go/#_ (accessed October 26, 2015).

Herr-Stephenson, Becky, and Alper, Meryll with Erin Reilly (2013, March 16) *T Is for Transmedia: Learning Through Transmedia Play*, USC Annenberg Innovation Lab. PDF, www.joanganzcooneycenter.org/wp-content/uploads/2013/03/t_is_for_transmedia.pdf (accessed October 26, 2015).

Hoops, Richard (2013, March 26) "Diving Into a Digital App., *USC News*, https://news.usc.edu/48592/diving-into-a-digital-app/ (accessed October 26, 2015).

Hutcheon, Linda (2006) *A Theory of Adaptation*, New York: Routledge.

IMAG-N-O-TRON: The Fantastic Flying Books of Mr. Morris Lessmore (2012) Los Angeles, CA: Moonbot Studios. App.

Jenkins, Henry (2007, March 22) "Transmedia Storytelling 101," Confessions of an Aca-Fan: The Official Weblog of Henry Jenkins, http://henryjenkins.org/2007/03/transmedia_storytelling_101.html (accessed October 26, 2015).

Jenkins, Henry (2008) *Convergence Culture: Where Old and New Media Collide*, 2nd ed. New York: New York University Press.

Joyce, William (2012) *The Fantastic Flying Books of Mr. Morris Lessmore*, illus. Joe Bluhm, New York: Atheneum Books for Young Readers.

Lemish, Dafna (ed.) (2013) *The Routledge International Handbook of Children, Adolescents and Media*, New York: Routledge.

Mackey, Margaret (2011) "The Case of the Flat Rectangles: Children's Literature on Page and Screen," *International Research in Children's Literature* 4: 99–114.

Maurice Sendak and Septime Webre's Where the Wild Things Are (2008) www.youtube.com/watch?v=Xt4bKj0Oowc (accessed October 26, 2015).

Moss, Geoff (1991) "The Film of the Picture Book: Raymond Briggs's 'The Snowman' as Progressive and Regressive Texts," *Children's Literature in Education* 22.3: 195–204.

Ott, Brian L., and Mack, Robert L. (2014) *Critical Media Studies: An Introduction*, 2nd ed., Chichester: John Wiley & Sons.

Raymond Briggs' The Snowman (1993/1982) film, directed by Dianne Jackson, Culver City, CA: Columbia TriStar Home Video (DVD).

Reilly, Erin B. (2012, March 8) "Flotsam: A Transmedia Play Experience," http://ebreilly.blogspot.ca/2012/03/flotsam-transmedia-play-experience.html, (accessed October 26, 2015).

Schwebs, Ture (2014) "Affordances of an App: A Reading of *The Fantastic Flying Books of Mr. Morris Lessmore*," *BLFT: Nordic Journal of ChildLit Aesthetics* 5: n.pag, www.childlitaesthetics.net/index.php/blft/article/view/24169/32840 (accessed October 18, 2015).

Sendak, Maurice (2013/1963) *Where the Wild Things Are*, New York: HarperCollins (first published 1963).

Stone, Jon, (1999/1971) *There's a Monster at the End of This Book*, illus. Michael Smollin, New York: Golden Books.

The Sweater (1980) Roch Carrier. Dir. Sheldon Cohen. Montreal: National Film Board of Canada.

Where the Wild Things Are (2010) film, dir. Spike Jonze, Burbank, CA: Warner Home Video (DVD).

Wiesner, David (2001) *The Three Pigs*, New York: Clarion Books.

Wiesner, David (2002) "2002 Caldecott Speech," *David Wiesner*, www.hmhbooks.com/wiesner/2002-speech.html (accessed October 26, 2015).

Wiesner, David (2006) *Flotsam*, New York: Clarion Books.

Wiesner, David (2015) *Spot*, New York: Houghton Mifflin Harcourt. App.

44

PICTUREBOOKS
AND TRANSLATION

Riitta Oittinen

Introduction

This chapter deals with picturebooks in translation with a special reference to the translator's child image and the relationship of the different modes of the verbal, the visual, and the aural. Such multimodality is of current interest in the modern world, where we meet with visual culture every day (Oittinen and Tuominen 2007; Oittinen and Ketola 2014; Oittinen 2014, 2015). In other words, a picturebook in translation may be depicted as a polyphonic form of art with many different voices to be heard and seen, those of the author, the illustrator, the translator, the editor, and the different readers, children as well as adults (Garavini 2014; Nodelman 1999).

In addition, picturebooks are usually directed toward children who cannot read by themselves (children below school age) and who are often read aloud to, which makes it important to create picturebook translations that roll off the aloud-reader's tongue (Nikolajeva and Scott 2001; Nikolajeva 2002; O'Connell 2006; O'Sullivan 2013). Moreover, a picturebook to be translated is interpreted in a certain context, in time, place, culture, and ideology. All these features make translating picturebooks a special field of translation (Oittinen, Garavini and Ketola, 2018).

Translating as domestication and foreignization

A translator's choices are based on the concrete works of art (the entity and the details) being translated as well as on the translator's child image (Oittinen 2000). On the other hand, the choices are also based on the norms and poetics prevailing in society (for norms in translation see Toury 1980; 1995; Chesterman 1997). While aiming their words toward a certain purpose and audience, translators adapt their texts according to that purpose with an appropriate style. Translating is also influenced by the conventions of the target culture (Lefevere 1992; Oittinen 2000).

Moreover, translators use different strategies, such as domestication and foreignization: foreignization refers to a translation strategy where some significant trace of the original 'foreign' text is retained; domestication in turn assimilates texts to linguistic and cultural values in the target culture/society (Venuti 1995; Paloposki and Oittinen 2001). Translators may domesticate several things (names, setting) for several reasons (censorship, moral values) and for different audiences, cultures, religions, and beliefs. Even choosing books for translation may be a form of domestication: such books are chosen that travel easily from one culture and language to another.

The strategies of domestication and foreignization are usually seen as concerning verbal language only. Yet, for example, the illustration in a book may give a foreign, even strange flavor to a book, which may have a strong influence on the translator's choices and strategies. Translators may interact with the illustration by giving the book a particular flavor verbally, too; they may also tone down the foreign in the verbal text and let the reader figure it out on the basis of what is seen in the illustration.

Translating the verbal and the visual

Translators of picturebooks need knowledge of the different ways of collaboration between the verbal and the visual (Doonan 1993; Kress and van Leeuwen 1996; Serafini 2010). In other words, translators interact with illustrations in many ways. In a concrete sense, translators try to make the written text and illustration match each other, and in another sense, translators have internalized the images from their reading of the words and illustrations. In the interaction of word, sound, and picture, each detail contributes to the whole. In the case of translating picturebooks, the unity of words and pictures is translated with the intent of producing (rewriting) a new iconotext in the target language (Happonen 2007; Garavini 2014).

Illustrations may help translators in many ways: they show the time and place where the story is situated; they also show the relations of the characters and how they look exactly. With the knowledge about the details given in the pictures, it is easier for the translator to describe what the characters do and how they sound. For example, the Finnish translator of the South African Niki Daly's *Jamela's Dress* (1999; 2001) faced a tough problem concerning one scene, "a teapots song," as the protagonist Jamela calls it: "'Let's do teapots, Mama!' cried Jamela. So Jamela taught Mama to do a little song about a teapot with a spout. They dipped and tipped and the tea poured out" (n. pag.). The scene is illustrated, so the translator's options were limited. In the end the translator decided to create a functional translation without diluting the foreign features shown in the verbal and the visual texts. In the Finnish version the mother and Jamela are dancing to the song *"Aamulla herätys, sängystä pois,"* which is a Finnish-language version of the song "Lou, Lou, skip to my Lou!"

In Jamela's case, the translator was given useful hints from the original illustration. Yet when the illustration shows scenes in great detail, the visual may also be a formidable opponent to translators. The hardest visual problems with picturebooks are due to co-prints: to reduce costs, versions in different languages are often printed at the same time and in the same place. This implies that no changes can be made in the illustrations or the layout; in principle, only the text in writing can be altered. This is why translators of picturebooks need to conform their verbal texts to what they see in the pictures. Even market forces, such as publishing houses, and the concrete ways of printing books have an influence.

Moreover, in every picturebook there is a certain kind of relationship between the verbal (written and/or spoken words) and the visual (illustration), which the translator needs to recognize. The translator then makes the decision to what extent she will follow the relationship in her own text. Furthermore, there are many constituents in picturebooks influencing how translators interpret the story told in words and pictures. For example, there are colors that are used for salience, underlining or focusing on objects and things, or toning them down. A bright color with a dull background stands out, and a figure with similar colors to the background is hard to notice. The use of color also depicts the atmosphere of scenes, which is relevant knowledge for translators from the angle of the importance and role of characters. For example, characters with similar colors may be interpreted as belonging to the same group or family (Oittinen 2004).

Colors are also culture-bound. For instance, the colors black and white symbolize different aspects in Europe and Asia: in the West, white is for purity and black for mourning; in Asia it can be the other way around. In such cases translators may choose to explain or let the child and adult readers figure out problems by themselves. In addition to cultural associations, translators need to be aware of metaphors such as 'red like fire' or 'black like dirt': nature is different and of different colors in different countries. Moreover, there are also ritual colors, such as the holy colors of churches, which again differ from one culture and religion to another (Schopp 2001).

In the same vein, translators need knowledge about how illustrators use lines to depict things; for instance, strong or weak characters are often depicted with strong or faint lines (Oittinen 2004). This happens in Langston's *Mile-High Apple Pie* (2004a; 2004b), which depicts the friendship of a grandmother and her little granddaughter. By changing the letter types and sizes, the illustrator describes a strong little girl and her fragile grandmother, whose face and hair are almost transparent. In this way the illustration influences the translator's choice of similarly fragile words in the target language.

Another example of how strong an influence the visual has on the translator's solutions and how existing earlier versions influence the translator's work is *To Every Thing There Is a Season* (1998) by the American artists Leo and Diane Dillon and the book's Finnish translation *Kaikella on määräai-kansa* (unpublished). All the passages of the book are from the Book of Ecclesiastes in the King James Version of the Bible (1611). On each page opening, there is one line with an illustration depicting different cultures, periods of time, and visual techniques. Toward the end of the book, the reader finds detailed information on the techniques used and cultures referred to.

The Finnish translator decided to use the most recent Finnish version of the Bible from 1992. However, the decision proved problematic on one page opening, whose (verbal) text goes like this: "A time to embrace, and a time to refrain from embracing." The Bible translators of the 1992 Finnish version had a different point of view than the translators of the King James Version. The Finnish 1992 version can be rendered in English as: "Time to embrace and time to be separated."

Now there was an unwanted contradiction in the stories told by the verbal and the visual modes. On the left-hand-page picture, the family members are embracing each other and leading a cozy family life in a private home. On the right-hand page, the family is working together, not embracing but still together and certainly not separated. Yet it says in the Finnish 1992 version that the family is "separated." To solve the contradiction between the verbal and the visual, the translator decided instead, at this part of the text, to use the older version of the Finnish Bible from 1933, where the translator's solution is very close to the King James Version: "A time to embrace, and a time to refrain from embracing." At the beginning of the target-language text, the translator has added a short expla-nation of the solution and the reasons for it.

Translating for read-aloud purposes and sentence structure

Reading is the key issue in translating for children with several readers at the different stages of the book creation process. There are readers such as the source-language authors and illustrators, the edi-tors, and the translators as well as the target-language readers, such as the audiences of children and their parents (Wall 1991). Moreover, when books with illustrations are read, the reading process gets even more complicated (Schiavi 1996; Galletti 2009; Garavini 2014).

One complicating factor is that translations of picturebooks often involve the aloud-reader's human voice, which is a powerful tool. As Dollerup argues, reading aloud is a continuation of the oral tradition: there is "interaction between a narrative [. . .] an (adult) person reading aloud, and a child audience" (2003: 82f.). Reading aloud goes together with the problem of readability, which is not only influenced by calculations of nouns and adjectives or other obvious factors like technical details, layout, and paper quality, but involves several factors such as the reader's motivation as well as the familiarity and emotional charge of the words (Spink 1990).

Tymoczko gives a piece of advice: "Before starting an actual translation, a translator should care-fully study the rhythm of the original, reading it aloud to catch the rhythm, intonation and tone of the story" (Tymoczko 1999: 43; see also 1990). The aloud-reader uses similar oral means such as into-nation, tempo, and tone while performing the story for the child, who is listening to and co-creating the story (Suojanen, Koskinen and Tuominen 2015).

In practice this would mean that translators use certain kinds of words, sentence length, smooth or abrupt transitions, active versus passive voice, pauses, stress, and punctuation to create a text that can easily be read aloud. For example, in different languages, commas and other such constituents are markers for the eye and reading aloud: they give a sign to the aloud-reader where to pause and inhale. All this has an effect on how the story is understood by the different readers involved.

Sendak's classic picturebook *Where the Wild Things Are* (1963), with its plentiful translations (for instance, the German translation (Sendak 1967) and the Finnish translation (Sendak 1970)), is another example of the importance of sentence structure and its influence on translation (Oittinen 2003: 135–139). The book structure is based on the variation of short and long sentences and small and big pictures. The first short sentences, with smaller pictures, describe the protagonist Max having an argument with his mother, who punishes her son and sends him to bed without any supper.

Then, in one long sentence, from one page opening to another, Max's room starts changing into a jungle and the pictures grow larger until they bleed over the edges and, all of a sudden, Max is sitting in a boat that is hitting the shore of a strange land. While the boat hits the shore, the long sentence ends in a period. In other words, when there is a full stop in the verbal text, there is also a visual 'full stop,' when the picture repeats what is said in words. Through punctuation and line breaks, Sendak forces the aloud-reader into a certain performance and reading rhythm.

Sendak's verbal and visual narration and the whole story rely on the child's angle and are experienced through the eyes of a small boy. Sendak himself finds the book's structure very important and mentions that the purpose of this technique is to keep the reader interested and curious about what happens next (Lanes 1980). The entire rhythm of the book is built on this structure, which translators need to study very carefully (Rhedin 1992; Oittinen 2004).

Translating for audiences and characterization

Since the (main) target audience of picturebooks and their translations is children, all choices made by picturebook translators are guided by their child images and the ways in which they understand the needs of the future reader (Oittinen 2004; Rudvin and Orlati 2006). Depending on the translator's child image, the translated text may be directed toward the able or unable child. As Oittinen and Ketola (2014) point out, a translator's child image also "resembles the sociolinguistic concept of *Audience Design*, a receiver-oriented approach to communication, according to which speakers modify their style of communication depending on what their audience is like" (Suojanen et al. 2015: 35; see Bell 2001).

Audience design or translating for a certain kind of audience is not far removed from Bakhtin's (1984) dialogics of the reading situation, where the words of the author, illustrator, and the reader meet, constantly creating new meanings. In the same way, the translation of picturebooks involves a so-called narrative contract between those involved in the read-aloud situation. Bakhtin would call them super-addresses: "they do not exist in the flesh but are authors' assumptions of the future readers of a story" (cited in Morson and Emerson 1990: 135). This depiction of readerships is close to Schiavi's (1996) views about the real and implied readers and authors of translations (see also O'Sullivan 2003).

Not only the child image of the author, illustrator, and different readers have an influence on the general storytelling, but the solutions of picturebook translators also represent both the child image and the characters in the stories translated (Bertills 2003). Moreover, translated personal names are of special importance for children's picturebooks for two reasons. First of all, names give the readers the possibility of identifying themselves with the characters (17–20). Another, even more important reason – as mentioned earlier – is that it is important to create read-aloudable picturebook translations: sometimes the proper names in originals to be translated are too complicated to pronounce in the target language.

In every case, the entity of a book – the verbal and the visual, and a story told silently or aloud to different readers and the underlying child images – has a strong influence on what translators do with names. Leppihalme lists different strategies: names can be maintained as such, or they may be substituted or deleted altogether. Translators may also add elements to names or make them shorter or closer to the target-language context. Names may also archaize or modernize, domesticate, or foreignize the story (Leppihalme 1994).

Cultural differences and censorship

Different child images are mirrored in translations through deletions, additions, and even different morals in stories, such as regarding ideological concerns about censorship (see for the translations of *Gulliver's Travels*, Shavit 1986; see also Oittinen 2006). In illustrated versions, including picturebooks, the translator's hands are tied as the pictures cannot normally be changed. Of course, even with illustrations, translators may in their verbal choices tone down or add to the influence of the visual text. The picturebooks by the Finnish artist Mauri Kunnas, with their many intertextual and cultural references to Finnish culture and art, give an insight into the challenges translators of picturebooks might face.

A case in point is *Koirien Kalevala* (The Canine Kalevala 1992), which is verbally and visually based on the stories from the Finnish epic *The Kalevala* as well as the paintings by Akseli Gallen-Kallela, a Finnish artist representing Finnish romanticism and symbolism (Oittinen 2005). First of all, the translator needs to consider carefully how well the target-language readers are able to deal with the culturally specific information given both verbally and visually: whether they know the original stories of *The Kalevala* and to what extent they are able to recognize the original paintings behind Kunnas's canine versions.

This knowledge is very important in interpreting such passages where old Finnish vocabulary is used, which has caused problems for the English translator. In the following example, the anti-hero Lemminkäinen tries to ski:

> Many a valiant hero had sought to capture the elk of Hiisi, but to no avail. Now it was Ahti Lemminkäinen's turn to try. Taking up **his skis, the long lyly and the short kalhu**, away he went.
>
> *My backtranslation, my bolding*

> Many a valiant hero had sought to capture the elk of Hiisi, but to no avail. Now it was Ahti Lemminkäinen's turn to try. Taking up **his skiing gear**, away he went.
>
> *n. pag., English version by Steffa, my bolding*

Even though the words referring to old-fashioned skis – the long *lyly* and the short *kalhu* – are not well known to average Finnish readers either, the Finnish reader will at least recognize the words. Again, Kunnas's original is based on the text from *The Kalevala*, where the skis are clearly described verbally.

There are several reasons for the different solutions, in particular cultural differences. The landscapes, the tools used, and the way the main protagonists, dogs, dress and act may be rather strange to English-speaking readers, which is probably why the English translator has excluded both the names and the descriptions of the skis. While the illustration both in the original and the translation gives most of the missing information, the English translator relies heavily on the picture, which shows the difference in the skis.

Yet, without any reference to the length of the skis, the English-language reader may just think that the skis are funny because the character, the cat Lemminkäinen, is funny. At this point in the original, the author-illustrator gives detailed folkloristic information about old Finnish traditions, which, however, are left out of the English translation.

Cultural differences can also be seen in the direction of writing: not only words but also pictures are read from different directions, which may create concrete problems to translators and editors. In the Islam religion, the right hand is the holy hand for eating and the left hand is for other everyday purposes (Hämeen-Anttila 2001). Jehan Zitawi (2004), who has carried out research on the Arabic translations of the Donald Duck comics for children, refers to a situation where Huey, Dewey, and Louie become left-handed when the reading direction is changed and the illustrations have become mirror images of themselves. This may cause a scene where a piece of bread is held in the 'wrong' hand, which may in the translation lead to a solution where the illustration needs to be changed or mirrored.

In addition to the reading direction, there may also be other problematic cultural issues. Zitawi shows several examples that, in the Arab world, are considered unsuitable for children because of their immorality, such as kissing in public and ladies not wearing black for the beach. Even certain animals like pigs are considered unholy (see also Kaindl 1997). All these examples are certainly due to a certain child image, to the will to protect the child (Oittinen 2004; for the importance of religion in Arabic children's literature and its translation, see Mdallel 2003).

Another striking example is the English translation of the Finnish illustrator-storyteller Louhi's first Aino story (Louhi 1985, 1987). During the translation process there were considerable problems concerning cultural differences in the presentation of daycare centers and other phenomena of every-day Finnish life, which were all domesticated in the British translation. This is already evident with the book covers. The original book cover depicts a little boy who has run out of the house into the cold snowy yard with nothing on except for a cap on his head. This picture, which illustrates the liberal attitude of the Scandinavian cultures, needed to be altered for the English translation so that the boy is properly dressed in the British edition. In Finland the original scene is regarded as funny as well as displaying young children's innocence and carefreeness. This book was not co-printed, which also makes it an example of the reillustrating of books for translation.

Conclusion

Translating picturebooks involves the modes of the verbal, the visual, and the aural, in other words, the whole performance of the story read silently and aloud. To produce a well-functioning translation, it is necessary for translators to be aware of the interaction of the verbal and the visual as well as the potentialities of verbal expression, thus contributing in every way possible to the aloud-reader's enjoyment of the story. Moreover, translators need to concentrate on punctuation in order to create a rhythm in the text for the listener's eyes and ears as well as for the aloud-reader's tongue.

What makes the picturebook translators' task very rewarding, but also very difficult, is that they have to orchestrate a number of different modes of expression: the verbal text, the illustration, and the sound (voice). In this situation translating picturebooks requires the ability to make choices between the relevant and the irrelevant: translators need to aim at creating an understandable story in the target language and for the read-aloud situation, which again is influenced by the child image of the translator and her/his culture.

References

Bakhtin, Mikhail (1984) *Rabelais and His World*, trans. Hélène Iswolsky, Bloomington: Indiana University Press.

Bell, Allan (2001) "Back in Style: Reworking Audience Design Applied to Translation Studies," in Penelope Eckert and John R. Rickford (eds) *Language and Society, Style and Sociolinguistic Variation*, Cambridge: Cambridge University Press, 139–169.

Bertills, Yvonne (2003) *Beyond Identification: Proper Names in Children's Literature*, Doctoral Dissertation, Åbo: Åbo Akademi University Press.

Chesterman, Andrew (1997) *Memes of Translation: The Spread of Ideas in Translation Theory*, Amsterdam: John Benjamins.

Daly, Niki (1999) *Jamela's Dress*, London: Frances Lincoln.

Daly, Niki (2001) *Jamelan leninki*, trans. Riitta Oittinen, Kärkölä: Pieni Karhu.

Dillon, Leo and Diane (1998) *To Every Thing There Is a Season*, New York: The Blue Skye Press.

Dillon, Leo and Diane (unpublished) *Kaikella on määräaikansa*, trans. Riitta Oittinen, Helsinki.

Dollerup, Cay (2003) "Translation for Reading Aloud," in Riitta Oittinen (ed.) *Translation for Children / Traduction pour les enfants*, special issue of *Meta* 48.1–2: 81–103.

Doonan, Jane (1993) *Looking at Pictures in Picture Books*, Stroud: Thimble Press.

Galletti, Chiara (2009) "The Voices of Enchantment in Translating for Children," in Stefania Cavagnoli, Elena Di Giovanni, and Raffaella Merlini (eds) *La ricerca nella comunicazione interlinguistica*, Milan: FrancoAngeli, 317–332.

Garavini, Melissa (2014) *La traduzione della letteratura per l'infanzia dal finlandese all'italiano: L'esempio degli albi illustrati di Mauri Kunnas*, Doctoral dissertation, Annales universitatis turkuensis, Turku: University of Turku.

Happonen, Sirke (2007) *Vilijonkka ikkunassa: Tove Janssonin muumiteosten kuva, sana ja liike*, Helsinki: WSOY.

The Holy Bible. Authorized King James Version (2001), New York: Harper Collins (first published 1611).

Hämeen-Anttila, Jaakko (2001) *Kuka murhasi Kyttyräselän? Tarinoita tuhannesta ja yhdestä yöstä*, trans. and ed. Jaakko Hämeen-Anttila, Helsinki: Basam Books.

Kaindl, Klaus (1997) "Warum sind alle Japaner Linkshänder? Zum Transfer von Bildern in der Übersetzung von Comics," *TextConText* 13.1: 1–24.

Kress, Gunther, and van Leeuwen, Theo (1996) *Reading Images: The Grammar of Visual Design*, London: Routledge.

Kunnas, Mauri (1992) *Koirien Kalevala*, Helsinki: Otava.

Kunnas, Mauri (2002) *The Canine Kalevala*, trans. Tim Steffa, Helsinki: Otava (first published in 1992).

Lanes, Selma G. (1980) *The Art of Maurice Sendak*, New York: Harry N. Abrams.

Langston, Laura (2004a) *Mile-High Apple Pie*, illus. Lindsey Gardiner, London: The Bodley Head, Random House Children's Books.

Langston, Laura (2004b) *Mummin mehevä omenapiirakka*, illus. Lindsey Gardiner, trans. Sanna Vehviläinen, Helsinki: Lasten Keskus.

Lefevere, André (1992) *Translation, Rewriting, and the Manipulation of Literary Fame*, London: Routledge.

Leppihalme, Ritva (1994) *Culture Bumps: On the Translation of Allusions*, London: Multilingual Matters.

Louhi, Kristiina (1985) *Aino ja pakkasen poika*, Espoo: Weilin + Göös.

Louhi, Kristiina (1987) *Annie and the New Baby*, trans. David Ross, London: Methuen Children's Books.

Mdallel, Sabeur (2003) "Translating for Children in the Arab World: The State of the Art," in Riitta Oittinen (ed.) *Translation for Children / Traduction pour les enfants*, special issue of *Meta* 48.1–2: 298–306.

Morson, Gary Saul, and Emerson, Caryl (eds) (1990) *Mikhail Bakhtin: The Creation of a Prosaics*, Stanford, CA: Stanford University Press.

Nikolajeva, Maria (2002) "The Verbal and the Visual. The Picturebook as a Medium," in Roger D. Sell (ed.) *Children's Literature as Communication*, Amsterdam: John Benjamins, 85–107.

Nikolajeva, Maria, and Scott, Carole (2001) *How Picturebooks Work*, New York: Garland.

Nodelman, Perry (1999) "Decoding the Images: Illustration and Picture Books," in Peter Hunt (ed.) *Children's Literature: The Development of Criticism*, London: Routledge, 69–80.

O'Connell, Eithne (2006) "Translating for Children," in Lathey, Gillian (ed.) *The Translation of Children's Literature. A Reader*, Clevedon, Buffalo, and Toronto: Multilingual Matters.

Oittinen, Riitta (2000) *Translating for Children*, New York: Garland.

Oittinen, Riitta (2003) "Where the Wild Things Are: Translating Picture Books," in Riitta Oittinen (ed.) *Translation for Children / Traduction pour les enfants*, special issue of *Meta* 48.1–2: 128–141.

Oittinen, Riitta (2004) *Kuvakirja kääntäjän kädessä*, Helsinki: Lasten Keskus.

Oittinen, Riitta (2005) "Translating Culture: Children's Literature in Translation," *Literatur zonder leeftijd* 67: 45–56.

Oittinen, Riitta (2006) "No Innocent Act: On the Ethics of Translating for Children," in Jan Van Coillie, and Walter P. Verschueren (eds) *Children's Literature in Translation*, Manchester and Kinderhook: St. Jerome, 35–45.

Oittinen, Riitta (2014) "Child and Child in Translation: On the Multimodality of Translating Picturebooks," in Brett J. Epstein (ed.) *True North: Literary Translation in the Nordic Countries*, Newcastle: Cambridge Scholars, 149–167.

Oittinen, Riitta (2015) "The Mélange of Multimodality: Picturebooks in Translation," in Annjo K. Greenal and Domhnall Mitchell (eds) *Cultural Mélange in Textual and Non-textual Aesthetic Practices*, Oslo: Akademika, 95–111.

Oittinen, Riitta, Garavini, Melissa, and Ketola, Anne (2018) *Revoicing Picturebooks*, New York: Routledge.

Oittinen, Riitta, and Ketola, Anne (2014) "Various Modes for Various Receivers – Audience Design in the Context of Picturebook Translation," in Mikko Höglund et al. (eds) *In Word and Image: Theoretical and Methodological Approaches*, Tampere: Tampere University, 107–125.

Oittinen, Riitta, and Tuominen, Tiina (eds) (2007) *Olennaisen äärellä: Johdatus audiovisuaaliseen kääntämiseen*, Tampere: Tampere University Press.

O'Sullivan, Emer (2003) "Narratology Meets Translation Studies, or, the Voice of the Translator in Children's Literature," in Riitta Oittinen (ed.) *Translation for Children / Traduction pour les enfants*, special issue of *Meta* 48.1–2: 197–207.

O'Sullivan, Emer (2013) "Children's Literature and Translation Studies," in Carmen Millán and Francesca Bartrina (eds) *The Routledge Handbook of Translation Studies*, London: Routledge, 451–462.

Paloposki, Outi, and Oittinen, Riitta (2001) "The Domesticated Foreign," in Andrew Chesterman, Natividad Gallardo, and Yves Gambier (eds) *Translation in Context: Proceedings of the 1998 EST Conference in Granada*, Amsterdam: John Benjamins, 373–390.

Rhedin, Ulla (1992) *Bilderboken på väg mot en teori*, Stockholm: Alfabeta.

Rudvin, Mette, and Orlati, Francesca (2006) "The Readership and Hidden Subtexts in Children's Literature: The Case of Salman Rushdie's *Haroun and the Sea of Stories*," in Jan Van Coillie and Walter P. Verschueren (eds) *Children's Literature in Translation*, Manchester and Kinderhook: St. Jerome, 157–184.

Schiavi, Giulietta (1996) "There Is Always a Teller in a Tale," *Target* 8.1: 1–21.

Schopp, Jürgen (2001) "Kuinka paljon typografiaa kääntäjä tarvitsee?" in Riitta Oittinen and Pirjo Mäkinen (eds) *Alussa oli käännös*, Tampere: Tampere University Press, 253–274.

Sendak, Maurice (1963) *Where the Wild Things Are*, New York: Harper and Row.

Sendak, Maurice (1967) *Wo die wilden Kerle wohnen*, trans. Claudia Schmölders, Zurich: Diogenes.

Sendak, Maurice (1970) *Hassut hurjat hirviöt*, trans. Heidi Järvenpää, Helsinki: Weilin + Göös.

Serafini, Frank (2010) "Reading Multimodal Texts: Perceptual, Structural and Ideological Perspectives," *Children's Literature in Education* 41: 85–104.

Shavit, Zohar (1986) *Poetics of Children's Literature*, Athens: University of Georgia Press.

Spink, John (1990) *Children as Readers. A Study*, London: Clive Bingley, Library Association.

Suojanen, Tytti, Koskinen, Kaisa, and Tuominen, Tiina (2015) *User-Centered Translation: Translation Practices Explained*, London: Routledge.

Toury, Gideon (1980) *In Search of a Theory of Translation*, Tel Aviv: The Porter Institute for Poetics and Semiotics, Tel Aviv University.

Toury, Gideon (1995) *Descriptive Translation Studies and Beyond*, Amsterdam: John Benjamins.

Tymoczko, Maria (1990) "Translation in Oral Tradition as a Touchstone for Translation Theory and Practice," in Susan Bassnett and André Lefevere (eds) *Translation, History, and Culture*, London: Pinter, 46–53.

Tymoczko, Maria (1999) *Translation in a Postcolonial Context*, Manchester: St. Jerome.

Venuti, Lawrence (1995) *The Invisibility of the Translator. A History of Translation*, London: Routledge.

Wall, Barbara (1991) *The Narrator's Voice: The Dilemma of Children's Fiction*, Basingstoke: Palgrave Macmillan.

Zitawi, Jehan (2004) *The Translation of Disney Comics in the Arab World: A Pragmatic Perspective*, PhD thesis, Manchester: University of Manchester, School of Modern Languages, CTIS.

PART V

Adaptations and remediation

45

PICTUREBOOKS AS ADAPTATIONS OF FAIRY TALES

Vanessa Joosen

Introduction

What does the wolf in "Little Red Riding Hood" look like in grandma's clothes? What dress does Cinderella wear to the ball? What is the color of Rapunzel's hair? How old are Hansel and Gretel? Countless illustrators have provided visual answers to these questions. Our mental images of fairy tales may have been influenced by television, theater, and film, but these compete with pictures that have been provided by illustrators for more than three centuries. The abundance of fairy tale illustrations may seem puzzling. Why do artists feel the need to illustrate the same handful of stories over and over again, when so many others have already done so? The mere popularity of fairy tales helps to explain this abundance in part. The widespread familiarity with a selection of stories and figures, as well as nostalgia, motivates the continued purchase of fairy tale volumes to date. Many titles will be remembered childhood reading for parents and grandparents, who in turn want to share those stories with the next generations. Moreover, the most popular narratives and figures have become stock knowledge in Western culture that many (grand)parents and teachers want to familiarize children with – if only to understand the recurrent allusions to fairy tales in books, films, cartoons, commercials, and expressions. Fairy tale illustrations help to keep the stories up to date, offering a commercially attractive combination of the old and the new. Fairy tale picture books and illustrated collections are steady sellers that many publishing houses actively commission.

In addition to the commercial reasons, artistic motivations also drive the vast numbers of illustrated fairy tales. Maria Nikolajeva highlights the freedom that they grant illustrators: "Folktales are usually scarce in details concerning settings and the appearance of characters [. . .], which allows a vast spectrum of pictorial solutions" (2008: 469). Moreover, because fairy tales are believed to have their roots in oral tradition and their authorship is often debatable (see also below), many translators and adapters do not feel inhibited to further shorten and alter the tales to fit their own, their audience's, and/or the illustrator's needs. Finally, various artists seem to feel challenged rather than put off by the abundance of former fairy tale editions. Many highly respected illustrators have produced illustrations to fairy tales – for instance, Walter Crane, George Cruikshank, Gustave Doré, and Arthur Rackham, or more recently, renowned Hans Christian Andersen Medal winners such as Anthony Browne, Quentin Blake, Roberto Innocenti, and Lisbeth Zwerger. Contemporary illustrators are faced with the challenge of finding an original approach that can add to the vast number of existing styles and images. Illustrations for fairy tales do not only enter into a dialogue with the text, but also with predecessors who have produced iconic images to the tales. In her study of illustrations for the

Grimms' "Goose Girl," Ruth Bottigheimer observes what she calls a striking "iconographic continuity," with countless artists focusing on the same two scenes over a period of more than 150 years. She concludes that "a firmly established iconographic tradition existed from a very early point" in the history of the Grimm tales, and "a departure from it represented a conscious choice on the part of the artist" (1985: 59). Some illustrators make their negotiation with this iconic tradition an overt theme in their work. Various illustrators of "Little Red Riding Hood," for example, include intervisual references to Gustave Doré's scene of the wolf in bed with Red Riding Hood (Beckett 2002: 41), and in *The Tunnel* (1989), Anthony Browne pays tribute to Walter Crane's influential "Little Red Riding Hood" illustrations by including a replica in the main character's bedroom (Figure 45.1).

Fairy tales do not really seem to need illustrations in the first place, as they have been performed orally, and as plain texts without illustrations, for example in the large editions of the Brothers Grimm's *Kinder- und Hausmärchen* (Children's and Household Tales, 1812–1815) or the first volumes of Hans Christian Andersen's *Eventyr* (Tales, 1835). In fact, one of the fairy tale's most influential critics, Bruno Bettelheim, argued against visuals. "[T]he illustrations direct the child's imagination away from how he, on his own, would experience the story," he claims in *The Uses of Enchantment* (1976). "The illustrated story is robbed of much content of personal meaning which it could bring to the child who applied only his own visual associations to the story, instead of those of the illustrator" (60). This fear of interfering with the child's imagination may have motivated some illustrators, such as Warja Lavater (1965) and Jean Ache (1974), to create abstract images, such as colored dots and squares, in their visual interpretation of the narratives (Beckett 2002: 57). Moreover, the minimalist visuals in these books mirror the brevity of some folktales' texts.

Figure 45.1 Illustration from Anthony Browne's *The Tunnel*. London: Julia McRae Books, 1989.
Used by permission of Anthony Browne.

Bettelheim's skepticism about visuals is opposed to the enthusiasm for visuals in children's literature studies, where pictures are deemed to enrich rather than limit the child's imagination. That is true for fairy tales as much as for any other story. As David Lewis argues: "the presence of pictures appears to loosen generic constraints and open up the text to alternative ways of looking and thinking" (2001:66). Fairy tales thus feature not only as plain texts, but more often as illustrated texts (both in the form of individual booklets and in volumes with several tales) and as picturebooks. The distinction between illustrated texts and picturebooks is not always easy to draw, but Maria Nikolajeva offers the following "rule of thumb":

> in illustrated tales, the text can stand on its own, without illustrations, as it once has been written or retold. Picture books offer new dimensions and interpretations that make the images an integral part of the story. Words and pictures in a true picture book are inseparable, and the meaning is created by the synergy of the verbal and the visual art.
>
> *2008: 473*

Whereas images in illustrated tales often remain limited to one or a few key scenes, in picturebooks, the number of visuals is more substantial. Moreover, picturebooks usually appear as separate publications, covering just one tale, or an amalgam of tales in one story. Illustrated tales, in contrast, often appear in collected volumes with several stories. That being said, the two formats function as key points on a continuum that ranges from non-illustrated fairy tales to wordless fairy tale picturebooks. Given the central theme of this volume, I will focus on picturebooks in this chapter, yet also highlight how picturebooks build on the tradition of illustration styles that was established in illustrated fairy tales in the nineteenth century.

The most popular subgenres of the fairy tale in the West are tales of magic (such as "Cinderella") and cautionary tales (such as "Little Red Riding Hood"), and in this chapter I will limit myself to examples that belong to these types. I also distinguish fairy tales from fantasy. Fairy tales are short stories which take place in one world: characters do not travel in time or from one dimension to another. Magic is a natural part of the fairy tale chronotope (Nikolajeva 1996: 122). Although stories such as Lewis Carroll's *Alice in Wonderland* (1865) or C.S. Lewis's *Narnia* books (1950–1956) are sometimes referred to as fairy tales in popular culture, scholars do not usually consider them as such – they belong to fantasy rather than fairy tales. In this chapter, I will not distinguish between fairy tales that most scholars believe to have emerged as oral folktales (such as "Little Red Riding Hood") and those that are generally considered literary products (such as Andersen's or Oscar Wilde's fairy tales). It suffices to note that the oral or literary roots of certain tales are heavily debated in fairy tale scholarship (see Bottigheimer 2009 and Zipes 2012: 157–173). For picturebook adaptations, however, this discussion is less relevant.

Within fairy tale picturebooks, a distinction must be made on the basis of the narrative and its relationship to older written sources. Some fairy tale picturebooks reprint the entire text of an older fairy tale, without any major cuts or revisions of style and content. Roberto Innocenti's illustrations to *Cendrillon* from 1983, for example, appear with the full text of Charles Perrault's "Cinderella," except for the moral at the end (Perrault 1983). In most other picturebooks, however, the text is substantially shortened and adapted to cater to what adults perceive as the needs of a young, contemporary audience. Jack Zipes uses the term "duplicates" (derived from Pierre Bourdieu's theories on education) for tales that "reproduce a set pattern of ideas and images that reinforce a traditional way of seeing, believing and behaving" (1994: 9). Most fairy tale picturebooks fit into this category, with frequent adaptations to style and content. In fact, few picturebooks based on tales by Perrault, the Grimms, or Andersen will reproduce the elaborate and archaic style that is typical of their fairy tales, but instead modernize the language and make cuts on both sentence and plot level. Repetitions or scenes that serve similar purposes are often deleted. For example, in the Grimms' "Snow White" (1857), the evil queen attempts to kill the eponymous heroine with tight laces, a poisoned comb, and a poisoned apple. In many duplicates, only the apple is retained. In addition, few picturebooks retain the Grimms' cruel ending to this tale, in which the stepmother is forced to dance in red-hot shoes that have been heated in the fire, until she drops dead. This ending is often deleted, so that she simply disappears from the story or receives a less cruel punishment. Although fairy tale picturebooks exist for various ages (Beckett 2012: 209), and the first literary collections of fairy tales by Giovanni Francesco Straparola and Giambattista Basile were written for adults rather than children, a particularly large group of duplicates seems aimed at what Charlotte Bühler (1918) called the typical "fairy tale age": children of four to eight years old. Adaptations to style and content in the so-called duplicates serve to make fairy tales more suitable to be read aloud to young children.

Duplicates are distinct from rewritings of fairy tales, in which authors and illustrators play intertextual games with the traditional fairy tales' plots and generic conventions. Various terms exist for this type of self-conscious adaption: Lawrence R. Sipe calls them "transformations" (1993: 18); Cristina Bacchilega (1997) uses the term "postmodern fairy tales"; Nikolajeva and Carole Scott label them "fractured fairy tales" (2001: 228); and other scholars use rewritings and retellings (Joosen 2011; Beckett 2014). Whereas duplicates can serve as a first introduction to a tale, rewritings are based on the presupposition that readers are already familiar with the tale as a pre-text and have acquired some intertextual competence. The reader can then engage in an intertextual comparison to tease out the way that the author and illustrator have adapted the story. Metafictional play with fairy tale and other literary conventions occurs frequently in these picturebooks. Given the different dynamics with the fairy tale tradition, as well as the different expectations that duplicates and rewritings raise in the implied reader, the two types also yield a different interaction with illustrations. In what follows, I will first discuss duplicates, and then move on to postmodern rewritings. It should be noted at this point that the role of publishers should not be underestimated in the entire process of initiating, guiding, and completing the creation of a picturebook (Fraustino 2004). Moreover, book designers often play a crucial part in combining text and images, selecting cover art, and developing endpapers (Martin 2004). Picturebooks should always be understood as the result of collaborative projects, even when I will mostly stress the role of the illustrator in my discussion.

Traditional tales and duplicates

Although cheaply produced pictorial broadsheets and booklets with illustrated fairy tales had been circulating in the eighteenth and early nineteenth centuries, it is in the second half of the nineteenth century that volumes with illustrated tales began to be produced on a large scale (Nikolajeva 2008: 469). At the end of the nineteenth century, various renowned and influential European artists started to engage with fairy tales to show off their skills (Lindenhovius 2003: 212) and try out new techniques (Hines 2014). Many nineteenth-century illustrations breathe the atmosphere of a medieval Europe, with traditional professions (millers, spinsters, and tailors), little technology, a powerful monarchy, and no industry. The illustrations to fairy tale duplicates often still help to maintain that atmosphere. Countless fairy tale picturebooks adopt a romantic and detailed, sometimes even photographic style, and set the tales in a pseudo-medieval context. In her extensive study of illustrations to the Grimm tales, Regina Freyberger (2009: 74–98) distinguishes a distinct idyllic tradition (with illustrators such as Franz von Pocci, Ludwig Emil Grimm, Ludwig Richter, and Ludwig Pietsch) in German fairy tale illustrations, which would become a popular style for duplicate picturebooks in the twentieth century. Freyberger describes Richter's fairy tale illustrations as follows: "In hilly meadows and light forests, in labyrinth-like villages with typically German half-timbered houses and modest rooms, Richter's fairy tale figures always move calmly and communicate with composed gestures" (79, my translation). They radiate a timeless, idyllic atmosphere. Also in the nineteenth century, a more comic strand characterized fairy tale illustrations. George Cruikshank's humorous illustrations to Edgar Taylor's first English translation of the Grimm tales, *German Popular Stories* (1823, re-issued 1994), contributed to the books' great success, and inspired the Brothers Grimm to produce an illustrated edition of their tales in German. Like the idyllic, the comic tradition has persisted in the twentieth and twenty-first centuries, in illustrated volumes as well as fairy tale picturebooks. Walt Disney can be said to combine the idyllic and comic traditions with particular commercial success. Disney's influence is unmistakable, especially in so-called supermarket editions – cheaply produced duplicates for mass-market sale which operate within strict boundaries of what is acceptable as children's literature.

Fairy tales pose particular challenges to illustrators, in addition to the iconic images that new artists have to negotiate or engage with when they embark on illustrating fairy tales. Some include magical transformations, for example, as well as anthropomorphized animals and other fantastical creatures which can be hard to visualize. In addition, fairy tales often deal with taboo subjects, in particular sex and violence, and sometimes criticize established authorities. Andersen's "The Emperor's New Clothes" is notorious for forcing its illustrators into making a decision about whether or not to include a visual representation of the emperor's nudity, which is so crucial to the story and mentioned explicitly in Andersen's text. Vilhelm Pedersen (1848), Andersen's personal favorite illustrator and an icon in Denmark, refrains from visualizing the naked body, depicting a rather modest emperor in a long nightshirt (Andersen 1955). As Heinz Wegehaupt explains, Pedersen did not feel comfortable illustrating irony, fantasy, and satire in Andersen's stories (1989: 24). Hans Tegner, who worked for ten years on 250 woodcuts for a luxury edition of Andersen's tales from 1900 (Andersen 1900), did include highly realistic images of existing houses in Copenhagen in his illustrations to the same tale (Dal 1975: 25), but also refrains from depicting the naked emperor, although his similarities with the French King Louis XIV are in line with Andersen's criticism of royal vanity. Others, such as the Czech illustrator Cyril Bouda (1956) or the Danish Ulf Löfgren (1980), further highlight the emperor's perversity by drawing attention to his overweight, comical, and even effeminate body. Depicting the naked emperor without showing his private parts is a challenge that many illustrators in the comic tradition have taken on. One of the tailors happens to bow in front of his waist in a picture by the French illustrator Bertall (pseudonym of Charles Albert d'Arnoux) from 1862 (Andersen 1862). Löfgren only shows his naked backside and obscures his body from view by strategically placing members of the crowd during the crucial parade.

As Nikolajeva and Scott argue, pictures in fairy tale books "do not only reflect the individual style of the artist and his or her response to the story, but also the general style in illustration at a particular period, ideology, pedagogical intentions, the society's views on certain things" (2001: 42). Having investigated the illustration history of Andersen's "Thumbelina," they found striking differences in the protagonists' characterization and in the emphasis on plot elements that illustrators place: "It is illuminating to see how some artists seem to deliberately emphasize Thumbelina's hardships, while others, more overtly addressing a young audience, subdue or omit them" (44). Similar research yields comparable results for other fairy tales. Striking is, for example, how the age of a character like Little Red Riding Hood differs in various illustrations, ranging from cute toddlers to young adult women. Of course, it makes a crucial difference to the interpretation of the story. Perrault's moral, which suggests that the tale is an allegory of a young girl being seduced by a man, has led to numerous interpretations of this story as a tale of sexual initiation and rape (Zipes 1993). Such a reading is made more difficult when the female protagonist appears as a small child in the visuals, as in the illustrations by Trina Schart Hyman (1983) (Figure 45.2).

Especially in the second half of the twentieth century, fairy tales have become the subject of a wide array of interpretations, from such diverse paradigms as structuralism, gender studies, Marxism, psychoanalysis, queer studies, religious interpretations, and disability studies. Their shortness, relative lack of detail, and wide popularity made them particularly exploitable for these critical paradigms. Some illustrators have engaged with these interpretations and included elements in their visuals. Although the text may present a traditional version or child-friendly adaptation of a fairy tale, the illustrations can add layers of interpretation to the narrative and thus transform the reading experience as a whole. In *Critical and Creative Perspectives on Fairy Tales* (2011), I argue that visuals can foreground an interpretation of a certain tale by adding aspects or drawing attention to aspects or

Figure 45.2 Illustration from Trina Schart Hyman's *Little Red Riding Hood*. New York: Holiday House, 1983.
Used by permission of Holiday House.

parallels in the story that might have otherwise escaped the reader's attention because they are not highlighted in the text. Illustrations should thus be considered as part of the fairy tale's reception, and as part of the intertextual range of certain critical texts as well.

For example, in his picturebook version of the Grimms' *Hansel and Gretel*, Anthony Browne offers a take on the tale that runs parallel to Bettelheim's psychoanalytic interpretation (see Joosen 2011: 140–157). In *The Uses of Enchantment*, he interprets the stepmother and the witch as two different appearances of the mother figure. "Hansel and Gretel," he argues, illustrates a child's frustration in the oral stage of childhood, when "Mother no longer serves him unquestioningly" (1976: 163). He links the children's home and the gingerbread house in a similar way as two different manifestations of the same latent content, claiming that "the parental home 'hard by a great forest' and the fateful house in the depths of the same woods are on an unconscious level but the two aspects of the parental home: the gratifying one and the frustrating one" (163). In his illustrations, Browne draws various visual parallels between Hansel and Gretel's home and the witch's house that support Bettelheim's interpretation. The differences in the child's perceptions of the two houses that Bettelheim addresses are reflected in the subtle variation of artistic styles that Browne uses to visualize the two locations: whereas the parental home is drawn in a realistic and detailed style, the gingerbread house looks fuzzier and is reminiscent of a child's drawing, as if it stems from Hansel and Gretel's imagination. More striking still is the visual analogy that Anthony Browne draws between the stepmother and the witch, who both look at the children from a window. Witch and stepmother appear as two people with strongly resembling facial characteristics: the bitter shape of their mouths, the black wart on their right cheek, and the triangular lines around their nose and mouth signal that they are identical. Moreover, both women are drawn in an ominous black triangle, which functions as a visual leitmotif that can be discerned whenever the stepmother or witch is present. No more of these black cones appear after Gretel has pushed the witch into the oven – they seem to have simultaneously disappeared from the parental home, as has the stepmother. The children learn upon their return home that she has died – a coincidence that endorses Bettelheim's interpretation that the two women are in fact one. Browne's illustrations offer the reader a visual interpretation of "Hansel and Gretel" that may be inspired by Bettelheim, or that at least has strong similarities to his theory (see also Freudenburg 1998).

Fairy tale rewritings

The fairy tale picturebooks discussed earlier all rely on a complete traditional or duplicate fairy tale text. In addition, a variety of postmodern picturebooks based on fairy tales has appeared, particularly since the 1990s. As Nikolajeva and Scott have noted, "[i]n picturebooks, intertextuality, as everything else, works on two levels, the verbal and the visual" (2001: 228), and it is no coincidence that they include illustrated fairy tale retellings to explore this thought. A variety of rewritings have appeared, with various types of revisions. There are prequels and sequels to the best known tales, such as Jon Scieszka and Steve Johnson's *The Frog Prince Continued* (1991). Highly popular were picturebooks which responded to the feminist interest in fairy tales, either with gender role reversals, such as Robert Munsch and Michael Martchenko's *The Paperbag Princess* (1980), and Babette Cole's *Princess Smartypants* (1986) and *Prince Cinders* (1987), or by giving the female protagonists more agency and portraying them in more profound relationships, such as Jane Yolen and Diane Stanley's *Sleeping Ugly* (1981) and Ellen Jackson and Kevin O'Malley's *Cinder Edna* (1994). In the former, the prince chooses not the most beautiful, but the kindest girl, and the second juxtaposes two Cinderella figures with a different approach to life. While one establishes a marriage with a prince based on beauty and richness, the other opts for a simple lifestyle with a man who can make her laugh. A disregard for royal status also lies at the basis of Mini Grey's *The Pea and the Princess* (2003). As the title suggests, the pea plays a leading role in this picturebook, which reflects a common practice in fairy tale rewritings to change the narrative perspective to that of a minor character in the traditional tale. After numerous princesses have failed the famous test from Andersen's tale, this pea helps to convince the queen that a simple female gardener is the 'princess' that her son needs as a wife. Grey's closing doublespread reveals that it is a happy match. In other rewritings, not only the content, but also the register is adapted – mostly to produce a comic effect. Roald Dahl's *Revolting Rhymes* (1982), for instance, has a saucy narrator describe how Red Riding Hood does not only turn the wolf into a fur coat, but also has a handbag made out of the skin of the three little pigs that call on her for help. Quentin Blake's illustrations add to the humor, depicting Red Riding Hood with a bag that has a small curly tail sticking out.

It is common in postmodern fairy tales for authors to diverge from the fairy tale's unspecified time and setting (once upon a time, in a kingdom far away). Dahl's Red Riding Hood answers the telephone, and Philip Pullman's sequel to "Cinderella," *I Was a Rat!* (1999), features such modern items as tabloids and electric fences. Various illustrators also engage in this game of relocating the tales to an unexpected time and setting to subvert the reader's expectations – either in combination with a text that endorses this shift in time and/or in place, or in combination with the traditional tale. Fiona French's *Snow White in New York* (1986) has become a classic in this respect because of its successful merging of a few changes to the Grimms' plot, including a relocation of the tale to New York in the Jazz age, and the stylistic features of the illustrations, which match the art of this period (Joosen 2014). The book radiates a fascination with the fashion of the past, an aspect that is also developed in Lynn and David Roberts's *Cinderella: An Art Deco Love Story* (2001). In the afterword, David Roberts explains how his "background in fashion design made it especially fun to research the wardrobe of Cinderella and her wicked stepfamily" (n. pag.). The architecture and interior design were all based on existing art deco objects. The timeless chronotope of the fairy tale allows these kinds of playful shifts, and the books offer the reader both recognition and surprise, in combining elements from specific time periods with the tale. In *Snow White in New York*, for example, Snow White is not poisoned with an apple, but with a cherry in a cocktail and the seven dwarves are replaced with seven trendy jazz musicians.

Particularly successful was Jon Scieszka and Lane Smith's *The Stinky Cheese Man* (1992), a collection of fairy tale parodies that works on various levels (Figure 45.3). A red thread is the metafictional play with the conventions of the book and the genre of the fairy tale in particular. The introduction, written by the fictional narrator "Jack," announces that the book contains "Fairly Stupid Tales" and discourages the reader from going on. The individual tales parody not only the fairy tale's predictability and sentimentalism, but also the romantic style of some illustrations. "The Really Ugly Duckling," for example, features a caricature of a mad-looking duck on the first page, and is framed by six more realistically drawn illustrations of birds and ducks. The intertextual link with Andersen creates the expectation of the protagonist's transformation into a beautiful swan, which also features as the visual climax to most illustrated versions of this tale. That is not what happens in *The Stinky Cheese Man*, though: the following page simply shows the same picture of the mad duckling, now enlarged. Elsewhere in the book, "Jack's Bean Problem" draws attention to the fairy tale genre's formulaic nature. A giant cuts up a fairy tale book and pastes together various phrases in a collage. Most can be attributed to different tales, such as "happily ever after" and "a spell had been cast by a wicked witch." The collage brings to the fore the structuralist idea – best known from Vladimir Propp's *Morphology of the Folktale* (1975) – that fairy tales are constructed from a recurrent set of roles and plotlines. The accompanying illustration is a visual collage, in which the variety of artistic styles stands out, and which again draws on some shared features of the tales, such as a magic wand or a prince in shining armour.

The Stinky Cheese Man is a so-called fairy tale amalgam, a type of rewriting which blends various fairy tale characters and episodes into one story. Perhaps even more than any other type of rewriting, the amalgam relies on the reader's advance knowledge of fairy tales to follow the plots and get the jokes – yet, because of the widespread knowledge of fairy tales via various media, readers from a very young age can be expected to recognize at least some intertextual references to fairy tales (see Sipe 2000). Not all amalgams involve the iconoclasm of fairy tales – some are simply playful without criticizing the traditional tales. In Janet and Allen Ahlbergh's *The Jolly Postman or Other People's Letters* (1986), the mere enjoyment of recognizing fairy tale figures in unexpected roles and combinations is an important reason for the book's success, as is the play with the physical format of the book, which contains slots with letters to various characters. Goldilocks, for example, apologizes with the three bears for coming into their house and invites baby bear to her party. The wolf – still dressed in Grandma's clothes – receives an official letter from "Meeny, Miny, Mo & Co. Solicitors" to inform him that "Three Little Pigs Ltd. are now firmly resolved to sue for damages." The humor in this

Figure 45.3 Illustration by Lane Smith from Jon Scieszka's *The Stinky Cheese Man and Other Fairly Stupid Tales*. London: Penguin, 1992.

Illustrations copyright © 1992 by Lane Smith. Used by permission of Viking Children's Books, a division of Penguin Random House LLC.

episode relies on the mismatch of registers, as well as on the visuals: the postman is looking very nervous when he sees "Grandma" reading the letter.

David Wiesner's Caldecott winning *The Three Pigs* (2001) does not only alter the traditional narrative, but plays with illustration styles to produce its postmodern, metafictional effect. The narrative starts in a cartoonlike style, until the wolf blows the pigs out of the story and they are drawn in a more detailed, realistic style. They navigate through various other stories, each with distinct illustrative styles, to finally return home with a dragon they borrowed from one of the narratives. This dragon ultimately helps them defeat the wolf and create an alternative happy ending. Sipe's reader response research with this particular book in a first grade at an American elementary school led to the conclusion that the "children were able to keep track of the entrances and exits of the pigs and the other creatures by noting that when they were 'in' the stories, they assumed the coloration and illustration style of the story" (2008b: 234). The child readers thus recognized the differences in illustration styles and understood how Wiesner employed them to create various dimensions in his story.

Conclusion

Fairy tale picturebooks — whether in the form of duplicates or postmodern rewritings — enter into a visual dialogue with the long traditions of both fairy tales and the various illustrations for these tales. Several of the titles mentioned in this chapter have won awards and become classics in their own right. In addition to their artistic quality, these picturebooks also possess didactic possibilities for teaching young readers about genre conventions and evolutions in art and illustration. As Sipe argues on the basis of his reader response research with children:

> Just as intertextual connections enabled the children to build up schemata for stories, connections between illustrations in different texts allowed them to *construct and refine their ideas of illustration style*. They could recognize the distinctive styles of particular artists: the scratchboard of Brian Pinkney, Eric Carle's collage, the watercolor style of Jerry Pinkney, or Tomie de Paola's soft colors and rounded outlined shapes.
>
> *2008a: 143*

The vast number of fairy tale picturebooks that are available on the market indeed provide a unique corpus to make children aware of the various approaches that different illustrators can apply to the same story by selecting certain scenes, shaping characters and settings in a certain way, highlighting interpretations or using different styles and techniques. Some metafictional retellings, such as Scieszka and Smith's, or Wiesner's, even encourage this type of comparison within the book itself. With the differing accents that illustrators put on the tales, their fairy tale illustrations contribute to the reception of this genre, making it relevant again for each new age. Not only duplicates, but also those picturebooks that parody or radically alter the tales contribute to the fairy tale's longevity, by drawing on reader's knowledge of the genre and acknowledging its relevance to date.

References

Ache, Jean (1974) *Des carrés et des ronds: Fables et contes*, Paris: Balland.

Ahlberg, Janet, and Ahlberg, Allan (1986) *The Jolly Postman or Other People's Letters*, London: Penguin.

Andersen, Hans Christian (1862) *Contes d'Andersen*, illus. Bertall, 2nd ed, Paris: Librairie de L. Hachette.

Andersen, Hans Christian Andersen (1900) *Sprookjes van H. C. Andersen: Werelduitgave*, illus. Hans Tegner, Amsterdam: Scheltema & Holkema.

Andersen, Hans Christian (1955) *De vliegende koffer en 17 andere sprookjes*, illus. Vilhelm Pedersen, Den Haag: Daamen (first published 1848).

Andersen, Hans Christian (1956) *Pohádky a povídky*, illus. Cyril Bouda, Prague: Státní nakladatelství krásné literatury, hudby a umění.

Andersen, Hans Christian (1980) *The Emperor's New Clothes*, illus. Ulf Löfgren, London: Hodder & Stoughton.

Bacchilega, Cristina (1997) *Postmodern Fairy Tales: Gender and Narrative Strategies*, Philadelphia: University of Pennsylvania Press.

Beckett, Sandra L. (2002) *Recycling Red Riding Hood*, New York: Routledge.

Beckett, Sandra L. (2012) *Crossover Picturebooks: A Genre for All Ages*, New York: Routledge.

Beckett, Sandra L. (2014) *Revisioning Red Riding Hood Around the World: An Anthology of International Retellings*, Detroit: Wayne State University Press.

Bettelheim, Bruno (1976) *The Uses of Enchantment: The Meaning and Importance of Fairy Tales*, London: Thames and Hudson.

Bottigheimer, Ruth (1985) "Iconographic Continuity in Illustrations of 'The Goosegirl,'" *Children's Literature* 13: 49–71.

Bottigheimer, Ruth (2009) *Fairy Tales: A New History*, Albany: State University of New York Press.

Browne, Anthony (1989) *The Tunnel*, London: Julia MacRae Books.

Bühler, Charlotte (1918) *Das Märchen und die Phantasie des Kindes*, Leipzig: Barth.

Cole, Babette (1986) *Princess Smartypants*, London: Hamish Hamilton.

Cole, Babette (1987) *Prince Cinders*, London: Puffin.

Dahl, Roald (1982) *Revolting Rhymes*, ill. Quentin Blake, London: Ted Smart.

Dal, Erik (1975) "The Emperor's Different Clothes," *Danish Journal* 78.3: 24–27.

Fraustino, Lisa Rowe (2004) "Children's Book Publishing," in Peter Hunt (ed.) *International Companion Encyclopedia of Children's Literature*, vol. II., London: Routledge, 647–665.

French, Fiona (1986) *Snow White in New York*, Oxford: Oxford University Press.

Freudenburg, Rachel (1998) "Illustrating Childhood – 'Hansel and Gretel,'" *Marvels and Tales* 12.2: 263–318.

Freyberger, Regina (2009) *Märchenbilder – Bildermärchen: Illustrationen zu Grimms Märchen 1819–1945*, Oberhausen: Athena.

Grey, Mini (2003) *The Pea and the Princess*, London: Red Fox.

Grimm, Jacob and Wilhelm (1981) *Hansel and Gretel*, illus. Anthony Browne, London: Walker Books.

Grimm, Jacob and Wilhelm (1994) *German Popular Stories*, trans. Edgar Taylor and David Jardine, illus. George Cruikshank, reprinted as *Grimm's Fairy Tales*, London: Puffin (first published 1823).

Hines, Sara (2014) "German Stories/British Illustrations: Production Technologies, Reception, and Visual Dialogue Across Illustrations from 'The Golden Bird' in the Grimms' Editions, 1823–1909," in Vanessa Joosen, and Gillian Lathey (eds) *Grimms' Tales Around the Globe: The Dynamics of Their International Reception*, Detroit: Wayne State University Press, 219–238.

Hyman, Trina Schart (1983) *Little Red Riding Hood*, New York: Holiday House.

Jackson, Ellen (1994) *Cinder Edna*, illus. Kevin O'Malley, New York: Lothrop, Lee & Shepard Books.

Joosen, Vanessa (2011) *Critical and Creative Perspectives on Fairy Tales: An Intertextual Dialogue Between Fairytale Scholarship and Postmodern Retellings*, Detroit: Wayne State University Press.

Joosen, Vanessa (2014) "Snow White and Her Dedicated Dutch Mothers: Translating in the Footsteps of the Brothers Grimm," *Marvels & Tales* 28.1: 88–103.

Lavater, Warja (1965) *Le Petit Chaperon Rouge: une imagerie d'après une conte de Perrault*, Paris: Adrien Maeght.

Lewis, David (2001) *Reading Contemporary Picturebooks: Picturing Text*, London: RoutledgeFalmer.

Lindenhovius, Willemijn (2003) "'Een prentenboek, waarvoor een half koninkrijk betaald was.' Over artistieke sprookjesprentenboeken," in Saskia de Bodt and Jeroen Kapelle (eds) *Prentenboeken: Ideologie en Illustratie 1890–1950*, Amsterdam: Ludion, 210–27.

Martin, Douglas (2004) "Children's Book Design," in Peter Hunt (ed.) *International Companion Encyclopedia of Children's Literature*, vol. II., London: Routledge, 635–646.

Munsch, Robert (1980) *The Paperbag Princess*, illus. Michael Martchenko, New York: Scholastic.

Nikolajeva, Maria (1996) *Children's Literature Comes of Age: Towards a New Aesthetic*, New York: Garland.

Nikolajeva, Maria (2008) "Illustration," in Donald Haase (ed.) *The Greenwood Encyclopedia of Folktales and Fairy Tales*, Vol. 2, Westport, CN: Greenwood Press, 468–478.

Nikolajeva, Maria, and Scott, Carole (2001) *How Picturebooks Work*, New York: Garland.

Perrault, Charles (1983) *Cendrillon*, illus. Roberto Innocenti, Paris: Grasset & Fasquelle.

Propp, Vladimir (1975) *Morphology of the Folktale*, trans. Svatava Pirkova-Jakobson, Austin: University of Texas Press.

Pullman, Philip (1999) *I Was a Rat!* New York: Dell Yearling.

Roberts, Lynn (2001) *Cinderella: An Art Deco Love Story*, illus. David Roberts, London: Pavilion.

Scieszka, Jon (1991) *The Frog Prince Continued*, illus. Steve Johnson, London: Puffin.

Scieszka, Jon (1992) *The Stinky Cheese Man and Other Fairly Stupid Tales*, illus. Lane Smith, London: Penguin.

Sipe, Lawrence R. (1993) "Using Transformations of Traditional Stories: Making the Reading-Writing Connection," *The Reading Teacher* 47.1: 18–26.

Sipe, Lawrence R. (2000) "'Those Two Gingerbread Boys Could Be Brothers': How Children Use Intertextual Connections During Storybook Readalouds," *Children's Literature in Education* 31.2: 73–90.

Sipe, Lawrence (2008a) *Storytime: Young Children's Literary Understanding in the Classroom*, New York: Teacher's College Press.

Sipe, Lawrence (2008b) "First Graders Interpret David Wiesner's *The Three Pigs*: A Case Study," in Lawrence R. Sipe and Sylvia Pantaleo (eds) *Postmodern Picturebooks: Play, Parody, and Self-Referentiality*, New York: Routledge, 223–236.

Wegehaupt, Heinz (1989) *Rose, Prinz und Nachtigall: Hundert Illustrationen aus anderthalb Jahrhunderten zu Märchen von Hans Christian Andersen*, Berlin: Kinderbuchverlag.

Wiesner, David (2001) *The Three Pigs*, New York: Clarion.

Yolen, Jane (1981) *Sleeping Ugly*, illus. Diane Stanley, New York: PaperStar.

Zipes, Jack (1993) *The Trials and Tribulations of Little Red Riding Hood*, New York: Routledge.

Zipes, Jack (1994) *Fairy Tales as Myth – Myth as Fairy Tale*, Lexington: University Press of Kentucky.

Zipes, Jack (2012) *The Irresistible Fairy Tale: The Cultural and Social History of a Genre*, Princeton, NJ: Princeton University Press.

46

PICTUREBOOKS AND ADAPTATIONS OF WORLD LITERATURE

Marlene Zöhrer

The term 'world literature' has oscillated between at least three different meanings/concepts since it was first mentioned more than two centuries ago by Johann Wolfgang von Goethe. Although Goethe himself never really defined the term *Weltliteratur* (world literature), his main ideas of world literature became distinctive. Broadly speaking, Goethe thought of world literature as the result of international exchange and mutual refinement. Furthermore, he referred to outstanding texts as world literature (cf. Damrosch 2003, 2014). Since then the theoretical concepts mostly range between archival and aesthetic ideas, and between coverage of all literature from all over the world and a selective canon of masterpieces. "Literature in general, and world literature in particular, has often been seen in one or more of three ways: as an established body of *classics*, as an evolving canon of *masterpieces*, or as multiple *windows on the world*" (Damrosch 2003: 9). Regarding contemporary adaptions of world literature for children, it is mainly the idea of timeless 'masterpieces' that is considered as well as an understanding that combines two or even all three mentioned concepts.

In children's literature theory the idea of a 'world literature for children' has been discussed since the early twentieth century. Also in this context, the concepts of world literature oscillate between a selective canon and the coverage of all children's literature. One aspect of the discussion is the question whether retellings of works originally written for adult readers can be children's classics and therefore part of a canon of world literature for children (cf. Kümmerling-Meibauer 2003: 169ff.). The retelling of stories for child and adolescent readers is fundamental to children's literature: "Throughout the world, literature for children originates with retelling and adapting the familiar stories of a culture – folktales, legends and stories about historical and fictional individuals memorialized for their heroism or holiness, adventurousness or mischief" (Stephens 2009: 181). Along with fairy tales, folktales, myths, and religious texts, adaptations of world literature, such as works written by Miguel de Cervantes, Daniel Defoe, Hermann Melville, William Shakespeare, and Jonathan Swift, have a strong tradition in children's literature. Charles and Mary Lamb's retellings of Shakespeare's plays, *Tales from Shakespeare* (1807), became a children's classic, just like retold versions of *Gulliver's Travels*, *Robinson Crusoe*, and *Moby Dick*.

Interestingly, in recent decades there has been an ever increasing number of plays, novels, and poems originally written for an adult audience which have been published as picturebooks. This observation goes hand in hand with the tendency for traditional stories and modern classics to no longer be exclusively retold as (illustrated) storybooks, but also to be published in a picturebook format. Using the term 'retelling' for these picturebooks may be misleading, as they are more than abridged text versions. By means of the illustrations and the unique interplay of the re-narrated text and newly added pictures, they offer a wide range of possible meanings and interpretations. In children's literature research there have been attempts to describe the multiple processes and different levels of bringing a text originally written for adult readers into a picturebook form as 'adaptation' (mostly used without a concrete definition) as well as 'transformation' (Zöhrer 2011). While the term 'retelling' refers to the intertextual relationship between at least two texts (Stephens 2009: 182; for intertextuality, cf. Allen 2000), 'transformation' includes both the re-narrated verbal text and the newly added visual codes. Considering the visual as well as the verbal narration is essential when analyzing world literature in picturebook format, not least because "illustrations themselves may function as retold stories" (Stephens 2009: 196).

Transferring an extensive text into a picturebook is not only pruning by presenting the pre-text in a condensed version (cf. Genette 1997a: 238). The re-narrating and illustrating process is always a selective, interpretative act. Especially the newly added illustrations and the distinct interplay between the verbatim text and the pictures offer various new possibilities in presenting well-known texts. Nearly every form of text-image relationship (cf. Nikolajeva and Scott 2001) can be found: some visual narrations stay close to the stories; others contain amplifications or modified ways of interpreting the pre-text. Besides the question of what is shown in the illustrations and how pictures and texts interact, it is important to consider the artistic style of the picturebook. Pictures not only show scenes, motifs, and characters that are related to the text and its story line, but illustrate them in their own specific way that derives from different factors, such as materials, coloring, layout, and composition. Therefore, the same text may appear different when illustrated by various artists. Johann Wolfgang von Goethe's famous ballad "*Der Erlkönig*" (The Erlking, 1782) was recently adapted by two German artists, Jens Thiele (2007) and Sabine Wilharm (2013). Wilharm's version picks up the common idea of the Erlking as a green creature. In her vivid colored drawings he appears as an unappealing clown who is scary but not really dangerous. To further diminish the ballad's threatening character – the father is not able to protect his child from the Erlking, so that his son is dead by the end of the text – Wilharm creates a visual frame narrative for the poem and its elaborating, symmetrical illustrations. The visual narrative already begins on the half-title page, showing a boy and his father on their way to the train station. The boy buys a comic book telling a story about an adventurous horse ride, which anticipates the story of the Erlking. Sitting in the train to Weimar, the boy falls asleep in his father's arms, while feeling observed by the man sitting across from them. Only now does the main narrative of the Erlking begin, presenting Goethe's verse. The Erlking resembles the mysterious man in the compartment, and the pictures of the main narrative recall the comic the boy just finished. Embedded like this, the poem and its tragic end appear as a dream. The motifs of child abuse and pedophilia that are discussed within the psychoanalyzing interpretations of Goethe's poem are implied in Wilharm's illustrations but not explicated. Her picturebook addresses children in the first instance, while offering adult readers different levels of meaning. In contrast, Thiele's collages appear very dark and drastic as he is not trying to weaken the possible interpretations that Goethe's ballad offers, but to find artistic resemblances (Figure 46.1). The collages, made of newspaper photographs of humans, fabrics, and textures, create a stage set within which the story is arranged and visualized from alternating perspectives. Thiele's figurative language blurs the boundaries with artists' books. Furthermore, the motif of child abuse is noticeably present in his collages. Among other aspects, these facts give the impression that this picturebook version targets (first and foremost) adults.

Crossover audience

Transformations of world literature into a picturebook format often address a dual audience: children and adults. These picturebooks transcend the boundaries between child and adult readers in different

Figure 46.1 Illustration by Jens Thiele from Johann Wolfgang von Goethe's *Der Erlkönig*. Weitra: Bibliothek der Provinz, 2007.

Reprinted by permission of Bibliothek der Provinz, Weitra.

ways and on multiple levels. First and foremost, the fact that a text originally written by authors such as Shakespeare or Goethe is presented in picturebook form attracts the adult reader's attention. Children, especially younger children for whom picturebooks have traditionally been considered, will not pay much or any attention to the author's name or reputation. But concerning the adult readers these famous authors evoke expectations that may be very high – considering the quality of the pre-text – or even quite low, since the prestige of retellings only seems to have improved within the last few decades. In both ways the author's name functions as an intertextual clue that addresses the adult reader, who is the intended buyer of the book for children or even himself. Contemporary picturebooks presenting illustrated texts of world literature are books for all ages, commonly called 'crossover picturebooks' (Beckett 2009), which support intergenerational communication. Adult readers who are familiar with the pre-text may profit from the artistic interpretations by contemporary authors and illustrators who offer new perspectives on literary classics. By contrast, children can come in contact with stories or unabridged texts of world literature, while adolescent readers may occasionally use these picturebooks for preparing literature classes. For all of them these special picturebooks, based on texts written for an adult audience, offer different forms of reading depending on their age, knowledge, and literary socialization.

In addition to the verbal and the visual text and their individual interplay, the paratextual matter also is a relevant issue in addressing transformations (cf. Genette 1997b). In many cases the peritext, such as the cover and title page, reveals the artists' and publishers' motives and strategies as well as the implied audience of the picturebook. For instance, the paperback edition of Shakespeare's *A Midsummer Night's Dream* (2003), retold by Andrew Matthews and illustrated by Tony Ross, quotes

The School Librarian on the back cover, saying "An excellent introduction to Shakespeare for the young reader." This quote is clearly addressed to the adult or adolescent reader who is looking for something for this purpose – a good introduction to Shakespeare. Besides promotional statements, the peritext also often features statements that focus on the value of the pre-text and the actual picturebook. As retellings have often been criticized in the past, authors and editors tend to defend their choices and decisions in advance. This strategy was already practiced by Charles and Mary Lamb, whose retellings are still popular when transforming Shakespeare's plays into picturebooks (cf. Miller 2009). Today there are several picturebooks using individual stories from *Tales from Shakespeare* as the basis for newly added illustrations, for instance *The Merchant of Venice* (1995), illustrated by Dusan Kalláy, *King Lear* (2002), with illustrations by Gary Andrews, and *Ein Sommernachtstraum* (A Midsummer Night's Dream 2014), illustrated by Friedrich Hechelmann. Apart from the fact that the Lambs' stories are regarded as children's classics, the fact that their texts are royalty-free is a valid economic reason for publishers and artists to adapt their retellings for picturebooks. Numerous editions also reprint the Lambs' foreword explaining that their retellings should be considered as an introduction to Shakespeare and are meant to inspire young readers to return to the original plays when they get older. This intention is still common today, as these two paratexts demonstrate:

> this volume, which, like all the others in this line, is meant to provide an enjoyable hint of the greater wonders still in store when Hamlet is seen in performance, or read in its entirety.
> *Bruce Coville in William Shakespeare's Hamlet 2004*

> "A poem deserves its title only inasmuch as it excites, by elevating the soul." Since Poe defined poetry in terms of its ability to excite the soul of the reader, we think he would probably approve of our approach. We suspect that he might even feel gratified to know that, in this way, the children of our generation can hear the full beauty of his poetic voice and come to love his poetry.
> *Brod Bagert in Poetry for Young People: Edgar Allen Poe 1995*

Only during the last decade have the paratexts started to focus more on the artistic value of the transformation as an original artwork. This tendency points to the fact that "[f]inally, the boundary between picturebooks and related book formats, such as artists' books, altered books, and graphic novels, is progressively becoming blurred" (Kümmerling-Meibauer 2015: 249). Nevertheless, the paratexts still address possible adult readers in order to position these picturebooks at the interface between children's literature and literature for adults, thus aspiring to raise the prestige of the picturebook as an art form.

Selection and canonization

One of the frequently mentioned reasons for retelling and illustrating familiar or classic texts for children is the idea of giving them the ability to gain easier access to literary heritage. By means of such picturebooks, young or inexperienced readers can get in touch with famous authors and their stories, so that they are able to experience 'world literature' at an early age and ideally re-read the pre-texts later on. Furthermore, these picturebook versions can be regarded as an active attempt at canonization, whereby literary traditions are kept alive over generations, times, and countries. Regarding retellings for children, Stephens states that these texts serve "important literary and social functions, inducting [their] audience into social, ethical and aesthetic values of producing culture. Retellings are thus marked by a strong sense that there is a distinct canon within any of the domains" (2009: 181). This statement can also be applied to transformations.

Taking a closer look at the canonical texts that have been transformed into picturebook versions, it is obvious that this canon arises from ideas of Western tradition and culture. In selecting texts written by Edgar Allan Poe, Friedrich Schiller, Theodor Fontane, Emily Dickinson, Nikolai Gogol, Franz Kafka, Pablo Neruda, Langston Hughes, E.E. Cummings, Martin Walser, and John Irving, the corpus shows obvious parallels to traditional literary canons built on the idea of collecting 'the best texts' of a particular style, genre, time, or nation. On the other hand, there are many texts and authors of high international esteem and timeless 'relevance,' such as Charles Baudelaire, Fedor Dostojevskij, and Orhan Pamuk, that cannot be found in children's literature, neither as retellings nor as transformations. Therefore, it is not an existing canon of world literature that is brought into children's literature but a selection that relies on certain criteria. Tellingly, the main selection process is derived by the question: which stories, themes, and motifs are 'appropriate' for children? The labeling 'appropriate' is indeed flexible, as it depends on various factors such as the socio-cultural context, contemporary ideas of childhood, educational and didactic norms and requirements, regulations of literary markets, the public interest, and political issues, as well as personal beliefs, interests, and preferences.

When reflecting upon the range of picturebooks published within the last decades, it is evident that the selected pre-texts tend to be adventurous, fantastic, or in some way related to the everyday life of children. Especially stories and motifs connected to magic, nature, and animals are very popular. Shakespeare's *A Midsummer Night's Dream* (1600) and *The Tempest* (1611) attract young readers with their magical characters such as fairies and wizards. Gogol's *Hoc* (The Nose, 1836) was chosen for its fantastical element of a lost nose turning into a character itself in Catherine Cowan's picturebook version *Nikolai Gogol's The Nose* (1994). Kafka's *Die Verwandlung* (The Metamorphosis 1916) is appealing with the main protagonist awakening as a giant beetle one morning, as Lawrence David's *Beetle Boy* (2002) convincingly shows. Goethe's famous poem "*Der Zauberlehrling*" (The Sorcerer's Apprentice 1827) covers both magical and didactic motifs. The poem was first published in the former East Germany as a picturebook in 1958 (*Der Zauberlehrling*), with illustrations by Attila Dargai, followed by an artistic, crossover interpretation by Richard Seewald (*Der Zauberlehrling* 1959). Both picturebooks reproduce Goethe's poem literally. Since then, Goethe's poem has been published as a picturebook in more than twenty different versions. While German-speaking publications tend to present the ballad verbatim, there are several English prose re-narrations focusing on the story of the young apprentice getting into trouble because he is using magic while his master is away. The international popularity of the story is closely linked to Walt Disney's animated film *Fantasia* (1940), wherein Mickey Mouse embodies the apprentice. Moreover, Goethe's ballad contains features that can be identified as fundamental motifs of children's classics: the absence of parents or persons of authority and the disobedience/refusal of the child protagonist that leads to a quest. In combination with the didactic message (not to ignore the rules and to be aware of personal knowledge and skills) and the fantastic setting, these features make "The Sorcerer's Apprentice" highly attractive and suitable for picturebook versions for children.

In addition to the idea of what is appropriate for children, it is the status of the author as an 'author of world literature' that particularly influences the selection process. This prominence is relevant for ideological as well as economic reasons in cultivating and promoting the idea of the canon (Neuhaus 2007: 143). By targeting adults as readers and consumers, the high esteem of an author functions as an emotional sales argument. Since also relatively unknown pre-texts of familiar authors are re-narrated and illustrated for picturebooks, it is the author's reputation and not the status of the specific text that appears to be the decisive selection criterion. Emilio Urberuaga, for example, illustrated Julio Cortázar's not so well-known philosophical short story *Discurso del Oso* (The Bear's Speech, German ed. *Die Rede des Bären* 2009), whose main protagonist is a bear who lives in the pipework of an apartment house.

Reduction and amplification

The transformation of world literature into a picturebook format often means the reduction of a text of 150 to 200 or even more pages to thirty-two or forty-eight pages. The only exceptions are those picturebook projects dealing with poems or short stories (up to 4,500 words), which can be adapted literally. But even in these cases, the reduction of the texts may be necessary or desired. In his collection *Edgar Allan Poe's Tales of Mystery and Madness* (2004), Gris Grimly shortens the original texts by deleting sentences and passages, or as he ironically explains in the paratext, "The original tales have been ever so slightly dismembered – but, of course, Poe understood dismemberment very well" (n. pag.). Although Poe's stories are basically reproduced verbatim, the abridgements are extensive as they cut them down to the plot. Consequently, Grimly tries to preserve the dark, mysterious, and sometimes grotesque atmosphere of Poe's short stories within his illustrations. While it is evident that Grimly shortened Poe's texts due to limitations of space, there may be various personal and editorial reasons that led Jeanette Winter to prune Emily Dickinson's poems in her picturebook *Emily Dickinson's Letters to the World* (2002). Embedded in a frame narrative that focuses on Dickinson's sister Lavinia, who discovered 1,775 unpublished poems Dickinson left behind, Winter presents a selection of twenty-one poems. Overall, twelve of these poems are abridged. In most of these cases the picturebook only displays the first, introductory stanza. The very brief and simple poem "I never saw a moor," for example, is missing four of eight lines: "I never saw a moor, I never saw the sea; Yet know I how the heather looks, And what a wave must be. / I never spoke with God, Nor visited in heaven; Yet certain am I of the spot As if the chart were given" (n. pag.). By cutting the second stanza, the poem loses its religious implications and powerful message of belief and is somehow changed into a neutral and naturalistic statement about imagination.

In his essay "Nutshells and Infinite Space: Stages of Adaptation," Bruce Coville writes about his experiences of retelling Shakespeare's plays in a picturebook format. After selecting an appropriate play in consultation with his editor and the marketing department of the publishing house, Coville started re-reading and analyzing the text, trying to find the "'bones' of the play" (2003: 64). Before transferring the drama into prose, he wrote "a line or two for each scene to explain the main thrust of the action" (64). Also at this stage he began to mark some lines that he wanted to "use verbatim in text, some simply because I love them, others because they are well-known enough that they are almost required for the adaptation" (65). Both considerations, the change of genre and the search for adequate quotes from the original text, are typical operations when adapting plays for children. While prose narrative helps to present the story in a short and plain manner, the citations attempt to preserve some of the pre-text's characteristics and original language. Sometimes the authors or editors reveal this hybridization of the text with typographic marks.

Another attempt to keep the genre of the pre-text 'alive' lies within the illustrations. Almud Kunert in *Ein Sommernachtstraum* (2005) and Marcia Williams in *Tales from Shakespeare* (2004) use theater settings as a leitmotif when illustrating Shakespeare's *A Midsummer Night's Dream*. By embedding typical elements from the stage into their visual narration, the illustrators build a direct link to the dramatic genre of the pre-text.

Kunert's illustrations complement Barbara Kindermann's prose retelling of Shakespeare's *A Midsummer Night's Dream*. In her version Kindermann focuses on the magical elements of the play, composing a "fantastisches Märchen" (fantastic fairy tale), as stated in the paratext. Kunert also embraces the idea of telling a fairy tale in her pictures, but goes far beyond what is told in the verbal text. Within her pictures she tells an amplifying story that is highly related to the motif of the theater: the visual narration is composed as a performance wherein the inhabitants of Athens are marionettes controlled by the fairies Oberon and Titania (Figure 46.2). By establishing the vision of a puppet show, Kunert is able to visualize several story lines at the same time. Furthermore, in showing actors, audience, stage, and curtains, the pictures enter into a dialogue with Shakespeare's play.

Figure 46.2 Illustration by Almud Kunert from Barbara Kindermann's *Ein Sommernachtstraum. Nach William Shakespeare neu erzählt.* Berlin: Kindermann Verlag, 2005.

Reprinted by permission of Kindermann Verlag, Berlin.

Variation

Besides those books which try to keep the re-narrated text as accurate and close as possible to the pre-text, there are some picturebooks that take a different approach. Instead of trying to adapt the story, language, and style in an applicable way, they present creative variations. Diegetic transpositions (Genette 1997a: 294ff.) such as changing the time or place of the story, or changing the sex of the protagonist are also common with picturebook versions of world literature. Nancy Willard (1993) as well as Mary Jane Begin (2005) present female apprentices in their re-narrations of Goethe's ballad *Der Zauberlehrling* (The Sorcerer's Apprentice). Ted Dewan transfers his version of the ballad to the late twentieth century, turning the sorcerer into a brilliant inventor: "Everyone thought the inventor's machines were magical, so they called him the Sorcerer" (1998: n. pag.). As the Sorcerer is busy with inventing new things, he does not have the time to clean up his workshop, so he invents a robot called Apprentice. But the robot, when left alone, clones himself to get some help with the vacuuming. And so does his clone and all the other clones. Soon there is an army of robots and the help of the Sorcerer is needed to sort out the mess. This contemporary version, or as it is called in the paratext 'electric retelling,' not only changes the characters and setting but the implications of the story as well. As magic becomes science Goethe's original ballad changes into a statement about artificial intelligence, computers, and cloning.

Another example of the mode of variation is *Beetle Boy* (2002) by Lawrence David, with illustrations by Delphine Durand. The picturebook clearly marks its pre-text within the paratext ("inspired by Franz Kafka's *The Metamorphosis*"), in the naming of its protagonist, and in the first sentence, which is reminiscent of Kafka's opening: "Gregory Sampson woke one morning to discover that he had become a giant beetle" (n. pag.). Nevertheless, this picturebook does not retell or recapitulate Kafka's famous novella, but creatively modifies its motifs and story line. Besides the fact that the story has been relocated into a contemporary setting, it changes the protagonist into a young boy, who is (in contrast to Gregor Samsa) able to leave his room. Gregory even goes to school, attends classes, and talks to his friends and teachers. But except for his friend Michael, nobody seems to care about Gregory's transformation into a beetle, which causes rather funny situations:

> In class, Miss Dobson asked what two times three equalled. "Six!" Gregory shouted. "Come up and show your work on the blackboard," Miss Dobson instructed. Gregory drew an oval beetle body with six legs, three on each side. "Two sets of three makes six," he explained. "Well done," Miss Dobson said. "Not fair," Michael told his friend. "You counted your legs."
>
> *n. pag.*

Moreover, the ending is modified compared to Kafka's short story. Gregory does not die but retransforms into a boy. This new happy ending is initiated by Gregory's ignorant family, which finally recognizes the boy's transformation:

> "Do you still love me now that I'm a beetle?" Gregory asked. "We'll always love you," Dad replied. "Be you boy or beetle," his mother added. [. . .] Gregory Sampson awoke the next morning to discover he was no longer a beetle. [. . .] Gregory Sampson's beetle day was over.
>
> *n. pag.*

Despite the differences between the pre-text and the picturebook version, there are essential correspondences between both texts. The verbal and the visual text, just as Kafka's pre-text, consistently refuse to differentiate between imagination and reality. There are no rational reasons given for what is happening to Gregory. Furthermore, the picturebook deals with a deeply disordered family structure and the question of identity and isolation (cf. Kaulen 2005: 65). As Heinrich Kaulen points out, it is the distance from the pre-text that constitutes this picturebook's advantage: as there is no need to imitate or surpass the original, the picturebook gains in originality and autonomy (66). Durand's humorous and at the same time touching gouaches accompany the story, which is told in a descriptive and rather unemotional but simple tone. The illustrations find a well-balanced way of presenting Gregory's strong emotions (astonishment, fear, self-doubt, despair) and the funny situations arising from the fact that the boy awakes and finds himself morphed into a giant beetle. The visual narration situates Gregory's adventure in a contemporary setting, showing present-day toys, furniture, and everyday objects, accompanied by humans wearing weird clothes. The comic-like style and the colorful compositions emphasize the fusion of real and surreal elements that is an essential aspect of Kafka's text.

In these two picturebooks, *Beetle Boy* and *The Sorcerer's Apprentice* by Dewan, the illustrations focus on the newly written story and therefore underscore the contemporary setting depicted in the text by providing congruent information. Overall there is a distinct tendency to concentrate on the current verbal text in these contemporary picturebooks, that is, the re-narrated story or the verbatim cited poem. But even though the verbal text dominates the production as well as the perception of these picturebooks, it is the visual text that invites young readers to get in touch with transformations of world literature. And that of course offers contemporary, artistic interpretations of as well as new perspectives on the pre-texts for all readers – children and adults.

References

Allen, Grahame (2000) *Intertextuality*, New York: Routledge.

Bagert, Brod (ed.) (1995) *Poetry for Young People: Edgar Allen Poe*, illus. Carolynn Cobleigh, New York: Sterling Pub.

Beckett, Sandra L. (2009) *Crossover Fiction*, New York: Routledge.

Begin, Mary Jane (2005) *The Sorcerer's Apprentice*, New York: Time Warner Book Group.

Cortázar, Julio (2009) *Die Rede des Bären*, illus. Emilio Urberuaga, Zurich: Bajazzo Verlag.

Coville, Bruce (2003) "Nutshells and Infinite Space: Stages of Adaptation," in Naomi Miller (ed.) *Reimagining Shakespeare for Children and Young Adults*, New York: Routledge, 56–66.

Coville, Bruce (2004) *William Shakespeare's Hamlet*, illus. Leonid Gore, New York: Dial Books.

Cowan, Catherine (1994) *Nikolai Gogol's The Nose*, illus. Kevin Hawkes, New York: Lothrop, Lee & Shepard Books.

David, Lawrence (2002) *Beetle Boy*, illus. Delphine Durand, London: Bloomsbury (first published 1999).

Damrosch, David (2003) "What Is World Literature?" *World Literature Today* 77.1: 9–14.

Damrosch, David (2014) *World Literature in Theory*, Chichester: John Wiley & Sons.

Dewan, Ted (1998) *The Sorcerer's Apprentice*, New York: Bantam Doubleday Dell.

Fantasia (1940) directed by Norman Ferguson, USA: Walt Disney.

Genette, Gérard (1997a) *Palimpsests: Literature in the Second Degree*, Lincoln: University of Nebraska Press.

Genette, Gérard (1997b) *Paratexts: Thresholds of Interpretation*, Cambridge: Cambridge University Press.

Goethe, Johann Wolfgang von (1958) *Der Zauberlehrling*, illus. Attila Dargai, Berlin: Junge Welt.

Goethe, Johann Wolfgang von [1959] *Der Zauberlehrling*, illus. Richard Seewald, Esslingen: Schreiber.

Goethe, Johann Wolfgang von (2007) *Der Erlkönig*, illus. Jens Thiele, Weitra: Bibliothek der Provinz.

Goethe, Johann Wolfgang von (2013) *Der Erlkönig*, illus. Sabine Wilharm, Berlin: Kindermann Verlag.

Hechelmann, Friedrich (2014) *Ein Sommernachtstraum*, München: Thiele Verlag.

Kaulen, Heinrich (2005) "Kafka für Kinder? Überlegungen zur Kafka-Rezeption in der aktuellen Erzählprosa für Kinder und Jugendliche," *Kinder- und Jugendliteraturforschung 2004/2005*, Frankfurt: Peter Lang, 61–75.

Kindermann, Barbara (2005) *Ein Sommernachtstraum: Nach William Shakespeare neu erzählt*, illus. Almud Kunert, Berlin: Kindermann Verlag.

Kümmerling-Meibauer, Bettina (2003) *Kinderliteratur, Kanonbildung und literarische Wertung*, Stuttgart and Weimar: Metzler.

Kümmerling-Meibauer, Bettina (2015) "From Baby Books to Picturebooks for Adults: European Picturebooks in the New Millennium," *Word & Image* 31.3: 249–264.

Lamb, Charles (2002) *King Lear*, illus. Gary Andrews, Edinburgh: Capercaillie.

Lamb, Charles, and Lamb, Mary (1988) *Tales From Shakespeare*, London: Puffin (first published 1807).

Lamb, Mary (1995) *The Merchant of Venice*, illus. Dusan Kállay, Taipei: Taiwan Mac Educational.

Matthews, Andrew (2003) *A Midsummer Night's Dream: A Shakespeare Story*, illus. Tony Ross, London: Orchard.

Miller, Naomi (ed.) (2009) *Reimagining Shakespeare for Children and Young Adults*, New York: Routledge.

Neuhaus, Stefan (2007) "Wie kommen die Klassiker ins Bilderbuch?" in Jens Thiele (ed.) *Neue Impulse der Bilderbuchforschung*, Baltmannsweiler: Schneider Verlag Hohengehren, 129–145.

Nikolajeva, Maria, and Scott, Carole (2001) *How Picturebooks Work*, New York: Garland.

Poe, Edgar Allan (2004) *Edgar Allan Poe's Tales of Mystery and Madness*, illus. Gris Grimly, London: Simon & Schuster.

Stephens, John (2009) "Retelling Stories Across Time and Cultures," in M.O. Grenby, and Andrea Immel (eds) *The Cambridge Companion to Children's Literature*, Cambridge: Cambridge University Press, 181–206.

Willard, Nancy (1993) *The Sorcerer's Apprentice*, illus. Leo and Diane Dillon, New York: The Blue Sky Press.

Williams, Marcia (2004) *Tales From Shakespeare: Seven Plays Presented and Illustrated by Marcia Williams*, Cambridge: Candlewick Press.

Winter, Jeanette (2002) *Emily Dickinson's Letters to the World: Story and Pictures by Jeanette Winter*, New York: Farrar, Straus and Giroux.

Zöhrer, Marlene (2011) *Weltliteratur im Bilderbuch*, Wien: Praesens.

47

FILM VERSIONS OF PICTUREBOOKS

Johanna Tydecks

Film adaptations of literature are far from being a new phenomenon. Since the invention of cinema, directors and producers have released films whose screenplays are based on literary texts, whether written for a child or an adult audience. Consequently, adaption studies have mostly focused on film adaptations of novels, but recently, also adaptations of comics and graphic novels have been in the spotlight of film studies and intermedia studies (Albrecht-Crane and Cutchins 2010; Bosch 2010). By contrast, just a few studies have focused on the investigation of film adaptations of picturebooks so far (Kurtz 2005; Aldred 2006; Tydecks 2013; Annunziato 2014; Barton and Unsworth 2014), although the first adaptations of picturebooks already appeared at the beginning of the 1940s. This chapter first presents a short overview of the history of film adaptations of picturebooks before turning to the specific narrative and medial changes that an adaptation of a picturebook into a film requires. These changes touch on different aspects, relating to the picturebook story, the text-picture relationship, and the paratext on the one hand, and to technical issues on the other. Finally, the chapter discusses the different target groups addressed in the film adaptations of picturebooks.

History of film adaptations of picturebooks

One of the first film adaptations of a picturebook was the Walt Disney production *Dumbo* (USA 1941), an animated version of *Dumbo, the Flying Elephant* (1939) by Helen Aberson and Harald Pearl. The original book was and still is not very well known, in contrast to the film and the subsequent film tie-in. However, the majority of film productions refer to already famous picturebooks such as Raymond Briggs's *The Snowman* (1978), John Burningham's *Granpa* (1984) or Chris Van Allsburg's *Jumanji* (1981). These filmic adaptations use different media forms, from animated half-hour films (such as *The Snowman*, UK 1982 and *Granpa*, UK 1989) to animated feature films (*Dumbo*, USA 1941) and live action feature films (*Der Struwwelpeter*, Germany 1955). In contrast to these early films, the digital postproduction developed significantly in the 1990s: computer graphic elements have increasingly emerged in film versions of picturebooks since the release of the live action feature film *Jumanji* (USA 1995), in which special effects play a dominant role in the filmic narration. Naturally, the further development of media has influenced the film versions of picturebooks since the 1980s as well. For instance, the song "Make Believe," composed by songwriter Howard Blake for the film *Granpa*, was released as a record at the same time as the film. But media launches like this one remain scarce in the twentieth century. Even though there may be many different intermedial references to the same picturebook, as several musical settings of *Der Struwwelpeter* or a video game of *The Snowman* show, they do not refer to the film version and vice versa.

From 2005 on, the production of picturebook adaptations has developed rapidly. Also, the appreciation of these film adaptations has increased. In the twentieth century, only *The Snowman* (UK 1982) had been nominated for an Oscar. This situation has completely changed since 2009, when films such as *The Gruffalo* (Germany/UK 2009) and *Where the Wild Things Are* (USA 2009) appeared on the Oscar shortlist, and *The Lost Thing* (Australia 2010) won an Oscar in the category of Best Animated Short Film in 2011. Elaborate postproduction of all these films is increasingly blurring the boundaries between animation and live action. In addition, the boundaries between book, film, and other media are changing, which is evident in the references of movies to TV series, which in turn refer to picturebooks. A prototypical example of this approach is the Swedish production *Petsson och Findus – Kattonauten* (2000). This movie combines the story lines of the picturebook series created by the Swedish author – illustrator Sven Nordqvist and the story lines of a TV series that is based on these picturebooks. For 2017, director Jake Kasdan has announced a "re-imagining" of the filmic picturebook adaptation *Jumanji*, which came out in 1995 (Gussen 2016). Also the picturebook's movie version Dr. Seuss' *How the Grinch Stole Christmas* (USA 2000) should be rebooted into a new animated feature film in 2017 (see Orange 2016). Apart from the interactions between the different media formats, an increasing effort in film merchandising on social media platforms such as Facebook, Twitter, or Pinterest can be observed, which serve as a new way to promote public interest in a movie (Asur and Huberman 2010). These placements of movies on social media as well as the multiple cinematic reboots (Tryon 2013) are increasingly shaping the film industry, including filmic adaptations of picturebooks.

Narrative changes

Although picturebooks, which are distinguished by an intricate relationship between text and images or a narrative picture sequence (in the case of wordless picturebooks), share some commonalities with comics and graphic novels, their adaptation into a screenplay is much more demanding, considering the format and length of a picturebook, which usually does not extend beyond the number of thirty-two pages. Turning a picture sequence and its accompanying text into a feature film demands a substantial extension of the story line. For this reason, some directors have decided to release short films that more or less rely on the picturebook story and images. A prominent example is *The Lost Thing*, a 15-minute animated short film. Most film adaptations stretch the book's story line to at least half an hour, as happened with the animated feature films *Granpa, The Snowman*, or *The Gruffalo*. However, the number of full-length feature films is increasing, due to the eminent success of picturebook adaptations such as *Where the Wild Things Are* and *Shrek* (USA 2001). In this regard, the scriptwriters as well as the directors chose different strategies in order to enhance the original picturebook story.

In many film versions, the plot is the same as in the picturebook(s) with only minor additions or changes. Therefore, these films are either short films, such as *The Lost Thing*, or they refer to a series of picturebooks, as in Daisy von Scherler Mayer's *Madeline* (USA 1998), which adapts four picturebooks of the Madeline series by Ludwig Bemelmans (1939). This procedure of putting the story lines of several picturebooks together into one movie is used in many films, for instance in the different film versions (*Petsson och Findus*, Sweden 2000; *Petterson und Findus*, Germany 2014) of Sven Nordquist's book series (1984–2000) or in the animated comedy-drama *Ernest et Célestine* (France, Belgium, and Luxembourg 2012), based on a book series of the same name by Gabrielle Vincent (1981–2000).

In contrast, there are also film versions of picturebooks that expand and change the books' plots. Consequently, the depiction of the time course changes: even though the narrative time has not been altered, the narrated time increases. This is obvious in the movies *The Polar Express* (USA 2004) and *Where the Wild Things Are*. Although the storyboards are based on the respective picturebook story, some events and minor characters that are only briefly mentioned in the picturebooks have been elaborated in the film adaptations. Furthermore, the film scripts introduce new events and characters that do not exist in the picturebooks at all.

The film version of *Where the Wild Things Are* gives more space to the depiction of the protagonists' feelings, which are highlighted by the different camera perspectives and the music score, which brings "childhood simplicity to a very grown-up set of emotions" (Chinen 2009: n. pag.; see also Staiger 2012). Close-ups of Max and the Wild Things focus on their facial expression and visualize the emotional rapprochement between the protagonists (Figure 47.1).

Some film adaptations not only add to but also heavily modify the picturebook plots. The storyboard of the movie *Shrek* basically refers to the story line of the picturebook by William Steig (1990): Shrek, an ugly ogre, is sent out into the world in order to scare people. A witch tells him about an even uglier ogre girl, whom he seeks and finds. In the end, the couple scares people together. This basic plot is changed and enriched by allusions to classic fairy tales, including an ironic version of a fabulous love story: Shrek travels a long way and finally finds Fiona locked up and sleeping in a tower. He kisses her, thereby referring to the popular tale of Sleeping Beauty. Other intertextual references are the seven dwarfs or the magic mirror from Snow White. The movie is replete with explicit references to Walt Disney's fairy tale film versions (Márquez Pérez 2003). Metafictional devices emphasize the postmodern appeal of *Shrek*. For instance, on a self-referential metalevel, Shrek is reading a fairy tale on the toilet at the very beginning of the movie and laughs about the story, because he considers this fairy tale to be unrealistic. In this way, the film adds new parts to the plot and offers other levels of interpretation. Considering these substantial changes, film versions that are merely inspired by the book's story line verge on "cinematic re-creation" (see Bosch and Duran 2010): new characters or an expanded plot turn the adaptation into a completely independent, autonomous work of art.

Apart from the story line, the paratext plays a significant role in the picturebook narration (Nikolajeva and Scott 2001). Therefore, it should be asked in what way film adaptations refer to the books' paratext. In picturebooks, the elements of this transition zone between the 'real' and the

Figure 47.1 Screenshot of *Where the Wild Things Are*, directed by Spike Jonze. USA 2009.

fictional worlds can be visibly separated as well as blurred within the fictional text (Kümmerling-Meibauer 2013b): in *The Lost Thing* (2000) by Shaun Tan, there is no clear boundary between the paratext – the title page in the book or the credits in the film – and the main text. Both are presented in the same visual style. The book plays with the conventions of the paratext by including information about the author on the back cover or the announcement of the genre in the subtitle. This playful approach possibly challenges the reader to recognize and identify these conventions and raises the expectation of reading an unconventional story. The movie in turn includes the title credits in the imagery of the fictional story, a common practice on the big screen. The movie's end credits, however, are presented differently: they roll in a bright type over a black background, clearly separated from the fictional story, which is a conventional form of end credits. Therefore, the viewer of the film can establish, recognize, or enhance his knowledge of the filmic structure. While the end credits of the short film *The Lost Thing* are quite conventional, the opening credits, in contrast, integrate the paratextual information into the fictional film world in a playful way, which is comparable to the approach of the book's paratext.

Another strategy is evident in the opening credits of the movie *Shrek*. They zoom in on the open pages of a fairy tale book, which is being read by the main protagonist while he is sitting on the toilet. In contrast to the picturebook's modest front page, which does not show any ironic allusions, the movie's opening credits raise a completely different expectation on behalf of the viewer by metafictionally referring to the fairy tale tradition. Therefore, the movie deviates not only from the original book's story line but also from its paratextual design.

Maurice Sendak's renowned picturebook *Where the Wild Things Are* (1963) and its movie adaptation are another interesting case in point. The endpapers of the book repeatedly show a specific visual element that is also depicted on the book cover. This visual element consists of overlapping shapes that resemble leaves, which "seem to function as stage curtains for the drama of Max's adventures in the land of the Wild Things" (Sipe and McGuire 2006: 298). In the film version, the film does not open with a reference to the theater stage, but with credits that look as if they had been scribbled by a child's hand, followed by a tumultuous exposition in which Max is chasing his dog. This episode is characterized by a rapid montage, a shaky hand camera, and a very dynamic soundscape. Although the film's opening credits do not refer to the picturebook's paratext, they visually foreshadow the upcoming story. These few examples indicate that the filmic paratext is very often just loosely connected to the picturebook's paratext. These changes are probably due to the change of media, but also reflect the increasing complexity of children's films, which touches on the construction of the filmic paratext.

Target groups

The target group of picturebooks is mostly, though not necessarily, children. The increasing number of crossover picturebooks and even picturebooks for adults indicates that the strict age boundaries are becoming progressively blurred. In the same line, film adaptations of picturebooks address different user communities. While most TV series and short animated films which are based on a picturebook story are intended for preschool and primary school children, other movies, such as *Where the Wild Things Are* and *Shrek*, address children as well as adults due to their multiple levels of meaning. In film studies, these movies are categorized as 'family films,' thus stressing their cross-generational appeal:

> The production of so-called family films, that is, films that address children and adults alike [. . .] demonstrate[s] that the typical properties of modern children's films are becoming increasingly similar to those of films targeted at an adult audience.
>
> *Kümmerling-Meibauer 2013a: 39*

It is no wonder, then, that the film versions of picturebook stories pay tribute to the expanding of the target group with a more complex story line, added characters, changed topics, and intertextual references. The film *Shrek*, for instance, focuses more on partnership and love than the original picturebook. Moreover, this film is filled with tongue-in-cheek references to other literary texts and movies, which are more or less addressed towards an older audience. Some film versions even change the age of the protagonists: while Max, the main character in the picturebook *Where the Wild Things Are*, is a preschool child, his age has been increased to nine years in the film version in order to create a higher identification potential for the intended target group.

Studies in media literacy in general and film literacy in particular have demonstrated that children have to acquire the relevant filmic codes in order to understand the film story. Consequently, the reception of a film demands different media skills, which partially rely on those skills already acquired when attentively looking at a picturebook. In movies, various sensual stimuli have to be processed at the same time, and the duration of the film usually demands a longer attention span in comparison to the joint reading of a picturebook. In this respect, scholars recommend that children should have their first contact with a children's film when they are slightly older and already accustomed to the visual codes of picturebooks. Therefore, the shift from looking at a picturebook to watching a children's film which is an adaptation of a picturebook might support the acquisition of the significant filmic codes (Kümmerling-Meibauer 2013a).

In order to reach a broader audience, many contemporary film versions of picturebooks are launched on their own websites, including a separate Facebook entry and a trailer on YouTube. These publicity campaigns also provoke newly published editions of the respective picturebooks, mostly in the form of film tie-ins with a cover that either announces the cinema release or shows a still from the movie.

Technical changes

Picturebooks and movies as multimodal art forms are distinguished by a close relationship between words and images, which touches on multiple aspects, such as form, color, and style (Jenkins 2008). Other elements exist solely in one of the two media: while picturebooks rely on haptic aspects, which refer to the materiality of the book as well as the activity of pageturning (Nikolajeva and Scott 2001), films usually include sound and music. Concerning the production of films, three possible techniques to present the story line are discernible: as an animated movie, as a mixed live action movie, or as a live action movie.

The simplest way to adapt a picturebook into a movie is a stop motion film or an animated movie. These types of films are preferably used in TV series, such as *The Very Hungry Caterpillar and Other Stories* (USA 1993). Apart from these TV series, there is a wealth of book-based audiovisual material available online: as interactive apps (for example, *Dr. Seuss Apps* by Oceanhouse Media 2015), as stimulus-low online series (for instance, www.pikcha.tv), as YouTube channels both for private and educational use, and as a merchandise product that accompanies a newly released picturebook (for instance, www.picklesadventures.com). Yet animation movies are much more complex than these filmed, read aloud, and partly animated pages with a very low degree of visual detail and precision. In contrast, the Australian short film *The Lost Thing* has been presented at numerous film festivals around the world, such as, for instance, the Festival d'Animation d'Annecy in 2010. A few months after its cinema release, it was shown on TV in different countries, and it can now be streamed on YouTube and other internet channels. Nevertheless, it was produced neither for television or YouTube nor as an app (in comparison to many other animated versions of picturebooks). The movie version tells almost the same story as the picturebook. The images and even the metadiegetic references of the picturebook have been cleverly adapted to the screen (Tydecks 2013). The characters and the setting are subtly different in their filmic representation, due to filmic elements such as positioning, gesture, and sound effects (Barton and Unsworth 2014). Particularly the sound level of the *The Lost Thing* exemplifies the intricate effects of sound, which contribute to the significance of the film as a "multimodal artifact" (Bateman and Schmidt 2012). Different musical motifs that symbolize friendship, caring, and belonging create a soundscape of tonal, rhythmic, and expressive features which impact on the meaning-making process (Barton and Unsworth 2014). The film narration thus offers a new interpretation, which is particularly evident in the depiction of the relationship between the boy and the Lost Thing. While "there is limited affective response on the part of the boy" (Barton and Unsworth 2014: 8) in the picturebook, the film version subtly changes the verbal and visual narration, which is additionally supported by a music score in a way that emphasizes the strong emotional bond between both protagonists. By means of the soundscape and the diverse points of view, expressed by camera movements, the film version displays an elaborate and rather complex representation of the boy's state of mind.

Apart from the dynamics and the sound, the media format is necessarily another aspect that distinguishes picturebooks and films. In *The Lost Thing*, the film shows step-by-step how the boy enters the living room at home, looks at his sleeping parents, and then turns on the television with its advertisements. By contrast, the book influences the reader's perception of the corresponding advertisement by a preceding page-turn and an unexpected scene-to-scene transition. Similarly, the brief scenes of the Lost Thing entering Utopia and of the door closing behind it are not shown in the picturebook (Figure 47.3). Instead, after turning the page, the depiction of Utopia comes as a sensational visual surprise (Figure 47.2).

Similar to animation, mixed live action movies, which fuse animation and live action, mostly rely on the original picturebook's visuals. This hybrid form is being used increasingly with the expanding possibilities of different computer-generated effects. Usually, animated images of single characters are inserted into the live action scenery, as is evident in the German production *Petterson und Findus* (2014). Findus the cat is an animated character which resembles the picturebook character, while the other characters and the setting are filmed in the live action manner. The movie *The Polar Express* is more complicated, as the illustrations of Chris Van Allsburg's same-named book (1985) have been transferred into a live action movie style with the motion capture technique. A computer records the real-life movements of a real live actor (Tom Hanks) while he wears a suit equipped with reflector dots. The actor performs on a blank stage and all his movements and facial expressions are recorded in detail. These recorded movements are applied to different digital characters. In this manner, Tom Hanks plays the boy, his father, the hobo, Santa Claus, and the conductor. But only the last one is given Hanks's features. Nevertheless, the original images of the picturebook are easily recognizable in the movie version. However, some critics have complained that the movie's visual aesthetic shows the impact of computer games: "The problem with the technique, at present, is that the characters do not appear truly human" (Kurtz 2005: 788; see also Aldred 2006).

Live action movies as adaptations of picturebooks usually retain the picturebook's illustrations as well, as can be seen in the American movie *Madeline*. The images from the picturebooks are filled in by adding further details, thus enabling the extension of the original story line (Tydecks 2012). In general, the illusion of reality is bigger in live action movies than in animation, since animation creates fictional worlds with their own rules and structure, which can be radically different to the "real world" (Wells 2007: 10). Yet the acoustic level is added, and by this, the story's characters, the setting, and the atmosphere are strongly influenced and newly interpreted. Furthermore, each adaptation necessarily changes the original level of visual detail. Depending on the chosen technique, the characters can appear more game-like or more realistic, and the shown setting can hide or add different details, but it never maintains the exact level of detail of the picturebook.

Figure 47.2 Illustration from Shaun Tan's *The Lost Thing*. Sydney: Hachette Australia, 2000.
Used by permission of Shaun Tan and Hachette Australia.

Figure 47.3 Screenshot of *The Lost Thing*, directed by Shaun Tan and Andrew Ruhemann. Australia 2010.

Conclusion

In comparison to a picturebook, the interaction between visual and verbal text is necessarily different in the filmic adaptation. Whether it is an animated version of one or a series of picturebooks, whether the plot has been changed or elaborated – the film is a new work of art whose story line, characters, and visual style refer to another work of art (Stam 2000: 54–76). Picturebooks and film adaptations differ from each other in various technical- and content-related aspects: the film narration not only adds sounds, music, and voices, but also changes the viewer's perspective, since the camera leads the eye in a different way than the printed pictures do (Painter, Martin and Unsworth 2013; Kress and van Leeuwen 2006). This transfer might be smoother when picturebooks display characteristics of film narration, such as montage, zooming, changing distances, and dynamic movement, as is discernible in the drawing style of Sven Nordquist, Dr. Seuss, or Raymond Briggs. Therefore, they seem particularly suitable for film adaptations.

Live action movies present the characters and the setting in a more realistic, detailed way than a picturebook. In a feature film, not only details but whole episodes have to be added in order to expand the length of the film. Thus, many gaps in the picturebook story are necessarily closed by the film narration, filling much of the picturebook's imagination space. A prominent example is Maurice Sendak's *Where the Wild Things Are*, in which Max's mother does not appear in the visuals, while she plays a prominent role in the film adaptation. Such a visualization of characters or events that are implied but not visualized in the picturebooks demonstrates that film adaptations of picturebooks mostly rely on the depiction of what happens between one image and the next. This strategy might run the risk of reducing the imaginative space and multiple meanings inherent in the original picturebook, but it might also enhance the picturebook's initial story line, characters, and atmosphere by invoking new possible interpretations. This is often achieved by a subjective camera perspective, the soundscape, and additional episodes and characters. How this specifically happens and in what manner picturebooks and their film versions may elicit children's media literacy have not been fully investigated yet, although these aspects certainly would give new insights into the child's developing sense of media awareness.

References

Aberson, Helen, and Pearl, Harald (1939) *Dumbo, the Flying Elephant*, New York: Roll-A-Book.

Albrecht-Crane, Christa, and Ray Cutchins, Dennis (2010) *Adaptation Studies: New Approaches*, Teaneck, MD: Fairleigh Dickinson University Press.

Aldred, Jessica (2006) "All Aboard *The Polar Express*: A 'Playful' Change of Address in the Computer-Generated Blockbuster," *Animation: An Interdisciplinary Journal* 1.2: 153–172.

Annunziato, Sara (2014) "A Child's Eye View of *Where the Wild Things Are*: Lessons from Spike Jonze's Film Adaptation of Maurice Sendak's Picture Book," *Journal of Children and Media* 8.3: 253–266.

Asur, Sitaram, and Huberman, Bernardo (2010) "Predicting the Future with Social Media," *WI-IAT 2010 Proceedings of the 2010 IEEE/WIC/ACM International Conference on Web Intelligence and Intelligent Agent Technology* 1: 492–499.

Barton, Georgina, and Unsworth, Len (2014) "Music, Multiliteracies and Multimodality: Exploring the Book and Movie Version of Shaun Tan's The Lost Thing," *Australian Journal of Language and Literacy* 37.1: 3–20.

Bateman, John, and Schmidt, Karl-Heinrich (2012) *Multimodal Film Analysis: How Films Mean*, London: Routledge.

Bemelmans, Ludwig (1939) *Madeline*, New York: Scholastic Book Services.

Bosch, Emma (2010) "Orígenes de originales: Del libro ilustrado al film y viceversa," *BLOC: Revista Internacional de Arte y Literatura Infantil* 5: 34–52.

Bosch, Emma, and Duran, Jaume (2010) "Re-creaciones cinematográficas a partir de libros ilustrados y álbumes," *Actas del 32 International Congress IBBY: The Strength of Minorities*, Santiago de Compostela, September 08–12.

Briggs, Raymond (1978) *The Snowman*, London: Hamish Hamilton.

Burningham, John (1984) *Granpa*, London: Jonathan Cape.

Chinen, Nate (2009) "Mature and Focused Sets, with Breaks for Playtime," www.nytimes.com (last accessed December 7, 2015).

Der Struwwelpeter (1955) film, dir. Fritz Genschow, Germany: Fritz Genschow Films.

Dr. Seuss' How the Grinch Stole Christmas (2000) film, dir. Ron Howard, USA: Imagine Entertainment.

Dr. Seuss Apps (2015) Encinitas: Oceanhouse Media. App.

Dumbo (1941) film, dir. Ben Sharpsteen, USA: Walt Disney Productions.

Ernest et Célestine (2012) film, dir. Stéphane Aubier, Vincent Patar, and Benjamin Renner, France, Belgium, and Luxembourg: La Parti Productions, Les Armateurs.

Granpa (1989) film, dir. Dianne Jackson, Great Britain: TVC Granpa, TVS Television, Channel 4 Television Corporation, TVC London.

The Gruffalo (2009) film, dir. Max Lang and Jakob Schuh, UK and Germany: Magic Light Pictures, Studio Soi, Orange Eye; Co-Production: British Broadcasting Corporation (BBC), Nick Jr., (ZDF).

Gussen, Jason (2016) "'Jumanji' Remake: 5 Things the 2017 Reboot Needs to Compete With the Original Movie," www.designntrend.com (last accessed April 3, 2016).

Jenkins, Henry (2008) *Convergence Culture: Where Old and New Media Collide*, New York: New York University Press.

Jumanji (1995) film, dir. Joe Johnston, USA: TriStar Pictures, Interscope Communications, Teitler Film.

Kress, Gunter, and van Leeuwen, Theo (2006) *Reading Images: The Grammar of Visual Design*, New York: Routledge.

Kümmerling-Meibauer, Bettina (2013a) "Introduction: New Perspectives in Children's Film Studies," *Journal of Educational Media, Memory and Society (JEMMS)* 5.2: 39–44.

Kümmerling-Meibauer, Bettina (2013b) "Paratexts in Children's Films and the Concept of Meta-filmic Awareness," *Journal of Educational Media, Memory and Society (JEMMS)* 5.2: 108–123.

Kurtz, Leslie A. (2005) "Digital Actors and Copyright – From 'The Polar Express' to 'Simone,'" *Santa Clara Computer and High Technology Law Journal* 21: 783–805.

The Lost Thing (2010) film, dir. Shaun Tan and Andrew Ruhemann, Australia: Passion Pictures Australia.

Madeline (1998) film, dir. Daisy von Scherler Mayer, USA: Jaffilms. Madeline Films, TriStar Pictures.

Márquez Pérez, Aida (2003) "Shrek: The Animated Fairytale Princess Re-invented," in Ignacio M. Paacios Martínez, María José López Couso, Patricia López, and Elena Seoane Posse (eds) *Fifty Years of English Studies in Spain (1952–2002). A Commemorative Volume*, Santiago de Compostela: Universidade, Servicio de Publicacións e Intercambio Científico, 281–286.

Nikolajeva, Maria, and Scott, Carole (2001) *How Picturebooks Work,* New York: Garland.

Nordqvist, Sven (1984) *Pannkakstårtan*, Bromma: Opal.

Nordqvist, Sven (1986) *Rävjagten*, Bromma: Opal.

Nordqvist, Sven (1996) *Tuppens minut*, Bromma: Opal.

Nordqvist, Sven (2001) *När Findus var liten och försvann*, Bromma: Opal.

Orange, Alan (2016) *'How the Grinch Stole Christmas' Gets Benedict Cumberbatch as the Grinch*, www.movieweb.com (last accessed April 13, 2016).

Painter, Claire, Martin, James R., and Unsworth, Len (2013) *Reading Visual Narratives: Image Analysis of Children's Picture Books*, Sheffield: Equinox.

Petterson und Findus: Kleiner Quälgeist, grosse Freundschaft (2014) film, dir. All Samadi Ahadi, Germany: Tradewind Pictures, Senator Film Produktion; Co-Production: Senator Film München, (ZDF).

Pettson och Findus – Kattonauten (2000) film, dir. Albert Hanan Kaminski and Torbjörn Jansson, Sweden: Happy Life Animation AB.

The Polar Express (2004) film, dir. Robert Zemeckis, USA: Castle Rock Entertainment, Shangri-La Entertainment, ImageMovers Playtone.

Sendak, Maurice (1963) *Where the Wild Things Are*, New York: Harper & Row.

Seuss, Dr. (1957) *The Grinch*, New York: Random House.

Shrek (2001) film, dir. Andrew Adamson and Vicky Jenson, USA: DreamWorks Animation, DreamWorks SKG, Pacific Data Images (PDI).

Sipe, Lawrence R., and McGuire, Caroline E. (2006) "Picturebook Endpapers: Resources for Literary and Aesthetic Interpretation," *Children's Literature in Education* 37.4: 291–304.

The Snowman (1982) film, dir. Dianne Jackson and Jimmy Murakami, UK: Snowman Enterprises, Channel 4 Television Corporation, TVC London.

Staiger, Michael (2012) "Wo die wilden Kerle wohnen und wie man dorthin kommt," in Christian Exner and Bettina Kümmerling-Meibauer (eds) *Von wilden Kerlen und wilden Hühnern: Perspektiven des modernen Kinderfilms*, Marburg: Schüren, 106–120.

Stam, Robert (2000) "Beyond Fidelity: The Dialogics of Adaptation," in James Naremore (ed.) *Film Adaptation*, New Brunswick, NJ: Rutgers University Press, 54–76.

Steig, William (1990) *Shrek!*, New York: Farrar, Straus and Giroux.

Tan, Shaun (2000) *The Lost Thing*, Sydney: Hachette Australia.

Tryon, Chuck (2013) "Reboot Cinema," *Convergence* 19.4: 432–437.

Tydecks, Johanna (2012) "Verfilmte Bilder, verfilmter Text: Zur typologischen Einordnung von Bilderbuchverfilmungen am Beispiel der filmischen Rezeption von 'Madeline'," in Christian Exner and Bettina Kümmerling-Meibauer (eds) *Von wilden Kerlen und wilden Hühnern: Perspektiven des modernen Kinderfilms*, Marburg: Schüren, 121–146.

Tydecks, Johanna (2013) "The Lost Thing: Moving Media Language From a Picture Book to a Short Film," *Journal of Educational Media, Memory and Society (JEMMS)* 5.2: 45–60.

Van Allsburg, Chris (1981) *Jumanji*, Boston, MA: Houghton Mifflin.

Van Allsburg, Chris (1985) *The Polar Express*, Boston, MA: Houghton Mifflin.

The Very Hungry Caterpillar and Other Stories (1993) TV series, dir. Andrew Goff, UK: GAGA, Illuminated Film Company, Scholastic Productions.

Vincent, Gabrielle (1981–2000) *Les albums d' Ernest et Célestine*, Tournai: Casterman.

Wells, Paul (2007) *Animation: Prinzipien, Praxis, Perspektiven*, Munich: Stiebner.

Where the Wild Things Are (2009) film, dir. by Spike Jonze, USA: Warner Bros. in Association With Legendary Pictures, and Village Roadshow Pictures, Playtone, Wild Things Productions.

48

PICTUREBOOKS, MERCHANDISING, AND FRANCHISING

Naomi Hamer

While many children's literature texts continue to be produced as isolated print texts, many recent picturebooks, particularly those published in the United States, are often designed and distributed as part of multimedia franchises that may include film and television adaptations, online fan clubs, video games, and a range of affiliated merchandise such as clothing, accessories, and toys. While the nature of merchandising of picturebooks has significantly changed over the last two decades with the increased influence of digital technologies and multimedia franchising practices, merchandising has historically played a role in the production and reception of picturebooks as a distinctive format in book publishing. This chapter addresses the role of merchandising in relation to popular picturebooks and their affiliated products as well as the role of picturebooks themselves that may be defined as merchandise items, specialized collectibles, or toys in the context of broader media franchises.

History of merchandising and licensing of picturebooks

Merchandise is defined (as a noun) by the Oxford English Dictionary as "the commodities of commerce; goods to be bought and sold" with the more specific definition of "Branded products used to promote a particular film, pop group etc., or linked to a particular fictional character" (OED). In reference to the history of American franchising, Thomas S. Dicke describes "modern franchising" as

> a method of organization that combines large and small business into a single administrative unit. In a franchise system one large firm, often called the parent company, grants or sells the right to distribute its products or use its trade name and processes to a number of smaller firms.
>
> *1992: 2*

In the study of children's literature, the practices of merchandising and franchising are often discussed in relation to the practices of marketing and commercialization of the children's book publishing industry. In her entry on "Marketing" for *Keywords for Children's Literature*, June Cummins argues that "marketing is as essential to the development and dissemination of children's literature as technology was" (2011: 146). The publisher John Newbery is often seen as a significant figure in the emergence of children's literature as a new market for specialized texts. Cummins observes that "Newbery may have been the first to use the 'tie-in' – that is, he would include playthings along with the books he sold" in addition to explicit advertising tactics including product placement within fictional narratives that advertised his patent medicines (147). The 1744 publication of *A Little Pretty Pocket Book* is identified as one of the first profitable children's texts, including a pincushion geared at female readers and a ball for male readers. These gendered tie-in toys were produced and distributed with the print text. The movable book constituted another popular format for texts geared at young people during the eighteenth and nineteenth centuries, blurring the lines between books, toys, and games. As Jacqueline Reid-Walsh observes in her analysis of eighteenth- and nineteenth-century flap books and paper doll books,

> [m]ovable books came to be associated with children in the period of burgeoning commercial publishing for children during the Enlightenment, partly through the popularity of John Locke's ideas concerning the importance of visual images and playthings in the promotion of literacy.
>
> *2015: 213*

Similar to Newbery's ball and pincushion, paper-doll books as well as toy theaters reflected and targeted traditionally gendered consumers for these hybrid texts. Movable books became more elaborate in the Victorian period and continue to exist in contemporary children's cultures through the production of various forms of pop-up texts, as well as digital paper doll games (213).

Newbery's marketing of children's books alongside toys in the eighteenth century was expanded upon through the merchandising and licensing of Beatrix Potter's *Peter Rabbit* books. The agreement made between Frederick Warne & Co. and Potter in 1902 established Peter Rabbit as the first licensed character, setting the stage for future merchandising of children's books particularly those with visual narratives. Potter's book series illustrates both the role of merchandising in the design of distinctive small format hardcover picturebooks, as well as the production of toys, clothes, and dishware in relation to a picturebook series. In addition, Beatrix Potter as author and illustrator was (and continues to be) marketed as a brand unto herself alongside the branding of the characters, particularly Peter Rabbit. Margaret Mackey observes that "(Frederick) Warne spokespeople are quick to cite Potter's personal interest in marketing," including her personal development of a Peter Rabbit doll, a board game, slippers, and wallpaper (1998: 104–105). Mackey builds on her discussion of this early merchandising with an examination of the more recent commodification and reworking of this franchise including animated video adaptations, a range of toys from the original to collectible figurines, and the CD-ROM editions (1998). In Beatrix Potter's *Peter Rabbit: A Classic at 100* (2002), Mackey's examination of the 'Peter Rabbit Barbie doll' reveals the continued significance of tie-in merchandising: "Her presentation box, decorated with Potteresque woodland scenes, also contains a small paperback of the book, and the whole kit is produced through cooperation between Frederick Warne and Mattel" (173–174). Mackey's analysis highlights issues of corporate ownership of copyright and licensing that are central to the merchandising of picturebook texts.

Other early Anglo-American illustrated and picturebook texts that established the relationship between character licensing include the soft doll of Johnny Gruelle's Raggedy Ann (1915) (Bernstein 2011); Paddington Bear (1958) as a stuffed toy in 1972 (Clarkson 2008); the *Thomas the Tank Engine* franchise (1945–1972) based on Awdry's series (Mackey 1995); and A.A. Milne's *Winnie-the-Pooh*, originally published in 1926 with merchandising rights purchased in the United States and Canada in 1930, followed by the Walt Disney Company ultimately acquiring the rights to the Pooh character in 1961. While Milne's original text is an illustrated children's novel rather than a picturebook, the success of Pooh's character licensing led to the extensive production of tie-in texts that included Disney brand picturebooks following the adventures of individual *Winnie-the-Pooh* characters such as Tigger and Piglet. Avi Santo observes that Slesinger [the property licensor] "was the one who dressed up Pooh in his iconic red shirt in an effort to distinguish the character from other teddy bears on the market, a tactical marketing decision with decidedly creative and cultural impact" (2015: 8). As a result, the licensing and merchandising of Pooh has been the subject of multiple legal disputes.

Nevertheless, the successful merchandising of *Winnie-the-Pooh* and other early illustrated children's books led to the licensing and merchandising of picturebook characters (particularly those in a series) including the Reys' *Curious George*, Jean de Brunhoff's *Babar*, and Ludwig Bemelmans's *Madeline*. The merchandising of products related to these picturebook series has developed further through animated television or film adaptations and their associated products. Most recently, character licensing of Eric Carle's *The Very Hungry Caterpillar* and the pigeon from Mo Willems's *Don't Let the Pigeon Drive the Bus!* has resulted in the development of mobile applications and games related to these picturebook characters such as *Don't Let the Pigeon Run this App!* and *Eric Carle's Counting with The Very Hungry Caterpillar*.

In addition to early examples of affiliated picturebook merchandise, since the late nineteenth century in Europe, illustrated children's literature texts have been sold as limited edition gift items, as a distinctive type of collectible merchandise for adult consumers. Jacqueline Rose notes that J.M. Barrie's 1906 publication, *Peter Pan of Kensington Gardens* (with Arthur Rackham's illustrations) "has always hovered on the edge of the children's book market as something of an art book – a collector's item destined less and less to be read and more and more to be cherished and preserved" (1984: 27). Limited editions and re-issues of out-of-print picturebooks, particularly those with tactile or special formats continue this trend of the picturebook positioned as a collectible merchandise item. For example, Margaret Wise Brown's *Little Fur Family*, first published in 1946 with illustrations by Garth Williams, included a patch of fur for the reader to touch. Moreover, the original edition was wrapped in a book jacket of real rabbit fur blurring the picturebook's role as a physical object for a child's sensory play, and a collectible art object with potential references to Surrealism (Mavor 2007). These original versions have been critiqued for their use of animal fur, but also sold as valuable collectibles. The book has been re-issued in other specialized formats, first in 2003 as a deluxe edition with the use of synthetic faux-fur fabric, and in 2005 as a tactile board book. The limited edition faux-fur cover of Dave Eggers's novel *The Wild Things* (2009), based on and released in tandem with the *Where the Wild Things Are* (2009) feature film adaptation of Maurice Sendak's (1963) picturebook of the same name, builds on this concept of children's literature texts as collectible items, providing not only a tie-in text for the film franchise, but a collectible item that references both Sendak's picturebook and Brown's collectible fur book jacket.

Mass market publishers and 'The Little Golden Books'

While there are many examples of the mass market production of chapter book series for children and adolescents, comic books, and film novelizations for young people produced by the Stratemeyer Syndicate and other mass market publishers in the late nineteenth and early twentieth century, 'The Little Golden Books' by Simon and Schuster (beginning in 1942) may be identified as the first mass market picturebooks produced for young readers (Cummins 2011: 148). These series texts were designed distinctively from the picturebooks produced as isolated literary and artistic texts by publishers. The Little Golden Books were produced and consumed at low cost, and sold primarily at grocery stores and department stores rather than bookstores and public libraries. Leonard S. Marcus interprets the commercial publishing success of 'The Little Golden Books' as a reflection of the successful pairing of New York publishing and Midwestern manufacturing industries, particularly with the emergence of increasingly sophisticated and less costly printing press technologies in the 1920s and 1930s (2007: 10–11). Building on the popularity of 'The Little Golden Books,' Disney (beginning with the licensing of Mickey Mouse), Warner Brothers (with *Looney Tunes*), and other entertainment companies from the 1930s until the present have produced low-cost picturebooks for young people based on the brand characters from popular films, comic books, and television programs. These picturebooks rely on partnerships and contracts between publishers and entertainment corporations for licensing and copyright of characters and other licensed images. In these cases, the picturebooks functioned primarily as tools for marketing of a brand, series, an entertainment company or an author. 'The Little Golden Books' texts have often been produced for popular film franchises with the most recent text released for the *Star Wars* franchise (2015). More recently, 'The Little Golden Books' are also sold as collectible merchandise in the form of re-issued texts for nostalgic adult collectors and consumers.

Commercialization and branding in picturebook publishing

'The Little Golden Books' and other franchise tie-in texts range from those with minimal written narratives that supplement a series of film stills to picturebooks with more complex visual/verbal dynamics that draw upon the characters of popular franchises. The nature of these low-cost commercial texts, much like the Stratemeyer series (Inness 1997) books and popular series such as *Goosebumps*, the *Captain Underpants* series, and others have often been challenged by librarians and educators who perceive these texts as solely commercial items defined by minimal literary and artistic value for young readers.

While many of these texts are often sold in department stores and chain grocery stores, many franchise texts are also sold in the context of educational children's book publishing companies such as Scholastic. Cummins references a recent study in 2009 by the Campaign for a Commercial-Free Childhood that reports "fully one-third of the items sold through Scholastic's book-buying club service, in which the huge publishing company distributes catalogues to children through their classrooms, were not books but toys, posters, makeup, jewelry, and other nonliterary products" (2011: 150; see also Marsh and Millard 2000). Similarly, Jack Zipes argues:

> Most publishing houses [. . .] are now part of huge conglomerates and are directed by business managers. Decisions to design and publish books are more often than not made by the marketing people in the firm. Editors are expected to acquire and shape good products in keeping with corporate guidelines. These days a publishing house will more than likely have ties to a food or toy company or will be part of a vast conglomerate that will expect to the book company to meet rigorous financial goals.
>
> *2001: 7–8*

Zipes's observations continue to be relevant with the simultaneous production of cross-media franchises including story apps and other tie-in media platforms that play significant roles in contemporary book publishing for young readers.

In their guidebook for packaging designers, Marianne Klimchuck and Sandra Krasovec outline the development of characters in the design of brand products: "[c]haracters can be developed to support brand communication, promote product attributes, and become the embodiment of the brand's personality" (2006: 28). The design of picturebooks themselves and their associated brand texts often exemplify the use of recognizable characters and repetitive visual images as part of a book series or broader media franchise. Moreover, many picturebook artists (Peter Sís, David Macaulay, and Chris Van Allsburg) were trained, or worked in graphic design or advertising and carry these experiences across work venues and contexts. The recognizable visual design of picturebooks by the same illustrator exemplifies the blurriness between visual branding and the visual style of an artist. The Very Hungry Caterpillar, the Cat in the Hat, Peter Rabbit, and the Pigeon (who shouldn't drive the bus) are all recognizable picturebook characters that function in conjunction with the characteristic visual styles of their illustrators: Eric Carle, Dr. Seuss, Beatrix Potter, and Mo Willems.

In relation to a film or television adaptations of children's literature texts, the design of collectible franchise texts tends to support the brand images for the film franchise, sometimes overshadowing the original illustrator's style. For example, the branded visual images of the central characters are integral to the transformation of the *Arthur* picturebook series by Marc Brown (1976) into the PBS television series *Arthur* (1996–present). The animated series focuses on the elementary school adventures and struggles of Arthur, the central protagonist, an anthropomorphic aardvark in his daily life with his friends and family including his sister D.W., and friends Buster, George, and Brain, among others. The adaptation from book to television has resulted in the visual emphasis on Arthur's human qualities, reducing the size of his aardvark nose from earlier picturebooks by Brown, and in turn emphasizing Arthur's round eyeglasses and signature clothing (yellow sweater, blue jeans, and red backpack) as key visual elements associated with his character. The animated representations, promotional images, and tie-in products for the *Arthur* television series illustrate each character in characteristic outfits and stylized pose to reinforce one or two specific traits, often reducing each character to a visual stereotype. In addition, on the affiliated website, when one taps each character with the cursor, a speech bubble appears with a short line from the character that indicates a selective element of their personality associated strongly with the character (Arthur and Friends Webpage 2016). These changes reflect similar choices made in the recent adaptation of canonical children's literature for film and television (see Hamer 2015 for a discussion of C.S. Lewis's *The Chronicles of Narnia* (1950–1956). Children's television series franchises based on picturebooks such as Lauren Child's *Charlie and Lola* (2005–2010; BBC 2005–2010), Rosemary Wells's *Max and Ruby* (1985–2010; Nickelodeon 2002–2016), and Paulette Bourgeois and Brenda Clark's *Franklin and Friends* (1987–2002; Nickelodeon 2011–2012) exemplify these branding practices that emphasize visual stereotypes of character from the design of products such as backpacks to the visual aesthetic of mobile apps affiliated with the franchises.

Transmedia storytelling and cross-media play with picturebook merchandise

Contemporary picturebooks are increasingly informed by the practices of transmedia storytelling. Henry Jenkins defines a 'transmedia story' as one that "unfolds across multiple media platforms with each new text making a distinctive and valuable contribution to the whole" (2006: 95–96). Within the context of a transmedia narrative, the visual and verbal elements of print picturebooks are not only adapted across multiple media platforms, but the design of each affiliated text (e.g., an interactive mobile app) meaningfully extends, informs, or potentially subverts the central discourses of the picturebook narrative. Mackey's work on *Thomas the Tank Engine* (1995) illustrates the transformations of discourse around nationhood, socio-economic status, and gender in the UK context and how these are dislocated and renegotiated when these texts are adapted and consumed in the US context across various modes and platforms. In this context, the design of the *Thomas* books and franchise merchandise reflects changes in their production and consumption as part of transmedia narratives.

Cross-media texts are designed not only in terms of what the textual narrative represents, but also in terms of how the book fits into the broader meanings of a brand, franchise or cross-media world. Thus, the design of books for readers addresses them as not only implied readers of the text but also as potential consumers of other products in a franchise. In addition, franchises and fandom exemplify various examples of engagement with textual meaning that may be defined in terms of hybrid forms of cross-media play. Digital technologies and cultures have become central to how young readers engage with older media forms such as books, films, and television. Marie-Louise Gay's *Stella and Sam* picturebook series exemplifies a distinctively Canadian example of transmedia storytelling through the cross-media adaptation, design, and franchising of a picturebook narrative that includes: print picturebooks (Groundwood) such as *Stella, Star of the Sea* (1999); an animated television series (Radical Sheep Productions 2010–2014); a stage adaptation, *Stella, Queen of the Snow* (Mermaid Theatre of Nova Scotia 2014); interactive mobile applications (zinc Roe Inc.) and collectible Canada Post stamps (2013). Each text contributes to the cross-media representation of Stella and Sam as hyperbolically curious siblings and child explorers involved in a series of whimsical adventures in natural settings often with their dog Fred. Mackey describes how

> Most readers, viewers, and players are familiar with two associated phenomena. One is the sensation of being completely absorbed in a fictional world. A different form of involvement includes the capacity to move in and out of that absorbed attention in order to consider wider questions about the fiction, yet without entirely leaving the "fiction zone."
>
> *2007: 177*

The two picturebook app types associated with this series invite readers to move in and out of the fiction zone in two distinct manners. The apps related to the Stella and Sam picturebooks include the *Stella and Sam Story Pack* and *Draw Along with Stella and Sam*. *The Story Pack* includes animated stories with short breaks or interruptions to the narrative, where young readers are invited to complete a task related to the story, like echo bird calls or dress a snowman. The second app, 'Draw Along with Stella and Sam' invites readers to make rudimentary animated drawings related to natural phenomenon in the stories such as frogs and birds. Thus, the picturebook apps seem to reinforce the picturebooks presented on a new platform with the potential to engage beyond the text but not to influence the direction of the story. Moreover, the activities are not explicitly didactic, but follow a pedagogic model of literacy education for early story time engagement, learning about story elements and anticipating elements of the story.

Critical perspectives on picturebooks, commercialization, and material cultures

Research on the marketing and merchandising of picturebooks often reflects a conflict similar to the public media discourse around young people and media discussed by David Buckingham in *After the Death of Childhood: Growing Up in the Age of Electronic Media* (2001). Following Buckingham, discourses around the merchandising of children's literature tends to vacillate between a perspective of children as passive victims in the rise of the commercially dominated multimedia age (Quart 2003), and a vision of children as active participants empowered through the opportunities of new technologies (Gee 2003; Tapscott 1998). Young people are often perceived as victims to the commercialization of the children's publishing and the children's culture industry more generally. Steven Kline's (1993) and Sharon Lamb and Lyn Mikel Brown's (2006) studies exemplify scholarly work that emphasizes the institutional forces of commercialization of children's media culture.

Marsha Kinder (1991) was the first to examine the significance of transmedia franchising in children's media cultures at the levels of production and consumption. Her observations about what she termed 'transmedia intertextuality' to describe how brand characters are adapted across modes and media, continue to resonate in the context of contemporary transmedia storytelling and multiplatform franchising geared at young consumers. Comparatively, Ellen Seiter discusses the role of consumer and material cultures in the contemporary social lives of children: "Consumer culture provides children with a shared repository of images, characters, plots, and themes: it proves the basis for small talk and play, and it does this on a national, even global scale" (1993: 297). She also observes how "children make meanings out of toys that are unanticipated by – perhaps indecipherable to – their adult designers," and, referencing British anthropologist Daniel Miller's work on material culture (1987), she argues that the significance of cultural artifacts lies in "their active participation in a process of social self-creation" (299). Similarly, Dan Fleming (1996) draws upon a range of toys and text, including play objects such as toy theaters prior to the twentieth century to explore the role of narrativization in play. He illustrates the tensions between the production of cultural and gendered meanings through the design of toys, and the potential for agentive and subversive play.

Robin Bernstein (2011) extends this earlier work in an examination of how the interpretation of material culture texts (often those that may be defined as franchise texts or merchandise) as "scriptive things" may offer opportunities for agentive play and social resistance (8). Significantly, she traces the blackface minstrel roots of Johnny Gruelle's *Raggedy Ann* and examines a variety of texts including performances, books, dolls, pincushions, and other associated merchandise. In addition, she re-examines the psychological tests with young people conducted in relation to Raggedy Ann dolls in the 1940s. Her analysis indicates the importance for critical examinations of the broader cultural contexts of picturebook texts and their affiliated merchandise products in order to dismantle historically entrenched discourses of race, gender, and identity.

Recent audience studies research aims to illustrate the agentive roles of young people as active consumers and negotiators of cross-media textual meanings, including those related to picturebook and other children's media franchises. David Buckingham and Julian Sefton-Green pose the question:

> So what is Pokémon in itself? It is clearly not just a 'text,' or even a collection of texts – a TV serial, a card game, toys, magazines or a computer game. It is not merely a set of objects that can be isolated for critical analysis, in the characteristic mode of academic Media Studies. It might more appropriately be described, in anthropological terms, as a 'cultural practice.' Pokémon is something you *do*, not just something you read or watch or 'consume.'
>
> *2003: 379*

The multiplicity, variety, and hybridity of picturebooks in contemporary children's media cultures raise significant methodological and theoretical challenges. Andrew Burn argues in reference to the *Harry Potter* book series phenomenon and its many textual incarnations across film, video game, and merchandise, "we can no longer afford to see literature as an entirely distinct mode and culture, with its own distinct literacy" (2004: 5). Moreover, he observes that

> [w]e need to think, then, how different literacies come into play, how they connect, what they have in common. We also need to consider how these are located in the context of children's contemporary media cultures – the games they play, the films and TV programmes they watch, the comics they read.
>
> 5

He examines micro-level moments in this cross-media phenomenon in order to understand broader meanings.

Research on the relationships between picturebooks, popular culture, new media and digital literacy in early childhood are addressed in a selection of research papers edited by Jackie Marsh (2005). Building on earlier work on using popular culture in the classroom context (with Millard 2000), Marsh's own chapter in this 2005 volume examines the findings from two extensive studies of home-based media-related literacies in England, drawing on questionnaires, field note observations, and interviews with parents and children aged two to four. Marsh employs a diagram to illustrate one girl's texts and artifacts related to "the narrative web" of *Winnie the Pooh* (36). The extensive range of texts in this diagram includes: an umbrella, computer game, tie-in picturebooks, video, hot water bottle cover, and nightdress, among other items. Alluding to Anne Haas Dyson (2003), she argues, "moving across modalities, children encounter key interruptions and questions which force them to reconsider perceptions and accommodate new learning about these semiotic systems" (37). Marsh envisions these artifacts and texts of popular culture as significant mediators of identity development and draws on a number of distinct research studies to apply to her analysis of literacy practice and identity (including Dyson 1997) beyond children's engagement with books, to an examination of affiliated texts and products.

More recent research on participatory and convergence cultures (Geraghty 2015) has explored the role of fan cultures in relation to children's book franchises, often with a focus on children's fiction such as *Harry Potter* (Jenkins 2006, 2015) or *Peter Pan* remediated through Disney's Tinkerbell franchise (Meyers et al. 2014). However, while research on audience play with material objects and picturebook merchandise is extensive, research into digital fan cultures with picturebooks by adults and children is still limited. In counterpoint, Derek Johnson (2013) examines the institutional dynamics that frame franchising in the media industries. He aims to challenge purely economic analyses of intellectual property holders such as Disney in order to explore "how media producers generate, hold investment in, and extract other kinds of value from creative resources" and to "highlight franchising not just as industry and business, but as shared and iterative culture" (8). This approach has particular relevance to the role played by transmedia franchising strategies in relation to contemporary picturebooks.

As examined in this chapter, while the nature of the merchandising of picturebooks has significantly changed with article: the expansion and solidification of multimedia franchising practices, merchandising has historically played a role in the production and reception of picturebooks as a distinctive format in book publishing, and in the role of picturebooks as merchandise texts themselves. Contemporary picturebooks are often designed, merchandised, and then simultaneously released and distributed across various platforms. While research examines the linkages between transmedia practices and children's cultures, the increasingly significant role of transmedia strategies demands further research into the role of transmedia practices in the production and consumption of picturebooks. These practices require research that examines the contexts of picturebook merchandising, a range of texts, and the engagements of young people with these texts.

References

Arthur (1996-present) Cinar, PBS, Television.

"Arthur and Friends Webpage" (2016) *PBS Kids*, http://pbskids.org/arthur/friends/index.html#1 WGBH Educational Foundation (last accessed April 1, 2016).

Awdry, Wilbert (1997) *Thomas the Tank Engine: The Complete Collection (Railway Series)*, illus. C. Reginald Dalby, New York: Random House (first published 1945–1972).

Bemelmans, Ludwig (1939) *Madeline*, New York: Penguin.

Bernstein, Robin (2011) *Racial Innocence: Performing American Childhood from Slavery to Civil Rights*, New York: New York University Press.

Bourgeois, Paulette (1986) *Franklin in the Dark*, illus. Brenda Clark, Toronto: Kids Can Press.

Brown, Marc (1976) *Arthur's Nose*, New York: Little Brown Books.

Brown, Margaret Wise (1946) *The Little Fur Family*, illus. Garth Williams, New York: HarperCollins (re-issued in 2003).

Brunhoff, Jean de (1933) *Story of Babar*, New York: Random House.

Buckingham, David (2001) *After the Death of Childhood: Growing up in the Age of Electronic Media*, Cambridge: Polity Press.

Buckingham, David, and Sefton-Green, Julian (2003) "Gotta catch 'em all: Structure, Agency and Pedagogy in Children's Media Culture," *Media, Culture & Society* 25.3: 379–399.

Burn, Andrew (2004) "Potterliteracy: Cross-Media Narratives, Cultures and Grammars," *Papers: Explorations in Children's Literature* 14.2: 5–17.

Carle, Eric (1969) *The Very Hungry Caterpillar*, New York: Putnam.

Charlie and Lola (2005–2010) Creator: Lauren Child, Tiger Aspect Productions, BBC, Television.

Child, Lauren (2005) *Charlie and Lola: But Excuse Me That Is My Book*, London: Puffin.

Clarkson, Shirley (2008) *Bearly Believable: My Part in the Paddington Bear Story*, Petersfield, UK: Harriman House.

Cummins, June (2011) "Marketing," in Philip Nel, and Lissa Paul (eds) *Keywords for Children's Literature*, New York: New York University Press, 146–150.

Dicke, Thomas S. (1992) *Franchising in America: The Development of a Business Method 1840–1080*, Chapel Hill: University of North Carolina Press.

Don't Let the Pigeon Run This App! (2013) Version 1.1, App for iPad, Disney.

Draw Along With Stella and Sam (2013) Version 1.3, App for iPad, zinc Roe Inc. (last accessed March 14, 2014).

Dyson, Anne Haas (1997) *Writing Superheros: Contemporary Childhood, Popular Culture, and Classroom Literacy*, New York: Teachers College Press.

Dyson, Anne Haas (2003) *The Brothers and Sisters Learn to Write: Popular Literacies in Childhood and School Cultures*, New York: Teachers College Press.

Eggers, Dave (2009) *The Wild Things*, New York: Random House.

Eric Carle's Counting With The Very Hungry Caterpillar (2012) Night & Day Studios, app for iPad.

Fleming, Dan (1996) *Powerplay: Toys as Popular Culture*, Manchester: Manchester University Press.

Franklin and Friends (1997–2014) Nelvana, Television.

Gay, Marie-Louise (1999) *Stella, Star of the Sea*, Toronto: Groundwood Books.

Gee, James Paul (2003) *What Video Games Have To Teach Us about Learning and Literacy*, New York: Palgrave Macmillan.

Geraghty, Lincoln (ed.) (2015) *Popular Media Cultures. Fans, Audiences and Paratexts*, Basingstoke: Palgrave Macmillan.

Hamer, Naomi (2015) "Re-mixing *The Chronicles of Narnia*: The Reimagining of Lucy Pevensie Through Film Franchise Texts and Digital Cultures," in Karin Beeler and Stan Beeler (eds) *Children's Film in the Digital Age: Essays on Audience, Adaptation and Consumer Culture*, Jefferson, NC: McFarland, 63–77.

Inness, Sherrie A. (1997) *Nancy Drew and Company: Culture, Gender, and Girls' Series*, Bowling Green, OH: Bowling Green State University Popular Press.

Jenkins, Henry (2006) *Convergence Culture: Where Old and New Media Collide*, New York: New York University Press.

Jenkins, Henry (2015) "'Cultural Acupuncture': Fan Activism and the Harry Potter Alliance," in Lincoln Geraghty (ed.) *Popular Media Cultures. Fans, Audiences and Paratexts*, Basingstoke: Palgrave Macmillan, 206–229.

Johnson, Derek (2013) *Media Franchising: Creative License and Collaboration in the Culture Industries*, New York: New York University Press.

Kinder, Marsha (1991) *Playing with Power in Movies, Television and Video Games: From Muppet Babies to Teenage Mutant Ninja Turtles*, Berkeley: University of California Press.

Klimchuk, Marianne Rosner, and Krasovec, Sandra A. (2006) *Packaging Design: Successful Product Branding from Concept to Shelf*, Hoboken, NJ: John Wiley & Sons.

Kline, Stephen (1993) *Out of the Garden: Toys, TV and Children's Culture in the Age of Marketing*, London: Verso.

Lamb, Sharon, and Brown, Lyn Mikel (2006) *Packaging Girlhood: Rescuing Our Daughters from Marketers' Schemes*, New York: St. Martin's Press.

Lewis, C.S. (1950) *The Lion, the Witch and the Wardrobe*, illus. Pauline Baynes, London: Geoffrey Bles.

Mackey, Margaret (1995) "Communities of Fiction: Story, Format, and *Thomas the Tank Engine*," *Children's Literature in Education* 26.1: 39–51.

Mackey, Margaret (1998) *The Case of Peter Rabbit: Changing Conditions of Literature for Children*, New York: Routledge.

Mackey, Margaret (ed.) (2002) *Beatrix Potter's Peter Rabbit: A Children's Classic at 100*, Lanham: Scarecrow Press.

Mackey, Margaret (2007) *Mapping Recreational Literacies: Contemporary Adults at Play*, New York: Peter Lang.

Marcus, Leonard S. (2007) *Golden Legacy: How Golden Books Won Children's Hearts, Changed Publishing Forever, and Became an American Icon Along the Way*, New York: Golden Books.

Marsh, Jackie (2005) "Ritual, Performance and Identity Construction: Young Children's Engagement with Popular Cultural and Media Texts," in Jackie Marsh (ed.) *Popular Culture, New Media and Digital Literacies in Early Childhood*, London: Routledge, 28–51.

Marsh, Jackie, and Millard, Elaine (2000) *Literacy and Popular Culture: Using Children's Culture in the Classroom*, London: Paul Chapman.

Mavor, Carol (2007) *Reading Boyishly: Roland Barthes, J.M. Barrie, Jacques Henri Lartigue, Marcel Proust, and D.W. Winnicott*, Durham, NC: Duke University Press.

"Merchandise," Oxford English Dictionary, www.oed.com.libproxy.uwinnipeg.ca/view/Entry/116642?result=1&rskey=GE7L3k& (last accessed June 17, 2015).

Meyers, Eric M., McKnight, Julia P., and Krabbenhoft, Lindsay M. (2014) "Remediating Tinker Bell: Exploring Childhood and Commodification Through a Century-Long Transmedia Narrative," *Jeunesse: Young People, Texts, Cultures* 6.1: 95–118.

Miller, Daniel (1987) *Material Culture and Mass Consumption*, Oxford: Basil Blackwell.

Milne, A.A. (1926) *Winnie-the Pooh*, illus. E.H. Shepard, London: Methuen.

Potter, Beatrix (2002) *The Tale of Peter Rabbit*, London: Penguin Books (first published 1902).

Quart, Alissa (2003) *Branded: The Buying and Selling of Teenagers*, London: Random House.

Reid-Walsh, Jacqueline (2015) "Movable Morals: Eighteenth-and Nineteenth-Century Flap Books and Paper Doll Books for Girls as Interactive 'Conduct Books,'" in Clare Bradford, and Mavis Reimer (eds) *Girls, Texts, Cultures*, Waterloo, ON: Wilfrid Laurier Press, 211–236.

Rey, Margret and Rey, H.A. (1941) *Curious George*, New York: Houghton Mifflin.

Rose, Jacqueline S. (1984) *The Case of Peter Pan or The Impossibility of Children's Fiction*, London: Macmillan.

Santo, Avi (2015) *Selling the Silver Bullet: The Lone Ranger and Transmedia Brand Licensing*, Austin: University of Texas Press.

Seiter, Ellen (1993) *Sold Separately: Children and Parents in Consumer Culture*, New Brunswick, NJ: Rutgers University Press.

Sendak, Maurice (1963) *Where the Wild Things Are*, New York: Harper & Row.

Seuss, Dr. (1957) *The Cat in the Hat*, New York: Random House.

Stella, Queen of the Snow (2014) Mermaid Theatre of Nova Scotia, 2014, theatrical production.

Stella and Sam (2010–2014) Radical Sheep Productions, Television.

Stella and Sam Story Pack (2013) Version 1.7, app for iPad, zinc Roe Inc. (last accessed March 14, 2014).

Tapscott, Don (1998) *Growing Up Digital: The Rise of the Net Generation*, New York: McGraw Hill.

The Chronicles of Narnia: The Lion, the Witch and the Wardrobe (2005) dir. Andrew Adamson, Walt Disney Pictures, Walden Media.

Wells, Rosemary (1985) *Max's Birthday*, New York: Macmillan.

Willems, Mo (2003) *Don't Let the Pigeon Drive the Bus!* New York: Hyperion.

Where the Wild Things Are (2009) dir: Spike Jonze, Warner Brothers.

Zipes, Jack (2001) *Sticks and Stones: The Troublesome Success of Children's Literature from Slovenly Peter to Harry Potter*, New York: Routledge.

INDEX

Taylor & Francis eBooks

Helping you to choose the right eBooks for your Library

Add Routledge titles to your library's digital collection today. Taylor and Francis ebooks contains over 50,000 titles in the Humanities, Social Sciences, Behavioural Sciences, Built Environment and Law.

Choose from a range of subject packages or create your own!

Benefits for you

» Free MARC records
» COUNTER-compliant usage statistics
» Flexible purchase and pricing options
» All titles DRM-free.

Benefits for your user

» Off-site, anytime access via Athens or referring URL
» Print or copy pages or chapters
» Full content search
» Bookmark, highlight and annotate text
» Access to thousands of pages of quality research at the click of a button.

REQUEST YOUR **FREE** INSTITUTIONAL TRIAL TODAY

Free Trials Available
We offer free trials to qualifying academic, corporate and government customers.

eCollections – Choose from over 30 subject eCollections, including:

Archaeology	Language Learning
Architecture	Law
Asian Studies	Literature
Business & Management	Media & Communication
Classical Studies	Middle East Studies
Construction	Music
Creative & Media Arts	Philosophy
Criminology & Criminal Justice	Planning
Economics	Politics
Education	Psychology & Mental Health
Energy	Religion
Engineering	Security
English Language & Linguistics	Social Work
Environment & Sustainability	Sociology
Geography	Sport
Health Studies	Theatre & Performance
History	Tourism, Hospitality & Events

For more information, pricing enquiries or to order a free trial, please contact your local sales team:
www.tandfebooks.com/page/sales

Routledge
Taylor & Francis Group

The home of
Routledge books

www.tandfebooks.com